1st Workshop on Challenges in Processing South Asian Languages (CHiPSAL 2025)

Abu Dhabi, United Arab Emirates
19 January 2025

ISBN: 979-8-3313-1360-9

Printed from e-media with permission by:

Curran Associates, Inc.
57 Morehouse Lane
Red Hook, NY 12571

CURRAN ASSOCIATES INC. proceedings .com

Some format issues inherent in the e-media version may also appear in this print version.

Association for Computational Linguistics
209 N. Eighth Street
Stroudsburg, Pennsylvania 18360

Phone: 1-570-476-8006
Fax: 1-570-476-0860

acl@aclweb.org

Additional copies of this publication are available from:

Curran Associates, Inc.
57 Morehouse Lane
Red Hook, NY 12571 USA
Phone: 845-758-0400
Fax: 845-758-2633
Email: curran@proceedings.com
Web: www.proceedings.com

COLING 2025

Proceedings of the First Workshop on Challenges in Processing South Asian Languages (CHiPSAL 2025)

Editors
Kengatharaiyer Sarveswaran
Surendrabikram Thapa
Sana Shams
Ashwini Vaidya
Bal Krishna Bal

CHiPSAL 2025 was co-located with the 31st International Conference on Computational Linguistics

January 19, 2025

Proceedings of the First Workshop on Challenges in Processing South Asian Languages (CHiPSAL 2025)

CHiPSAL 2025 was co-located with the 31st International Conference on Computational Linguistics (COLING 2025) and held virtually on 19 January 2025.

Message from the Organizing Chairs

Welcome to the proceedings of CHiPSAL 2025, the First Workshop on Challenges in Processing South Asian Languages (CHiPSAL), held as part of the 31st International Conference on Computational Linguistics (COLING 2025) in Abu Dhabi, UAE, on January 19, 2025. This inaugural workshop, conducted in virtual mode, served as a platform to explore challenges and foster collaboration in processing South Asian languages.

The proceedings include highlights, challenges, and future directions from the workshop, presented in "A Brief Overview of the First Workshop on Challenges in Processing South Asian Languages (CHiPSAL)."

CHiPSAL featured regular papers, invited keynotes, and shared task papers, with a focus on Devanagari-script language understanding. Subtasks included language identification, hate speech detection, and target classification. These contributions reflect the workshop's mission to address linguistic and cultural nuances, resource constraints, and orthographic complexities in low-resource South Asian languages while advancing multilingual NLP research.

We extend our heartfelt thanks to the program committee members worldwide for their rigorous reviews, ensuring three reviews per submission. We also express gratitude to the authors for their valuable contributions, as well as the COLING workshop chairs and the COLING 2025 organizing committees for their support in making this workshop a success.

We congratulate all authors on their accepted papers and are proud to note that CHiPSAL was a highly competitive workshop. We hope it provided a meaningful platform for discussing the challenges and future directions in South Asian language processing.

Thank you for being part of this inaugural event.

Kengatharaiyer Sarveswaran
Ashwini Vaidya
Bal Krishna Bal
Sana Shams
Surendrabikram Thapa

`https://sites.google.com/view/chipsal/`

Workshop Chairs

Kengatharaiyer Sarveswaran, University of Jaffna, Sri Lanka.
Ashwini Vaidya, Indian Institute of Technology, Delhi, India.
Bal Krishna Bal, Kathmandu University, Kathmandu, Nepal.
Sana Shams, University of Engineering and Technology, Lahore, Pakistan.
Surendrabikram Thapa, Virginia Tech, USA.

Program Committee Members (Alphabetical Order)

A M Abirami, Thiagarajar College of Engineering, India.
Abhai Pratap Singh, Amazon, USA.
Akaash Vishal Hazarika, Splunk, USA.
Aloka Fernando, University of Moratuwa, Sri Lanka.
Aman Shakya, Institute of Engineering, Pulchowk, Tribhuvan University, Nepal.
Anitha Dhakshina Moorthy, Thiagarajar College of Engineering, India.
Ann Sinthusha Anton Vijeevaraj, University of Vavuniya, Sri Lanka.
Annette Hautli-Janisz, University of Passau, Germany.
Ashwini Vaidya, IIT Delhi, India.
Bal Krishna Bal, Kathmandu University, Nepal.
Balaram Prasain, Tribhuvan University, Nepal.
Bareera Sadia, Al-Khawarizmi Institute of Computer Science, UET, Lahore, Pakistan.
Brinda Gurusamy, Cisco, USA.
Buddhika Karunarathne, University of Moratuwa, Sri Lanka.
Eugene Y A Charles, University of Jaffna, Sri Lanka.
Farah Adeeba, University of Engineering and Technology, KSK, Pakistan.
Farhan Jafri, Jamia Millia Islamia, India.
Gihan Dias, University of Moratuwa, Sri Lanka.
H N D Thilini, University of Colombo School of Computing, Sri Lanka.
Hariram Veeramani, UCLA, USA.
Hassan Sajjad, Dalhousie University, Canada.
Jayeeta Putatunda, Fitch Ratings, USA.
Kengatharaiyer Sarveswaran, University of Jaffna, Sri Lanka.
Krishna Chalise, Tribhuvan University, Nepal.
Kritesh Rauniyar, IIMS College, Nepal.
Lekhnath Pathak, Tribhuvan University, Nepal.
Lynnette Hui Xian Ng, CMU, USA.
Mahak Shah, Columbia University, USA.
Manjunath Chandrashekaraiah, Astera Labs, USA.
Menan Velayuthan, University of Moratuwa, Sri Lanka.
Munief Tahir, Al-Khawarizmi Institute of Computer Science, UET, Lahore, Pakistan.
Parameswari Krishnamurthy, IIIT Hyderabad, India.
Paritosh Katre, PayPal, USA.
Prakash Poudyal, Kathmandu University, Nepal.
Preetish Kakkar, Adobe, USA.
Qurat-ul-Ain Akram, University of Engineering and Technology, KSK, Pakistan.
Randil Pushpananda, University of Colombo School of Computing, Sri Lanka.
Sahar Rauf, Al-Khawarizmi Institute of Computer Science, UET, Lahore, Pakistan.
Sana Shams, Al-Khawarizmi Institute of Computer Science, UET, Lahore, Pakistan.

Shuvam Shiwakoti, Virginia Tech, USA.
Siddhant Bikram Shah, Northeastern University, USA.
Sinnathamby Mahesan, University of Jaffna, Sri Lanka.
Suganya Ramamoorthy, Vellore Institute of Technology University, India.
Surabhi Adhikari, Columbia University, USA.
Surangika Ranathunga, Massey University, New Zealand.
Surendrabikram Thapa, Virginia Tech, USA.
Tafseer Ahmed, Alexa Translations, Canada.
Toqeer Ehsan, Mohamed bin Zayed University of Artificial Intelligence, United Arab Emirates.
Usman Naseem, Macquarie University, Australia.
Uthayasanker Thayasivam, University of Moratuwa, Sri Lanka.
Vijayrajsinh Gohil, New York University, USA.

Volunteers (alphabetical order)

Ahrane Mahaganapathy, Unversity of Jaffna, Sri Lanka.
Menan Velayuthan, Unversity of Moratuwa, Sri Lanka.
Suthakar Sivashanth, Unversity of Jaffna, Sri Lanka.

Table of Contents

CHiPSAL 2025 Program

Sunday, January 19, 2025

(GMT+4)

8:30–10:30 Morning Oral Presentations

8:30–8:50 *A Brief Overview of the First Workshop on Challenges in Processing South Asian Languages (CHiPSAL)*
Kengatharaiyer Sarveswaran, Surendrabikram Thapa, Sana Shams, Ashwini Vaidya and Bal Krishna Bal

8:50–9:10 *Development of Pre-Trained Transformer-based Models for the Nepali Language*
Prajwal Thapa, Jinu Nyachhyon, Mridul Sharma and Bal Krishna Bal

9:10–9:30 *Benchmarking the Performance of Pre-trained LLMs across Urdu NLP Tasks*
Munief Hassan Tahir, Sana Shams, Layba Fiaz, Farah Adeeba and Sarmad Hussain

9:30–9:50 *Bengali ChartSumm: A Benchmark Dataset and study on feasibility of Large Language Models on Bengali Chart to Text Summarization*
Nahida Akter Tanjila, Afrin Sultana Poushi, Sazid Abdullah Farhan, Abu Raihan Mostofa Kamal, Md. Azam Hossain and Md. Hamjajul Ashmafee

9:50–10:10 *DweshVaani: An LLM for Detecting Religious Hate Speech in Code-Mixed Hindi-English*
Varad Srivastava

10:10–10:30 *Improving Accuracy of Low-resource ASR using Rule-Based Character Constituency Loss (RBCCL)*
Rupak Raj Ghimire, Prakash Poudyal and Bal Krishna Bal

10:30–12:00 Break

12:00–14:50 Afternoon Oral Presentations

12:00–12:20 *Natural Language Understanding of Devanagari Script Languages: Language Identification, Hate Speech and its Target Detection*
Surendrabikram Thapa, Kritesh Rauniyar, Farhan Ahmad Jafri, Surabhi Adhikari, Kengatharaiyer Sarveswaran, Bal Krishna Bal, Hariram Veeramani and Usman Naseem

12:20–12:40 *SiTa - Sinhala and Tamil Speaker Diarization Dataset in the Wild*
Uthayasanker Thayasivam, Thulasithan Gnanenthiram, Shamila Jeewantha and Upeksha Jayawickrama

12:40–13:00 *Sandhi Splitting in Tamil and Telugu: A Sequence-to-Sequence Approach Leveraging Transformer Models*
Priyanka Dasari, Mupparapu Sohan Gupta, Nagaraju Vuppala, Pruthwik Mishra and Parameswari Krishnamurthy

13:00–13:20 *Bridge the GAP: Multi-lingual Models For Ambiguous Pronominal Coreference Resolution in South Asian Languages*
Rahothvarman P, Adith John Rajeev, Kaveri Anuranjana and Radhika Mamidi

13:20–13:50 Poster spotlights

14:00–15:00 Poster Presentations

Poster papers

A Dual Contrastive Learning Framework for Enhanced Hate Speech Detection in Low-Resource Languages
Krishan Chavinda and Uthayasanker Thayasivam

Abstractive Summarization of Low resourced Nepali language using Multilingual Transformers
Prakash Dhakal and Daya Sagar Baral

Structured Information Extraction from Nepali Scanned Documents using Layout Transformer and LLMs
Aayush Neupane, Aayush Lamichhane, Ankit Paudel and Aman Shakya

Domain-adaptative Continual Learning for Low-resource Tasks: Evaluation on Nepali
Sharad Duwal, Suraj Prasai and Suresh Manandhar

A Brief Overview of the First Workshop on Challenges in Processing South Asian Languages (CHiPSAL)

Kengatharaiyer Sarveswaran
University of Jaffna
Sri Lanka
sarves@univ.jfn.ac.lk

Surendrabikram Thapa
Virginia Tech, Blacksburg
United States of America
surendrabikram@vt.edu

Sana Shams
Al-Khawarizmi Institute
of Computer Science
UET, Pakistan
sana.shams@kics.edu.pk

Ashwini Vaidya
Indian Institute of Technology, Delhi
India
avaidya@iitd.ac.in

Bal Krishna Bal
Kathmandu University
Nepal
bal@ku.edu.np

Abstract

In this paper, we provide a brief summary of the inaugural workshop on Challenges in Processing South Asian Languages (CHiPSAL) held as part of COLING 2025. The workshop included regular papers, invited keynotes, and shared task papers, fostering a collaborative platform for exploring challenges in processing South Asian languages. The shared task focused on Devanagari-script language understanding, encompassing subtasks on language identification, hate speech detection, and target classification. This workshop series aims to address linguistic and cultural nuances, resource constraints, and orthographic complexities in low-resource South Asian languages while advancing NLP research and promoting multilingual inclusivity.

1 Introduction

South Asia, encompassing Afghanistan, Bangladesh, Bhutan, India, Maldives, Nepal, Pakistan, and Sri Lanka, is one of the world's most populous regions, accounting for nearly a quarter of the global population (see Table 1). The region is linguistically diverse, featuring languages from at least four major language families and several potential linguistic isolates. (Hock and Bashir, 2016; Arora et al., 2022) With over 700 languages and approximately 25 major scripts, South Asia boasts a rich cultural and linguistic heritage. Furthermore, over 50 million South Asians reside abroad. Despite this remarkable diversity, South Asian languages remain significantly underrepresented in language technology.

Recent large language models (LLMs) incorporate limited data from South Asia, and the processing of South Asian languages presents significant challenges, starting with encoding issues. Although most scripts are standardized in Unicode, many applications fail to render them accurately due to orthographic complexities. Additionally, input methods for these languages remain a persistent barrier in the region. The linguistic complexity of South Asian languages, characterized by diverse writing systems and extensive literary traditions, further complicates natural language processing (NLP) tasks. Dialectal and cultural variations, along with the close linguistic relationships among these languages, introduce additional layers of complexity.

This workshop addresses the multifaceted challenges in processing South Asian languages, focusing on linguistic and cultural factors, encoding and orthographic issues, and resource constraints. By tackling these issues, we aim to advance NLP for South Asian languages while preserving and promoting their rich linguistic and cultural heritage. In this paper, we provide a brief overview of our accepted papers, shared tasks, and the workshop's future directions.

2 Submission and Review

We received 46 long papers, 13 short papers for the main track of CHiPSAL workshop, and 20 shared-task papers which is organised as the part of the workshop. Twelve papers were later withdrawn by authors, and two papers were desk-rejected.

We accepted a total of 38 papers for the work-

Proceedings of the First Workshop on Challenges in Processing South Asian Languages (CHiPSAL 2025), pages 1–8
January 19, 2025.

Country	Population (millions)	Living Languages	Literacy Rate (%)
Afghanistan	38.347	33	43
Bangladesh	166.303	36	74
Bhutan	0.772	21	67
India	1380	424	74
Maldives	0.541	1	98
Nepal	30.226	109	68
Pakistan	225.2	68	59
Sri Lanka	22.156	5	92
Total	**1863.549**	**697**	-
	(23.43% of World)	(10.07% of World)	

Table 1: South Asian Languages and Literacy Data (Eberhard et al., 2024)

shop, including 3 short papers, 17 long papers, and 18 shared task papers. For the main workshop track, 48 submissions were considered for review, of which 20 were accepted, resulting in an acceptance rate of approximately 41.7%. Of these, 8 papers were selected for oral presentations, while the remaining 12 were designated for poster presentations. The selection for oral and poster presentations aimed to ensure coverage of diverse tasks and languages while accommodating all presentations within a single day. Each submission underwent a rigorous review process, with three program committee members evaluating each paper to ensure a fair and thorough assessment. Overall, 55 program committee members from around the world, representing both academia and industry, contributed to the review process.

The submissions cover research on Bengali, English, Hindi, Kannada, Malayalam, Nepali, Pashto, Punjabi, Sinhala, Tamil, Telugu and Urdu languages on topics e.g. low-resource language challenges, script and linguistic complexity, speech processing and recognition, hate speech and code-mixing, and linguistic resource development.

3 Accepted papers

3.1 Long papers

Thapa et al. (2025a), in *Development of Pre-Trained Transformer-based Models for the Nepali Language*, highlight the under-representation of Nepali in NLP due to limited resources and monolingual corpora. They address this by collecting 27.5 GB of Nepali text data and pre-training BERT, RoBERTa, and GPT-2 models. They also explore instruction tuning, improving performance on Nepali datasets. Their models surpass the NepgLUE benchmark by 2 points, scoring 95.60, and perform better on text generation tasks, advancing Nepali text processing.

Chavinda and Thayasivam (2025), in *A Dual Contrastive Learning Framework for Enhanced Hate Speech Detection in Low-Resource Languages*, address hate speech detection in Sinhala and Tamil. They introduce a framework combining Multilingual Large Language Models (MLLMs) with Dual Contrastive Learning (DCL) to enhance detection. Using datasets from Facebook and Twitter, their approach outperforms traditional models, with the Twitter/twhin-bert-base model showing the best results. This study advances hate speech detection in low-resource languages.

Dhakal and Baral (2025), in *Abstractive Summarization of Low-Resourced Nepali Language Using Multilingual Transformers*, apply mBART and mT5 models to summarize Nepali news headlines. They create a headline corpus and fine-tune the models with Low-Rank Adaptation (LoRA) and quantization. Evaluations show the 4-bit quantized mBART model performs best. This work advances abstractive summarization and NLP for Nepali.

Neupane et al. (2025), in *Structured Information Extraction from Nepali Scanned Documents Using Layout Transformer and LLMs*, develop methods for extracting information from Nepali documents. They use the Language Independent Layout Transformer (LiLT), achieving an F1 score of 0.87, and compare it with LLMs like GPT-4o and Llama 3.1 8B. Their findings provide a foundation for digitizing Nepali texts.

Duwal et al. (2025), in *Domain-Adaptive Continual Learning for Low-Resource Tasks: Evaluation on Nepali*, explore domain-adaptive pre-training

(DAPT) to improve Llama 3 8B for Nepali. Using synthetic data and 4-bit QLoRA, they evaluate performance and knowledge retention, finding a 19.29% improvement in higher-shot evaluations. This study highlights DAPT's potential for low-resource tasks.

Rahothvarman et al. (2025), in *Bridge the GAP: Multi-Lingual Models for Ambiguous Pronominal Coreference Resolution in South Asian Languages*, address coreference resolution in Dravidian languages by creating the mGAP dataset. They develop joint embedding and cross-attention models, demonstrating the latter's effectiveness in capturing pronoun-candidate relations and leveraging transfer learning for low-resource languages.

Dasari et al. (2025), in *Sandhi Splitting in Tamil and Telugu: A Sequence-to-Sequence Approach Leveraging Transformer Models*, tackle sandhi splitting by creating annotated corpora and implementing sequence-to-sequence transformers. Their models, evaluated on the IN22-Conv Benchmark, improve preprocessing for morphologically rich languages like Tamil and Telugu.

James and Krishnamurthy (2025), in *POS-Aware Neural Approaches for Word Alignment in Dravidian Languages*, explore neural methods like SimAlign and AWESOME-align for Tamil and Telugu. They show that POS-tag fine-tuning improves alignment accuracy by 6–7% and investigate cross-linguistic mappings with English, highlighting the complexities of low-resource language alignment.

Pokharel and Agrawal (2025), in *neDIOM: Dataset and Analysis of Nepali Idioms*, introduce a Nepali idioms dataset and evaluate multilingual models on processing figurative language. They find that smaller models outperform larger ones, offering a resource for advancing idiom processing in low-resource languages.

Tahir et al. (2025), in *Benchmarking the Performance of Pre-Trained LLMs Across Urdu NLP Tasks*, benchmark seven pre-trained LLMs across 17 Urdu NLP tasks. They find models with richer language-specific data, like Llama 3.1-8B, often outperform larger models in tasks, emphasizing the importance of linguistic diversity in NLP research.

Khalid et al. (2025), in *Bridging the Bandwidth Gap: A Mixed Band Telephonic Urdu ASR Approach with Domain Adaptation for Banking Applications*, presents a telephonic Urdu ASR system using a corpus of 445 speakers. Comparing GMM-HMM and TDNN models, they find TDNN outperforms GMM-HMM. Mixing narrow-band and wide-band speech reduces Word Error Rates (WER), and domain adaptation with a specialized lexicon enhances performance for banking applications.

Chhetri and Poudyal (2025), in *Impacts of Vocoder Selection on Tacotron-Based Nepali Text-To-Speech Synthesis*, evaluate WaveNet and MelGAN vocoders for Nepali TTS. The study uses Nepali OpenSLR and News male voice datasets. They find that Tacotron2 + MelGAN consistently outperforms Tacotron2 + WaveNet in naturalness and higher Mean Opinion Score (MOS).

Thevakumar et al. (2025), in *EmoTa: A Tamil Emotional Speech Dataset*, introduce a dataset of 936 utterances from 22 Tamil speakers expressing five emotions. Fleiss' Kappa shows substantial agreement (0.74), and machine learning models achieve F1-scores above 0.90 for emotion classification. EmoTa supports Tamil speech emotion recognition research.

Ghimire et al. (2025), in *Improving Accuracy of Low-Resource ASR Using Rule-Based Character Constituency Loss (RBCCL)*, introduce RBCCL to improve transcription in Devanagari script. Combining RBCCL with cross-entropy loss reduces Word Error Rate (WER) from 47.1% to 23.41%, enhancing low-resource ASR performance.

Thayasivam et al. (2025), in *SiTa - Sinhala and Tamil Speaker Diarization Dataset in the Wild*, introduce a dataset addressing the lack of conversational data for speaker diarization in Sinhala and Tamil. They benchmark existing models, providing a resource for advancing speaker diarization in low-resource languages.

Srivastava (2025), in *DweshVaani: An LLM for Detecting Religious Hate Speech in Code-Mixed Hindi-English*, proposes Dwesh-Vaani, a fine-tuned Gemma-2 model outperforming other approaches for detecting hate speech and religion-specific targets in code-mixed Hindi-English. The study highlights challenges and opportunities in this domain.

Tanjila et al. (2025), in *Bengali ChartSumm: A Benchmark Dataset and Study on Feasibility of Large Language Models on Bengali Chart-to-Text Summarization*, introduce a dataset with 4,100 Bengali charts and summaries. Evaluating models like mT5 and BanglaT5, they establish baselines to support low-resource NLP research.

3.2 Short papers

Karim and Uzuner (2025), in *Leveraging Machine-Generated Data for Joint Intent Detection and Slot Filling in Bangla: A Resource-Efficient Approach*, generated a Bangla dataset for Natural Language Understanding (NLU) by translating the English SNIPS dataset (Coucke et al., 2018) using the LLaMA-3 model, focusing on intent detection and slot-filling tasks. They evaluated both separate and joint modeling approaches using different BERT variants, finding that the multilingual BERT (mBERT) achieved the best performance, with 97.83% intent accuracy and 91.03% slot-filling F1 score.

Sehar et al. (2025), in *Benchmarking Whisper for Low-Resource Speech Recognition: An N-Shot Evaluation on Pashto, Punjabi, and Urdu*, benchmarked the Whisper ASR model's performance on three low-resource languages - Pashto, Punjabi, and Urdu - by first evaluating its zero-shot performance and then fine-tuning the Whisper Small model on domain-specific datasets. They found that few-shot fine-tuning significantly reduced the Word Error Rate (WER), with improvements ranging from 6-19 percentage points across different languages and datasets, demonstrating the potential of adapting Whisper to low-resource language contexts.

Khade et al. (2025), in *Challenges in Adapting Multilingual LLMs to Low-Resource Languages using LoRA PEFT Tuning*, investigated the challenges of adapting Large Language Models (LLMs), specifically Gemma models, to Marathi, a low-resource language, using Low-Rank Adaptation (LoRA) Parameter-Efficient Fine-Tuning (PEFT). While automated evaluation metrics suggested a performance decline after fine-tuning, manual assessments revealed that the fine-tuned models often outperformed their original versions, particularly in generating contextually relevant responses.

4 Shared Task on Natural Language Understanding of Devanagari Script Languages

This shared task (Thapa et al., 2025b) aimed to address critical challenges in understanding Devanagari-script languages, which include Hindi, Nepali, Marathi, Sanskrit, and Bhojpuri. By focusing on language identification, hate speech detection, and target classification, the task sought to develop robust and generalizable NLP models for these linguistically rich but underrepresented languages. The task attracted widespread participation with 113 participants.

4.1 Shared Task Description

The shared task comprised three subtasks to explore different aspects of Devanagari-script language understanding. **Subtask A** focused on identifying the language of a given text among five Devanagari-script languages. **Subtask B** involved detecting whether a given text contained hate speech. **Subtask C** required identifying the target of hate speech, categorizing it as directed toward an individual, a community, or an organization. These tasks encouraged the development of models capable of addressing linguistic complexity and cultural nuances in diverse contexts.

4.2 Winning Team Performances

The winning teams employed innovative methodologies and domain-specific adaptations to achieve state-of-the-art performance across all three subtasks, showcasing the potential of multilingual and low-resource NLP research. Below, we give a short description of the approaches for winning teams in each subtask.

4.2.1 Subtask A

Team **CUFE** (Ibrahim, 2025) utilized fastText classifier for language identification, leveraging its subword modeling capabilities through n-grams along with systematic token generation using the tokenizer vy Team et al. (2022). The proposed system achieves a near-perfect F1 score of 0.9997 on the test set and secures the first position in the shared task.

4.2.2 Subtask B

Team **Paramananda** (Acharya et al., 2025) utilized FastText and demonstrated superior performance, particularly with data augmentation, achieving an F1 score of 81.39% and scoring first position on the leaderboard. This outperformed BERT, which struggled with an F1 score of 0.5763. Despite its contextual embedding strengths, BERT's underperformance was attributed to overfitting on sparse datasets, as evidenced by a higher evaluation score that did not generalize to test data.

4.2.3 Subtask C

Team **MDSBots** (Thapaliya et al., 2025) used a hybrid approach for the detection of the targets of hate speech. Their approach involved augmenting the data with synthetic examples using synonym replacement and GPT-4, addressing class imbalance for minority categories like ‘community’. Additionally, a rule-based Named Entity Recognition (NER) tagger was applied to identify entities such as individuals, organizations, and groups within tweets. These NER tags were incorporated into the model’s input to improve performance, resulting in the highest F1 score in the competition. NER has historically shown good performance in target identification (Thapa et al., 2023).

5 Discussion on Challenges in Processing South Asian Languages

South Asian language processing poses significant challenges that stem from the region’s linguistic diversity, complex scripts, and limited availability of resources. These challenges are compounded by the region’s rich cultural and dialectal variations, creating additional obstacles for NLP applications. In this section, we examine several of these key challenges, drawing insights from accepted papers.

5.1 Low-Resource Nature and Data Scarcity

One of the foremost challenges is the lack of adequate linguistic resources, including annotated datasets, corpora, and pre-trained models for many South Asian languages. As highlighted by Thapa et al. (2025a), the scarcity of monolingual corpora and benchmarks limits the development of robust language models. For example, Nepali has limited large-scale datasets, and efforts such as pretraining language models on collected corpora are necessary to bridge this gap. Similarly, the lack of datasets for figurative language processing, such as idioms in Nepali (Pokharel and Agrawal, 2025), highlights the need for resource development to tackle specific linguistic phenomena.

5.2 Script and Orthographic Complexity

The South Asian linguistic landscape includes over 25 major scripts, many of which have complex orthographic rules that challenge standard encoding and rendering systems. Issues such as conjunct consonants, diacritical marks, and inconsistent Unicode implementation often lead to errors in text representation. As discussed by Ghimire et al. (2025), the Devanagari script, used in Nepali, Hindi, and Marathi, presents unique challenges for automatic speech recognition (ASR) and transcription due to its character-level complexities. Solutions like Rule-Based Character Constituency Loss (RBCCL) show promise in addressing transcription errors in Devanagari script (Ghimire et al., 2025).

5.3 Dialectal and Cultural Variations

South Asian languages often have multiple dialects with significant lexical and syntactic variations, making the development of universal models difficult. This diversity is further complicated by the lack of standardization in data collection and annotation. Papers like Chavinda and Thayasivam (2025) demonstrate how multilingual models must account for these variations to improve tasks like hate speech detection in south Asian languages like Tamil and Sinhala. Data augmentation and domain adaptation are critical for enhancing model performance across diverse dialectal contexts.

5.4 Linguistic Challenges

Languages like Tamil and Telugu, with their agglutinative morphology and intricate sandhi rules, challenge tokenization and translation systems. Specialized algorithms are required to address these linguistic features effectively (Dasari et al., 2025).

5.5 Code-Mixing and Multilinguality

Code-mixing, or the blending of languages within the same text, is a prevalent phenomenon in South Asia, particularly in social media and informal communication. This introduces additional challenges for NLP tasks like hate speech detection and sentiment analysis. The work by Srivastava (2025) exemplifies this issue by focusing on code-mixed Hindi-English hate speech detection. Fine-tuning multilingual models for such mixed-language contexts is an ongoing research challenge.

5.6 Speech and Text Processing

Speech recognition and text-to-speech systems face unique difficulties in South Asian languages due to phonetic richness and resource constraints. The lack of diverse speech datasets, as addressed by Chhetri and Poudyal (2025), limits the development of robust models. Similarly, the introduction of datasets like EmoTa for Tamil speech emotion recognition (Thevakumar et al., 2025) is a step forward in addressing the need for expanding resources in underrepresented languages.

5.7 Bias and Evaluation Limitations

The inherent biases in multilingual pre-trained models pose another significant challenge. Models trained on limited or skewed data often fail to generalize across different languages and tasks. Tahir et al. (2025) emphasize the need for benchmarking models on diverse set of tasks and languages, such as Urdu, to identify and mitigate these biases effectively.

5.8 Resource and Infrastructure Constraints

Unlike high-resource languages, South Asian languages suffer from limited computational and financial resources, which hampers the development of advanced models. The use of parameter-efficient fine-tuning methods like LoRA (Khade et al., 2025) offers a promising direction to address these constraints, enabling efficient model adaptation for low-resource settings.

5.9 Future Directions

While some progress has been made, addressing these challenges requires a multifaceted approach. Collaborative resource creation, the development of domain-specific models, and culturally informed annotation practices are critical for advancing NLP in South Asian languages. Furthermore, as demonstrated by CHiPSAL shared tasks (Thapa et al., 2025b), targeted competitions and benchmarks can drive innovation and foster community-driven solutions to these complex problems. In summary, addressing the challenges in processing South Asian languages requires a combination of innovative methods, resource development, and community collaboration. By tackling these issues, we can enhance inclusivity and robustness of NLP systems for the diverse linguistic landscape of South Asia.

6 Future Directions of the Workshop

In the future, the CHiPSAL workshop aims to expand its role as a leading platform for addressing the challenges and opportunities in South Asian language processing. Building upon the success of its inaugural workshop, the organizers plan to diversify the workshop's activities to foster deeper engagement and collaboration within the community. To encourage active participation and knowledge exchange, we aim to introduce interactive sessions such as expert panels, hands-on tutorials, and focused round-table discussions. These sessions will highlight emerging issues, including improving low-resource NLP methods, mitigating biases in multilingual and multimodal systems, and advancing cultural and linguistic inclusivity in AI.

Future workshops will place a strong emphasis on resource creation and open collaboration. We plan to organize dedicated tracks for dataset curation, multilingual benchmarking, and model development tailored to South Asian languages. These initiatives will address the lack of publicly available resources and benchmarks, empowering researchers and practitioners to develop state-of-the-art solutions for underrepresented languages. We also intend to expand the scope of shared tasks, introducing new challenges that encompass speech processing, code-mixing, figurative language understanding, and cross-modal applications. These tasks will encourage participants to tackle diverse linguistic phenomena and real-world scenarios unique to South Asia.

As NLP evolves, future CHiPSAL workshops will focus on leveraging advances in LLMs and multimodal systems for South Asian languages. This will include exploring innovative techniques such as continual learning, low-resource fine-tuning, and transfer learning, ensuring that state-of-the-art technologies are effectively adapted to the linguistic diversity of the region. Additionally, the workshop will continue to address ethical considerations, such as mitigating biases and ensuring fair representation in AI systems for South Asian languages. By promoting community-driven solutions and interdisciplinary collaboration, we aim to establish CHiPSAL as a key platform for the development of inclusive and impactful NLP in South Asia.

7 Conclusion

The inaugural CHiPSAL workshop provided a platform to address the challenges and opportunities in processing South Asian languages, emphasizing their linguistic diversity, script complexity, and low-resource nature. With contributions ranging from new datasets and benchmarks to advanced model fine-tuning, the workshop welcomed innovative approaches to tackle issues like code-mixing, dialectal variation, and linguistic resource constraints. Our shared task, which was participated by over 100 participants, also helped students and early-career researchers to understand and work on the problems within Devanagari NLU. Moving forward, CHiPSAL aims to expand its scope, foster greater collaboration, and address emerging issues, with a focus on resource creation, ethical AI practices, and equitable access. By driving impactful research and fostering community engagement, CHiPSAL aspires to create lasting contributions that empower both academic and applied NLP for South Asia's rich linguistic and cultural heritage.

References

Darwin Acharya, Sundeep Dawadi, Shivram Saud, and Sunil Regmi. 2025. Paramananda@NLU of Devanagari Script Languages 2025: Detection of Language, Hate Speech and Targets using FastText and BERT. In *Proceedings of the First Workshop on Challenges in Processing South Asian Languages (CHiPSAL)*, Abu Dhabi. International Committee on Computational Linguistics (ICCL).

Aryaman Arora, Adam Farris, Samopriya Basu, and Suresh Kolichala. 2022. Computational historical linguistics and language diversity in South Asia.

Krishan Chavinda and Uthayasanker Thayasivam. 2025. A Dual Contrastive Learning Framework for Enhanced Hate Speech Detection in Low-Resource Languages. In *Proceedings of the First Workshop on Challenges in Processing South Asian Languages (CHiPSAL)*, Abu Dhabi, UAE. International Committee on Computational Linguistics (ICCL).

Ganesh Dhakal Chhetri and Prakash Poudyal. 2025. Impacts of Vocoder Selection on Tacotron-based Nepali Text-To-Speech Synthesis. In *Proceedings of the First Workshop on Challenges in Processing South Asian Languages (CHiPSAL)*, Abu Dhabi, UAE. International Committee on Computational Linguistics (ICCL).

Alice Coucke, Alaa Saade, Adrien Ball, Théodore Bluche, Alexandre Caulier, David Leroy, Clément Doumouro, Thibault Gisselbrecht, Francesco Caltagirone, Thibaut Lavril, et al. 2018. Snips voice platform: an embedded spoken language understanding system for private-by-design voice interfaces. *arXiv preprint arXiv:1805.10190*.

Priyanka Dasari, Mupparapu Sohan Gupta, Nagaraju Vuppala, Pruthwik Mishra, and Parameswari Krishnamurthy. 2025. Sandhi Splitting in Tamil and Telugu: A Sequence-to-Sequence Approach Leveraging Transformer Models. In *Proceedings of the First Workshop on Challenges in Processing South Asian Languages (CHiPSAL)*, Abu Dhabi, UAE. International Committee on Computational Linguistics (ICCL).

Prakash Dhakal and Daya Sagar Baral. 2025. Abstractive Summarization of Low Resourced Nepali Language using Multilingual Transformers. In *Proceedings of the First Workshop on Challenges in Processing South Asian Languages (CHiPSAL)*, Abu Dhabi, UAE. International Committee on Computational Linguistics (ICCL).

Sharad Duwal, Suraj Prasai, and Suresh Manandhar. 2025. Domain-Adaptive Continual Learning for Low-Resource Tasks: Evaluation on Nepali. In *Proceedings of the First Workshop on Challenges in Processing South Asian Languages (CHiPSAL)*, Abu Dhabi, UAE. International Committee on Computational Linguistics (ICCL).

David M. Eberhard, Gary F. Simons, and Charles D. Fennig. 2024. *Ethnologue: Languages of the World*, 27th edition. SIL International, Dallas, TX, USA.

Rupak Raj Ghimire, Prakash Poudyal, and Bal Krishna Bal. 2025. Improving Accuracy of Low-resource ASR using Rule-Based Character Constituency Loss (RBCCL). In *Proceedings of the First Workshop on Challenges in Processing South Asian Languages (CHiPSAL)*, Abu Dhabi, UAE. International Committee on Computational Linguistics (ICCL).

Hans Henrich Hock and Elena Bashir, editors. 2016. *The Languages and Linguistics of South Asia*. De Gruyter Mouton, Berlin, Boston.

Michael Ibrahim. 2025. CUFE@NLU of Devanagari Script Languages 2025: Language Identification using fastText. In *Proceedings of the First Workshop on Challenges in Processing South Asian Languages (CHiPSAL)*, Abu Dhabi. International Committee on Computational Linguistics (ICCL).

Antony Alexander James and Parameswari Krishnamurthy. 2025. POS-Aware Neural Approaches for Word Alignment in Dravidian Languages. In *Proceedings of the First Workshop on Challenges in Processing South Asian Languages (CHiPSAL)*, Abu Dhabi, UAE. International Committee on Computational Linguistics (ICCL).

A H M Rezaul Karim and Ozlem Uzuner. 2025. Leveraging machine-generated data for joint intent detection and slot filling in bangla: A resource-efficient approach. In *Proceedings of the First Workshop on Challenges in Processing South Asian Languages (CHiPSAL)*.

Omkar Khade, Shruti Jagdale, Abhishek Phaltankar, Gauri Takalikar, and Raviraj Joshi. 2025. Challenges in adapting multilingual llms to low-resource languages using lora peft tuning. In *Proceedings of the First Workshop on Challenges in Processing South Asian Languages (CHiPSAL)*.

Ayesha Khalid, Farah Adeeba, Najm Ul Sehar, and Sarmad Hussain. 2025. Bridging the Bandwidth Gap: A Mixed Band Telephonic Urdu ASR Approach with Domain Adaptation for Banking Applications. In *Proceedings of the First Workshop on Challenges in Processing South Asian Languages (CHiPSAL)*, Abu Dhabi, UAE. International Committee on Computational Linguistics (ICCL).

Aayush Neupane, Aayush Lamichhane, Ankit Paudel, and Aman Shakya. 2025. Structured Information Extraction from Nepali Scanned Documents using Layout Transformer and LLMs. In *Proceedings of the First Workshop on Challenges in Processing South Asian Languages (CHiPSAL)*, Abu Dhabi, UAE. International Committee on Computational Linguistics (ICCL).

Rhitabrat Pokharel and Ameeta Agrawal. 2025. neDIOM: Dataset and Analysis of Nepali Idioms. In *Proceedings of the First Workshop on Challenges in Processing South Asian Languages (CHiPSAL)*, Abu Dhabi, UAE. International Committee on Computational Linguistics (ICCL).

P Rahothvarman, Adith John Rajeev, Kaveri Anuranjana, and Radhika Mamidi. 2025. Bridge the GAP: Multi-lingual Models For Ambiguous Pronominal Coreference Resolution in South Asian Languages. In *Proceedings of the First Workshop on Challenges in Processing South Asian Languages (CHiPSAL)*, Abu Dhabi, UAE. International Committee on Computational Linguistics (ICCL).

Najm Ul Sehar, Ayesha Khalid, Farah Adeeba, and Sarmad Hussain. 2025. Benchmarking whisper for low-resource speech recognition: An n-shot evaluation on pashto, punjabi, and urdu. In *Proceedings of the First Workshop on Challenges in Processing South Asian Languages (CHiPSAL)*.

Varad Srivastava. 2025. DweshVaani: An LLM for Detecting Religious Hate Speech in Code-Mixed Hindi-English. In *Proceedings of the First Workshop on Challenges in Processing South Asian Languages (CHiPSAL)*, Abu Dhabi, UAE. International Committee on Computational Linguistics (ICCL).

Munief Hassan Tahir, Sana Shams, Layba Fiaz, Farah Adeeba, and Sarmad Hussain. 2025. Benchmarking the Performance of Pre-trained LLMs across Urdu NLP Tasks. In *Proceedings of the First Workshop on Challenges in Processing South Asian Languages (CHiPSAL)*, Abu Dhabi, UAE. International Committee on Computational Linguistics (ICCL).

Nahida Akter Tanjila, Afrin Sultana Poushi, Sazid Abdullah Farhan, Abu Raihan Mostofa Kamal, Md. Azam Hossain, and Md. Hamjajul Ashmafee. 2025. Bengali ChartSumm: A Benchmark Dataset and Study on Feasibility of Large Language Models on Bengali Chart to Text Summarization. In *Proceedings of the First Workshop on Challenges in Processing South Asian Languages (CHiPSAL)*, Abu Dhabi, UAE. International Committee on Computational Linguistics (ICCL).

NLLB Team, Marta R. Costa-jussà, James Cross, Onur Çelebi, Maha Elbayad, Kenneth Heafield, Kevin Heffernan, Elahe Kalbassi, Janice Lam, Daniel Licht, Jean Maillard, Anna Sun, Skyler Wang, Guillaume Wenzek, Al Youngblood, Bapi Akula, Loic Barrault, Gabriel Mejia Gonzalez, Prangthip Hansanti, John Hoffman, Semarley Jarrett, Kaushik Ram Sadagopan, Dirk Rowe, Shannon Spruit, Chau Tran, Pierre Andrews, Necip Fazil Ayan, Shruti Bhosale, Sergey Edunov, Angela Fan, Cynthia Gao, Vedanuj Goswami, Francisco Guzmán, Philipp Koehn, Alexandre Mourachko, Christophe Ropers, Safiyyah Saleem, Holger Schwenk, and Jeff Wang. 2022. No Language Left Behind: Scaling Human-Centered Machine Translation.

Prajwal Thapa, Jinu Nyachhyon, Mridul Sharma, and Bal Krishna Bal. 2025a. Development of Pre-Trained Transformer-based Models for the Nepali Language. In *Proceedings of the First Workshop on Challenges in Processing South Asian Languages (CHiPSAL)*, Abu Dhabi, UAE. International Committee on Computational Linguistics (ICCL).

Surendrabikram Thapa, Farhan Ahmad Jafri, Ali Hürriyetoğlu, Francielle Vargas, Roy Ka Wei Lee, and Usman Naseem. 2023. Multimodal Hate Speech Event Detection-Shared Task 4. In *CASE 2023-Proceedings of the 6th Workshop on Challenges and Applications of Automated Extraction of Socio-Political Events from Text, associated with 14th International Conference on Recent Advances in Natural Language Processing, RANLP 2023*, pages 151–159. Association for Computational Linguistics.

Surendrabikram Thapa, Kritesh Rauniyar, Farhan Ahmad Jafri, Surabhi Adhikari, Kengatharaiyer Sarveswaran, Bal Krishna Bal, Hariram Veeramani, and Usman Naseem. 2025b. Natural language understanding of devanagari script languages: Language identification, hate speech and its target detection. In *Proceedings of the First Workshop on Challenges in Processing South Asian Languages (CHiPSAL)*.

Anish Thapaliya, Prabhat Ale, and Suman Paudel. 2025. MDSBots@NLU of Devanagari Script Languages 2025: Detection of Language, Hate Speech, and Targets using MURTweet. In *Proceedings of the First Workshop on Challenges in Processing South Asian Languages (CHiPSAL)*, Abu Dhabi. International Committee on Computational Linguistics (ICCL).

Uthayasanker Thayasivam, Thulasithan Gnanenthiram, Shamila Jeewantha, and Upeksha Jayawickrama. 2025. SiTa - Sinhala and Tamil Speaker Diarization Dataset in the Wild. In *Proceedings of the First Workshop on Challenges in Processing South Asian Languages (CHiPSAL)*, Abu Dhabi, UAE. International Committee on Computational Linguistics (ICCL).

Jubeerathan Thevakumar, Luxshan Thavarasa, Thanikan Sivatheepan, Sajeev Kugarajah, and Uthayasanker Thayasivam. 2025. EmoTa: A Tamil Emotional Speech Dataset. In *Proceedings of the First Workshop on Challenges in Processing South Asian Languages (CHiPSAL)*, Abu Dhabi, UAE. International Committee on Computational Linguistics (ICCL).

Development of Pre-Trained Transformer-based Models for the Nepali Language

Prajwal Thapa*, **Jinu Nyachhyon***, **Mridul Sharma***, **Bal Krishna Bal**

Information and Language Processing Research Lab (ILPRL), Kathmandu University,
prazzwalthapa87@gmail.com, nyachhyonjinu@gmail.com, mridulsharma3301@gmail.com, bal@ku.edu.np

Abstract

Transformer-based pre-trained language models have dominated the field of Natural Language Processing (NLP) for quite some time now. However, the Nepali language, spoken by approximately 32 million people worldwide, remains significantly underrepresented in this domain. This underrepresentation is primarily attributed to the scarcity of monolingual data corpora and limited available resources for the Nepali language. While existing efforts have predominantly concentrated on basic encoder-based models, there is a notable gap in the exploration of decoder-based architectures. To address this gap, we have collected 27.5 GB of Nepali text data, approximately 2.4x larger than any previously available Nepali language corpus. Leveraging this data, we pre-trained three different models i.e., BERT, RoBERTa, and GPT-2, exclusively for the Nepali Language. Furthermore, we performed instruction tuning and explored its potential for monolingual Nepali data, providing a foundation for future research. Our models outperformed the existing best model by 2 points on Nep-gLUE benchmark, scoring 95.60 and also outperformed existing models on text generation tasks, demonstrating improvements in both understanding and generating Nepali text.

1 Introduction

In recent years, Natural Language Processing (NLP) has undergone a remarkable evolution, transitioning from traditional rule-based to statistical methods to sophisticated deep learning architectures. The initial approaches, such as n-grams (Goodman, 2001) and rule-based systems, laid the groundwork for understanding language. But these methods faced significant limitations in handling the complexities of natural language and general human communication, which often involves subtle nuances, contextual dependencies, and varying linguistic structures.

The introduction of Recurrent Neural Networks (RNNs) (Mikolov et al., 2010) and Long Short-Term Memory networks (LSTMs) (Sundermeyer et al., 2012) for language modeling marked a significant advancement, allowing models to process sequential data more effectively. RNNs and LSTMs brought notable improvements in tasks like language modeling and sequence prediction. However, they still encountered challenges with long-range dependencies and computational efficiency, which limited their scalability and performance. These models require substantial computational resources and face difficulties in maintaining consistent performance across varying lengths of text and contexts. The development of the self-attention mechanism (Vaswani et al., 2017) marked a pivotal moment in NLP, enabling models to capture dependencies in text more effectively. The self-attention mechanism, integral to the Transformer architecture, allows models to weigh the importance of different words in a sequence, facilitating a more nuanced understanding of context. This was further enhanced by the concept of self-supervised model pre-training, where models like ELMo (Peters et al., 2018), BERT (Devlin et al., 2019) and GPT (Radford et al., 2018), leveraged vast amounts of unlabeled text data to learn general language representations. These models demonstrated unprecedented performance improvements across a range of NLP tasks.

Further advancements in NLP include instruction tuning (Wei et al., 2021; Wang et al., 2022), which trains models on instruction-output pairs to improve their ability to follow user commands.This method enhances the model's ability to follow specific user commands and adapt to diverse application scenarios. Instruction tuning has proven effective in improving the versatility and responsiveness of models, allowing them to better handle varied tasks and user interactions. Models, through unsupervised pre-training on large corpora, and

Proceedings of the First Workshop on Challenges in Processing South Asian Languages (CHiPSAL 2025), pages 9–16
January 19, 2025.

instruction-tuning have demonstrated the ability to generalize across various tasks, achieving state-of-the-art results.

Nepali is spoken by over 32 million people worldwide. Syntactically, the Nepali language differs significantly from English. In English, the typical sentence structure follows a Subject-Verb-Object (SVO) order whereas Nepali employs a Subject-Object-Verb (SOV) structure (Timilsina et al., 2022). Nepali language incorporates a complex system of noun, adjective and verb inflections. Nouns have a system of gender, case and number (Bal, 2004). This fundamental difference in syntactic arrangement highlights the unique characteristics of Nepali and underscores the challenges pertinent to natural language processing tasks in the Nepali language.

Our motivation for developing a monolingual language model for Nepali language comes from recent advancements in natural language processing, particularly the success of large-scale pre-trained models. However, the majority of these developments have focused on high-resource languages, leaving a gap in the availability of robust models for low-resource languages like Nepali. To address this disparity, we developed pre-trained monolingual language models for the Nepali language. Our first steps included compiling a dataset, large enough to develop pre-trained language models. We assembled approximately 27.5 GB of text data by scraping the top 99 Nepali news websites, representing the largest Nepali language dataset to date. We also used an instruction-tuning dataset to explore the potential of instruction-tuned models for Nepali, providing a foundation for future advancements.

This paper outlines our methods for developing pre-trained models and presents a thorough evaluation of their performance and comparison with existing models, setting new standards for Nepali NLP and contributing significantly to research on low-resource languages.

2 Related Works

The development of pre-trained language models has been foundational in advancing NLP, and a variety of approaches have emerged over the years. In this section, we briefly review the key methods that have influenced the creation and evolution of language models.

2.1 Unsupervised Pre-training Approaches

Early methods for developing pre-training language models utilized unsupervised learning to create generalized representations, with word embeddings like Word2Vec (Mikolov et al., 2013) and GloVe (Pennington et al., 2014) establishing the foundation by learning vector representations of words from large text corpora. These embeddings enhanced performance across various NLP tasks by capturing semantic relationships in a continuous vector space. The advent of contextualized word embeddings marked a significant advancement, exemplified by (Peters et al., 2018), which generated dynamic embeddings based on surrounding text using bidirectional LSTM networks, leading to improved results in benchmarks such as Question Answering and Named Entity Recognition. The introduction of the Transformer architecture (Vaswani et al., 2017) further revolutionized the field, giving rise to models like BERT (Devlin et al., 2019), RoBERTa (Liu et al., 2019), ELECTRA (Clark et al., 2020), DeBERTa (He et al., 2020) and GPT (Radford et al., 2018). BERT and other encoder model's bidirectional training approach allowed it to predict masked words by considering both left and right context, achieving state-of-the-art results across numerous NLP tasks, while GPT's autoregressive method excelled in text generation and completion.

2.2 Multilingual and Monolingual Language Models

The release of multilingual models, such as m-BERT (Pires et al., 2019), XLM (Lample and Conneau, 2019) and XLM RoBERTa (Conneau et al., 2020) which includes support for languages like Nepali, has further expanded the accessibility of NLP tools across different languages. While these models offer impressive results for many languages, their performance for languages other than English is still not up to the mark due to limited training data, issues with tokenization, lack of adequate vocabulary, and absence of techniques to handle linguistic diversity.

Recently, numerous powerful monolingual models for languages other than English have emerged showing promising results such as NorBERT (Kutuzov et al., 2021) for Nordic languages, FinBERT (Virtanen et al., 2019) for Finnish language, HerBERT (Mroczkowski et al., 2021) for Polish language, GBERT (Chan et al., 2020) for German language, Chinese BERT (Cui et al., 2021) for Chinese language, NepBERTa (Timilsina et al., 2022) for Nepali language etc. These models have demonstrated that optimizing tokenizers and architectures for specific languages can lead to substantial improvements in performance.

Few of the models have also focused on the Nepali language. IndicBERT (Doddapaneni et al., 2022) focused on several Indic languages, including Nepali, and demonstrated that language-specific models could outperform their multilingual counterparts on specialized tasks. NepBERTa (Timilsina et al., 2022) introduced a BERT-based language model specifically for the Nepali language, trained on the largest monolingual Nepali corpus with 0.8 billion words collected from various sources. They also established the first Nepali Language Understanding Evaluation benchmark (Nep-gLUE). Similarly, NepaliBERT (Pudasaini et al., 2023) also developed a monolingual BERT model specifically for the Nepali language. These models demonstrate the importance of optimizing tokenizers and architectures for addressing the unique characteristics of individual languages, especially those with complex syntactic and morphological structures like Nepali.

2.3 Instruction Tuning on Low-Resource Language Models

Instruction tuning has recently gained attention as a technique to substantially improve zero-shot performance on unseen tasks (Wei et al., 2021; Wang et al., 2022; Ouyang et al., 2022). This method involves fine-tuning pre-trained models on tasks that require the model to understand and execute explicit instructions, thereby increasing its adaptability and effectiveness across a variety of tasks. While this approach has been widely explored for high-resource languages, its potential in low-resource languages, such as Nepali, remains unexplored.

3 Dataset

This section describes the dataset used in our study, focusing on the methodologies implemented for data collection and preprocessing. Given the necessity for extensive training data in transformer-based language models, we compiled a dataset that is by far the largest one for the Nepali language.

3.1 Dataset Collection

Recently, the rise in digital content in Nepali has led to the increasing number of Nepali-language websites. This has opened doors to creating a comprehensive Nepali language corpus for which we performed web scraping across 99 Nepali news websites. As a result, we were able to gather a dataset totaling 30.4 GB of text data, which is significantly larger than existing resources.

We made a deliberate decision not to include existing datasets, such as the Nepali Wikipedia (Arora, 2020) dataset which is less than 1GB, the OSCAR dataset (Suarez et al., 2019) which is approximately 3GB, and the 12.5 GB dataset from NepBERTa (Timilsina et al., 2022). This choice was based on the fact that all these existing datasets were also scraped from news websites, which overlapped with our sources. To avoid duplication and ensure the uniqueness of our dataset, we opted to scrape all content from scratch.

For Instruction Tuning, we utilized the publicly available Nepali alpaca dataset (Kafley, 2024)) containing 52k rows of instructions. We cleaned the data by removing/translating all the non-Nepali texts. After the cleaning process, we achieved 40k rows of instructions.

3.2 Dataset Preprocessing

Following the data collection phase, we implemented a preprocessing pipeline to enhance the quality of the dataset. First, we implemented a deduplication process to remove redundant content, which was essential due to the extensive nature of our data collection. To address the challenge of multilingual content often found on news websites, we removed or translated the languages other than Nepali depending upon the context. We also developed specialized scripts to remove noise, eliminating non-textual elements such as HTML tags, special characters, and formatting artifacts common in web-scraped data. Additionally, text normalization techniques, including Unicode normalization, were applied to standardize character representation and maintain consistency. After these preprocessing steps, the dataset was refined and reduced to 27.5 GB, ensuring it was clean and well-suited for model training.

3.3 Tokenization

Tokenization is a crucial preprocessing step in natural language processing that breaks text into smaller units, such as words or subwords, enabling effective processing by language models. Traditional word piece tokenization methods (Wu et al., 2016) rely on splitting text based on spaces and punctuation and often encounter limitations with out-of-vocabulary (OOV) words and morphological variations, leading to potential information loss. In contrast, Byte-Pair Encoding (BPE) (Sennrich et al., 2016) tokenization addresses these limitations by segmenting words into subword units. BPE improves the handling of rare or unseen words by breaking them down into more manageable subword units, which helps in retaining meaningful information and maintaining consistency across different word forms. This method provides optimal balance between vocabulary size and coverage, which is particularly beneficial for morphologically rich languages like Nepali, where word forms can vary significantly.

For our study, we utilized the entire dataset to create two different BPE tokenizers, one with a vocabulary size of 30,522 and another with a vocabulary size of 50,256. These tokenizers were designed to optimize the balance between computational efficiency and linguistic coverage, ensuring that our language models could effectively process and understand Nepali text.

4 BERT & RoBERTa

BERT and RoBERTa are both built upon the transformer encoder architecture, which serves as the foundation for their robust natural language processing capabilities. While they share this common architecture, they differ significantly in their training methodologies and objectives. BERT, introduced by (Devlin et al., 2019), employs two distinct pretraining objectives: Masked Language Modeling (MLM) and Next Sentence Prediction (NSP). In the MLM task, certain words within a sentence are intentionally masked, and the model's goal is to predict these masked words using the context provided by the surrounding words. Similarly, in the NSP task, the model is presented with pairs of sentences and must determine whether the second sentence logically follows the first or if it is a random, unrelated sentence. In contrast, RoBERTa(Liu et al., 2019) focuses solely on the MLM objective, excluding the NSP task altogether, which has been shown to perform better in various benchmarks.

For our study. we pretrained single BERT (Devlin et al., 2019) variant comprising 110 million parameters using the tokenizer of vocabulary size 30,522. Similarly, we also pretrained the single RoBERTa(Liu et al., 2019) variant, also comprising 110 million parameters, using the tokenizer of vocabulary size 50,257.

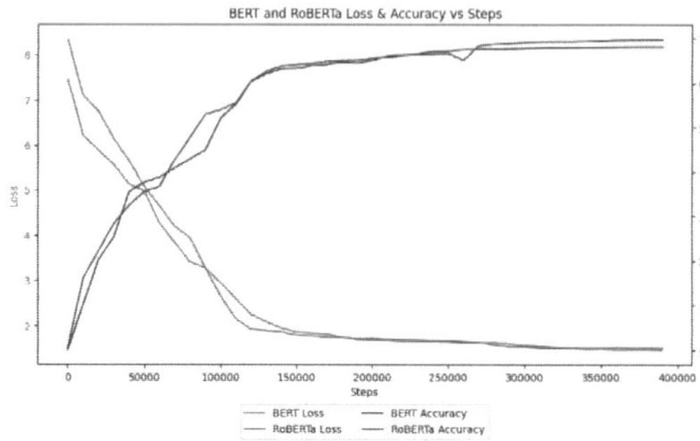

Figure 1: Loss and accuracy of the BERT and RoBERTA model compared with steps

In the case of both BERT (Devlin et al., 2019) (Devlin et al., 2019) and RoBERTa (Liu et al., 2019), we used a batch size of 256 and trained for 400k steps. We chose the Adam optimizer (Kingma and Ba, 2014) with a learning rate of 1×10^{-4}, $\beta_1 = 0.9$, $\beta_2 = 0.999$, and included an L2 weight decay of 0.01. We also implemented a learning rate warmup for the first 10,000 steps, followed by a linear decay to ensure smooth training. To improve generalization, we set a dropout probability of 0.1 on all layers. For activation, we used the Gaussian Error Linear Unit (GELU) (Hendrycks and Gimpel, 2016) function.

The training loss and accuracy trends for BERT and RoBERTa models are illustrated in Figure 1. For BERT, the training loss starts at 8.34 and gradually decreases to 1.51 after 400k steps, while accuracy improves from 3% to 68.11%. In comparison, RoBERTa begins with a training loss of 7.45, which steadily drops to 1.47 by 400k steps, achieving a slightly higher accuracy of 69.72%. The figure underscores RoBERTa's faster convergence and marginally better performance than BERT.

5 GPT-2

In the case of GPT-2 (Radford et al., 2019), we pretrained the 124M parameter model using the causal language modeling (CLM) objective, as described in the original GPT-2 paper (Radford et al., 2019). CLM, as outlined in the original GPT-2 paper (Radford et al., 2019), is designed to predict the next word in a sequence given the preceding con-

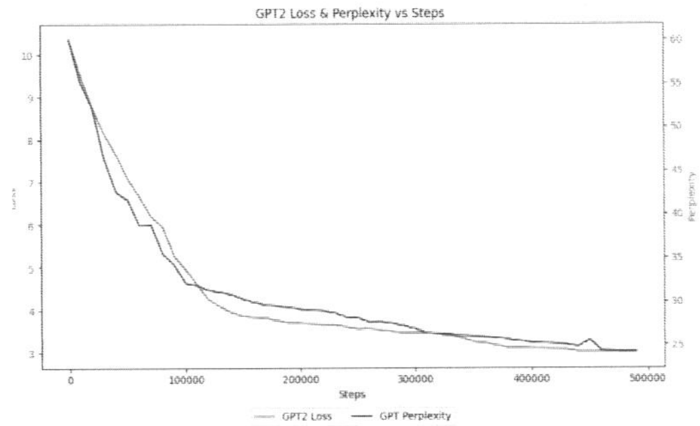

Figure 2: Loss and Perplexity of the GPT2 model compared with steps

text. Unlike BERT's masked language modeling, which predicts masked words from the surrounding context, CLM operates in a left-to-right manner. This means that the model generates text sequentially, using only the preceding words to predict the next word in the sequence. We used a batch size of 256 and trained for 500k steps. We used the Adam optimizer with a learning rate of 1×10^{-4}, $\beta_1 = 0.9$, $\beta_2 = 0.98$, and an L2 weight decay of 0.01. Similar to BERT (Devlin et al., 2019) and RoBERTa (Liu et al., 2019), we implemented a learning rate warmup over the first 10,000 steps, followed by a linear decay. To regularize the model, we set the dropout probability to 0.1 across all layers. This model was also trained using the GELU activation function (Hendrycks and Gimpel, 2016). Furthermore, we performed instruction tuning on the pretrained model using supervised fine-tuning. We used a batch size of 16, the Adam optimizer with a learning rate of 1×10^{-4}, and an attention dropout probability of 0.01. The training loss and perplexity trends for GPT-2 are shown in Figure 2. Initially, the training loss starts at 10.34 and steadily decreases to 3.001 after 500k steps. Similarly, perplexity drops from 60.03 to 24.13 over the same period. The figure illustrates GPT-2's significant improvement in model performance, with both loss and perplexity showing a consistent downward trend, reflecting the model's enhanced ability to predict the next token with greater accuracy as training progresses.

6 Evaluation

We conducted a thorough evaluation across several NLP tasks. Our evaluation includes both Natural Language Understanding (NLU) for encoder models and Natural Language Generation (NLG) tasks for decoder models.

6.1 Evaluating BERT & RoBERTa

For the evaluation of encoder-based models (BERT & RoBERTa) (Devlin et al., 2019; Liu et al., 2019), we used the Nepali Language Evaluation Benchmark, or Nep-gLUE (Timilsina et al., 2022). It consists of four tasks, including Named Entity Recognition (NER), Part-of-Speech (POS) Tagging, text classification, and categorical pair similarity. We used a batch size of 32 and fine-tuned for 3-10 epochs with multiple learning rates (5e-5, 4e-5, 3e-5, 2e-5, and 1e-5) over the data for all Nep-gLUE tasks. For each task, we selected the best-performing model on the test set.

Our models outperformed all existing models across all tasks, scoring 95.60 on Nep-gLUE (Timilsina et al., 2022) benchmark, a result that can be primarily attributed to the large and diverse training corpus we used. The scale of the data allowed the models to generalize better and capture a broader range of linguistic patterns, leading to improved performance.

6.2 Evaluating GPT-2

There were no existing benchmarks for NLG tasks, so we used abstractive summarization for the evaluation of GPT-2 (Radford et al., 2019). We used a publicly available summarization dataset (Bhandari, 2024) and fine-tuned both the GPT-2 model and GPT-2 Instruct model. The dataset consists of 7,258 data points, where we used 5,806 (80%) data points for training and the remaining 1,452 (20%) data points for evaluation. For finetuning, we used a batch size of 8 and trained for 3,000 steps. We used the ROUGE score (Lin, 2004) (Lin and Och, 2004) as our evaluation metric.

One of the things we observed was that the model tends to hallucinate when given very long contexts, and it did not perform well on long inputs, typically those exceeding 400 tokens. A key reason for this behavior can be traced to the model's training. The model was originally trained on sequences of 512 tokens, which limits its ability to handle longer sequences effectively, resulting in average ROGUE scores.

7 Results

We evaluated our pretrained Nepali language models on various Natural Language Processing tasks, comparing their performance with existing models. The results of the evaluation are summarized in table 1 and table 2.

Model	PARAMS	NER	POS	CC	CPS	Nep-GLUE Score
multilingual BERT (Devlin et al., 2019)	172M	85.45	94.65	91.08	93.60	91.19
XLM-Rbase (Conneau et al., 2020)	270M	87.59	94.88	92.33	93.65	92.11
NepBERT (Pudasaini et al., 2023)	110M	79.12	90.63	90.98	91.05	87.94
NepaliBERT (Rajan, 2021)	110M	82.45	91.67	90.10	89.46	88.42
NepBERTa (Timilsina et al., 2022)	110M	91.09	95.56	93.13	94.42	93.55
BERT (Ours)	110M	93.57	96.94	94.47	95.72	95.18
RoBERTa (**Ours**)	125M	**93.74**	**97.52**	**94.68**	**96.49**	**95.60**

Table 1: Nep-gLUE Test Result

Model	PARAMS	ROUGE-1	ROUGE-2	ROUGE-L
distilgpt-nepali (Maskey, 2022)	88.2M	10.16	8.63	9.19
GPT-2 (Ours)	124M	19.66	14.51	16.84
GPT-2-Instruct (**Ours**)	124M	**20.42**	**15.89**	**17.76**

Table 2: Performance comparision on summarization task

For BERT and RoBERTa in table 1, we used the NepGLUE benchmark and evaluated models, against existing monolingual and multilingual models. Both of our models outperformed the previous state-of-the-art, with RoBERTa achieving the highest overall NepGLUE score of 95.60. In particular, our models demonstrated superior performance on every task, reflecting the effectiveness of our models.

In the summarization task in table 2, we compared our GPT-2 models, including an instruction-tuned variant with existing (Maskey, 2022) model. Our GPT-2 models demonstrated substantial improvements across all ROUGE metrics, with the GPT-2-Instruct model achieving the highest scores of 20.42 (ROUGE-1), 15.89 (ROUGE-2), and 17.76 (ROUGE-L).

8 Conclusion

Our study reports significant progress in the field of Natural Language Processing (NLP) for the Nepali language, achieved through the development and evaluation of pre-trained large language models. Our key contributions include the development of by far the largest monolingual corpus for Nepali language and the pretraining of RoBERTa and BERT variants, as well as the introduction of the first GPT-2 model specifically designed for Nepali.

Extensive evaluations conducted on the NepGLUE benchmark and abstractive summarization tasks reveal that our models outperform existing state-of-the-art methods, demonstrating substantial improvements across a range of NLP tasks. By addressing both encoder and decoder architectures, our research emphasizes the potential for optimizing language models tailored to low-resource languages. Our findings not only contribute to the existing body of knowledge but also lay the groundwork for future research and applications in low-resource settings. We anticipate that these insights and benchmarks will inspire further innovations in the field, ultimately resulting in more effective and inclusive NLP research.

9 Acknowledgement

We extend our sincere gratitude to Google's TPU Research Cloud program for granting us free and unlimited access to TPU v4-8 for 30 days and School of Engineering, Kathmandu University for providing us with Nvidia GeForce RTX 3090 GPUs. This research would not have been possible without the unwavering support of the TPU Research Cloud team and School of Engineering, Kathmandu University.

References

Gaurav Arora. 2020. inltk: Natural language toolkit for indic languages. In *Proceedings of Second Workshop for NLP Open Source Software (NLP-OSS)*, pages 66–71. Association for Computational Linguistics.

Bal Krishna Bal. 2004. *Structure of Nepali Grammar*.

Sanjeev Bhandari. 2024. Xlsum-nepali-summerization-dataset.

Branden Chan, Stefan Schweter, and Timo Möller. 2020. German's next language model. In *Proceedings of the 28th International Conference on Computational Linguistics*, pages 6788–6796. International Committee on Computational Linguistics.

Kevin Clark, Minh-Thang Luong, Quoc V. Le, and Christopher D. Manning. 2020. Electra: Pre-training text encoders as discriminators rather than text generators. In *International Conference on Learning Representations (ICLR)*.

Alexis Conneau, Kartikay Khandelwal, Naman Goyal, Vishrav Chaudhary, Guillaume Wenzek, Francisco Guzmán, Edouard Grave, Myle Ott, Luke Zettlemoyer, and Veselin Stoyanov. 2020. Unsupervised cross-lingual representation learning at scale. *arXiv preprint arXiv:1911.02116v2*.

Yiming Cui, Wanxiang Che, Ting Liu, Bing Qin, and Ziqing Yang. 2021. Pre-training with whole word masking for chinese bert. *IEEE/ACM Transactions on Audio, Speech, and Language Processing*.

Jacob Devlin, Ming-Wei Chang, Kenton Lee, and Kristina Toutanova. 2019. Bert: Pre-training of deep bidirectional transformers for language understanding. In *Proceedings of the 2019 Conference of the North American Chapter of the Association for Computational Linguistics: Human Language Technologies, Volume 1 (Long and Short Papers)*, pages 4171–4186. Association for Computational Linguistics.

Sumanth Doddapaneni, Rahul Aralikatte, Gowtham Ramesh, Shreya Goyal, Mitesh M. Khapra, Anoop Kunchukuttan, and Pratyush Kumar. 2022. Towards leaving no indic language behind: Building monolingual corpora, benchmark and models for indic languages. *arXiv preprint arXiv:2212.05409*.

Joshua Goodman. 2001. A bit of progress in language modeling. *Expert Systems with Applications*, 41(3):853–860.

Pengcheng He, Xiaodong Liu, Jianfeng Gao, and Weizhu Chen. 2020. Deberta: Decoding-enhanced bert with disentangled attention. *arXiv preprint arXiv:2006.03654*.

Dan Hendrycks and Kevin Gimpel. 2016. Gaussian error linear units. *arXiv preprint arXiv:1606.08415*.

Saugat Kafley. 2024. alpaca-nepali-sft.

Diederik P. Kingma and Jimmy Lei Ba. 2014. Adam: A method for stochastic optimization. *arXiv preprint arXiv:1412.6980*.

Andrey Kutuzov, Jeremy Barnes, Erik Velldal, Lilja Øvrelid, and Stephan Oepen. 2021. Large-scale contextualised language modelling for norwegian. *arXiv preprint arXiv:2104.06546*.

Guillaume Lample and Alexis Conneau. 2019. Cross-lingual language model pre-training. In *Advances in Neural Information Processing Systems (NeurIPS)*.

Chin-Yew Lin and Franz Josef Och. 2004. Automatic evaluation of machine translation quality using longest common subsequence and skip-bigram statistics. In *Proceedings of the 42nd Annual Meeting of the Association for Computational Linguistics (ACL-04)*, pages 605–612.

Yinhan Liu, Myle Ott, Naman Goyal, Jingfei Du, Mandar Joshi, Danqi Chen, Omer Levy, Mike Lewis, Luke Zettlemoyer, and Veselin Stoyanov. 2019. Roberta: A robustly optimized bert pretraining approach. *arXiv preprint arXiv:1907.11692*.

Utsav Maskey. 2022. Distilgpt2-nepali.

Tomas Mikolov, Kai Chen, Greg Corrado, and Jeffrey Dean. 2013. Efficient estimation of word representations in vector space. *arXiv preprint arXiv:1301.3781*.

Tomaš Mikolov, Martin Karafiát, Lukáš Burget, Jan "Honza" Černocký, and Sanjeev Khudanpur. 2010. Recurrent neural network based language model. In *Interspeech*.

Robert Mroczkowski, Piotr Rybak, Alina Wróblewska, and Ireneusz Gawlik. 2021. Herbert: Efficiently pretrained transformer-based language model for polish. In *Proceedings of the 8th Workshop on Balto-Slavic Natural Language Processing*, pages 1–10. Association for Computational Linguistics.

Long Ouyang, Jeff Wu, Xu Jiang, Diogo Almeida, Carroll L. Wainwright, Pamela Mishkin, Chong Zhang, Sandhini Agarwal, Katarina Slama, Alex Ray, John Schulman, Jacob Hilton, Fraser Kelton, Luke Miller, Maddie Simens, Amanda Askell, Peter Welinder, Paul Christiano, Jan Leike, and Ryan Lowe. 2022. Training language models to follow instructions with human feedback. In *Advances in Neural Information Processing Systems (NeurIPS)*, volume 35, pages 27730–27744.

Jeffrey Pennington, Richard Socher, and Christopher Manning. 2014. Glove: Global vectors for word representation. In *Proceedings of the 2014 Conference on Empirical Methods in Natural Language Processing (EMNLP)*, pages 1532–1543. Association for Computational Linguistics.

Matthew E. Peters, Mark Neumann, Mohit Iyyer, Matt Gardner, Christopher Clark, Kenton Lee, and Luke Zettlemoyer. 2018. Deep contextualized word representations. *arXiv preprint arXiv:1802.05365*.

Telmo Pires, Eva Schlinger, and Dan Garrette. 2019. How multilingual is multilingual bert? *arXiv preprint arXiv:1906.01502*.

Shushanta Pudasaini, Subarna Shakya, Aakash Tamang, Sajjan Adhikari, Sunil Thapa, and Sagar Lamichhane. 2023. Nepalibert: Pre-training of masked language model in nepali corpus. In *7th International Conference on IoT in Social, Mobile, Analytics and Cloud*.

Alec Radford, Karthik Narasimhan, Tim Salimans, and Ilya Sutskever. 2018. Improving language understanding with unsupervised learning. *OpenAI Blog*.

Alec Radford, Jeffrey Wu, Rewon Child, David Luan, Dario Amodei, and Ilya Sutskever. 2019. Language models are unsupervised multitask learners. *OpenAI blog*.

Rajan. 2021. Nepalibert.

Rico Sennrich, Barry Haddow, and Alexandra Birch. 2016. Neural machine translation of rare words with subword units. In *Proceedings of the 54th Annual Meeting of the Association for Computational Linguistics (Volume 1: Long Papers)*, pages 1715–1725. Association for Computational Linguistics.

Pedro Ortiz Suarez, Benoît Sagot, and Laurent Romary. 2019. Asynchronous pipeline for processing huge corpora on medium to low resource infrastructures. In *7th Workshop on the Challenges in the Management of Large Corpora (CMLC-7)*. Leibniz-Institut für Deutsche Sprache.

Martin Sundermeyer, Ralf Schlüter, and Hermann Ney. 2012. Lstm neural networks for language modeling. In *Interspeech*.

Sulav Timilsina, Milan Gautam, and Binod Bhattarai. 2022. Nepberta: Nepali language model trained in a large corpus. In *Proceedings of the 2nd Conference of the Asia-Pacific Chapter of the Association for Computational Linguistics and the 12th International Joint Conference on Natural Language Processing*. Association for Computational Linguistics (ACL).

Ashish Vaswani, Noam Shazeer, Niki Parmar, Jakob Uszkoreit, Llion Jones, Aidan N. Gomez, Łukasz Kaiser, and Illia Polosukhin. 2017. Attention is all you need. In *Advances in Neural Information Processing Systems*, volume 30.

Antti Virtanen, Jenna Kanerva, Rami Ilo, Jouni Luoma, Juhani Luotolahti, Tapio Salakoski, Filip Ginter, and Sampo Pyysalo. 2019. Multilingual is not enough: Bert for finnish. *arXiv preprint arXiv:1912.07076*.

Yizhong Wang, Yeganeh Kordi, Swaroop Mishra, Alisa Liu, Noah A. Smith, Daniel Khashabi, and Hannaneh Hajishirzi. 2022. Self-instruct: Aligning language models with self-generated instructions. *arXiv preprint arXiv:2212.10560*.

Jason Wei, Maarten Bosma, Vincent Y. Zhao, Kelvin Guu, Adams Wei Yu, Brian Lester, Nan Du, Andrew M. Dai, and Quoc V. Le. 2021. Finetuned language models are zero-shot learners. *arXiv preprint arXiv:2109.01652*.

Yonghui Wu, Mike Schuster, Zhifeng Chen, Quoc V. Le, Mohammad Norouzi, Wolfgang Macherey, Maxim Krikun, Yuan Cao, Qin Gao, Klaus Macherey, et al. 2016. Google's neural machine translation system: Bridging the gap between human and machine translation. *arXiv preprint arXiv:1609.08144*.

Benchmarking the Performance of Pre-trained LLMs across Urdu NLP Tasks

Munief Hassan Tahir, Sana Shams, Layba Fiaz, Farah Adeeba, Sarmad Hussain

Center for Language Engineering, Al-Khawarizmi Institute of Computer Science
University of Engineering and Technology, Lahore, Pakistan
firstname.secondname@kics.edu.pk

Abstract

Large Language Models (LLMs) pre-trained on multilingual data have revolutionized natural language processing research, by transitioning from languages and task specific model pipelines to a single model adapted on a variety of tasks. However majority of existing multilingual NLP benchmarks for LLMs provide evaluation data in only few languages with little linguistic diversity. In addition these benchmarks lack quality assessment against the respective state-of the art models. This study presents an in-depth examination of 7 prominent LLMs: GPT-3.5-turbo, Llama 2-7B-Chat, Llama 3.1-8B, Bloomz 3B, Bloomz 7B1, Ministral-8B and Whisper (Large, medium and small variant) across 17 tasks using 22 datasets, 13.8 hours of speech, in a zero-shot setting, and their performance against state-of-the-art (SOTA) models, has been compared and analyzed. Our experiments show that SOTA models currently outperform encoder-decoder models in majority of Urdu NLP tasks under zero-shot settings. However, comparing Llama 3.1-8B over prior version Llama 2-7B-Chat, we can deduce that with improved language coverage, LLMs can surpass these SOTA models. Our results emphasize that models with fewer parameters but richer language-specific data, like Llama 3.1-8B, often outperform larger models with lower language diversity, such as GPT-3.5, in several tasks.

1 Introduction

The rapid increase in the application of Artificial Intelligence (AI) across a diverse spectrum of research areas including machine translation, natural language understanding and question answering can be attributed to the remarkable performances exhibited by Foundation Models (FM) (Bommasani et al., 2021). Based on the framework of transformers (Vaswani et al., 2017), multilingual large language models (LLM) are a prominent category of foundation models that can be utilized in multiple downstream tasks. A number of studies have have evaluated the potential of LLMs on various Natural Language Processing (NLP) tasks. LLMRec, a LLM-based recommender system (Liu et al., 2023) evaluated 3 LLMs including Llama, ChatGPT and ChatGLM on 5 recommendation tasks. (Zhong et al., 2021) conducted a human evaluation encompassing 10 LLMs with variations in pre-training methods, prompts, and model scales evaluated the zero-shot summarization capability. (Bian et al., 2023) used 11 datasets covering 8 domains to evaluate the LLMs' ability in answering common sense questions. (Hendy et al., 2023) conducted evaluations on 3 GPT models: ChatGPT, GPT3.5 (text-davinci-003), and text-davinci002 using 9 language pairs including low resource languages, to evaluate 18 machine translation directions. Holistic Evaluation of Language Models (HELM) project (Liang et al., 2023) evaluated 30 LLMs (open, limited-access, and closed models) for English across 42 NLP tasks. (Ahuja et al., 2023) conducted a multilingual evaluation of GPT 2.5 and Bloomz, comparing their performance with SOTA on 8 NLP tasks involving 33 languages. (Srivastava et al., 2023) conducted a comprehensive evaluation of 214 tasks, including 48 non-English low-resource languages using 13 transformer models and 8 GPT-3 series models with varying parameters from 125 million to 175 billion. Another notable effort was conducted by (Abdelali et al., 2024) for evaluation of 3 LLMs on 33 unique tasks for Arabic Language.

Our study, focuses on evaluating the potential of both closed and open LLMs for supporting Urdu, a low resource language with limited data coverage in LLM's pre-training. In our experiments we utilize GPT3.5 turbo by OpenAI, Llama 2 and Llama 3.1 by Meta , Bloomz 3B and 7B1 by Big Science, Ministral 8B by Mistral AI and Whisper by OpenAI in zero-shot setting, and perform evaluation on 17 Urdu NLP tasks analyzing their performances

Proceedings of the First Workshop on Challenges in Processing South Asian Languages (CHiPSAL 2025), pages 17–34
January 19, 2025.

with the existing SOTA models. To the best of our knowledge, this is the first in depth evaluation of prominent LLMs in Urdu Language context.

2 Approach

For benchmarking of Urdu NLP tasks, we perform experiments using GPT 3.5, Bloomz 3B and Bloomz 7B1 , Llama 2 and Llama 3.1, Ministral 8B and Whisper in zero-shot setting and comparatively analyse the results with the respective SOTA models. Model selection was based on factors like accessibility (open/closed), infrastructure requirement, performance and language support. GPT 3.5 was selected because of its superior performance on English tasks. Among open models, popular multilingual models i.e. Llama 2 , Llama 3.1, Ministral 8B and Bloomz were evaluated for text processing tasks and Whisper models were evaluated for speech recognition task. Due to budget limitations and lack of Urdu data in the pre-training, other closed LLMs models were not investigated.

The evaluation of LLMs involved prompting and significant post-processing to extract the output in desired format. A number of prompts were curated for all NLP tasks following the recommended format and instruction pattern proposed by LAraBench (Abdelali et al., 2024). The prompts for each model were optimized after testing them on a few samples for each task. These prompts have been reported in Appendix. A After obtaining a reasonable prompt, we used the LLM models in different settings. OpenAI's API was used for GPT 3.5. For Bloomz, we ran the model on Google Colab utilizing 16GB GPU and for Llama 2, Llama 3.1 and Ministral 8B, we used on premises hosted versions utilizing 2X40GB A100 GPUs. Results were post-processed in all cases to align with the test set's output. The following section elaborates the LLMs (including prompting and post-processing details), NLP Tasks, Datasets, SOTA Models and evaluation metrics, used in the study.

2.1 Models

2.1.1 GPT 3.5

GPT 3.5 Turbo has been trained on 175B parameters, encompassing both text and code data. GPT 3.5 despite being closed-source and less powerful than GPT-4 (OpenAI and et al., 2023), is more cost-effective, as its provides free access for experimentation. Additionally, at the time of research it was the most advanced model available from OpenAI for fine-tuning.

2.1.2 Bloomz 3B and 7.1B

Bloomz (Muennighoff et al., 2023), a Multitask Prompting Fine Tuned (MTF) version of the BLOOM (BigScienceWorkshop and et al., 2023), is trained on ROOTS corpus (Laurençon et al., 2023) covering 59 languages (including 13 programming languages, and 2.59TB of Urdu language data). For evaluation, the Bloomz 3B and 7.1B models from HuggingFace were used due to their open-source availability, and optimal balance between size and computational resources.

2.1.3 Llama 2 and Llama 3.1

Llama 2 (Touvron et al., 2023), released by Meta, is trained on 2 trillion tokens, with 89.70% of its content in English. Llama 3.1 (AI@Meta, 2024), available in three variants with 8 billion, 70 billion and 405 billion parameters, is trained on over 15 trillion tokens. Both models support 8k context lengths. For evaluation, the Llama 2-7b and Llama 3.1-8b models were used due to their open-source availability and potential for transfer learning and generalization to languages with limited data.

2.1.4 Ministral 8B

The Ministral 8B (Mistral AI Team, 2024) is trained on a mixture of multilingual and code datasets, supporting a context window of up to 128k facilitated by an interleaved sliding-window attention mechanism and a vocabulary of 131k. We benchmarked this model due to its open-source availability and its capability for low-memory inference, and its ability to be fine-tuned and adapted to a variety of tasks.

2.1.5 Whisper

Whisper (Radford et al., 2022), an Automatic Speech Recognition (ASR) model developed by OpenAI, is trained on an extensive dataset comprising 680,000 hours of multilingual and multitask supervised data collected from the web. Among the diverse languages included, Whisper incorporates only 104 hours of Urdu speech corpus. For inference , we utilized the small, medium and large variants of the pre-trained Whisper model. The small variant has 12 layers, 12 attention heads, a width of 768 with 244 million parameters. The medium variant is characterized by 24 layers, 16 attention heads, a width of 1024, and consists of 769 million parameters while, the large variant features

Task	Dataset	Dataset Size	Testset Size
Name Entity Recognition	MK-PUCIT (Kanwal et al., 2019)	99718	4165
News Categorization	COUNTER (Sharjeel et al., 2017)	1200	360
Intent Detection	Urdu Web Queries Dataset (UWQ-22) (Shams and Aslam, 2022)	6819	850
Hate Speech Detection	ISE-Hate corpus (Akram et al., 2023)	21759	2176
Hate Speech Detection	CLE-Hatespeech dataset (Ali et al., 2021)	5432	1087
Propaganda Detection	ProSOUL (Kausar et al., 2020)	11574	1737
Abusive Language Detection	HASOC - Task A(Das et al., 2021)	2400	240
Threat Detection	HASOC - Task B(Das et al., 2021)	9950	1975
Cyber Bullying Identification	Cyberbullying corpus (Adeeba et al., 2024)	12759	2480
Fake News Detection	(Khan et al., 2023)	4097	820
Hate Speech Categorization	ISE-Hate corpus(Akram et al., 2023)	8702	871
Text Summarization	CORPURES (Humayoun and Akhtar, 2022)	2649	311
Sentiment Analysis	(Muhammad and Burney, 2023)	10008	2002
Sentiment Analysis	Corpus of Aspect-based Sentiment for Urdu Political Data (ul Haq et al., 2020)	8760	1450
Multi-label Emotion Classification	Overview of EmoThreat (Task A) (Ashraf et al., 2022)	9750	1950
Emotion Classification	Urdu Nastalique Emotions Dataset (UNED) (Bashir et al., 2023)	4000	397
Machine Translation(Quran)	English-Urdu Religious Parallel Corpus (Jawaid and Zeman, 2011)	6414	200
Machine Translation(Bible)	English-Urdu Religious Parallel Corpus (Jawaid and Zeman, 2011)	7957	257
Abstractive Summarization	CLE Meeting Corpus (Sadia et al., 2024)	240	10
POS Tagging	Sense Tagged CLE Urdu Digest Corpus (Urooj et al., 2014)	100000	22522
ASR (Read Speech)	Urdu Speech Corpus (Farooq et al., 2019)	-	9.5 hours
ASR (Broadcast)	Urdu Broadcast (BC) Corpus(Khan et al., 2021)	-	4.3 hours

Table 1: NLP Tasks and Dataset Statistics

32 layers, 20 attention heads, a width of 1280, and comprises 1550 million parameters.

2.2 Tasks and Datasets

This study has focused on a comprehensive evaluation of pre-trained open and closed LLMs on Urdu NLP tasks. This study utilizes 22 publicly available datasets (see Table 1) to evaluate 17 Urdu NLP tasks as discussed in the following sections.

2.2.1 Name Entity Recognition

Name Entity Recognition (NER) is a sequence tagging task that involves identifying entities, such as names of people, organizations, locations, dates, etc. For its evaluation, we used the MK-PUCIT dataset and its SOTA model reported in (Kanwal et al., 2019).

2.2.2 News Categorization

News categorization classify news articles into topics based on their content. For its evaluation, COUNTER dataset (Sharjeel et al., 2017) was used that consisted of articles from 5 different domains and its SOTA is reported in (Khan et al., 2023).

2.2.3 Intent Detection

Intent detection focuses on determining the communicative intent behind a user's input query in the form of text or speech. For our evaluation, we used the UWQ-22 dataset and SOTA model reported in (Shams and Aslam, 2022).

2.2.4 Ethics and NLP: Factuality and Harmful Content Detection

These tasks aim to evaluate the accuracy of information, identify and combat misinformation, and detect harmful content. We benchmark several tasks such as i) Hate Speech Detection using the ISE-Hate corpus by (Akram et al., 2023) and CLE-Hatespeech dataset (Ali et al., 2021). ii) Propaganda Detection on the ProSOUL dataset developed by (Kausar et al., 2020). iii) Abusive Language Detection in Urdu, on the dataset by (Das et al., 2021) for their Subtask A. iv) Threat Detection on the dataset of (Das et al., 2021) for Subtask B. v) Cyber Bullying Identification using Cyberbullying corpus (Adeeba et al., 2024) vi) Fake News Detection using dataset prepared by (Khan et al., 2023) vii) Hate Speech Categorization using ISE-Hate corpus by (Akram et al., 2023).

2.2.5 Text Summarization

Text summarization involves extracting the most important sentences from a document to create a condensed version retaining essential information. We evaluated the LLMs on:

- **Extractive Summarization**

  Extractive summarization condenses text by

Task	Dataset	Metric	GPT 3.5	Bloomz 3B	Bloomz 7B1	Llama 2	Llama 3.1	Ministral 8B	SOTA	Delta
Name Entity Recognition	MK-PUCIT	Macro-F1	**0.55**	0.25	0.27	0.15	0.41	0.25	0.77	0.22
News Categorization	COUNTER	Macro-F1	**0.87**	0.58	0.48	0.13	0.64	0.67	0.70	-0.17
Intent Detection	Urdu Web Queries Dataset (UWQ-22)	Macro-F1	0.30	0.22	0.18	0.07	**0.42**	0.34	0.90	0.56
Hate Speech Detection	ISE-Hate corpus	Macro-F1	**0.72**	0.52	0.53	0.48	0.70	0.53	0.83	0.11
Hate Speech Detection	CLE-Hatespeech dataset	Macro-F1	0.67	0.35	0.43	0.51	**0.72**	0.54	0.98	0.26
Propaganda Detection	ProSOUL	Macro-F1	0.31	0.47	0.47	0.44	**0.66**	0.53	0.83	0.17
Abusive Language Detection	HAOSOC - Task A	Macro-F1	0.23	**0.51**	0.47	0.44	0.50	0.48	0.88	0.37
Threat Detection	HAOSOC - Task B	Macro-F1	**0.49**	0.35	0.20	0.21	0.40	0.46	0.54	0.05
Cyber Bullying Identification	(Adeeba et al., 2024)	Macro-F1	0.19	0.15	0.10	0.06	**0.22**	0.08	0.84	0.41
Fake News Detection	(Khan et al., 2023)	Macro-F1	0.55	0.52	0.51	0.47	**0.72**	0.57	0.93	0.21
Hate Speech Categorization	ISE-Hate corpus	Macro-F1	**0.40**	0.28	0.15	0.21	0.30	0.22	0.83	0.43
Extractive Summarization	CORPURES	Average Rouge-2 F1 score	0.54	0.46	0.55	0.59	**0.62**	0.52	0.57	-0.04
Abstractive Summarization	CLE Meeting Corpus	Rouge-1 Score (Avg)	0.22	0.02	0.07	0.006	**0.24**	0.06	0.31	0.07
Sentiment Analysis	(Muhammad and Burney, 2023)	Macro-F1	**0.62**	0.35	0.33	0.3	0.44	0.36	0.88	0.26
Sentiment Analysis	Corpus of Aspect-based Sentiment for Urdu Political Data	Macro-F1	0.31	0.20	0.21	0.13	**0.37**	0.28	0.70	0.37
Multi-label Emotion Classification	Overview of EmoThreat (Task A)	Macro-F1	0.20	0.17	0.26	–	**0.40**	0.29	0.68	0.28
Emotion Classification	Urdu Nastalique Emotions Dataset (UNED)	Macro-F1	0.32	0.25	0.21	0.18	0.24	**0.41**	0.87	0.46
Machine Translation (Quran)	English-Urdu Religious Parallel Corpus	BLEU	**3.75**	1.91	2.36	2.49e-78	3.44	0.004	13.24	9.49
Machine Translation(Bible)	English-Urdu Religious Parallel Corpus	BLEU	5.96	2.28	2.47	0.097	**6.43**	1.31e-78	13.99	8.03
POS Tagging	CLE Urdu POS Tagset	Accuracy	**0.49**	0.11	0.06	0.09	0.31	0.14	0.96	0.47

Table 2: Results from zero-shot experiments of GPT 3.5, Bloomz 3B, Bloomz 7B1, Llama 2, Llama 3.1 and Ministral 8B Models Compared to SOTA over NLP tasks. **Bold** text indicates the best score among models.

selecting and combining key sentences directly from the original content. For the evaluation of this task, we used the CORPURES dataset by (Humayoun and Akhtar, 2022).

- **Abstractive Summarization**

  Abstractive summarization generates concise summaries by understanding and paraphrasing the core meaning of a text into new, shorter sentences. For its evaluation, we have used CLE Meeting Corpus and its SOTA available in (Sadia et al., 2024).

2.2.6 Sentiment and Emotion Analysis

These tasks include understanding and interpreting human expressions in textual data. For Sentiment analysis, datasets from (Muhammad and Burney, 2023) and CLE (ul Haq et al., 2020) are used. For emotion analysis we used dataset from (Ashraf et al., 2022) for their Task A: Multi-label Emotion Detection consisted of "Neutral" label and Ekman's six basic emotions (Ekman, 1999). The other dataset used was Urdu Nastalique Emotions Dataset (UNED) by (Bashir et al., 2023).

2.2.7 Machine Translation

Machine translation of Urdu is challenging due to its morphological complexity. To evaluate the translation capabilities of LLMs for English Urdu pair, we utilized the dataset by (Jawaid and Zeman, 2011) for Quran and Bible translations containing 200 and 257 testing samples respectively.

2.2.8 Part of Speech (POS) Tagging

POS tagging is a fundamental task in NLP that involves labeling each word in a sentence with its corresponding part of speech, such as noun, verb, adjective, etc. To evaluate this task we have used the CLE Urdu POS Tagset with the SOTA reported in (Ahmed et al., 2014).

2.2.9 Automatic Speech Recognition (ASR)

ASR automatically converts spoken language into text. For its evaluation, we utilized the small, medium and large variant of the pre-trained Whisper model (Radford et al., 2022). We benchmarked this model against the SOTA models using its pre-trained weights for both broadcast and read speech recognition tasks using following two corpora:

- Urdu Broadcast (BC) corpus: A broadcast speech corpus (Khan et al., 2021) with 4.3 hours of data from 25 speakers (14 males and 11 females). This dataset includes recordings from five different broadcast channels and YouTube, covering genres such as entertainment, health and science, current affairs, and politics.
- Urdu Speech corpus: A read speech corpus (Farooq et al., 2019) consisting of 9.5 hours of Urdu speech from 62 speakers. The dataset is balanced in terms of gender and recording channels.

2.3 Zero-Shot Setup

For all LLMs; GPT 3.5, Bloomz 3b and 7b, Llama 2 and Llama 3.1 and Ministral 8B we use zero-shot prompting giving natural language instructions describing the task and specify the expected output. Prompts allow LLMs to learn context and narrows the inference space to produces accurate output as further elaborated in the section 2.5.

2.4 Inference Settings

The inference experiments for Llama 2, Llama 3.1 and Ministral 8B were conducted using two parallel NVIDIA A100-PCIE-40GB GPUs, providing a combined computational capacity of 80GB. During the inference, nearly 90 percent of the total GPU capacity was utilized. For experiments of GPT-3.5, API from OpenAI was utilized. Inference experiments with GPT-3.5 were conducted using Google Colab. Inference experiments with Bloomz's 3B and 7.1B models, available on huggingface, were also conducted using Google Colab. For Speech processing experiments using Whisper, two NVIDIA RTX3060-12GB GPUs were employed, providing a combined computational capacity of 24GB.

2.5 Prompt Engineering and Post Processing

In our experimentation with different LLMs, we tweaked the prompts based on the models input. Prompts for tasks such as News categorization A.2 and Hate speech Categorization A.11 were challenging because they required outputs from predefined ground-truth categories. Prompts for Machine Translation task A.19 had to be engineered so that the model's output only includes the translated text. Thus optimal prompts were curated by testing against each model on few samples, while ensuring no bias in decision-making.

Despite careful prompting, model responses required post-processing to align with desired outcomes e.g. capitalization ("fake" vs. "Fake"), standardizing output formats ("1. Propaganda" to "1"), and omitting "explanations" and "note" produced with the models' responses, specifically in Hate speech detection A.5 task. Some model outputs didn't match desired outcomes, e.g. News categorization included 5 domains i.e. sports, showbiz, foreign , national , business however the models output out of context domains such as "politics" and "entertainment". Among all the models, Llama 2 required the most output post-processing.

For a thorough description of the prompts crafted for each LLM, please refer to Appendix A.

2.6 SOTA Models

In this study, we benchmark the capabilities of LLMs in a zero-shot scenario by comparing them with SOTA models as reported in respective studies. These SOTA models employed diverse architectures including Capsule NN, Support Vector Machine (SVM), Random Forest (RF), Decision Tree (J48), Sequential Minimal Optimization (SMO), Convolutional Neural Networks (1D-CNN), LSTM with CNN features , Naive Bayes classifier and various multilingual transformer models such as m-BERT and frameworks like XGboost and LGBM.

2.7 Evaluation Metrics

The evaluation metrics used for the experiments have been kept identical to the one used in the respective state of the art references. They are Macro-F1, Rouge 2 F1 score, BLEU [1], accuracy and Word Error Rate (WER). We have also computed the delta to highlight the differential between best performing LLM's output with the SOTA model.

[1] https://www.nltk.org/api/nltk.translate.bleu

Task	Domain	Metric	Whisper (Large)	Whisper (Medium)	Whisper (Small)	SOTA	Delta
ASR	Read Speech	WER	**23.51**	27.88	36.90	16.94	-6.57
ASR	Broadcast	WER	**27.97**	35.57	42.57	18.59	-9.38

Table 3: Performance Metrix of ASR for Whisper Large, Medium and Small Models Compared to SOTA.

3 Results and Discussion

The results on text processing tasks of our experimentation have been summarized in Figure 1. The Figure presents a grid of bar graphs for each NLP task, with the y-axis showing evaluation metrics specific to each task. For classification and detection tasks, the y-axis represents the macro F1 score. For summarization tasks, it shows the average ROUGE-2 score, while for machine translation tasks, it displays the BLEU score. Each model is represented by a distinct color bar , as indicated in the Figure's legend, which is kept consistent across all tasks, with the bar of SOTA providing a reference point for comparison. Missing bars in certain tasks indicate that the model outputs were effectively zero (e.g., in Table 2 value is 2.49e-78 for Llama 2 on the Machine Translation (Quran) task, and 1.31e-78 for Mistral 8B on the Machine Translation (Bible) task), reflecting negligible performance.

Our results show that LLMs differ in their applicability to different data regimes and tasks. LLM models were able to surpassed the SOTA model for news categorization with GPT 3.5 and Llama 3.1 for Extractive Summarization. In all other experiments, LLMs remained lower than the SOTA models (reference Table 2). Across all experiments, Llama 3.1 outperformed in 10 of the 17 tasks, while GPT-3.5 excelled in 8 tasks. In comparison, Bloomz and Ministral 8B each led in only one task. The minimum delta obtained was 0.05 between GPT 3.5 and SOTA model for threat detection task. In comparison with other the open LLMs, Llama 3.1 performed better in majority of the NLP tasks which is due to its extensive multilingual data, architecture and advanced training techniques, enabling it to effectively generalize across languages and tasks.

In choice and evaluation of LLMs, Bloomz 3B and Bloomz 7B1 were initially chosen for experimentation due to their early introduction and multilingual capabilities. However, they have not kept pace with advancements seen in other models like Llama. Analysis reveals that there is no significant performance efficiency gained from transitioning from Bloomz-3B to Bloomz-7B1 as evident from Table 2. In contrast, the performance of Llama models has notably improved, particularly from Llama 2 to Llama 3.1, indicating a more effective evolution in their design and capabilities.

Based on our evaluations, the top two performing models for NLP tasks are GPT-3.5 and Llama 3.1 with comparable performances as evident from Figure 1. Llama 3.1 outperformed GPT 3.5 in 11 NLP tasks and was even better than SOTA in Extractive Summarization. On the other hand, GPT 3.5 was better than Llama 3.1 in 8 tasks and surpassed SOTA in News Categorization task. Llama 3.1's superior performance is due to the increased coverage of Non-English data in the model as well as increased amount of pretraining data i.e. 15 trillion tokens.

The performance of Ministral 8B is comparable to GPT 3.5 and Llama 3.1. It outperformed GPT 3.5 in 6 NLP Tasks i.e. Intent Detection, Propaganda Detection, Abusive Language Detection, Fake News Detection, Multi Label Emotion Classification and Emotion Classification. And outperformed Llama 3.1 in News Categorization and it was best among all models in Emotion Classification. However its performance was quite inadequate on generation tasks like Machine Translation (reference Figure 1). Overall its performance is good in detection tasks and is attributed to its interleaved sliding-window attention mechanism, which enables it to efficiently handle extended contexts with reduced memory usage. Detection tasks such as Fake News Detection and Propaganda Detection often require recognizing patterns across longer texts. This enhanced ability to retain and utilize extended contextual information allowed Ministral 8B to excel in detection tasks.

The results of Speech Processing tasks are summarized in Table 3. The analysis of the results indicates that the SOTA models, which were trained

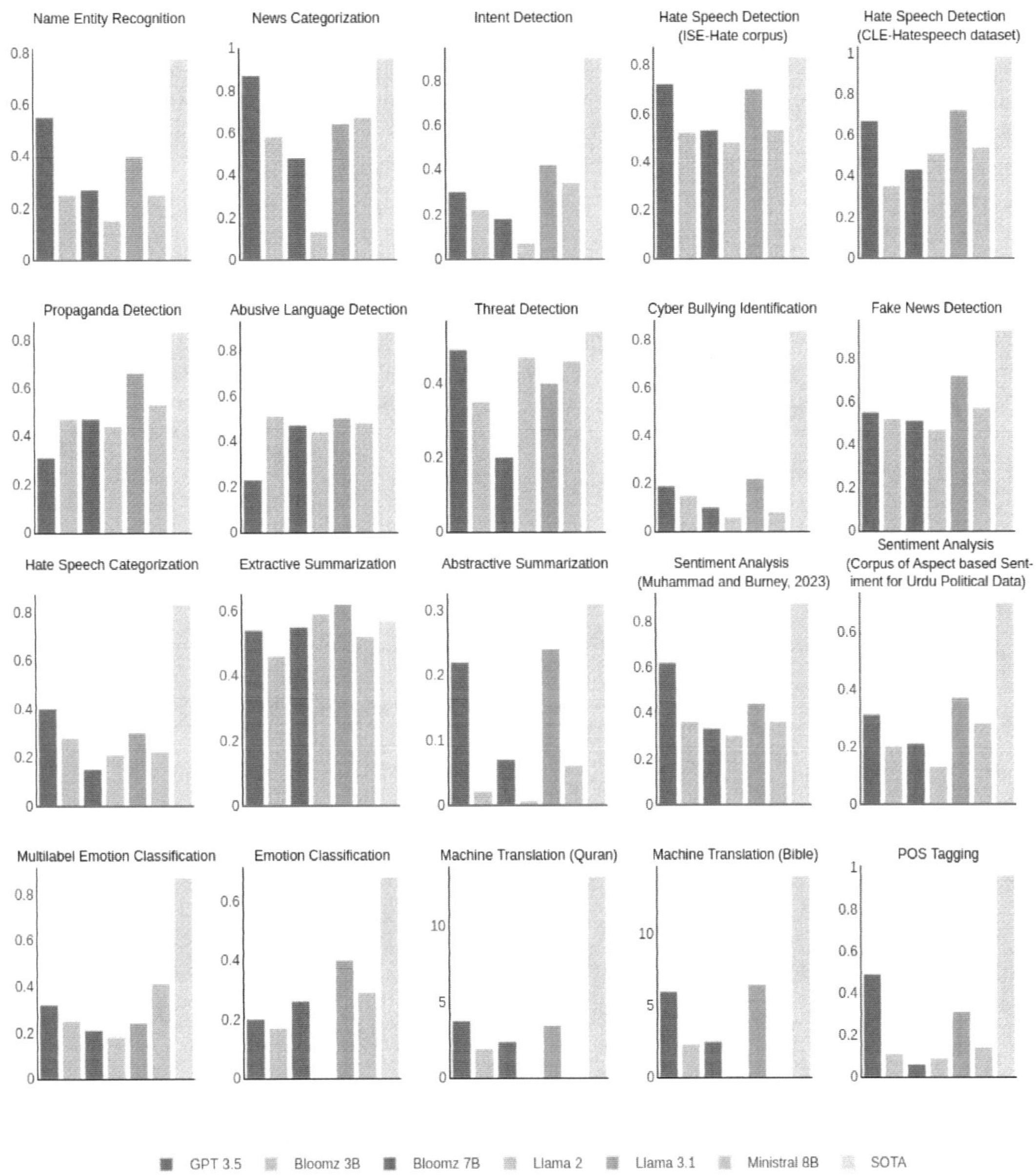

Figure 1: The performance of different models in zero-shot scenario as compared to SOTA. Missing bars in some tasks mean that the specific model cannot perform the specified task.

on a larger corpus of Urdu data, outperformed all variants of the Whisper model across the evaluated datasets. These findings suggest that while the SOTA models trained on more extensive Urdu datasets exhibited superior performance, the larger variant of the Whisper also demonstrated improved performance compared to its medium and small counterpart, underscoring the importance of model size and complexity in ASR tasks. The negative delta values indicate that the model's performance falls below the SOTA benchmarks, highlighting a gap to be addressed.

Error analysis of the LLMs' output against the ground truth revealed two main factors that account for the decline in overall F1 scores of LLMs. The factors include i) discrepancies in the output format, where the output contained extra or omitted tokens, and ii) the generation of out-of-scope labels. These observations imply that the seamless deployment of LLMs may be challenging, requiring substantial efforts either in formulating precise prompts for accurate outputs or engaging in post-processing to align the outputs with reference labels.

Thus, performance of LLMs significantly depends on well-curated prompts and intelligent post-processing of the outputs. While Llama 2 and Bloomz show a notable performance deficit compared to the SOTA, the newer Llama version i.e. Llama 3.1 and GPT 3.5 succeeds in mitigating this gap to a considerable extent.

4 Conclusion and Future Work

In this study, we benchmark the potential of both open and closed LLMs on 17 Urdu NLP tasks employing a substantial number of publicly accessible datasets. Through our experiments we provide a comparative performance analysis for each task and dataset against the SOTA. These findings will assist the Urdu NLP community in selecting suitable models for usage and fine-tuning within specific contexts. As future work, we aim to develop a public leader board for Urdu benchmarking and explore integration of additional models, tasks, and datasets. Also, after evaluating multiple models, we are focusing on pretraining Llama 3.1 to enhance Urdu language support and expand token coverage for greater adaptability across diverse languages and domains. This will also includes domain-specific fine-tuning to further boost performance, leveraging Llama 3.1's compact size, active community, and robust results.

Limitations

Our study is confined to seven LLMs and does not include the heavier versions of models such as Bloomz-170B or Llama 3.1 405B due to hardware and computational resource limitations which may impact the comprehensiveness of the analysis. This limitation may affect the generalization of the findings to models with higher parameters, potentially missing insights into the performance of more robust versions of these language models. Our study also primarily concentrates on evaluating the models in a zero-shot setting. While this setting provides valuable insights into the models' out-of-the-box performance, it may not capture the full potential of fine-tuned models for specific tasks. Our study also does not extensively delve into the quality and representativeness of the training data for Urdu language used in these models.

Acknowledgments

We would like to express our sincere gratitude to Dr. Miriam Butt for allowing us to utilize the infrastructure at the University of Konstanz for our benchmarking experiments. Additionally, we extend our acknowledgment to Miss Ayesha Khalid for supplying the ASR dataset and corresponding SOTA techniques.

References

Ahmed Abdelali, Hamdy Mubarak, Shammur Absar Chowdhury, Maram Hasanain, Basel Mousi, Sabri Boughorbel, Yassine El Kheir, Daniel Izham, Fahim Dalvi, Majd Hawasly, Nizi Nazar, Yousseif Elshahawy, Ahmed Ali, Nadir Durrani, Natasa Milic-Frayling, and Firoj Alam. 2024. Larabench: Benchmarking arabic ai with large language models.

Farah Adeeba, Muhammad Irfan Yousuf, Izza Anwer, Sardar Umair Tariq, Abdullah Ashfaq, and Malik Naqeeb. 2024. Addressing cyberbullying in urdu tweets: a comprehensive dataset and detection system. *PeerJ Comput. Sci.*, 10:e1963.

Tafseer Ahmed, Saba Urooj, Sarmad Hussain, Asad Mustafa, Rahila Parveen, Farah Adeeba, Annette Hautli, and Miriam Butt. 2014. The cle urdu pos tagset.

Kabir Ahuja, Harshita Diddee, Rishav Hada, Millicent Ochieng, Krithika Ramesh, Prachi Jain, Akshay Nambi, Tanuja Ganu, Sameer Segal, Maxamed Axmed, Kalika Bali, and Sunayana Sitaram. 2023. Mega: Multilingual evaluation of generative ai.

AI@Meta. 2024. Llama 3 model card.

Muhammad Akram, Khurram Shahzad, and Maryam Bashir. 2023. Ise-hate: A benchmark corpus for inter-faith, sectarian, and ethnic hatred detection on social media in urdu. *Information Processing & Management*, 60.

Muhammad Ali, Ehsan Ul Haq, Sahar Rauf, Kashif Javed, and Sarmad Hussain. 2021. Improving hate speech detection of urdu tweets using sentiment analysis. *IEEE Access*, PP:1–1.

Noman Ashraf, lal khan, Sabur Butt, Hsien-Tsung Chang, Grigori Sidorov, and Alexander Gelbukh. 2022. Multi-label emotion classification of urdu tweets. *PeerJ Computer Science*, 8:e896.

Muhammad Farrukh Bashir, Abdul Rehman Javed, Muhammad Umair Arshad, Thippa Reddy Gadekallu, Waseem Shahzad, and Mirza Omer Beg. 2023. Context-aware emotion detection from low-resource urdu language using deep neural network. *ACM Trans. Asian Low-Resour. Lang. Inf. Process.*, 22(5).

Ning Bian, Xianpei Han, Le Sun, Hongyu Lin, Yaojie Lu, and Ben He. 2023. Chatgpt is a knowledgeable but inexperienced solver: An investigation of commonsense problem in large language models.

BigScienceWorkshop and et al. 2023. Bloom: A 176b-parameter open-access multilingual language model.

Rishi Bommasani, Drew A. Hudson, Ehsan Adeli, Russ B. Altman, Simran Arora, Sydney von Arx, Michael S. Bernstein, Jeannette Bohg, Antoine Bosselut, Emma Brunskill, Erik Brynjolfsson, Shyamal Buch, Dallas Card, Rodrigo Castellon, Niladri S. Chatterji, Annie S. Chen, Kathleen Creel, Jared Quincy Davis, Dorottya Demszky, Chris Donahue, Moussa Doumbouya, Esin Durmus, Stefano Ermon, John Etchemendy, Kawin Ethayarajh, Li Fei-Fei, Chelsea Finn, Trevor Gale, Lauren Gillespie, Karan Goel, Noah D. Goodman, Shelby Grossman, Neel Guha, Tatsunori Hashimoto, Peter Henderson, John Hewitt, Daniel E. Ho, Jenny Hong, Kyle Hsu, Jing Huang, Thomas Icard, Saahil Jain, Dan Jurafsky, Pratyusha Kalluri, Siddharth Karamcheti, Geoff Keeling, Fereshte Khani, Omar Khattab, Pang Wei Koh, Mark S. Krass, Ranjay Krishna, Rohith Kuditipudi, and et al. 2021. On the opportunities and risks of foundation models. *CoRR*, abs/2108.07258.

Mithun Das, Somnath Banerjee, and Punyajoy Saha. 2021. Abusive and threatening language detection in urdu using boosting based and BERT based models: A comparative approach. *CoRR*, abs/2111.14830.

Paul Ekman. 1999. *Basic Emotions*, chapter 3. John Wiley & Sons, Ltd.

Muhammad Farooq, Farah Adeeba, Sahar Rauf, and Sarmad Hussain. 2019. Improving large vocabulary urdu speech recognition system using deep neural networks. pages 2978–2982.

Amr Hendy, Mohamed Abdelrehim, Amr Sharaf, Vikas Raunak, Mohamed Gabr, Hitokazu Matsushita, Young Jin Kim, Mohamed Afify, and Hany Awadalla. 2023. How good are gpt models at machine translation? a comprehensive evaluation.

Muhammad Humayoun and Naheed Akhtar. 2022. Corpures: Benchmark corpus for urdu extractive summaries and experiments using supervised learning. *Intelligent Systems with Applications*, 16:200129.

Bushra Jawaid and Daniel Zeman. 2011. Word-order issues in english-to-urdu statistical machine translation. *The Prague Bulletin of Mathematical Linguistics*, 95.

Safia Kanwal, Kamran Malik, Khurram Shahzad, Faisal Aslam, and Zubair Nawaz. 2019. Urdu named entity recognition: Corpus generation and deep learning applications.

Soufia Kausar, Bilal Tahir, and Amir Mehmood. 2020. Prosoul: A framework to identify propaganda from online urdu content.

E. Khan, S. Rauf, F. Adeeba, and S. Hussain. 2021. A multi-genre urdu broadcast speech recognition system. In *Proceedings of The O-COCOSDA 2021*, Singapore.

Sajid Khan, Mehmoon Anwar, Huma Ayub, Farooq Ali, and Marriam Nawaz. 2023. Fake news classification using machine learning: Count vectorizer and support vector machine. *Journal of Computing & Biomedical Informatics*, 4.

Hugo Laurençon, Lucile Saulnier, Thomas Wang, Christopher Akiki, Albert Villanova del Moral, Teven Le Scao, Leandro Von Werra, Chenghao Mou, Eduardo González Ponferrada, Huu Nguyen, Jörg Frohberg, Mario Šaško, Quentin Lhoest, Angelina McMillan-Major, Gerard Dupont, Stella Biderman, Anna Rogers, Loubna Ben allal, Francesco De Toni, Giada Pistilli, Olivier Nguyen, Somaieh Nikpoor, Maraim Masoud, Pierre Colombo, Javier de la Rosa, Paulo Villegas, Tristan Thrush, Shayne Longpre, Sebastian Nagel, Leon Weber, Manuel Muñoz, Jian Zhu, Daniel Van Strien, Zaid Alyafeai, Khalid Almubarak, Minh Chien Vu, Itziar Gonzalez-Dios, Aitor Soroa, Kyle Lo, Manan Dey, Pedro Ortiz Suarez, Aaron Gokaslan, Shamik Bose, David Adelani, Long Phan, Hieu Tran, Ian Yu, Suhas Pai, Jenny Chim, Violette Lepercq, Suzana Ilic, Margaret Mitchell, Sasha Alexandra Luccioni, and Yacine Jernite. 2023. The bigscience roots corpus: A 1.6tb composite multilingual dataset.

Percy Liang, Rishi Bommasani, Tony Lee, Dimitris Tsipras, Dilara Soylu, Michihiro Yasunaga, Yian Zhang, Deepak Narayanan, Yuhuai Wu, Ananya Kumar, Benjamin Newman, Binhang Yuan, Bobby Yan, Ce Zhang, Christian Cosgrove, Christopher D. Manning, Christopher Ré, Diana Acosta-Navas, Drew A. Hudson, Eric Zelikman, Esin Durmus, Faisal Ladhak, Frieda Rong, Hongyu Ren, Huaxiu Yao, Jue Wang, Keshav Santhanam, Laurel Orr, Lucia Zheng, Mert Yuksekgonul, Mirac Suzgun, Nathan Kim, Neel Guha, Niladri Chatterji, Omar Khattab, Peter Henderson, Qian Huang, Ryan Chi, Sang Michael Xie, Shibani Santurkar, Surya Ganguli, Tatsunori Hashimoto, Thomas Icard, Tianyi Zhang, Vishrav Chaudhary, William Wang, Xuechen Li, Yifan Mai, Yuhui Zhang, and Yuta Koreeda. 2023. Holistic evaluation of language models.

Junling Liu, Chao Liu, Peilin Zhou, Qichen Ye, Dading Chong, Kang Zhou, Yueqi Xie, Yuwei Cao, Shoujin Wang, Chenyu You, and Philip S. Yu. 2023. Llmrec: Benchmarking large language models on recommendation task.

Mistral AI Team. 2024. Un ministral, des ministraux. Accessed: 2024-10-29.

Niklas Muennighoff, Thomas Wang, Lintang Sutawika, Adam Roberts, Stella Biderman, Teven Le Scao, M Saiful Bari, Sheng Shen, Zheng-Xin Yong, Hailey Schoelkopf, Xiangru Tang, Dragomir Radev, Alham Fikri Aji, Khalid Almubarak, Samuel Albanie, Zaid Alyafeai, Albert Webson, Edward Raff, and Colin Raffel. 2023. Crosslingual generalization through multitask finetuning.

Khalid Bin Muhammad and S. M. Aqil Burney. 2023. Innovations in urdu sentiment analysis using machine and deep learning techniques for two-class classification of symmetric datasets. *Symmetry*, 15(5).

OpenAI and et al. 2023. Gpt-4 technical report.

Alec Radford, Jong Wook Kim, Tao Xu, Greg Brockman, Christine McLeavey, and Ilya Sutskever. 2022. Robust speech recognition via large-scale weak supervision.

Bareera Sadia, Farah Adeeba, Sana Shams, and Kashif Javed. 2024. Meeting the challenge: A benchmark corpus for automated urdu meeting summarization. *Information Processing & Management*, 61(4):103734.

Sana Shams and Muhammad Aslam. 2022. Improving user intent detection in urdu web queries with capsule net architectures. *Applied Sciences*, 12:11861.

Muhammad Sharjeel, Rao Nawab, and Paul Rayson. 2017. Counter: corpus of urdu news text reuse. *Language Resources and Evaluation*, 51.

Aarohi Srivastava, Abhinav Rastogi, Abhishek Rao, Abu Awal Md Shoeb, Abubakar Abid, Adam Fisch, Adam R. Brown, Adam Santoro, Aditya Gupta, Adrià Garriga-Alonso, Agnieszka Kluska, Aitor Lewkowycz, Akshat Agarwal, Alethea Power, Alex Ray, Alex Warstadt, Alexander W. Kocurek, Ali Safaya, Ali Tazarv, Alice Xiang, Alicia Parrish, Allen Nie, Aman Hussain, Amanda Askell, Amanda Dsouza, Ambrose Slone, Ameet Rahane, Anantharaman S. Iyer, Anders Andreassen, Andrea Madotto, Andrea Santilli, B. Ryan Roberts, Bao Sheng Loe, Barret Zoph, Bartłomiej Bojanowski, Batuhan Özyurt, Behnam Hedayatnia, Behnam Neyshabur, Benjamin Inden, Benno Stein, Berk Ekmekci, Hana Galijasevic, Hannah Kim, Hannah Rashkin, Hannaneh Hajishirzi, Harsh Mehta, Hayden Bogar, Henry Shevlin, Hinrich Schütze, Hiromu Yakura, Hongming Zhang, Hugh Mee Wong, Ian Ng, Isaac Noble, Jaap Jumelet, Jack Geissinger, Jackson Kernion, Jacob Hilton, Jaehoon Lee, Jaime Fernández Fisac, James B. Simon, James Koppel, James Zheng, James Zou, Jan Kocoń, Jana Thompson, Janelle Wingfield, Jared Kaplan, Jarema Radom, Noah Fiedel, Nuan Wen, Oliver Zhang, Omar Agha, Omar Elbaghdadi, Omer Levy, Owain Evans, Pablo Antonio Moreno Casares, Parth Doshi, Pascale Fung, Paul Pu Liang, Paul Vicol, Pegah Alipoormolabashi, Peiyuan Liao, Percy Liang, Peter Chang, Peter Eckersley, Phu Mon Htut, Pinyu Hwang, Piotr Miłkowski, Piyush Patil, Pouya Pezeshkpour, Priti Oli, Qiaozhu Mei, Qing Lyu, Qinlang Chen, Rabin Banjade, Rachel Etta Rudolph, Raefer Gabriel, Rahel Habacker, Ramon Risco, Raphaël Millière, Rhythm Garg, Richard Barnes, Rif A. Saurous, Riku Arakawa, Robbe Raymaekers, Robert Frank, Rohan Sikand, Roman Novak, Roman Sitelew, Ronan LeBras, Rosanne Liu, Rowan Jacobs, Rui Zhang, Ruslan Salakhutdinov, Ryan Chi, Ryan Lee, Ryan Stovall, Ryan Teehan, et al. 2023. Beyond the imitation game: Quantifying and extrapolating the capabilities of language models.

Hugo Touvron, Louis Martin, Kevin Stone, Peter Albert, Amjad Almahairi, Yasmine Babaei, Nikolay Bashlykov, Soumya Batra, Prajjwal Bhargava, Shruti Bhosale, Dan Bikel, Lukas Blecher, Cristian Canton Ferrer, Moya Chen, Guillem Cucurull, David Esiobu, Jude Fernandes, Jeremy Fu, Wenyin Fu, Brian Fuller, Cynthia Gao, Vedanuj Goswami, Naman Goyal, Anthony Hartshorn, Saghar Hosseini, Rui Hou, Hakan Inan, Marcin Kardas, Viktor Kerkez, Madian Khabsa, Isabel Kloumann, Artem Korenev, Punit Singh Koura, Marie-Anne Lachaux, Thibaut Lavril, Jenya Lee, Diana Liskovich, Yinghai Lu, Yuning Mao, Xavier Martinet, Todor Mihaylov, Pushkar Mishra, Igor Molybog, Yixin Nie, Andrew Poulton, Jeremy Reizenstein, Rashi Rungta, Kalyan Saladi, Alan Schelten, Ruan Silva, Eric Michael Smith, Ranjan Subramanian, Xiaoqing Ellen Tan, Binh Tang, Ross Taylor, Adina Williams, Jian Xiang Kuan, Puxin Xu, Zheng Yan, Iliyan Zarov, Yuchen Zhang, Angela Fan, Melanie Kambadur, Sharan Narang, Aurelien Rodriguez, Robert Stojnic, Sergey Edunov, and Thomas Scialom. 2023. Llama 2: Open foundation and fine-tuned chat models.

Ehsan ul Haq, Sahar Rauf, Sarmad Hussain, and Kashif Javed. 2020. Corpus of aspect-based sentiment for urdu political data.

Saba Urooj, Sana Shams, Sarmad Hussain, and Farah Adeeba. 2014. Sense tagged cle urdu digest corpus.

Ashish Vaswani, Noam Shazeer, Niki Parmar, Jakob Uszkoreit, Llion Jones, Aidan N. Gomez, Lukasz Kaiser, and Illia Polosukhin. 2017. Attention is all you need. *CoRR*, abs/1706.03762.

Ming Zhong, Da Yin, Tao Yu, Ahmad Zaidi, Mutethia Mutuma, Rahul Jha, Ahmed Hassan Awadallah, Asli Celikyilmaz, Yang Liu, Xipeng Qiu, and Dragomir Radev. 2021. QMSum: A new benchmark for query-based multi-domain meeting summarization. In *Proceedings of the 2021 Conference of the North American Chapter of the Association for Computational Linguistics: Human Language Technologies*, pages 5905–5921, Online. Association for Computational Linguistics.

A Appendix

A.1 Prompts - Name Entity Recognition

A.1.1 Bloomz

Perform Name Entity Recognition for the words using the following technique: - Mark names, nicknames, cast, family, and relational names as Person. - Mark names of companies, media groups, teams, and political parties as Organization. - Mark all man-made structures and politically defined locations, such as names of countries, cities, and places like railway stations, as Location. - Mark all remaining words, such as prepositions, adjectives, adverbs, and names of books and movies, as Other. No explanation is required. Just output the Entity name.Word: Entity:

A.1.2 GPT 3.5

Perform Name Entity Recognition corresponding to each word using the following annotation technique: Person : name,nickname,cast,family,relational names and titles. God's name should NOT be marked as Person. Organization : name of company, media group, team,political party. Name of product or brand should NOT be marked as Organization. Location : all man-made structures and politically defined locations such as names of countries,city and places like railway station etc. A generic reference to location should NOT be marked as Location. Other : all remaining words, such as prepositions, adjectives, adverbs, names of books and movies etc. No explanation is required. Just output the tag name. word =

A.1.3 Llama 2

You are Performing Name Entity Recognition for the urdu words.«/SYS» Human: Word: Please select one of the following entity: Person Organization Location Other No explanation or further assistance is required. Only entity name is required Assistant: The entity is

A.1.4 Llama 3.1

You are a name entity recognition model. Your task is to mark the entity as Person, Organization, Location, or Other in Urdu text samples. Ensure that your outputs are Person, Organization, Location, or Other. No explanation is required.

A.1.5 Ministral 8B

Perform Name Entity Recognition for the words using the following technique: - Mark names, nicknames, cast, family, and relational names as Person. - Mark names of companies, media groups, teams, and political parties as Organization. - Mark all man-made structures and politically defined locations, such as names of countries, cities, and places like railway stations, as Location. - Mark all remaining words, such as prepositions, adjectives, adverbs, and names of books and movies, as Other. No explanation is required. Just output the Entity name.Word: Entity:

A.2 Prompts - News Categorization

A.2.1 Bloomz

News: Classify the given news into one of the following category 0. sports 1. national 2. foreign 3. showbiz 4. business Choose the best suited label from above. Your output should be 0-4 only. No explanation. Only 0-4. No other label or additional text. Label (0,1,2,3,4):

A.2.2 GPT 3.5

News: Classify the given news into one of the following category 0. sports 1. national 2. foreign 3. showbiz 4. business Choose the best suited label from above. Your output should be the name of the category only. No explanation.No other label or additional text. Category:

A.2.3 Llama 2

Provide the label of the above news from the following: 0. sports 1. national 2. foreign 3. showbiz 4. business No explanation. Please answer in numbers News : Answer:

A.2.4 Llama 3.1

News: Classify the given news into one of the following category 0. sports 1. national 2. foreign 3. showbiz 4. business Choose the best suited label from above. Your output should be 0-4 only. No explanation. Only 0-4. No other label or additional text. Label (0,1,2,3,4):

A.2.5 Ministral 8B

News: Classify the given news into one of the following category 0. sports 1. national 2. foreign 3. showbiz 4. business Choose the best suited label from above. Your output should be 0-4 only. No explanation. Only 0-4. No other label or additional text. Label (0,1,2,3,4):

A.3 Prompts - Intent Detection

A.3.1 Bloomz

You are an intent classification model. Your task is to identify the intent in the following urdu sentence. Intents are: 0. Informational 1. Navigational 2. Transitional Output (0,1,2):

A.3.2 GPT 3.5

"system": "You are an intent detection classification model. You are an intent classification model. Your task is to identify the intent in the following urdu sentence. Intents are: 0. Informational 1. Navigational 2. Transitional Output (0,1,2):

A.3.3 Llama 2

You are an intent classification model. Your task is to identify the intent in the following urdu sentence. Intents are: 0. Informational 1. Navigational 2.

Transitional Dont write any explanation or reason for answer. Output (0,1,2):

A.3.4 Llama 3.1

You are an intent classification model. Your task is to mark the intent as 0 or 1 or 2 in Urdu text samples. Ensure that the model outputs '0' for Informational intent , '1' for Navigational intent and '2' for Transitional intent. Ensure that your outputs 0 or 1 or 2 only. No explanation is required.

A.3.5 Ministral 8B

You are an intent classification model. Your task is to identify the intent in the following urdu sentence. Intents are: Informational Navigational Transitional Only output the name of the intent. No explanation is required.

A.4 Prompts - Hate Speech Detection ISE-Hate corpus

A.4.1 Bloomz

Classify the hate sentence into the category it falls: Ethnic Interfaith Sectarian Other Output "0" for Other, "1" for "Sectarian", "2" for "Interfaith" and "3" for "Ethnic" Sentence: Class:

A.4.2 GPT 3.5

"system": "You are an expert in detecting hate speech in the urdu samples " Classify the hate sentence into the category it falls: Ethnic Interfaith Sectarian Other Output "0" for Other, "1" for "Sectarian", "2" for "Interfaith" and "3" for "Ethnic". No explanation is required Sentence: Output (0,1,2,3):

A.4.3 Llama 2

You are a hate speech classification model. Labels: 1: Sectarian hate 2: Interfaith hate 3: Ethnic hate 0: None of the above Instructions: To distinguish between hate speech and non-hate speech in text samples. Ensure that the model outputs "1" for hate related to "Sectarian", "2" for hate related to "Interfaith" and "3" for hate related to "Ethnic" and "0" if you think it does not fall in these three categories. Your output should be only 0, 1, 2 or 3. No explanation is required. Sentence: Label(0,1,2,3):

A.4.4 Llama 3.1

You are a hate speech classification model. Your task is to mark 0 or 1 or 2 or 3 in Urdu text samples. Ensure that the model outputs '1' for Sectarian hate text , '2' for Interfaith hate text , '3' for Ethnic hate text and '0' for any other hate text. Ensure that your outputs 0 or 1 or 2 or 3 only. No explanation is required.

A.4.5 Ministral 8B

You are a hate speech classification model. Labels: 1: Sectarian hate 2: Interfaith hate 3: Ethnic hate 0: None of the above Instructions: To distinguish between hate speech and non-hate speech in text samples. Ensure that the model output "1" for hate related to "Sectarian", "2" for hate related to "Interfaith" and "3" for hate related to "Ethnic" and "0" if you think it does not fall in these three categories. Your output should be only 0, 1, 2 or 3. No explanation is required. Sentence: Label(0,1,2,3):

A.5 Prompts - Hate Speech Detection CLE corpus

A.5.1 Bloomz

Classify the sentence as hate speech or non-hate speech. Output "1" for non-hate speech and "-1" for hate speech. No explanation is required. Sentence: Output(1 or -1):

A.5.2 GPT 3.5

"system": "You are an expert in detecting hate speech in the urdu samples" Classify the sentence as hate speech or non-hate speech. Output "1" for non-hate speech and "-1" for hate speech. No explanation is required. Sentence:

A.5.3 Llama 2

You are a hate speech classification model. Labels: 1: Non-hate speech -1: Hate speech Instructions: To distinguish between hate speech and non-hate speech in text samples. Ensure that the model outputs 1 for non-hate speech and -1 for hate speech. Your output should be only 1 or -1. No explanation is required Sentence: Label(1 or -1):

A.5.4 Llama 3.1

You are a hate speech classification model. Your task is to mark 0 or 1 in Urdu text samples. Ensure that the model outputs '0' for Non-hate text and '1' for Hate text. Ensure that your outputs 0 or 1 only. No explanation is required.

A.5.5 Ministral 8B

You are a hate speech classification model. Labels: 0: Non-hate speech 1: Hate speech Instructions: To distinguish between hate speech and non-hate speech in text samples. Ensure that the model outputs 0 for non-hate speech and 1 for hate speech. Your output should be only 0 or 1 Sentence: Label:

A.6 Prompts - Propaganda Detection

A.6.1 Bloomz

Classify the article as Propaganda or Non-Propaganda. Output '1' for Propaganda and '0' for Non-Propaganda. Don't concatenate input with output. No explanation is required. The article is: . Class(0 or 1):

A.6.2 GPT 3.5

Classify the article as Propaganda or Non-Propaganda. Output '1' for Propaganda and '0' for Non-Propaganda. No explanation is required. The article is: . Class(0 or 1):

A.6.3 Llama 2

Classify the article as Propaganda or Non-Propaganda. Output '1' for Propaganda and '0' for Non-Propaganda. Don't concatenate input with output. No explanation is required. The article is: . Class(0 or 1):

A.6.4 Llama 3.1

Classify the article as Propaganda or Non-Propaganda. Output '1' for Propaganda and '0' for Non-Propaganda. Don't concatenate input with output. No explanation is required. The article is: . Class(0 or 1):

A.6.5 Ministral 8B

Classify the article as Propaganda or Non-Propaganda. Output '1' for Propaganda and '0' for Non-Propaganda. No explanation is required. The article is: . Class (0 or 1):

A.7 Prompts - Abusive Language Detection

A.7.1 Bloomz

You are an abusive language detection model. Labels: 0: non-abusive language 1: abusive language Instructions: To distinguish between abusive and non-abusive language in text samples. Ensure that the model outputs 0 for non-abusive language and 1 for abusive language. Your output should be only 0 or 1 Sentence: Label:

A.7.2 GPT 3.5

"system": "You are an expert in detecting abusive language in the urdu samples Classify the sentence as abusive language or non-abusive language. Output "1" for non-abusive language and "0" for abusive language. No explanation is required. Sentence:

A.7.3 Llama 2

You are a abusive language detection model. Labels: 0: non-abusive language 1: abusive language Instructions: To distinguish between abusive and non-abusive language in text samples. Ensure that the model outputs 0 for non-abusive language and 1 for abusive language. Your output should be only 0 or 1. No explanation Sentence: Label(0 or 1):

A.7.4 Llama 3.1

You are a abusive language detection model.

Labels:

0: non-abusive language 1: abusive language Instructions: To distinguish between abusive and non-abusive language in text samples. Ensure that the model outputs 0 for non-abusive language and 1 for abusive language. Your output should be only 0 or 1. No explanation Sentence: Label(0 or 1):

A.7.5 Ministral 8B

You are a abusive language detection model. Labels: 0: non-abusive language 1: abusive language Instructions: To distinguish between abusive and non-abusive language in text samples. Ensure that the model outputs 0 for non-abusive language and 1 for abusive language. Your output should be only 0 or 1. No explanation Sentence: Label(0 or 1):

A.8 Prompts - Threat Detection

A.8.1 Bloomz

Classify the sentence as threatening or non threatening. Output class "1" for threatening and "0" for non threatening. Sentence: Class(1 or 0):

A.8.2 GPT 3.5

system: You are an expert in detecting threat in the urdu samples Classify the sentence as threatening or non threatening. Output "1" for threatening and "0" for non threatening. Sentence: :

A.8.3 Llama 2

Classify the sentence as threatening or non threatening. Output class "1" for threatening and "0" for non threatening. No explanation required. Sentence: Output(1 or 0):

A.8.4 Llama 3.1

You are a classification model. Your job is to classify the sentences as threatening or non-threatening. Output "1" if the sentence is threatening and "0" if it is non-threatening. No explanation is required

A.8.5 Ministral 8B

Classify the sentence as threatening or non threatening. Output "1" for threatening and "0" for non threatening. No explanation is required. Sentence:

A.9 Prompts - Cyber Bullying Identification

A.9.1 Bloomz

Your task is to classify the nature of cyberbullying with one of the labels: INSULT OFFENSIVE NAMECALLING PROFANE THREAT CURSE NONE Output only label name. no explanation is required. Sentence . Output label:

A.9.2 GPT 3.5

Your task is to classify the nature of cyberbullying with one of the labels: INSULT OFFENSIVE NAMECALLING PROFANE THREAT CURSE NONE Output only label name. no explanation is required. Sentence . Output label:

A.9.3 Llama 2

You are a helpful assistant in classification of cyberbullying. You should always provide answer from given labels without explanation. «/SYS» Human: Sentence . classify the nature of cyber bullying present in sentence with one of the following label: INSULT OFFENSIVE NAMECALLING PROFANE THREAT CURSE NONE Assitant:

A.9.4 Llama 3.1

You are a cyberbullying classification model. Your task is to mark the input as INSULT or OFFENSIVE or NAMECALLING or PROFANE or THREAT or CURSE or NONE in Urdu text samples. Ensure that your output is INSULT or OFFENSIVE or NAMECALLING or PROFANE or THREAT or CURSE or NONE. No explanation is required.

A.9.5 Ministral 8B

Your task is to classify the nature of cyberbullying with one of the labels: INSULT OFFENSIVE NAMECALLING PROFANE THREAT CURSE NONE Output only label name. no explanation is required. Sentence . Output label:

A.10 Prompts - Fake News Detection

A.10.1 Bloomz

You are a fake news detection model. Labels: fake real Instructions: To distinguish between fake news and real news in text samples. Ensure that the model outputs 'fake' for fake news and 'real' for real news. No explanation is required Sentence: Label(fake or real):

A.10.2 GPT 3.5

"system": "You are an expert in detecting fake news in the urdu samples" You are a fake news detection model. Labels: fake real Instructions: To distinguish between fake news and real news in text samples. Ensure that the model outputs 'fake' for fake news and 'real' for real news. No explanation is required Sentence: Label(fake or real):

A.10.3 Llama 2

You are a fake news detection model. Labels: fake real Instructions: To distinguish between fake news and real news in text samples. Ensure that the model outputs 'fake' for fake news and 'real' for real news. No explanation is required Sentence: Label(fake or real):

A.10.4 Llama 3.1

You are a fake news detection model.Output "fake" for fake news and "real" for real news. No explanation is required.

A.10.5 Ministral 8B

You are a fake news detection model. Labels: fake real Instructions: To distinguish between fake news and real news in text samples. Ensure that the model outputs 'fake' for fake news and 'real' for real news. No explanation is required Sentence: Label(fake or real):

A.11 Prompts - Hate Speech Categorization

A.11.1 Bloomz

You are a hate speech classification model. Labels: 0: Non-hate speech 1: Hate speech Instructions: To distinguish between hate speech and non-hate speech in text samples. Ensure that the model outputs 0 for non-hate speech and 1 for hate speech. Your output should be only 0 or 1 Sentence: Label:

A.11.2 GPT 3.5

You are a hate speech classification model. Labels: 0: Non-hate speech 1: Hate speech Instructions: To distinguish between hate speech and non-hate speech in text samples. Ensure that the model outputs 0 for non-hate speech and 1 for hate speech. Your output should be only 0 or 1 Sentence:

A.11.3 Llama 2

You are a hate speech classification model. Labels: 0: Non-hate speech 1: Hate speech Instructions:

To distinguish between hate speech and non-hate speech in text samples. Ensure that the model outputs 0 for non-hate speech and 1 for hate speech. Your output should be only 0 or 1. No explanation is required Sentence: Label(0 or 1):

A.11.4 Llama 3.1

You are a hate speech classification model. Your task is to mark 0 or 1 in Urdu text samples. Ensure that the model outputs '0' for Non-hate text and '1' for Hate text. Ensure that your outputs 0 or 1 only. No explanation is required.

A.11.5 Ministral 8B

You are a hate speech classification model. Your task is to mark 1 or -1 in Urdu text samples. Ensure that the model outputs '1' for Non-hate text and '-1' for hate text. Ensure that your outputs 1 or -1 only. No explanation is required.

A.12 Prompts - Extractive Summarization

A.12.1 Bloomz

You are an extractive summarization model. Label the sentence that you considered is important for Summarization as "1". If you think sentence should not be kept for extractive summary, label it as "0". Sentence Label:

A.12.2 GPT 3.5

"system": "You are an extractive summarization model for Urdu language" You are an extractive summarization model. Label the sentence that you considered is important for Summarization as "1". If you think sentence should not be kept for extractive summary, label it as "0". Sentence Label:

A.12.3 Llama 2

Passage: For extractive summarization, should this passage be kept or discarded? Act as a summarization model. Provide answer only (0 or 1) without explanation. Answer:

A.12.4 Llama 3.1

You are an extractive summarization model. You have to decide whether the given passage should be kept or discarded for summary? Output "1" if the passage should be kept and "0" for discarding (0 or 1) without explanation

A.12.5 Ministral 8B

You are an extractive summarization model. You have to decide whether the given passage should be kept or discarded for summary? Output "1" if the passage should be kept and "0" for discarding (0 or 1) without explanation

A.13 Prompts - Abstractive Summarization

A.13.1 Bloomz

Write summary of the given Urdu meeting. Meeting: . Summary:

A.13.2 GPT 3.5

You are a summarization model. Generate summary for the given meeting minutes in Urdu. Prompt: Meeting minutes: Summary:

A.13.3 Llama 2

You are a summarization model. Your job is to summarize the urdu meeting minutes. Meeting minutes: Summary:

A.13.4 Llama 3.1

You are a summarization model. Generate the summary for the meeting minutes in Urdu.

A.13.5 Ministral 8B

You are a summarization model. Generate the summary for the meeting minutes in Urdu.

A.14 Prompts - Sentiment Analysis

A.14.1 Bloomz

Do the sentimental analysis. Output should be "pos" for positive sentence , "neu" for neutral sentence and "neg" for negative sentence. No explanation is required. Sentence: Label:

A.14.2 GPT 3.5

Do the sentiment analysis. Output should be "pos" for positive sentences , "neu" for neutral sentences and "neg" for negative sentences. No explanation is required. Sentence:

A.14.3 Llama 2

You are a helpful assistant in sentiment analysis. You should always provide answer from given labels without explanation. Human: Do the sentiment analysis. Output "neu" for neutral sentence, "pos" for positive sentence , and "neg" for negative sentence. No explanation is required. Sentence: Assistant:

A.14.4 Llama 3.1

Perform sentiment analysis. Your output should be "pos" for positive sentence , "neu" for neutral sentence and "neg" for negative sentence. No explanation is required.

A.14.5 Ministral 8B

You are a helpful assistant in sentiment analysis. You should always provide answer from given labels without explanation. Tweet: . Perform sentiment analaysis on the tweet and answer with one of the following label: -2 for Highly negative -1 for Negative 0 for Neutral 1 for Positive 2 for Highly positive No explanation is required. Output (-2,-1,0,1,2):

A.15 Prompts - Sentiment Analysis (CLE)

A.15.1 Bloomz

Your task is to perform sentiment analysis on the tweets. Labels are: -2 : Highly negative -1 : Negative 0 : Neutral 1 : Positive 2 : Highly positive Output only label name. no explanation is required. Tweet . Output label:

A.15.2 GPT 3.5

"system": "You are an expert in sentiment analysis on urdu tweets Your task is to perform sentiment analysis on the tweets. Labels are: -2 : Highly negative -1 : Negative 0 : Neutral 1 : Positive 2 : Highly positive Output only label name. no explanation is required. Tweet . Output label:

A.15.3 Llama 2

You are a helpful assistant in sentiment analysis. You should always provide answer from given labels without explanation.

Human: Tweet: . Perform sentiment analysis on the tweet and answer with one of the following label: -2 : Highly negative -1 : Negative 0 : Neutral 1 : Positive 2 : Highly positive Assitant:

A.15.4 Llama 3.1

You are a helpful assistant in performing sentiment analysis. Perform sentiment analaysis on the tweet and answer with one of the following label: -2 for Highly negative -1 for Negative 0 for Neutral 1 for Positive 2 for Highly positive Only output -2 to 2 based on the above mentioned scale. No explanation is required

A.15.5 Ministral 8B

You are a helpful assistant in performing sentiment analysis. Perform sentiment analaysis on the tweet and answer with one of the following label: -2 for Highly negative -1 for Negative 0 for Neutral 1 for Positive 2 for Highly positive Only output -2 to 2 based on the above mentioned scale. No explanation is required

A.16 Prompts - Multi-label Emotion Classification

A.16.1 Bloomz

Output the emotion or emotions(if multiple) for the sentence. Emotions: anger, disgust, fear, sadness, surprise, happiness, neutral. You can output multiple emotions as well but should only be the name of the emotions. Output:

A.16.2 GPT 3.5

Output the emotion or emotions(if multiple) for the sentence. Emotions: anger, disgust, fear, sadness, surprise, happiness, neutral. You can output multiple emotions as well but should only be the name of the emotions. Output:

A.16.3 Llama 2

Output the emotion or emotions(if multiple) for the sentence. Emotions: anger, disgust, fear, sadness, surprise, happiness, neutral. You can output multiple emotions as well but should only be the name of the emotions. Output:

A.16.4 Llama 3.1

Output the emotion or emotions(if multiple) for the sentence. Emotions: anger, disgust, fear, sadness, surprise, happiness, neutral. You can output multiple emotions as well but should only be the name of the emotions. No explanation is required.

A.16.5 Ministral 8B

Output the emotion or emotions for the paragraph. Emotions: neutral, happy, fear, sad, anger, love. Your output should only be the name of one of the emotions. Output:

A.17 Prompts - Emotion Classification

A.17.1 Bloomz

Output the emotion or emotions for the paragraph. Emotions: neutral, happy, fear, sad, anger, love. Your output should only be the name of one of the emotions. Output:

A.17.2 GPT 3.5

"system", "content": "You are an expert in emotion recognition in the urdu samples " Output the emotion or emotions for the paragraph. Emotions: neutral, happy, fear, sad, anger, love. Your output should only be the name of one of the emotions. Output:

A.17.3 Llama 2

Output the emotion or emotions for the paragraph. Emotions: neutral, happy, fear, sad, anger, love. Your output should only be the name of only one of the emotions. Output:

A.17.4 Llama 3.1

Output the emotions for the paragraph from one of the following: neutral, happy, fear, sad, anger, love. Your output should only be the name of one of the given emotions. Don't provide any other apart from these six emotions. No explanation is required

A.17.5 Ministral 8B

Output the emotions for the paragraph from one of the following: neutral, happy, fear, sad, anger, love. Your output should only be the name of one of the given emotions. Don't provide any other apart from these six emotions. No explanation is required

A.18 Prompts - Machine Translation

A.18.1 Bloomz

You are an expert translator specialized in translating texts from English to Urdu .Translate the following English sentence to Urdu:

A.18.2 GPT 3.5

"system": "You are an expert translator specialized in translating texts from English to Urdu " Translate the following English sentence to Urdu:

A.18.3 Llama 2

No explanation or notes required. Just translate. English: Urdu:

A.18.4 Llama 3.1

You are an English to Urdu translator. Translate the english sentences into Urdu. No explanation is required. Just translate into Urdu

A.18.5 Ministral 8B

You are an expert translator specialized in translating texts from English to Urdu. Translate the following English sentence to Urdu: "". Provide only the Urdu translation, without any additional text or explanations.

A.19 Prompts - POS Tagging

A.19.1 Bloomz

Your task is to tag POS in input. You will use following Taggig scheme: Tag Proper Noun as NNP ,Tag Common Noun as NN,Tag Personal pronoun as PRP,Tag Demonstrative as PDM,Tag Possessive pronouns as PRS,Tag Reflexive pronouns as PRF,Tag Reflexive Apna as APNA,Tag Relative Personal as PRR,Tag Relative Demonstrative as PRD,Tag Main Verb Infinitive as VBI,Tag Main Verb Finite as VB,Tag Aspectual auxiliaries as AUXA,Tag Progressive auxiliaries as AUXP,Tag Tense auxiliaries as AUXT,Tag Modals auxiliaries as AUXM,Tag Foreign Fragment as FF,Tag Interjection as INJ,Tag Preposition as PRE,Tag Postposition as PSP,Tag Common as SYM,Tag Punctuation as PU,Tag Common as RB,Tag Negation as NEG,Tag Common as PRT,Tag Vala as VALA,Tag Coordinate Conjunction as CC,Tag Subordinate Conjunction as SC,Tag SC Kar as SCK,Tag Presentential as SCP,Tag Ordinal as OD,Tag Fraction as FR,Tag Multiplicative as QM,Tag Adjective as JJ,Tag Quantifier as Q,Tag Cardinal as CD. Your Output should be only one tag corrosponding to input word. no explaination is required. input:

A.19.2 GPT 3.5

"system": "You are an expert in Urdu pos tagging " Your task is to tag POS in input. You will use following Taggig scheme: Tag Proper Noun as NNP ,Tag Common Noun as NN,Tag Personal pronoun as PRP,Tag Demonstrative as PDM,Tag Possessive pronouns as PRS,Tag Reflexive pronouns as PRF,Tag Reflexive Apna as APNA,Tag Relative Personal as PRR,Tag Relative Demonstrative as PRD,Tag Main Verb Infinitive as VBI,Tag Main Verb Finite as VB,Tag Aspectual auxiliaries as AUXA,Tag Progressive auxiliaries as AUXP,Tag Tense auxiliaries as AUXT,Tag Modals auxiliaries as AUXM,Tag Foreign Fragment as FF,Tag Interjection as INJ,Tag Preposition as PRE,Tag Postposition as PSP,Tag Common as SYM,Tag Punctuation as PU,Tag Common as RB,Tag Negation as NEG,Tag Common as PRT,Tag Vala as VALA,Tag Coordinate Conjunction as CC,Tag Subordinate Conjunction as SC,Tag SC Kar as SCK,Tag Presentential as SCP,Tag Ordinal as OD,Tag Fraction as FR,Tag Multiplicative as QM,Tag Adjective as JJ,Tag Quantifier as Q,Tag Cardinal as CD. Your Output should be only one tag corrosponding to input word. no explaination is required. input:

A.19.3 Llama 2

Your task is to tag POS in input. You will use following Taggig scheme: Tag Proper Noun as NNP ,Tag Common Noun as NN,Tag Personal pronoun as PRP,Tag Demonstrative as PDM,Tag Possessive pronouns as PRS,Tag Reflexive pronouns as PRF,Tag Reflexive Apna as APNA,Tag Relative Personal as PRR,Tag Relative Demonstrative as PRD,Tag Main Verb Infinitive as VBI,Tag Main Verb Finite as VB,Tag Aspectual auxiliaries as AUXA,Tag Progressive auxiliaries as AUXP,Tag Tense auxiliaries as AUXT,Tag Modals auxiliaries as AUXM,Tag Foreign Fragment as FF,Tag Interjection as INJ,Tag Preposition as PRE,Tag Postposition as PSP,Tag Common as SYM,Tag Punctuation as PU,Tag Common as RB,Tag Negation as NEG,Tag Common as PRT,Tag Vala as VALA,Tag Coordinate Conjunction as CC,Tag Subordinate Conjunction as SC,Tag SC Kar as SCK,Tag Presentential as SCP,Tag Ordinal as OD,Tag Fraction as FR,Tag Multiplicative as QM,Tag Adjective as JJ,Tag Quantifier as Q,Tag Cardinal as CD. Your Output should be only one tag corrosponding to input word. no explaination is required. input:

A.19.4 Llama 3.1

Your task is to tag POS in input. You will use following Taggig scheme: Tag Proper Noun as NNP ,Tag Common Noun as NN,Tag Personal pronoun as PRP,Tag Demonstrative as PDM,Tag Possessive pronouns as PRS,Tag Reflexive pronouns as PRF,Tag Reflexive Apna as APNA,Tag Relative Personal as PRR,Tag Relative Demonstrative as PRD,Tag Main Verb Infinitive as VBI,Tag Main Verb Finite as VB,Tag Aspectual auxiliaries as AUXA,Tag Progressive auxiliaries as AUXP,Tag Tense auxiliaries as AUXT,Tag Modals auxiliaries as AUXM,Tag Foreign Fragment as FF,Tag Interjection as INJ,Tag Preposition as PRE,Tag Postposition as PSP,Tag Common as SYM,Tag Punctuation as PU,Tag Common as RB,Tag Negation as NEG,Tag Common as PRT,Tag Vala as VALA,Tag Coordinate Conjunction as CC,Tag Subordinate Conjunction as SC,Tag SC Kar as SCK,Tag Presentential as SCP,Tag Ordinal as OD,Tag Fraction as FR,Tag Multiplicative as QM,Tag Adjective as JJ,Tag Quantifier as Q,Tag Cardinal as CD. Your Output should be only one tag corrosponding to input word. no explaination is required. input:

A.19.5 Ministral 8B

Your task is to tag POS in input. You will use following Taggig scheme: Tag Proper Noun as NNP ,Tag Common Noun as NN,Tag Personal pronoun as PRP,Tag Demonstrative as PDM,Tag Possessive pronouns as PRS,Tag Reflexive pronouns as PRF,Tag Reflexive Apna as APNA,Tag Relative Personal as PRR,Tag Relative Demonstrative as PRD,Tag Main Verb Infinitive as VBI,Tag Main Verb Finite as VB,Tag Aspectual auxiliaries as AUXA,Tag Progressive auxiliaries as AUXP,Tag Tense auxiliaries as AUXT,Tag Modals auxiliaries as AUXM,Tag Foreign Fragment as FF,Tag Interjection as INJ,Tag Preposition as PRE,Tag Postposition as PSP,Tag Common as SYM,Tag Punctuation as PU,Tag Common as RB,Tag Negation as NEG,Tag Common as PRT,Tag Vala as VALA,Tag Coordinate Conjunction as CC,Tag Subordinate Conjunction as SC,Tag SC Kar as SCK,Tag Presentential as SCP,Tag Ordinal as OD,Tag Fraction as FR,Tag Multiplicative as QM,Tag Adjective as JJ,Tag Quantifier as Q,Tag Cardinal as CD. Your Output should be only one tag corrosponding to input word. no explaination is required. input:

Bengali ChartSumm: A Benchmark Dataset and Study on Feasibility of Large Language Models on Bengali Chart to Text Summarization

Nahida Akter Tanjila, Afrin Sultana Poushi, Sazid Abdullah Farhan, Abu Raihan Mostofa Kamal, Md. Azam Hossain, Md. Hamjajul Ashmafee
NDAG Research Lab, Department of CSE,
Islamic University of Technology, Gazipur, Bangladesh
{nahidaakter, afrinsultana, sazidabdullah, raihan.kamal, azam, ashmafee}@iut-dhaka.edu

Abstract

In todays data-driven world, effectively organizing and presenting data is challenging, particularly for non-experts. Although tables organize data systematically, they often fall short in conveying intuitive insights; in contrast, charts provide clear and compelling visual summaries. Although recent advances in NLP, powered by large language models (LLMs), have primarily benefited high-resource languages such as English, low-resource languages such as Bengali spoken by millions worldwide still face significant data limitations. This research addresses this gap by introducing "Bengali ChartSumm," a benchmark dataset with 4,100 Bengali chart images, metadata, and summaries. This dataset facilitates the analysis of LLMs (mT5, BanglaT5, Gemma) in Bengali chart-to-text summarization, offering essential baselines and evaluations that enhance NLP research for low-resource languages.

1 Introduction

In today's data-driven world, enormous amounts of data are generated every second, presenting unique challenges in organizing and presenting it effectively. Although tabular formats can organize data, they are often inadequate for complex datasets, particularly for non-experts who may find it challenging to identify essential insights. This difficulty arises because tables lack intuitive trends or highlights, making it challenging to extract valuable information. To address this, various tools and methods have been developed to uncover hidden patterns in data efficiently. Among these, specialized visualizations, particularly charts, stand out as powerful tools for translating complex information. By blending numerical data, text, and visual elements, these visualizations communicate intricate information in a clear and accessible way, making data insights more understandable and impactful (Islam et al., 2021).

The emergence of deep learning-driven artificial neural networks has significantly enhanced Natural Language Processing (NLP), boosting the efficiency and accuracy of textual data processing. However, this progress has been largely limited to high-resource languages like English, which benefit from vast amounts of labeled and unlabeled data from sources such as books, social media, websites, and academic publications. This data-intensive environment allows NLP models to be more optimized for specific tasks, resulting in improved accuracy. In contrast, low-resource languages lack this support, making it challenging to develop the NLP domain due to the absence of even baseline datasets, models, and evaluation benchmarks. Essential resources like tokenizers, parsers, part-of-speech taggers, and dependency grammars are often missing or underdeveloped for these languages, and creating them from scratch requires substantial linguistic expertise and time.

Bengali is one of the most widely spoken languages in the world, with approximately one in eight people worldwide using it but research resources for this language are still scarce in comparison to its substantial population (Ekram et al., 2022). Although English has made significant advances in the field of natural language processing (NLP) in various chart-related downstream tasks such as question answering, summarization, and the mathematical analysis of chart images, Bengali and other low-resource languages are facing severe data limitations. Although Bengali speakers frequently employ Bengali charts in a variety of contexts, these constraints impede the efficient training and fine-tuning of NLP models. Text summaries, in particular, can enhance the comprehension and interpretation of charts by highlighting key elements like temporal trends, causal relationships, and evaluative aspects (Bhattacharjee et al., 2023). Given the abundant resources available in English, there is an opportunity to leverage them to address this

Proceedings of the First Workshop on Challenges in Processing South Asian Languages (CHiPSAL 2025), pages 35–45
January 19, 2025.

research gap and create data repositories that will allow domain experts to access and utilize chart data more effectively in the Bengali language.

Large Language Models (LLMs) have made remarkable progress in natural language processing (NLP), particularly in language generation and other language-centric tasks. Multimodal LLMs, specifically vision-language models trained on chart data, excel at tackling the challenges of integrating visual and textual information, making them highly effective in tasks that require comprehensive understanding across modalities. These vision-language models undergo extensive pre-training on chart-related tasks, involving multitask instructional tuning and task-specific fine-tuning, which equips them to perform well across a range of downstream tasks.

However, most of the research in this field focuses on high-resource languages such as English, leaving low-resource languages like Bengali underrepresented (Kabir et al., 2023). This lack of research and the absence of baseline models and evaluation benchmarks make it challenging to develop effective NLP models for these languages. Recently, multilingual models have been introduced to address these limitations, but they still suffer from the under-representation of low-resource languages, highlighting a significant opportunity to explore and establish robust baseline research for these languages.

To the best of our knowledge, large language models (LLMs) have not yet been specifically applied to the task of chart-to-text summarization in Bengali. This is primarily due to the lack of extensive, well-defined datasets that include chart images, metadata, and detailed summaries in Bengali. In this work, we have addressed the scarcity of public datasets in the automatic chart summarization task. We have proposed a benchmark dataset - Bengali ChartSumm comprising 4,100 chart images with corresponding chart metadata and summaries and conducted a study on large language models' feasibility on Bengali Chart Summarization. A sample from the curated dataset is shown in Figure: 1 as an example.

2 Literature Review

The task of generating descriptive summaries from non-linguistic structured data, such as tables or charts, is referred to as "chart-to-text summarization." This falls within the broader domain of natural language generation (NLG) and involves converting data visualizations (like line, bar, bubble, and pie charts) into textual descriptions. Current chart-to-text summarization systems produce summaries based either on the chart image itself (Hsu et al., 2021) or on the metadata associated with the chart (Obeid and Hoque, 2020; Kantharaj et al., 2022).

Several datasets have been developed to support research in English chart to text summarization, including SciCap (Tan et al., 2022), Chart2Text (Obeid and Hoque, 2020), AutoChart (Zhu et al., 2021), and Chart-To-Text (Kantharaj et al., 2022). These datasets vary in their formulation, ranging from table to text descriptions, image to extracted metadata using OCR to text descriptions, and system-generated short summaries to descriptive human-written summaries. The development of these datasets reflects the growing interest in exploring automatic chart summarization techniques and evaluating their performance across different types of charts and data sources (Rahman et al., 2023).

Deep learning-based techniques have recently gained substantial attention (Obeid and Hoque, 2020; Zhu et al., 2021; Kantharaj et al., 2022) due to their improved performance over traditional template-based approaches. However, the lack of datasets for chart-to-text summarization poses a significant challenge: not only do models for this task need refinement, but also their overall effectiveness has yet to be fully assessed. Most multimodal foundation models (Li et al., 2023) are focused on natural images and have achieved remarkable progress in fields like image captioning (Vinyals et al., 2015) and visual question answering (Johnson et al., 2017).

Some approaches have adapted vision-language models for chart-related tasks (Han et al., 2023) or created plugins enabling large language models (LLMs) to interpret charts (Xia et al., 2023). Transfer learning, facilitated through learned language representations in models like T5 and GPT that use transformer architectures, has become integral to NLP, allowing language models to be adapted for a range of downstream tasks (summarization, question-answering, inference, etc.) (Raffel et al., 2020). Nevertheless, challenges persist for low-resource languages, which face underrepresentation, biases, lack of required datasets for downstream tasks, and limited evaluation benchmarks for such models (Pires et al., 2019).

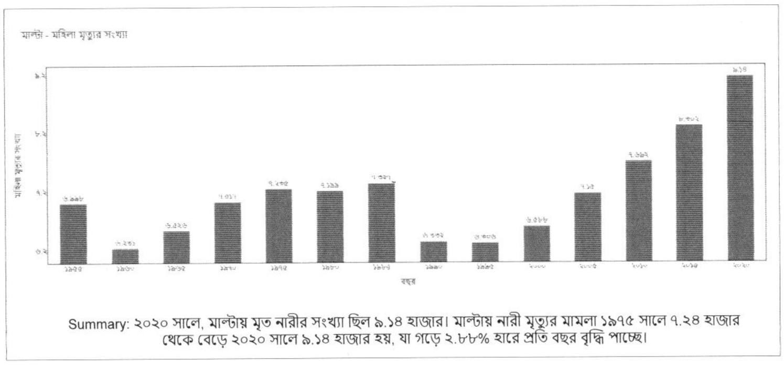

Figure 1: An example of the Bengali Chart image and corresponding summary.

3 Bengali Chart-to-text dataset

The lack of benchmark chart-to-text datasets in Bengali has compelled us to utilize language translation services for transforming existing chart-to-text datasets from resource-abundant English into Bengali, as illustrated in Figure: 2 mostly extending the work by (Rahman et al., 2023). By translating a part of their dataset to Bengali, we developed a resource tailored for Bengali language processing. Subsequently, we executed further steps to finalize the curation of this dataset, preparing it for the fine-tuning and evaluation of large language models.

3.1 Data Collection

Finding an appropriate data source is the first step in this research as it is essential to compile an extensive dataset for the low-resource Bengali language. As an available resource for summarization tasks from chart images, our first step was to utilize an English chart-to-text dataset (Rahman et al., 2023) collected from different public online repositories, including both long and short summaries. Although this repository includes bar, line, and pie charts, we chose to include only line and bar charts in our dataset for ease of curation and model fine-tuning. In our next phase, we will include pie charts and other common charts in Bengali from many more public repositories to make it diverse, realistic, and challenging for research. We started translating about 4,100 samples from the original dataset covering diverse topics while maintaining fidelity to the original content as well as ensuring linguistic and cultural accuracy. These translations included both titles and captions, indicating a substantial increase in the dataset's usefulness.

3.2 Data Annotation

Following machine translation, the annotation process was meticulously performed by human annotators (Munaf et al., 2023). We selected undergraduate students with STEM backgrounds, specifically those with strong chart analysis skills and fluency in both English and Bengali. From a group of interested candidates (19 students), we conducted a controlled assessment to evaluate one's competency in translating and analyzing charts and identify expert annotators, ultimately selecting five students based on their performance. To ensure the dataset's quality and relevance for the intended audience, random samples of their annotations were reviewed, verifying the accuracy and cultural appropriateness of translations. The use of a relatively small group of annotators from similar educational backgrounds introduces the potential for biases. To mitigate this, random quality checks were performed on their annotations to verify accuracy and cultural appropriateness. In addition, random samples of annotations were periodically reviewed to ensure that translated summaries preserved the intent and tone of the original dataset while being accessible to a Bengali-speaking audience. Some samples are shown in Appendix A.1.

3.3 Dataset Preparation

After annotating the dataset, we conducted several **data preprocessing** steps to prepare it for analysis (Meng et al., 2024). This process included cleaning the data by removing whitespace, newlines, and irrelevant content, as well as converting metadata into a format compatible with language models. Additionally, heuristic rules were applied to generate x-labels and y-labels where the originals were corrupted. In the following **tokenization**

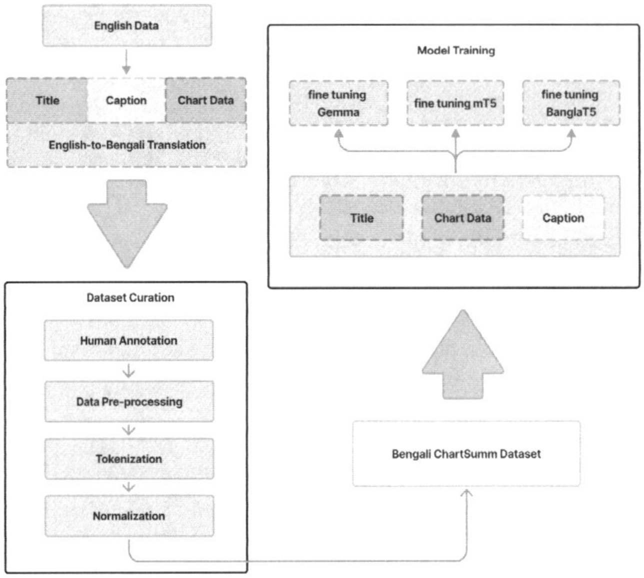

Figure 2: A comprehensive overview of this research.

LLM Models	Number of Parameters
Google/mT5-small[1]	300 Millions
BanglaT5[2]	247 Millions
Google/gemma-2b[3]	2.5 Billions[4]

Table 1: LLM models used for this experiment and corresponding number of parameters in the models.

step, we used customized tokenizers tailored to the pre-trained models (as detailed in Table 1) to stem and tokenize the text data, ensuring it was ready for subsequent analysis (Rahman et al., 2023).

Data normalization was done as Bengali words have many characters whereas English has only 26 characters. As a result, a word could have different forms having identical appearances and meanings. In Bengali, a special character "'়'" having the symbol called "Nukta" which can alter the meaning of a character depending on its inclusion or absence. Various tokenizers approach this issue differently to minimize confusion caused by multiple representations of the same word. To resolve this, we utilized a Bengali text normalizer (Hasan et al., 2020), which effectively handles these challenges, including the accurate processing of Bengali numerical entities.

[1] https://huggingface.co/google/mt5-small
[2] https://huggingface.co/csebuetnlp/banglat5
[3] https://huggingface.co/google/gemma-2-2b-it
[4] Both embedding and non-embedding parameters

3.4 Dataset Analysis

We analyzed the text length distribution which gives useful information about the dataset's features. The visualization aids in understanding the variety in text lengths among different types of content in the training data, which is critical for model tuning which is seen in Figure 3. The distribution is relatively narrow, with 50% of titles falling between 39 and 60 tokens. The histogram shows a peak in frequency of around 50 tokens, indicating that most titles are of moderate length, likely brief descriptions or names. Summaries exhibit a wider distribution, suggesting varying levels of detail in the chart descriptions. The middle 50% of summaries fall between 138 and 255 tokens. The histogram indicates a concentration of around 200 tokens, with a somewhat even spread, showing summaries are typically more detailed and descriptive than titles but less than the chart data.

In our chart dataset, text length shows the greatest variability, with an average length of approximately 586 tokens but a very high standard deviation. The histogram reveals a multi-modal distribution, with peaks around both lower and higher text lengths,

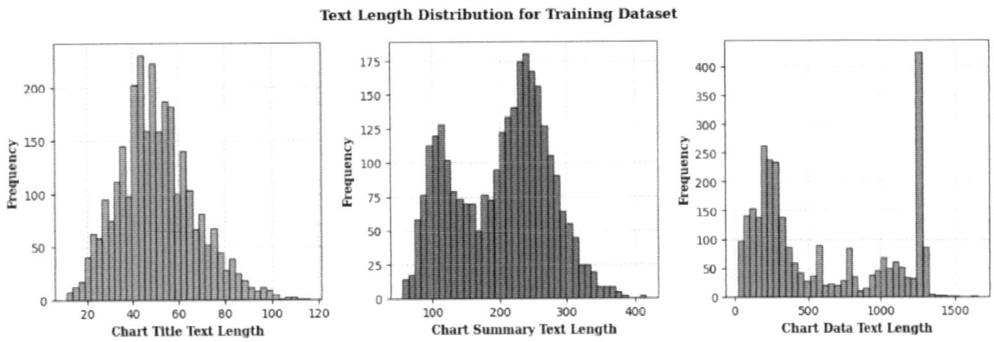

Figure 3: Visualize text length distribution for Training dataset

indicating that some charts have very concise data, while others provide extensive details, which is why we have handpicked the text with a stable and average number of tokens that will help in our model to not be over-fitting. Addressing this variability could improve the feasibility of applying LLMs to this complex task, making it an essential consideration in developing *Bengali ChartSumm* as a benchmark dataset.

4 Methodology

This section outlines the process of fine-tuning, training, and evaluating our selected models (shown in Figure: 2) for the Bengali chart-to-text summarization task. The primary focus is on the setup of the evaluation metrics and the rationale for their selection, ensuring a robust assessment framework.

4.1 Problem Formulation

The overall process of our Bengali Chart-to-Text Summarization system is shown in Figure 2. We consider the problem setting for Bengali chart summarization assuming that the underlying data table of the chart image is available. Formally, we are given a dataset with N examples $D = \{m_i, s_i\}_{i=1}^{N}$, where m_i represents the underlying metadata for a given chart image and s_i represents the target summary text for m_i. The Bengali Chart Summarization models learn to predict the summary s_i given the metadata m_i.

4.2 Model Training and Fine-tuning

Each model was fine-tuned on our prepared *Bengali ChartSumm* dataset to optimize its performance for generating Bengali text summaries from chart metadata. For this task, we utilized three models: mT5 (Xue et al., 2020), BanglaT5 (Bhattacharjee et al., 2023), and Gemma (Team et al., 2024), each with unique architectures and strengths for multilingual and Bengali text generation (listed in Table 1).

For the models mt5 and banglat5, the input format was structured as "title + chart metadata", with the output targeted as the "caption". We defined a custom PyTorch *Dataset* class, *Seq2SeqDataset*, which tokenizes and processes input data. The dataset class concatenates the chart title and chart data into a single input text sequence with the format <Title> "চার্ট তথ্য:" <Chart Data>. The summary column serves as the target sequence.

For the Gemma model, we used prompting and context to structure the dataset to get the summary as a prompt answer. We proceeded by loading the Bengali chart data, which consisted of three text files: titles, summaries, and chart data. The data was organized into a DataFrame with three columns: *title*, *summary*, and *chart_data*. We created a custom template to serve as an instruction for the model. This template was designed to instruct the model to provide chart summarization in Bengali, with a format that included the chart title, and chart data as `<input_sequence>`. The complete prompt template was like this -

```
"Instruction: Your task is to give chart
summarization in Bengali language:
(এই চার্টটি বাংলা ভাষায় সারাংশ কর):"
"Given data: চার্ট তথ্য:" <input_sequence>
"Summary: সারাংশ:"
```

Each data line was modified to add labels for the x-axis and y-axis, making it easier for the model to understand the context. A regular expression function, *modify_data_line*, was used to add these labels to the data points, creating a standardized input format. Using this template, the chart titles, data, and corresponding captions were combined into structured prompts and stored in a list format suitable for model fine-tuning.

4.3 Evaluation Metrics

To rigorously evaluate the quality of the generated summaries, we employed a set of commonly used metrics in natural language processing for summarization and translation tasks (Rahman et al., 2023; Meng et al., 2024). These metrics assess various aspects of model performance by measuring both n-gram overlaps and error rates. **BLEU** (Bilingual Evaluation Understudy) (Post, 2018) measures n-gram precision between machine-generated and reference texts, emphasizing precision to evaluate how closely the generated summaries align with the reference summaries. **ROUGE** (Recall-Oriented Understudy for Gisting Evaluation) (Lin, 2004), often used in text summarization and longer text generation tasks, focuses on recall by measuring the overlap of n-grams or sequences between machine-generated and reference texts. We report three variants of **ROUGE**: **ROUGE-1**, which assesses unigram recall; **ROUGE-2**, which evaluates bigram recall, reflecting phrase-level accuracy; and **ROUGE-L**, which captures the longest common subsequence, providing a measure of structural similarity. **CER** (Character Error Rate) (Wang et al., 2016) calculates the ratio of character-level errors (insertions, deletions, substitutions) to the total characters in the reference text, making it especially important in Bengali text generation, where small character variations can significantly alter meaning. **WER** (Word Error Rate) (Ali and Renals, 2018) measures word-level accuracy by calculating insertions, deletions, and substitutions relative to the reference text, with a lower WER indicating fewer errors in capturing the intended word sequence. Together, these metrics offer a comprehensive understanding of the models summarization quality, highlighting both precise word matching and broader structural accuracy, laying the groundwork for a thorough performance comparison of the models, which is presented in the following section.

5 Experimental Setup

To aid model training, we normalized the text input with the normalize function from the normalizer library (Hasan et al., 2020), which is specially developed for Bengali language processing. Each input sequence is tokenized with a maximum length of 256 tokens converted into PyTorch tensors. Training configurations for each model included 15 epochs, a learning rate of 1e-3, epsilon of 1e-8, weight decay of 0.01, AdamW[1] optimizer and a batch size of 16, optimized for the given dataset and task requirements. The dataset was split into a Training set: 70%, a Validation set: 10.5%, and a Test set: 19.5%. We also applied appropriate approaches for the remaining model configurations. For evaluation, we loaded the fine-tuned model and tokenizer and generated summaries for the test dataset. We used the generate function with num_beams (4) to apply beam search and set max_length (512) for generated summaries. To avoid overly short summaries, we omitted any length penalty and removed early stopping to ensure complete generation.

6 Evaluation

6.1 Results and Discussions

In this section, we analyze the performance of three distinct Large Language Models: mT5, BanglaT5, and Gemma using several key evaluation metrics. These models were tested on their ability to generate coherent and accurate text based on given reference texts. The evaluation metrics considered include ROUGE (ROUGE-1, ROUGE-2, ROUGE-L), which measures the recall of n-grams and the longest common subsequence, BLEU (Bilingual Evaluation Understudy), which focuses on n-gram precision, and two error rates: CER (Character Error Rate) and WER (Word Error Rate)which gauge the accuracy of the generated text at the character and word levels, respectively. The summary of this evaluation is shown in Table 2.

6.1.1 ROUGE Scores

BanglaT5 outperforms mT5 and Gemma in ROUGE-1, achieving a score of 0.0678 compared to mT5's 0.0422, marking a significant 63% improvement. This suggests that BanglaT5 is better at recalling individual words (unigrams) from the reference text. However, when examining ROUGE-2 and ROUGE-L, all models exhibit lower scores, indicating struggles with recalling bigrams and maintaining the overall structure of the reference text.

[1] https://pytorch.org/docs/stable/generated/torch.optim.AdamW.html

Models	Rouge-1	Rouge-2	Rouge-L	BLEU	CER ↓	WER ↓
mT5	0.0422	0.0015	0.0397	**0.2779**	**0.5295**	**0.7189**
BanglaT5	**0.0678**	**0.0016**	**0.0592**	0.0505	0.9681	1.1530
Gemma	0.0227	0.0008	0.0204	0.2153	0.7828	1.0653

Table 2: Experiment results on Large Language Models

These low scores highlight the challenges faced by the models in producing text that accurately mirrors the phrasal patterns and the longest common subsequences found in the reference material.

6.1.2 BLEU Score

In contrast to the ROUGE scores, mT5 shows a significant advantage in the BLEU score, with 0.2779 compared to BanglaT5's 0.0505 and Gemma's 0.2153. The BLEU metric emphasizes n-gram precision, suggesting that mT5 is more successful at generating text with sequences of words that exactly match those in the reference text. Despite this, the low ROUGE-L score indicates that while mT5 may produce some n-gram matches, it may still struggle with overall fluency and faithfulness to the reference text's structure.

6.1.3 CER and WER

When considering CER (Character Error Rate) and WER (Word Error Rate), BanglaT5 displays higher error rates (0.9681 for CER and 1.1530 for WER) compared to mT5 (0.5295 for CER and 0.7189 for WER) and Gemma (0.7828 for CER and 1.0653 for WER). These metrics reflect the tendency to introduce more character and word errorssuch as insertions, deletions, or substitutions when generating text, leading to a higher deviation from the reference for BanglaT5 and Gemma.

6.1.4 Overall Comparison

The comparative analysis of the models suggests a trade-off between recall and precision. BanglaT5, while better at recalling individual words, struggles with n-gram precision, fluency, and overall correctness, as evidenced by its lower BLEU score and higher error rates. On the other hand, mT5, despite its lower ROUGE-1 score, performs better in BLEU, CER, and WER, indicating fewer errors and better n-gram precision, although it may lack in producing text that fully captures the structure of the reference text. These results imply that the training data for BanglaT5 might have been less comprehensive or diverse, limiting its ability to generate text with complex phrasings and structures. While all models have their respective shortcomings, mT5 demonstrates a more balanced performance, particularly in generating summaries that are more precise and contain fewer errors. The findings underscore the importance of model training on diverse and high-quality datasets to improve the overall performance of text generation models. Appendix A.2 provides a sample summary generated by Gemma as part of a qualitative comparison.

7 Conclusion

Our study on Bengali chart-to-text summarization establishes a strong foundation for future research and development in automatic chart summarization, particularly for under-resourced languages like Bengali. The primary objectives were to create a dataset specifically designed for Bengali chart summarization and to evaluate the applicability of Large Language Models (LLMs) in this context. By addressing the resource gap and demonstrating the potential of LLMs in Bengali chart summarization, this work not only advances the field but also paves the way for further research and development. Showing the feasibility of using language models for Bengali chart-to-text summarization represents a significant step in applying these powerful models to underrepresented languages and tasks, ultimately promoting inclusivity and accessibility in NLP technology.

Future research could focus on integrating Bengali-specific Optical Character Recognition (OCR) technology to enhance the accuracy of reading both handwritten and printed Bengali text in charts, thereby expanding the scope of chart formats our dataset and models can handle. Expanding the dataset to include a broader range of common chart types (e.g., pie charts, bubble charts, etc.) could increase its diversity and complexity. Additionally, utilizing state-of-the-art large language models (LLMs), such as LLaMA and Mistral, could significantly enhance the performance of chart summarization. On the other hand, translating the dataset and models into other languages would broaden their linguistic applicability and enable cross-lingual comparisons, paving the way for universally applicable chart summarization methods. Another promising avenue is the development of interactive platforms or chatbots that use these models to provide real-time interpretation of Bengali charts, increasing accessibility for users. Despite these advancements, further work is needed to address the technical challenges associated with OCR technology tailored for Bengali and other languages.

Limitations and Ethical Considerations

While Bangla and English include various chart types, for this research, we focused on bar and line charts due to the availability of public English datasets and the relative simplicity of these chart types. Our LLM models are trained with limited resources, which restricts their efficiency in generating complex, detailed summaries. Increasing dataset diversity and sizes, along with more intensive training on state-of-the-art multimodal LLMs, could better support complex reasoning across visual and textual features, leading to improved summarization performance.

We addressed several ethical considerations during the dataset collection and annotation stages. To respect the intellectual property rights of dataset sources, we exclusively used publicly available charts that comply with their terms and conditions. Our annotators were compensated above the minimum wage in Bangladesh (12,500 taka, or approximately \$113 USD per month). Each task was estimated to take 3-5 minutes, and annotators were paid 2.5 taka (\$0.021 USD) per task. Additionally, to protect their privacy, all annotations were anonymized. For reproducibility, our experimental hyperparameter settings are provided in Section 5.

Acknowledgment

This work was supported by the supported by the Islamic University of Technology Research Seed Grants (IUT RSG) (Ref: REASP/IUT-RSG/2022/OL/07/013). We extend our sincere gratitude to our annotators for their invaluable support in creating the dataset. We are also deeply thankful to Raian Rahman and Ishmam Tashdeed, alumni of the NDAG Research Lab, for their constructive feedback. Additionally, we appreciate the thoughtful comments and suggestions from the anonymous reviewers, which greatly contributed to improving this paper.

References

Ahmed Ali and Steve Renals. 2018. Word error rate estimation for speech recognition: e-WER. In *Proceedings of the 56th Annual Meeting of the Association for Computational Linguistics (Volume 2: Short Papers)*, pages 20–24, Melbourne, Australia. Association for Computational Linguistics.

Abhik Bhattacharjee, Tahmid Hasan, Wasi Ahmad, and Rifat Shahriyar. 2023. Banglanlg and banglat5: Benchmarks and resources for evaluating low-resource natural language generation in bangla. In *Findings of the Association for Computational Linguistics: EACL 2023*, pages 714–723.

Syed Mohammed Sartaj Ekram, Adham Arik Rahman, Md. Sajid Altaf, Mohammed Saidul Islam, Mehrab Mustafy Rahman, Md Mezbaur Rahman, Md Azam Hossain, and Abu Raihan Mostofa Kamal. 2022. BanglaRQA: A benchmark dataset for under-resourced Bangla language reading comprehension-based question answering with diverse question-answer types. In *Findings of the Association for Computational Linguistics: EMNLP 2022*, pages 2518–2532, Abu Dhabi, United Arab Emirates. Association for Computational Linguistics.

Yucheng Han, Chi Zhang, Xin Chen, Xu Yang, Zhibin Wang, Gang Yu, Bin Fu, and Hanwang Zhang. 2023. Chartllama: A multimodal LLM for chart understanding and generation. *CoRR*, abs/2311.16483.

Tahmid Hasan, Abhik Bhattacharjee, Kazi Samin, Masum Hasan, Madhusudan Basak, M Sohel Rahman, and Rifat Shahriyar. 2020. Not low-resource anymore: Aligner ensembling, batch filtering, and new datasets for bengali-english machine translation. *arXiv preprint arXiv:2009.09359*.

Ting-Yao Hsu, C. Lee Giles, and Ting-Hao Kenneth Huang. 2021. Scicap: Generating captions for scientific figures. In *Findings of the Association for Computational Linguistics: EMNLP 2021, Virtual Event / Punta Cana, Dominican Republic, 16-20 November, 2021*, pages 3258–3264. Association for Computational Linguistics.

Md. Rafiqul Islam, Jiaming Zhang, Md. Hamjajul Ashmafee, Imran Razzak, Jianlong Zhou, Xianzhi Wang, and Guandong Xu. 2021. Exvis: Explainable visual decision support system for risk management. In *8th International Conference on Behavioral and Social Computing, BESC 2021, Doha, Qatar, October 29-31, 2021*, pages 1–5. IEEE.

Justin Johnson, Bharath Hariharan, Laurens van der Maaten, Li Fei-Fei, C. Lawrence Zitnick, and Ross B. Girshick. 2017. CLEVR: A diagnostic dataset for compositional language and elementary visual reasoning. In *2017 IEEE Conference on Computer Vision and Pattern Recognition, CVPR 2017, Honolulu, HI, USA, July 21-26, 2017*, pages 1988–1997. IEEE Computer Society.

Mohsinul Kabir, Mohammed Saidul Islam, Md Tahmid Rahman Laskar, Mir Tafseer Nayeem, M Saiful Bari, and Enamul Hoque. 2023. Benllmeval: A comprehensive evaluation into the potentials and pitfalls of large language models on bengali nlp. *arXiv preprint arXiv:2309.13173*.

Shankar Kantharaj, Rixie Tiffany Ko Leong, Xiang Lin, Ahmed Masry, Megh Thakkar, Enamul Hoque, and Shafiq Joty. 2022. Chart-to-text: A large-scale benchmark for chart summarization. *arXiv preprint arXiv:2203.06486*.

Junnan Li, Dongxu Li, Silvio Savarese, and Steven Hoi. 2023. Blip-2: Bootstrapping language-image pre-training with frozen image encoders and large language models. *Preprint*, arXiv:2301.12597.

Chin-Yew Lin. 2004. Rouge: A package for automatic evaluation of summaries. In *Text summarization branches out*, pages 74–81.

Fanqing Meng, Wenqi Shao, Quanfeng Lu, Peng Gao, Kaipeng Zhang, Yu Qiao, and Ping Luo. 2024. Chartassisstant: A universal chart multimodal language model via chart-to-table pre-training and multitask instruction tuning. *CoRR*, abs/2401.02384.

Mubashir Munaf, Hammad Afzal, Naima Iltaf, and Khawir Mahmood. 2023. Low resource summarization using pre-trained language models. *CoRR*, abs/2310.02790.

Jason Obeid and Enamul Hoque. 2020. Chart-to-text: Generating natural language descriptions for charts by adapting the transformer model. In *Proceedings of the 13th International Conference on Natural Language Generation*, pages 138–147, Dublin, Ireland. Association for Computational Linguistics.

Telmo Pires, Eva Schlinger, and Dan Garrette. 2019. How multilingual is multilingual bert? In *Proceedings of the 57th Conference of the Association for Computational Linguistics, ACL 2019, Florence, Italy, July 28- August 2, 2019, Volume 1: Long Papers*, pages 4996–5001. Association for Computational Linguistics.

Matt Post. 2018. A call for clarity in reporting bleu scores. *arXiv preprint arXiv:1804.08771*.

Colin Raffel, Noam Shazeer, Adam Roberts, Katherine Lee, Sharan Narang, Michael Matena, Yanqi Zhou, Wei Li, and Peter J. Liu. 2020. Exploring the limits of transfer learning with a unified text-to-text transformer. *J. Mach. Learn. Res.*, 21:140:1–140:67.

Raian Rahman, Rizvi Hasan, Abdullah Al Farhad, Md Tahmid Rahman Laskar, Md Hamjajul Ashmafee, and Abu Raihan Mostofa Kamal. 2023. Chartsumm: A comprehensive benchmark for automatic chart summarization of long and short summaries. *arXiv preprint arXiv:2304.13620*.

Hao Tan, Chen-Tse Tsai, Yujie He, and Mohit Bansal. 2022. Scientific chart summarization: Datasets and improved text modeling. In *SDU@ AAAI*.

Gemma Team, Thomas Mesnard, Cassidy Hardin, Robert Dadashi, Surya Bhupatiraju, Shreya Pathak, Laurent Sifre, Morgane Rivière, Mihir Sanjay Kale, Juliette Love, et al. 2024. Gemma: Open models based on gemini research and technology. *arXiv preprint arXiv:2403.08295*.

Oriol Vinyals, Alexander Toshev, Samy Bengio, and Dumitru Erhan. 2015. Show and tell: A neural image caption generator. In *IEEE Conference on Computer Vision and Pattern Recognition, CVPR 2015, Boston, MA, USA, June 7-12, 2015*, pages 3156–3164. IEEE Computer Society.

Weiyue Wang, Jan-Thorsten Peter, Hendrik Rosendahl, and Hermann Ney. 2016. Character: Translation edit rate on character level. In *Proceedings of the First Conference on Machine Translation: Volume 2, Shared Task Papers*, pages 505–510.

Renqiu Xia, Bo Zhang, Haoyang Peng, Ning Liao, Peng Ye, Botian Shi, Junchi Yan, and Yu Qiao. 2023. Structchart: Perception, structuring, reasoning for visual chart understanding. *CoRR*, abs/2309.11268.

Linting Xue, Noah Constant, Adam Roberts, Mihir Kale, Rami Al-Rfou, Aditya Siddhant, Aditya Barua, and Colin Raffel. 2020. mt5: A massively multilingual pre-trained text-to-text transformer. *arXiv preprint arXiv:2010.11934*.

Jiawen Zhu, Jinye Ran, Roy Ka wei Lee, Kenny Choo, and Zhi Li. 2021. Autochart: A dataset for chart-to-text generation task. *Preprint*, arXiv:2108.06897.

A Appendix

A.1 Human Annotations

Table 3 presents a qualitative comparison highlighting specific tasks performed by our human annotators to capture and preserve the nuances of the language.

English Summary	Machine Translation	Human Annotation	Comments
Between 1965 and 2014, Guinea Bissau CO2 emissions from gas flaring remained stable at around 0 thousand metric tons.	১৯৬৫ থেকে 2014 সালের মধ্যে, গিনি বিসাউ এর উদ্দীপ্ত গ্যাস থেকে CO2 নির্গমন প্রায় ০ হাজার মেট্রিক টনে স্থিতিশীল ছিল।	১৯৬৫ থেকে ২০১৪ সালের মধ্যে, গিনি বিসাউ এর উদ্দীপ্ত গ্যাস থেকে কার্বন ডাই অক্সাইড নির্গমন প্রায় ০ হাজার মেট্রিক টনে স্থিতিশীল ছিল	Replace “CO2” with its full form and the year “2014” with its proper Bengali number (in summary)
Italy - Total population aged 25-49 years	ইতালি - মোট জনসংখ্যা ২৫-৪৯ বছর বয়সী	ইতালি - ২৫-৪৯ বছর বয়সী মোট জনসংখ্যা	Rearrange words to clarify in natural Bengali (in title)
In 2019, female life expectancy for Australia was 85 years. Female life expectancy of Australia increased from 74.4 years in 1970 to 85 years in 2019 growing at an average annual rate of 0.27%.	২০১৯ সালে, অস্ট্রেলিয়ায় মহিলাদের আয়ু ছিল ৮৫ বছর। অস্ট্রেলিয়ার মহিলাদের আয়ু ১৯৭০ সালে ৭৪.৪ বছর থেকে বেড়ে ২০১৯ সালে ৮৫ বছর হয়েছে যা বার্ষিক গড় ০.২৭% হারে বৃদ্ধি পেয়েছে।	২০১৯ সালে, অস্ট্রেলিয়ায় মহিলাদের প্রত্যাশিত আয়ুষ্কাল ছিল ৮৫ বছর। অস্ট্রেলিয়ার মহিলাদের প্রত্যাশিত আয়ুষ্কাল ১৯৭০ সালে ৭৪.৪ বছর থেকে বেড়ে ২০১৯ সালে ৮৫ বছর হয়েছে যা বার্ষিক গড় ০.২৭% হারে বৃদ্ধি পেয়েছে।	Use "প্রত্যাশিত আয়ুষ্কাল" instead of "আয়ু," to translate the word "life expectancy" more precisely (in summary)
Monthly oil production in Angola 2019-2021	অ্যাঙ্গোলা ২০১৯-২০২১ এ মাসিক তেল উত্পাদন	অ্যাঙ্গোলা ২০১৯-২০২১ এ মাসিক তেল উৎপাদন	Refine Bengali spelling (in title)
The Christmas of 2020 is being perceived differently among all the people celebrating it. According to a survey conducted in Italy, 85 percent of the respondents strongly agreed or agreed that this Christmas is going to be different from former Christmases. Some 66 percent believed it is going to be sadder, while 25 percent thought it would be more simple.	২০২০ এর ক্রিসমাস এটি উদযাপন করা সমস্ত লোকের মধ্যে আলাদাভাবে বিবেচিত হচ্ছে। ইতালিতে পরিচালিত একটি সমীক্ষা অনুসারে, ৮৫ শতাংশ উত্তরদাতারা দৃ strongly ়ভাবে সম্মত বা সম্মত হয়েছেন যে এই ক্রিসমাসটি প্রাক্তন ক্রিসমাস থেকে আলাদা হতে চলেছে। প্রায় ৬৬ ৬৬ শতাংশ বিশ্বাস করেছিলেন যে এটি দুঃখজনক হতে চলেছে, যখন ২৫ শতাংশ ভেবেছিলেন এটি আরও সহজ হবে।	২০২০ এর ক্রিসমাস এটি উদযাপন করা সমস্ত লোকের মধ্যে আলাদাভাবে বিবেচিত হচ্ছে। ইতালিতে পরিচালিত একটি সমীক্ষা অনুসারে, ৮৫ শতাংশ উত্তরদাতারা দৃঢ়ভাবে সম্মত বা সম্মত হয়েছেন যে এই ক্রিসমাসটি প্রাক্তন ক্রিসমাস থেকে আলাদা হতে চলেছে। প্রায় ৬৬ শতাংশ বিশ্বাস করেছিলেন যে এটি দুঃখজনক হতে চলেছে, যখন ২৫ শতাংশ ভেবেছিলেন এটি আরও সহজ হবে।	Refine to preserve the intent (in summary)

Table 3: Tasks done by human annotators.

A.2 Chart Summarization by LLM

Figure 4 presents a sample summary generated from the provided chart data and a prompt by Gemma, alongside its corresponding gold label. This demonstrates that straightforward trends are readily identified by the models and effectively represented in the Bengali summary.

```
Instruction: Your task is to give chart summarizaton in Bengali language
(এই চার্টটি বাংলা ভাষায় সারাংশ কর):

চার্ট তথ্য: জর্জিয়া - সম্পূর্ণ নিয়ন্ত্রণে সেচের জন্য সজ্জিত এলাকা x-axis: বছর y-axis:
সম্পূর্ণ_নিয়ন্ত্রণে_সেচের_জন্য_সজ্জিত_এলাকা chart_data: ১৯৯৬.০ ৪৩৭.৫ ১৯৯৭.০ ৪৩
৮.১ ২০০২.০ ৪৪১.০ ২০০৭.০ ৪৭২.২ ২০১২.০ ৪৭২.২ ২০১৭.০ ৪৭২.২ ২০১৮.০ ৪৭
২.২

সারাংশ: ৪৭২.২ বর্গ কিলোমিটার জমিতে ১৯৯৬ থেকে ২০১৮ সাল পর্যন্ত সম্পূর্ণ নিয়ন্ত্রণে
সেচের জন্য সজ্জিত এলাকা ছিল জর্জিয়াতে।

Gold label: ২০১৮ সালে সম্পূর্ণ নিয়ন্ত্রণে সেচের জন্য সজ্জিত জর্জিয়া এলাকা ৪৭২.২
কিলোমিটার স্তরে ছিল, যা আগের বছরের থেকে অপরিবর্তিত ।
```

Figure 4: A Bengali chart summary generated by Gemma.

DweshVaani: An LLM for Detecting Religious Hate Speech in Code-Mixed Hindi-English

Varad Srivastava
Barclays
varadsrivastava.iitdelhi@gmail.com

Abstract

Traditional language models in NLP have been extensively made use of, in hateful speech detection problems. With the growth of social media, content in regional languages has grown exponentially. However, use of language models as well as LLMs on code-mixed Hindi-English hateful speech detection is under-explored. Our work addresses this gap by investigating both cutting-edge LLMs by Meta, Google, OpenAI, Nvidia as well as Indic-LLMs like Sarvam, Indic-Gemma, and Airavata on hateful speech detection in code-mixed Hindi-English languages in a comprehensive set of few-shot scenarios which include examples selected randomly, as well as with retrieval-augmented generation (RAG) based on MuRIL language model. We observed that Indic-LLMs which are instruction tuned on Indian content fall behind on the task. We also experimented with finetuning approaches, where we use knowledge-distillation based-finetuning by using rationale behind hate speech. Finally, we also propose Dwesh-Vaani, an LLM based on fine-tuned Gemma-2, that out-performs all other approaches at the task of religious hateful speech detection as well as targeted religion identification in code-mixed Hindi-English languages. Black-box functionality testing is used to establish its robustness and stability.

1 Introduction

Due to the exponential growth of internet, social media has become a preferred medium for individuals to share their views and thoughts. According to some estimates, more than half of the world now actively use social media, with this number growing by around 260 million, just over the last year. While social media has undoubtedly brought people closer and made access to information easy, it has also been used over the years to spread hate and misinformation. Social media is used by individuals with malicious intents to spread hate by amplifying their stereotypical and derogatory views expressing hate or encouraging violence at an individual or community (based on their race, religion, sex etc.), which can reach audience in all corners of the world in a matter of seconds. The presence and generation of such negative contents can create divide within individuals and communities within society and lead to conflicts and hostility. Previous studies have also pointed out the urgency to address this issue, in order to maintain a peaceful and inclusive society.

Over the past few years, numerous research studies have examined different aspects of hate speech and offensive language detection, including related topics such as identifying abusive content (Nobata et al., 2016; Sazzed, 2021), cyberbullying detection (Paul et al., 2022; Iwendi et al., 2020) and detecting hostility (Bagora et al., 2022; Kamal et al., 2021; Raha et al., 2021). Some of these studies have specifically concentrated on targeted hate speech (Chiril et al., 2021; ElSherief et al., 2018; Sharma et al., 2023), while others have explored issues related to vulnerable communities, such as detecting homophobia and transphobia (Sharma et al., 2022; Chakravarthi et al., 2022)

In spite of recent research, the incidences of religious hate speech are continuously rising every day. Additionally, we have started to see drastic real-world consequences of hate speech targeting religious groups, one prominent example being the Rohingya crisis in Myanmar, where social media was used extensively to spread misinformation and incite violence against the minority Rohingya Muslim community. Similarly, anti-Semitic hate speech surged across the social media during

Proceedings of the First Workshop on Challenges in Processing South Asian Languages (CHiPSAL 2025), pages 46–60
January 19, 2025.

the conflict between Hamas and Israel, inciting violence. Given the huge volumes of hate speech content that is generated on social media, language models have been used extensively in previous studies for automatic detection of harmful content.

Most of the existing research works focus on content in English language, and there is relatively less study on hateful content on social media in low-resource languages like Hindi. Hindi is spoken across 20 countries with 577 million native speakers and now has a significant amount of content available online, as people are increasingly expressing themselves on social media in regional or code-mixed languages. However, lack of suitable datasets for targeted hate speech against religion in Hindi or Hindi-English code-mixed languages, had rendered the progress slow. Recently, Targeted Hate Speech Against Religion (THAR) dataset (Sharma et al., 2024) was curated, in a step towards building language models to bridge this gap. Additionally, given the language understanding prowess of LLMs, they have been under-explored on tasks like hate speech detection, with a scarcity of research in this area.

In this paper, we bridge the aforementioned gap by evaluating both Multi-lingual Masked Language Model (like MuRIL) and few-shot learning techniques with cutting-edge LLMs like Llama-3.1, Gemma-2, and GPT-4o Mini as well as Indic LLMs like Sarvam, Nemotron, Airavata, and IndicGemma.

Therefore, we perform analyses and evaluations in following four different approaches. Firstly, we evaluate a multilingual masked language model on the task of religious hate speech detection in YouTube comments and identification of religion that the comment hatefully targets.

Secondly, we make use of in-context learning using state-of-the-art open-source Instruction-tuned LLMs, to evaluate their performance on zero-shot and few-shot (1 and 2 examples per class) learning and Retrieval-Augmented Generation (RAG). Thirdly, we experiment with fine-tuning and knowledge-distillation approaches using the LLMs.

Finally, we propose DweshVaani, an LLM based on Gemma-2, that can be used as state-of-the-art model for religious hate speech detection in Hindi and Hindi-English code-mixed languages. We show that this model is able to outperform all other approaches, as well black-box testing shows it to be more robust. Additionally, we also perform extensive error analysis of the best performing model.

2 Related Work

2.1 Hate-Speech Detection

Previous studies have focused on different facets of hate speech detection, like abusive comments (Nobata et al., 2016; Sazzed, 2021; Zia Ur Rehman et al., 2023), offensive content (Salaam et al., 2022; Saumya et al., 2021; Chen et al., 2012), toxic speech (D'Sa et al., 2020; Nguyen et al., 2021), including transphobia (Chakravarthi et al., 2022; Sharma et al., 2022) and misogyny detection (Nozza et al., 2019; Pamungkas et al., 2020). Hate speech concerning religion is a sensitive topic as it has the power to create divide in societies, as recently observed in the Delhi riots. There do exist studies on religious hate speech detection but have often not been comprehensive in covering major religions, for example, some cover only Islamophobia detection (Mehmood et al., 2021). Due to lack of suitable datasets and generalized models, religious hate speech detection in low-resource languages remains under-explored.

Despite a significant amount of population speaking Hindi, datasets for religious hate-speech detection in Hindi or code-mixed Hindi-English were largely absent. Targeted Hate Speech Against Religion (THAR) dataset (Sharma et al., 2024) was recently released which aimed to address this gap. It not only has information about whether a comment was hatefully targeting a religion, but also encompasses information about which religion it was targeting. We make use of this dataset in our study.

2.2 Using LLMs for Hate Speech Detection

There has been some focus on using LLMs to generate datasets on hateful speech. Hartvigsen et al. (2022) used demonstration-based prompting for LLMs, to encourage it to generate both toxic and benign sentences that talk about minority groups without any sort of explicit words or language. In this way they created the TOXIGEN dataset which encompasses implicit toxicity which can be used to train language models to detect subtle toxicity rather than getting confised with any mentions of minorities. Some works like that by Das et al. (2022a) have even constructed evaluation sets (HateCheckHIn) in Hindi for testing multilingual functionalities of hate speech detection models. In a further work, Das et al. (2024) evaluated ChatGPT 3.5 on these functionality tests and observed that it performs inferior on Hindi as compared to other languages.

Guo et al. (2023) assessed the ability of LLMs in hate speech detection by employing them on five datasets, namely - HateXplain, COVID-HATE, CallMeSexist, USElectionHate and SWSR. They used few-shot learning and chain-of-thought prompting techniques with GPT3.5-Turbo along with fine-tuned BERT, and RoBERTa models, and observed that ChatGPT consistently out-performs both of them. Additionally, when they tested ChatGPT on multilingual hate speech detection in Chinese language, it was observed that ChatGPT performs significantly poor than expected. Roy et al. (2023) evaluated GPT3.5, flan-T5-large and text-davinci, across three datasets - HateXplain, implicit hate, and Toxic-Spans, which contain the ground truth explanations as well. Using vanilla prompts, flan-T5-large came out to be the best performing model among the three. Additionally, when the prompt included information about the target community, performance gains of upto 30% are obtained. Sen et al. (2024) explored use of Tiny LLMs like TinyLlama, phi-2 and opt-1.3B on two hate-speech datasets, namely - DynaHate and hateeval. They observed significant gains in performance across all models for both datasets, when they fine-tuned the models using LoRa, with opt-1.3b model coming out as the best performing model.

These works have multiple gaps - they do not either assess LLMs on religious hateful speech in code-mixed Hindi-English languages, or do not present the targeted religion, which is a more challenging task than hate identification.

3 Task and Dataset

Hateful speech detection in Code-mixed Hindi-English languages is a challenging problem because of scarcity of appropriate datasets. For this work, we used the recently released Targeted Hate Speech Against Religion (THAR) dataset (Sharma et al., 2024). It consists of comments from YouTube videos scraped from videos discussing controversial topics in religious contexts, including political discussions. Two sub-tasks are proposed by the creators for this dataset:

Subtask 1 (Binary Classification): In this, the comments are classified into two categories - Anti-religion and Non-Anti-religion.

1. *Anti-religion*: A comment falls under the anti-religion class if it meets one or more of the following criteria:
   - Show hostility towards religious beliefs and their sacred elements.
   - Attack or belittle any religious faith.
   - Critique the practices and rituals associated with a specific religion.
   - Exhibit hate towards spiritual leaders or celebrities who promote a particular religion and its cultural aspects.
2. *Non-Anti-religion*: A comment falls under the non-anti-religion class if it is not hostile in nature and does not promote any religious hate or any form of hatred.

Subtask 2 (Multi-class Classification): In this, the comments are classified into four categories:

1. *Christianity*: A comment falls under this class if it spreads hate or attack on missionaries, the church, their religious customs, and seek to diminish or undervalue their faith or beliefs.
2. *Hinduism*: A comment falls under this class if it is hostile directed at Hindus, their religious beliefs, cultural practices, sacred elements, and places; criticizes their spiritual leaders, uses abusive language towards them for their speeches, or insults their deities.
3. *Islam*: A comment falls under this class if it promotes hatred towards Muslims, their religious beliefs, culture, and sacred elements, as well as criticisms directed at their religious leaders and disrespectful language regarding their teachings.

4. *None*: A comment falls under this class if it does not promote religious hate or any form of hatred, maintains a non-hostile and respectful tone towards all beliefs and faiths.

In this work, we utilize the *Subtask 2*, considering that it encompasses the non-anti-religion hateful speech detection task as well as it includes the problem of identification of the targeted religion, which is a more challenging task. Details of the dataset are shown in Table 1. Some examples from the dataset are shown below. A few other examples are added in Appendix A.

1. **Christianity**:
   - ***Comment***: Chrtitan log convent school kholte h Waha bachho ko convert karte
     Explanation: The comment suggests that Christians open convent schools where they convert the religion of children, implying a negative view of Christianity.

2. **Hinduism**:
   - ***Comment***: Bharat main pahle Hindu hi the lekin woh sab kalma padh kar Musalman huye aur hindu kisi layak nahi
     Explanation: This comment implies a derogatory assertion about Hindus by suggesting a superiority of another group, which can be interpreted as an attack on Hindu identity and beliefs.

3. **Islam**:
   - ***Comment***: Yeh hain peace wala religion musalman 😂😂😂
     Explanation: This comment appears to mock a religious group, implying a negative view of Islam.

4. **None**:
   - ***Comment***: हिंदू और मुसलमान बनने से पहले इंसान बनो ! देश में अभी भी इंसानियत जिंदा है !
     Explanation: This comment suggests to put humanity first before religion, and does not express hatred towards any religion.

	Train	Test	Whole
Christianity	360	31	391
Hinduism	1,217	132	1,349
Islam	3,326	388	3,714
None	5,491	604	6,095
Total	10394	1155	11549

Table 1: THAR Dataset statistics

- ***Comment***: Inke na khane se sach khane se sach jhuth to nhi bn sakta sach to sach hi rhega 🙏🙏😂
  Explanation: This comment expresses a general opinion that not saying anything would not affect the truth.

4 Methodology

4.1 In-Context Learning

For in-context learning, we use LLMs like:

- `Llama`: We used Meta's Llama-3.1 8B model (AI@Meta, 2024). Llama-3 has 2 other variants at the time of writing - 70B and 405B parameter models, all of which have context length of 128k.
- `GPT`: We used OpenAI's GPT-4o Mini (OpenAI et al., 2024) which has a context window of 128k.
- `Gemma`: We used Gemma-2 9B model (Google) (Gemma Team, 2024), which has context length of 8,192.
- `Sarvam-1`: We used Sarvam AI's Sarvam-1 (Sarvam, 2024) 2B model.
- `Nemotron-Hindi`: We used Nvidia's Nemotron-4-Hindi (Joshi et al., 2024) 4B Instruct-tuned model.
- `Indic-Gemma`: We used Telugu LLM Labs' Indic-Gemma (TeluguLLM-Labs), which is fine-tuned on Gemma 7B model.
- `Airavata`: We used AI4Bharat's Airavata model (Gala et al., 2024) which is a IndicInstruct dataset fine-tuned version of OpenHanthi 7B model.
- `Project Indus`: We used TechMahindra's Project Indus LLM (Malhotra et al., 2024), which is a 7B parameter model.

These pre-trained chat models have been further fine-tuned to follow instructions (except Sarvam-1) with Reinforcement Learning from Human Preferences (RLHF) (Ouyang et al., 2024). Therefore, we use the Instruction-tuned versions of each of the models. For Sarvam-1, we do not perform in-context learning, and directly fine-tune the model on our instruction dataset to perform inference. We perform inference using a Nvidia L4 GPU with upto 22.5 GB of GPU memory. We experiment with 4-bits quantized versions of the models.

4.2 Prompt Engineering

Articulate prompt engineering is crucial in steering behaviour and response of the LLMs, by providing them the appropriate instructions and context for a task. The prompt template is shown in B.1.

The prompt starts with an instruction which encompasses the context of the task including a knowledge base detailing the classification criteria and names of the classes. The test statement is then provided as an input by the user.

4.2.1 Zero Shot and Random Few Shot Learning

For our initial approach, we experimented with zero-shot learning and in-context learning with 1 and 2 examples per class, chosen randomly from the training set.

4.2.2 Retrieval Augmented Generation: Semantically Similar Few Shot Learning

In this approach, we select those examples for in context learning from the training set, which are semantically similar to the test statement at inference. This is achieved by first training a sentence transformer (MuRIL) (Khanuja et al., 2021) on the training set, which learns to encode the statements in the embedding space, based on whether their class is similar or dissimilar. Details of MuRIL model are given in Appendix C.

In this work, we select one of its variations-'muril-large-cased', which is based on the BERT Large model. Therefore based on this idea, for each test sentence to be classified, we use the muril-large-cased vector embeddings and the cosine similarity metric (for distance calculation) to retrieve the 1, 4 and 8 most similar examples at inference time, while performing in-context learning (as shown in Figure 1).

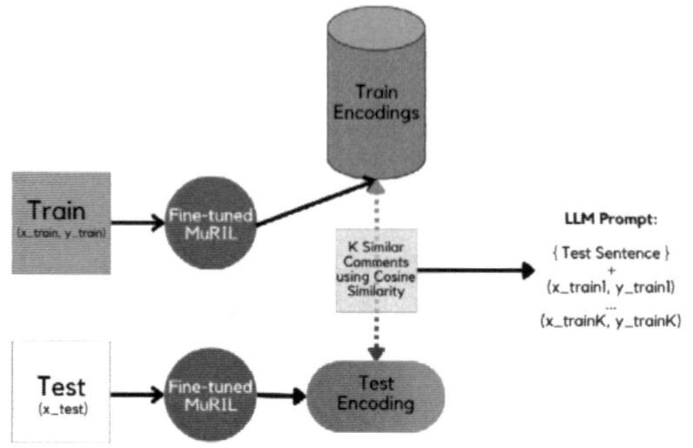

Figure 1: Dynamic LLM prompt construction through Retrieval-Augmented Generation (RAG), using cosine similarity for in-context data selection. We use K=1, 4, 8.

5 Experiments and Results

5.1 Experimental Setup

We perform fine-tuning of the Sentence Transformers model using PyTorch and HuggingFace libraries. For in-context learning, the prompt is described in Section 4.2.

5.2 Hyper-parameter tuning of MuRIL

MuRIL was fine-tuned using Optuna framework. Over 10 trials, validation micro-F1 was maximized by having search spaces over body's learning rate (1e-6, 1e-3), and weight decay (1e-3, 1e-1). Tuning and deployment of the model was performed on an Nvidia L4 GPU with 22.5 GB memory.

5.3 Results

We report the performance of the models through the metrics: micro-F1 (μ-F1) and macro-F1 (m-F1), as shown in Table 2.

On zero-shot learning, GPT-4o-Mini is the best performing model, followed by Gemma-2. On one-shot learning as well, GPT-4o-Mini significantly out-performs all other models, however, we see a significant increase in performance of all models when RAG-based one similar example is presented. For e.g., here, for the second best performing model Airavata, μ-F1 increases from 34.03 to 55.58, which is an increment of more than 20 percentage points (pp).

When presented with RAG-based 4 similar examples, GPT-4o-Mini still is the best performing mode, however, Airavata appears to close in on the gap. Interestingly, when RAG-based 8 most similar examples are provided, GPT-4o-Mini's performance appears to plateau indicating that more examples are contributing to noise, rather than helping in model's understanding of hateful comment. We observed a similar trend for the next best model here - Gemma-2, which only had a 1 pp increase in µ-F1, from the 4-shot learning (similar) setting, as well as Airavata - whose performance actually declines (from 60.43 to 58.96 µ-F1).

Additionally, even when presented with upto RAG-based 8 similar examples, the best performing model (GPT-4o-Mini), still lags upto 10 percentage points compared to the MuRIL language model, which was fine-tuned on the whole dataset, but is much smaller in size. This could be attributed to the challenging nature of the dataset, where the samples have been picked up from Youtube comments, and include real-world noise - emojis, slangs, typos etc. Due to this, it must be difficult for the LLMs to excel at the task, given that they are generally pre-trained on curated and processed datasets.

Another open-source LLM that we employed - Project Indus, performed poorly with gibberish outputs, even when one example was provided. Therefore, we omitted the model while presenting the results.

Therefore, in general we observed that using our RAG-approach based similar samples lead to better in-context learning results for all the models, across all the settings. Although there's a threshold of examples, beyond which the performance for the LLMs seems to either plateau or decline, on the task.

6 Fine-Tuning of Instruction Tuned LLMs

Based on the performance of models during in-context learning, we select Gemma-2 model for fine-tuning to investigate if model performance could be enhanced further. Each sample from the training set was converted into a prompt which included the test statement as a user input and the true label as the reply expected from the chat assistant. The prompt template used was exactly the same as depicted in Section 4.2. QLoRA (Quantized Low-Rank Adaptation) (Dettmers et al., 2023) was used to efficiently fine-tune the model. We first quantized the pre-trained model to 4-bit and then added a set of learnable low-rank adapter weight matrices with rank 64, that are tuned using backpropagation for upto 3 epochs. This was able to significantly reduce trainable parameters to 216M, hence significantly reducing GPU memory requirements. The details of hyper-parameters are shown in Table 5 in Appendix D. We compared the performance with the Sarvam-1 2B model, which we instruct-tuned on this task.

We observed that with just three epochs of fine-tuning, it is able to achieve a µ-F1 score of 76.19%, which significantly out-performs few-shot learning based approaches in LLMs as well as MuRIL (as shown in Table 3). Therefore, we propose this fine-tuned model, namely Dwesh-Vaani LLM as state-of-the-art language model for hateful speech detection as well as targeted religion identification.

7 Knowledge Distillation based Fine-tuning

Considering the challenging nature of the task, we investigated if incorporating additional information like rationale during the fine-tuning process can help improve the model's understanding of hateful speech. To test this, we experimented with dynamically augmenting training prompts during the fine-tuning process with the rationale behind each of the classifications, i.e. why or why not a particular comment is hatefully targeting a religion, and in case it is - why is it targeting that particular religion. We generated these rationale using the GPT-4o-Mini LLM, and the prompt templates are shown in B.2.

Some examples of generated rationale:

- ***Comment***: आपकी आवाज दूरदर्शन के TV ANCHOR की तरह है,लाइक your voice

  Targeted Religion: None

  Generated Rationale: The comment expresses a positive comparison of someone's voice to that of a TV anchor, without any derogatory or negative implications towards any religion.

- ***Comment***: Bhai Muslim sb ko jhagra kar ke kya milta ha jaha dekho hindu sb ko marte rhete ha akhir kya bigara hindu sb

  Targeted Religion: Islam

  Generated Rationale: The comment expresses hostility towards Muslims by suggesting they are instigating conflict with Hindus, which perpetuates negative stereotypes and incites division between the two religious communities.

- ***Comment***: दुनिया के सबसे पहले इंसान आदम अलैहिस्सलाम थे और वो मुसलमान थे तो हिंदुओं का पूर्वज भी मुसलमान ही हुए थोड़ा दिमाग लगाओ सालों अकल है या नहीं

  Targeted Religion: Hinduism

  Generated Rationale: The comment dismissively asserts that the first human was a Muslim, implying that Hindu beliefs about their own origins are inferior or incorrect, which can be seen as an attack on Hinduism and its cultural identity.

- ***Comment***: Mujhe 5 baar kosis ki gai thi Christianity me convert karne ki.

  Targeted Religion: Christianity

  Generated Rationale: The comment expresses frustration about repeated attempts to convert the speaker to Christianity, which can imply a negative sentiment towards the religion and its practices, potentially reflecting a broader disdain or hostility towards Christianity.

Therefore, we essentially used rationale knowledge distilled from the GPT-4o-Mini LLM in the Gemma-2 model and used it to dynamically augment the training prompts during the fine-tuning process. We trained this model for one epoch, while keeping all the other hyper-parameters same as shown in Table 5. We name the resulting model, DweshVaani-X (experimental). Contrary to our hypothesis, we achieved significantly poor results (shown in Table 3) as compared to both in-context learning, as well as Dwesh-Vaani, which was directly fine-tuned without using any additional knowledge.

Models	$\mu-F_1$	m$-F_1$
GPT-4o (8-shot RAG)	63.03	53.14
Gemma-2 (8-shot RAG)	59.83	51.64
MuRIL	73.33	61.31
Sarvam-1	51.86	44.98
DweshVaani	**76.19**	**64.27**
DweshVaani-X	60.69	41.92

Table 3: Comparison of our model's performance against other other approaches

Methods	Setting	$\mu-F_1$	m$-F_1$
MuRIL	Full-Data	73.33	61.31
Llama-3.1	0-shot	44.68	40.17
Gemma-2	0-shot	45.97	40.16
GPT-4o	0-shot	**49.96**	**44.17**
Nemotron	0-shot	41.13	34.76
Airavata	0-shot	34.03	32.17
Indic-Gem	0-shot	45.63	36.56
Llama-3.1	1-shot (sim)	55.50	47.44
Gemma-2	1-shot (sim)	54.03	47.02
GPT-4o	1-shot (sim)	**59.39**	**50.72**
Nemotron	1-shot (sim)	49.87	41.78
Airavata	1-shot (sim)	55.58	49.03
Indic-Gem	1-shot (sim)	44.16	36.77
Llama-3.1	4-shot (sim)	56.36	39.35
Llama-3.1	4-shot (ran)	49.78	41.65
Gemma-2	4-shot (sim)	58.87	51.08
Gemma-2	4-shot (ran)	56.19	47.54
GPT-4o	4-shot (sim)	**63.03**	**52.86**
GPT-4o	4-shot (ran)	54.89	46.12
Nemotron	4-shot (sim)	57.66	44.67
Nemotron	4-shot (ran)	54.89	40.56
Airavata	4-shot (sim)	60.43	52.80
Airavata	4-shot (ran)	43.46	39.63
Indic-Gem	4-shot (sim)	54.03	41.75
Indic-Gem	4-shot (ran)	54.03	40.53
Llama-3.1	8-shot (sim)	57.23	48.64
Llama-3.1	8-shot (ran)	49.52	41.64
Gemma-2	8-shot (sim)	59.83	51.64
Gemma-2	8-shot (ran)	54.72	46.70
GPT-4o	8-shot (sim)	**63.03**	**53.14**
GPT-4o	8-shot (ran)	56.97	47.43
Airavata	8-shot (sim)	58.96	51.73
Airavata	8-shot (ran)	37.49	33.60
Indic-Gem	8-shot (sim)	59.05	46.55
Indic-Gem	8-shot (ran)	50.65	39.12

Table 2: Classification results for all models on the test data, with N-Shot indicating the number of samples used during training. Sim: Similar examples and Ran: Random examples

Gold Label	Misclassifications
Christianity	54.84%
Hinduism	55.30%
Islam	20.62%
None	17.38%

Table 4: Misclassified labels along with their misclassification percentages, for the DweshVaani (zero-shot) LLM

8 ERROR ANALYSIS

We performed an error analysis of our top model DweshVaani (zero-shot), to understand the model's behaviour based on what it gets wrong. The misclassified labels along with the percentage errors in each are shown in Table 4. The model made 105 errors on 'None', 80 on 'Islam', 73 on 'Hinduism' and 17 on 'Christianity' class.

Upon inspecting the samples and their predicted labels, we observe that the all the comments for "Christianity" were classified as "None". We noticed that some comments like "हिंदू धर्म मानने वाले लोग कान खोल कर सुन लीजिए ईसाई धर्म जैसे कोई धर्म नहीं है", were labelled as targeting religions like "Christianity" and classified as "None". Another example of such an error is "Vo pati Patni ke beech ki ladai thi fir sb thik hogaya". These errors point to labelling errors, and provide belief in robustness of our model, which is able to still classify as the right label.

For the class "Hinduism", we observed ambiguity with respect to targeting "Islam", confusing the model into misclassifying one into another. For example, "हमारे ही परिवार के लोग मुस्लिम बन गए", was labelled as targeting "Hinduism", but classified as "Islam". Here too, we observed labelling errors. We see a similar trend for "Islam" class as well.

Overall, we observed that the incorrect labeling could be attributed to most of the errors and an analysis and correction of labels is required.

9 FUNCTIONALITY BLACK-BOX TESTING

Higher values of the metrics used (like $\mu - F_1$) indicate more desirable performance (as shown in Table 3). Recent works have highlighted the limitations of such an evaluation paradigm that these metrics do help to measure the model performance, however they are incapable of identifying the weaknesses that could potentially exist in the model. Therefore, we perform additional functionality black-box testing using the HateCheckHIn (Das et al., 2022b) evaluation dataset to find out weaknesses present in our multilingual hate speech detection model - DweshVaani. Functionality testing results are shown and discussed in detail in Appendix E. Overall, we show that our model provides more stable and robust performance on religious hateful speech than the baseline.

10 CONCLUSION

We leveraged LLMs for hateful speech detection against religions in code-mixed Hindi-English languages. For this, we conducted a comprehensive few-shot text classification study based on random examples as well as using a RAG-based approach. We demonstrated that using semantically similar examples, LLMs can surpass zero-shot and other few-shot learning approaches. We also experimented with QLoRA-based fine-tuning approaches, where we used two approaches - one, where the model was directly fine-tuned without providing any additional information; and two - where the model was fine-tuned based on knowledge about rationale distilled from the GPT model. Interestingly, the latter could only perform at par with the 8-shot RAG setting. We did extensive qualitative analysis of the errors made by our model. Finally, we proposed Dwesh-Vaani LLM, based on fine-tuned Gemma-2, which surpasses all other approaches in performance on hateful speech detection on code-mixed Hindi-English languages.

11 LIMITATIONS

We have identified the following limitations of this work. First, the counter-intuitive results with knowledge distilled model need to be further investigated. Second, there are some refinements that need to be performed on the dataset. And finally, in an aim towards comprehensive models targeting detection of hate-speech, datasets corresponding to other aspects like gender, misogyny etc. could also be included.

References

AI@Meta. 2024. Llama 3 model card.

Aditi Bagora, Kamal Shrestha, Kaushal Maurya, and Maunendra Sankar Desarkar. 2022. Hostility detection in online hindi-english code-mixed conversations. In *Proceedings of the 14th ACM Web Science Conference 2022*, WebSci '22, page 390–400, New York, NY, USA. Association for Computing Machinery.

Bharathi Raja Chakravarthi, Adeep Hande, Rahul Ponnusamy, Prasanna Kumar Kumaresan, and Ruba Priyadharshini. 2022. How can we detect homophobia and transphobia? experiments in a multilingual code-mixed setting for social media governance. *International Journal of Information Management Data Insights*, 2(2):100119.

Ying Chen, Yilu Zhou, Sencun Zhu, and Heng Xu. 2012. Detecting offensive language in social media to protect adolescent online safety. In *2012 International Conference on Privacy, Security, Risk and Trust and 2012 International Confernece on Social Computing*, pages 71–80.

Patricia Chiril, Endang Wahyu Pamungkas, Farah Benamara, Véronique Moriceau, and Viviana Patti. 2021. Emotionally informed hate speech detection: A multi-target perspective. *Cognitive Computation*, 14:322 – 352.

Mithun Das, Saurabh Kumar Pandey, and Animesh Mukherjee. 2024. Evaluating ChatGPT against functionality tests for hate speech detection. In *Proceedings of the 2024 Joint International Conference on Computational Linguistics, Language Resources and Evaluation (LREC-COLING 2024)*, pages 6370–6380, Torino, Italia. ELRA and ICCL.

Mithun Das, Punyajoy Saha, Binny Mathew, and Animesh Mukherjee. 2022a. HateCheckHIn: Evaluating Hindi hate speech detection models. In *Proceedings of the Thirteenth Language Resources and Evaluation Conference*, pages 5378–5387, Marseille, France. European Language Resources Association.

Mithun Das, Punyajoy Saha, Binny Mathew, and Animesh Mukherjee. 2022b. HateCheckHIn: Evaluating Hindi hate speech detection models. In *Proceedings of the Thirteenth Language Resources and Evaluation Conference*, pages 5378–5387, Marseille, France. European Language Resources Association.

Tim Dettmers, Artidoro Pagnoni, Ari Holtzman, and Luke Zettlemoyer. 2023. Qlora: Efficient finetuning of quantized llms. *arXiv preprint arXiv:2305.14314*.

Jacob Devlin, Ming-Wei Chang, Kenton Lee, and Kristina Toutanova. 2018. BERT: pre-training of deep bidirectional transformers for language understanding. *CoRR*, abs/1810.04805.

Ashwin Geet D'Sa, Irina Illina, and Dominique Fohr. 2020. Bert and fasttext embeddings for automatic detection of toxic speech. In *2020 International Multi-Conference on: "Organization of Knowledge and Advanced Technologies" (OCTA)*, pages 1–5.

Mai ElSherief, Vivek Kulkarni, Dana Nguyen, William Yang Wang, and Elizabeth Belding. 2018. Hate lingo: A target-based linguistic analysis of hate speech in social media. In *Proceedings of the international AAAI conference on web and social media*, volume 12.

Jay Gala, Thanmay Jayakumar, Jaavid Aktar Husain, Aswanth Kumar M, Mohammed Safi Ur Rahman Khan, Diptesh Kanojia, Ratish Puduppully, Mitesh M. Khapra, Raj Dabre, Rudra Murthy, and Anoop Kunchukuttan. 2024. Airavata: Introducing hindi instruction-tuned llm. *arXiv preprint arXiv: 2401.15006*.

Google DeepMind Gemma Team. 2024. Gemma 2: Improving open language models at a practical size. `https://storage.googleapis.com/deepmind-media/gemma/gemma-2-report.pdf`.

Keyan Guo, Alexander Hu, Jaden Mu, Ziheng Shi, Ziming Zhao, Nishant Vishwamitra, and Hongxin Hu. 2023. An investigation of large language models for real-world hate speech detection. In *2023 International Conference on Machine Learning and Applications (ICMLA)*, pages 1568–1573.

Thomas Hartvigsen, Saadia Gabriel, Hamid Palangi, Maarten Sap, Dipankar Ray, and Ece Kamar. 2022. ToxiGen: A large-scale machine-generated dataset for adversarial and implicit hate speech detection. In *Proceedings of the 60th Annual Meeting of the Association for Computational Linguistics (Volume 1: Long Papers)*, pages 3309–3326, Dublin, Ireland. Association for Computational Linguistics.

Celestine Iwendi, Gautam Srivastava, Suleman Khan, and Praveen Kumar Reddy Maddikunta. 2020. Cyberbullying detection solutions based on deep learning architectures. *Multimedia Systems*, 29:1839–1852.

Raviraj Joshi, Kanishk Singla, Anusha Kamath, Raunak Kalani, Rakesh Paul, Utkarsh Vaidya, Sanjay Singh Chauhan, Niranjan Wartikar, and Eileen Long. 2024. Adapting multilingual llms to low-resource languages using continued pre-training and synthetic corpus. *arXiv preprint arXiv:2410.14815*.

Divyanshu Kakwani, Anoop Kunchukuttan, Satish Golla, Gokul N.C., Avik Bhattacharyya, Mitesh M. Khapra, and Pratyush Kumar. 2020. IndicNLPSuite: Monolingual Corpora, Evaluation Benchmarks and Pre-trained Multilingual Language Models for Indian Languages. In *Findings of EMNLP*.

Ojasv Kamal, Adarsh Kumar, and Tejas Vaidhya. 2021. Hostility detection in hindi leveraging pre-trained language models. *ArXiv*, abs/2101.05494.

Simran Khanuja, Diksha Bansal, Sarvesh Mehtani, Savya Khosla, Atreyee Dey, Balaji Gopalan, Dilip Kumar Margam, Pooja Aggarwal, Rajiv Teja Nagipogu, Shachi Dave, Shruti Gupta, Subhash Chandra Bose Gali, Vish Subramanian, and Partha Talukdar. 2021. Muril: Multilingual representations for indian languages. *Preprint*, arXiv:2103.10730.

Nikhil Malhotra, Nilesh Brahme, Satish Mishra, and Vinay Sharma. 2024. Project indus: A foundational model for indian languages. *Tech Mahindra Makers Lab.*

Qasim Mehmood, Anum Kaleem, and Imran Siddiqi. 2021. Islamophobic hate speech detection from electronic media using deep learning. In *Mediterranean conference on pattern recognition and artificial intelligence*, pages 187–200. Springer.

Luan Thanh Nguyen, Kiet Van Nguyen, and Ngan Luu-Thuy Nguyen. 2021. Constructive and toxic speech detection for open-domain social media comments in vietnamese. In *Advances and Trends in Artificial Intelligence. Artificial Intelligence Practices: 34th International Conference on Industrial, Engineering and Other Applications of Applied Intelligent Systems, IEA/AIE 2021, Kuala Lumpur, Malaysia, July 26–29, 2021, Proceedings, Part I*, page 572–583, Berlin, Heidelberg. Springer-Verlag.

Chikashi Nobata, Joel Tetreault, Achint Thomas, Yashar Mehdad, and Yi Chang. 2016. Abusive language detection in online user content. In *Proceedings of the 25th International Conference on World Wide Web*, WWW '16, page 145–153, Republic and Canton of Geneva, CHE. International World Wide Web Conferences Steering Committee.

Debora Nozza, Claudia Volpetti, and Elisabetta Fersini. 2019. Unintended bias in misogyny detection. In *IEEE/WIC/ACM International Conference on Web Intelligence*, WI '19, page 149–155, New York, NY, USA. Association for Computing Machinery.

OpenAI, Josh Achiam, Steven Adler, Sandhini Agarwal, Lama Ahmad, Ilge Akkaya, Florencia Leoni Aleman, Diogo Almeida, Janko Altenschmidt, Sam Altman, Shyamal Anadkat, Red Avila, Igor Babuschkin, Suchir Balaji, Valerie Balcom, Paul Baltescu, Haiming Bao, Mohammad Bavarian, Jeff Belgum, Irwan Bello, Jake Berdine, Gabriel Bernadett-Shapiro, Christopher Berner, Lenny Bogdonoff, Oleg Boiko, Madelaine Boyd, Anna-Luisa Brakman, Greg Brockman, Tim Brooks, Miles Brundage, Kevin Button, Trevor Cai, Rosie Campbell, Andrew Cann, Brittany Carey, Chelsea Carlson, Rory Carmichael, Brooke Chan, Che Chang, Fotis Chantzis, Derek Chen, Sully Chen, Ruby Chen, Jason Chen, Mark Chen, Ben Chess, Chester Cho, Casey Chu, Hyung Won Chung, Dave Cummings, Jeremiah Currier, Yunxing Dai, Cory Decareaux, Thomas Degry, Noah Deutsch, Damien Deville, Arka Dhar, David Dohan, Steve Dowling, Sheila Dunning, Adrien Ecoffet, Atty Eleti, Tyna Eloundou, David Farhi, Liam Fedus, Niko Felix, Simón Posada Fishman, Juston Forte, Isabella Fulford, Leo Gao, Elie Georges, Christian Gibson, Vik Goel, Tarun Gogineni, Gabriel Goh, Rapha Gontijo-Lopes, Jonathan Gordon, Morgan Grafstein, Scott Gray, Ryan Greene, Joshua Gross, Shixiang Shane Gu, Yufei Guo, Chris Hallacy, Jesse Han, Jeff Harris, Yuchen He, Mike Heaton, Johannes Heidecke, Chris Hesse, Alan Hickey, Wade Hickey, Peter Hoeschele, Brandon Houghton, Kenny Hsu, Shengli Hu, Xin Hu, Joost Huizinga, Shantanu Jain, Shawn Jain, Joanne Jang, Angela Jiang, Roger Jiang, Haozhun Jin, Denny Jin, Shino Jomoto, Billie Jonn, Heewoo Jun, Tomer Kaftan, Łukasz Kaiser, Ali Kamali, Ingmar Kanitscheider, Nitish Shirish Keskar, Tabarak Khan, Logan Kilpatrick, Jong Wook Kim, Christina Kim, Yongjik Kim, Jan Hendrik Kirchner, Jamie Kiros, Matt Knight, Daniel Kokotajlo, Łukasz Kondraciuk, Andrew Kondrich, Aris Konstantinidis, Kyle Kosic, Gretchen Krueger, Vishal Kuo, Michael Lampe, Ikai Lan, Teddy Lee, Jan Leike, Jade Leung, Daniel Levy, Chak Ming Li, Rachel Lim, Molly Lin, Stephanie Lin, Mateusz Litwin, Theresa Lopez, Ryan Lowe, Patricia Lue, Anna Makanju, Kim Malfacini, Sam Manning, Todor Markov, Yaniv Markovski, Bianca Martin, Katie Mayer, Andrew Mayne, Bob McGrew, Scott Mayer McKinney, Christine McLeavey, Paul McMillan, Jake McNeil, David Medina, Aalok Mehta, Jacob Menick, Luke Metz, Andrey Mishchenko, Pamela Mishkin, Vinnie Monaco, Evan Morikawa, Daniel Mossing, Tong Mu, Mira Murati, Oleg Murk, David Mély, Ashvin Nair, Reiichiro Nakano, Rajeev Nayak, Arvind Neelakantan, Richard Ngo, Hyeonwoo Noh, Long Ouyang, Cullen O'Keefe, Jakub Pachocki, Alex Paino, Joe Palermo, Ashley Pantuliano, Giambattista Parascandolo, Joel Parish, Emy Parparita, Alex Passos, Mikhail Pavlov, Andrew Peng, Adam Perelman, Filipe de Avila Belbute Peres, Michael Petrov, Henrique Ponde de Oliveira Pinto, Michael, Pokorny, Michelle Pokrass, Vitchyr H. Pong, Tolly Powell, Alethea Power, Boris Power, Elizabeth Proehl, Raul Puri, Alec Radford, Jack Rae, Aditya Ramesh, Cameron Raymond, Francis Real, Kendra Rimbach, Carl Ross, Bob Rotsted, Henri Roussez, Nick Ryder, Mario Saltarelli, Ted Sanders, Shibani Santurkar, Girish Sastry, Heather Schmidt, David Schnurr, John Schulman, Daniel Selsam, Kyla Sheppard, Toki Sherbakov, Jessica Shieh, Sarah Shoker, Pranav

Shyam, Szymon Sidor, Eric Sigler, Maddie Simens, Jordan Sitkin, Katarina Slama, Ian Sohl, Benjamin Sokolowsky, Yang Song, Natalie Staudacher, Felipe Petroski Such, Natalie Summers, Ilya Sutskever, Jie Tang, Nikolas Tezak, Madeleine B. Thompson, Phil Tillet, Amin Tootoonchian, Elizabeth Tseng, Preston Tuggle, Nick Turley, Jerry Tworek, Juan Felipe Cerón Uribe, Andrea Vallone, Arun Vijayvergiya, Chelsea Voss, Carroll Wainwright, Justin Jay Wang, Alvin Wang, Ben Wang, Jonathan Ward, Jason Wei, CJ Weinmann, Akila Welihinda, Peter Welinder, Jiayi Weng, Lilian Weng, Matt Wiethoff, Dave Willner, Clemens Winter, Samuel Wolrich, Hannah Wong, Lauren Workman, Sherwin Wu, Jeff Wu, Michael Wu, Kai Xiao, Tao Xu, Sarah Yoo, Kevin Yu, Qiming Yuan, Wojciech Zaremba, Rowan Zellers, Chong Zhang, Marvin Zhang, Shengjia Zhao, Tianhao Zheng, Juntang Zhuang, William Zhuk, and Barret Zoph. 2024. Gpt-4 technical report. *Preprint*, arXiv:2303.08774.

Long Ouyang, Jeff Wu, Xu Jiang, Diogo Almeida, Carroll L. Wainwright, Pamela Mishkin, Chong Zhang, Sandhini Agarwal, Katarina Slama, Alex Ray, John Schulman, Jacob Hilton, Fraser Kelton, Luke Miller, Maddie Simens, Amanda Askell, Peter Welinder, Paul Christiano, Jan Leike, and Ryan Lowe. 2024. Training language models to follow instructions with human feedback. In *Proceedings of the 36th International Conference on Neural Information Processing Systems*, NIPS '22, Red Hook, NY, USA. Curran Associates Inc.

Endang Wahyu Pamungkas, Valerio Basile, and Viviana Patti. 2020. Misogyny detection in twitter: a multilingual and cross-domain study. *Inf. Process. Manag.*, 57:102360.

Sayanta Paul, Sriparna Saha, and Jyoti Prakash Singh. 2022. Covid-19 and cyberbullying: deep ensemble model to identify cyberbullying from code-switched languages during the pandemic. *Multimedia Tools Appl.*, 82(6):8773–8789.

Tathagata Raha, Sayar Ghosh Roy, Ujwal Narayan, Zubair Abid, and Vasudeva Varma. 2021. Task adaptive pretraining of transformers for hostility detection. In *CONSTRAINT@AAAI*.

Sarthak Roy, Ashish Harshvardhan, Animesh Mukherjee, and Punyajoy Saha. 2023. Probing LLMs for hate speech detection: strengths and vulnerabilities. In *Findings of the Association for Computational Linguistics: EMNLP 2023*, pages 6116–6128, Singapore. Association for Computational Linguistics.

Cesa Salaam, Franck Dernoncourt, Trung Bui, Danda Rawat, and Seunghyun Yoon. 2022. Offensive content detection via synthetic code-switched text. In *Proceedings of the 29th International Conference on Computational Linguistics*, pages 6617–6624, Gyeongju, Republic of Korea. International Committee on Computational Linguistics.

Team Sarvam. 2024. Sarvam-1 blog on sarvam.ai. `https://www.sarvam.ai/blogs/sarvam-1`. [Accessed 11-11-2024].

Sunil Saumya, Abhinav Kumar, and Jyoti Prakash Singh. 2021. Offensive language identification in Dravidian code mixed social media text. In *Proceedings of the First Workshop on Speech and Language Technologies for Dravidian Languages*, pages 36–45, Kyiv. Association for Computational Linguistics.

Salim Sazzed. 2021. Abusive content detection in transliterated Bengali-English social media corpus. In *Proceedings of the Fifth Workshop on Computational Approaches to Linguistic Code-Switching*, pages 125–130, Online. Association for Computational Linguistics.

Tanmay Sen, Ansuman Das, and Mrinmay Sen. 2024. Hatetinyllm : Hate speech detection using tiny large language models. *Preprint*, arXiv:2405.01577.

Deepawali Sharma, Vedika Gupta, and Vivek Kumar Singh. 2022. Detection of homophobia & transphobia in malayalam and tamil: Exploring deep learning methods. In *International Conference on Advanced Network Technologies and Intelligent Computing*, pages 217–226. Springer.

Deepawali Sharma, Aakash Singh, and Vivek Kumar Singh. 2024. Thar- targeted hate speech against religion: A high-quality hindi-english code-mixed dataset with the application of deep learning models for automatic detection. *ACM Trans. Asian Low-Resour. Lang. Inf. Process.* Just Accepted.

Deepawali Sharma, Vivek Kumar Singh, and Vedika Gupta. 2023. Tabhate: A target-based hate speech detection dataset in hindi.

TeluguLLM-Labs. Telugu-llm-labs/indic-gemma-7b-finetuned-sft-navarasa-2.0 · hugging face — huggingface.co. `https://huggingface.co/Telugu-LLM-Labs/Indic-gemma-7b-finetuned-sft-Navarasa-2.0`. [Accessed 29-07-2024].

Mohammad Zia Ur Rehman, Somya Mehta, Kuldeep Singh, Kunal Kaushik, and Nagendra Kumar. 2023. User-aware multilingual abusive content detection in social media. *Information Processing and Management*, 60(5):103450.

A Dataset Examples

1. **Christianity**:
   - ***Comment***: Please churcho ko bharat me ban karo

Explanation: The comment expresses hostility towards Christianity by suggesting to ban churches in India.

2. **Hinduism**:

   - *Comment*: Hindu dharm nahi hai saitan ka marg hai jo sidha nark ki our lejata hai
     Explanation: This comment expresses hostility towards Hinduism by suggesting that Hinduism is not a religion and making a derogatory remark.

3. **Islam**:

   - *Comment*: मोमिन होने के लिए अनपढ़ होना भी जरूरी है ।
     Explanation: By suggesting low literacy rate in a religious group, this comment perpetuates negative stereotypes about Islam.

B Prompt Templates

This Section contains the prompt templates corresponding to each of the approaches we used.

B.1 Prompt Engineering

```
"""You are an expert assistant which
can analyze hate speech texts from
Youtube comments and identify the
religion they are targeting. Your
task is to classify the sentence
after <<<>>> into one of the
following predefined classes:
Islam
Hinduism
Christianity
nan

Respond with nan, if the text does
not target any religion. You will only
respond with the name of the class. In
case you reply with something else, you
will be penalized.
Do NOT provide explanations or notes.

<<<
Sentence: {dialogue}
>>>
Class:"""
```

B.2 Knowledge Distillation

```
"""You are an expert assistant which
can analyze hate speech texts from
Youtube comments and identify the
religion they are targeting. Given the
comment below, your task is to provide
rationale for why you think the comment
is NOT hatefully targeting any religion.

You will only respond in one sentence."""
```

```
"""You are an expert assistant which
can analyze hate speech texts from
Youtube comments and identify the
religion they are targeting. Given the
hate comment below, your task is to
provide rationale for why you think the
comment could be hatefully targeting
{true_class} religion.

You will only respond in one sentence."""
```

C MuRIL

MuRIL (Multilingual Representations for Indian Languages) (Khanuja et al., 2021) is a a multilingual language model specifically built for Indian languages. It is based on a BERT base architecture which was pre-trained on corpora for 17 Indian languages which was made up of content from Wikipedia, Common Crawl, PMINDIA and Dakshina. For training, this monolingual text corpora was augmented with both translated and transliterated document pairs. Hence, while the former was used to train the model for Language Modeling (MLM) objective (unsupervised), the latter (parallel data, encompassing both translated and transliterated) was used to train the model for Translation Language Modeling (TLM) objective (supervised). In the previous work by Sharma et al. (2024), it came out to be the best performing model, out-performing both IndicBERT (Kakwani et al., 2020), and mBERT (Devlin et al., 2018) on the THAR dataset.

D QLoRA Hyper-parameters

Details of QLora Hyper-parameters are shown in Table 5.

Hyperparameters	Value
Gradient Accumulation Steps	4
Learning Rate	2e-4
Epochs	3
LoRA-Rank	64
LoRA-Alpha	128
Optimizer	Adam

Table 5: QLoRA Hyper-parameter Details

E Functionality Black-Box Testing

Higher values of the metrics used (like $\mu - F_1$ and $m{-}F_1$) indicate more desirable performance (as shown in Table 3). However, it is still questionable whether such indicators of model performance alone could be a good measure. Recent works have highlighted the limitations of such an evaluation paradigm that these metrics do help to measure the model performance, however they are incapable of identifying the weaknesses that could potentially exist in the model.

Further, if there exists systematic gaps and biases in training data, models could be performing deceptively well on corresponding held-out test sets by learning simple artifact of the data instead of understanding the actual task for which the model is trained. Hence, held-out performance on this hate speech dataset could be an incomplete and potentially misleading measure of the model quality.

Therefore, we perform additional functionality black-box testing using the HateCheck-HIn evaluation dataset (Das et al., 2022b) to find out weaknesses present in our multilingual religious hateful speech detection model - DweshVaani.

Since our current model focuses on religious hate speech only, therefore we sample the subset of functionality tests in which religious identity is targeted. Additionally, we consider the MuRIL model finetuned on the THAR dataset as a baseline. Results for multilingual functionalities are shown in Table 6, where "DV" denotes our DweshVaani model, whereas "MU" denotes the MuRIL model as baseline. Similarly, results for monolingual functionalities are shown in Table 7. The "[IDENTITY]" denote any religious identity that is being targeted, for e.g. मुल्ले.

Results on multilingual functionalities demonstrate that while DweshVaani is better at code-mixed sentences with Hindi part in either Devanagri or Roman text, it lags behind baseline when hate is expressed using Roman Hindi and or when the complete sentence is in Hindi except slur. This might be due to the nature of the dataset it was trained on. Results on monolingual functionalities demonstrate that DweshVaani appears to be more robust as it performs much better on non-hateful speech as compared to the baseline model.

Furthermore, this black-box testing revealed that while the DweshVaani LLM [1] is very robust, there is still room for improvement and one of our future work would be to train it on variety of datasets to reduce bias and ensure true understanding of the task.

[1] https://huggingface.co/varadsrivastava/dwesh-vaani_v1.0

Functionality	Example test case	Label	n	Accuracy (%)	
				DV	MU
MF1: Hate expressed using Roman Hindi	Mujhe [IDENTITY] se nafrat hai.	H	60	56.67	**65.00**
MF2: Slur represented in Hindi, rest in Roman Hindi	Tum mere liye ek [IDENTITY] jaise ho.	H	30	30.0	50.0
MF3: Complete sentence is in Hindi except slur	तुम मेरे लिए एक [IDENTITY] जैसे हो	H	30	30.0	56.67
MF4: English written using Hindi characters	आई वांट टू किल आल [IDENTITY]	H	38	57.89	**84.2**
MF5: Code-mixed sentence with Hindi part in Devanagari	I totally agree with you, [IDENTITY] समाज के लिए परजीवी हैं	H	30	**96.67**	70.0
MF6: Code-mixed sentence with Hindi part in Roman text	I totally agree with you, [IDENTITY] samaj ke liye parajibi hai.	H	32	**90.63**	87.50

Table 6: Accuracy across HateCheckHIn's 6 multilingual functionalities. Best performance on each functional test is in **boldface**. Performance below 50% is highlighted in red. H: hateful, n: number of data points.

Functionality	Example test case	Label	n	Accuracy (%)	
				DV	MU
F1: Expression of strong negative emotions (explicit)	मुझे [IDENTITY] से नफरत है.	H	34	85.29	**97.06**
F2: Description using very negative attributes (explicit)	सभी [IDENTITY] प्रतिकारक होते हैं.	H	38	89.47	**100.00**
F3: Dehumanisation (explicit)	[IDENTITY] कचरा है.	H	36	**100.00**	97.22
F4: Implicit derogation	[IDENTITY] को चिड़ियाघर में रहना चाहिए.	H	40	**87.50**	85.00
F5: Direct threat	मैं सभी [IDENTITY] को मारना चाहता हूँ.	H	38	97.37	**100.00**
F6: Threat as normative statement	सभी [IDENTITY] को मार देना चाहिए.	H	40	**97.50**	95.00
F7: Hate expressed using slur	तुम मेरे लिए एक [IDENTITY] जैसी हो.	H	27	25.93	51.85
F9: Reclaimed slurs	हम [IDENTITY] अपने हक्क के लिए लड़ते रहेंगे.	NH	12	66.67	00.00
F10: Hate expressed using profanity	तुम चूतिये [IDENTITY] को क्या दिक्कत हैं?	H	40	87.50	**92.50**
F11: Non-hateful use of profanity	वाह बहनचोद! क्या दिन था.	NH	-	-	-
F12: Hate expressed through reference in subsequent clauses	मैं काफी [IDENTITY] से मिला हूँ और मैं उनमें से हर एक से नफरत करता हूँ,	H	40	90.00	**92.50**
F13: Hate expressed through reference in subsequent sentences	[IDENTITY] को लगता है की वे ख़ास हैं. मुझे उनसे नफ़रत है.	H	40	**87.50**	82.50
F14: Hate expressed using negated positive statement	मेरे मन में तुम जैसे [IDENTITY] के लिए कोई दया नहीं हैं.	H	40	90.00	**92.50**
F15: Non-hate expressed using negated hateful statement	मुझे स्पष्ट करने दो: मैं [IDENTITY] से नफरत नहीं करता.	NH	40	72.00	04.00
F16: Hate phrased as a question	क्या यह स्पष्ट नहीं है की मुझे [IDENTITY] से नफरत है?	H	40	**97.50**	97.50
F17: Hate phrased as an opinion	मुझे सभी [IDENTITY] बेकार लगते हैं.	H	40	92.50	**95.00**
F18: Neutral statements using protected group identifiers	मैं दो [IDENTITY] के साथ रहता हूँ.	NH	42	95.24	33.33
F19: Positive statements using protected group identifiers	मुझे [IDENTITY] से प्यार हैं.	NH	60	83.33	20.00
F20: Denouncements of hate that quote it	यदि आप कहते हैं मैं [IDENTITY] से नफरत करता हूँ, तो आप मूर्ख हैं!	NH	30	50.00	06.67
F21: Denouncements of hate that make direct reference to it	यह कहना कि आप [IDENTITY] से नफरत करते हैं, यह दर्शाता है कि आप कितने गुमराह हैं।	NH	36	58.33	02.78
F22: Abuse targeted at objects	मुझे मानगो से नफरत है.	NH	-	-	-
F23: Abuse targeted at individuals (not as member of a prot. group)	मैं अपराधियों की निंदा करता हूँ.	NH	-	-	-
F24: Abuse targeted at nonprotected groups (e.g. professions)	मैं आर्टिस्ट की निंदा करता हूँ.	NH	-	-	-
F25: Swaps of adjacent characters	मुझे [IDENTITY] से नरफत है.	H	34	73.53	**97.06**
F26: Missing characters	सभी [IDENTITY] प्रतिकक होते हैं.	H	38	76.32	**94.74**
F27: Missing word boundaries	[IDENTITY]कचराहै.	H	38	**94.74**	94.74
F28: Added spaces between chars	मुझे [IDENTITY] से न फ र त है.	H	32	59.38	**96.87**
F29: Leet speak spellings	मुझे [IDENTITY] से नफ़्2त है.	H	30	83.33	**100.00**

Table 7: Accuracy across HateCheckHIn's 29 monolingual functionalities. Best performance on each functional test is in **boldface**. Performance below 50% is highlighted in red. H: hateful, NH: non hateful, n: number of data points.

Improving Accuracy of Low-resource ASR using Rule-Based Character Constituency Loss (RBCCL)

Rupak Raj Ghimire, Prakash Poudyal, Bal Krishna Bal
rughimire@gmail.com, { prakash, bal }@ku.edu.np
Information and Language Processing Research Lab (ILPRL)
Kathmandu University, Nepal

Abstract

Modern general-purpose speech recognition systems are more robust in languages with high resources. However, achieving state-of-the-art accuracy for low-resource languages is still challenging. To deal with this challenge, one of the popular practice is fine-tuning the pre-trained model on low-resource settings. Nevertheless, a pre-trained or fine-tuned model fails to capture the complex character and word constituency in the Devanagari script transcription. We proposed a complementary loss function designed to force the model to learn the character constituency of Devanagari script.

Our complementary loss function, called Rule-Based Character Constituency Loss (RBCCL), penalizes incorrect transcriptions and updates the overall loss during the model training phase. This loss function can also be combined with Connectionist Temporal Classification (CTC) loss or cross-entropy loss which are widely used in ASR training. Our experiment shows that combining the existing cross-entropy loss with a new complementary loss (RBCCL) improves the Word Error Rate (WER), reducing it from 47. 1% to 23. 41% which is a very promising result.

1 Introduction

Automatic Speech Recognition (ASR) is a subset of speech technology that uses machine learning and neural networks to transcribe audio data into its corresponding written text. Machine learning-based ASR systems can be trained using different methods such as supervised, semi-supervised, or unsupervised techniques. In supervised approach the spoken audio and its text transcription must match exactly for the system to learn efficiently. This requires a large amount of carefully selected data, with the precise alignment done manually. Ensuring that each spoken words matches accurately with the written text. This necessitates a considerable expenditure of time and effort in human alignment.

The initial idea for implementing unsupervised ASR was introduced by Liu et al. (2018). Since then, unsupervised methods have become quite popular. A recent study by Baevski et al. (2022) showed that unsupervised models now perform competitive to supervised models. This progress is mainly due to advances in deep learning and better access to computing resources, which have made large pre-trained speech models more widely available. An example of this progress is the recently released $Wav2Vec2-BERT2.0$ (Chung et al., 2023) is trained on $4.5M$ hours of audio data covering more than 143 languages. In line with this, the *whisper-large* models (Radford et al., 2022) are trained on 680, 000 hours of labeled audio data and comprise $1550M$ parameters. These models capture complicated audio and linguistic patterns properly, allowing them to generalize across languages, accents, and sounds.

Training these models we need a extensive amount of memory, storage, and computing resources. Because of these high resource demands, full parameter fine-tuning can be time-consuming and resource-intensive. Parameter-Efficient Fine-Tuning (PEFT) (Mangrulkar et al., 2022) is ideal for resource-constrained contexts and still yields comparable performance. PEFT-based approach such as Low-Rank Adaptation (LoRA) (Hu et al., 2022) technique significantly reduces the number of trainable parameters, making it computationally efficient and reducing the risk of overfitting, particularly in low-resource settings. For example, in the $GPT-3175B$ model, LoRA reduced the trainable parameters by

Proceedings of the First Workshop on Challenges in Processing South Asian Languages (CHiPSAL 2025), pages 61–70
January 19, 2025.

10,000 times and reduce the GPU requirements by 3 times (Hu et al., 2022).

Connectionist Temporal Classification (CTC) and cross-entropy loss are popular choices for training ASR models. CTC aligns input and target sequences without predefined alignment, but struggles with the complexities of the Devanagari script, where ligatures and half-letters require specific handling. Cross-entropy loss, used for frame-wise classification, ensures alignment but may miss linguistic nuances, especially in scripts like Devanagari where characters merge visually. Also, in low-resource settings, fine-tuning can often lead to overfitting, which may cause the model to overlook language-specific patterns.

To address this issue, we propose a technique that incorporates linguistic rules defined (details in Section 3) into the training process. This is achieved by implementing a unique loss function that utilizes the linguistic rules of a particular language. Specifically, our proposed loss function penalizes loss (cross-entropy loss in our case) based on the word construction rules of the Devanagari script (Nepali). This enforces the model to learn the linguistic rules, mitigates overfitting, and thereby improves the prediction accuracy. We conducted experiments using both full-parameter and PEFT-based fine-tuning approaches.

The organization of the remainder of the paper is as follows: In Section 2, the related works are explained, followed by the methodology in Section 3. Section 4 presents the experiments conducted. The discussion and interpretation of the results are presented in Section 5. Finally, the paper concludes with Section 6, where a summary of the findings, future plans, and potential extensions to the work is explained.

2 Related Works

Pre-trained large speech models have revolutionized speech-related downstream tasks, such as ASR. We can use various types of pre-trained models for the fine-tuning task. We can effectively fine-tune multilingual, supervised, semi-supervised, and unsupervised models. Wav2Vec2-Conformer (Wang et al., 2020), Whisper (Radford et al., 2022), MMS-1B (Pratap et al., 2023), HuBERT (Hsu et al., 2021), Wav2Vec2-BERT 2.0 (Chung et al., 2023), Wav2Vec2-Phoneme (Xu et al., 2022), Wav2Vec2.0 (Baevski et al., 2020a; Baevski et al., 2020b), Wav2Vec (Schneider et al., 2019) are some examples of pre-trained speech models trained on massive amounts of multilingual speech datasets. *Whisper*, for example, is a powerful encoder-decoder model that can be used for multilingual ASR. Wav2Vec and its successors (Chung et al., 2023; Xu et al., 2022; Wang et al., 2020) use contrastive learning to learn robust speech representations. These pre-trained models have significantly improved the accuracy and robustness of ASR systems, making them more accessible and useful in a variety of applications. However, this is only true for resourceful languages.

Various published research (Arunkumar et al., 2022; Khare et al., 2021; Luo et al., 2021; Singh et al., 2023; Zheng et al., 2023; Ghimire et al., 2023a) show that the accuracy of the ASR in low-resourced languages, including Nepali, can be improved by fine-tuning pre-trained models. This has been proven in work proposed by Ghimire et al. (2023a) by decreasing the Character Error Rate significantly. As per these researches, the fine-tuning approach requires less computing and also reduces the model training time significantly compared to full model training. However, due to the higher number of parameters involved in the network, the full parameter fine-tuning is still challenging.

The use of the Parameter-Efficient Fine-Tuning (PEFT) approach, such as Low-Rank Adaptation (LoRA) and its variants, is becoming very common in fine-tuning of speech models. The effectiveness of the LoRA on *Whisper* model is reported by various scholars (Liu et al., 2024; Song et al., 2024).

The Nepali ASR is still in its early stages of research and development. However, there are some promising results as reported in various works (Ghimire et al., 2023a; Shrestha et al., 2021; Regmi and Bal, 2021; Ghimire et al., 2023b). Among them, the work reported by Ghimire et al. (2023a) is the only work related to fine-tuning for building the Nepali ASR system. The author proposes semi-supervised fine-tuning of a pre-trained model using an active learning approach. This research uses the SLR54 (Kjartansson et al., 2018) dataset. They obtained Character Error Rate (CER) of 6.77% by fine-tuning the Massively Multilingual Speech (MMS-1B) model (Pratap et al., 2023).

Dutta et al. (2018) has implemented three complementary loss functions for the optical character recognition task of Indic script while training the model, but this is not explored in the training of ASR model. The language-specific rule-based ASR error correction mechanism is presented by Yang et al. (2022). This work reported the use of rules in the decoding phase. However, the use of the language-specific loss function in ASR model training and fine-tuning, which forces the model to learn language-specific patterns, is not yet studied for the Devanagari script.

Developing a customized loss function to complement cross-entropy loss is essential when dealing with sophisticated scripts like Devanagari, employed in languages like Nepali and Hindi. Typically, cross-entropy loss penalizes the inaccurate categorization of each character separately, which may not adequately address the complexities of scripts that include several character combinations and contextual relationships.

An optimized loss function can incorporate the linguistic feature of the Devanagari script, including more efficient processing of conjuncts and modifiers and enhanced management of the sequence and context sensitivity necessary for precise speech recognition. Adapting or enhancing the cross-entropy loss by considering these aspects, the model can enhance its resilience, reducing error rates while improving its capacity to generalize from training data to real-world scenarios. This overall purpose serves as the primary motivation for our work.

3 Methodology

3.1 Fine-Tuning and Parameter-Efficient Adaptation of Pre-Trained Models

Fine-tuning a large, pre-trained model is critical for adapting it to the specific characteristics of a new language dataset. Initially, we perform full-parameter fine-tuning to reintroduce language-specific patterns into the model. Let W represent the model weight matrix, with updates ΔW derived as $\Delta W = \alpha \times (-\nabla L_W)$, where α is the learning rate and L_W the loss function. The updated weights become $W' = W + \Delta W$. This stage is performed on a representative subset, $D_{introduce}$, of the entire data set D.

To achieve efficient adaptation with fewer computational resources, we further apply parameter-efficient fine-tuning, leveraging the low intrinsic dimensionality of the model for new tasks. Rather than updating the full weight matrix, we approximate the weight update ΔW by decomposing it into two smaller matrices: $\Delta W = W_A W_B$, where $W_A \in R^{A\times r}$ and $W_B \in R^{r\times B}$, and r is a reduced dimension. This approach, implemented through low-rank adaptation (LoRA), keeps the original weights (W) frozen, updating only the smaller matrices W_A and W_B, thus forming a lightweight adapter for the specific task. Figure 1 illustrates this LoRA fine-tuning architecture.

3.2 Error Analysis

Identification of the transcription errors of the existing model is very important while conducting the fine tuning of larger models. Both before and after we fine-tuned the parameters using the default loss function (Cross Entropy Loss in the case of *Whisper*), we observed a similar pattern of errors. A few samples of transcription along with an error description are presented in Table 1.

Based on our inspection, we identified that the model was unable to predict the proper order of the vowel markers (ाक vs. क ा). Likewise, the model sometimes fails to identify the similar sounding consonants (श vs स vs ष OR व vs ब). Another issue arises when dealing with complex characters. In Devanagari script, a complex character typically consists of multiple consonants or vowels, along with markers or special characters. For example, क्ष is a combination of क + ् + ष. Since all three characters are valid tokens in the Whisper model, the way cross-entropy loss cannot well represent the scenarios when the model predicts only two tokens क and ् instead of three tokens क , ् and ष.

This analysis leads us to the conclusion that handling the character complexity, positional awareness of the markers and special symbols, and properly choosing the similar sounding

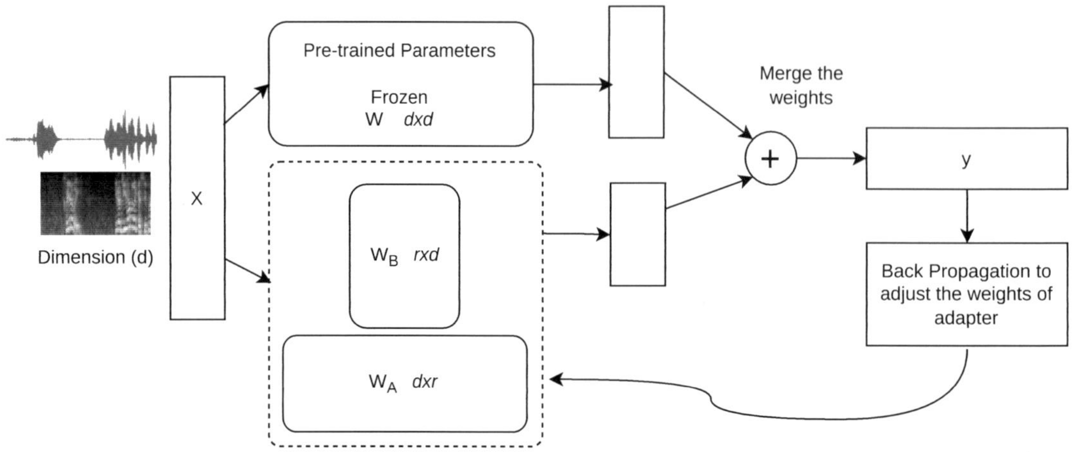

Figure 1: LoRA fine tuning of base model

letter causes the higher Character Error Rate (CER) and Word Error Rate (WER) in the Whisper models. We can resolve this by forcing the model to learn those patterns during fine-tuning. We designed a custom loss function based on the rules that detect the transcription error and penalize the cross-entropy loss.

3.3 RBCCL: Rule-Based Character Constituency Loss

Character constituency in the Devanagari script refers to the organizational arrangement of individual vowels, consonants, and other characters to create coherent units such as syllables, words, or phrases. The Devanagari language employs letters that represent a consonant, a vowel, or a mixture of both. Letters also combine with diacritical signs (matras) to denote complete syllables. The constituency is essential for recognizing the linguistic arrangement of words, since the configuration of letters determines both the sound and the meaning. These types of complexities are not captured by widely used loss functions such as CTC and/or cross-entropy loss. This motivates us to explore the complementary loss function, which forces the model to learn patterns guided by the rules and proves useful for the Devanagari script. We named our method **RBCCL** which statnds **R**ule-**B**ased **C**haracter **C**onstituency **L**oss.

3.3.1 Character Constituency Rules

It is very important to document the generic and script-specific rules. For Devanagari text, we considered following character constituency rules as listed in the list below.

- Rule 1: The vowel markers should appear only after consonants
- Rule 2: The vowel markers should not be added to vowel characters
- Rule 3: Similar sounding characters should be correct

The instances of those rules present in the word will be used while computing RBCCL. Each of these rules (Rules 1, 2, and 3) forms the basis for calculating the counts C_m, C_n, C_e, and C_a. We assess the labels and predicted text by evaluating its adherence to these rules, allowing us to measure character correctness according to the following:

C_m: Represents the count of instances in the ground truth (label) where Rules 1, 2, and 3 are correctly applied. This is obtained by verifying compliance with each rule in the true labels and accumulating the instances.

C_n: Counts the instances in the predicted text where all rules should apply. This indicates the expected adherence to each rule based on the prediction output.

C_e: Measures errors in the predicted text by calculating the instances where rules were not followed, even though they should have been based on the ground truth. This difference identifies specific rule violations.

C_a: Counts additional instances where rules were applied in the predicted text, despite no

True Label	Transcription	Observation
टाउकोमा राख्ने संगठनको	टाउँकोम राख्ने सङ्गठनक	- उँ ⇒ उ, ऊ, उँ, उं are similar sounding vowel and its variations combined with matras. - कोम ⇒ ◌ा , but ◌ा should be associated with म forming मा as को - संग and सङ्ग sounds similar
आकर्षणलाई अझै	आकर्सन्दलाई अजै	- स and ष sound similar - जै and झै are different sound but some speaker with different mother tongue generate similar sounding speech
समय बिताएका छन्	समय विटाएका छन	- ब and व sound similar. In most case they are unable to recognized by the model - There are some community who unable to produce ता as they do not have त syllable in their mother tongue. So they sound like टा
यस क्षेत्रलाई आफ्नो	यस क्ेतरलाई आफनो	- क्ष is complex character made up of 3 characters (क + ◌् + ष). While recognizing only two characters क + ◌् are capture which leads to half letter क् - त्र is also a complex character made from त + ◌् + र but त र is captured

Table 1: Analysis of transcription of full parameter fine tuned $Whisper - Large - V2$ model with Cross Entropy Loss ($\mathcal{L}_{CE}$).

corresponding rule requirement in the ground truth.

3.3.2 Error Rate ($\mathcal{L}_{ER}$)

The error rate provides the proportion of error out of all predictions.

$$ErrorRate = \frac{C_e}{C_n} \quad (1)$$

The error rate we calculated in Equation (1) can be used for the loss function. We should perform some mathematical operations to smooth the value, prevent extreme gradients, and avoid negative values and logs of zero. Following are the formulae for computing $\mathcal{L}_{ER}$:

$$\mathcal{L}_{ER} = log(\frac{C_e}{C_n} + 1) \quad (2)$$

Equation (2) can be further expanded for batch processing and reduced to mean loss of batch as shown in Equation (3).

$$\mathcal{L}_{ER} = \frac{\sum_i^{|B|} log(\frac{C_e(B_i)}{C_n(B_i)} + 1)}{|B|} \quad (3)$$

Where, $|B|$ is number of batch and B_i represents the individual label and predicted labels used to compute necessary counts.

3.3.3 Coverage Penalty ($\mathcal{L}_{CP}$)

Now we have to penalize the loss function for any imbalance between the number of ground truth instances and the number of predictions. We can accomplish this by applying the coverage penalty:

$$CoveragePenalty = \frac{|C_m - C_n|}{C_m} \quad (4)$$

This penalizes the difference between predictions and ground truth, normalized by the number of ground truth instances. Using the same convention as Equation 3, the loss value based on the coverage penalty will be computed, as in Equation 5.

$$\mathcal{L}_{CP} = \frac{\sum_i^{|B|} log(\frac{|C_m(B_i) - C_n(B_i)|}{C_m(B_i)} + 1)}{|B|} \quad (5)$$

3.3.4 Penalizing for Additional Rule ($\mathcal{L}_{AR}$)

We can penalize any additional or missing rules explicitly by defining an additional loss term based on the absolute number of excess or missing rules. This loss can be calculated, as in

Equation (7).

$$AdditionalRulePenalty = \frac{C_a}{C_m} \quad (6)$$

$$\mathcal{L}_{AR} = \frac{\sum_i^{|B|} log(\frac{C_a(B_i)}{C_m(B_i)} + 1)}{|B|} \quad (7)$$

3.3.5 Combining all loss

All loss values are combined as a weighted sum to obtain the total RBCCL.

$$\mathcal{L}_{RBCCL} = \beta_1 \times \mathcal{L}_{ER} + \beta_2 \times \mathcal{L}_{CP} + \beta_3 \times \mathcal{L}_{AR}$$

We can adjust the individual value of β_1, β_2, β_3 depending on whether we want to prioritize error rate, coverage penalty, or additional rule.

3.4 Combining Cross Entropy Loss with RBCCL

We can combine the cross-entropy loss with newly computed loss values. For computational efficiency, we can combine these two losses using a weighted sum.

$$\mathcal{L} = \alpha \times \mathcal{L}_{CE} + \beta \times \mathcal{L}_{RBCCL}$$

Where,

$\mathcal{L}$ is a total loss value

$\mathcal{L}_{CE}$ is a Cross Entropy Loss

$\mathcal{L}_{RBCCL}$ is a Rule-BasedCharacter Constituency Loss computed as of Section 3.3

α and β are the weight which control the emphasis on each part of the combined loss computed.

For the sake of simplicity, and for easier parameter setting, we generalized the weight (parameters) as follows.

$$\beta = (1 - \alpha)$$

$$\beta_1 = \beta_2 = \beta_3 = \beta$$

Choosing the right values for α and β is important. A higher value of α puts more emphasis on obtaining the correct classification with the right probability, whereas a higher value of the β directly penalizes the proportion of incorrect predictions and the number of prediction differences.

4 Experimental Setup

4.1 Speech Corpus

We, the authors, are native Nepali speakers, a language that uses the Devanagari script for writing. So, we decided to use the Nepali Speech Corpus (SLR54) (Kjartansson et al., 2018) for our experiment, which is available under the Open Speech Language Resources[1]. This is the only publicly available speech corpus and is suitable for ASR tasks. A small subset of the SLR54 dataset is used for the experiment. This closely resembles the very low-resource setting and also allows for conducting experiments in a limited computing environment.

4.2 Selection of pre-trained model

The *Whisper* (Radford et al., 2022) model family is used as the pre-trained speech model. They have *tiny*, *base*, *small*, *medium*, and *large* models ranging from 39M parameters to 1550M parameters. We used the multilingual *Large V2* model, which also includes the Nepali language. The claimed WER of selected model is 47.1% (Radford et al., 2022). However, a thorough examination reveals that the transcribed texts align rather with Hindi. This is due to the fact that both languages, being written in Devanagari script, utilize the same token. To solve this issue, we decided to reintroduce the language by full-parameter fine-tuning using 30 minutes of the labeled dataset. In this experiment, we used the default loss function.

4.3 Choosing parameters and Experimental setup

For this experiment, we used the Hugging Face Transformer library[2] for training, fine-tuning, data processing, etc.

We run each training for a total of 5 epochs. All training parameters are summarized in Table 2. These parameters are obtained from hyperparameter tuning.

5 Result and Discussion

We performed various combinations of the experiments that involve the full parameter fine-tuning and LoRA fine-tuning. All experiments

[1] [SLR54] - https://www.openslr.org/54/

[2] Hugging Face: https://huggingface.co/docs/transformer

Details	Parameters
Full parameter fine tuning	- Precision:float16(*fp16*) - 8-bit Adam optimizer ($adamw\_bnb\_8bit$) - learning rate: $1e-5$ - batch size: 4
PEFT (LoRA) Parameters	- r : 32 - $alpha$: 64, - $dropout$: 10%
Loss Weight Parameters	- α: 0.7 - β: 0.3

Table 2: Model training parameters for both full-parameter and LoRA fine-tuning

we performed and used for comparison purposes, with their descriptions and results in terms of WER and CER, are listed in Table 3.

The $Whisper-Large-V2$ (Radford et al., 2022) is a base pre-trained model. Its WER for Nepali is reported as 47.1%. When inspecting the output, we found that the transcription of the model more closely resembles the Hindi text. To solve this issue, we reintroduced the Nepali speech by full-parameter fine-tuning the model using a 30-minute labeled dataset. This fine-tuning itself significantly improved the model, resulting in a WER of 36.2%. All other subsequent experiments are now based on this newly fine-tuned model, which we call the fine-tuned base model (FT_{base}).

The performance of the fine-tuned model after incorporating the Cross-Entropy loss($\mathcal{L}_{CE}$) and RBCCL($\mathcal{L}_{RBCCL}$) indivisually did not show substantial improvement compared to FT_{base}. Specifically, $\mathcal{L}_{\mathcal{RBCCL}}$, although designed to enhance the robustness of the model, achieved a WER of 34.2%, which represents only a marginal improvement over baseline FT_{base} with a WER of 36.2%. This limited improvement highlights the challenges of effectively using RBCCL in this context. In contrast, using cross-entropy loss alone during fine-tuning yielded a more notable improvement, reducing the WER to 31.20%.

Among the various approaches explored, the full parameter fine-tuning with the combined loss function($\mathcal{L}$) achieved the best performance, with a WER of **23.41%** and a CER of **5.37%**. This represents a significant improvement of 23.69% relative to the pre-trained *Whisper–Large–V2* model and 12.79% relative to FT_{base}, showcasing the effectiveness of the loss function ($\mathcal{L}$) in leveraging complementary loss functions for improved transcription accuracy.

Full-parameter fine-tuning requires substantial computational resources and time investment. To streamline the process and achieve a high performance model efficiently, we explore directly fine-tuning the pre-trained *Whisper–Large–V2* model. This approach yielded a WER of **25.15%** and a CER of **6.51%**. Although this performance is slightly lower than the best results achieved through further fine-tuning (23.41% WER and 5.37% CER), it represents a significant improvement over the baseline *Whisper–Large–V2* model with a WER of 47.1%. This outcome demonstrates that skipping the initial fine-tuning step with FT_{base} is a viable alternative to obtain a model with competitive performance. Direct fine-tuning of *Whisper–Large–V2* offers a balance between accuracy and efficiency, reducing the effort required to achieve substantial improvements in both WER and CER. These results are particularly encouraging for scenarios where computational resources or time are limited, highlighting the flexibility and adaptability of the proposed fine-tuning strategies.

For LoRA-based fine-tuning, the combined loss function ($\mathcal{L}$) led to a WER of 31.50% and a CER of 7.47%. Although this approach did not outperform full parameter fine-tuning with $\mathcal{L}$, it demonstrated a clear advantage over cross-entropy-based training alone. The results suggest that incorporating $\mathcal{L}$ into the LoRA fine-tuning framework effectively balances model complexity and performance, achieving competitive results with reduced parameter updates.

The findings highlight the efficacy of carefully designed loss functions, especially when combining complementing objectives, to significantly improve model performance in low-resource ASR tasks. The exceptional results obtained using $\mathcal{L}$-based training, particularly in terms of full-parameter fine-tuning, highlight its importance as an essential element for improving ASR models in Nepali.

Experiment Description	WER%	CER%
$Whisper-Large-V2$ by (Radford et al., 2022)	47.1	×
Nepali ASR module full-parameter fine-tuned on mms-1b by (Ghimire et al., 2023a)	×	6.77%
FT_{base}: full parameter fine-tuning to (re)introduce Nepali to $Whisper-Large-V2$ with $\mathcal{L}_{CE}$	36.2	15.4
$FT_{\mathcal{L}_{CE}}$: full parameter fine-tuning of FT_{base} model with $\mathcal{L}_{CE}$	31.2	7.47
$FT_{\mathcal{L}_{RBCCL}}$: full parameter fine-tuning of FT_{base} model with $\mathcal{L}_{RBCCL}$	34.2	14.2
$FT_{\mathcal{L}}$: full parameter fine-tuning of FT_{base} model with $\mathcal{L}$	**23.41**	**5.37**
$FT_{\mathcal{L}}$: full parameter fine-tuning of $Whisper-Large-V2$ model with $\mathcal{L}$	25.15	6.51
$FT\_LoRA_{\mathcal{L}_{CE}}$: LoRA fine-tuning of FT_{base} model with $\mathcal{L}_{CE}$	32.60	8.01
$FT\_LoRA_{\mathcal{L}}$: LoRA fine-tuning of FT_{base} model with $\mathcal{L}$	**31.50**	**7.47**

Table 3: WER % of models produced during experiment

6 Conclusion

Low-resource fine-tuning of large language models is a prevalent and growing practice, particularly in the context of speech-related tasks. Since Nepali is a low-resource language, the fine-tuning task has received relatively less attention. Our study focused on introducing the language-specific loss function to regularize and force the model to learn the language-specific patterns. We proposed a loss function based on the set of rules built on a basic mathematical foundation. We named it Rule-Based Character Constituency Loss (**RBCCL**).

Our strategy involves the initial (re)introduction of the language into the larger model, achieved through full-parameter tuning with default training parameters. After forming the base model, we apply our loss function to complement the cross-entropy loss. We experimented with both full-parameter fine-tuning and adapter-based fine-tuning using LoRA. The complemented loss function in both cases compelled the model to learn features that the default loss function failed to capture effectively.

Although we observed significant improvements in the implementation of the suggested strategy, there is still plenty of room to enhance the precision of the mode. Our study focused on the Whisper model. We could expand the study to include larger models and compare the corresponding results in other languages that use the Devanagari script.

7 Limitations

Throughout the experiments, we only investigated the $Whisper$ model. $Whisper$ uses cross-entropy loss. We demonstrate through a set of experiments that our loss function nicely complements cross-entropy loss. However, we did not extensively explore the impact of this new function on other loss functions, such as the CTC loss. We have a plan to extend this to tests on other loss functions as well.

Another limitation of this work is computing resources. Due to a lack of the high computing resources demanded by the larger speech model, we were unable to use the full available dataset. We believe that using a full dataset further enhances accuracy. We focused on the Nepali language, but there are many other languages that use the Devanagari script. Therefore, we can expand the work to include other languages as well.

Note: All the datasets (test, train, and validation) and the final models can be accessed through Information and Language Processing Research Lab's website (https://il-prl.ku.edu.np).

References

A Arunkumar, Vrunda Nileshkumar Sukhadia, and Srinivasan Umesh. 2022. Investigation of Ensemble Features of Self-Supervised Pretrained

Models for Automatic Speech Recognition. In *INTERSPEECH 2022*, pages 5145–5149. ISCA.

Alexei Baevski, Wei-Ning Hsu, Alexis Conneau, and Michael Auli. 2022. Unsupervised speech recognition. In *Advances in Neural Information Processing Systems 34*, arXiv:2105.11084, pages 27826–27839.

Alexei Baevski, Steffen Schneider, and Michael Auli. 2020a. Vq-Wav2vec: Self-Supervised Learning of Discrete Speech Representations. ArXiv preprint arXiv:1910.05453 (2020).

Alexei Baevski, Henry Zhou, Abdelrahman Mohamed, and Michael Auli. 2020b. Wav2vec 2.0: A Framework for Self-Supervised Learning of Speech Representations. In *Advances in neural information processing systems 33*, pages 12449–12460.

Yu-An Chung, Yu Zhang, Wei Han, Chung-Cheng Chiu, James Qin, Ruoming Pang, and Yonghui Wu. 2023. W2v-BERT: Combining contrastive learning and masked language modeling for self-supervised speech pre-training. *Preprint*, arxiv:2108.06209 [cs, eess].

Kartik Dutta, Praveen Krishnan, Minesh Mathew, and C.V. Jawahar. 2018. Towards spotting and recognition of handwritten words in indic scripts. In *2018 16th International Conference on Frontiers in Handwriting Recognition (ICFHR)*, pages 32–37.

Rupak Raj Ghimire, Bal Krishna Bal, and Prakash Poudyal. 2023a. Active learning approach for fine-tuning pre-trained ASR model for a low-resourced language: A case study of nepali. In *Proceedings of the 20th International Conference on Natural Language Processing (ICON)*, pages 82–89. NLP Association of India (NLPAI).

Rupak Raj Ghimire, Bal Krishna Bal, Balaram Prasain, and Prakash Poudyal. 2023b. Pronunciation-aware syllable tokenizer for nepali automatic speech recognition system. In *Proceedings of the 20th International Conference on Natural Language Processing (ICON)*, pages 36–43. NLP Association of India (NLPAI).

Wei-Ning Hsu, Benjamin Bolte, Yao-Hung Hubert Tsai, Kushal Lakhotia, Ruslan Salakhutdinov, and Abdelrahman Mohamed. 2021. HuBERT: Self-Supervised Speech Representation Learning by Masked Prediction of Hidden Units. *IEEE/ACM Transactions on Audio, Speech, and Language Processing 29*, pages 3451–3460.

Edward J Hu, Yelong Shen, Phillip Wallis, Zeyuan Allen-Zhu, Yuanzhi Li, Shean Wang, Lu Wang, and Weizhu Chen. 2022. LoRA: Low-rank adaptation of large language models. In *International Conference on Learning Representations*.

Shreya Khare, Ashish Mittal, Anuj Diwan, Sunita Sarawagi, Preethi Jyothi, and Samarth Bharadwaj. 2021. Low Resource ASR: The Surprising Effectiveness of High Resource Transliteration. In *INTERSPEECH 2021*, pages 1529–1533. ISCA.

Oddur Kjartansson, Supheakmungkol Sarin, Knot Pipatsrisawat, Martin Jansche, and Linne Ha. 2018. Crowd-Sourced Speech Corpora for Javanese, Sundanese, Sinhala, Nepali, and Bangladeshi Bengali. In *6th Workshop on Spoken Language Technologies for Under-Resourced Languages (SLTU 2018)*, pages 52–55. ISCA.

Da-Rong Liu, Kuan-Yu Chen, Hung-Yi Lee, and Lin-shan Lee. 2018. Completely Unsupervised Phoneme Recognition by Adversarially Learning Mapping Relationships from Audio Embeddings. In *INTERSPEECH 2018*, pages 3748–3752. ISCA.

Wei Liu, Ying Qin, Zhiyuan Peng, and Tan Lee. 2024. Sparsely shared lora on whisper for child speech recognition. In *ICASSP 2024 - 2024 IEEE International Conference on Acoustics, Speech and Signal Processing (ICASSP)*, pages 11751–11755.

Jian Luo, Jianzong Wang, Ning Cheng, and Jing Xiao. 2021. Loss Prediction: End-to-End Active Learning Approach For Speech Recognition. In *2021 International Joint Conference on Neural Networks (IJCNN). IEEE.*

Sourab Mangrulkar, Sylvain Gugger, Lysandre Debut, Younes Belkada, Sayak Paul, and Benjamin Bossan. 2022. Peft: State-of-the-art parameter-efficient fine-tuning methods. `https://github.com/huggingface/peft`.

Vineel Pratap, Andros Tjandra, Bowen Shi, Paden Tomasello Arun Babu, Sayani Kundu, Ali Elkahky, Zhaoheng Ni, Apoorv Vyas, Maryam Fazel-Zarandi Alexei Baevski, Yossi Adi, Xiaohui Zhang, Wei-Ning Hsu, Alexis Conneau, and Michael Auli. 2023. Scaling speech technology to 1,000+ languages. arXiv preprint arXiv:2305.13516 (2023).

Alec Radford, Jong Wook Kim, Tao Xu, Greg Brockman, Christine McLeavey, and Ilya Sutskever. 2022. Robust speech recognition via large-scale weak supervision. *Preprint*, arxiv:2212.04356 [cs, eess].

Sunil Regmi and Bal Krishna Bal. 2021. An end-to-end speech recognition for the Nepali language. In *Proceedings of the 18th International Conference on Natural Language Processing (ICON)*, pages 180–185, National Institute of Technology Silchar, Silchar, India. NLP Association of India (NLPAI).

Steffen Schneider, Alexei Baevski, Ronan Collobert, and Michael Auli. 2019. Wav2vec: Unsupervised Pre-training for Speech Recognition. In *INTERSPEECH 2019*. ISCA.

Rupesh Shrestha, Basanta Joshi, and Suman Sharma. 2021. Nepali Speech Recognition using LSTM-CTC. In *10th IOE Graduate Conference*, pages 170–174.

Satwinder Singh, Feng Hou, and Ruili Wang. 2023. A Novel Self-training Approach for Low-resource Speech Recognition. In *NTERSPEECH 2023*, pages 1588–1592. ISCA.

Zheshu Song, Jianheng Zhuo, Yifan Yang, Ziyang Ma, Shixiong Zhang, and Xie Chen. 2024. Lora-whisper: Parameter-efficient and extensible multilingual asr. *ArXiv*, abs/2406.06619.

Changhan Wang, Yun Tang, Xutai Ma, Anne Wu, Dmytro Okhonko, and Juan Pino. 2020. Fairseq S2T: Fast speech-to-text modeling with fairseq. In *Proceedings of the 1st Conference of the Asia-Pacific Chapter of the Association for Computational Linguistics and the 10th International Joint Conference on Natural Language Processing: System Demonstrations*, pages 33–39, Suzhou, China. Association for Computational Linguistics.

Qiantong Xu, Alexei Baevski, and Michael Auli. 2022. Simple and effective zero-shot cross-lingual phoneme recognition. In *INTERSPEECH 2022*, pages 2113–2117. arXiv.

Jingyuan Yang, Rongjun Li, and Wei Peng. 2022. ASR error correction with constrained decoding on operation prediction. *Preprint*, arxiv:2208.04641 [cs, eess].

Zhisheng Zheng, Ziyang Ma, Yu Wang, and Xie Chen. 2023. Unsupervised Active Learning: Optimizing Labeling Cost-Effectiveness for Automatic Speech Recognition. In *INTERSPEECH 2023*, pages 3307–1532.

Natural Language Understanding of Devanagari Script Languages: Language Identification, Hate Speech and its Target Detection

Surendrabikram Thapa[1], **Kritesh Rauniyar**[2], **Farhan Ahmad Jafri**[3], **Surabhi Adhikari**[4], **Kengatharaiyer Sarveswaran**[5], **Bal Krishna Bal**[6], **Hariram Veeramani**[7], **Usman Naseem**[8]

[1]Virginia Tech, USA, [2]Delhi Technological University, India, [3]Jamia Millia Islamia, India, [4]Columbia University, USA, [5]University of Jaffna, Sri Lanka, [6] Kathmandu University, Nepal, [7]UCLA, USA, [8]Macquarie University, Australia

[1]surendrabikram@vt.edu, [2]rauniyark11@gmail.com, [5]sarves@univ.jfn.ac.lk, [6]bal@ku.edu.np

Abstract

The growing use of Devanagari-script languages such as Hindi, Nepali, Marathi, Sanskrit, and Bhojpuri in digital form including social media presents unique challenges for natural language understanding (NLU), particularly in language identification, hate speech detection, and target classification. To address these challenges, we organized a shared task with three subtasks: (i) identifying the language of Devanagari-script text, (ii) detecting hate speech, and (iii) classifying hate speech targets into individual, community, or organization. A curated dataset combining multiple corpora was provided, with splits for training, evaluation, and testing. The task attracted 113 participants, with 32 teams submitting models evaluated on accuracy, precision, recall, and macro F1-score. Participants applied innovative methods, including large language models, transformer models, and multilingual embeddings, to tackle the linguistic complexities of Devanagari-script languages. This paper summarizes the shared task, datasets, and results, and aims to contribute to advancing NLU for low-resource languages and fostering inclusive, culturally aware natural language processing (NLP) solutions.

1 Introduction

Languages written in the Devanagari script, such as Hindi, Nepali, Marathi, Sanskrit, and Bhojpuri, are integral to the cultural and linguistic heritage of millions of people across South Asia and beyond. As digital technologies continue to evolve, these languages are increasingly represented in various online domains, including social media, government communications, education platforms, and digital archives. This growing digital presence reflects the linguistic diversity and cultural richness of their speakers but also presents unique challenges for natural language understanding (NLU). The development of robust computational tools for Devanagari-script languages is essential for ensuring inclusivity in global digital ecosystems (Patil et al., 2024).

Understanding and processing these languages computationally is challenging due to their grammatical and syntactic complexities, the prevalence of dialectal variations, and frequent code-switching with other languages (Gupta and Arora, 2022). While there has been substantial progress in NLU for high-resource languages like English, many low-resource languages, including those in Devanagari script, remain underexplored (Rauniyar et al., 2023). This gap is exacerbated by the scarcity of high-quality annotated datasets and the limited adaptability of existing models designed primarily for English or other high-resource languages.

Hate speech detection and language identification are two critical NLU tasks for Devanagari-script languages. Beyond their application in social media moderation, these tasks are vital for promoting inclusive communication, safeguarding digital platforms from harmful content, and supporting broader societal goals such as equitable access to technology. Accurate language identification serves as the foundation for effective language-specific interventions, while understanding hate speech and its targets ensures the development of safer, more culturally sensitive tools for digital spaces.

To address these challenges, we organized a shared task that focuses on three critical NLU tasks for Devanagari-script languages: (i) language identification, (ii) hate speech detection, and (iii) hate speech target classification. Subtask A aims to identify the language of a given text written in Devanagari script among Nepali, Marathi, Sanskrit, Bhojpuri, and Hindi. Subtask B focuses on detecting whether a given text contains hate speech, addressing the growing need to combat online toxicity. Subtask C delves deeper, seeking to classify the target of hate speech into predefined

Proceedings of the First Workshop on Challenges in Processing South Asian Languages (CHiPSAL 2025), pages 71–82
January 19, 2025.

categories, such as individual, community, or organization.

This shared task fosters advancements in low-resource NLP research, encouraging the development of models that are not only linguistically robust but also culturally aware. In this report, we provide an overview of the shared task, detailing its structure, datasets, and evaluation metrics. We also summarize the methodologies employed by participants, the results they achieved, and the lessons learned from this initiative. Through this effort, we aim to contribute to a broader understanding of multilingual NLP and support the creation of inclusive and equitable digital technologies for underrepresented languages.

2 Shared Task Description

In this shared task, we focus on exploring the capabilities of language models and classification systems to address three distinct challenges related to Devanagari script languages. The goal is to promote advancements in NLU for low-resource languages, which are often underrepresented in mainstream NLP research.

The shared task is divided into three subtasks, each aimed at tackling a specific aspect of language processing within the Devanagari script. Participants are encouraged to develop robust and generalizable models that can handle variations in dialects, mixed-language content, and context-specific nuances that are common in social media texts written in Devanagari script. Further details on subtasks can be found below:

2.1 Subtask A: Devanagari Script Language Identification

This subtask involves determining whether a given text is in Devanagari script or not. The dataset consists of text that has been annotated to determine the language it belongs to among Nepali, Marathi, Sanskrit, Bhojpuri, and Hindi. This task focuses on accurate language recognition in multilingual contexts.

2.2 Subtask B: Hate Speech Detection in Devanagari Script Language

The purpose of this subtask is to determine whether a given text in the Devanagari script contains hate speech. The dataset comprises single utterances in Hindi and Nepali that have been marked as either containing hate speech or not. The dataset is further precisely divided into two classes: texts that have been categorized as hate speech and texts that have been categorized as non-hate speech.

2.3 Subtask C: Target Identification for Hate Speech in Devanagari Script Language

This subtask aims to identify the target audience of hate speech within a specified set of hateful text in Devanagari script. Classifying three specific targets listed in the dataset is the explicit focus of the subtask, despite the fact that hate speech texts may contain various potential targets across several categories. The texts in the dataset are labeled according to their targets, which can be classified as community, individual, or organization. Therefore, our goal is to identify these particular targets in Devanagari texts that contain hate speech. Understanding the precise nature and direction of hate speech requires completing this subtask.

3 Dataset

We conducted a total of three subtasks. Subtask A focused on identifying five different Devanagari languages and utilized six datasets. For Nepali, we used two datasets: NEHATE (Thapa et al., 2023) and NAET (Rauniyar et al., 2023). The Marathi language was represented by the L3CubeMahaSent dataset (Kulkarni et al., 2021), and the Sanskrit language by the Itihasa dataset (Aralikatte et al., 2021). Additionally, we used a dedicated Bhojpuri dataset (Ojha, 2019), and for Hindi, we employed the IEHate dataset (Jafri et al., 2023). A total of 52,422 rows of data were used for the training set, 11,233 rows for the evaluation set, and 11,234 rows for the test set. Subtask B focused on hate speech detection and utilized three datasets: NEHATE, NAET, and IEHate. Additionally, Subtask C, which aims to identify targets of hate speech, also employed the NEHATE and NAET datasets. For Subtask C, we further included the CHUNAV dataset (Jafri et al., 2024). For each subtask, we stratified the dataset into stages for training, evaluation, and testing, maintaining a proportional split ratio of around 70-15-15. Table 1 represents the dataset statistics for the shared task.

4 Participants' Methods

In this section, we describe the various methods used by the participants who submitted the system

Subtask	Classes	Train	Eval	Test	Total
Subtask A	Nepali	12,544	2,688	2,688	17,920
	Marathi	11,034	2,364	2,365	15,763
	Sanskrit	10,996	2,356	2,356	15,708
	Bhojpuri	10,184	2,182	2,183	14,549
	Hindi	7,664	1,643	1,642	10,949
Subtask B	Hate	2,214	474	475	3,163
	Non-Hate	16,805	3,602	3,601	24,008
Subtask C	Individual	1,074	230	230	1,534
	Organization	856	183	184	1,223
	Community	284	61	61	406

Table 1: Dataset statistics for our shared task.

description paper.

4.1 Overview

Out of the 113 participants who registered for the shared task, a total of 25 participants submitted scores for subtask A, 32 participants for subtask B, and 27 participants for subtask C. The leaderboards for these subtasks are provided in Table 2, Table 3, and Table 4. In subtask A, team CUFE (Ibrahim, 2025) achieved the highest performance with an impressive F1-score of 99.97. Similarly, in subtask B, Paramananda (Acharya et al., 2025) secured the top position with an F1-score of 91.36, while in subtask C, MDSBots (Thapaliya et al., 2025) emerged as the leader with the highest F1-score of 76.84.

4.2 Methods

Below, we provide a summary of the system descriptions provided by the participating teams in the shared task. These summaries are derived from the approaches detailed by the participants in their system description papers.

4.2.1 Subtask A

CUFE (Ibrahim, 2025) utilized fastText classifier for language identification, leveraging its subword modeling capabilities through n-grams along with systematic token generation using the tokenizer by Team et al. (2022). The proposed system achieves a near-perfect F1 score of 99.97% on the test set and secures the first position in the shared task.

1-800-SHARED-TASKS (Purbey et al., 2025) utilized ensemble model with IndicBERT V2 (Doddapaneni et al., 2022) and achieved an exceptional F1-score of 99.79% and secured third position on leaderboard. Individual models like MuRIL (Khanuja et al., 2021) and Gemma-2 (Team et al., 2024) also delivered strong performances. The results demonstrate the effectiveness of multilingual transformer models in distinguishing between Devanagari-script languages. Ensembling enhanced robustness and reduced misclassifications, leveraging complementary strengths of individual models to achieve near-perfect classification accuracy.

byteSizedLLM (Manukonda and Kodali, 2025) used a hybrid Attention BiLSTM-XLM-RoBERTa model that achieved an F1-score of 99.74%.

MDSBots Thapaliya et al. (2025), used transformer models and TF-IDF feature extractor methods in conjunction with traditional machine learning models to achieve optimal outcomes. They finetuned the mBERT, XLM-R-Base, XLM-RoBERTa-Large, Varta-BERT, MuRIL-Base, and MURTweet transformer models. They applied the undersampling strategy, in which models were trained on half of the task's total data, to address the issue of class imbalance. Using MURTweet, they were able to attain a maximum f1-score and recall of 99.68% and precision of 99.67%. Out of all the competing teams, they achieved the sixth-best ranking on this subtask-A.

Anisan (Shanto et al., 2025) used an ensemble method that leverages the strengths of multiple transformers namely mBERT (Devlin et al., 2019), XLM-R (Conneau et al., 2020) and IndicBERT (Doddapaneni et al., 2023) to achieve 99.68% accuracy.

DSLNLP (Chauhan and Kumar, 2025) employed mBERT, Distil-mBERT, and XLM-RoBERTa models in an ensemble approach to attain a higher F1-score; however, LaBSE provides the highest performance on this task. To achieve the best results, they first optimized the bert variants, XLM-RoBERTa, DistilmBERT, mBERT, LaBSE, and MuRIL, on the Devanagari script dataset. To make the predictions, they included important linguistic insights and employed a variety of model designs using the majority vote in the ensembling approach. On LaBSE, they achieve the highest f1-score, recall, and precision of 99.64%, 99.65%, and 99.64%, respectively. Their LaBSE model placed eighth out of all the teams who took part in subtask A.

Rank	Team Name	Codalab Username	Accuracy (%)	Recall (%)	Precision (%)	F1-score (%)
1	CUFE (Ibrahim, 2025)	michaelibrahim	99.97	99.97	99.97	99.97
2	CLTL	Yestin	99.82	99.82	99.82	99.84
3	1-800-SHARED-TASKS (Purbey et al., 2025)	jebish7	99.79	99.81	99.80	99.82
4	1-800-SHARED-TASKS (Purbey et al., 2025)	lazyboy.blk	99.76	99.76	99.76	99.79
5	byteSizedLLM (Manukonda and Kodali, 2025)	mdp0999	99.75	99.73	99.74	99.76
6	MDS Bots (Thapaliya et al., 2025)	sumanpaudel	99.68	99.67	99.68	99.72
7	AniSan (Shanto et al., 2025)	Priya57	99.66	99.64	99.65	99.69
8	DSLNLP (Chauhan and Kumar, 2025)	Abhinav05	99.65	99.64	99.65	99.68
9	-	sandeep_S	99.58	99.59	99.58	99.63
10	Nepali Transformers (Khadka et al., 2025)	Pilot-Khadka	99.56	99.54	99.55	99.60
11	-	decem	99.56	99.55	99.55	99.60
12	-	jerrytomy	99.50	99.55	99.53	99.57
13	CUET_Big_O (Hossan et al., 2025)	dark_shadow	99.40	99.41	99.41	99.47
14	SKPD Emergency (Shakya et al., 2025)	shubham_shakya	99.44	99.38	99.41	99.48
15	Paramananda (Acharya et al., 2025)	sure	99.39	99.40	99.39	99.46
16	Nitro NLP	menta27	99.38	99.37	99.38	99.46
17	NLP Champs	abhay-43	99.34	99.34	99.34	99.40
18	Paramananda (Acharya et al., 2025)	fulbutte	99.18	99.18	99.18	99.26
19	-	samanjoy2	99.11	99.10	99.11	99.18
20	AGRJ	getabhi89	96.78	96.43	96.49	96.90
21	-	Tanvir_77	96.30	96.19	96.14	96.44
22	-	RohanR	95.69	95.77	95.72	95.99
23	CUET_Big_O (Hossan et al., 2025)	sakib07	94.24	95.11	94.54	95.08
24	CipherLoom	Nikhil_7280	65.72	57.19	59.71	69.87
25	CNLP-NITS	advaitha	56.70	67.72	50.46	53.53

Table 2: Sub-task A (Devanagari Script Language Identification) Leaderboard, Ranked by Macro F1-score. All scores are presented as percentages (%). It is to be noted that this leaderboard contains the score till the test deadline and does not consider further runs done by participants as a part of the system description paper.

Nepali Transformers (Khadka et al., 2025) used the Twitter-trained multilingual RoBERTa (Barbieri et al., 2020) and achieved exceptional results, with F1-score reaching 99.55%, outperforming other baseline models, including general-purpose and Devanagari-specific architectures. This approach secured tenth position on the leaderboard, demonstrating the model's effectiveness in handling the linguistic diversity and complexity of the Devanagari script.

CUET_Big_O (Hossan et al., 2025) used Traditional ML models such as Logistic Regression, SVM, Multinomial Naive Bayes, Random Forest and Deep Learning models such as CNN, LSTM, BiLSTM, along with the aggregation of models like CNN+GRU, CNN+BiLSTM. The best-performing model was CNN with BiLSTM which achieved an F1-score of 99.41%.

SKPD Emergency (Shakya et al., 2025), used an innovative approach using Continuous Bag of Words (CBOW) embeddings and an attention-enhanced Bidirectional Long Short-Term Memory (BiLSTM) neural network to identify languages written in Devanagari script. The results were impressive, with the model achieving a remarkable 99% overall accuracy. Sanskrit was perfectly classified, while some challenges remained in differentiating between highly similar languages like Hindi and Bhojpuri. The CBOW embeddings significantly outperformed character-level encoding, demonstrating their ability to capture semantic relationships and linguistic subtleties that character-based approaches miss.

Paramananda (Acharya et al., 2025) employed the FastText and BERT models, achieving exceptional performance with F1-scores of 99.17% and 99.39%, respectively, securing the seventeenth position on the leaderboard. While BERT marginally outperformed FastText by leveraging its deep contextual embeddings to capture nuanced linguistic differences, FastText demonstrated higher computational efficiency, making it more suitable for large-scale applications.

CUET_Big_O (Hossan et al., 2025) used CNN with BiLSTM to obtain F1-score of 99.41%. This however differs from the official leaderboard.

4.2.2 Subtask B

Paramananda Acharya et al. (2025) utilized FastText and demonstrated superior performance, particularly with data augmentation, achieving an F1 score of 81.39% and scoring first position on the leaderboard. This outperformed BERT, which struggled with an F1 score of 0.5763. Despite its contextual embedding strengths, BERT's underperformance was attributed to overfitting on sparse

Rank	Team Name	Codalab Username	Accuracy (%)	Recall (%)	Precision (%)	F1-score (%)
1	Paramananda (Acharya et al., 2025)	fulbutte	85.52	78.47	81.39	91.36
2	CLTL	Yestin	81.27	74.61	77.3	89.35
3	MDS Bots (Thapaliya et al., 2025)	sumanpaudel	76.94	76.32	76.63	90.26
4	1-800-SHARED-TASKS (Purbey et al., 2025)	jebish7	74.41	79.25	76.52	91.12
5	1-800-SHARED-TASKS (Purbey et al., 2025)	lazyboy.blk	73.6	78.95	75.88	90.97
6	-	MuhammadArham	72.61	78.14	74.94	90.68
7	byteSizedLLM (Rohith Gowtham Kodali and Iglesias, 2025)	mdp0999	77.45	72.86	74.81	88.57
8	Dll5143A (Yadav and Singh, 2025)	Dll5143A	75.76	73.45	74.52	88.98
8	Dll5143A (Yadav and Singh, 2025)	Dll5143	75.76	73.45	74.52	88.98
9	LLMsAgainstHate (Sidibomma et al., 2025)	rushendra910	71.19	78.84	74.19	90.75
10	-	jerrytomy	73.14	74.12	73.61	89.35
11	1-800-SHARED-TASKS (Purbey et al., 2025)	Siddartha-10	70.34	78.95	73.59	90.7
12	-	sandeep_S	74.63	72.56	73.52	88.59
13	CUET_HateShield Aodhora et al. (2025)	Sumaiya_127	73.52	72.38	72.93	88.57
14	Nepali Transformers (Khadka et al., 2025)	Pilot-Khadka	73.24	72	72.59	88.4
15	-	srikarkashyap	73.29	71.87	72.54	88.32
16	-	decem	66.5	76.64	69.89	89.89
17	NLPineers (Guragain et al., 2025)	anmol2059	77.62	66.39	69.14	82.58
18	CUET_823	ratnajit_dhar	67.28	71.6	69.07	88.52
19	NLP_Ninjaas	Nadika	68.77	69.34	69.04	87.44
20	CUFE (Ibrahim, 2025)	michaelibrahim	65.45	73.12	68.17	89.01
21	CIOL (Gupta et al., 2025)	azminewasi	65.47	71.06	67.62	88.4
22	NLP Champs	abhay-43	68.16	64.77	66.14	84.42
23	DSLNLP (Chauhan and Kumar, 2025)	Abhinav05	62.57	76.49	66.13	89.57
24	CUET_Big_O (Hossan et al., 2025)	dark_shadow	67.98	63.48	65.1	83.15
25	SKPD Emergency (Shakya et al., 2025)	shubham_shakya	62.62	64.03	63.26	85.62
26	AniSan (Shanto et al., 2025)	Priya57	59.47	70.69	62.06	88.44
27	-	RohanR	58.22	66.37	60.2	87.54
28	-	Tanvir_77	66.66	58.62	58.94	74.19
29	Paramananda (Acharya et al., 2025)	sure	55.9	73.77	57.63	88.76
30	CNLP-NITS	advaitha	50	44.17	46.91	88.35
31	Nitro NLP	menta27	51.84	50.81	46.49	60.28

Table 3: Sub-task B (Hate Speech Detection) Leaderboard, Ranked by Macro F1-score. All scores are presented as percentages (%). It is to be noted that this leaderboard contains the score till the test deadline and does not consider further runs done by participants as a part of the system description paper.

datasets, as evidenced by a higher evaluation score that did not generalize to test data.

MDSBots Thapaliya et al. (2025), experimented with identical transformer and classical models that were used in subtask-A. In order to reduce class imbalance, samples from the non-hate class were prioritized above samples from the majority class. They achieved a maximum f1-score, recall, and precision of 76.62%, 76.87%, and 76.38%, respectively, using MURTweet. Out of all the participating teams, they ranked third on this subtask-B.

1-800-SHARED-TASKS (Purbey et al., 2025) opted for the same ensemble technique as Subtask A and the ensemble of models achieved the highest F1-score of 0.7588 and placed fifth position on the leaderboard. Fine-tuning with focal loss (Lin, 2017) was instrumental in addressing class imbalance, and improving the detection of minority instances.

byteSizedLLM (Rohith Gowtham Kodali and Iglesias, 2025) focused on a hybrid Attention BiLSTM-XLM-RoBERTa architecture which utilized BiLSTM's sequential processing, attention mechanisms for contextual emphasis, and XLM-RoBERTa embeddings for multilingual adaption. The model attained an F1-score of 74.81% and secured seventh position on the leaderboard, surpassing other models.

Dll5143A (Yadav and Singh, 2025) used the Hierarchical Gated Adaptive Attention (HGAA) model, leveraging XLM-RoBERTa embeddings, achieved a competitive F1-score of 74.52% and securing an eighth position on the leaderboard. This model balanced precision and recall, demonstrating its robustness in detecting hate speech in Devanagari-scripted languages. Comparatively, the non-gated architecture showed lower performance. The introduction of gating mechanisms significantly improved the models ability to handle class imbalance, enhancing minority class detection at the cost of some false positives.

LLMsAgainstHate (Sidibomma et al., 2025) used Nemo-Instruct-2407 model (AI and NVIDIA) and achieved the highest performance with an F1-score of 74.52%, outperforming alternatives such as Phi-3-medium (Abdin et al., 2024) and Llama-3.1. Despite significant class imbalance favoring non-hate class, Nemo demonstrated robust detection capabilities, particularly benefiting from Parameter-Efficient Fine-Tuning using Low-Rank Adaptation (Hu et al., 2021).

CUETHateShield Aodhora et al. (2025) used the classical, deep learning, and transformer models to experiment with this task. In classical machine learning models, they incorporated the Logistic Regression, Support Vector Machine, and Random Forest model with TF-IDF feature extractor, and for deep learning models, they used CNN, Bi-LSTM, and CNNBiLSTM model with fastText and keras embedding. In transformer model, they used mBERT, MuRIL, IndicBERT, Indic-SBERT, and XLM-RoBERTa. To obtain higher-quality data, they eliminated noise in the preprocessing step, which included punctuation, emojis, hyperlinks, alphanumeric letters, and special symbols (such as slashes, brackets, and ampersands). They obtain an f1-score of 74% on XLM-RoBERTa, recall of 75% on Indic-SBERT, and precision of 72% on MuRIL.After competing against all teams, they came in at number eleven on this subtask.

Nepali Transformers (Khadka et al., 2025) deployed the Twitter-trained multilingual RoBERTa model (Barbieri et al., 2020), which achieved an F1-score of 72.93% and secured the fourteenth position on the leaderboard, outperforming general-purpose and Devanagari-specific models. This model excelled due to its domain-specific pretraining on social media datasets, effectively capturing nuanced hate speech patterns in Devanagari-scripted languages.

NLPineers (Guragain et al., 2025) used an ensemble of multilingual BERT to achieve a recall of 77.62% (ranked 3rd out of 31 in terms of recall and 17th out of 31 for an F1 score of 69.14%). To address the class imbalance, the authors used back-translation for data augmentation and cosine similarity to preserve label consistency after augmentation.

IITR-CIOL (Gupta et al., 2025) developed a model called *MultilingualRobertaClass*, which is a deep neural network built on the pre-trained IBM transformer model "ia-multilingual-transliterated-roberta". The model achieved an accuracy of 82.21%, a weighted precision of 79.84%, a weighted Recall of 82.21%, and a weighted F1 Score of 80.97%.

DSLNLP (Chauhan and Kumar, 2025), XLM-RoBERTa performs the best on this problem despite using the same ensembling algorithm as subtask-A. For the best results on hate speech recognition on Devanagari scripts, they refined the same models of Bert variations on all of the scripts, just like in the prior task. They achieved the highest precision of 78.9% by LaBSE, whereas the maximum f1-score and recall on XLM-RoBERTa were 66.13% and 62.57%, respectively. In subtask B, their XLM-RoBERTa model ended at number 23 out of all the teams that took part.

4.2.3 Subtask C

MDSBots (Thapaliya et al., 2025), employed the same models as the previous tasks, but they added a hybrid model in this task. In the hybrid model, they integrated named entity information (NER) into features produced by BERT models and used open-source large language models to reclassify samples with low confidence scores by prompting. They employed data augmentation to address the class disparity, by augmenting the minority class to represent community targets. Their best f1-score, recall, and precision on NERMURTweet were 70.98%, 70.38%, and 71.75%, respectively. Out of all the teams, they won first place for this subtask-C.

CUET_INSights (Tofa et al., 2025) combine traditional ML and Deep Learning Techniques while leveraging the multilingual capabilities of Indic-BERT & m-BERT with the adoption of Bhojpuri-to-Hindi translation along with class weights to mitigate imbalance. By utilizing these techniques including the almost perfect blend of deeper embeddings with shallow ML (TFIDF) features, the authors achieve a high F1 score of 69.17% thereby securing the third spot in the leaderboard.

CUET_Big_O (Hossan et al., 2025) used GridSearchCV for hyperparameter tuning and tested different kernels (linear, RBF) for SVM. They also tested multiple transformers: m-BERT, Indic-BERT, MuRIL-BERT, XLM-R, and Verta-BERT. The best performer was MuRIL-BERT with an F1-score of 68.32%.

1-800-SHARED-TASKS (Purbey et al., 2025) employed Gemma-2 27B model, fine-tuned using

Rank	Team Name	Codalab Username	Accuracy (%)	Recall (%)	Precision (%)	F1-score (%)
1	MDS Bots (Thapaliya et al., 2025)	sumanpaudel	70.38	71.75	70.98	76.84
2	-	Siddartha-10	68.73	74.11	70.33	77.89
3	CUET_INSights (Tofa et al., 2025)	Tofa	67.17	74.18	69.17	76.63
4	CUET_Big_O (Hossan et al., 2025)	sakib07	68.13	68.61	68.32	74.53
5	1-800-SHARED-TASKS (Purbey et al., 2025)	jebish7	66.69	71.83	68.04	76.63
6	One_by_zero (Chakraborty et al., 2025)	Dola_Chakraborty	68.1	67.88	67.98	73.68
7	byteSizedLLM (Rohith Gowtham Kodali and Iglesias, 2025)	mdp0999	66.89	67.44	67.15	74.11
8	-	jerrytomy	66.68	66.29	66.41	73.05
9	-	sandeep_S	65.72	67.54	66.37	73.89
10	CLTL	Yestin	65.46	67.4	66.12	74.53
11	Dll5143A (Yadav and Singh, 2025)	Dll5143A	65.37	66.38	65.76	71.37
12	-	srikarkashyap	64.78	67.58	65.69	72.42
13	Dll5143	Dll5143	64.75	64.76	64.74	72.21
14	LLMsAgainstHate (Sidibomma et al., 2025)	rushendra910	63.36	65.29	64.08	72
15	CipherLoom	Nikhil_7280	61.4	64.47	62.37	71.16
16	Nepali Transformers (Khadka et al., 2025)	Pilot-Khadka	62.36	61.57	61.83	68.63
17	DSLNLP (Chauhan and Kumar, 2025)	Abhinav05	60.61	61.98	61.01	68.42
18	-	decem	59.39	63.81	59.96	71.16
19	CUET_SSTM	aref111n	59.39	64.39	59.73	69.89
20	CIOL (Gupta et al., 2025)	azminewasi	58.39	59.1	58.16	66.11
21	Paramananda (Acharya et al., 2025)	sure	57.44	58.57	57.85	66.95
22	Paramananda (Acharya et al., 2025)	fulbutte	53.3	56.67	53.74	63.58
23	NLP Champs	abhay-43	50.77	51.16	50.57	58.32
24	CUFE	michaelibrahim	50.27	54.55	50.08	62.53
25	-	RohanR	45.77	56.41	44.22	60.42
26	-	Tanvir_77	46.85	41.1	43.74	61.68
27	AniSan (Shanto et al., 2025)	Priya57	45.33	44.94	42.07	61.68

Table 4: Sub-task C (Target Identification for Hate Speech) Leaderboard, Ranked by Macro F1-score. All scores are presented as percentages (%). It is to be noted that this leaderboard contains the score till the test deadline and does not consider further runs done by participants as a part of the system description paper.

ORPO (Hong et al., 2024), achieved the highest F1-score of 68.04%, with recall and precision scores of 66.69% and 71.83%, respectively. This model outperformed alternatives like Gemma-2 9B and XLM-RoBERTa, which scored lower due to challenges in detecting nuanced targets like "community". The results highlighted the model's strong performance in identifying targets such as "individual" and "organization," while community-target detection remained a challenge, underscoring the need for richer datasets.

One_by_zero (Chakraborty et al., 2025) utilized traditional machine learning models such as Logistic Regression, SVM leveraging TF-IDF Feature Extraction, deep learning (DL) architectures such as CNN, BiLSTM, CNN+BiLSTM hybrid) utilizing Word2Vec and FastText embeddings and Transformer-based architectures such as IndicBERT, MuRIL, XLM-R while adopting oversampling for underrepresented classes. Specifically, along with IndicBERT they achieve a notable high score of 67.85% percentage securing the sixth spot in the leaderboard.

byteSizedLLM (Rohith Gowtham Kodali and Iglesias, 2025) opted Attention BiLSTM-XLM-RoBERTa architecture achieved a macro F1-score of 67.15% and also secured a seventh position on the leaderboard, effectively categorizing hate speech targets as individual, organization, or community. This model outperformed baseline approaches, with the BiLSTM-XLM-RoBERTa variant scoring 63.56% and the XLM-RoBERTa base scoring 61.47%. The attention mechanism improved focus on critical context, enhancing accuracy for complex multilingual tasks.

Dll5143A (Yadav and Singh, 2025) implemented the HGAA model which achieved a macro F1-score of 65.76% and eleventh position on the leaderboard, demonstrating effective classification for individual and organizational targets. Community target detection remained challenging due to nuanced language and class imbalance. The inclusion of gating mechanisms improved performance compared to simpler architectures, particularly in minority class detection, showcasing the model's ability to balance precision and recall across diverse linguistic contexts.

LLMsAgainstHate (Sidibomma et al., 2025), the Nemo-Instruct-2407 model (AI and NVIDIA) delivered the strongest results with an F1-score of 64.08%. It outperformed models like Phi-3-medium and Qwen2.5 (Yang et al., 2024), showcasing its robustness in handling target-specific classifications. However, a detailed class-wise breakdown revealed a notable performance disparity, with high accuracy in detecting

"Individual" and "Organization" targets, but a significant drop for "Community". This discrepancy underscores the challenge posed by imbalanced datasets and under-represented categories.

For **Nepali Transformers** (Khadka et al., 2025), the Twitter-trained multilingual RoBERTa (Barbieri et al., 2020) demonstrated competitive performance, achieving an F1-score of 61.83%. While the model excelled in identifying "Individual" and "Organization" targets, it struggled with "Community" due to the scarcity of labeled examples. Augmentation strategies using multilingual embeddings provided modest improvements but did not fully resolve the imbalance challenges.

DSLNLP (Chauhan and Kumar, 2025), their MuRIL model performs the best on this task. In order to achieve the greatest results on target identification for hate speech on Devanagari scripts, they improved the same models of Bert variations and applied the same ensembling techniques as in the prior tasks. The ensemble method with a majority voting strategy yielded the highest precision of 63.91%, whereas the maximum F1-score and recall on MuRIL were 61.01% and 60.60%, respectively. Their MuRIL model came in at number seventeen out of all the teams who took part in subtask C.

IITR-CIOL (Gupta et al., 2025) built a model that was pre-trained on a multilingual transformer model to handle the linguistic diversity and complexity of South Asian languages. While the model performed exceptionally well in Subtask B (hate speech detection), achieving an accuracy of 88.40%, its performance in Subtask C was notably lower, with an accuracy of 66.11%. The ablation studies revealed that sequence length was the most critical factor in model performance, with longer sequences providing better context and more accurate predictions.

Paramananda (Acharya et al., 2025) used BERT which demonstrated superior performance with an F1 score of 53.74%. BERT's success is attributed to its ability to leverage deep contextual embeddings, enabling the identification and differentiation of nuanced targets such as individuals, organizations, and communities.

5 Discussion

The shared task on Devanagari-script languages offered unique insights into the complexities of NLU for low-resource languages. Participants showcased a diverse range of approaches, from classical machine learning models to transformer-based architectures and large language models, each with distinct strengths and limitations. Success of models like IndicBERT and XLM-RoBERTa in Subtask A underscores importance of multilingual and domain-specific embeddings in effectively distinguishing between linguistically similar languages.

However, the results also illuminate several challenges. Despite achieving high overall accuracy, many models struggled with underrepresented classes, such as 'Community' in Subtask C, pointing to limitations of existing datasets and the need for better class balance and data augmentation techniques. Additionally, while transformer-based models excelled in capturing contextual nuances, their reliance on large-scale training data highlights the necessity of domain-specific pretraining and fine-tuning strategies tailored for low-resource languages. Moving forward, fostering collaboration within the NLP community and developing more comprehensive datasets will be crucial to addressing these challenges and advancing research in Devanagari-script languages.

6 Conclusion

This shared task on NLU for Devanagari-script languages addressed critical challenges in language identification, hate speech detection, and target classification. Through the participation of diverse teams and methodologies, the task highlighted the potential of transformer-based models, ensemble approaches, and hybrid architectures in tackling the linguistic and contextual intricacies of low-resource languages. Substantial progress was demonstrated, particularly in language identification, where models achieved near-perfect scores, showcasing the effectiveness of multilingual embeddings and pretraining on diverse datasets. Nevertheless, challenges such as class imbalance, underrepresentation of specific categories, and the need for domain-specific pretraining were identified as key areas requiring further research. This task has laid the groundwork for future exploration and highlighted the importance of more research in inclusive and culturally aware NLP solutions.

References

Marah Abdin, Jyoti Aneja, Hany Awadalla, Ahmed Awadallah, Ammar Ahmad Awan, Nguyen Bach, Amit Bahree, Arash Bakhtiari, Jianmin Bao, Harkirat Behl, et al. 2024. Phi-3 technical report: A highly capable language model locally on your phone. *arXiv preprint arXiv:2404.14219*.

Darwin Acharya, Sundeep Dawadi, Shivram Saud, and Sunil Regmi. 2025. Paramananda@nlu of devanagari script languages 2025: Detection of language, hate speech and targets using fasttext and bert. In *Proceedings of the First Workshop on Challenges in Processing South Asian Languages (CHiPSAL)*, Abu Dhabi. International Committee on Computational Linguistics (ICCL).

Mistral AI and NVIDIA. Title of webpage. https://huggingface.co/mistralai/Mistral-Nemo-Instruct-2407. Accessed: 2024.

Sumaiya Rahman Aodhora, Shawly Ahsan, and Mohammed Moshiul Hoque. 2025. Cuet_hateshield @ nlu of devanagari script languages 2025: Transformer-based hate speech detection in devanagari script languages. In *Proceedings of the First Workshop on Challenges in Processing South Asian Languages (CHiPSAL)*, Abu Dhabi. International Committee on Computational Linguistics (ICCL).

Rahul Aralikatte, Miryam De Lhoneux, Anoop Kunchukuttan, and Anders Søgaard. 2021. Itihasa: A large-scale corpus for sanskrit to english translation. In *Proceedings of the 8th Workshop on Asian Translation (WAT2021)*, pages 191–197.

Francesco Barbieri, Jose Camacho-Collados, Leonardo Neves, and Luis Espinosa-Anke. 2020. Tweeteval: Unified benchmark and comparative evaluation for tweet classification. *arXiv preprint arXiv:2010.12421*.

Valerio Basile, Cristina Bosco, Elisabetta Fersini, Debora Nozza, Viviana Patti, Francisco Manuel Rangel Pardo, Paolo Rosso, and Manuela Sanguinetti. 2019. Semeval-2019 task 5: Multilingual detection of hate speech against immigrants and women in twitter. In *Proceedings of the 13th international workshop on semantic evaluation*, pages 54–63.

Dola Chakraborty, Jawad Hossain, and Mohammed Moshiul Hoque. 2025. One_by_zero@nlu of devanagari script languages 2025: Target identification for hate speech leveraging transformer-based approach. In *Proceedings of the First Workshop on Challenges in Processing South Asian Languages (CHiPSAL)*, Abu Dhabi. International Committee on Computational Linguistics (ICCL).

Shraddha Chauhan and Abhinav Kumar. 2025. Dslnlp@nlu of devanagari script languages 2025: Leveraging bert-based architectures for language identification, hate speech detection and target classification. In *Proceedings of the First Workshop on Challenges in Processing South Asian Languages (CHiPSAL)*, Abu Dhabi. International Committee on Computational Linguistics (ICCL).

Alexis Conneau, Kartikay Khandelwal, Naman Goyal, Vishrav Chaudhary, Guillaume Wenzek, Francisco Guzmán, Edouard Grave, Myle Ott, Luke Zettlemoyer, and Veselin Stoyanov. 2020. Unsupervised cross-lingual representation learning at scale. In *Proceedings of the 58th Annual Meeting of the Association for Computational Linguistics*, pages 8440–8451, Online. Association for Computational Linguistics.

Jacob Devlin, Ming-Wei Chang, Kenton Lee, and Kristina Toutanova. 2019. BERT: Pre-training of deep bidirectional transformers for language understanding. In *Proceedings of the 2019 Conference of the North American Chapter of the Association for Computational Linguistics: Human Language Technologies, Volume 1 (Long and Short Papers)*, pages 4171–4186, Minneapolis, Minnesota. Association for Computational Linguistics.

Sumanth Doddapaneni, Rahul Aralikatte, Gowtham Ramesh, Shreya Goyal, Mitesh M Khapra, Anoop Kunchukuttan, and Pratyush Kumar. 2022. Towards leaving no indic language behind: Building monolingual corpora, benchmark and models for indic languages. *arXiv preprint arXiv:2212.05409*.

Sumanth Doddapaneni, Rahul Aralikatte, Gowtham Ramesh, Shreya Goyal, Mitesh M. Khapra, Anoop Kunchukuttan, and Pratyush Kumar. 2023. Towards leaving no Indic language behind: Building monolingual corpora, benchmark and models for Indic languages. In *Proceedings of the 61st Annual Meeting of the Association for Computational Linguistics (Volume 1: Long Papers)*, pages 12402–12426, Toronto, Canada. Association for Computational Linguistics.

Samridhi Gupta and Bhavna Arora. 2022. Stemming techniques on english language and devanagari script: A review. *Recent Innovations in Computing: Proceedings of ICRIC 2021, Volume 1*, pages 541–550.

Siddhant Gupta, Siddh Singhal, and Azmine Toushik Wasi. 2025. Iitr-ciol@nlu of devanagari script languages 2025: Multilingual hate speech detection and target identification in devanagari-scripted languages. In *Proceedings of the First Workshop on Challenges in Processing South Asian Languages (CHiPSAL)*, Abu Dhabi. International Committee on Computational Linguistics (ICCL).

Vikram Gupta, Sumegh Roychowdhury, Mithun Das, Somnath Banerjee, Punyajoy Saha, Binny Mathew, Animesh Mukherjee, et al. 2022. Multilingual abusive comment detection at scale for indic languages. *Advances in Neural Information Processing Systems*, 35:26176–26191.

Anmol Guragain, Nadika Poudel, Rajesh Piryani, and Bishesh Khanal. 2025. Nlpineers@ nlu of devanagari script languages 2025: Hate speech detection using ensembling of bert-based models. In *Proceedings of the First Workshop on Challenges in Processing South Asian Languages (CHiPSAL)*, Abu Dhabi. International Committee on Computational Linguistics (ICCL).

Jiwoo Hong, Noah Lee, and James Thorne. 2024. Reference-free monolithic preference optimization with odds ratio. *arXiv e-prints*, pages arXiv–2403.

Md. Refaj Hossan, Nazmus Sakib, Md. Alam Miah, Jawad Hossain, and Mohammed Moshiul Hoque. 2025. Cuet_big_o@nlu of devanagari script languages 2025: Identifying script language and detecting hate speech using deep learning and transformer model. In *Proceedings of the First Workshop on Challenges in Processing South Asian Languages (CHiPSAL)*, Abu Dhabi. International Committee on Computational Linguistics (ICCL).

Edward J Hu, Yelong Shen, Phillip Wallis, Zeyuan Allen-Zhu, Yuanzhi Li, Shean Wang, Lu Wang, and Weizhu Chen. 2021. Lora: Low-rank adaptation of large language models. *arXiv preprint arXiv:2106.09685*.

Michael Ibrahim. 2025. Cufe@nlu of devanagari script languages 2025: Language identification using fasttext. In *Proceedings of the First Workshop on Challenges in Processing South Asian Languages (CHiPSAL)*, Abu Dhabi. International Committee on Computational Linguistics (ICCL).

Farhan Ahmad Jafri, Kritesh Rauniyar, Surendrabikram Thapa, Mohammad Aman Siddiqui, Matloob Khushi, and Usman Naseem. 2024. Chunav: Analyzing hindi hate speech and targeted groups in indian election discourse. *ACM Transactions on Asian and Low-Resource Language Information Processing*.

Farhan Ahmad Jafri, Mohammad Aman Siddiqui, Surendrabikram Thapa, Kritesh Rauniyar, Usman Naseem, and Imran Razzak. 2023. Uncovering political hate speech during indian election campaign: A new low-resource dataset and baselines.

Pilot Khadka, Ankit BK, Ashish Acharya, Bikram K.C., Sandesh Shrestha, and Rabin Thapa. 2025. Nepali transformersnlu of devanagari script languages 2025: Detection of language, hate speech and targets. In *Proceedings of the First Workshop on Challenges in Processing South Asian Languages (CHiPSAL)*, Abu Dhabi. International Committee on Computational Linguistics (ICCL).

Simran Khanuja, Diksha Bansal, Sarvesh Mehtani, Savya Khosla, Atreyee Dey, Balaji Gopalan, Dilip Kumar Margam, Pooja Aggarwal, Rajiv Teja Nagipogu, Shachi Dave, et al. 2021. Muril: Multilingual representations for indian languages. *arXiv preprint arXiv:2103.10730*.

Atharva Kulkarni, Meet Mandhane, Manali Likhitkar, Gayatri Kshirsagar, and Raviraj Joshi. 2021. L3cubemahasent: A marathi tweet-based sentiment analysis dataset. In *Proceedings of the Eleventh Workshop on Computational Approaches to Subjectivity, Sentiment and Social Media Analysis*, pages 213–220.

T Lin. 2017. Focal loss for dense object detection. *arXiv preprint arXiv:1708.02002*.

Vidula Magdum, Omkar Dhekane, Sharayu Hiwarkhedkar, Saloni Mittal, and Raviraj Joshi. 2023. mahanlp: A marathi natural language processing library. *arXiv preprint arXiv:2311.02579*.

Durga Prasad Manukonda and Rohith Gowtham Kodali. 2025. bytesizedllm@nlu of devanagari script languages 2025: Language identification using customized attention bilstm and xlm-roberta base embeddings. In *Proceedings of the First Workshop on Challenges in Processing South Asian Languages (CHiPSAL)*, Abu Dhabi. International Committee on Computational Linguistics (ICCL).

Binny Mathew, Punyajoy Saha, Seid Muhie Yimam, Chris Biemann, Pawan Goyal, and Animesh Mukherjee. 2021. Hatexplain: A benchmark dataset for explainable hate speech detection. In *Proceedings of the AAAI conference on artificial intelligence*, volume 35, pages 14867–14875.

Ioannis Mollas, Zoe Chrysopoulou, Stamatis Karlos, and Grigorios Tsoumakas. 2022. Ethos: a multi-label hate speech detection dataset. *Complex & Intelligent Systems*, 8(6):4663–4678.

Atul Kr Ojha. 2019. English-bhojpuri smt system: Insights from the karaka model. *arXiv preprint arXiv:1905.02239*.

Nedjma Ousidhoum, Zizheng Lin, Hongming Zhang, Yangqiu Song, and Dit-Yan Yeung. 2019. Multilingual and multi-aspect hate speech analysis. *arXiv preprint arXiv:1908.11049*.

Sanika Patil, Shraddha Nandvikar, Aakash Pardeshi, and Swapnali Kurhade. 2024. Automatic devanagari text summarization for youtube videos. In *2024 International Conference on Emerging Innovations and Advanced Computing (INNOCOMP)*, pages 16–21. IEEE.

Jebish Purbey, Siddartha Pullakhandam, Kanwal Mehreen, Muhammad Arham, Drishti Sharma, Ashay Srivastava, and Ram Mohan Rao Kadiyala. 2025. 1-800-shared-tasks@nlu of devanagari script languages 2025: Detection of language, hate speech, and targets using llms. In *Proceedings of the First Workshop on Challenges in Processing South Asian Languages (CHiPSAL)*, Abu Dhabi. International Committee on Computational Linguistics (ICCL).

Kritesh Rauniyar, Sweta Poudel, Shuvam Shiwakoti, Surendrabikram Thapa, Junaid Rashid, Jungeun Kim, Muhammad Imran, and Usman Naseem.

2023. Multi-aspect annotation and analysis of nepali tweets on anti-establishment election discourse. *IEEE Access*.

Durga Prasad Manukonda Rohith Gowtham Kodali and Daniel Iglesias. 2025. bytesizedllm@nlu of devanagari script languages 2025: Hate speech detection and target identification using customized attention bilstm and xlm-roberta base embeddings. In *Proceedings of the First Workshop on Challenges in Processing South Asian Languages (CHiPSAL)*, Abu Dhabi. International Committee on Computational Linguistics (ICCL).

Shubham Shakya, Saral Sainju, Subham Krishna Shrestha, Prekshya Dawadi, and Shreya Khatiwada. 2025. Skpd emergency @ nlu of devanagari script languages 2025: Devanagari script classification using cbow embeddings with attention-enhanced bilstm. In *Proceedings of the First Workshop on Challenges in Processing South Asian Languages (CHiPSAL)*, Abu Dhabi. International Committee on Computational Linguistics (ICCL).

Anik Mahmud Shanto, Mst. Sanjida Jamal Priya, and Mohammad Shamsul Arefin. 2025. Anisan@nlu of devanagari script languages 2025: Optimizing language identification with ensemble learning. In *Proceedings of the First Workshop on Challenges in Processing South Asian Languages (CHiPSAL)*, Abu Dhabi. International Committee on Computational Linguistics (ICCL).

Arpit Sharma and BN Mithun. 2023. Deep learning character recognition of handwritten devanagari script: A complete survey. In *2023 IEEE International Conference on Contemporary Computing and Communications (InC4)*, volume 1, pages 1–6. IEEE.

Deepawali Sharma, Aakash Singh, and Vivek Kumar Singh. 2024. Thar-targeted hate speech against religion: A high-quality hindi-english code-mixed dataset with the application of deep learning models for automatic detection. *ACM Transactions on Asian and Low-Resource Language Information Processing*.

Rushendra Sidibomma, Pransh Patwa, Parth Patwa, Aman Chadha, Vinija Jain, and Amitava Das. 2025. Llmsagainsthate@nlu of devanagari script languages 2025: Hate speech detection and target identification in devanagari languages via parameter efficient fine-tuning of llms. In *Proceedings of the First Workshop on Challenges in Processing South Asian Languages (CHiPSAL)*, Abu Dhabi. International Committee on Computational Linguistics (ICCL).

Akshay Singh and Rahul Thakur. 2024. Generalizable multilingual hate speech detection on low resource indian languages using fair selection in federated learning. In *Proceedings of the 2024 Conference of the North American Chapter of the Association for Computational Linguistics: Human Language Technologies (Volume 1: Long Papers)*, pages 7204–7214.

Sukhjinder Singh, Naresh Kumar Garg, and Munish Kumar. 2023. Feature extraction and classification techniques for handwritten devanagari text recognition: a survey. *Multimedia Tools and Applications*, 82(1):747–775.

Gemma Team, Thomas Mesnard, Cassidy Hardin, Robert Dadashi, Surya Bhupatiraju, Shreya Pathak, Laurent Sifre, Morgane Rivière, Mihir Sanjay Kale, Juliette Love, et al. 2024. Gemma: Open models based on gemini research and technology. *arXiv preprint arXiv:2403.08295*.

NLLB Team, Marta R. Costa-jussà, James Cross, Onur Çelebi, Maha Elbayad, Kenneth Heafield, Kevin Heffernan, Elahe Kalbassi, Janice Lam, Daniel Licht, Jean Maillard, Anna Sun, Skyler Wang, Guillaume Wenzek, Al Youngblood, Bapi Akula, Loic Barrault, Gabriel Mejia Gonzalez, Prangthip Hansanti, John Hoffman, Semarley Jarrett, Kaushik Ram Sadagopan, Dirk Rowe, Shannon Spruit, Chau Tran, Pierre Andrews, Necip Fazil Ayan, Shruti Bhosale, Sergey Edunov, Angela Fan, Cynthia Gao, Vedanuj Goswami, Francisco Guzmán, Philipp Koehn, Alexandre Mourachko, Christophe Ropers, Safiyyah Saleem, Holger Schwenk, and Jeff Wang. 2022. No language left behind: Scaling human-centered machine translation.

Surendrabikram Thapa, Kritesh Rauniyar, Shuvam Shiwakoti, Sweta Poudel, Usman Naseem, and Mehwish Nasim. 2023. Nehate: Large-scale annotated data shedding light on hate speech in nepali local election discourse. In *ECAI 2023*, pages 2346–2353. IOS Press.

Anish Thapaliya, Prabhat Ale, and Suman Paudel. 2025. Mdsbots@nlu of devanagari script languages 2025: Detection of language, hate speech, and targets using murtweet. In *Proceedings of the First Workshop on Challenges in Processing South Asian Languages (CHiPSAL)*, Abu Dhabi. International Committee on Computational Linguistics (ICCL).

Sulav Timilsina, Milan Gautam, and Binod Bhattarai. 2022. Nepberta: Nepali language model trained in a large corpus. In *Proceedings of the 2nd conference of the Asia-pacific chapter of the association for computational linguistics and the 12th international joint conference on natural language processing*. Association for Computational Linguistics (ACL).

Farjana Alam Tofa, Lorin Tasnim Zeba, Md Osama, and Ashim Dey. 2025. Cuet_insights@nlu of devanagari script languages 2025: Leveraging transformer-based models for target identification in hate speech. In *Proceedings of the First Workshop on Challenges in Processing South Asian Languages (CHiPSAL)*, Abu Dhabi. International Committee on Computational Linguistics (ICCL).

Abhishek Velankar, Hrushikesh Patil, Amol Gore, Shubham Salunke, and Raviraj Joshi. 2022. L3cube-mahahate: A tweet-based marathi hate speech detection dataset and bert models. *arXiv preprint arXiv:2203.13778*.

Ashok Yadav and Vrijendra Singh. 2025. Dll5143a@nlu of devanagari script languages 2025: Detection of hate speech and targets using hierarchical attention network. In *Proceedings of the First Workshop on Challenges in Processing South Asian Languages (CHiPSAL)*, Abu Dhabi. International Committee on Computational Linguistics (ICCL).

An Yang, Baosong Yang, Binyuan Hui, Bo Zheng, Bowen Yu, Chang Zhou, Chengpeng Li, Chengyuan Li, Dayiheng Liu, Fei Huang, et al. 2024. Qwen2 technical report. *arXiv preprint arXiv:2407.10671*.

A Related Works

Identifying Devanagari script in social media is an increasingly challenging task that requires the attention of scholars, policymakers, and society (Sharma and Mithun, 2023; Singh et al., 2023). Hate speech detection has been a prominent research domain, with numerous studies concentrating on English and other widely spoken languages (Basile et al., 2019; Ousidhoum et al., 2019). However, efforts to identify hate speech in Devanagari-script languages, including Hindi, Nepali, and Marathi, are still insufficient (Sharma et al., 2024; Velankar et al., 2022; Singh and Thakur, 2024). Few studies have made substantial progress in identifying the targets of hate speech. Current studies generally expand hate speech classification to identify targets as persons or groups based on established criteria (Mathew et al., 2021; Mollas et al., 2022). Nevertheless, these approaches often rely primarily on English-centric models, with minimal adaptations for Devanagari script. Few studies have begun to fill the gap by leveraging multilingual embeddings to identify Devanagari script and its applications (Magdum et al., 2023; Timilsina et al., 2022; Gupta et al., 2022). Despite these advancements, the domain continues to encounter obstacles due to the varied linguistic attributes of the Devanagari script and the restricted availability of high-quality labeled datasets. To overcome the problem of reliable annotated datasets, researchers curated the corpus specifically focused on Devanagari languages like Hindi, Marathi, Bhojpuri, Sanskrit and Nepali (Jafri et al., 2024; Kulkarni et al., 2021; Ojha, 2019; Aralikatte et al., 2021; Rauniyar et al., 2023). This shared task utilizes the Devanagari dataset to engage scholars and professionals in addressing the problem of language identification, hate speech, and its target identification in the corpus.

B Evaluation and Competition

This section explains the nature of our competition, including the system for calculating rankings and other important details.

B.1 Evaluation Metrics

We employed accuracy, precision, recall, and macro F1-score to evaluate the performance. The macro F1-score sorting method was used to establish the participants' rank.

B.2 Competition Setup

We used the Codalab[1] to organize our competition. There were two stages to the competition: an evaluation stage where participants were introduced to the Codalab system, and a testing phase where the ultimate leaderboard ranking was established based on performance.

Registration: The shared task attracted 113 participants. Our shared task had interest from a diverse range of backgrounds and regions as anticipated by the email domains they registered with. Of these, 32 teams submitted their predictions.

Competition Timelines: On August 19, 2024, participants received access to the training and evaluation data, marking the beginning of the task. This initial phase aimed to help participants become familiar with the dataset and task requirements. The test phase started on September 27, 2024, when test data was made available without ground truth labels. Originally scheduled to end on October 17, 2024, the testing period was extended to October 27, 2024, in response to requests from participants, allowing additional time to complete submissions. The deadline for system description paper submissions was also extended from November 3 to November 10, 2024, providing more time for participants to document their methods. This structured timeline allowed participants to fully engage with each phase. We also ensured that support was provided to the participants in case of technical difficulties.

[1]The competition page can be found here: `https://codalab.lisn.upsaclay.fr/competitions/20000`.

SiTa - Sinhala and Tamil Speaker Diarization Dataset in the Wild

Uthayasanker Thayasivam, Thulasithan Gnanenthiram, Shamila Jeewantha, Upeksha Jayawickrama
Department of Computer Science and Engineering
University of Moratuwa
Sri Lanka
{rtuthaya,thulasithan.20,shamila.20,kasuni.20}@cse.mrt.ac.lk

Abstract

The dynamic field of speaker diarization continues to present significant challenges, despite notable advancements in recent years and the rising focus on complex acoustic scenarios emphasizes the importance of sustained research efforts in this area. While speech resources for speaker diarization are expanding rapidly, aided by semi-automated techniques, many existing datasets remain outdated and lack authentic real-world conversational data. This challenge is particularly acute for low-resource South Asian languages, due to limited public media data and reduced research efforts. Sinhala and Tamil are two such languages with limited speaker diarization datasets. To address this gap, we introduce a new speaker diarization dataset for these languages and evaluate multiple existing models to assess their performance. This work provides essential resources, a novel dataset[1] and valuable insights from model benchmarks to advance speaker diarization for low-resource languages, particularly Sinhala and Tamil.

1 Introduction

The history of speaker diarization dates back to the early 1990s (Park et al., 2022), primarily driven by the need to enhance Automatic Speech Recognition (ASR) systems. Early diarization systems focused on tasks such as transcribing radio broadcasts, conference calls, and speech communication systems, with a major emphasis on improving the accuracy of ASR in multi-speaker environments (Jain et al., 1996; Padmanabhan et al., 1996; Gish et al., 1991). Since then, speaker diarization has been extensively researched over the last few decades, leading to significant advancements in its techniques and applications. Initially, basic clustering (Ng et al., 2001; Tung et al., 2010) and segmentation algorithms were used, but over time, more sophisticated methods, such as deep learning-based approaches, have emerged to perform single-module optimizations (Xie et al., 2016; Lin et al., 2020; Wang et al., 2020), as well as completely end-to-end neural diarization (EEND) systems (Fujita et al., 2019a,b; Horiguchi et al., 2022), pushing the boundaries of diarization performance.

When examining state-of-the-art diarization models, the requirement for large, well-developed diarization datasets can be identified as one of the major factors contributing to the performance of these models. While diarization datasets for languages such as English, Spanish, French, German, and other European languages, along with Asian languages such as Chinese, Japanese, and Korean, possess significantly larger volumes of content, the available datasets for low-resource languages frequently prove inadequate. This scarcity of data often leads to suboptimal performance in speaker diarization models for low-resource languages, where the lack of diversity and size in datasets becomes a major hindrance to model training and evaluation.

The South Asian region is home to many languages that are natively spoken but are often classified as low-resource, resulting in a significant lack of available datasets. Among these languages, Sinhala and Tamil are the two most widely spoken languages in Sri Lanka. Sinhala is an Indo-Aryan language, primarily used by the Sinhalese population of more than 15 million, and Tamil is a Dravidian language, spoken by more than 3 million Tamils in Sri Lanka (Department of Census and Statistics, Sri Lanka, 2012). Despite their large speaker bases, there is a significant lack of rich, diverse linguistic datasets for both languages, especially in fields like speech processing and speaker diarization. Developing diarization datasets for Sinhala and Tamil is essential to advancing speech recognition and diarization systems, which will, in

[1]The dataset is available at https://github.com/SiTa-SpeakerDiarization/SiTa

Proceedings of the First Workshop on Challenges in Processing South Asian Languages (CHiPSAL 2025), pages 83–92
January 19, 2025.

turn, improve digital accessibility and linguistic resources for these populations.

In this paper, we introduce SiTa, a speech dataset specifically curated for speaker diarization tasks in Tamil and Sinhala languages. We detail the methodology utilized in developing this dataset, which includes data collection, preprocessing, and the annotation pipeline. Additionally, we present experimental results obtained from applying SiTa to state-of-the-art diarization models. Our efforts aim to address the scarcity of resources for low-resource languages like Sinhala and Tamil, thereby contributing to the advancement of multilingual speaker diarization research.

2 Related Work

Over the years, many speaker diarization datasets have been released, particularly in English language. The NIST SRE 2000 (Przybocki and Martin, 2001) or more commonly known as CALLHOME dataset has been the most commonly used speaker diarization dataset, especially for benchmarking purposes. This dataset consists of approximately 500 recordings of multilingual telephone conversations with each session containing two to seven speakers. The CHiME-5/6 challenge (Barker et al., 2018; Watanabe et al., 2020) contains a 50 hour dataset of casual conversations recorded in homes with multi-array microphones that focused on overlapping speech and noisy environments.

The DIHARD Challenges (Ryant et al., 2018, 2019, 2020) are a series of annual events designed to tackle "hard" diarization scenarios where existing systems frequently underperform. The evaluation dataset spans complex domains, including clinical interviews, child language acquisition recordings, restaurant conversations, and online videos. In scoring, overlapped speech was accounted for, and no forgiveness collar was applied, making the challenge even more rigorous.

Following advancements in audio-only diarization, a new frontier opened in audio-visual diarization aimed at enhancing robustness and accuracy. This shift has been facilitated by the introduction of comprehensive multimodal datasets such as the AMI (Mccowan et al., 2005) and AVDIAR (Gebru et al., 2017) corpora. A common characteristic of these datasets is that they are recorded in controlled indoor environments, featuring scripted conversations performed by actors, which contrasts with more naturalistic settings typically encountered in real-world interactions. The AMI (Augmented Multi-party Interaction) Corpus contains 100 hours of meeting recordings captured across multiple locations, offering multi-microphone audio and multi camera video. This dataset also provides synchronized audio-visual streams and transcriptions, enabling the development of sophisticated Automatic Speech Recognition (ASR) systems integrated with speaker diarization. The AVDIAR dataset is designed to encompass a wide variety of multi-speaker scenarios, featuring diverse configurations such as static and moving participants, which facilitate the benchmarking of audio-visual diarization methods in complex interaction settings.

The REPERE (Giraudel et al., 2012) corpus is a multimodal French video dataset developed for advancing automatic people recognition systems, featuring annotated news and debate segments from French television with a focus on varied audio-visual conditions. The RTVE datasets (Lleida et al., 2019, 2020; Ortega et al., 2022) comprising 6 hours, 33 hours, and 25 hours of annotated Spanish speech data respectively, primarily focus on speaker diarization and include enrollment material for speaker identification. These datasets cover diverse accents, spontaneous speech, and overlapping dialogues across various broadcast scenarios.

Having utilized TV shows, meetings, and telephonic data, datasets began incorporating "in the wild" data, primarily from publicly available YouTube videos, to address challenges such as the limited diversity of speech patterns, low presence of overlapping conversations, and the limited variability in background noise that can compromise model performance in real-world applications. The first significant effort in this direction was the VoxCeleb Speaker Recognition Challenge (VoxSRC) series (Chung et al., 2019; Nagrani et al., 2020; Brown et al., 2022; Huh et al., 2023), which initially focused solely on speaker verification tasks; however, the diarization task was later introduced as Track 4 in subsequent iterations. Following this initiative, several novel "in the wild" speaker diarization datasets were created. Voxconverse (Chung et al., 2020) is one of the first dedicated large-scale diarization datasets, containing 64 hours of diverse YouTube videos which included a test set of 232 videos and a dev set of 216 videos. Its contributions also include a semi-automatic dataset creation pipeline, which significantly reduces the time required to annotate videos with speaker labels. This innovation addresses a key reason for the scarcity of large-scale diarization datasets derived from natural conversations such as those in YouTube videos. Atomic Visual Action Audio-Visual Diarization (AVA-AVD) dataset (Xu et al., 2022) is another comparable multilingual speaker diarization dataset developed based on the AVA-Active Speaker dataset (Roth et al., 2020), which focuses on detecting active speakers in audiovisual contexts but excluding the videos with dubbed scenes, as dubbing can disrupt the audio-visual synchronization. The AVA-AVD dataset consists of 351 videos totaling 29 hours of content, extracted from movies produced worldwide with diversity in ethnicity, language, accents, dialects, and age. Similarly, MSDWild (Liu et al., 2022) is a large multilingual speaker diarization dataset, featuring 3,143 YouTube videos with an emphasis on daily conversations, totaling 80 annotated hours.

During the early development of speaker diarization, publications focusing on low-resource speaker diarization datasets were limited, as initial research efforts primarily concentrated on larger corpora in English. Nonetheless, attempts to create non-English diarization datasets were made during the late 1990s and early 2000s, coinciding with the expanding interest in speech recognition. Among these early initiatives were the CALLHOME collections (Canavan and Zipperlen, 1996; Wheatley, 1996), which includes multilingual telephone conversational data for both diarization and speaker identification. In 2002, the Karlsruhe Institute of Technology introduced the GlobePhone corpus (Schultz, 2002), encompassing audio recordings and transcriptions in 20 languages, including Hausa, Swahili, and Vietnamese. Additionally, in 2005, the International Institute of Information Technology in India developed speech corpora for Tamil, Telugu, and Marathi languages (Chitturi et al., 2005). Released in 2021, AISHELL-4 (Fu et al., 2021) provided a Mandarin Chinese meeting corpus of 118 hours. In addition, AliMeeting (Yu et al., 2022) and RAMC (Yang et al., 2022) datasets feature meeting scenarios in distinct room environments and Mandarin phone call recordings respectively. The Corpus of Spontaneous Japanese (Maekawa, 2003) offered 12 hours of dialogue data captured using headset microphones, highlighting natural, spontaneous conversations between two speakers.

In the scope of South Asian languages, the DIarization of SPeaker and LAnguage in Conversational Environments (DISPLACE) challenge (Baghel et al., 2023) introduced a unique dataset for diarization tasks in multilingual, multi-speaker conversational contexts, highlighting the challenges posed by code-mixed and code-switched speech. In the second DISPLACE challenge (Kalluri et al., 2024), three tasks were introduced: speaker diarization (SD), identifying "who spoke when"; language diarization (LD), determining "which language was spoken when"; and automatic speech recognition (ASR), all of which are complicated by speaker overlaps and frequent language transitions. The dataset includes recorded conversations in various room settings, covering topics such as culture, lifestyle, entertainment, and sports. It spans nine Indian languages such as Hindi, Kannada, Bengali, Malayalam, Telugu, Tamil, and Indian English totaling 38 hours of conversational speech across 197 speakers. CONVURL (Zaheer et al., 2025) is a 24-hour dataset that consists of natural spontaneous conversations in Urdu, featuring 212 unique speakers. The dataset includes 38 clips sourced from YouTube videos, primarily encompassing scholarly debates and political talk shows. In 2022, another YouTube-based Tamil diarization dataset (Jarashanth et al., 2022) was published focusing more on overlapped speech. The development of speech corpora for Sinhala language has also gained attention, particularly within the domain of automatic speech recognition (ASR). Notable efforts include the publication of a 65-hour speech corpus in 2013 (Nadungodage et al., 2013), and the release of a 4.15-hour Sinhala speech corpus (Dinushika et al., 2019) in 2019. However, research literature on speaker diarization in Sinhala remains limited, indicating an insufficient focus in this domain. This study seeks to address this gap by introducing a speaker diarization corpus in the Sinhala and Tamil language to support further research and development in this area.

3 SiTa

3.1 Dataset Description

SiTa is an audio-only speaker diarization dataset for Sinhala and Tamil languages, comprising two distinct subsets: one for Sinhala speech and the other for Tamil. The Sinhala subset includes 60 videos totaling approximately 600 minutes (10 hours) of audio, while the Tamil subset contains 14 videos, accounting for around 120 minutes (2 hours) of audio. SiTa features multi-speaker conversations

set	# videos	# mins	# speakers	video durations (min)	speech %	overlap %
Sinhala	60	602	1 / 3.4 / 10	5.1 / 10.0 / 16.6	37.3 / 88.6 / 99.1	0 / 1.5 / 9.2
Tamil	14	121	2 / 3.0 / 6	5.0 / 8.7 / 14.5	78.6 / 92.7 / 97.4	0 / 3.3 / 14.21

Table 1: Statistics of the SiTa Dataset. Each entry with three values represents the minimum, mean, and maximum. speech %: is the proportion of audio time that contains speech. overlap %: is the proportion of speech occurring when two or more speakers are active simultaneously.

captured "in the wild" and encompasses a range of conversation types, from controlled settings with few speakers, slow-paced dialogue, minimal noise, and negligible speaker overlap such as panel discussions and interviews to more dynamic and challenging contexts. These include political debates, quiz programs, and lively discussions with numerous speaker turns, background noise, and frequent overlaps among a larger group of speakers. A unique aspect of SiTa is its inclusion of code-mixing, where English terms appear interspersed within native Tamil and Sinhala sentences. This phenomenon, common in South Asian languages, introduces an additional layer of complexity absent in most English speaker diarization datasets. Table 1 provides a comprehensive statistical overview of the Tamil and Sinhala subsets within the SiTa dataset.

3.2 Data Collection

In line with approaches used in in-the-wild datasets, YouTube videos were manually selected from diverse domains, including intellectual discussions, education, morning shows, celebrity interviews, political debates, and children's programs. Figure 1 illustrates the distribution percentages of video types selected for data collection in the Sinhala and Tamil languages. To ensure a broad selection, keywords from Sinhala, Tamil, and English were used in the search, as many content creators use English titles regardless of the content's spoken language. Videos were sourced from independent YouTube channels as well as the official YouTube channels of public television networks. Additionally, videos with extensive code-switching, those containing full sentences in English rather than isolated terms were avoided to allow for a focused study of language-specific dynamics in Sinhala and Tamil. Only one excerpt from each of these videos were carefully chosen for the dataset to maximize speech activity, speaker turns, and instances of overlapping speech. Videos with excessive noise or crowd laughter were avoided to ensure label clarity, although segments with applause were included without explicit labeling. All selected video excerpts were converted to a mono-channel waveform audio (WAV) format with a sampling rate of 16 kHz.

3.3 Annotation

A semi-automated, two-stage pipeline was implemented in the development of both Sinhala and Tamil subsets of SiTa. In the Initial stage, speaker labels and timestamps were generated using Pyannote 3.1[2], which were then manually reviewed and corrected using VGG Image Annotator (VIA) (Dutta and Zisserman, 2019), a standalone annotation tool for images, audio, and video during the second stage. VIA facilitates the addition of multiple timelines for different speakers, adjustable playback speeds, timeline zooming, selective playback of labeled segments, and the seamless insertion of new labels at the current playback position without manual adjustments. Figure 2 illustrates the user-friendly interface employed for the manual annotation of audio files.

3.3.1 Guidelines

Annotation guidelines and verification protocols were adopted from established datasets such as VoxConverse (Chung et al., 2020), MSDWild (Liu et al., 2022), and AVA-AVD (Xu et al., 2022). Minor non-verbal sounds, such as short utterances ("mmm", "ooo"), were ignored unless they were at least 100 ms in duration and clearly audible. Within a speech segment from the same speaker, pauses were not treated as split points unless the pause duration exceeded 250 ms. Additionally, annotators were instructed to ensure that label timestamp boundaries did not deviate from the actual speech boundaries by more than 100 ms to maintain precision. Music segments were excluded from labeling. In instances where speaker distinction was challenging based solely on audio, annotators referred to the corresponding YouTube video to accurately identify each speaker. The average time required for annotating an audio file, adhering to aforementioned guidelines, was approximately 8–10 times

[2]https://huggingface.co/pyannote/speaker-diarization-3.1

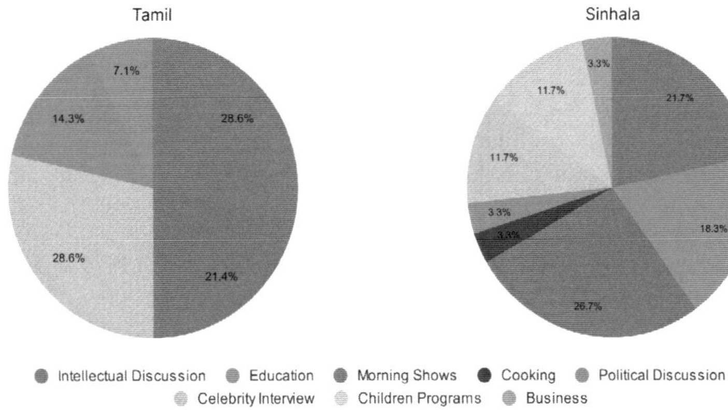

Figure 1: Percentage distribution of video types selected for data collection in Sinhala and Tamil languages.

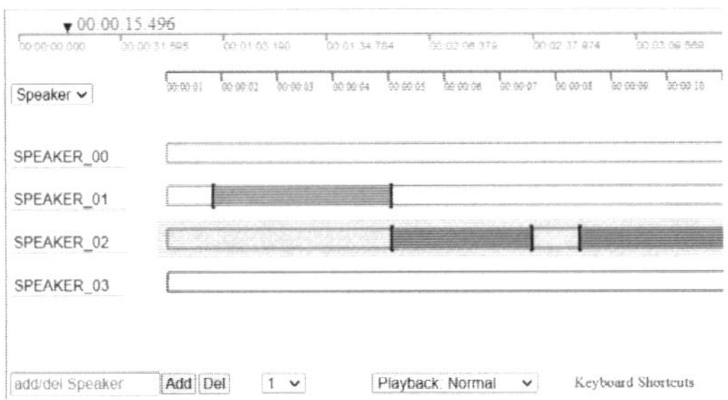

Figure 2: The user interface of the VGG Image Annotator (VIA), showing the audio playback timeline, speaker timelines, and temporal segments representing speaker labels.

the duration of the original audio. This duration could be reduced for audio clips with fewer speakers and minimal overlap.

3.3.2 Quality Assurance

To ensure consistency and maintain high-quality annotations, periodic double-annotations were conducted during which annotators independently annotated the same video, and the diarization error between the two annotations was calculated using one as the reference and the other as the hypothesis. This diarization error rate was maintained below 1%, and annotators were reminded to strictly follow the guidelines if this threshold was exceeded. Finally, a separate reviewer, distinct from the initial annotator, verified that the annotations accurately matched the WAV files and confirmed the overall quality and consistency of the annotations.

4 Experiments

4.1 Evaluation Metric

In this study, we used the Diarization Error Rate (DER) as our primary evaluation metric to assess the performance of speaker diarization. DER is defined as the sum of missed speech (MS), false alarm (FA), and speaker confusion (SC), normalized by the total duration of speech. Mathematically, it can be expressed as:

$$DER = \frac{MS + FA + SC}{Total\ Speech} \tag{1}$$

Consistent with prior research, the DER is calculated with a forgiveness collar of 0.25 seconds around each detected speech segment to account for slight temporal discrepancies in speaker labeling.

4.2 Baseline Models

We evaluated three baseline models to test our proposed SiTa dataset. These models include both modular and end-to-end (EEND) systems. The modular systems allow for distinct components to be developed and optimized separately, while the EEND systems aim to streamline the process by integrating all stages of speaker diarization into a single framework. This diversity in model architectures chosen enables a comprehensive assessment of our dataset's performance across different approaches to speaker diarization. All selected models utilized publicly available pre-trained versions, and their corresponding results on SiTa dataset are presented in Table 2.

Set	Model	MS	FA	SC	DER
Sinhala	End-to-End Segmentation (Bredin and Laurent, 2021)	2.5	12.9	9.5	**6.4**
	Powerset Cross-Entropy Diarization (Plaquet and Bredin, 2023)	1.6	12.0	9.7	**6.0**
	DiaPer (Landini et al., 2024)	19.4	6.8	42.4	**14.3**
Tamil	End-to-End Segmentation (Bredin and Laurent, 2021)	3.9	10.0	11.2	**6.0**
	Powerset Cross-Entropy Diarization (Plaquet and Bredin, 2023)	1.9	9.3	16.1	**6.6**
	DiaPer (Landini et al., 2024)	14.0	6.3	30.1	**11.5**

Table 2: Performance Metrics of Speaker Diarization Models on the SiTa Dataset. MS: Missed Speech; FA: False Alarms; SC: Speaker Confusion; DER: Diarization Error Rate.

4.2.1 End-to-End Speaker Segmentation with Overlap-Aware Re-segmentation

The End-to-End Speaker Segmentation model[3] (Bredin and Laurent, 2021) integrates voice activity, speaker change, and overlap detection into a single architecture by modeling it as a multi-label classification problem incorporating permutation-invariant training. The second contribution of this model is the incorporation of overlap-aware re-segmentation, which refines the initial segmentation output by based on contextual and temporal information across segments, ultimately enabling accurate assignment of overlapping speech segments to their corresponding speakers.

4.2.2 Powerset Cross-Entropy Diarization

The Powerset Cross-Entropy diarization model[4] (Plaquet and Bredin, 2023) uses the concept of assigning unique label combinations to overlapping speakers, using a powerset approach replacing the existing multi label classification approach. By representing all possible speaker combinations as distinct classes, this method allows for the removal of the detection threshold hyperparameter and thereby accurately handling overlaps in speech.

4.2.3 DiaPer: Perceiver-based Diarization

DiaPer[5] (Landini et al., 2024) introduces a novel architecture that replaces the encoder-decoder attractor component of the EEND-EDA (Horiguchi et al., 2022) with a Perceiver-based module. This new design, features a decoder that generates speaker attractors using a transformer-based Perceiver with fixed-size latent representations and cross-attention mechanisms, thereby eliminating the sequential processing typically associated with the LSTM-based EEND-EDA. Ultimately, DiaPer enhances speaker count estimation, accelerates inference speed, and improves diarization accuracy through this innovative module.

4.3 Results and Discussion

For both modular systems (End-to-End Segmentation and Powerset Cross-Entropy Diarization), the Diarization Error Rate (DER) for the Sinhala and Tamil sets in our SiTa dataset closely aligns with the values reported by the original authors of each model for the VoxConverse dataset. The lower DER observed for the SiTa dataset, compared to the reported DER for VoxConverse by the authors, in the EEND model, DiaPer, can be attributed to the training approach. While DiaPer was primarily trained on simulated speech data for its evaluation on VoxConverse, the version used for evaluating our dataset was fine-tuned on the MSDWild dataset. Additionally, when compared to the other two modular systems, DiaPer exhibits a relatively higher DER. This can be attributed to its lack of Voice Activity Detection (VAD) or other pre-processing steps, making it more susceptible to noise. Moreover, EEND models, including DiaPer, are empirically known to overfit more than other diarization approaches, further contributing to the higher DER observed.

Apart from that, the DER is closely influenced by the percentage of overlapping speech within each dataset. According to the statistics, the Sinhala set has an average overlap of 1.5%, while the Tamil set exhibits a higher mean overlap of 3.3%. This difference results in higher speaker confusion in the two modular diarization systems on the Tamil set, as increased overlap poses challenges in accurately distinguishing between speakers. This suggests that overlap handling is crucial for improving DER in multi-speaker environments. Code-mixing, however, shows minimal impact on DER across our dataset. Common issues observed in the generated diarization results included excessive speaker la-

[3]https://huggingface.co/pyannote/segmentation

[4]https://github.com/FrenchKrab/IS2023-powerset-diarization

[5]https://github.com/BUTSpeechFIT/DiaPer

bels in non-speech segments, missing labels for speech segments, omitted speaker timelines resulting in fewer identified speakers, and instances of swapped speaker labels. Specifically, male speakers with similarly rough voices were frequently assigned identical labels. Female speakers were often mislabeled, with extreme cases where all female speech segments were assigned the same speaker label. In some cases, even though the labeling was mostly correct, short utterances such as 'mmmm's and 'aaah's were mislabeled. Non-speech sounds, such as chimes in quiz programs, were occasionally mislabeled as speakers. In children's speech segments, the initial utterances of female child voices were often misattributed to the wrong female child speaker, similar to cases in clips with only adult female speakers. Male child voices were sometimes misattributed to female child speakers or even to adult female speakers if present. Additionally, segments of speech, which preceded or followed music, exhibited slight misalignments in timestamps. Furthermore, the staccato rhythm of the Sinhala language was particularly prominent in intellectual discussions. In such cases, continuous speech from a single speaker was often fragmented into multiple segments.

5 Limitations

The size of the Sinhala and Tamil subsets in our SiTa dataset is limited to around 12 hours, which restricts its use for reliably training speaker diarization models from scratch. As a result, these subsets were only used as test sets to evaluate the models' performance. Furthermore, the amount of overlapping speech in the larger Sinhala subset is relatively low, as the annotation of such segments is an error-prone and time-intensive process. While the dataset does encompass a range of domains, the number of audio samples from each domain remains limited, which could affect the robustness of model evaluation across different contexts. We did not intentionally include all regional dialects present in Sinhala and Tamil in the SiTa dataset and the selected YouTube videos primarily consisted of the standard language typically spoken in TV broadcasts, as well as in formal and urban settings. Even in more casual videos, this was largely the case. As a result, the dataset lacks representation of regional dialectal diversity, and we are unable to evaluate the potential dynamics or impacts of it on speaker diarization performance.

6 Conclusion

In this study, we introduced SiTa, a speaker diarization dataset comprising subsets in Sinhala and Tamil languages. Through evaluations using diverse baseline models, including modular and end-to-end (EEND) approaches, we observed the effects of language-specific characteristics, overlap levels, and continuous speech patterns on diarization performance. Our results reveal that overlapping speech significantly impacts DER, highlighting the need for effective overlap handling in speaker diarization. For the Sinhala subset, we found that increasing gap tolerance before segmenting speech can mitigate over-segmentation, thereby enhancing diarization accuracy.

Though the dataset size limits its use to testing rather than training, SiTa serves as a valuable benchmark for evaluating diarization in low-resource languages and presents a first step towards more comprehensive multilingual diarization datasets. Future work could focus on expanding SiTa and improving overlap annotation to enable training applications and further insights into language-specific diarization challenges.

References

Shikha Baghel, Shreyas Ramoji, Sidharth, Ranjana H, Prachi Singh, Somil Jain, Pratik Roy Chowdhuri, Kaustubh Kulkarni, Swapnil Padhi, Deepu Vijayasenan, and Sriram Ganapathy. 2023. The displace challenge 2023 - diarization of speaker and language in conversational environments. In *INTERSPEECH 2023*, pages 3562–3566.

Jon Barker, Shinji Watanabe, Emmanuel Vincent, and Jan Trmal. 2018. The fifth 'chime' speech separation and recognition challenge: Dataset, task and baselines. In *Interspeech 2018*, pages 1561–1565.

Hervé Bredin and Antoine Laurent. 2021. End-to-end speaker segmentation for overlap-aware resegmentation. *arXiv preprint arXiv:2104.04045*.

Andrew Brown, Jaesung Huh, Joon Son Chung, Arsha Nagrani, Daniel Garcia-Romero, and Andrew Zisserman. 2022. Voxsrc 2021: The third voxceleb speaker recognition challenge. *arXiv preprint arXiv:2201.04583*.

Alexandra Canavan and George Zipperlen. 1996. Callhome japanese speech. Web Download.

Rahul Chitturi, Sachin Joshi, Rohit Kumar, Satinderpal Singh, R. N. V. Sitaram, and S. P. Kishore. 2005. Development of indian language speech databases for large vocabulary speech recognition systems.

Joon Son Chung, Jaesung Huh, Arsha Nagrani, Triantafyllos Afouras, and Andrew Zisserman. 2020. Spot the conversation: speaker diarisation in the wild. *arXiv preprint arXiv:2007.01216*.

Joon Son Chung, Arsha Nagrani, Ernesto Coto, Weidi Xie, Mitchell McLaren, Douglas A Reynolds, and Andrew Zisserman. 2019. Voxsrc 2019: The first voxceleb speaker recognition challenge. *arXiv preprint arXiv:1912.02522*.

Department of Census and Statistics, Sri Lanka. 2012. Census of population and housing of sri lanka, 2012 – table a3: Population by district, ethnic group and sex. `http://203.94.94.83:8041/Pages/Activities/Reports/SriLanka.pdf`. Additional data available at `https://www.statistics.gov.lk/PopHouSat/CPH2012Visualization/htdocs/index.php?action=Map&indId=10&usecase=indicator` and `https://www.statistics.gov.lk/pophousat/cph2012visualization/htdocs/index.php?usecase=indicator&action=Data&indId=10`.

Thilini Dinushika, Lakshika Kavmini, Pamoda Abeyawardhana, Uthayasanker Thayasivam, and Sanath Jayasena. 2019. Speech command classification system for sinhala language based on automatic speech recognition. *2019 International Conference on Asian Language Processing (IALP)*, pages 205–210.

Abhishek Dutta and Andrew Zisserman. 2019. The VIA annotation software for images, audio and video. In *Proceedings of the 27th ACM International Conference on Multimedia*, MM '19, New York, NY, USA. ACM.

Yihui Fu, Luyao Cheng, Shubo Lv, Yukai Jv, Yuxiang Kong, Zhuo Chen, Yanxin Hu, Lei Xie, Jian Wu, Hui Bu, et al. 2021. Aishell-4: An open source dataset for speech enhancement, separation, recognition and speaker diarization in conference scenario. *arXiv preprint arXiv:2104.03603*.

Yusuke Fujita, Naoyuki Kanda, Shota Horiguchi, Kenji Nagamatsu, and Shinji Watanabe. 2019a. End-to-end neural speaker diarization with permutation-free objectives. *arXiv preprint arXiv:1909.05952*.

Yusuke Fujita, Naoyuki Kanda, Shota Horiguchi, Yawen Xue, Kenji Nagamatsu, and Shinji Watanabe. 2019b. End-to-end neural speaker diarization with self-attention. In *2019 IEEE Automatic Speech Recognition and Understanding Workshop (ASRU)*, pages 296–303.

Israel D Gebru, Sileye Ba, Xiaofei Li, and Radu Horaud. 2017. Audio-visual speaker diarization based on spatiotemporal bayesian fusion. *IEEE transactions on pattern analysis and machine intelligence*, 40(5):1086–1099.

Aude Giraudel, Matthieu Carré, Valérie Mapelli, Juliette Kahn, Olivier Galibert, and Ludovic Quintard. 2012. The repere corpus : a multimodal corpus for person recognition. In *Proceedings of the Eight International Conference on Language Resources and Evaluation (LREC'12)*, Istanbul, Turkey. European Language Resources Association (ELRA).

H. Gish, M.-H. Siu, and R. Rohlicek. 1991. Segregation of speakers for speech recognition and speaker identification. In *[Proceedings] ICASSP 91: 1991 International Conference on Acoustics, Speech, and Signal Processing*, pages 873–876 vol.2.

Shota Horiguchi, Yusuke Fujita, Shinji Watanabe, Yawen Xue, and Paola Garcia. 2022. Encoder-decoder based attractors for end-to-end neural diarization. *IEEE/ACM Transactions on Audio, Speech, and Language Processing*, 30:1493–1507.

Jaesung Huh, Andrew Brown, Jee-weon Jung, Joon Son Chung, Arsha Nagrani, Daniel Garcia-Romero, and Andrew Zisserman. 2023. Voxsrc 2022: The fourth voxceleb speaker recognition challenge. *arXiv preprint arXiv:2302.10248*.

Udeeta Jain, Matthew Siegler, Sam-Joo Doh, Evandro Gouvea, Juan Huerta, Pedro Moreno, Bhiksha Raj, and Richard Stern. 1996. Recognition of continuous broadcast news with multiple unknown speakers and environments.

S.T. Jarashanth, K. Ahilan, R. Valluvan, T. Thiruvaran, and A. Kaneswaran. 2022. Overlapped speech detection for improved speaker diarization on tamil dataset. In *2022 6th SLAAI International Conference on Artificial Intelligence (SLAAI-ICAI)*, pages 1–5.

Shareef Babu Kalluri, Prachi Singh, Pratik Roy Chowdhuri, Apoorva Kulkarni, Shikha Baghel, Pradyoth Hegde, Swapnil Sontakke, Deepak K T, S.R. Mahadeva Prasanna, Deepu Vijayasenan, and Sriram Ganapathy. 2024. The second displace challenge: Diarization of speaker and language in conversational environments. In *Interspeech 2024*, pages 1630–1634.

Federico Landini, Themos Stafylakis, Lukáš Burget, et al. 2024. Diaper: End-to-end neural diarization with perceiver-based attractors. *IEEE/ACM Transactions on Audio, Speech, and Language Processing*.

Qingjian Lin, Yu Hou, and Ming Li. 2020. Self-attentive similarity measurement strategies in speaker diarization. In *Interspeech 2020*, pages 284–288.

Tao Liu, Shuai Fan, Xu Xiang, Hongbo Song, Shaoxiong Lin, Jiaqi Sun, Tianyuan Han, Siyuan Chen, Binwei Yao, Sen Liu, Yifei Wu, Yanmin Qian, and Kai Yu. 2022. Msdwild: Multi-modal speaker diarization dataset in the wild. In *Interspeech 2022*, pages 1476–1480.

Eduardo Lleida, Alfonso Ortega, Antonio Miguel, Virginia Bazán, Carmen Pérez, Manuel Gómez, and Alberto de Prada. 2020. Albayzin evaluation: Iberspeech-rtve 2020 multimodal diarization and scene description challenge.

Eduardo Lleida, Alfonso Ortega, Antonio Miguel, Virginia Bazán-Gil, Carmen Pérez, Manuel Gómez, and Alberto de Prada. 2019. Albayzin 2018 evaluation: The iberspeech-rtve challenge on speech technologies for spanish broadcast media. *Applied Sciences*, 9(24).

Kikuo Maekawa. 2003. Corpus of spontaneous japanese : Its design and evaluation.

Iain Mccowan, J Carletta, Wessel Kraaij, Simone Ashby, S Bourban, M Flynn, M Guillemot, Thomas Hain, J Kadlec, V Karaiskos, M Kronenthal, Guillaume Lathoud, Mike Lincoln, Agnes Lisowska Masson, Wilfried Post, Dennis Reidsma, and P Wellner. 2005. The ami meeting corpus. *Int'l. Conf. on Methods and Techniques in Behavioral Research*.

Thilini Nadungodage, Viraj Welgama, and Ruvan Weerasinghe. 2013. Developing a speech corpus for sinhala speech recognition.

Arsha Nagrani, Joon Son Chung, Jaesung Huh, Andrew Brown, Ernesto Coto, Weidi Xie, Mitchell McLaren, Douglas A Reynolds, and Andrew Zisserman. 2020. Voxsrc 2020: The second voxceleb speaker recognition challenge. *arXiv preprint arXiv:2012.06867*.

Andrew Ng, Michael Jordan, and Yair Weiss. 2001. On spectral clustering: Analysis and an algorithm. In *Advances in Neural Information Processing Systems*, volume 14. MIT Press.

Alfonso Ortega, Antonio Miguel, Eduardo Lleida, Virginia Bazán, Carmen Pérez, and Alberto de Prada. 2022. Iberspeech-rtve 2022 speaker diarization and identity assignment. In *Albayzin Evaluation*. Accessed: 2024-11-05.

M. Padmanabhan, L.R. Bahl, D. Nahamoo, and M.A. Picheny. 1996. Speaker clustering and transformation for speaker adaptation in large-vocabulary speech recognition systems. In *1996 IEEE International Conference on Acoustics, Speech, and Signal Processing Conference Proceedings*, volume 2, pages 701–704 vol. 2.

Tae Jin Park, Naoyuki Kanda, Dimitrios Dimitriadis, Kyu J Han, Shinji Watanabe, and Shrikanth Narayanan. 2022. A review of speaker diarization: Recent advances with deep learning. *Computer Speech & Language*, 72:101317.

Alexis Plaquet and Hervé Bredin. 2023. Powerset multi-class cross entropy loss for neural speaker diarization. *arXiv preprint arXiv:2310.13025*.

Mark Przybocki and Alvin Martin. 2001. 2000 nist speaker recognition evaluation. Web Download. LDC2001S97.

Joseph Roth, Sourish Chaudhuri, Ondrej Klejch, Radhika Marvin, Andrew Gallagher, Liat Kaver, Sharadh Ramaswamy, Arkadiusz Stopczynski, Cordelia Schmid, Zhonghua Xi, et al. 2020. Ava active speaker: An audio-visual dataset for active speaker detection. In *ICASSP 2020-2020 IEEE International Conference on Acoustics, Speech and Signal Processing (ICASSP)*, pages 4492–4496. IEEE.

Neville Ryant, Kenneth Church, Christopher Cieri, Alejandrina Cristia, Jun Du, Sriram Ganapathy, and Mark Liberman. 2019. The second dihard diarization challenge: Dataset, task, and baselines. *arXiv preprint arXiv:1906.07839*.

Neville Ryant, Mark Liberman, James Fiumara, and Christopher Cieri. 2018. First dihard challenge evaluation - nine sources. Web Download. LDC Catalog No. LDC2019S12, DOI: 10.35111/1bsf-4c55.

Neville Ryant, Prachi Singh, Venkat Krishnamohan, Rajat Varma, Kenneth Church, Christopher Cieri, Jun Du, Sriram Ganapathy, and Mark Liberman. 2020. The third dihard diarization challenge. *arXiv preprint arXiv:2012.01477*.

Tanja Schultz. 2002. Globalphone: a multilingual speech and text database developed at karlsruhe university. In *7th International Conference on Spoken Language Processing (ICSLP 2002)*, pages 345–348.

Frederick Tung, Alexander Wong, and David A. Clausi. 2010. Enabling scalable spectral clustering for image segmentation. *Pattern Recognition*, 43(12):4069–4076.

Jixuan Wang, Xiong Xiao, Jian Wu, Ranjani Ramamurthy, Frank Rudzicz, and Michael Brudno. 2020. Speaker diarization with session-level speaker embedding refinement using graph neural networks. In *ICASSP 2020-2020 IEEE International Conference on Acoustics, Speech and Signal Processing (ICASSP)*, pages 7109–7113. IEEE.

Shinji Watanabe, Michael Mandel, Jon Barker, Emmanuel Vincent, Ashish Arora, Xuankai Chang, Sanjeev Khudanpur, Vimal Manohar, Daniel Povey, Desh Raj, David Snyder, Aswin Shanmugam Subramanian, Jan Trmal, Bar Ben Yair, Christoph Boeddeker, Zhaoheng Ni, Yusuke Fujita, Shota Horiguchi, Naoyuki Kanda, Takuya Yoshioka, and Neville Ryant. 2020. Chime-6 challenge: Tackling multispeaker speech recognition for unsegmented recordings. In *6th International Workshop on Speech Processing in Everyday Environments (CHiME 2020)*, pages 1–7.

Barbara Wheatley. 1996. Callhome mandarin chinese transcripts. Web Download.

Junyuan Xie, Ross Girshick, and Ali Farhadi. 2016. Unsupervised deep embedding for clustering analysis. In *International conference on machine learning*, pages 478–487. PMLR.

Eric Zhongcong Xu, Zeyang Song, Satoshi Tsutsui, Chao Feng, Mang Ye, and Mike Zheng Shou. 2022. Ava-avd: Audio-visual speaker diarization in the wild. In *Proceedings of the 30th ACM International Conference on Multimedia*, pages 3838–3847.

Zehui Yang, Yifan Chen, Lei Luo, Runyan Yang, Lingxuan Ye, Gaofeng Cheng, Ji Xu, Yaohui Jin, Qingqing Zhang, Pengyuan Zhang, Lei Xie, and Yonghong Yan. 2022. Open source magicdata-ramc: A rich annotated mandarin conversational(ramc) speech dataset. pages 1736–1740.

Fan Yu, Shiliang Zhang, Yihui Fu, Lei Xie, Siqi Zheng, Zhihao Du, Weilong Huang, Pengcheng Guo, Zhijie Yan, Bin Ma, Xin Xu, and Hui Bu. 2022. M2MeT: The ICASSP 2022 multi-channel multi-party meeting transcription challenge. In *Proc. ICASSP*. IEEE.

Nimra Zaheer, Agha Ali Raza, and Mudassir Shabbir. 2025. Conversations in the wild: Data collection, automatic generation and evaluation. *Computer Speech Language*, 89:101699.

Sandhi Splitting in Tamil and Telugu: A Sequence-to-Sequence Approach Leveraging Transformer Models

Priyanka Dasari[1], Nagaraju Vuppala[1], Mupparapu Sohan Gupta[1], Pruthwik Mishra[2], Parameswari Krishnamurthy[1]
[1]IIIT Hyderabad; [2]SVNIT Surat
{dasari.priyanka, nagaraju.vuppala, sohan.mupparapu}@research.iiit.ac.in
pruthwikmishra@aid.svnit.ac.in, param.krishna@iiit.ac.in,

Abstract

Dravidian languages like Tamil and Telugu are agglutinative languages, they form wordforms by combining two or more elements into a single string with morphophonemic changes at the point of concatenation, known as *sandhi*. This linguistic feature adds complexity to automatic language processing, making the preprocessing of sandhi words essential for NLP applications. We developed extensive sandhi-annotated corpora of 15K for Telugu and Tamil, focusing on the systematic application of sandhi rules which explains the word formation patterns by showing how lexical and functional categories combine to create composite non-compound words. We implemented compact sequence-to-sequence transformer networks for the automatic sandhi processing. To evaluate our models, we manually annotated Telugu and Tamil IN22-Conv Benchmark datasets (Gala et al., 2023) with sandhi annotations. Our experiments aim to enhance the language processing tasks like machine translation in morphologically rich languages.

1 Introduction

In a text, the identification of individual words is necessary for the computational processing of the text. Due to the high agglutinative nature of Dravidian languages, word identification often becomes complex because of *Sandhi*. *Sandhi*, in linguistics, is a process in which two or more morphemes or word forms unite to form a complex word. It involves the alteration of sounds at word boundaries when two words are combined to form a new word (Uma Maheshwar Rao, 2012). *Sandhi*, as derived from Sanskrit, means 'join together'. It refers to the natural phonetic transformations that occur when two or more words are juxtaposed. These transformations are often guided by a particular language's phonological rules. These phenomena can include merging phonemes (units of sound), omitting phonemes, and adding phonemes to facilitate smooth word transitions.

The task of sandhi splitting becomes complex in agglutinative languages as tokens obtained through tokenization can contain more than one morphological word within them. Shallow parsers (Abney, 2022), which are useful in both text (Collins, 1996), and speech processing domains (Wahlster, 2013) is a task of automatic identification of correlated groups of words or chunks. A shallow parser is not a single module but is a set of modules with a tokenizer, parts-of-speech tagger, and chunker or phrase identifier which are put in a pipeline that can be affected by the sandhi words. Tokenization serves as the initial step before engaging in sandhi splitting. Hence, sandhi splitting must be done as part of the tokenization step, as composite words cause the fusion of tokens. This sequential approach ensures that the text is appropriately structured and analyzed, thus facilitating a deeper understanding of the intricate morphological processes.

We conduct our experiments on sandhi splitting in Tamil and Telugu using the OpenNMT framework, (Open-Source Neural Machine Translation) (Klein et al., 2017) which is a popular open-source toolkit for building and training neural machine translation models. It is a deep learning framework designed specifically for seq2seq modeling tasks, such as machine translation (Bahdanau et al., 2014), text summarization (Nenkova et al., 2011), and speech recognition (Yu and Deng, 2016). We utilized this framework for simulating the task of sandhi splitting as it can be modeled as a Seq2Seq task.

Proceedings of the First Workshop on Challenges in Processing South Asian Languages (CHiPSAL 2025), pages 93–103
January 19, 2025.

This study evaluates the effectiveness of transformer architectures in handling sandhi splitting for Tamil and Telugu texts. We trained our models using the datasets of 15K sandhi annotated sentences per language, which encompasses both splitting and non-splitting sentences to enable the model to discern when to split words. We evaluated our approach using two distinct test sets: a held-out portion of our 15K annotated corpus and the sandhi-annotated IN22-Conv benchmark dataset (Gala et al., 2023). Through this study, we seek to enhance sandhi splitting accuracy in text processing, ultimately contributing to the advancement of NLP applications in morphologically rich languages.

2 Sandhi Splitting in Dravidian languages

Dravidian languages like Tamil and Telugu are agglutinative languages as they form words by attaching various morphemes (meaningful word units) as suffixes to a root or base word (Krishnamurti and Gwynn, 1985). These morphemes can convey grammatical information such as gender, number, person, case markers, tense, aspect, mood, and more. In these languages, nouns can be highly inflected to indicate case and number. And verbs are also richly inflected, with extensive conjugation patterns for tense, aspect, mood, gender, person, and number.

Sandhi can be understood in two ways. Internal sandhi refers to different types of sound changes that occur within words (internally) in the word-formation processes, such as inflection and derivation, whereas external sandhi refers to sound changes that happen between two or more fully-formed word boundaries (externally). In our study compound words are considered as single tokens and can not be split because as they derive new lexical sense on combining. The composite words which are non-compound words in external sandhi do not derive new meanings on combining, these word forms are considered as multiple different tokens and we consider these to be the split points in our model.

1. **Telugu**

   īMṭikoccāḍu = *īMṭiki* + *occāḍu* (*He came home*)
   home + come-PST.SG.3.M

2. **Tamil**

   camayttukkoṭuttāṉ = *camayttuk* + *koṭuttāṉ* (*Cooked and gave*)
   cook + give-PST.SG.3.M

Further detailed explanations of the various types of sandhi and the rules for sandhi splitting are provided in Appendix **A**, which formed the basis for constructing our datasets.

Sandhi Splitting is the process of splitting a given composite word into its constituent word forms[1]. This explicit study on splitting composite words is essential as it necessitates a deep understanding of morphological distinctions, syntactic variations, and semantic clarity. Composite words are usually formed with multiple word forms with different roots including suffixes and their grammatical features. Along with morphological distinctions, they exhibit various syntactic relationships that affect overall sentence structure and meaning. They may also carry multiple lexical senses and splitting them into constituent parts clarifies their individual contributions to the overall context. These linguistic aspects are interconnected and essential for understanding the complexity of language.

3 Challanges in downstream tasks:

Machine Translation (MT) systems often struggle with accurate translations, particularly when handling morphologically complex languages. One of such challenge arises from sandhi formations - where two distinct words combine with phonological changes at their boundaries. This phenomenon is especially prevalent in Dravidian languages like Telugu and Tamil. Table[1] compares translation outputs for the same sentences under two conditions: before and after applying sandhi splitting.

As shown in Table[1], in Telugu-English translation, the Telugu sandhi word 'māyiṃṭikocci - *to come our home*' is transliterated in translation output as 'Maintikochi'.

[1]the first wordform is termed as W1, the second wordform as W2, and subsequent words are termed W3... Wn.

Language	Sandhi Splitting	Source	Google-Translate
Telugu-English	Before	మాయింటికొచ్చి నాలుగు జానపద గేయాలు పాడేసి వెళ్ళవా? 'māyiṃṭikocci nālugu jānapada gēyālu pāḍēsi veḷḷavā? '	Shall we sing four folk songs in Maintikochi?
	After	మా ఇంటికి వచ్చి నాలుగు జానపద గేయాలు పాడేసి వెళ్ళవా? 'mā iṃṭiki vacci nālugu jānapada gēyālu pāḍēsi veḷḷavā? '	*Will you* ***come to my house*** *and sing four folk songs and leave?*
Telugu-Tamil	Before	లక్ష్మీదేవి, చోళరాజుకు కూతురైయ్యింది. 'lakṢmīdēvi, cōḻarājuku kŪturayyiṃdi '	லட்சுமி தேவி சோழராஜாவின் மகள் ஆவார். 'Laxmi devi will become Chola Raja's daughter.'
	After	లక్ష్మీదేవి, చోళరాజుకు కూతురు అయ్యింది 'lakṢmīdēvi, cōḻarājuku kŪturu ayyiṃdi' .	லட்சுமி தேவி சோழராஜாவின் மகள் ஆனார். *'Laxmi devi* ***became*** *the daughter of Chola Raja.'*

Table 1: Differences in translation outputs in before and after sandhi splitting

However, after sandhi splitting, 'māyiṃṭikocci' is splitted into 'mā iṃṭiki vacci' gives the accurate translation. Here, the sandhi word combines; pronoun (mā- *our*) + noun (iṃṭiki- *home*) + verb (vacci - *to come*), providing the correct syntactic structure for a meaningful translation.

In Telugu-Tamil translation example, the Telugu word 'kŪturayyyiṃdi - *became daughter*' is translated incorrectly in the future tense as 'makaḷ āvār - *will become daughter*'. After sandhi splitting 'kŪturu ayyiṃdi' produces the correct translation. In this case, the sandhi word combines the noun (kŪturu - *daughter*) with verb (**ayyiṃdi** - *became*), accurately conveying the intended past tense in translation.

4 Related Work

A significant amount of research has focused on sandhi splitting in Indian languages. However, most of this research has concentrated on internal sandhi phenomena. Our study, in contrast, addresses the splitting of external sandhi words where two or more fully formed composite words are combined. Among the traditional approaches, a rule-based sandhi splitter was developed as part of a morphological analyzer and spell checker tool for Telugu (Uma Maheshwar Rao, 2012). However, this method fails to split new words not covered by the predefined rules.

Kuncham et al. (2015) employs a statistical method to perform sandhi splitting in Telugu and Malayalam languages. The testing results indicated an accuracy of 89.07% for Telugu and 90.50% for Malayalam, demonstrating the effectiveness of this approach. This methodology comprised two main components: segmentation and word generation, both of which utilized Conditional Random Fields (CRFs) as a key tool. Devadath et al. (2014) devise a hybrid method that leverages the phonological changes occurring when words are joined together in the context of external sandhi. This approach combines the statistical identification of split points with the application of predefined character-level linguistic rules. As a result, their system currently achieves an accuracy rate of 91.1%. The study by Devadath and Sharma (2016) addresses issues related to the Malayalam Dependency Treebank in the context of external sandhi explaining the challenges posed by external sandhi in the syntactic annotation of Malayalam sentences. Their experiment uses a statistical parser to empirically validate the improvements made to the treebank, stating that even the separation of a single type of external sandhi significantly enhances overall parsing accuracy.

Vempaty and Nagalla (2011) introduce a method that employs finite state automata to identify possible words within compound words in Telugu. It is built using the syllables of base words, enabling the recognition of candidate words within compound structures. Nair and Peter (2011) design an algorithm aimed at breaking down Malayalam compound words into a series of morphemes by employing multiple levels of finite state automata. Shree et al. (2016) have adopted an approach to the internal sandhi splitting technique in the Kannada language. Gupta and Goyal (2009) conduct Sandhi-Vicheda on Hindi words and assess their software using a dataset of over 200 words through their rule-based algorithm. The studies highlighted employ a variety of approaches, including rule-based methods, statistical techniques, finite state automata, and hybrid approaches combining rules and statistics for tackling the sandhi splitting problem in different Indian languages like Telugu, Malayalam, Kannada, and Hindi.

More recent studies indicate that neural network approaches perform well for sandhi splitting implemented for Sanskrit. The work by Hellwig (2015) is the first in formulating the problem as a neural sequence labeling task, and this was further improved upon by Hellwig and Nehrdich (2018). Hellwig and Nehrdich (2018) introduce end-to-end neural network models that tokenize Sanskrit words by jointly separating compound words and resolving phonetic merge (sandhi) cases. These models do not require hand-crafted features or external linguistic resources, operating solely on parallel data of raw and segmented text.

Additionally, Reddy et al. (2018); Aralikatte et al. (2018) propose Seq2Seq models for this task. Aralikatte et al. (2018) treat word segmentation as a multi-task problem, using a shared encoder with two decoders, where one decoder predicts the split locations and the other generates the characters in the split words. Unlike earlier rule-based or statistical methods, these studies demonstrate the application of neural architectures like sequence labeling and Seq2Seq models to tackle the sandhi splitting problem in an end-to-end fashion directly from data.

5 Need for Sandhi Splitting

This explicit focus on the sandhi split of composite words is essential for several key reasons:

1. **Morphological Distinctions:** Composite words are often formed by joining distinct roots, each with its own grammatical and morphological properties. By splitting these words, the language retains clarity in morphological structure, enabling a precise understanding of the constituent roots and their individual roles within the word.

2. **Syntactic Variations:** In composite words, the constituent word forms can display various syntactic relationships. These relationships help in understanding the overall sentence structure and meaning. Splitting these word forms helps disambiguate syntactic relationships and ensure the sentence retains its intended syntax.

3. **Semantic Clarity:** Composite words may convey multiple, distinct lexical senses when examined as separate components. Splitting them into their constituent parts enables a clearer understanding of the individual lexical meanings they contribute to the overall context. Combining multiple roots and grammatical features often leads to nuanced and context-specific meanings. Sandhi rules help in preserving and revealing these semantic nuances, ensuring that the intended message is conveyed accurately.

6 Implementation

6.1 Data Collection and Annotations

Experiments are conducted on Tamil and Telugu sandhi data using Transformer models at both sentence and character levels to capture morphological patterns effectively. For each language, we developed a dataset comprising 15,000 manually annotated sandhi sentences. Tamil data was sourced from diverse online repositories, including Wikipedia and the Tamil Nadu Tourism website[2], while

[2]https://www.tamilnadutourism.tn.gov.in/tamil

Telugu data was gathered from Wikimedia and publicly available datasets on GitHub[3]. The models were trained and evaluated on both levels to compare their performance and efficacy in handling sandhi variations.

We created two test sets to evaluate model performance on sandhi detection and splitting. The first set was randomly sampled from the 15,000 annotated sentences, while the second set is from the IN22-Conv benchmark dataset (Gala et al., 2023), chosen over FLORES-200(NLLB Team, 2022) for its higher frequency of sandhi splits. In each test set, we formatted the data so that each line in the source side consists of a single sentence, while the target side contains either the single equivalent word or its sandhi form(s), with components separated by a '+' symbol when applicable. The annotations are carried in accordance with sandhi guidelines as mentioned in Appendix **A**. To ensure accuracy, the annotations were thoroughly reviewed and verified by expert linguists proficient in the respective languages. Our curated datasets include both sandhi and non-sandhi sentences, allowing the model to distinguish contexts where splitting is required from those where it is not, promoting a balanced understanding of natural language structure.

Splits of Dataset	No. of sentneces
Train	10000
Valid	3000
Test	2000
IN22-Conv	1503

Table 2: Statistics of Dataset

Splits	Tamil	Telugu
Train and Valid	3200	4002
Testset	853	809
IN22-Conv	145	374

Table 3: Statistics of sandhi split

The dataset is divided into training, validation, and test sets. The statistics for each split are presented in Table[2], while the number of sandhi occurrences within each split is shown in Table[3]. Careful measures have been taken to ensure that the test set remains entirely separate from the training data, eliminating any risk of data leakage and ensuring unbiased predictions.

6.2 Experiments

We employ the Transformer architecture (Vaswani et al., 2017), a state-of-the-art deep learning model with proven success across numerous natural language processing tasks. Transformer's capacity to capture contextual information makes it especially suitable for sandhi splitting. Our model follows the typical encoder-decoder structure: the encoder processes input text, and the decoder predicts sandhi splits upon detecting sandhi words. We implement the Transformer model using the PyTorch-based OpenNMT toolkit (Klein et al., 2018).

The first set of experiments is conducted on sentence-level data, where the source sentences are non-sandhi split sentences, and the target sentences are sandhi-annotated, with sandhi words marked using the '+' symbol. We refer to this as the *Sentence Level Model* (SLM).

In a variation of this experiment, we used *subword-nmt* (Sennrich et al., 2016) to apply byte-pair encoding (BPE) on the training data, creating the *Sentence Level Subword Model* (SLSM). This approach allowed us to evaluate the impact of subword tokenization on the model's performance.

In the character-level experiment, we have arranged the sentence-level data such that every single character is separated by a space. This structure enables the model to process the text at a granular, character-by-character level, which is particularly useful for capturing detailed morphological patterns in sandhi splits. We refer to this setup as the *Character Level Model* (CLM).

In addition to our custom models, we fine-tuned the mt5-small model (Xue, 2020) for the task of sandhi splitting in Tamil and Telugu . mT5 (multilingual T5) is a variant of the T5 (Text-To-Text Transfer Transformer) architecture specifically designed to handle 101 languages, including low-resource ones. Fine-tuning on our annotated dataset refines the model's focus on the sandhi splitting task, improving its ability to identify and split sandhi words accurately. Results are discussed

[3]https://github.com/AnushaMotamarri/Telugu-Books-Dataset?tab=readme-ov-file

Gloss	*Mom, let's go for a movie tomorrow.*		
Input Type	**Sentence Level**	**Sentence Level Subword Model**	**Character Model**
Telugu	అమ్మా, రేపు సినిమాకి వెళ్దాం.	అ@@ మ్మా@@ , రే@@ పు సి@@ ని@@ మా@@ కి వె@@ ళ్@@ దా@@ ◌ం.	అ మ ◌్మ ◌ా , # ర ◌ే ప ◌ు # స ◌ి న ◌ి మ ◌ా క ◌ి # వ ◌ె ళ ◌్ద ◌ా ◌ం .
Tamil	அம்மா, நாம் நாளைக்கு சினிமா பார்க்கப் போகலாமா?	அ@@ ம்@@ மா@@, ந@@ ◌ாம@@ ◌்ந@@ ◌ாள@@ ◌ை க்க@@ ◌ுச@@ ◌ின@@ ◌ிம@@ ◌ாப@@ ◌ார@@ ◌்க்க@@ப@@ ◌்போ@@க@@ லாம@@ ◌ா@@?	அ ம ◌் ம ◌ா , # ந ◌ா ம ◌் # ந ◌ா ள ◌ை க ◌் க ◌ு # ச ◌ி ன ◌ி ம ◌ா # ப ◌ா ர ◌் க ◌் க ப ◌் # ப ◌ோ க ல ◌ா ம ◌ா ?

Table 4: Illustration of the sample input format used for the models.

Testset	Character		Sentence		Sentence-subword		mT5	
Metrics	**Tamil**	**Telugu**	**Tamil**	**Telugu**	**Tamil**	**Telugu**	**Tamil**	**Telugu**
Precision	0.8076	0.7832	0.7715	0.7351	0.8124	0.7639	0.8045	0.7568
Recall	0.7384	0.731	0.7423	0.6924	0.7532	0.745	0.7862	0.731
F1 Score	0.7714	0.7562	0.7566	0.7133	0.7818	0.7544	0.8132	0.7437
Accuracy	**0.8205**	0.7485	0.7902	0.7319	0.7841	**0.7832**	0.7917	0.7742

Table 5: Evaluation metrics on Testset

IN22-Conv	Character		Sentence		Sentence-subword		mT5	
Metrics	**Tamil**	**Telugu**	**Tamil**	**Telugu**	**Tamil**	**Telugu**	**Tamil**	**Telugu**
Precision	0.7532	0.7413	0.7398	0.6774	0.7856	0.7559	0.7583	0.7553
Recall	0.7421	0.6754	0.7123	0.6342	0.7521	0.7221	0.7245	0.7218
F1 Score	0.7476	0.7075	0.7256	0.6551	0.7685	0.7383	0.7408	0.7384
Accuracy	0.7595	0.6912	0.7451	0.6653	**0.7793**	**0.7625**	0.7632	0.7496

Table 6: Evaluation metrics on IN22-Conv

in next section 6.3. Table [4] illustrates the sample input format sentence taken from the IN22-conv test set used for three models: sentence-level, sentence-level subword, and character-level. For the mT5 model, the standard sentence-level data format is utilized during training.

6.3 Results

Our experiments treat sandhi splitting as a Seq2Seq task, evaluating our models using precision, recall, f1 score, and accuracy. We define true positives as correctly split sandhis and true negatives as accurately identified non-sandhis. False positives count when non-sandhis are incorrectly predicted as sandhis, while false negatives represent instances where fewer sandhi splits are predicted than expected. Our performance evaluation is based on these definitions.

Across all models, Tamil character-level models achieve higher accuracy, with 82% as shown in Table [5]. This is due to the character-level nature of sandhi, where conjugation occurs within the characters of words. On the IN22-Conv test set, sentence-level subword models outperform others, as shown in Table [6] due to their ability to capture broader contextual information and handle diverse sandhi constructions effectively. We also considered a rule-based sandhi splitter for Telugu (Uma Maheshwar Rao, 2012) as a baseline model, which resulted in 65% accuracy on our test set and 59% on the IN22-Conv set. This method struggles to split new words not covered by the predefined rules, limiting its performance compared to the learned models.

Overall, Tamil models achieve higher accuracy than Telugu models, likely because Telugu, being more agglutinative, requires larger datasets to capture its complex linguistic intricacies. Furthermore, the greater number of sandhi splits in Telugu as in

Table [3] increases the challenge. The higher number of true negatives, representing correctly predicted non-sandhi sentences, also contributes to the improved performance of Tamil models.

7 Observations and Limitations

Our findings indicate that the effectiveness of sandhi splitting techniques varies between languages, with Telugu resulting in lower accuracies as it exhibits more sandhi words naturally as shown in Table [3].

In some cases, the model tended to overgenerate or hallucinate outputs. However, it performed well in sandhi splitting for functional category contexts, as detailed in Section B. For example, in Telugu, the model correctly split combinations like అదేమిటంటే 'adēmiṭaṃṭē' (*what it means*) into అది 'adi' (*it*') + ఏమిటి 'ēmiṭi' (*what*) + అంటే 'aṃṭē' (*means*) and మానేద్దమని 'mānēddamani' (*to quit*) into మానేద్దాము 'mānēddāmu' (*quit*) + అని 'ani' (*particle*). Similarly, in Tamil, examples like பிறகெங்கே 'pirakeṅke' (*then where*) into பிறகு 'piraku' (*then*) + எங்கே 'eṅke' (*where*) and இலங்கையாகும் 'ilaṅkayyākum' (Srilanka) into இலங்கை 'ilaṅkay' (*Srilanka*) + ஆகும் 'ākum' (*be-copula*).

Functional categories are typically finite, shorter (mono or bisyllabic), and easier for the model to generalize, especially when paired with longer, non-monosyllabic lexical categories. However, the model faced difficulties with more complex lexical category combinations, such as in Telugu, ప్రోత్సహిస్తారనుకుంటావా? 'prōtsahistāranukuṃṭāvā?' (*Do you think they will encourage?*) should be split as ప్రోత్సహిస్తారు 'prōtsahistāru' (*encourage*) + అనుకుంటావా? 'anukuṃṭāvā' (*do you think*) — and in Tamil, ஆட்டமிழந்து 'āṭṭamilantu' (*lost the game*) split as ஆட்டம் 'āṭṭam' (*game*) +இழந்து 'ilantu' (*lost*). These longer and different lexical category combinations posed greater challenges for the model, making accurate splitting more difficult.

To address this, more high-quality data with richer sandhi splits is needed and due to limited computational resources couldn't fine-tune the model for more epochs. We attempted to train a language model, specifically, Llama-3.1-8B (Touvron et al., 2023), which requires substantial datasets and higher computational power. However, our efforts using the comparatively smaller dataset did not yield higher accuracies, as the outcomes were very low.

8 Conclusion and Future work

This study examined the challenges of sandhi splitting in Dravidian languages, focusing on Tamil and Telugu. Future work will extend this research to other Dravidian languages, such as Kannada and Malayalam, and fine-tune additional large language models (LLMs) with more data to address issues of overgeneration and hallucination. Additionally, by fine-tuning machine translation (MT) systems using sandhi-split annotated datasets, we aim to assess their performance on existing benchmarks. This approach will enhance translation evaluation metrics and contribute to the advancement of MT systems for more accurate translations across Dravidian languages.

References

Steven P Abney. 2022. Principle-based parsing. In *12th Annual Conference. CSS Pod*, pages 1021–1021. Psychology Press.

Rahul Aralikatte, Neelamadhav Gantayat, Naveen Panwar, Anush Sankaran, and Senthil Mani. 2018. Sanskrit sandhi splitting using seq2 (seq)^ 2. *arXiv preprint arXiv:1801.00428*.

Dzmitry Bahdanau, Kyunghyun Cho, and Yoshua Bengio. 2014. Neural machine translation by jointly learning to align and translate. *arXiv preprint arXiv:1409.0473*.

Michael Collins. 1996. A new statistical parser based on bigram lexical dependencies. *arXiv preprint cmp-lg/9605012*.

VV Devadath, Litton J Kurisinkel, Dipti Misra Sharma, and Vasudeva Varma. 2014. A sandhi splitter for malayalam. In *Proceedings of the 11th International Conference on Natural Language Processing*, pages 156–161.

VV Devadath and Dipti Misra Sharma. 2016. Significance of an accurate sandhi-splitter in shallow parsing of dravidian languages. In *Proceedings of the ACL 2016 Student Research Workshop*, pages 37–42.

Jay Gala, Pranjal A Chitale, A K Raghavan, Varun Gumma, Sumanth Doddapaneni, Aswanth Kumar M, Janki Atul Nawale, Anupama Sujatha,

Ratish Puduppully, Vivek Raghavan, Pratyush Kumar, Mitesh M Khapra, Raj Dabre, and Anoop Kunchukuttan. 2023. Indictrans2: Towards high-quality and accessible machine translation models for all 22 scheduled indian languages. *Transactions on Machine Learning Research.*

Priyanka Gupta and Vishal Goyal. 2009. Implementation of rule based algorithm for sandhi-vicheda of compound hindi words. *arXiv preprint arXiv:0909.2379.*

Oliver Hellwig. 2015. Using recurrent neural networks for joint compound splitting and sandhi resolution in sanskrit. In *4th Biennial workshop on less-resourced languages.*

Oliver Hellwig and Sebastian Nehrdich. 2018. Sanskrit word segmentation using character-level recurrent and convolutional neural networks. In *Proceedings of the 2018 Conference on Empirical Methods in Natural Language Processing*, pages 2754–2763, Brussels, Belgium. Association for Computational Linguistics.

Guillaume Klein, Yoon Kim, Yuntian Deng, Vincent Nguyen, Jean Senellart, and Alexander M. Rush. 2018. Opennmt: Neural machine translation toolkit.

Guillaume Klein, Yoon Kim, Yuntian Deng, Jean Senellart, and Alexander M. Rush. 2017. Opennmt: Open-source toolkit for neural machine translation. In *Proc. ACL.*

Bhadriraju Krishnamurti and John Peter Lucius Gwynn. 1985. *A grammar of modern Telugu.* Oxford University Press, USA.

Prathyusha Kuncham, Kovida Nelakuditi, Sneha Nallani, and Radhika Mamidi. 2015. Statistical sandhi splitter for agglutinative languages. In *Computational Linguistics and Intelligent Text Processing: 16th International Conference, CICLing 2015, Cairo, Egypt, April 14-20, 2015, Proceedings, Part I 16*, pages 164–172. Springer.

Latha Ravindran Nair and S. David Peter. 2011. Development of a rule based learning system for splitting compound words in malayalam language. *2011 IEEE Recent Advances in Intelligent Computational Systems*, pages 751–755.

Ani Nenkova, Kathleen McKeown, et al. 2011. Automatic summarization. *Foundations and Trends® in Information Retrieval*, 5(2–3):103–233.

James Cross Onur Çelebi Maha Elbayad Kenneth Heafield Kevin Heffernan Elahe Kalbassi Janice Lam Daniel Licht Jean Maillard Anna Sun Skyler Wang Guillaume Wenzek Al Youngblood Bapi Akula Loic Barrault Gabriel Mejia Gonzalez Prangthip Hansanti John Hoffman Semarley Jarrett Kaushik Ram Sadagopan Dirk Rowe Shannon Spruit Chau Tran Pierre Andrews Necip Fazil Ayan Shruti Bhosale Sergey Edunov Angela Fan Cynthia Gao Vedanuj Goswami Francisco Guzmán Philipp Koehn Alexandre Mourachko Christophe Ropers Safiyyah Saleem Holger Schwenk Jeff Wang NLLB Team, Marta R. Costa-jussà. 2022. No language left behind: Scaling human-centered machine translation.

Vikas Reddy, Amrith Krishna, Vishnu Dutt Sharma, Prateek Gupta, Pawan Goyal, et al. 2018. Building a word segmenter for sanskrit overnight. *arXiv preprint arXiv:1802.06185.*

Rico Sennrich, Barry Haddow, and Alexandra Birch. 2016. Neural machine translation of rare words with subword units. In *Proceedings of the 54th Annual Meeting of the Association for Computational Linguistics (Volume 1: Long Papers)*, pages 1715–1725, Berlin, Germany. Association for Computational Linguistics.

M Rajani Shree, Sowmya Lakshmi, and BR Shambhavi. 2016. A novel approach to sandhi splitting at character level for kannada language. In *2016 International Conference on Computation System and Information Technology for Sustainable Solutions (CSITSS)*, pages 17–20. IEEE.

Hugo Touvron, Thibaut Lavril, Gautier Izacard, Xavier Martinet, Marie-Anne Lachaux, Timothée Lacroix, Baptiste Rozière, Naman Goyal, Eric Hambro, Faisal Azhar, et al. 2023. Llama: Open and efficient foundation language models. *arXiv preprint arXiv:2302.13971.*

Amba P. Kulkarni Parameshwari K. Uma Maheshwar Rao, G. 2012. Telugu spell-checker. *Vaagartha, First edition.*

Ashish Vaswani, Noam Shazeer, Niki Parmar, Jakob Uszkoreit, Llion Jones, Aidan N Gomez, Ł ukasz Kaiser, and Illia Polosukhin. 2017. Attention is all you need. In *Advances in Neural Information Processing Systems*, volume 30. Curran Associates, Inc.

Phani Chaitanya Vempaty and Satish Chandra Prasad Nagalla. 2011. Automatic sandhi spliting method for telugu, an indian language. *Procedia-Social and Behavioral Sciences*, 27:218–225.

Wolfgang Wahlster. 2013. *Verbmobil: foundations of speech-to-speech translation.* Springer Science & Business Media.

L Xue. 2020. mt5: A massively multilingual pre-trained text-to-text transformer. *arXiv preprint arXiv:2010.11934.*

Dong Yu and Lin Deng. 2016. *Automatic speech recognition*, volume 1. Springer.

A Appendix

A.1 Types of Sandhi

Sandhi is realized in two ways: Internal Sandhi and External Sandhi. Detailed explanations of Internal sandhi and External sandhi are given here:

Internal Sandhi:
Internal Sandhi, also known as *antar* sandhi, refers to phonological changes that occur within a single word, typically due to morphological processes like inflection and derivation.

1. **Inflections:** Inflected words are base words that undergo grammatical changes to convey different meanings, such as verb conjugations, noun plurals, prepositions or postpositions, and case markers are considered inflectional markers. Tables[7] and [8] explain the inflectional suffixes in Telugu and Tamil.

Wordforms	Inflections	Gloss
kattitō	*katti + tō* knife + INS	'with the knife'
gul̤l̤ō	*guḍi + lo* temple + LOC	'in the temple'
ūllu	*uru + lu* village + PL	'villages'
cēstāḍu	*ces + tā + ḍu* come+will -FUT+SG.3.M	'he will do'

Table 7: Inflectional Suffixes of Telugu

Wordforms	Inflections	Gloss
pēn̠āvaykkoṇṭu	*pēn̠āvayk+koṇṭu* pen + INS	'with pen'
*valatupur̠*attil	*valatupur̠am+il* right side + LOC	'towards right side'
par̠kaḷ	*pal+kaḷ* tooth + PL	'teeth'
āṭuvāḷ	*āṭu+vā+ḷ* dance +will -FUT+SG.3.F	'she will dance'

Table 8: Inflectional Suffixes of Tamil

2. **Derivations:** Derivation involves creating new words or modifying the meaning of existing words by adding prefixes, suffixes or infixes. These affixes alter the root word's meaning or grammatical category. Tables [9] and [10] explain the derivational suffixes in Telugu and Tamil.

Wordforms	Derivations	Gloss
aṃdamayna	*aṃdam+ ayna* pleasant + ADJV	'beauteous'
vēgaṃgā	*vēgaṃ+ gā* fast + ADV	'fastly'
cēyavaddu	*cēyu + vaddu* do + not-AUX	'do not do'

Table 9: Derivational Suffixes in Telugu

Wordforms	Derivations	Gloss
ar̠ivān̠a	*ar̠ivu+ān̠a* Intelligent + ADJ	'intelligent'
nērāka	*nēr+āka* Straight + ADV	'straightly'
pārkkakkūṭātu	*pārkkak + kūṭātu* see + not-AUX	'do not see'

Table 10: Derivational Suffixes in Tamil

External Sandhi:
External sandhi, also known as *bahya* sandhi, involves phonological changes that occur at the boundaries of words when they come into contact, either due to word combination or sentence formation as a result of stylistic variation. External sandhi can be divided into two types.

1. **Compound Words:** Compound words are formed by combining two or more complete words to create a new word with a distinct meaning.
   Examples in Telugu:
   (a) *rāmālayaM* 'Rama's temple' = *rāmā* + *ālayaM*
   (b) *paramārdhaM* 'great meaning' = *parama* + *ardhaM*

   Examples in Tamil:
   (a) *matiyavēḷay* "afternoon" = *matiya* + *veḷay*
   (b) *tuvaramparuppu* 'toor dal' = *tuvaram* + *paruppu*

2. **Composite words or Non-compound Words:** Composite words, also known as Non-compound words, contain two or

more complete words within them but do not derive new or distinct meanings from this combination. Since these composite words do not derive new meanings on combining, these word forms are considered as two different tokens and hence to be split.

Examples in Telugu

(a) *īMṭikoccāḍu* = *īMṭiki* + *occāḍu*
home + come-PST.SG.3.M

(b) *vaccānannāḍu* = *vaccānu* + *annāḍu*
come-PST.SG.3 + say-PST.SG.3.M

(c) *atanoccāḍēmō* = *atanu* + *occāḍu* + *ēmō*
'he + come-PST.SG.3.M + emo-ADV

Examples in Tamil

(a) *camayttukkoṭuttāṉ* = *camayttu* + *koṭuttāṉ*
cook + give-PST.SG.3.M

(b) *koṭumayceyvāḷ* = *koṭumay* + *ceyvāḷ*
torture + do-FUT.SG.3.F

(c) *virayvākappo* = *virayvāka* + *pō*
fast -ADV +go

B Contexts for Sandhi Splitting

Sandhi rules allow us to unravel the complexities of composite words, leading to a deeper comprehension of their structure, syntax, and meaning in language analysis and interpretation. These rules for sandhi are made based on the distinction between the lexical and functional categories. lexical categories such as nouns (N), verbs (V), pronouns (PR), adjectives (JJ), and number words, can take inflectional and derivational suffixes and often carry the core meaning in a sentence. Functional categories in Telugu, including quantifiers (QT), particles (RP), quotatives (UT), intensifiers (INTF), negations (NEG), etc., are often considered as closed-class words, and they are more stable in their form and do not readily take inflections or any derivational suffixes. We identify four major contexts in which word forms are conjoined that need to be split. The contexts are:

1. **Lexical Categories + Lexical Categories:**
This combination involves sandhi between two lexical categories of words. Examples are given in Tables [11] and [12].

W1+W2	W1	W2
dēvuḍiccina	*dēvuḍu*(N) 'god'	*iccina*(V) 'given'
mēmanukōvaccu	*mēmu*(PR) 'we'	*anukōvaccu*(V) 'thought'
vaccāḍokasāri	*vaccāḍu*(V) 'come-PST.M.SG'	*okasāri*(N) 'once'
aydaMtasthula	*aydu*(N) 'five'	*aMtasthula*(N) 'floors'

Table 11: Lexical Categories (W1) + Lexical Categories (W2) in Telugu

W1+W2	W1	W2
aḷavilirukkum	*aḷavil*(N) 'in amount'	*irukkum*(N) 'be-FUT.3.NEU'
atikamāṉavay	*atikam*(N) "More"	*āṉavay*(V) 'become-PST.PL.3.NEU'
aticayamākum	*aticayam*(N) 'miracle'	*ākum* (V) 'is'
ataṟkuḷḷākave	*ataṟku*(N) 'for that'	*uḷḷākave*(ADV) "within"
ārampakālaṅkaḷ	*ārampam*(ADJ) "begin"	*kālaṅkaḷ*(N) "seasons"

Table 12: Lexical Categories (W1) + Lexical Categories (W2) in Tamil

2. **Functional Categories + Functional Categories:**
This combination involves sandhi between two functional categories of words. Examples are given in Tables [13] and [14].

W1+W2	W1	W2
lēḍakkaḍa	*lēḍu* 'not'	*akkaḍa* 'there'
ippuḍakkaḍa	*ippuḍu* 'now'	*akkaḍa* 'there'
appuḍaMdarikī	*appuḍu* 'then'	*aMdarikī* 'all'
ekkaḍikaMṭe	*ekkaḍiki* 'where'	*aMṭe* 'means'

Table 13: Functional Categories (W1) + Functional Categories (W2) in Telugu

W1+W2	W1	W2
avvārillay	*avvāru* 'like that'	*illay* 'not'
piṟakaṅke	*piṟaku* 'then'	*aṅke* 'there'
vēṟellām	*vēṟu* 'something else'	*ellām* 'all'
eppaṭiyeṉṟāl	*eppaṭi* 'how'	*eṉṟāl* 'means'

Table 14: Functional Categories (W1) + Functional Categories (W2) in Tamil

3. **Lexical Categories + Functional Categories:**
This combination is the interaction between lexical categories and functional categories. Lexical categories provide the core meaning, while functional categories modify the sense of the sentence being in

the W2 position. Examples are given in Tables [15] and [16].

W2 Type	**W1+W2**	**W1**	**W2**
Concessive	*koMḍalaynā*	*koMḍalu* (N) ‘mountains’	*ayinā* ‘ even though’
Conditional	*pillalayite*	*pillalu* (N) ‘children’	*ayite* ‘if’
Quantifiers	*abhivr̲ddhaMtā*	*abhivr̲ddhi* (N) ‘development’	*aMtā/aMta* ‘all (that much)‘
Interogatives	*āhārālēmī*	*āhārālu*(N) ‘food’	*ēmī* ‘What’
Distals	*vāḷlakkaḍa*	*vāḷlu* (PR) ‘they’	*akkaḍa* ‘place’
Proximals	*pillalitlA*	*pillalu* (N) ‘children’	*iṭlā* ‘manner’

Table 15: Lexical Categories (W1) + Functional Category (W2) in Telugu

W2 Type	**W1+W2**	**W1**	**W2**
Concessive	*taṭaṅkaliruppin̲um*	*taṭan̲kal* (N) ‘obstacles’	*iruppin̲um* ’in spite of’
Conditional	*avan̲iruntāl*	*avan̲* (PRON) ‘he’	*iruntāl* ‘if’
Quantifiers	*kavalayyan̲ayttum*	*kavalay* (N) ‘worries’	*an̲ayttum* ‘all (that much)‘
Interogatives	*paṭuvateṅkē?*	*pāṭuvatu*(N) ‘to sing’	*eṅkē?* ‘Where’
Distals	*avan̲aṅku*	*avan̲* (PR) ‘he’	*aṅku* ‘there’
Proximals	*ivan̲iṅku*	*ivan̲* (PR) ‘he’	*iṅku* ‘here’

Table 16: Lexical Categories (W1) + Functional Category (W2) in Tamil

4. **Functional Categories + Lexical Categories:**
   In this combination, functional categories are supplementary to Lexical categories, often modifying or specifying the meaning of the lexical category word in the W2 position. Examples are given in Tables [17] and [18].

W1 Type	**W1+W2**	**W1**	**W2**
Quantifiers	*aṃḍarunna*	*aṃḍaru* ‘that many /so many (people)’	*unna* (V) ‘to be’
Interogatives	*ēmiṭammāyi*	*ēmiṭi* ‘What’	*ammāyi* (N) ‘girl’
Distals	*akkaḍokaru*	*akkaḍa* ‘place’	*okaru* (N) ‘one person’
Proximals	*ikkaḍunnavāḷlu*	*ikkaḍa* ‘place’	*unnavāḷlu* (N) ‘people’

Table 17: Functional Categories + Lexical Categories in Telugu

W1 Type	**W1+W2**	**W1**	**W2**
Quantifiers	*palapēr*	*pala* ‘many’	*pēr* ‘members’
Interogatives	*ekkāriyam?*	*enta* ‘Which’	*kāriyam?* ‘matter’
Distals	*aṅkuḷḷōr*	*aṅku* ‘there’	*uḷḷōr* ‘people-be’
Proximals	*iṅkuḷḷōr*	*iṅku* ‘here’	*uḷḷōr* ‘people-be’

Table 18: Functional Categories + Lexical Categories in Tamil

Bridge the GAP: Multi-lingual Models For Ambiguous Pronominal Coreference Resolution in South Asian Languages

Rahothvarman P*
IIIT Hyderabad
rahothvarman.p@research.iiit.ac.in

Adith John Rajeev*
IIIT Hyderabad
adith.r@research.iiit.ac.in

Kaveri Anuranjana
IIIT Hyderabad
kaveri.a@research.iiit.ac.in

Radhika Mamidi
IIIT Hyderabad
radhika.mamidi@iiit.ac.in

Abstract

Coreference resolution, the process of determining what a referring expression (a pronoun or a noun phrase) refers to in discourse, is a critical aspect of natural language understanding. However, the development of computational models for coreference resolution in low-resource languages, such as the Dravidian (and more broadly all South Asian) languages, still remains a significant challenge due to the scarcity of annotated corpora in these languages. To address this data scarcity, we adopt a pipeline that translates the English GAP dataset into various South Asian languages, creating a multi-lingual coreference dataset mGAP. Our research aims to leverage this dataset and develop two novel models, namely the joint embedding model and the cross attention model for coreference resolution with Dravidian languages in mind. We also demonstrate that cross-attention captures pronoun-candidate relations better leading to improved coreference resolution. We also harness the similarity across South Asian languages via transfer learning in order to use high resource languages to learn coreference for low resource languages.

1 Introduction

Coreference resolution involves identifying and linking referring expressions (pronouns or noun phrases) to their respective referents. Accurate resolution is essential for discourse-level tasks such as dialogue understanding (Tseng et al., 2021), machine translation (Stojanovski and Fraser, 2019), summarization (Steinberger et al., 2007), question answering (Castagnola, 2002) and sentiment analysis (De Clercq and Hoste, 2020). Prominent datasets such as OntoNotes 5.0 (Pradhan et al., 2013a) (English, Chinese & Arabic), ParCorFull (Lapshinova-Koltunski et al., 2018) (English & German) and TransMuCoRes (Mishra et al., 2024) (31 South Asian languages) have focused on multilingual coreference resolution.

Transformer-based methods have been proposed for multilingual coreference resolution (Martinelli et al., 2024; Liu et al., 2022). Additionally, ChatGPT (Chen, 2024), despite its advances on the WinoGrand Challenge, could not learn linguistic features of Chinese such as zero pronouns. South Asian languages (SALs) exhibit similar unique traits which we investigate in this paper.

Pronominal coreference resolution, the most common type of coreference (Lappin and Leass, 1994), identifies the referents of pronouns. In languages with complex grammatical structures such as pro-drop, gender-neutral pronouns or elaborate gender agreement — resolving pronominal coreference is quite challenging. Indo-European and Sino-Tibetan are the two largest language families with 4.7 billion speakers together (eth, 2024). Despite its prevalance, pronominal coreference resolution remains unexplored in SALs. Addressing this gap is crucial for the growing need for NLP solutions tailored to these populations. We aim to bridge this gap by making the following key contributions:

1. **Multilingual GAP (mGAP)**: mGAP is a multilingual ambiguous pronoun resolution corpus of 8,908 ambiguous pronoun-name pairs derived from the GAP Coreference Dataset for 27 SALs. This includes a manually translated **Gold** subset for few languages to address automatic translation errors and a pronoun lexicon, **PronounLex**.

2. **Coreference Resolution Multilingual Models**: We develop multilingual models for coreference resolution and train them on mGAP. We also demonstrate that cross-attention improves pronoun resolution.

3. **Transfer Learning for South Asian languages**: We explore transfer learning by train-

*These authors contributed equally to this work.

Proceedings of the First Workshop on Challenges in Processing South Asian Languages (CHiPSAL 2025), pages 104–114

ing our models on one language and testing on other SALs. This provides insights into the cross-lingual adaptability of coreference resolution systems and the similarity between various languages.

2 Related Work

Several datasets have been developed for coreference resolution. OntoNotes (Pradhan et al., 2013b) spans English, Chinese, and Arabic, providing coreference annotations along with syntactic, semantic, and discourse-level information. It adopts a span-detection approach, where models identify text spans referring to the same entity, offering a comprehensive framework for coreference resolution. LitBank (Bamman et al., 2019) contains longer documents annotated with ACE entity categories, including person, location, geopolitical entity, facility, organization, and vehicle. The Winograd Schema Challenge (WSC) (Levesque et al., 2012) serves as a key benchmark for evaluating models under ambiguous pronoun resolution scenarios that demand contextual reasoning beyond simple linguistic cues to handle complex pronoun disambiguation.

The GAP Coreference Dataset (Webster et al., 2018) contains 8,908 coreference-labeled pairs of ambiguous pronouns and candidate names, sampled from Wikipedia. It provides a gender-balanced dataset designed to evaluate gender bias in language models. The current state-of-the-art on the GAP dataset is achieved by the Coref-MTL(Liu et al., 2023) model, which attains an overall score of 92.72 and demonstrates a bias score of 99.76. This model jointly learns to identify mentions and establish coreferential links.

Cross-attention enables deeper interactions between pronouns, candidates and surrounding context, addressing limitations of dual-encoder models that rely on fixed vector representations (Agarwal and Bikel, 2020; Li and Zhang, 2024). It also captures dependencies across discourse in linguistically rich contexts (Liu et al., 2022). Inspired by recent advances in entity linking using cross-attention encoders, we propose applying cross-attention mechanisms to pronoun resolution.

2.1 SAL Coreference Resolution

In the context of SALs, coreference resolution has traditionally relied on rule-based approaches, which require extensive linguistic analysis and manual annotation. Initial work on Hindi (Dakwale et al., 2013) and Telugu (Jonnalagadda and Mamidi, 2015) made use of manually-crafted rules. Further strategies involved the integrating of Gender-Number-Person (GNP) features and using Conditional Random Fields (CRFs). These approaches were investigated in Hindi (Lalitha Devi et al., 2014) and Tamil (A and Lalitha Devi, 2012) to ascertain coreference relationships. Nevertheless, the application of GNP features in SALs presents a challenge due to their highly unique and intricate inflectional system, and thus would limit the scalability of such rule-based approaches.

Meanwhile, recent work on Chinese anaphora resolution demonstrated the ability of ChatGPT to accurately resolve anaphora on a Chinese Winograd Schema (Chen, 2024), thereby illustrating the significant potential of transformer-based models for non-English languages.

Despite these advancements, there is a significant gap in resources and models for South Asian languages especially those that are low resource. Previous efforts by Mishra et al. (2024) address this gap by introducing a dataset encompassing 31 South Asian languages, created using translation and word-alignment tools from OntoNotes and LitBank. The study demonstrates that 75% of the English references align with their predicted translations, showing promise in the accuracy of the dataset.

2.2 Transfer Learning

Major pre-trained multilingual models like mBERT (Devlin et al., 2019) and XLM-R (Conneau et al., 2020) learn language agnostic representations and have set strong baselines across benchmarks like XGLUE (Liang et al., 2020), XCOPA (Edoardo M. Ponti and Korhonen, 2020) and XNLI (Conneau et al., 2018).

Radford (2018) highlight that complete fine-tuning of language models utilizing task-aware input transformations can enhance performance across diverse natural language understanding benchmarks, outperforming traditional discriminatively trained models. Additionally, Hu et al. (2020) demonstrate the effectiveness of zero-shot learning for cross-lingual transfer across diverse NLP tasks and languages, highlighting its potential in low-resource settings. Models jointly trained on multiple datasets with sampling for data augmentation outperform those trained on individual ones, achieving robust and state-of-the-art coreference resolution across varied domains (Toshniwal et al., 2021).

3 Dataset

In this research, we incorporate the human annotated corpus on gendered ambiguous pronoun, GAP (Webster et al., 2018) to create mGAP. The GAP dataset, sourced from Wikipedia consists of the following attributes, the **text**, **pronoun**, **candidateA** and **candidateB** along with their character offsets in the text. There are 4,454 contexts (a balanced set between masculine and feminine contexts) each of which contains two annotated names, this results in 8,908 pronoun–candidate pair labels.

3.1 Dataset creation

We follow a slightly modified version of the pipeline proposed by Mishra et al. (2024) to create mGAP. The pipeline consists of the following tasks: machine translation and alignment.

3.1.1 Machine Translation

nllb-200-1.3B (Costa jussà et al., 2022) an MT model based on Sparsely Gated Mixture of Experts based approach which has been trained on more than 200 languages. It's high coverage makes it suitable for translating even low resource languages. For the GAP dataset, we translate the text, pronoun and the candidates to the target language using nllb-200-1.3B model.

3.1.2 Text Alignment

The GAP dataset also annotated the character offsets of the the pronoun and candidates for each text. These offsets facilitated evaluation of additional span-based models. Section 4.2 also presents a span-based model which harnesses coreference cross-attention using these spans. To obtain the offsets in the target languages, we use **awesome-align** (Dou and Neubig, 2021), a multilingual BERT-based aligner. It leverages mBERT's rich multilingual representations, fine-tuning it for alignment resulting in broad language support and high-quality alignments.

However, the model was built to only return "positive" alignments based on a confidence threshold, which often excluded essential alignments, particularly for the pronouns and nouns. To resolve this issue, we modified the architecture to prioritize recall over precision, selecting the highest alignment for each word regardless of a threshold. While this approach could be more noisy for the general task of alignment, it effectively improved the identification of pronouns and nouns. Furthermore, analysis of the aligned data revealed that the model makes fewer errors with pronouns and nouns compared to other grammatical categories, underscoring the effectiveness of this approach.

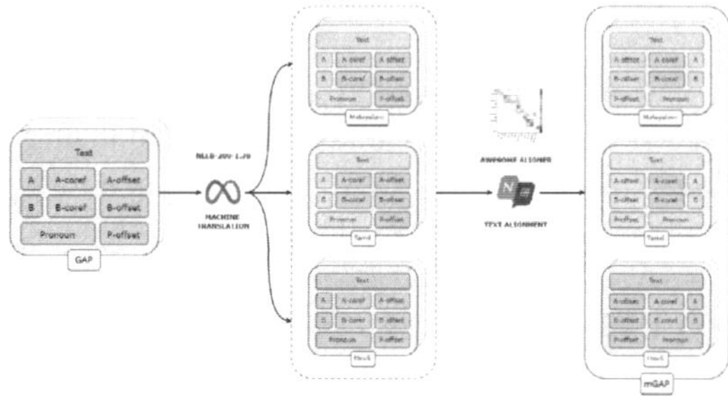

Figure 1: Translate and align pipeline used to generate mGAP. **nllb** (Costa jussà et al., 2022) translates the English sentences to respective SAL and **awesome-align** (Dou and Neubig, 2021) generates the candidate and pronoun span indices.

3.1.3 PronounLex

We used hand curated lexicon of pronouns for a specific SAL, PronounLex to perform a sanity check on the alignments to see how well the Aligner performs before and after the change in architecture of the Aligner. This step helps us gauge whether the system is correctly identifying and aligning pronouns in the target languages. This acts as a safeguard to ensure that the system has at least identified and aligned a pronoun, it is not foolproof since although the pronoun could be pointing to a word that belongs in the lexicon in the target language, it need not be the right pronoun. This approach still provides a simple check to monitor the aligner's accuracy and identify potential areas for improvement.

3.2 Gold Dataset

To scale the dataset across many SALs, we rely on nllb and awesome-align. However, errors can accumulate across translation and alignment stemming from each model's errors, affecting the final output. To address this, we include gold test sets by taking a subset of 200 random samples from the test split and manually cleaning the translations and alignments for a few key languages (Tamil, Malayalam, Kannada, Hindi and Bengali).

During the manual dataset creation, we observed certain linguistic phenomena that make mGAP challenging. One such feature is pro-drop, which omits the pronoun entirely. However, this was observed in a negligible fraction of samples across languages. Additionally, longer sentences often undergo phrase rearrangement. For Hindi, pronouns sometimes align with the object's gender instead of the subject's. Moreover, certain honorific pronouns lose gender distinction while verbs become gendered. These linguistic variations illustrate the unique challenges involved in resolving ambiguous pronouns in SALs.

4 Model Architecture

We introduce two coreference resolution models, each targeting distinct challenges. The Joint Embedding Model (JEM) is centered on harnessing the efficacy of the multilingual embeddings across multiple languages. The goal of this model is to investigate how pronoun resolution in multilingual contexts can be improved by leveraging shared representations across languages.

In contrast, the Cross Attention Model (CAM) relies on a cross-attention mechanism to capture the relationships between pronouns and the potential candidates. CAM investigates how architectural improvements can improve the coreference resolution procedure by specifically attending to candidate spans inside phrases, whereas JEM highlights the effectiveness of multilingual embeddings.

4.1 Joint Embedding Model (JEM)

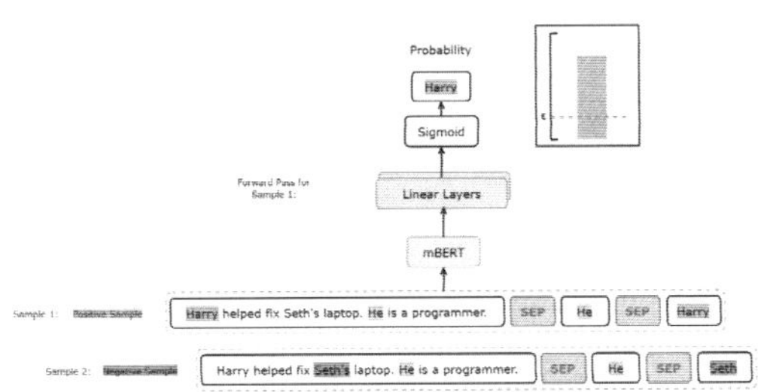

Figure 2: Architecture of Joint Embedding Model (JEM). Each sentence is passed twice with a positive and negative sample during training. The model outputs the probability of the pronoun referring to sampled candidate thresholded by ϵ.

Our Joint Embedding Model leverages multilingual BERT fine-tuned for coreference resolution (see Figure 2). We reformulate GAP's three-way classification task (candidate A, candidate B or neither (ϕ)) to a binary classification task that predicts whether the candidate present in the data point either corresponds to the pronoun or not. We selected this objective because our experiments revealed that the three-way classification objective led to suboptimal performance.

In this binary framework, each data point is sampled twice: once with the pronoun paired with its correct candidate (positive sample) and once with an incorrect candidate (negative sample). Cases where the pronoun refers to neither candidate are excluded during training and handled via a threshold-based mechanism at inference. We hypothesize that in the three-way setup, by focusing on a direct relationship between the pronoun and a single candidate, the model can learns relevant features without the distraction of multiple competing candidates (or even learning to predict neither). Additionally an increased number of samples further leads to better results.

We format the input sequence as follows:

$$x = [\text{[CLS]} ; S ; \text{[SEP]} ; P ; \text{[SEP]} ; C_i]$$

where x is the input to the model, S is the context sentence containing the ambiguous pronoun, P is the target pronoun requiring resolution, C_i are possible candidates ($C_i \in \{A, B\}$).

During training, we perform the binary classification by obtaining the probabilities for each candidate using the following formula:

$$\hat{y} = \sigma(W_2 \cdot \text{ReLU}(W_1 \cdot h + b_1) + b_2)$$

where h is the $[CLS]$ token output from mBERT for the concatenated input, W_1 and W_2 are the weights of the linear layers, and b_1 and b_2 are the biases.

During inference, we implement the 3-way classification as follows. For each data point, the model evaluates the label l, by computing the probabilities for both candidates A and B (using their respective BERT representations h_a and h_b) and comparing them with the threshold:

$$\hat{y_a} = \sigma(W_2 \cdot \text{ReLU}(W_1 \cdot h_a + b_1) + b_2)$$

$$\hat{y_b} = \sigma(W_2 \cdot \text{ReLU}(W_1 \cdot h_b + b_1) + b_2)$$

$$l = \begin{cases} A, & \text{if } \hat{y_a} \leq \hat{y_b} \text{ and } \hat{y_a} > \epsilon \\ B, & \text{if } \hat{y_b} > \hat{y_a} \text{ and } \hat{y_b} > \epsilon \\ \phi, & \text{if } \hat{y_a} \leq \epsilon \text{ and } \hat{y_b} \leq \epsilon \end{cases}$$

If the probabilities for both candidates are below a pre-defined threshold ϵ (0.2 in our case), the model classifies the pronouns as referring to "neither". Otherwise, it classifies the pronoun to the candidate with the higher probability.

This architecture enables the model to effectively resolve ambiguous pronouns by leveraging contextual information. In the future, this approach could be also implemented for more than 3 classes, or can be implemented after identifying possible candidate spans within the sentence.

4.2 Cross Attention Model (CAM)

We present our other approach, a multi-headed cross attention network that computes the similarity between the candidates and pronouns from the underlying vector representations of the pronouns and candidates. This architecture consists of two main components, namely the candidate / pronoun encoders and the coreference resolver. Figure 3, illustrates the architecture.

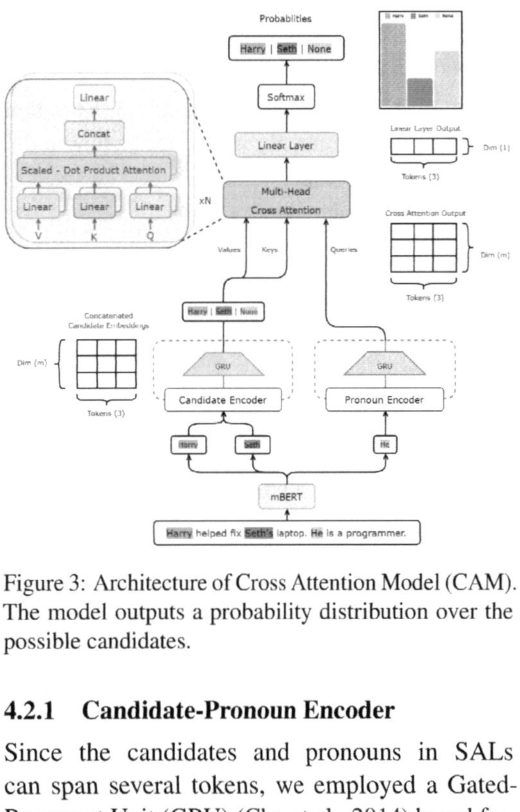

Figure 3: Architecture of Cross Attention Model (CAM). The model outputs a probability distribution over the possible candidates.

4.2.1 Candidate-Pronoun Encoder

Since the candidates and pronouns in SALs can span several tokens, we employed a Gated-Recurrent Unit (GRU) (Cho et al., 2014) based feature aggregation layer for the candidate-pronoun encoder to address this variation in token length for the candidates-pronouns between language. This application case is well suited to the GRU's capacity to maintain sequential information while aggregating the embeddings into a fixed-length representation. It efficiently condenses the multiple-token words $\in R^{N_t \text{ x } m}$ (where N_t represents the token length) into a single, cohesive vector so that the resolver can process it more easily.

While the pronoun encoder encodes the pronoun P as $E_p \in R^{1 \text{ x } m}$, the candidate A, B are independently encoded as $E_a \in R^{1 \text{ x } m}$, $E_b \in R^{1 \text{ x } m}$ respectively. The "neither" class $E_n \in R^{1 \text{ x } m}$ is represented with a zero vector. It is then concatenated with the candidate embeddings as shown below. Since all three potential outputs (A, B or neither) will now be represented consistently as E_t, this should simplify the categorization work. By relying on the model to learn this structure, we avoid arbitrary threshold-based cutoffs methods which were proposed in the previous sections.

$$E_t = [[E_a] : A; [E_b] : B; [E_n] : N]$$

4.2.2 Coreference Resolver

The network is given the concatenated candidate embeddings $E_t \in R^{3 \text{ x } m}$ as Key K and value V, and the pronoun embedding $E_p \in R^{1 \text{ x } m}$ as query Q. The cross attention is defined as follows :

$$\sigma(x_i) = \frac{e^{x_i}}{\sum_{j=1}^{m} e^{x_j}}, \ \sigma(x_i) \in (0, 1)^m \quad (1)$$

$$Sim(Q, K) = \sigma(\frac{QK^T}{\sqrt{d_k}}), \ d_k = \frac{m}{n_{heads}} \quad (2)$$

$$Attn = Sim(Q, K) * V \quad (3)$$

This attention mechanism allows the model to attend to the most relevant parts of the concatenated candidate representations in relation to the pronoun's representation. The model dynamically focuses on the specific features of candidate A, candidate B and even the absence of an appropriate candidate (indicated by the zero vector for "neither").

4.3 Implementation & Hyper-parameters

For JEM, the models were trained on a single NVIDIA GTX 1080Ti for 40 epochs, using a batch size of 8. For optimizer, we used the Adam optimizer with a learning rate of 10^{-5} and Binary Cross Entropy (BCE) loss. We used early stopping to prevent overfitting.

For CAM, the models were trained on a single NVIDIA RTX 2070 Super Max-Q GPU for 100 epochs, using a batch size of 64. We employed the Adam optimizer with a learning rate of 10^{-5} and Categorical Cross Entropy (CCE) loss. Early stopping was used to prevent overfitting, and the best model was selected based on its performance on the validation set.

5 Results and Discussions

We trained our proposed approaches on the development sets of the mGAP dataset (28 languages) and evaluated it on the test sets of mGAP. The evaluation metrics used were F1 and Bias (Table 1). As reported by Webster et al. (2018), bias is the ratio of F1 scores of the female to male pronouns. A bias of less than one indicates the model predicts masculine pronouns better. Additionally, we assess the zero-shot transfer performance of both the models across various SALs.

5.1 Comparison of the Proposed Approaches

The Joint Embedding Model (JEM) and Cross-Attention Model (CAM) present two distinct approaches to pronominal anaphora resolution, each with different parameter footprints and computational requirements. JEM, which utilizes mBERT's CLS token through fully connected layers, requires training both the mBERT backbone and the additional FC layers. In contrast, CAM maintains a frozen mBERT backbone and only trains the cross-attention layer. Training only the Cross Attention layer significantly reduces the number of trainable parameters, leading to faster convergence, lower memory requirements and shorter training times.

With an average F1 score of 62.23 across all languages, CAM performs marginally better than JEM, which averages 60.94. With JEM at 0.97 and CAM at 0.99, the bias levels of the two models are comparable. In terms of F1 scores, CAM often outperforms JEM, particularly for languages with less resources. With a large difference between its best score (76.13 for English) and lowest score (42.95 for Chhattisgarhi), JEM exhibits a greater variance in F1 scores across languages. CAM performs more consistently across languages and exhibits less variation in F1 score. CAM's greatest score (71.06 for English) and lowest score (55.06 for Burmese) fall within a more constrained range than JEM's.

Language	**JEM**		**CAM**	
	F1	**Bias**	**F1**	**Bias**
English	76.13	1.02	71.06	1.03
Assamese	49.27	0.99	57.08	0.98
Awadhi	67.7	0.98	61.81	0.97
Bengali	66.99	1.00	67.08	1.00
Bhojpuri	62.32	1.00	60.71	1.00
Burmese	56.24	0.95	55.06	1.02
Chhattisgarhi	42.95	0.98	63.46	0.95
Gujarati	65.92	0.95	66.48	0.97
Hindi	70.74	0.94	67.66	1.00
Kannada	68.38	0.98	65.30	1.03
Kashmiri	58.5	0.93	57.38	0.96
Magahi	65.84	0.97	62.21	0.96
Maithili	66.57	0.95	62.47	1.01
Malayalam	64.75	0.95	60.11	1.02
Marathi	64.65	0.95	65.32	1.02
Meitei	52.55	0.97	57.79	0.96
Nepali	62.89	1.04	65.16	0.98
Pashto	44.6	0.97	56.27	0.99
Persian	68.09	0.98	65.56	1.01
Punjabi	64.44	0.99	69.44	1.00
Santali	50.9	0.91	55.66	0.96
Sindhi	44.26	0.98	57.37	1.01
Tajik	56.42	0.92	59.23	1.03
Tamil	65.73	0.95	64.30	0.99
Telugu	70.02	1.04	66.84	1.00
Urdu	66.89	0.95	66.47	0.98
Uyghur	52.5	0.95	54.76	1.05
Uzbek	60.10	0.96	60.36	1.02
Average	60.94	0.97	62.23	0.99

Table 1: Results of our proposed approaches across English and 27 South Asian languages of mGAP

5.2 Transfer Learning in SALs

In our research on zero-shot transfer learning, we looked at 27 different South Asian languages including English. In order to evaluate the model's cross-lingual generalization and pronominal anaphora resolution capabilities, we trained the models on one language and tested it on the remaining 27 languages for each experiment. With this setup, we were able to investigate the efficacy of

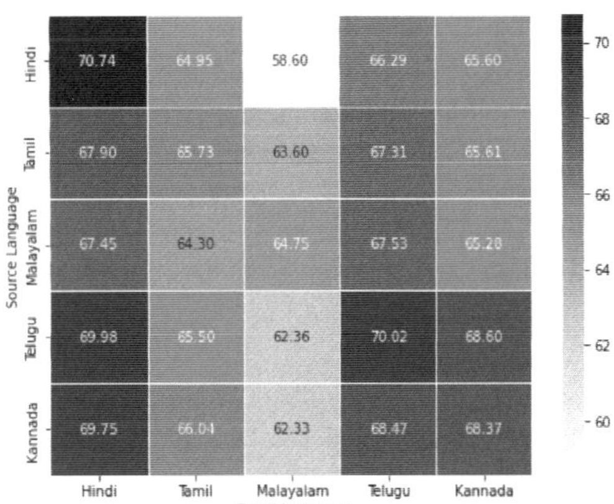

Figure 4: F1 scores of the Zero-Shot Transfer Experiments on JEM for a subset of languages in mGAP

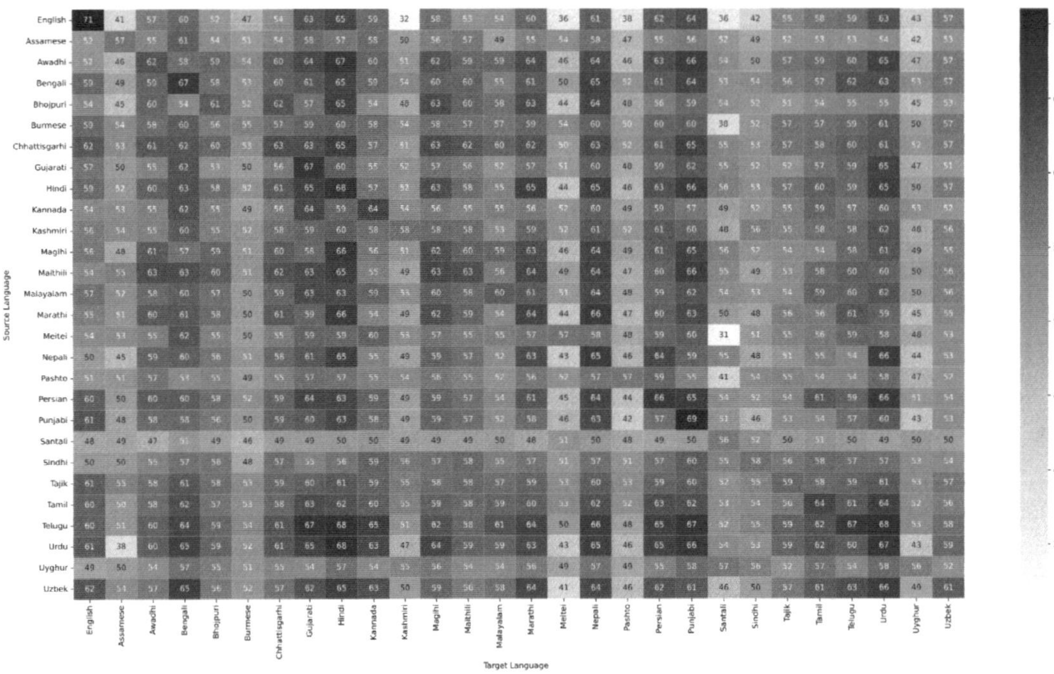

Figure 5: F1 scores of the Zero-Shot Transfer Experiments on CAM for all languages in mGAP

mBERT embeddings and the cross-lingual robustness of our architecture in a range of script-based and linguistic challenges.

5.2.1 JEM

Due to the large memory footprint of JEM, we limited our transfer learning trials to only five languages as it requires fine-tuning of mBERT (Figure 4). Consequently, we focused the assessment of the model's cross-lingual performance only on the Dravidian languages and Hindi.

In our experiments, we observed the models perform best when trained and evaluated on the same languages, with Telugu (70.02) and Hindi (70.74) exhibiting the highest self-performance. The high adaptability of Telugu and Kannada with one another (68.47 and 68.60) and with other languages is probably caused by the common Dravidian linguistic traits that mBERT has identified. Despite having a lower overall cross-lingual transferability, Malayalam outperforms Hindi (58.6) in other Dravidian languages like Tamil (63.6) and Telugu (62.36). These findings demonstrate the efficacy of mBERT in cross-lingual transfer learning, particularly among linguistically related populations.

5.2.2 CAM

With CAM, we were able to perform transfer learning for every language pair, enabling a comprehensive evaluation of cross-lingual performance across all 28 languages (Figure 5).

The analysis of CAM's zero shot transfer matrix reveals that the performance is relatively symmetric - if language A transfers well to language B, the reverse is often true as well. Similar to JEM, the model works better when trained and tested on the same language, as seen by the higher F1 scores along the diagonal for several languages. The languages (like Santali, Sindhi, Ughyur) that make poor sources and target are those that which mBERT isn't trained on. Indo-Aryan languages (Hindi, Bengali, Urdu, Punjabi, Marathi, and Gujarati) have high mutual scores (60–68%), particularly as pairings between Hindi and Urdu and Bengali and Hindi. Punjabi shows decent transfer with Hindi, Urdu, and Persian and vice-versa, likely because of its less rigid gender system, especially for loanwords. Tamil, Telugu and Kannada are all Dravidian languages that fare well together (58–65%), despite variations in script. Telugu has a high degree of cross-family transmission with Indo-Aryan languages. Persian and Tajik have higher scores because of script alignment, but Pashto, Persian, and Tajik all perform moderately (56–61%). It is evident that common linguistic traits have a greater impact than script similarity alone because Santali, which is linguistically and script-wise isolated, routinely ranks lower (48–50%). In general, cross-lingual performance is improved by shared scripts, such as Devanagari across Indo-Aryan languages. Nevertheless, it appears that language family predicts transfer success more accurately than script sharing.

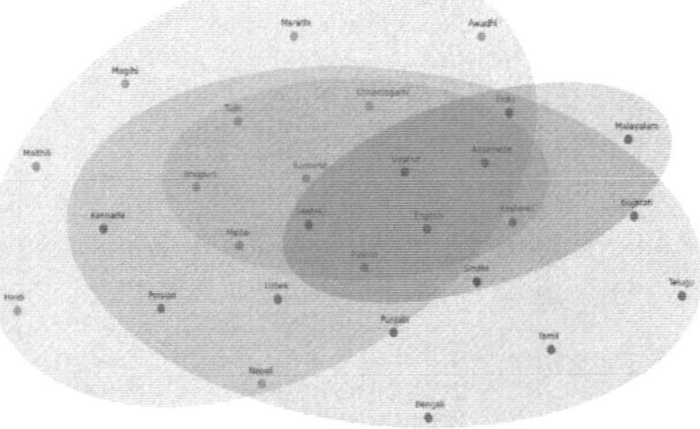

Figure 6: t-SNE Projections of Spectral Language Clusters obtained from Figure 5

We employed spectral clustering to find language groupings based on CAM's zero-shot pronominal coreference resolution performance (Figure 5). Groups were identified by t-SNE visualization (Figure 6): The clustering of the Dravidian languages (Kannada, Tamil, and Telugu) suggests that they have many structural traits and are highly transferable. Bengali, Marathi, and Hindi are Indo-Aryan languages that also clustered, indicating linguistic commonality. On the periphery, Malayalam implies less cross-lingual flexibility because of its distinct linguistic characteristics. This analysis highlights CAM's ability to capture nuanced cross-lingual relationships, enabling interpretation of model performance through a linguistic lens.

5.3 Gender Bias across SALs

As indicated in Table 1, JEM demonstrated gender bias that favours female pronouns in 5 out of the 28 languages. In contrast, CAM shows a preference for female pronouns in a broader range - 16 out of 28 languages. This could be attributed to CAM's ability to capture better representations from the dataset. Furthermore, CAM's average bias score is closer to 1 than JEM's, suggesting a more equitable performance across genders.

6 Conclusion and Future Work

In this study, we addressed data limitations and used multilingual transfer learning techniques to propose a comprehensive approach to resolving coreference in South Asian Languages that are severely under-resourced. We implement a pipeline that allowed us to produce a multilingual coreference dataset - mGAP, for 27 languages, with an addition manually-curated gold subset for a few key languages like Tamil, Malayalam, Hindi and Kannada. This dataset enabled us to test two novel model architectures, namely the Joint Embedding Model (JEM) and the Cross-Attention Model (CAM).

We evaluated the performance of multilingual embeddings and cross-attention architecture using JEM and CAM respectively. Strong zero shot transfer learning potential between a number of South Asian languages was validated by our results. The scores were also significantly impacted by the linguistic and cultural proximity of these languages. Additionally, we demonstrated the potential benefits of sequentially fine-tuning two languages, especially those with limited resources.

Ultimately, this work suggests practical methods for model adaption and offers insightful multilingual resources for coreference resolution in under-represented languages. Future research may expand on these findings by including additional under-resourced languages and exploring language-specific fine-tuning strategies for improved cross-lingual efficacy.

7 Limitations

Our approaches face a few constraints, primarily originating from limitations in the dataset and the challenges inherent in creating high-quality multilingual resources. We worked with only 27 out of the 31 languages used in Mishra et al. (2024) due to missing support for certain scripts in mBERT like Odia, Tibetan and Sinhalese.

Another significant limitation is the potential for error propagation throughout the dataset creation process, as each stage- translation and alignment- carries a risk of introducing inaccuracies. Although we modified the **awesome-align** model to enhance recall rather than precision, this adjustment may introduce further noise. Errors can accumulate through all these stages, affecting the overall quality of the dataset, and any model trained on this data.

Lastly, our gold standard dataset consists of merely 200 samples from the original dataset, which were manually annotated. Since creating gold data requires skilled annotators, the number of languages we currently cover, and the number of samples we annotate is greatly limited. The small size implies that it may not be able to cover all the linguistic and syntactical diversity found in larger, more varied datasets. While it provides a valuable benchmark for quality control, its limited scope may not fully capture the complexity of larger corpora.

References

2024. What are the largest language families? https://www.ethnologue.com/insights/largest-families/.

Akilandeswari A and Sobha Lalitha Devi. 2012. Resolution for pronouns in Tamil using CRF. In *Proceedings of the Workshop on Machine Translation and Parsing in Indian Languages*, pages 103–112, Mumbai, India. The COLING 2012 Organizing Committee.

Oshin Agarwal and Daniel M. Bikel. 2020. Entity linking via dual and cross-attention encoders. *Preprint*, arXiv:2004.03555.

David Bamman, Sejal Popat, and Sheng Shen. 2019. An annotated dataset of literary entities. In *Proceedings of the 2019 Conference of the North American Chapter of the Association for Computational Linguistics: Human Language Technologies, Volume 1 (Long and Short Papers)*, pages 2138–2144, Minneapolis, Minnesota. Association for Computational Linguistics.

Luciano Castagnola. 2002. *Anaphora resolution for question answering*. Ph.D. thesis, Massachusetts Institute of Technology.

Shuangshuang Chen. 2024. Resolving chinese anaphora with chatgpt. In *2024 International Conference on Asian Language Processing (IALP)*, pages 31–36.

Kyunghyun Cho, Bart van Merrienboer, Caglar Gulcehre, Dzmitry Bahdanau, Fethi Bougares, Holger Schwenk, and Yoshua Bengio. 2014. Learning phrase representations using rnn encoder-decoder for statistical machine translation. *Preprint*, arXiv:1406.1078.

Alexis Conneau, Kartikay Khandelwal, Naman Goyal, Vishrav Chaudhary, Guillaume Wenzek, Francisco Guzmán, Edouard Grave, Myle Ott, Luke Zettlemoyer, and Veselin Stoyanov. 2020. Unsupervised cross-lingual representation learning at scale. In *Proceedings of the 58th Annual Meeting of the Association for Computational Linguistics*, pages 8440–8451, Online. Association for Computational Linguistics.

Alexis Conneau, Ruty Rinott, Guillaume Lample, Adina Williams, Samuel R. Bowman, Holger Schwenk, and Veselin Stoyanov. 2018. Xnli: Evaluating cross-lingual sentence representations. In *Proceedings of the 2018 Conference on Empirical Methods in Natural Language Processing*. Association for Computational Linguistics.

Marta R. Costa jussà, James Cross, Onur Çelebi, Maha Elbayad, Kenneth Heafield, Kevin Heffernan, Elahe Kalbassi, Janice Lam, Daniel Licht, Jean Maillard, Anna Y. Sun, Skyler Wang, Guillaume Wenzek, Al Youngblood, Bapi Akula, Loïc Barrault, Gabriel Mejia Gonzalez, Prangthip Hansanti, John Hoffman, Semarley Jarrett, Kaushik Ram Sadagopan, Dirk Rowe, Shannon Spruit, Chau Tran, Pierre Andrews, Necip Fazil Ayan, Shruti Bhosale, Sergey Edunov, Angela Fan, Cynthia Gao, Vedanuj Goswami, Francisco Guzmán, Philipp Koehn, Alexandre Mourachko, Christophe Ropers, Safiyyah Saleem, Holger Schwenk, and Jeff Wang. 2022. No language left behind: Scaling human-centered machine translation. *CoRR*, abs/2207.04672.

Praveen Dakwale, Vandan Mujadia, and Dipti Misra Sharma. 2013. A hybrid approach for anaphora resolution in hindi. In *International Joint Conference on Natural Language Processing*.

Orphee De Clercq and Veronique Hoste. 2020. It's absolutely divine! can fine-grained sentiment analysis benefit from coreference resolution? In *Proceedings of the Third Workshop on Computational Models of Reference, Anaphora and Coreference*, pages 11–21, Barcelona, Spain (online). Association for Computational Linguistics.

Jacob Devlin, Ming-Wei Chang, Kenton Lee, and Kristina Toutanova. 2019. BERT: Pre-training of deep bidirectional transformers for language understanding. In *Proceedings of the 2019 Conference of the North American Chapter of the Association for Computational Linguistics: Human Language Technologies, Volume 1 (Long and Short Papers)*, pages 4171–4186, Minneapolis, Minnesota. Association for Computational Linguistics.

Zi-Yi Dou and Graham Neubig. 2021. Word alignment by fine-tuning embeddings on parallel corpora. In *Proceedings of the 16th Conference of the European Chapter of the Association for Computational Linguistics: Main Volume*, pages 2112–2128, Online. Association for Computational Linguistics.

Olga Majewska Qianchu Liu Ivan Vulić Edoardo M. Ponti, Goran Glavaš and Anna Korhonen. 2020. XCOPA: A multilingual dataset for causal commonsense reasoning. In *Proceedings of the 2020 Conference on Empirical Methods in Natural Language Processing (EMNLP)*.

Junjie Hu, Sebastian Ruder, Aditya Siddhant, Graham Neubig, Orhan Firat, and Melvin Johnson. 2020. XTREME: A massively multilingual multi-task benchmark for evaluating cross-lingual generalisation. In *Proceedings of the 37th International Conference on Machine Learning*, volume 119 of *Proceedings of Machine Learning Research*, pages 4411–4421. PMLR.

Hemanth Reddy Jonnalagadda and Radhika Mamidi. 2015. Resolution of pronominal anaphora for Telugu dialogues. In *Proceedings of the 12th International Conference on Natural Language Processing*, pages 183–188, Trivandrum, India. NLP Association of India.

Sobha Lalitha Devi, Vijay Sundar Ram, and Pattabhi RK Rao. 2014. A generic anaphora resolution engine for Indian languages. In *Proceedings of COLING 2014, the 25th International Conference on Computational Linguistics: Technical Papers*, pages 1824–1833, Dublin, Ireland. Dublin City University and Association for Computational Linguistics.

Shalom Lappin and Herbert J Leass. 1994. An algorithm for pronominal anaphora resolution. *Computational linguistics*, 20(4):535–561.

Ekaterina Lapshinova-Koltunski, Christian Hardmeier, and Pauline Krielke. 2018. ParCorFull: a parallel corpus annotated with full coreference. In *Proceedings of the Eleventh International Conference on Language Resources and Evaluation (LREC 2018)*, Miyazaki, Japan. European Language Resources Association (ELRA).

Hector J. Levesque, Ernest Davis, and Leora Morgenstern. 2012. The winograd schema challenge. In *KR*. AAAI Press.

Shi Li and Yongkang Zhang. 2024. Improving entity linking by combining semantic entity embeddings and cross-attention encoder. *J. Intell. Fuzzy Syst.*, 46(1):2899–2910.

Yaobo Liang, Nan Duan, Yeyun Gong, Ning Wu, Fenfei Guo, Weizhen Qi, Ming Gong, Linjun Shou, Daxin Jiang, Guihong Cao, Xiaodong Fan, Ruofei Zhang, Rahul Agrawal, Edward Cui, Sining Wei, Taroon Bharti, Ying Qiao, Jiun-Hung Chen, Winnie Wu, Shuguang Liu, Fan Yang, Daniel Campos, Rangan Majumder, and Ming Zhou. 2020. Xglue: A new benchmark dataset for cross-lingual pre-training, understanding and generation. *arXiv*, abs/2004.01401.

Ruicheng Liu, Guanyi Chen, Rui Mao, and E. Cambria. 2023. A multi-task learning model for gold-two-mention co-reference resolution. *2023 International Joint Conference on Neural Networks (IJCNN)*, pages 1–8.

Tianyu Liu, Yuchen Eleanor Jiang, Nicholas Monath, Ryan Cotterell, and Mrinmaya Sachan. 2022. Autoregressive structured prediction with language models. In *Findings of the Association for Computational Linguistics: EMNLP 2022*, pages 993–1005, Abu Dhabi, United Arab Emirates. Association for Computational Linguistics.

Giuliano Martinelli, Edoardo Barba, and Roberto Navigli. 2024. Maverick: Efficient and accurate coreference resolution defying recent trends. In *Proceedings of the 62nd Annual Meeting of the Association for Computational Linguistics (Volume 1: Long Papers)*, pages 13380–13394, Bangkok, Thailand. Association for Computational Linguistics.

Ritwik Mishra, Pooja Desur, Rajiv Ratn Shah, and Ponnurangam Kumaraguru. 2024. Multilingual coreference resolution in low-resource south asian languages. *Preprint*, arXiv:2402.13571.

Sameer Pradhan, Alessandro Moschitti, Nianwen Xue, Hwee Tou Ng, Anders Björkelund, Olga Uryupina, Yuchen Zhang, and Zhi Zhong. 2013a. Towards robust linguistic analysis using OntoNotes. In *Proceedings of the Seventeenth Conference on Computational Natural Language Learning*, pages 143–152, Sofia, Bulgaria. Association for Computational Linguistics.

Sameer Pradhan, Alessandro Moschitti, Nianwen Xue, Hwee Tou Ng, Anders Björkelund, Olga Uryupina, Yuchen Zhang, and Zhi Zhong. 2013b. Towards robust linguistic analysis using OntoNotes. In *Proceedings of the Seventeenth Conference on Computational Natural Language Learning*, pages 143–152, Sofia, Bulgaria. Association for Computational Linguistics.

Alec Radford. 2018. Improving language understanding by generative pre-training.

Josef Steinberger, Massimo Poesio, Mijail A. Kabadjov, and Karel Ježek. 2007. Two uses of anaphora resolution in summarization. *Information Processing Management*, 43(6):1663–1680. Text Summarization.

Dario Stojanovski and Alexander Fraser. 2019. Improving anaphora resolution in neural machine translation using curriculum learning. In *Proceedings of Machine Translation Summit XVII: Research Track*, pages 140–150, Dublin, Ireland. European Association for Machine Translation.

Shubham Toshniwal, Patrick Xia, Sam Wiseman, Karen Livescu, and Kevin Gimpel. 2021. On generalization in coreference resolution. In *Proceedings of the Fourth Workshop on Computational Models of Reference, Anaphora and Coreference*, pages 111–120, Punta Cana, Dominican Republic. Association for Computational Linguistics.

Bo-Hsiang Tseng, Shruti Bhargava, Jiarui Lu, Joel Ruben Antony Moniz, Dhivya Piraviperumal, Lin Li, and Hong Yu. 2021. CREAD: combined resolution of ellipses and anaphora in dialogues. *CoRR*, abs/2105.09914.

Kellie Webster, Marta Recasens, Vera Axelrod, and Jason Baldridge. 2018. Mind the gap: A balanced corpus of gendered ambiguous pronouns. *Preprint*, arXiv:1810.05201.

A Appendix: Transfer Learning

We experiment with a sequential transfer learning methodology where we initially fine-tune a coreference resolution model using a source language, followed by additional finetuning on the target language. We aim to determine if this two-step process would improve cross-lingual performance.

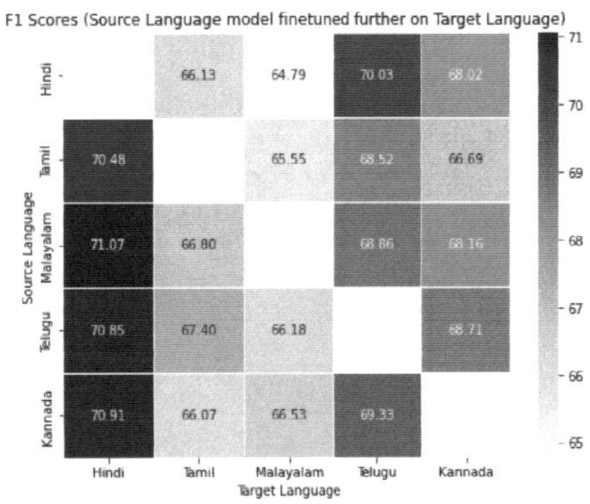

Figure 7: F1 Scores of JEM on a subset of the languages first finetuned on the source language, and then further on the target language.

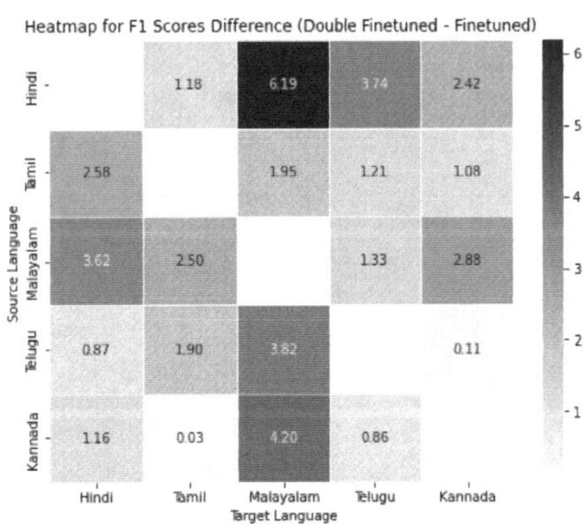

Figure 8: Difference in F1 scores from zero shot setting. (ref Fig. 4)

These experiments show us patterns in the cross-lingual training that highlight the impact of language families and linguistic distance between languages. The improvement from Hindi to the Dravidian languages show substantial growth with the double finetuning approach, with gains up to 6.19 F1 points (Hindi $\rightarrow$ Malayalam). This improvement suggests that zero shot transfer across these language families could be challenging due to the linguistic distance, and this gap could be effectively bridged by finetuning on the target language as well.

The case for Malayalam is especially interesting as a target language, as it consistently demonstrates the highest average improvements across various language sources. The significant enhancements noted when transitioning to Malayalam (6.19 from Hindi, 4.20 from Kannada) suggests that Malayalam could be distinct in its structural characteristics that render zero-shot transfer particularly difficult; however, these obstacles can be effectively mitigated through further finetuning. This observation has important implications for the allocation of resources in multilingual NLP initiatives that involve Malayalam.

In the context of the Dravidian language family, we observe more modest improvements resulting from double finetuning. These lesser gains likely indicate the stronger initial zero-shot transfer capabilities among these languages, which can be attributed to their shared linguistic traits and close linguistic distance. These results align with linguistic reasoning, indicating that models are more capable of transferring knowledge between closely related languages, even in zero-shot scenarios, thereby leaving limited opportunities for enhancement through additional fine-tuning. They also highlight the necessity of considering language family relationships when formulating transfer learning strategies for low-resource languages.

A Dual Contrastive Learning Framework for Enhanced Hate Speech Detection in Low-Resource Languages

Krishan Chavinda
Department of Computer Science & Engineering
University of Moratuwa
Sri Lanka
krishan.19@cse.mrt.ac.lk

Uthayasanker Thayasivam
Department of Computer Science & Engineering
University of Moratuwa
Sri Lanka
rtuthaya@cse.mrt.ac.lk

Abstract

Hate speech on social media platforms is a critical issue, especially in low-resource languages such as Sinhala and Tamil, where the lack of annotated datasets and linguistic tools hampers the development of effective detection systems. This research introduces a novel framework for detecting hate speech in low resource languages by leveraging Multilingual Large Language Models (MLLMs) integrated with a Dual Contrastive Learning (DCL) strategy. Our approach enhances detection by capturing the nuances of hate speech in low-resource settings, applying both self-supervised and supervised contrastive learning techniques. We evaluated our framework using datasets from Facebook and Twitter, demonstrating its superior performance compared to traditional deep learning models such as CNN, LSTM, and BiGRU. The results highlight the efficacy of DCL models, particularly when fine-tuned on domain-specific data, with the best performance achieved using the TwHIN-BERT model. This study underscores the potential of advanced machine learning techniques in improving hate speech detection for under-resourced languages, paving the way for further research in this domain.

1 Introduction

Hate speech has become a significant problem in the digital age, particularly on social media platforms where communication is fast, widespread, and often anonymous. The rise of online platforms has not only enhanced global connectivity but has also provided a fertile ground for the dissemination of harmful content, including hate speech.We adopt the definition by Lu et al. (2023): "Hate speech is subjective and derogatory speech towards protected characteristics expressed directly or indirectly to such groups in textual form". This form of expression, which targets individuals or groups based on attributes such as race, religion, ethnicity, gender, or sexual orientation, has severe societal impacts, including the escalation of violence, promotion of discrimination, and deepening of social divides. The urgency to address hate speech is further underscored by its ability to rapidly spread and amplify through social networks, making it a formidable challenge for regulatory bodies and social media companies alike.

In multicultural societies, hate speech has been a particular concern due to its potential to incite ethnic and religious violence. However, while considerable research has been devoted to hate speech detection in languages like English, less attention has been given to low-resource languages such as Sinhala and Tamil. The lack of resources, such as annotated datasets and linguistic tools, has posed significant challenges to developing robust hate speech detection systems in low-resource languages.

Despite the growing interest in using advanced technologies to combat hate speech, the application of Large Language Models (LLMs) in this domain remains underexplored, particularly in the context of Sinhala. LLMs, with their ability to understand and generate human-like text, offer a promising avenue for improving hate speech detection. However, existing studies (Munasinghe and Thayasivam, 2022) (Samarasinghe et al., 2020) (Hettiarachchi et al., 2020) (Sandaruwan et al., 2019) in Sinhala have predominantly relied on traditional machine learning models, which, while effective, may not capture the nuances of the language or the context of the speech as effectively as LLMs. Therefore, this research aims to bridge this gap by exploring the potential of LLMs for detecting hate speech in Sinhala as well as providing a different approach for hate speech detection in low resource languages, focusing specifically on content generated on social media platforms.

This study aims to contribute to the field by developing and evaluating a hate speech detection model for Sinhala and Tamil, two low-resource languages, utilizing the capabilities of large language

Proceedings of the First Workshop on Challenges in Processing South Asian Languages (CHiPSAL 2025), pages 115–123
January 19, 2025.

models (LLMs). The findings of this research could provide valuable insights into the effectiveness of LLMs in low-resource languages and offer a foundation for future work in this critical area of study.

2 Related Work

We have conducted an extensive literature review, primarily focused on hate speech detection in Sinhala, a low-resource language, as our main focus lies within this linguistic domain. The research into hate speech detection in the Sinhala language, particularly in the context of social media, has garnered significant attention due to the growing prevalence of online abusive content. Various studies have employed different machine learning techniques and natural language processing (NLP) methods to address this issue, highlighting the unique challenges presented by the Sinhala language and its Romanized form.

In the study by Munasinghe and Thayasivam (2022), a deep learning ensemble method was introduced to detect hate speech in Sinhala tweets. Their approach contrasts with previous models that primarily relied on traditional machine learning methods like Naive Bayes, Support Vector Machines (SVM), and Random Forest classifiers, which often struggled to generalize due to limited dataset sizes and suboptimal results. By creating a new dataset using Twitter API and applying techniques such as stop word removal, stemming, and tokenization, they were able to develop a deep learning model based on convolutional neural networks (CNN), Long Short-Term Memory (LSTM), and Bi-GRU models. This ensemble method yielded superior performance, achieving over 90% accuracy, precision, recall, and F-scores. The ensemble's ability to outperform individual models demonstrates the potential of deep learning for hate speech detection in low-resource languages like Sinhala.

The research by Samarasinghe et al. (2020) focused on the detection of hate speech in Sinhala Unicode text, utilizing a CNN model with FastText word embeddings. This study introduced a two-stage classification process where the first step identified hate speech, and the second classified it according to the severity of the hate. While the study achieved high accuracy in the hate speech classification (83%), it highlighted the challenges in identifying varying levels of hate speech, particularly due to the imbalanced dataset. The difficulty in accessing larger, more diverse datasets further limited the model's ability to generalize, underlining a significant barrier in hate speech detection for Sinhala.

Hettiarachchi et al. (2020) extended the scope of hate speech detection by focusing on Romanized Sinhala, a unique form of Sinhala written using the English script. Their research applied a variety of machine learning algorithms, including Logistic Regression, Naive Bayes, SVM, and Random Forest, to a dataset of Facebook comments written in Romanized Sinhala. Despite the language's complexities, including inconsistencies in spelling and grammar, the study found that the Naive Bayes classifier performed best with bigram features, achieving an accuracy of 71%. This research emphasized the potential of applying machine learning methods to non-standard linguistic forms, particularly for low-resource languages like Sinhala.

Further research conducted by Dias et al. (2018) explored racist comments in Sinhala social media using text analytics models. They experimented with a Support Vector Machine (SVM) classifier using a set of Facebook comments labeled as either racist or non-racist. Their results, with a 70.8% accuracy, highlighted the challenges of detecting racist comments specifically, which share many linguistic traits with general offensive comments. The imbalanced dataset and the difficulty of separating intent from context were key hurdles. The study recommended that future research use more sophisticated NLP techniques to improve detection rates.

In a similar vein, Fernando and Deng (2023) introduced a novel approach that enhanced hate speech detection in Sinhala by applying feature selection techniques. Their study proposed a global feature selection process to tackle high-dimensional input data challenges, using classifiers such as SVM, Multinomial Naive Bayes (MNB), and Random Forest. The research demonstrated that advanced feature selection could significantly improve detection performance in the sparse and noisy datasets typical of Sinhala social media, particularly when combined with character and word n-grams. This approach also revealed improvements in model generalization across training and testing datasets.

Moreover, Sandaruwan et al. (2019) explored the lexicon-based and machine learning approaches for hate speech detection in Sinhala social media, where they used a corpus of 3,000 comments. Their study revealed that the Multinomial Naive Bayes classifier, when combined with character trigrams, achieved the highest accuracy of 92.33%. This lexicon-based approach also showed promise in identifying hate, offensive, and neutral speech categories, though the study underlined the need for better feature engineering and larger datasets to improve the model's scalability.

Across these studies, common themes emerge, including the importance of dataset size, feature engineering, and model selection. Traditional machine learning models, while effective in certain cases, struggle with generalization when faced with small or imbalanced datasets, as evidenced by the drop in performance in various studies. Deep learning models, particularly those that leverage ensemble techniques, have demonstrated more robust performance, although they require significantly more data and computational resources. Moreover, the detection of hate speech in Romanized Sinhala adds another layer of complexity, necessitating the exploration of feature extraction methods that can handle linguistic variations. In conclusion, the advancement of hate speech detection in the Sinhala language relies heavily on the availability of large, annotated datasets and the continued development of sophisticated NLP models.

3 Methodology

In this research, we introduce a novel framework designed specifically for hate speech detection in low-resource languages, by leveraging multilingual Large Language Models (MLLMs). This framework adapts and extends the Dual Contrastive Learning (DCL) strategy proposed by Lu et al. (2023), integrating enhancements suitable for handling the nuances of low resource language hate speech on social media platforms.

3.1 Dual Contrastive Learning Framework for Low Resource Languages

The framework depicted in figure 1 represents a novel Dual Contrastive Learning (DCL) approach specifically tailored for hate speech detection in low resource languages, leveraging multilingual Large Language Models (MLLMs) that support low-resource languages. The overall framework involves the following steps:

1. Embedding Generation with Multilingual LLM: Input sentences, including both hate and non-hate speech, are processed using a pre-trained multilingual LLM that supports low-resource languages. This model generates contextual embeddings that capture the semantic meaning of the input text.

2. Data Augmentation through Dropout: To enhance the training data, dropout-based data augmentation is applied to the embeddings generated by the LLM. This process creates multiple augmented views of each input, which are used in subsequent contrastive learning stages.

3. Dual Contrastive Learning Mechanisms: The proposed framework employs two stages of contrastive learning:

   - **Self-Supervised Contrastive Learning:** This stage focuses on learning invariant representations by creating positive pairs from augmented views of the same hate speech sample. Strong data augmentation techniques are used to generate these pairs, aiming to maximize the separation between these positive pairs and negative pairs (non-hate speech) in the embedding space.
   - **Supervised Contrastive Learning:** This stage utilizes label information to refine the representation space by pulling samples from the same class closer together while pushing apart those from different classes. This clustering effect improves the model's ability to distinguish between hate and non-hate speech effectively.

The integration of these stages allows the framework to capture both intrinsic patterns within hate speech and the discriminative features between hate and non-hate content, thereby enhancing the detection capabilities for low resource language hate speech on social media platforms. For the above learning, there will be losses to identify the performance of the Model.

3.2 Self-Supervised Contrastive Learning

Considering the complexity and ambiguity of hate speech expressions, we use self-supervised contrastive learning for data augmentation and deeper semantic feature extraction. By constructing positive and negative

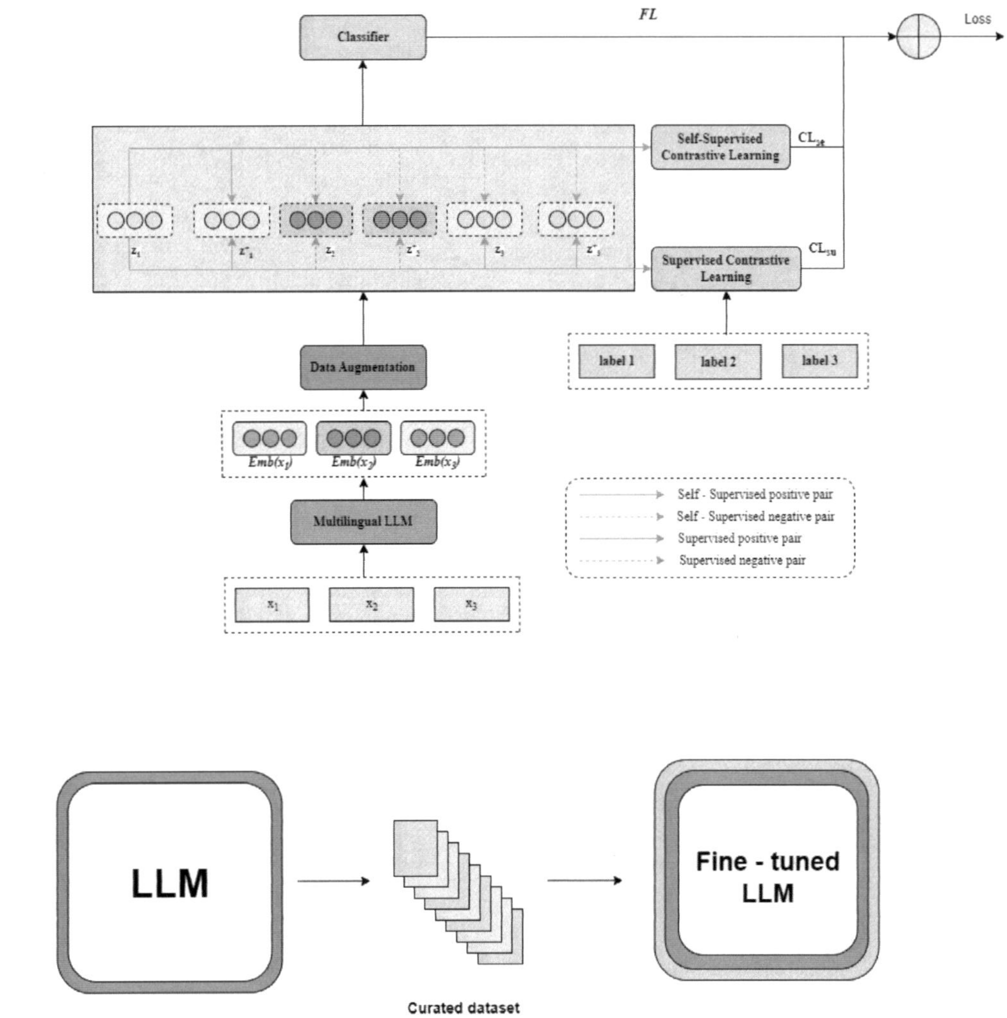

Figure 1: Dual Contrastive Learning Framework for Low Resource Languages

samples, this approach captures more comprehensive span-level features, going beyond token-level semantics, to better distinguish subtle differences (Gao et al., 2021).

$$\text{CL}_{se} = -\sum_{j=1}^{2N} log \frac{e^{sim(z_j, z_j^+)/\Gamma_{se}}}{\sum_{k=1}^{2N} 1_{[j \neq k]} \cdot e^{sim(z_j, z_k)/\Gamma_{se}}}, \tag{1}$$

CL_{se} represent the Self-Supervised Contrastive Learning loss and for a given input sentence x_i, standard dropout is applied twice to create the sentence embedding $Emb(x_i)$ that retains maximum semantic information (Srivastava et al., 2014). This embedding is then used to generate two augmented samples, z_j and z_j^+, through independently sampled dropout masks on fully-connected layers. The pair (z_j, z_j^+) serves as positive samples, while other samples in the batch are treated as negatives. The parameters include N for batch size before data augmentation and τ_{se} as a non-negative temperature hyperparameter. The function $sim(\cdot)$ calculates the similarity scoring between z_j and z_j^+ using cosine similarity to guide the contrastive objective, encouraging similar embeddings for augmented variants of the same input and contrasting them against others.

3.3 Supervised Contrastive Learning

To improve hate speech detection, we first apply self-supervised contrastive learning to highlight important span-level semantics within the data. Next, we incorporate label information through supervised contrastive learning. This approach ensures that examples sharing the same label (positive samples) are drawn closer together in the embedding space, while those with different labels (negative samples) are pushed apart. By doing so, the model benefits from both the self-supervised augmentation and the explicit label guidance.

Given a batch of N samples, the supervised contrastive loss CL_{su} is defined as:

$$\mathrm{CL}_{su} = -\sum_{i=1}^{N} \frac{1}{N_{y_i}-1} \sum_{j=1}^{N} 1_{[i \neq j]} \cdot 1_{[y_i \neq y_j]} \cdot \log \frac{e^{\mathrm{sim}(z_j, z_j)/\Gamma_{su}}}{\sum_{k=1}^{N} 1_{[i \neq k]} e^{\mathrm{sim}(z_j, z_k)/\Gamma_{su}}} \quad (2)$$

Here, (z_i, z_j) is a pair of positive samples (with the same label),and (z_i, z_k) represents a comparison to a randomly chosen sample.The labels of z_i and z_j are denoted by y_i and y_j, respectively, with N_{y_i} representing the count of samples sharing the same label as z_i. The non-negative temperature coefficient Γ_{su} modulates the supervised contrastive loss.

3.4 Dual Contrastive and Focal losses Integration

To jointly integrate both self-supervised and supervised signals, we define our overall loss function for contrastive learning as follows:

$$CL = CL_{se} + CL_{su} \quad (3)$$

Dual contrastive learning objectives (losses) are then integrated with the focal loss(Ross and Dollár, 2017) function which addresses data imbalance issues in hate speech detection to obtain the total loss function, which will be optimized to obtain the fine-tuned DCL model.

The Focal loss is defined as follows:

$$FL = -\sum_{i=1}^{N} \alpha_i (1 - \hat{p_i})^{\gamma} log(\hat{p_i}) \quad (4)$$

The parameter γ, a non-negative tuning factor, distinguishes between easy and challenging samples in the context of model's learning. A lower γ encourages the model to prioritize misclassified instances, diminishing the impact of well-classified samples. Additionally, α, ranging from 0 to 1, serves as a weighting factor, ensuring a balance in the significance attributed to positive and negative samples, which is defined as,

$$\alpha_i = \begin{cases} \alpha, & \text{if } y_i = 1 \\ 1 - \alpha, & \text{otherwise} \end{cases} \quad (5)$$

$\hat{p_i}$ in (4) reflects the relationship between the estimated probability and the target class.

$$\hat{p_i} = \begin{cases} p_i & \text{if } y_i = 1 \\ 1 - p_i & \text{otherwise} \end{cases} \quad (6)$$

$p_i \in [0, 1]$ is the estimated probability for the class with the label $y_i = 1$ in each sentence embedding z_i.

This adaptive approach enhances the model's ability to focus on challenging instances and effectively balances the influence of different sample types in the learning process.

The Total Loss function is defined as follows:

$$Loss = FL + \lambda \cdot CL \quad (7)$$

A weighting coefficient λ is used to balance the impact of these two losses, where $\lambda \in [0, 1]$.

4 Experiments

In this section, we evaluate the performance of our DCL Framework for low-resource languages using two multilingual LLMs: xlm-roberta-base (Conneau et al., 2019) and twhin-bert-base (Zhang et al., 2022), both of which support Sinhala and Tamil. We introduce three publicly available datasets, describe our experimental setups, and present evaluation results that compare our model with other baseline deep learning models. We then analyze these results in detail.

For hyperparameter tuning, we employed Optuna (Akiba et al., 2019), and for improved experiment tracking and monitoring, we incorporated Neptune.ai. Our experiments primarily focus on the Sinhala language, providing a comparative analysis of model performance. We also conducted experiments for the Tamil language, but without a comparative perspective.

4.1 Datasets

For our research, we used the following three publicly available datasets. [1]

4.1.1 Facebook Sinhala Hate Speech Dataset

This dataset contains a total of 6,345 samples, sourced from Facebook. It features a near-balanced distribution with 3,455 instances of hate speech (54.45%) and 2,890 instances of non-hate speech (45.55%). The balanced nature of this dataset, combined with its real-world context from Facebook, makes it highly applicable for developing and assessing hate speech detection models tailored for social media platforms. Its comprehensive representation of both hate and non-hate speech ensures that models trained on this data can effectively generalize to similar scenarios on Facebook.

4.1.2 Twitter Sinhala Hate Speech Dataset

Comprising 4,502 samples collected from Twitter, this dataset includes 1,108 instances of hate speech (24.62%) and 3,394 instances of non-hate speech (75.38%). The dataset's higher proportion of non-hate speech mirrors the typical distribution on Twitter, providing valuable insights for detecting hate speech in real-world social media environments. Its focus on the Twitter platform allows for effective training and evaluation of hate speech detection models, particularly in handling imbalanced data and adapting to the nuances of Twitter's social media interactions.

4.1.3 Tamil Hate Speech Dataset

The Tamil hate speech dataset consists of a total of 5,503 labeled instances, with 3,573 classified as non-hate speech and 1,930 as hate speech. This distribution indicates that approximately 64.9% of the dataset is non-hate speech, while 35.1% is hate speech. The dataset is slightly imbalanced, with a higher proportion of non-hate speech compared to hate speech, though the imbalance is not extreme.

4.2 Experimental Settings

In this section, we describe the experimental setup for our framework. We conducted experiments using two multilingual large language models (LLMs) integrated with our framework and evaluated their performance on the datasets. These experiments demonstrate that our approach outperforms traditional state-of-the-art deep learning methods. The datasets were divided into training and test sets, and we employed 5-fold cross-validation for each dataset to assess model performance on the test set.

For training, we used a dropout rate of 0.5 and the AdamW optimizer (Kingma and Ba, 2014). Hyperparameter tuning was performed to optimize the batch size, learning rate, number of epochs, and additional parameters such as λ, τ_{se}, τ_{su}, as well as the focal loss parameters α and γ.

Model performance was primarily assessed using the weighted F1 score with cross-validation. We selected the models and hyperparameters that achieved the best validation results and further evaluated these on the test set using metrics such as accuracy, weighted F1 score, precision, and recall.

All models were trained on an NVIDIA T4 GPU to ensure efficient computation.

5 Results & Analysis

The performance metrics of several deep learning models, including CNN, LSTM, BiGRU, an ensemble of these models, and DCL models($DCL_{XLM-RoBERTa}$ and $DCL_{TwHIN-BERT}$), were evaluated on two sinhala datasets: the Twitter Sinhala Hate Speech Dataset and the Facebook Sinhala Hate Speech Dataset. The results are presented in Table 1 and Table 2. In addition, the results presented in Table 3 show the performance of the DCL models on the Tamil Hate Speech Dataset.

Based on the results, our $DCL_{TwHIN-BERT}$ model outperformed on both Sinhala datasets (Table 1 and Table 2). This highlights the importance of employing advanced machine learning techniques to address challenges in hate speech detection within under-resourced language contexts.

The $DCL_{TwHIN-BERT}$ model achieved the highest performance on the Twitter Sinhala Hate Speech Dataset, with 94.00% accuracy and balanced F1, recall, and precision scores, highlighting its robustness. The $Ensemble_{(CNN,LSTM,BiGRU)}$ model slightly surpassed in accuracy (94.10%) but underperformed in F1 score, recall and precision, suggesting less balanced generalization. On the Facebook Sinhala Hate Speech Dataset, the $DCL_{TwHIN-BERT}$ model again excelled, achieving 87.29% accuracy, outperforming the ensemble model (85.70%) and other models.

[1]Here are the publicly available Datasets: (1) Facebook Sinhala Hate Speech (2) Twitter Sinhala Hate Speech (3) Tamil Hate Speech

Table 1: Performance Metrics for Deep Learning Models on the Twitter Sinhala Hate Speech Dataset

Model	Accuracy	F1 Score	Recall	Precision
CNN[2]	90.10%	90.10%	90.10%	90.10%
LSTM[2]	91.90 %	91.90%	91.90%	91.90%
BiGRU[2]	92.80%	92.80%	92.80%	92.80%
$Ensemble_{(CNN,LSTM,BiGRU)}$[2]	**94.10%**	91.90%	93.00%	90.10%
$DCL_{XLM-RoBERTa}$	91.50%	91.60%	91.50%	91.90%
$DCL_{TwHIN-BERT}$	94.00%	**94.00%**	**94.00%**	**94.00%**

[2]denotes results obtained from the literature

Table 2: Performance Metrics for Deep Learning Models on the Facebook Sinhala Hate Speech Dataset

Model	Accuracy	F1 Score	Recall	Precision
CNN[3]	84.80 %	84.80%	84.80%	84.80%
LSTM[3]	83.10%	83.10%	83.10%	83.10%
BiGRU[3]	85.10%	85.10%	85.10%	85.10%
$Ensemble_{(CNN,LSTM,BiGRU)}$[3]	85.70%	85.70%	85.70%	85.70%
$DCL_{XLM-RoBERTa}$	85.82%	85.85%	85.82%	86.08%
$DCL_{TwHIN-BERT}$	**87.29%**	**87.19%**	**87.29%**	**87.61%**

[3]denotes results obtained from the literature

5.1 Key Observations

- $DCL_{TwHIN-BERT}$ model was the top performer across all datasets, highlighting the power of DCL-based approach in detecting hate speech on low resource languages.
- $Ensemble_{(CNN,LSTM,BiGRU)}$ model showed competitive results, particularly on the Twitter dataset, but were outperformed by the DCL model, especially in terms of F1 score, recall, and precision.
- The traditional models (CNN, LSTM, BiGRU) demonstrated reasonable performance but did not reach the level of the DCL models, emphasizing the importance of pre-trained language models fine-tuned for specific tasks such as hate speech detection.

5.2 Performance Comparison between XLM-RoBERTa and TwHIN-BERT based DCL Models

The XLM-RoBERTa model is pre-trained on the CommonCrawl Corpus (CC-100), which primarily comprises data collected from open web pages (Conneau et al., 2019). In particular, this corpus excludes social media data. Consequently, the model lacks exposure to social media-specific patterns, trends, and expressions, which are often informal, context-specific, and culturally nuanced. Furthermore, low-resource languages such as Sinhala and Tamil have limited representation in digital content (Joshi et al., 2020), making it challenging for the model to capture the unique linguistic characteristics of these languages as they appear in social media contexts.

We hypothesize that this limitation in XLM-RoBERTa's pre-training significantly restricts the potential performance gains achievable through its integration with the DCL framework. This stands in contrast to the DCL framework employing TwHIN-BERT, a model pre-trained on 7 billion tweets across 100 languages. TwHIN-BERT leverages textual data alongside social engagement signals through the Twitter Heterogeneous Information Network (TwHIN) (Zhang et al., 2022). This socially enriched pretraining enables TwHIN-BERT to better understand the informal and context-specific linguistic expressions prevalent on social media platforms.

Given these differences, our results demonstrate that the $DCL_{TwHIN-BERT}$ model excels in hate speech detection, which requires social media-specific linguistic understanding. The inclusion of social media data during TwHIN-BERT's pre-training enables it to capture cultural nuances and informal language variations more effectively than XLM-RoBERTa. This advantage is reflected in the observed superior performance of TwHIN-BERT-based implementations compared to their XLM-RoBERTa counterparts in hate speech detection for

Table 3: Performance Metrics for Deep Learning Models on a Tamil Hate Speech Dataset

Model	Accuracy	F1 Score	Recall	Precision
$DCL_{XLM-RoBERTa}$	65.86%	56.32%	65.86%	63.86%
$DCL_{TwHIN-BERT}$	74.58%	74.38%	74.58%	74.26%

low-resource languages on social media.

5.3 Limitations

Our work primarily focuses on hate speech in the Sinhala language, with limited exploration of Tamil among low-resource languages. Experiments were conducted exclusively with XLM-RoBERTa and TwHIN-BERT models, leaving scope for future exploration of other multilingual large language models (MLLMs).

Conclusion

This study highlights the potential of advanced machine learning techniques, particularly use of dual contrastive learning with pre-trained multilingual LLMs like XLM-RoBERTa and TwHIN-BERT, for hate speech detection in low-resource languages such as Sinhala and Tamil.Our DCL framework-based model outperformed existing state-of-the-art traditional deep learning models, with the TwHIN-BERT-based DCL model consistently achieving superior performance across both Sinhala datasets.In addition, our findings reveal the critical importance of domain-specific pretraining on social media data, as demonstrated by TwHIN-BERT, in addressing the challenges of informal and context-dependent expressions prevalent on social media platforms, particularly for hate speech detection in low-resource languages. These results lay a strong foundation for future research in hate speech detection for low-resource languages using Multilingual Large Language Models.

References

Takuya Akiba, Shotaro Sano, Toshihiko Yanase, Takeru Ohta, and Masanori Koyama. 2019. Optuna: A next-generation hyperparameter optimization framework. In *Proceedings of the 25th ACM SIGKDD International Conference on Knowledge Discovery and Data Mining*.

Alexis Conneau, Kartikay Khandelwal, Naman Goyal, Vishrav Chaudhary, Guillaume Wenzek, Francisco Guzmán, Edouard Grave, Myle Ott, Luke Zettlemoyer, and Veselin Stoyanov. 2019. Unsupervised cross-lingual representation learning at scale. In *Annual Meeting of the Association for Computational Linguistics*.

Dulan S Dias, Madhushi D Welikala, and Naomal GJ Dias. 2018. Identifying racist social media comments in sinhala language using text analytics models with machine learning. In *2018 18th International Conference on Advances in ICT for Emerging Regions (ICTer)*, pages 1–6. IEEE.

Eranga N Fernando and Jeremiah D Deng. 2023. Enhancing hate speech detection in sinhala language on social media using machine learning.

Tianyu Gao, Xingcheng Yao, and Danqi Chen. 2021. Simcse: Simple contrastive learning of sentence embeddings. *arXiv preprint arXiv:2104.08821*.

Nimali Hettiarachchi, Ruvan Weerasinghe, and Randil Pushpanda. 2020. Detecting hate speech in social media articles in romanized sinhala. In *2020 20th International Conference on Advances in ICT for Emerging Regions (ICTer)*, pages 250–255. IEEE.

Pratik Joshi, Sebastin Santy, Amar Budhiraja, Kalika Bali, and Monojit Choudhury. 2020. The state and fate of linguistic diversity and inclusion in the nlp world. *arXiv preprint arXiv:2004.09095*.

Diederik P. Kingma and Jimmy Ba. 2014. Adam: A method for stochastic optimization. *CoRR*, abs/1412.6980.

Junyu Lu, Hongfei Lin, Xiaokun Zhang, Zhaoqing Li, Tongyue Zhang, Linlin Zong, Fenglong Ma, and Bo Xu. 2023. Hate speech detection via dual contrastive learning. *IEEE/ACM Transactions on Audio, Speech, and Language Processing*.

Sidath Munasinghe and Uthayasanker Thayasivam. 2022. A deep learning ensemble hate speech detection approach for sinhala tweets. In *2022 Moratuwa Engineering Research Conference (MERCon)*, pages 1–6. IEEE.

T-YLPG Ross and GKHP Dollár. 2017. Focal loss for dense object detection. In *proceedings of the IEEE conference on computer vision and pattern recognition*, pages 2980–2988.

SWAMD Samarasinghe, RGN Meegama, and M Punchimudiyanse. 2020. Machine learning approach for the detection of hate speech in sinhala unicode text. In *2020 20th International Conference on Advances in ICT for Emerging Regions (ICTer)*, pages 65–70. IEEE.

HMST Sandaruwan, SAS Lorensuhewa, and MAL Kalyani. 2019. Sinhala hate speech detection in social media using text mining and machine learning. In *2019 19th international conference on advances in ICT for emerging regions (ICTer)*, volume 250, pages 1–8. IEEE.

Nitish Srivastava, Geoffrey Hinton, Alex Krizhevsky, Ilya Sutskever, and Ruslan Salakhutdinov. 2014. Dropout: a simple way to prevent neural networks from overfitting. *The journal of machine learning research*, 15(1):1929–1958.

Xinyang Zhang, Yury Malkov, Omar U. Florez, Serim Park, Brian McWilliams, Jiawei Han, and Ahmed El-Kishky. 2022. Twhin-bert: A socially-enriched pre-trained language model for multilingual tweet representations at twitter. *Proceedings of the 29th ACM SIGKDD Conference on Knowledge Discovery and Data Mining*.

Abstractive Summarization of Low resourced Nepali language using Multilingual Transformers

Prakash Dhakal[1], Daya Sagar Baral[1]
[1]Department of Electronics and Computer Engineering,
Institute of Engineering, Pulchowk Campus,
Tribhuvan University, Nepal
Correspondence: 079msdsa016.prakash@pcampus.edu.np

Abstract

Nepali, one of the prominent languages of South Asia, remains underrepresented in natural language processing (NLP) research, particularly in the domain of abstractive summarization. While significant progress has been made in extractive summarization, the complexity of generating coherent, human-like summaries from low-resource languages like Nepali is still largely unexplored. This paper introduces the first comprehensive study on applying multilingual transformer-based models, specifically mBART and mT5, to the task of generating headlines for Nepali news articles through abstractive summarization. To address the absence of large-scale datasets for this task, we developed a Nepali news headline summarization corpus by aggregating data from multiple online news portals. Leveraging this dataset, we fine-tuned multilingual transformer models, mBART and mT5, using Low-Rank Adaptation (LoRA) and quantization techniques to optimize computational efficiency without sacrificing performance. Comprehensive evaluations were conducted using ROUGE scores to measure the models' output quality, complemented by a detailed human evaluation to select the best summary overall based on relevance, fluency, conciseness, informativeness, factual accuracy, and coverage. Notably, the 4-bit quantized mBART model demonstrated superior performance, significantly reducing computational costs while maintaining high-quality results. This work not only underscores the feasibility of applying transformer-based approaches to Nepali abstractive summarization but also provides a scalable solution to advancing NLP capabilities for underrepresented South Asian languages.

Keywords: Nepali Abstractive text summarization, Transformers, Natural language processing, Low-Rank Qdaptation (LoRA), Quantization, ROUGE, Human evaluation

1 Introduction

The exponential growth of digital content, such as news articles, blogs, and social media, has made automatic text summarization a critical task in Natural Language Processing (NLP). This involves generating concise summaries that capture the main ideas of the original text while maintaining its meaning. Summarization is generally performed in two ways: extractive summarization and abstractive summarization. Abstractive summarization generates new sentences to convey the original text's meaning, requiring sophisticated language generation, while extractive summarization involves the extraction of key sentences or phrases from the original text.

Summarization in Nepali language plays a crucial social and practical role, particularly in areas such as education, news aggregation, and information access. In rural communities and underserved populations, where internet infrastructure is limited, concise and relevant summaries can help bridge the information gap. Additionally, in the context of education, this technology can generate brief and informative content summaries to aid students and educators. This research not only contributes to enhancing the digital content accessibility for Nepali speakers but also highlights the potential for large-scale deployment in sectors that rely heavily on information dissemination, making it highly relevant to the region's linguistic needs.

Transformer models such as mBART (Liu et al., 2020) and mT5 (Xue et al., 2021) have proven to be highly effective for a variety of NLP tasks in low-resource languages, offering state-of-the-art performance in text generation and summarization tasks. These models utilize the transformer architecture, which is adept at capturing long-range dependencies in text, making them particularly suitable for abstractive summarization where the model must generate coherent, novel sentences rather than merely extracting phrases from the

Proceedings of the First Workshop on Challenges in Processing South Asian Languages (CHiPSAL 2025), pages 124–133
January 19, 2025.

source text. Compared to earlier approaches that relied on recurrent neural networks (RNNs) like GRU (Gated Recurrent Units) or LSTMs (Long Short-Term Memory networks), transformers are able to process input sequences in parallel, making them more efficient and scalable for large datasets.

This study represents the first known application of transformer models, specifically mBART(Liu et al., 2020) and mT5(Xue et al., 2021), for abstractive summarization in the Nepali language. It introduces a novel dataset, and by leveraging LoRA with quantization techniques to optimize performance for low-resource settings. This research marks a crucial step forward for underrepresented Nepali languages in NLP. A novel Nepali news summarization dataset had to be created by scraping data from various news portals due to lack of dataset for this particular task. The multilingual models were then fine-tuned with this dataset using Low-Rank Adaptation (Hu et al., 2021) and quantization techniques as suggested in (Dettmers et al., 2023), making the training process more computationally efficient and faster. The performance of these models were then evaluated using ROUGE scores (Lin, 2004) and human evaluation following winner-take-all approach based on criteria such as relevance, fluency, conciseness, informativeness, factual accuracy, and coverage to ensure the generated summaries were coherent and conveyed the original meaning.

2 Related Work

With the rise of transformer-based models (Vaswani et al., 2023), various research works have been carried out using them for text summarization. Many studies focus on English, while research on the Nepali language is limited and primarily based on extractive summarization approaches.

(Ranabhat et al., 2019) introduced extractive summarization to produce summaries from multiple Nepali sentences by selecting a subset from the original text using TextRank (Mihalcea and Tarau, 2004). These summaries contained the most important sentences of the input. They utilized TextRank for sentence scoring and topic modeling for summary evaluation.

(Mishra et al., 2020) generated Nepali news headlines using GRU (Chung et al., 2014) in an encoder-decoder fashion, taking the news content as input and generating a headline as output. The news was converted into word tokens and vectorized using FastText (Bojanowski et al., 2017), trained on a corpus of Nepali news articles and headlines collected from several web portals.

(Khanal et al., 2022) employed an extractive method for Nepali text summarization using TextRanking (Mihalcea and Tarau, 2004) and LSTM (Hochreiter and Schmidhuber, 1997). They trained a Nepali news corpus with GloVe embeddings using different window sizes (10, 12, 15) and vector sizes (100, 200, 300). For extractive text summarization, they used Text Ranking and an attention-based LSTM model (Wang et al., 2016).

(Timalsina et al., 2022) introduced an attention-based RNN for abstractive Nepali text summarization. They first created a Nepali text dataset by scraping Nepali news from online portals, then designed a deep learning-based summarization model using an encoder-decoder recurrent neural network with attention. Specifically, Long Short-Term Memory (LSTM) (Hochreiter and Schmidhuber, 1997) cells were used in both the encoder and decoder layers. They built nine models by varying hyperparameters and reported Recall-Oriented Understudy for Gisting Evaluation (ROUGE) scores (Lin, 2004) to evaluate performance.

3 Methodology

3.1 Data Collection

A comprehensive dataset of Nepali news articles, was created with web scraping from various online news portals like BBC Nepali (Hasan et al., 2021) and others. A sample of the dataset obtained through this process is illustrated in Figure 1, and a link to the full dataset generated in this study is provided in the annexes.

3.2 Data Preprocessing

In this step, we have removed HTML tags, special characters, and irrelevant sections of the text (such as advertisements and navigation links). As the data was collected in two steps, the headlines and their corresponding article bodies had to be joined to create the complete dataset.

The collected dataset still had numerous characters that were not part of the Nepali Devanagari Character Set. These extraneous characters would have degraded the overall text quality and negatively impacted model performance. Specifically, the unwanted characters including Latin letters (a-z, A-Z), Arabic numerals (0-9), etc. To mitigate these issues, these characters have been removed from the dataset. A prefix was also added to the start of each input text to indicate the summarization task to the model and it helped the model to better understand the context and the task it needs to perform.

learn the mapping from the input text to the target headlines during training. A data collator was also used after the tokenization, in order to dynamically pad the inputs and labels to the maximum length during the batching process, ensuring the efficient utilization of the model's capabilities.

S.N	Article	Headline
1.	काठमाडौँ — १३ औं सागमा नेपालले अहिलेसम्मकै ठूलो सफलता पाएपछि सरकारले खेलाडीलाई प्रोत्साहन गर्न पुरस्कार घोषणा गर्यो । पुरस्कार घोषणा गरेको ४० दिन बितिसक्यो । पदक विजेता खेलाडीहरुलाई सरकारले दिने भनेको पुरस्कार रकम हालसम्म पनि सरकारी प्रक्रियामै अल्झिरहेको छ । ...	अर्थमन्त्रालय गएर रोकियो सागको पुरस्कार रकम
2.	काठमाडौं, पुस ६ गते । साताको दुई दिन लगातार रुपमा बढेको नेप्से बुधबार सामान्य अङ्कले गिरावट आएको छ । आज नेप्से परिसूचक ५.८९ अङ्क घटेर १८६७.२२ बिन्दुमा झरेको छ । त्यस्तै, सेन्सेटिभ इण्डेक्स १.३१ अङ्कले घटेको छ भने फ्लोट इण्डेक्स ०.११ अङ्क र सेन्सेटिभ फ्लोट इण्डेक्स ०.४० अङ्कले घटेको छ । ...	नेप्से परिसूचक ५.८९ अङ्कले गिरावट
3.	काठमाडौँ — श्रीलंकामा हुने काभा पुरुष भलिबल च्यालेन्ज कपमा सहभागी हुने नेपाली खेलाडीलाई बिदाइ गरिएको छ । शुक्रबार काठमाडौंमा एक कार्यक्रमबीच खेलाडीहरुको बिदाइ गरिएको हो ।अर्को हप्तादेखि कोलम्बोमा सुरु हुने प्रतियोगितामा नेपालसहित श्रीलंका, माल्दिभ्स, बंगलादेश, अफगानिस्तान, साउदी अरब, तुर्केमिनिस्तान र उज्वेकिस्तान समावेश छन् । ...	काभा भलिबल च्यालेन्ज कपमा सहभागी हुने नेपाली खेलाडीको बिदाइ
4.	रियो डे जेनेरियो — कोपा अमेरिकाको सेमिफाइनलमा दुई पुराना प्रतिद्वन्द्वी अर्जेन्टिना र ब्राजिल भिड्ने भएका छन् । अर्जेन्टिनाले शुक्रबारको क्वाटरफाइनलमा भेनेजुएलालाई २–० ले हरायो । त्यसमा लउतारो र जियोभानी लोलो गोल गरे । आयोजक ब्राजिल यसअघि नै सेमिफाइनल पुगिसकेको छ । ...	अर्जेन्टिना र ब्राजिल भिड्ने
5.	राष्ट्रपति विद्यादेवी भण्डारीले नेपालको संविधान २०७२ को धारा ७६ (२) अनुसार नयाँ सरकारको गठनका निम्ति राजनीतिक दलहरूलाई आह्वान गर्नुभएको छ। संविधानको धारा ७६ (१) अनुसार प्रतिनिधि सभामा कुनै पनि एक दलसित आवश्यक बहुमत नरहेका कारण राष्ट्रपतिले धारा ७६ को उपधारा (२) अनुसार नयाँ सरकार गठनको निम्ति आह्वान गर्नुको विकल्प थिएन। ...	गठबन्धनको पक्षमा जनमत
6.	काठमाडौँ, भदौ २ गते ।बाढीपहिरोले क्षति पुर्याउने भन्दै मेलम्ची खानेपानी आयोजनाको पानी बन्द गरिएपछि काठमाडौँमा बागमतीको पानी वितरण गरिएको छ । बाढीपहिरोले विगतका वर्ष झैँ आयोजनाको हेडवक्र्स र सुरुङमा क्षति पुर्याउन नदिन पूर्वतयारीस्वरूप असारको पहिलो हप्तादेखि मेलम्चीको पानी वितरण प्रणाली बन्द गरिएको छ ।...	बागमतीको पानी वितरण
7	विश्वका हरेक भागको समग्र भूगोलमै विभिन्न प्राकृतिक प्रकोपको सम्भाव्य जोखिम छ । मानवीय क्रियाकलाप, प्राकृतिक सम्पदाको अविवेकी दोहन, जलवायु परिवर्तन आदिले प्राकृतिक प्रकोपको जोखिम बढाएको सर्वविदितै छ । प्राकृतिक प्रकोप न्यूनीकरण गर्न पूर्वतयारी तथा सतर्कता अपनाउन जरुरी छ ।...	विपत् न्यूनीकरणको पूर्वतयारी
8	बागलुङ — झन्डै तीन दशकअघि । जिल्लामा सडक सञ्जालमा समेत जोडिएको थिएन । भलिबल र फुटबललाई मात्रै खेल भनिन्थ्यो । मार्सल आर्टबारे जिल्लावासीमा थाहै थिएन । ललितपुरको ठेचोमा जन्मेका धनदास महर्जनले पहिलोपल्ट बागलुङ आएर मार्सल आर्ट्स चिनाए । २७ वर्षदेखिको उनको सक्रियताले अहिले बागलुङ मार्सल आर्ट्सको उत्कृष्ट जिल्लामा गनिन्छ। ...	बागलुङमा जसले कराते सिकाए
9	जनकपुर — प्रदेश सरकारको अर्थ विविध शीर्षकमा रहेको ३ अर्ब ३४ करोड २३ लाख ८ हजार ३ सय ४१ रुपैयाँ आर्थिक वर्षको अन्त्यतिर विभिन्न मन्त्रालय र स्थानीय तहमा गरेको रकमान्तरमा 'चलखेल' भएको भन्दै विशेष संसदीय छानबिन समितिले मधेश प्रदेशका दुई मन्त्रीसँग आइतबार बयान लिएको छ ।...	३ अर्ब ३४ करोड रकमान्तर, मधेशका दुई मन्त्रीसँग संसदीय समितिको बयान
10.	काठमाडौँ — नेपाली कांग्रेसका महामन्त्री एवम् प्रतिनिधिसभा सदस्य गगनकुमार थापाले अहिले विश्वविद्यालयलाई राजनीतिक भागबण्डाको दलदलबाट निकाल्ने मौका रहेको बताएका छन् । त्रिभुवन विश्वविद्यालयका नवनियुक्त उपकुलपतिले रेक्टर र रजिष्टार नियुक्त गर्न प्रयास गरेकोमा प्रधामन्त्री पुष्पकमल दाहालले अवरोध गरेको सुनिएको भन्दै नेता थापाले त्रिविलाई राजनीतिक दलदलबाट बाहिर निकाल्ने उपकुलपतिको प्रयासमा अवरोध नबन्ने आग्रह गरेका छन् । ...	प्रधानमन्त्रीलाई थापाको आग्रह- 'त्रिविलाई दलीय भाडबण्डाको दलदलबाट निकाल्न अवरोध नगर्नुहोस्

Figure 1: Data Sample

The input texts (articles) and the target texts (headlines) were then, tokenized to a maximum length of 1024 and 20 tokens respectively, ensuring that longer texts were truncated. The tokenized headlines from the previous step were then, set as labels in the model inputs. This helped the model to

3.3 Exploratory Data Analysis

The dataset, meticulously compiled from various news portals, encapsulated a total of 70,769 articles, categorized into ten distinct thematic areas: News, Sports, Opinion, Entertainment, Feature, Diaspora, World, Education, Blog and Others(Mix). The dataset had more data related to News category, while blog category had the least amount of data. The average length of title and the text of the articles were found to be approximately 6 and 390 respectively. The dataset were, then splitted into training, validation, and test sets in an 70-20-10 ratio to ensure robust model evaluation.

Dataset type	Count
Training Set	49,538
Validation Set	14,154
Test Set	7,076

Table 1: Data distribution in training, validation and testing dataset

S.N	Category	Count
1	News	36798
2	Sports	18767
3	Others(Mix)	7258
4	Opinion	2358
5	Entertainment	2144
6	Feature	2014
7	Diaspora	750
8	World	462
9	Education	188
10	Blog	30
	Total	70,769

Table 2: Data Statistics

3.4 Model Selection and Fine-Tuning

3.4.1 Model Selection

In this study, we chose to use transformer-based models, specifically mBART (Liu et al., 2020) and mT5 (Xue et al., 2021), for abstractive summarization in Nepali. These models were selected over alternatives, due to their demonstrated effectiveness in multilingual settings and their ability to handle long-range dependencies in text as presented in (Taunk and Varma, 2023)(Baykara and Gungor, 2022)(Kahla et al., 2022). Both models have been pre-trained on large-scale multilingual datasets, making them particularly suitable for low-resource languages like Nepali, where language-specific data is limited.

- mBART: This model is a denoising autoencoder designed for multilingual machine translation and text generation. Its architecture is based on BART(Lewis et al., 2019), which reconstructs corrupted text sequences, allowing it to learn complex text representations across languages. We opted for mBART-large-50, which has around 600 million parameters, as it strikes a balance between performance and computational feasibility. Its ability to handle diverse languages makes it ideal for abstractive summarization in Nepali, where linguistic resources are scarce.

- mT5: As a text-to-text transformer model, mT5 is capable of handling a wide variety of NLP tasks, including summarization, translation, and classification. With 598 million parameters, mT5-base was selected due to its ability to perform multilingual tasks efficiently without requiring massive datasets for each language. The text-to-text approach allows for consistent handling of inputs and outputs, making it adaptable for low-resource languages like Nepali.

Both mBART and mT5 are well-suited for abstractive summarization because they generate new text rather than merely extracting parts of the source document, making them superior to earlier extractive methods. Given the size and complexity of these models, fine-tuning them with limited computational resources poses significant challenges. To address this, we incorporated two key techniques:

- Quantization (Dettmers et al., 2023): This technique reduces the precision of the weights in the model from 32-bit floating points to lower precisions, such as 4-bit or 8-bit. Quantization significantly reduces memory usage and accelerates computation by enabling faster arithmetic operations. In our study, 4-bit and 8-bit quantization was used for mBART, which allowed for a substantial reduction in computational cost without significantly compromising performance. This was crucial for making the model feasible to train in a low-resource setting.

- Low-Rank Adaptation (LoRA) (Hu et al., 2021): This method drastically reduces the number of trainable parameters by introducing low-rank updates to the model weights, rather than fully updating the entire model during fine-tuning. By applying LoRA, we were able to fine-tune large models like mBART and mT5 on Nepali text while using significantly fewer resources. This approach not only made the fine-tuning process more efficient but also enabled faster convergence with fewer training steps.

Together, these techniques allowed us to fine-tune transformer models on relatively modest hardware, such as NVIDIA Tesla P100 GPUs provided by Kaggle, and enabled us to process our dataset efficiently for continuous 12hours.

3.4.2 Fine-Tuning

To enhance efficiency, we stored the dataset on Hugging Face. During the fine-tuning process, the model weights and configurations obtained after each training session were also pushed to Hugging Face for every model.

The following training arguments were set in the trainer and in the LoRA for the training in each models:

Parameters	Value
evaluation_strategy	epoch
learning_rate	5e-4
per_device_train_batch_size	5
per_device_eval_batch_size	5
weight_decay	0.01
num_train_epochs	3
per_device_train_batch_size	5

Table 3: Training arguments for trainer

Parameters	Value
r	32
lora-alpha	32
lora-dropout	0.1
bias	lora_only

Table 4: Training arguments for LoRA

The pre-trained models were then, adapted using the LoRA configuration. This involved updating the model's weights based on the low-rank adaptations, making it more efficient for the specific task of Nepali news headline generation. Finally, the adapted model were fine-tuned using the same training process as described earlier. The low-rank update enabled faster and more efficient training, resulting in a model that could generate high-quality headlines.

3.5 Evaluation

The evaluation strategy was set to run at the end of each epoch, allowing for periodic assessment of the model's performance during training. A custom function to compute evaluation metrics was provided to the trainer. This function calculated ROUGE scores to evaluate the quality of the generated headlines. The model's performance was finally assessed on the testing set using the custom evaluation function and helped in understanding the model's ability to generate accurate and coherent headlines from Nepali news articles.

To assess the models' performance, a survey was conducted with 62 participants, all of whom had at least 12 years of formal education in Nepali. They were asked to evaluate summaries of 10 different sentences from various categories for the evaluation. Each sentence had summaries generated by six different models. Participants were tasked with selecting the best summary overall based on criteria such as relevance, fluency, conciseness, informativeness, factual accuracy, and coverage.

4 Experimental Setup

For the execution of this experiment, the following setup was created:

4.1 Environment Configuration:

4.1.1 Hardware and Software Setup:

Given the substantial computational demands of fine-tuning our language models, we found Kaggle to be the most suitable platform. It offered free access to the NVIDIA TESLA P100 GPU (16GB), allowing us to conduct uninterrupted training sessions for up to 12 hours. For storing the data, the model weights and the configurations obtained after each training session, Hugging Face was used.

The experiments were ran using Python 3.12.3 along with key libraries such as PyTorch, BeautifulSoup, Selenium, Pandas, Numpy, Matplotlib, Plotly etc.

4.2 Experimental Workflow:

4.2.1 Dataset Handling:

The dataset was processed in batches of approximately 10,000 samples during training. For this experiment, 50,000 news articles along with their corresponding summaries were utilized for training, while 14,000 were reserved for validation. At the start of each training session, the entire dataset was loaded into memory to facilitate efficient access for the models.

4.2.2 Batch processing and training time:

Batch processing was implemented to streamline training and evaluation. Training was performed with a batch size of 5 and ran for 3 epochs and validation was carried out at regular intervals to track performance improvements.

The total time taken to train each model was approximately 12 hours.

4.2.3 Optimization and Hyperparameters:

Hyperparameter tuning plays a vital role in optimizing the model's performance. While we set certain key hyperparameters such as learning rate (5e-4), weight decay (0.01), and batch size (5), additional tuning was performed to ensure optimal training efficiency.

- Learning Rate: The learning rate was selected based on experimentation. We observed that higher learning rates led to instability during fine-tuning, while lower learning rates slowed convergence. The value of 5e-4 was found to provide a good balance between fast convergence and model stability.

- Batch Size: A batch size of 5 was chosen due to memory constraints on the available GPUs. Larger batch sizes led to out-of-memory errors, while smaller batch sizes resulted in slower training. Using a batch size of 5 allowed for efficient utilization of GPU resources while maintaining training speed.

- Number of Epochs: We fine-tuned the model over three epochs, which was determined based on validation set performance. During early experimentation, we noticed that performance improvements plateaued after the third epoch, making additional epochs unnecessary.

4.3 Evaluation Setup:

4.3.1 Automated Evaluation:

In this study, we chose to use ROUGE (Recall-Oriented Understudy for Gisting Evaluation)(Lin, 2004) as the primary metric for evaluating the performance of the abstractive summarization models. Given the nature of our task—summarizing Nepali news articles—ROUGE is particularly well-suited for evaluating how well the models capture the key content of the source text. While additional metrics such as BLEU(Papineni et al., 2002) and METEOR(Lavie and Agarwal, 2007) could offer complementary insights, we determined that ROUGE alone provides sufficient coverage for the following reasons:

- Focus on Content Overlap: The goal of summarization is to ensure that the key ideas from the original text are preserved in the summary. ROUGE is highly effective in measuring this by quantifying the overlap of n-grams between the generated and reference summaries. This makes ROUGE particularly useful when the emphasis is on recall, as it ensures that the model does not miss critical information from the original text.

- Simplicity and Interpretability: ROUGE scores are widely accepted in the NLP community and offer a simple, interpretable way to measure performance. Introducing additional metrics may complicate the evaluation without necessarily providing new insights for the particular task of summarizing low-resource language texts like Nepali. The ROUGE metric's emphasis on recall and precision has proven reliable in many summarization tasks, and it correlates well with human judgment when the goal is content preservation.

- Alignment with Task Goals: The objective of this work is to generate coherent and concise summaries that faithfully represent the original content. Given that ROUGE scores provide a strong indicator of how much content overlap exists between the generated and reference summaries, they align well with our goals for content retention and accuracy. While BLEU and METEOR focus on fluency and sentence-level correctness, these aspects are already partially captured in human evaluation.

4.3.2 Human Evaluation:

For human evaluation, winner-takes-it-all approach was considered, where the human evaluators were asked to select the best summary overall based on factors such as relevance, fluency, conciseness, informativeness, factual accuracy, and coverage among different summaries generated from different models for different sentences. A simple Google form was created and used to streamline the collection of feedback, ensuring that responses were gathered efficiently.

5 Results

The ROUGE scores for precision, recall, and F1-scores across all models are summarized in Table 6. These metrics provide a comprehensive evaluation of the summarization performance. Based on the results in the table, the 4-bit quantized mBART model with LoRA emerged as the best-performing model, consistently achieving the highest ROUGE scores in all categories. This indicates that the model was able to retain a higher degree of the original text's meaning while generating concise and fluent summaries.

Model	Number of votes received	Percentage of votes (%)
4bit quantized mBART + LoRA	235	34.06
8bit quantized mBART + LoRA	191	27.68
mBART + LoRA	164	23.77
mT5 + LoRA	100	14.49
4bit quantized mT5 + LoRA	000	00.00
8bit quantized mT5 + LoRA	000	00.00

Table 5: Results from the Human Evaluation

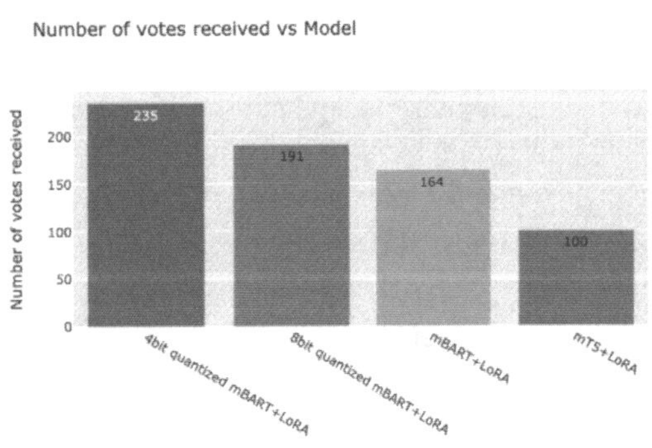

Figure 2: Results from the Human Evaluation

In addition to the automatic evaluation, the human evaluation results are presented in Table 5. These results further validate the performance of the 4-bit quantized mBART with LoRA, as it was selected the most (34.06%) by human evaluators. The model's summaries were consistently rated higher overall based on relevance, fluency, and factual accuracy compared to the other models. This strong alignment between the ROUGE scores and human preferences reinforces the model's ability to generate high-quality summaries that resonate with both automatic metrics and human judgment. The mT5 model, particularly in its quantized form, struggled with articles containing complex sentence structures or domain-specific terminology, such as those in the 'Politics' categories. This underperformance may be attributed to the model's sensitivity to quantization and its limited adaptation to the intricacies of the Nepali language. An example of a successful summary generated by mBART involved summarizing a political article where the model effectively captured the key points while maintaining fluency. In contrast, the mT5 model produced an incoherent summary with incomplete sentences, highlighting the model's challenges in handling complex topics.

mBART+LoRA	4bit quantized mBART+LoRA	8bit quantized mBART+LoRA	mT5+LoRA
पदक विजेता खेलाडीलाई दिने भनिएको पुरस्कार रकम अझै पनि सरकारी प्रक्रियामै अल्झिदै	पुरस्कार घोषणा गरेको ४० दिन बितिसक्यो, तर रकम अझै अल्झिरहेको छ : प्रशिक्षक न्यौपाने	पुरस्कार घोषणा ४० दिन ४० दिन बित्यो, अहिलेसम्म पनि रकमको छिनोफानो भएन	सरकारले दिने भनेको पुरस्कार रकम सरकारी प्रक्रियामै अल्झिरहेको
सामान्य अङ्कले घट्यो नेप्से	सामान्य अङ्कले घट्यो नेप्से	नेप्सेमा ५.८९ अङ्कको गिरावट	नेप्से परिसूचक ५.८९ अङ्कले गिरावट
काभा पुरुष भलिबल च्यालेन्ज कपमा सहभागी हुने नेपाली खेलाडीको बिदाइ	काभा पुरुष भलिबल च्यालेन्ज कपमा सहभागी हुने नेपाली खेलाडीको बिदाइ	काभा पुरुष भलिबल च्यालेन्ज कपमा सहभागी हुने नेपाली खेलाडीको बिदाइ	काभा पुरुष भलिबल च्यालेन्ज कप : नेपाललाई बिदाइ
कोपा अमेरिका : अर्जेन्टिना र ब्राजिल भिड्ने	कोपा अमेरिका : सेमिफाइनलमा अर्जेन्टिना र ब्राजिल भिड्ने	कोपा अमेरिका : अर्जेन्टिना र ब्राजिल सेमिफाइनलमा	अर्जेन्टिना र ब्राजिल भिड्ने
राजनीतिक स्थायित्वको सुनिश्चितता	राजनीतिक स्थायित्वका चुनौती	राजनीतिक स्थायित्वको खाँचो	नयाँ सरकारको दाबी गर्न दलहरु आह्वान

Figure 3: Summaries generated by different models (1-5)

Note: The highlighted entries in the above and below table received the maximum number of votes in the survey.

mBART+LoRA	4bit quantized mBART+LoRA	8bit quantized mBART+LoRA	mT5+LoRA
मेलम्चीको पानी वितरण सुरु	मेलम्चीको पानी काठमाडौंमा वितरण सुरु	बागमतीको पानी वितरण सुरु	मेलम्चीको पानी बन्द गरिएपछि काठमाडौंमा बागमतीको
प्राकृतिक प्रकोप न्यूनीकरणका उपाय	प्राकृतिक प्रकोपको जोखिम	प्राकृतिक प्रकोपको जोखिम न्यूनीकरण	विपत्को पूर्वतयारी
बागलुङ मार्सल आर्ट्सको उत्कृष्ट जिल्ला	' बागलुङ मार्सल आर्ट्सको उत्कृष्ट जिल्ला	'राजधानीमै बसेको भए यस्तो अवसर पाइने थिएन'	बागलुङमा करातेको चहलपहल
मधेशका दुई मन्त्रीसित छुट्टाछुट्टै बयान	मधेशका दुई मन्त्रीले लिए बयान	मधेश प्रदेशका दुई मन्त्रीसित छुट्टाछुट्टै बयान	मधेश प्रदेशका दुई मन्त्रीसँग विशेष संसदीय छानबिन समिति
विश्वविद्यालयलाई राजनीतिक भागबण्डाको दलदलबाट निकाल्ने मौका हो : महामन्त्री थापा	विश्वविद्यालयलाई राजनीतिक भागबण्डाको दलदलबाट निकाल्ने मौका छ : महामन्त्री थापा	अहिले विश्वविद्यालयलाई राजनीतिक भागबण्डाको दलदलबाट निकाल्ने मौका छ : महामन्त्री थापा	विश्वविद्यालयलाई दलीय भागबण्डाको दलदलबाट निकाल्ने मौ

Figure 4: Summaries generated by different models (6-10)

Model	ROUGE-1			ROUGE-2			ROUGE-L		
	P	R	F1	P	R	F1	P	R	F1
mBART+LoRA	0.3797	0.3517	0.355	0.211	0.196	0.1964	0.3684	0.3411	0.3443
4-bit quantized mBART+LoRA	0.3865	**0.354**	**0.359**	**0.2163**	**0.1984**	**0.1999**	**0.3754**	**0.344**	**0.3488**
8-bit quantized mBART+LoRA	**0.3871**	0.35	0.3574	0.2141	0.1941	0.1969	0.3754	0.3395	0.3466
mT5+LoRA	0.335	0.3248	0.3218	0.1746	0.1701	0.1675	0.3252	0.3154	0.3123

Table 6: ROUGE scores of different models on the test dataset

Note: The scores of the 4-bit quantized mT5+LoRA and 8-bit quantized mT5+LoRA models are not presented in the table as they produced zero scores across all calculated metrics, indicating that these configurations were not effective for the task at hand.

6 Conclusion

This study represents a significant step forward in addressing the challenges of abstractive summarization for low-resource languages like Nepali. By leveraging state-of-the-art multilingual transformer models, mBART and mT5, alongside innovative techniques such as Low-Rank Adaptation (LoRA) and quantization, the research successfully generated high-quality Nepali news headlines. The creation of a novel Nepali news dataset further supports the advancement of NLP resources for underrepresented languages.

The results demonstrated the superior performance of the 4-bit quantized mBART model with LoRA, which achieved high ROUGE scores and received the most favorable responses in human evaluations. This highlights its potential to deliver efficient and coherent summarization while addressing computational constraints. However, the mT5 model underperformed, indicating opportunities for further optimization tailored to Nepali's linguistic characteristics.

This work not only provides a practical framework for summarization in low-resource settings but also opens avenues for future exploration. Enhancements in quantization strategies, integration of diverse datasets, and the adoption of alternative evaluation metrics can further refine summarization models. Moreover, expanding this research to other South Asian languages can contribute to creating inclusive NLP tools that cater to diverse linguistic needs.

7 Limitations:

While this study provides significant insights into the potential of multilingual transformer models for abstractive summarization of low-resource languages like Nepali, it is not without its limitations. These constraints highlight areas where further improvements and investigations are necessary to enhance the effectiveness and applicability of the proposed methods. Below, we discuss the key limitations and outline directions for future research:

1. While LoRA and quantization techniques effectively reduce computational costs, their specific impact on linguistic characteristics, such as Nepali syntax and orthography, remains underexplored. Future studies could analyze how these techniques influence language-specific features and propose improvements for better adaptability.

2. The reliance on specific portals during dataset creation may have introduced domain bias, potentially limiting linguistic diversity. Expanding the dataset to include a wider range of sources across different domains could improve model generalization and adaptability in real-world applications.

3. The performance of mT5 models in this study underscores the need for customized fine-tuning and quantization approaches. Future research could experiment with advanced quantization levels, parameter-efficient tuning methods, or hybrid models tailored to Nepali's linguistic complexities.

4. While ROUGE scores were utilized effectively, additional metrics such as semantic coherence and logical consistency could enrich the evaluation. Future studies should employ more comprehensive metrics to better capture the quality and depth of model-generated summaries.

Acknowledgment

The authors thank the faculty members and staff of the Department of Electronics and Computer Engineering, Institute of Engineering, Pulchowk Campus, Tribhuvan University, Nepal, for their invaluable guidance and support.

References

Batuhan Baykara and Tunga Gungor. 2022. Turkish abstractive text summarization using pretrained sequence-to-sequence models. *Natural Language Engineering*, 29:1–30.

Piotr Bojanowski, Edouard Grave, Armand Joulin, and Tomas Mikolov. 2017. Enriching word vectors with subword information. *Preprint*, arXiv:1607.04606.

Junyoung Chung, Caglar Gulcehre, KyungHyun Cho, and Yoshua Bengio. 2014. Empirical evaluation of gated recurrent neural networks on sequence modeling. *Preprint*, arXiv:1412.3555.

Tim Dettmers, Artidoro Pagnoni, Ari Holtzman, and Luke Zettlemoyer. 2023. Qlora: Efficient finetuning of quantized llms. *ArXiv*, abs/2305.14314.

Tahmid Hasan, Abhik Bhattacharjee, Md. Saiful Islam, Kazi Mubasshir, Yuan-Fang Li, Yong-Bin Kang, M. Sohel Rahman, and Rifat Shahriyar. 2021. XL-sum: Large-scale multilingual abstractive summarization for 44 languages. In *Findings of the Association for Computational Linguistics: ACL-IJCNLP 2021*, pages 4693–4703, Online. Association for Computational Linguistics.

Sepp Hochreiter and Jürgen Schmidhuber. 1997. Long short-term memory. *Neural Comput.*, 9(8):1735–1780.

Edward J. Hu, Yelong Shen, Phillip Wallis, Zeyuan Allen-Zhu, Yuanzhi Li, Shean Wang, Lu Wang, and Weizhu Chen. 2021. Lora: Low-rank adaptation of large language models. *Preprint*, arXiv:2106.09685.

Mram Kahla, Attila Novák, and Zijian Yang. 2022. Fine-tuning and multilingual pre-training for abstractive summarization task for the arabic language. *Annales Mathematicae et Informaticae*, Accepted manuscript.

Rishi Khanal, Smita Adhikari, and Sharan Thapa. 2022. Extractive method for nepali text summarization using text ranking and lstm.

Alon Lavie and Abhaya Agarwal. 2007. Meteor: An automatic metric for mt evaluation with high levels of correlation with human judgments. pages 228–231.

Mike Lewis, Yinhan Liu, Naman Goyal, Marjan Ghazvininejad, Abdelrahman Mohamed, Omer Levy, Ves Stoyanov, and Luke Zettlemoyer. 2019. Bart: Denoising sequence-to-sequence pre-training for natural language generation, translation, and comprehension. *Preprint*, arXiv:1910.13461.

Chin-Yew Lin. 2004. Rouge: A package for automatic evaluation of summaries. page 10.

Yinhan Liu, Jiatao Gu, Naman Goyal, Xian Li, Sergey Edunov, Marjan Ghazvininejad, Mike Lewis, and Luke Zettlemoyer. 2020. Multilingual denoising pre-training for neural machine translation. *Transactions of the Association for Computational Linguistics*, 8:726–742.

Rada Mihalcea and Paul Tarau. 2004. TextRank: Bringing order into text. In *Proceedings of the 2004 Conference on Empirical Methods in Natural Language Processing*, pages 404–411, Barcelona, Spain. Association for Computational Linguistics.

Kaushal Mishra, Jayshree Rathi, and Janardan Banjara. 2020. Encoder decoder based nepali news headline generation. *International Journal of Computer Applications*, 175:975–8887.

Kishore Papineni, Salim Roukos, Todd Ward, and Wei Jing Zhu. 2002. Bleu: a method for automatic evaluation of machine translation.

Robin Ranabhat, Amit Upreti, Bidhan Sangpang, and Shoaib Manandhar. 2019. Salient sentence extraction of nepali online health news texts.

Dhaval Taunk and Vasudeva Varma. 2023. Summarizing indian languages using multilingual transformers based models.

Bipin Timalsina, Nawaraj Paudel, and Tej Shahi. 2022. Attention based recurrent neural network for nepali text summarization. *Journal of Institute of Science and Technology*, 27:141–148.

Ashish Vaswani, Noam Shazeer, Niki Parmar, Jakob Uszkoreit, Llion Jones, Aidan N. Gomez, Lukasz Kaiser, and Illia Polosukhin. 2023. Attention is all you need. *Preprint*, arXiv:1706.03762.

Yequan Wang, Minlie Huang, Xiaoyan Zhu, and Li Zhao. 2016. Attention-based lstm for aspect-level sentiment classification. pages 606–615.

Linting Xue, Noah Constant, Adam Roberts, Mihir Kale, Rami Al-Rfou, Aditya Siddhant, Aditya Barua, and Colin Raffel. 2021. mt5: A massively multilingual pre-trained text-to-text transformer. *Preprint*, arXiv:2010.11934.

A Appendix

A.1 Dataset Details

The dataset created as part of this study is available at the following link.
https://www.kaggle.com/datasets/dhakal2444/nepali-news-dataset

A.2 Models

- **Pre-trained models:**
  The pre-trained models used as part of this study is available at the following link.
  mBART: *https://huggingface.co/facebook/mbart-large-50*
  mT5:*https://huggingface.co/google/mt5-base*

- **Fine-tuned models:**
  The fine-tuned models created as part of this study is available at the following link. *https://huggingface.co/collections/caspro/summarization-models-for-nepali-language-66c209bfac74db25dee47759*

Structured Information Extraction from Nepali Scanned Documents using Layout Transformer and LLMs

Aayush Neupane **Aayush Lamichhane** **Ankit Paudel** **Aman Shakya**
Pulchowk Campus, Institute of Engineering, Tribhuvan University
{075bct006.aayush, 075bct004.aayush, 075bct013.ankit}@pcampus.edu.np
aman.shakya@ioe.edu.np

Abstract

Despite growing global interest in information extraction from scanned documents, there is still a significant research gap concerning Nepali documents. This study seeks to address this gap by focusing on methods for extracting information from texts with Nepali typeface or Devanagari characters. The primary focus is on the performance of the Language Independent Layout Transformer (LiLT), which was employed as a token classifier to extract information from Nepali texts. LiLT achieved F1 score of approximately 0.87. Complementing this approach, large language models (LLMs), including OpenAI's proprietary GPT-4o and the open-source Llama 3.1 8B, were also evaluated. The GPT-4o model exhibited promising performance, with an accuracy of around 55-80% accuracy for a complete match, accuracy varying among different fields. Llama 3.1 8B model achieved only 20-40% accuracy. For 90% match both GPT-4o and Llama 3.1 8B had higher accuracy by varying amounts for different fields. Llama 3.1 8B performed particularly poorly compared to the LiLT model. These results aim to provide a foundation for future work in the domain of digitization of Nepali documents.

1 Introduction

As the development on complex NLP techniques has progressed, Information Extraction from the documents has also seen lots of development. Both private as well as public companies are using different types of information extraction algorithms to streamline their business processes. Development of word representation techniques like Word2vec (Mikolov et al., 2013). and self attention mechanism (Vaswani et al., 2017) has highly impacted information extraction.These advancements allow for a more nuanced understanding of language by capturing semantic relationships and contextual information. However, there are few challenges in extracting information accurately from the documents. The challenges include first, information present in the complex document can be present in various places, there are many possible ways in which information can be organized in 2d plane, important information can be also represented in document in visual way like by underlining the words, italics word and bold word may represent different meaning, even the size of the different text can vary within single documents. Thereby making information extraction from so called Visually Rich Document (VRD) more challenging. While a good model for information extraction uses visual and layout information, along with a deeper understanding of the language, to extract information effectively, large language models like GPT (Radford, 2018) and LLaMA (Touvron et al., 2023) excel as well. Their vast scale and deep linguistic understanding allow them to perform exceptionally, even when faced with minor OCR errors, as they can often correct these mistakes seamlessly (Zhang et al., 2024).

Most of the document information extraction (IE) systems today use either sequence-tagging or sequence-generation methods. In sequence-tagging (Wang et al., 2023; Rasmus Berg Palm and Winther, 2017), each word is labeled with Inside-Outside-Begin (IOB) tags (Ramshaw and Marcus, 1995). This method helps to find and locate simple entities in the text. But, it is not easy to use these methods for extracting complex, nested entities. Pre-training of transformer based models with text and layout information (Xu et al., 2020) has been proven to be effective in a variety of visually-rich document understanding tasks due to its effective model architecture and the advantage of large-scale unlabeled scanned/digital-born documents.Models like LayoutLMv2 (Xu et al., 2022) are trained on the interaction among text, layout, and image in a single multi-modal framework. Specifically, with a two-stream multi-modal Transformer encoder.

Proceedings of the First Workshop on Challenges in Processing South Asian Languages (CHiPSAL 2025), pages 134–143
January 19, 2025.

On the other hand, sequence-generation methods (Kim et al., 2022; Powalski et al., 2021) treat extraction like generating text using autoregressive decoders (Sutskever et al., 2014). These methods can handle complex entities but cannot tell where exactly the entities are located in the document. Also, both methods need a lot of human effort to label the data correctly, which makes the process expensive.

The purpose of this study is to examine and evaluate few approaches for extracting key information from these documents. To achieve this, we experimented with LiLT (Wang et al., 2022) , which is a transformer-based model that uses layout information as well visual clues in addition to textual content. Large language models like GPT4-o (OpenAI, 2023) and Llama3.1 8b (LLaMA Team, AI @ Meta, 2024) were also evaluated, comparing the results and assessing the extraction quality.

The Language-Independent Layout Transformer (LiLT) is a model designed for structured document understanding, independent of language constraints. LiLT decouples text and layout information, optimizing them jointly during pre-training and re-coupling them during fine-tuning. This approach allows the model to learn and integrate both textual and layout features effectively. LiLT's Bi-directional Attention Complementation Mechanism (BiACM) enhances the interaction between text and layout modalities, ensuring efficient cross-modality cooperation.

We chose LiLT due to its robust pre-training on tasks like key point location, cross-modal alignment, and masked visual-language modeling. This enables it to effectively understand document layouts and content. LiLT's modular design allows for seamless integration with various pre-trained textual models, making it versatile for multilingual structured document tasks.

This work aims to improve accessibility and preservation of Nepali documents by facilitating their digitization. We hope this work lays the groundwork for future research and the development of more accurate and efficient extraction methods for Nepali texts.

2 Related Works

The field of information extraction has seen significant advancements from early rule-based systems to sophisticated machine learning and deep learning models. Initial approaches relied on rule-based methods, utilizing extensive lexicons and rules for tasks such as Named Entity Recognition (NER) and Part-Of-Speech (POS) tagging (Sarawagi, 2008; Falk Brauer and Barczynski, 2011; Deckert et al., 2011; Bertin Klein, 2019). The evolution to machine learning techniques, and subsequently deep learning models, introduced more nuanced approaches by leveraging learned token representations and reducing the need for manual feature engineering.

Information extraction from VRD is a difficult task, and there are many ways to approach it. A lot of methods break the problem into two steps. First, they use an Optical Character Recognition (OCR) service to recognize the text in the document. Then, they parse the text to find the important entities. (Xu et al., 2022) and (Appalaraju et al., 2021) handle this parsing step by using Named Entity Recognition (NER). They use a transformer encoder to label each token in the text with IOB tags, which helps to extract and locate simple entities in the document.

Other methods treat extraction as a sequence generation problem. For example, (Powalski et al., 2021) adds an auto-regressive decoder on top of a text-layout-image encoder, which is based on T5 (Raffel et al., 2023). This method helps to predict complex, hierarchical entities but does not tell us exactly where the entities are located in the document.

Self-supervised learning methods have seen a lot of development in the last several years, it is especially true in the area of natural language processing (NLP) pre-trained language models. Building on these achievements, a substantial amount of recent research has been done on structured document pre-training. For example, by adding 2D spatial coordinate embeddings to the BERT model, LayoutLM (Xu et al., 2020) improved document understanding. LayoutLMv2 (Xu et al., 2022) investigated additional pre-training tasks to better use unlabeled document data and treated visual features as unique tokens, thus improving upon the original LayoutLM model. Furthermore, LiLT introduced a more flexible and reliable way to comprehend multilingual documents that contains information in a structured format. Another notable model, LayoutXLM, extends these capabilities to multiple languages by incorporating cross-lingual embeddings to handle diverse document layouts (Xu et al., 2021). Despite these advancements, all these models have predominantly focused on English and other major languages, with limited research addressing their performance on Nepali documents.

In addition to specialized models like LiLT, Large Language Models (LLMs) are also being used for information extraction task (Perot et al., 2024) LLMs such as GPT-4o and Llama 3.1 8B offer valuable alternatives. These models provide flexibility and ease of implementation, making them useful for initial extraction tasks. One of the great advantages of using LLMs is that they are trained on large corpus of data and they understand multiple languages making them highly suitable for document understanding task. While LLMs may not achieve the same level of accuracy as specialized models in token classification, they offer scalable solutions and can adapt to various languages with minimal retraining (Naveed et al., 2023; Brown et al., 2020).

Despite significant advancements in information extraction techniques, research focusing on Nepali documents remains sparse. Most existing studies and models, including LayoutLM (Xu et al., 2020), LayoutLMv2 (Xu et al., 2022), and LayoutXLM (Xu et al., 2021), have predominantly addressed languages with extensive resources and research focus, such as English. To address this gap, we developed a custom dataset comprising 600 scanned Nepali notices, sourced from various governmental and non-governmental institutions. This dataset includes images and manually annotated text files, providing a unique resource for evaluating information extraction techniques on Nepali documents. The creation of this dataset is crucial for assessing the performance of existing models on Nepali texts and for exploring new approaches tailored to this linguistic context.

3 Methodology

In this section, we present a systematic methodology for extracting structured data from scanned Nepali notices. We explore two distinct approaches: the first leverages the Language-Independent Layout Transformer (LiLT) model fine-tuned for token classification, and the second utilizes Large Language Models (LLMs) for information extraction. Each approach employs different techniques and tools to convert unstructured text data into a structured JSON format, which is useful for various applications such as digital archiving and data analysis.

3.1 Dataset

For evaluating the processes, we prepared a dataset of 600 notices using images and PDF downloaded from various governmental and non-governmental institutions like the Institute of Engineering, Institute of Medicine, Department of Transportation, Department of Land Management and Affairs, Ministry of Home Affairs, National Examination Board, National Disaster Risk Reduction and Management Authority, Department of Transportation Management, Ministry of Finance, and Nepal Police Personnel Record. These images were publicly available on the internet. Only the first page of the PDF was taken and converted to an image.

These documents are typically formatted in a visually structured yet information-rich manner. Most of these documents contain headers that prominently feature the issuing authority name/logo at the top, often alongside a date and authority who signed a document at the bottom. The content is predominantly textual, written in formal Nepali language, and includes specific sections such as the subject line and detailed body text. Their visual richness lies in the consistent use of logos, stamps, and proper alignment, while the textual content is dense and context-specific. These characteristics make them suitable for evaluating and comparing different information extraction techniques, especially when dealing with Nepali text, semi-structured layouts, and a mix of numeric and textual information.

We chose Subject, Date, and Signed By because they cover key information in the document. The Subject explains the purpose, the Date shows when it was issued, and Signed By identifies the authority behind it. These fields represent both structured and semi-structured data, making them useful for testing how well models extract important details.

Google OCR was used to get the text and the bounding boxes from the images. All images were manually annotated. The dataset consists of images of scanned receipts and the following text files.

- dataset_bbox.txt contains the normalized bounding boxes for the text detected by OCR.
- dataset_labels.txt contains the labels for the "signed_by", "date" and "subject" field in the IOBES format.
- dataset.txt contains the mapping between the text detected by OCR and the labels.

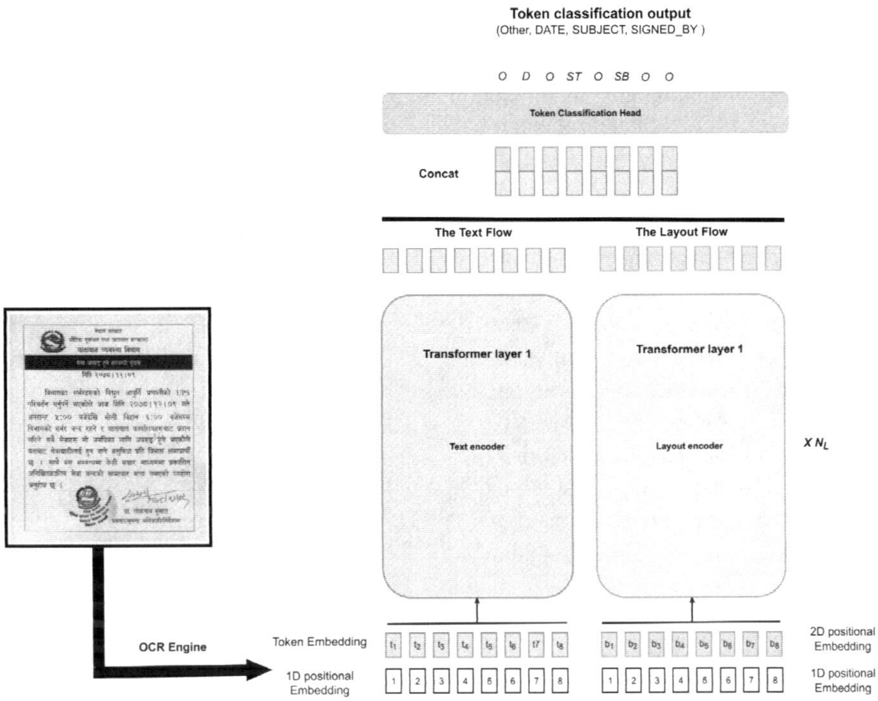

Figure 1: LiLT as a token classifier

- dataset_image.txt contains the mapping between the text detected by OCR, the bounding boxes and the original image names.

Each text file has empty newlines that separate the details of each individual image.

3.2 LiLT-based Token Classification

The LiLT-based approach is our primary methodology and focuses on leveraging the Language Independent Layout Transformer model. This model is fine-tuned specifically for the token classification task using a custom dataset of Nepali notice documents. The process involves several critical steps:

3.2.1 Model Fine-tuning

The fine-tuning of the Language Independent Layout Transformer (LiLT) model is performed with key parameters to optimize performance. Data exported after annotation were pre-processed before using it for finetuning. This pre-processing involved normalizing bounding box coordinates on a scale of 0 to 1000. The normalization of X and Y values was performed using the following equations:

$$\mathrm{X}_{norm} = \frac{X}{imagewidth} \times 1000,$$

$$\mathrm{Y}_{norm} = \frac{Y}{imageheight} \times 1000$$

For tokenization, the tokenizer from nielsr/lilt-xlm-roberta-base was utilized due to its support for multiple languages. This tokenizer specifically handles multilingual text, making it particularly suitable for scenarios that involve processing text in various languages such as low-resource Nepali language text. This tokenizer combines the Language-Independent Layout Transformer (LiLT) with XLM-RoBERTa (Conneau et al., 2019), which is a RoBERTa model trained on 100 languages. After pre-processing the data and choosing the tokenizer that supports texts in the Nepali language, model weights from the pre-trained LiLT model were loaded and the model was trained for 15 epochs with a learning rate of 5×10^{-5}. A batch size of 4 was used for both training and evaluation, considering memory constraints. The final model selected is the one with the highest F1 score on the validation set, ensuring optimal performance in token classification tasks.

3.2.2 Token Classification

After fine-tuning, the LiLT model is employed for token classification on new Nepali notice documents. In this phase, the model processes text that has been digitized through OCR. Each token in the OCR-processed text is classified into specific categories that were learned during the fine-tuning phase. This classification involves identifying tokens relevant to different information fields such as dates, subjects, and signatories. The output of this process is a set of labeled tokens, which are then used to extract and organize structured information from the raw text. We noticed that an error introduced while performing OCR is also propagated to the token classification step, as the token that has an error can sometimes be wrongly classified as a different label. This structured data is crucial for transforming unstructured documents into a format that supports efficient data organization, retrieval, and subsequent analysis. By leveraging the model's ability to classify tokens accurately, we can effectively automate the extraction of meaningful information from Nepali documents.

3.3 Large Language Model (LLM) Based Approach

The LLM-based approach represents an alternative method for information extraction, utilizing large pre-trained language models. Use of LLM falls under the sequence generator approach for information extraction. LLMs work like autoregressive decoders but modern LLMs are trained to follow instructions provided in the form of text which is also called prompt. An autoregressive decoder refers to a type of model in machine learning, particularly in sequence generation tasks, where each output token is predicted sequentially based on the previous tokens. This approach is characterized by its ease of implementation and reliance on the natural language understanding capabilities of models such as OpenAI's ChatGPT 4o and the Llama 3.1 8 billion parameter model. The methodology consists of the following stages:

3.3.1 Optical Character Recognition (OCR)

The process begins with OCR technology to extract the textual as well as layout information of scanned Nepali notices. This step converts images of text into machine-encoded text, which is necessary for further processing. Google OCR is used to ensure accurate text recognition of the Devanagari script. Google OCR works very well with documents having both English and Devnagari characters. OCR that supports both types of text in a single document is required as we have such documents in our dataset. In addition to these Google OCR also detects text that is at some angle instead of a completely horizontal text segment. Furthermore, We observed that Tesseract OCR struggled with processing documents featuring white text on a black background, while Google OCR performed effectively under these conditions. This is the reason we ended up using Google OCR for our research and it has positively impacted the performance of our extraction system.

3.3.2 Prompt Generation

Following OCR, a structured prompt is created to guide the extraction process. The prompt is designed to instruct the LLM to identify and extract key pieces of information, including the date of publication, subject matter, and signatory details. This prompt ensures that the LLM can focus on extracting relevant data accurately. Listing 1 shows the exact prompt that we used for extracting information from the document. Note that 'OCR' is a placeholder that will contain the OCR of the document that we want to extract. Moreover, it is to be noted that there is no specific reason for using this exact prompt, we tried and tested different prompts and this was a relatively good result, hence was used for our task. For instance, specifying a datatype as a comment in the SCHEMA section yielded better results.

Listing 1: Extraction Instructions

```
Please extract the following
   information from the provided
   notice: the date, subject, and
    signed_by fields. The final
   result should be in JSON
   format. The date refers to the
    publication date of the
   notice, the subject represents
    the main topic or title of
   the notice, and signed_by
   refers to the person who
   signed the notice. The keys
   should be in English, and the
   values should be in Devanagari
    script. Your output should
   strictly follow this format:

SCHEMA:
```

```
{
    "date": "",            //string
    "subject":"",          //string
    "signed_by": ""        //string
}

IMPORTANT NOTES:
If any of the fields are not
   present in the notice, you
   must leave the corresponding
   value empty.

OCR text:
{OCR}

Extraction Results:
```

3.3.3 Language Model Inference (LLM Inference)

In this stage, the LLM processes the OCR text and infers the required information based on the structured prompt. The LLM's advanced language understanding capabilities enable it to parse the text and extract relevant data points with high precision. Models like ChatGPT 4o and Llama 3.1 are employed for this inference task. To ensure consistent and accurate results, the temperature parameter for both ChatGPT 4o and Llama 3.1 was set to zero. This setting minimizes the model's randomness, leading to more deterministic and predictable outputs.

3.3.4 Decoding

The final stage involves decoding the information inferred by the LLM into a structured JSON format. JSON is chosen for its ease of use in data interchange and integration with various applications. As we can see in Figure 2, the output of LLM may contain irrelevant text in addition to the extracted information. We use a simple algorithm to detect the start and end of the JSON and extract the relevant part from this text. The structured JSON output provides a clear representation of the extracted data, facilitating its use in digital systems and databases.

4 Results

Two approaches were used for evaluating the performance of our system. For the fine-tuned LiLT model, we used classification metrics as we modeled the information extraction task as a token classification problem.

The final results, as summarized in Table 1 and Table 2, demonstrate the effectiveness of the LiLT model in accurately extracting information from Nepali scanned documents. The model achieved a precision of 89.69%, a recall of 88.20%, and an F1 score of 87.65%.

Table 1: Final Performance Metrics of the Fine-Tuned LiLT Model

Metric	Value
Precision (%)	89.69
Recall (%)	88.20
F1 Score (%)	87.65

Moreover, to effectively evaluate the information extraction system using LLMs, for each output generated by the model, a score of 0 is assigned for no match and 1 for a complete match. The Levenshtein distance is used to calculate the similarity score. Levenshtein distance is the minimum number of edits, deletions, and substitutions needed to transform one string into another.

$$similarity = 1 - \frac{L(a,b)}{max(|a|,|b|)} \qquad (1)$$

where a and b are strings and L is the Levenshtein function.

The matching algorithm is especially useful for evaluating text extraction systems, as it allows for a nuanced assessment of the system's output by quantifying the degree of similarity to the expected result. We evaluated our model by taking 0.9 as a threshold and again taking a complete match. These metrics are mentioned in Table 3

These metrics reflect the overall accuracy and reliability of our information extraction system when applied to the dataset of 600 documents collected from institute notice boards.

To compare the result of LiLT model with the LLMs, we transformed the output of token classification to match the JSON output extracted using LLMs. Table 3 shows that LiLT outperforms LLMs on our dataset.

We observe that the Llama model, with its 8 billion parameters, doesn't perform as good as the GPT-4o model, which boasts a massive 200 billion parameters. This performance gap might be due to the large disparity in the size of the models,

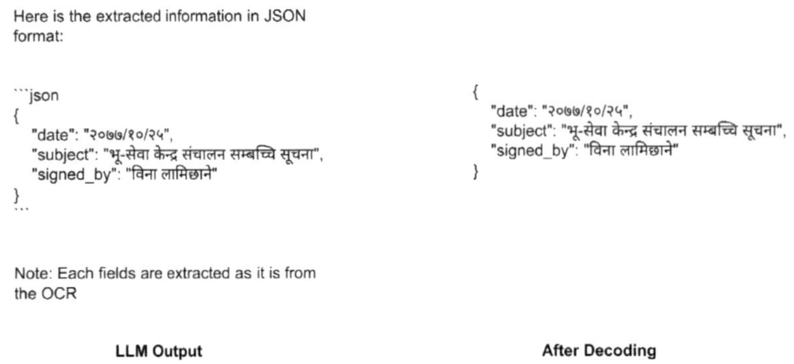

Figure 2: Filtering out JSON from LLM Output

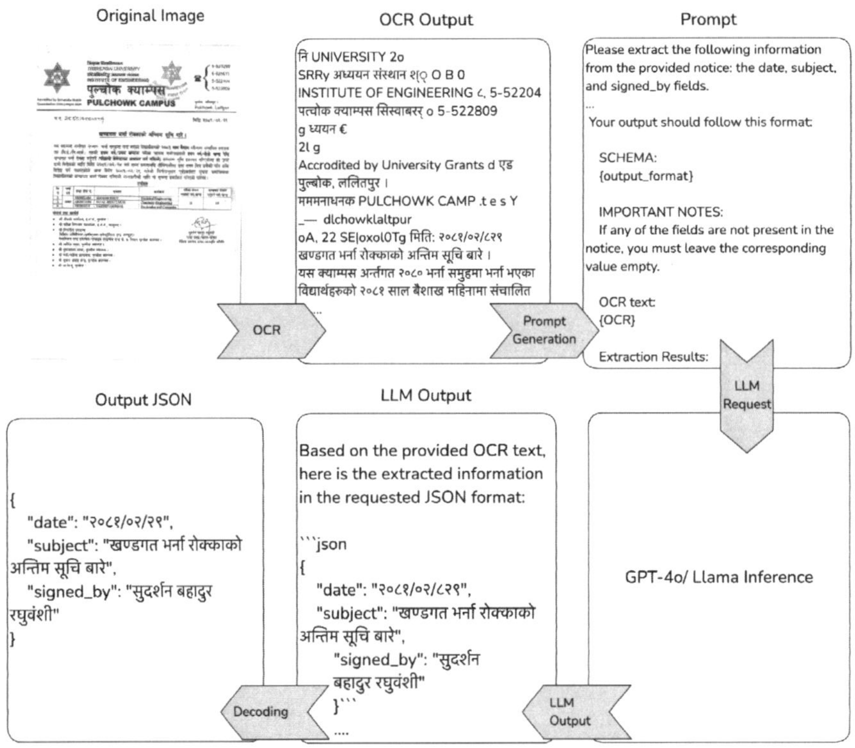

Figure 3: LLM System Process Flow Diagr In our framework, the text and layout information is first decoupled and jointly optimized during pre-training, and then re-coupled for fine-tuning

Table 2: Entity-Wise Performance Metrics of the Fine-Tuned LiLT Model

Entity	Precision (%)	Recall (%)	F1 Score (%)
Date	91.80	94.12	92.95
Signed By	90.12	89.02	89.57
Subject	87.18	84.30	85.71

the volume of training data, and the computational resources used.

Table 3: **Match Accuracy on Notices Dataset**

Label	90% Match			100% Match		
	LiLT	GPT-4o	Llama-8B	LiLT	GPT-4o	Llama-8B
Date	**0.81**	0.56	0.44	**0.78**	0.55	0.42
Subject	**0.93**	0.81	0.62	**0.27**	0.25	0.20
Signed By	**0.87**	0.85	0.37	**0.71**	0.66	0.30

5 Limitation

In this study, our method heavily relies on the input of text lines and bounding boxes, often generated through Optical Character Recognition (OCR) systems. This presents certain limitations, particularly in its inability to handle non-textual entities, such as images embedded within documents, which our approach does not account for. Additionally, the system is sensitive to common OCR challenges, including misinterpretations of reading order, incorrect grouping of text lines, and recognition errors. These OCR-related inaccuracies can adversely affect the performance of our model, especially in data-rich environments where precision in text extraction is critical. In addition to the Layout transformer, our approach leverages a Large Language Model (LLM) as an autoregressive decoder to extract information from the document. The LLM predicts tokens sequentially, generating outputs based on the given context. While this generative capability enables effective information extraction, it introduces a significant challenge: difficulty in localizing the extracted tokens back to their exact positions in the original document. Since LLMs are designed for token generation rather than precise token localization, mapping the output directly to specific document sections becomes complex, potentially affecting the interpretability and traceability of the extracted information.

With the LiLT transformer model, we have a limit of 512 tokens, which forces us to leave out tokens from the middle part of documents. This decision was made because, in most cases, the key information we need is found at the top or bottom of the document, while the middle part tends to be less useful for our task. By focusing on these sections, we ensure the model concentrates on what's important, though there is a chance that we might miss some relevant information in the middle. On the other hand, using LLM-based methods requires much larger models that can handle thousands of tokens to cover the whole document. While this leads to better extraction results, it also increases computational costs significantly, making these methods more difficult to scale or apply in high-volume situations. Finding a balance between token limitations and computational resources remains a challenge for our approach.

6 Conclusion and Future Works

In conclusion, our research demonstrates the effectiveness of two distinct approaches for extracting structured information from Nepali scanned documents. The fine-tuned Language Independent Layout Transformer (LiLT) model achieved high performance with a precision of 89.69%, recall of 88.20%, and an F1 score of 87.65%, indicating its robust capability in token classification and information extraction. In comparison, the large language models (LLMs) GPT-4o and Llama 3.1 8B showed variable accuracy, with GPT-4o performing generally better than Llama 3.1 8B and both GPT-4o and Llama 3.1 8B performing not as good as LiLT model. Despite their lower accuracy, LLM-based methods offer advantages such as ease of implementation and flexibility, which can be valuable for initial information extraction tasks. Integrating human feedback could further enhance the performance of LLMs and improve the overall accuracy of the system.

Thus, while the LiLT model provides higher precision, LLMs present a practical alternative with the potential for refinement and adaptation. To improve the overall accuracy of the LLM system, we can try several other methods. For instance, in the decoding phase of the LLM-based approach, we can use other approaches for example, instead of guiding the model to get the data that matches the schema provided in the prompt, we can ask the model to get all possible key-value pairs, and then pick the value corresponding to the key we are interested in.

References

Srikar Appalaraju, Bhavan Jasani, Bhargava Urala Kota, Yusheng Xie, and R. Manmatha. 2021. Docformer: End-to-end transformer for document understanding. *Preprint*, arXiv:2106.11539.

Andreas R Dengel Bertin Klein. 2019. An adaptive system for document analysis and understanding. in reading and learning. pages 166–186.

Tom B. Brown, Benjamin Mann, Nick Ryder, Melanie Subbiah, Jared Kaplan, Prafulla Dhariwal, Arvind Neelakantan, Pranav Shyam, Girish Sastry, Amanda Askell, Sandhini Agarwal, Ariel Herbert-Voss, Gretchen Krueger, Tom Henighan, Rewon Child, Aditya Ramesh, Daniel M. Ziegler, Jeffrey Wu, Clemens Winter, Christopher Hesse, Mark Chen, Eric Sigler, Mateusz Litwin, Scott Gray, Benjamin Chess, Jack Clark, Christopher Berner, Sam McCandlish, Alec Radford, Ilya Sutskever, and Dario Amodei. 2020. Language models are few-shot learners. *Preprint*, arXiv:2005.14165.

Alexis Conneau, Kartikay Khandelwal, Naman Goyal, Vishrav Chaudhary, Guillaume Wenzek, Francisco Guzmán, Edouard Grave, Myle Ott, Luke Zettlemoyer, and Veselin Stoyanov. 2019. Unsupervised cross-lingual representation learning at scale. *CoRR*, abs/1911.02116.

Florian Deckert, Benjamin Seidler, Markus Ebbecke, and Michael Gillmann. 2011. Table content understanding in smartfix. in 2011 international conference on document analysis and recognition. *IEEE*, pages 488–492.

Adrian Mocan Falk Brauer, Robert Rieger and Wojciech M Barczynski. 2011. Enabling information extraction by inference of regular expressions from sample entities. page 1285–1294.

Geewook Kim, Teakgyu Hong, Moonbin Yim, Jeongyeon Nam, Jinyoung Park, Jinyeong Yim, Wonseok Hwang, Sangdoo Yun, Dongyoon Han, and Seunghyun Park. 2022. Ocr-free document understanding transformer. *Preprint*, arXiv:2111.15664.

LLaMA Team, AI @ Meta. 2024. The llama 3 herd of models. *Preprint*, arXiv:2407.21783.

Tomas Mikolov, Kai Chen, Greg Corrado, and Jeffrey Dean. 2013. Efficient estimation of word representations in vector space. *Preprint*, arXiv:1301.3781.

Humza Naveed, Asad Ullah Khan, Shi Qiu, Muhammad Saqib, Saeed Anwar, Muhammad Usman, Naveed Akhtar, Nick Barnes, and Ajmal Mian. 2023. A comprehensive overview of large language models. *arXiv preprint arXiv:2307.06435*.

OpenAI. 2023. Gpt-4 technical report. Accessed: 2024-10-15.

Vincent Perot, Kai Kang, Florian Luisier, Guolong Su, Xiaoyu Sun, Ramya Sree Boppana, Zilong Wang, Zifeng Wang, Jiaqi Mu, Hao Zhang, Chen-Yu Lee, and Nan Hua. 2024. Lmdx: Language model-based document information extraction and localization. *Preprint*, arXiv:2309.10952.

Rafał Powalski, Łukasz Borchmann, Dawid Jurkiewicz, Tomasz Dwojak, Michał Pietruszka, and Gabriela Pałka. 2021. Going full-tilt boogie on document understanding with text-image-layout transformer. *Preprint*, arXiv:2102.09550.

Alec Radford. 2018. Improving language understanding by generative pre-training.

Colin Raffel, Noam Shazeer, Adam Roberts, Katherine Lee, Sharan Narang, Michael Matena, Yanqi Zhou, Wei Li, and Peter J. Liu. 2023. Exploring the limits of transfer learning with a unified text-to-text transformer. *Preprint*, arXiv:1910.10683.

Lance Ramshaw and Mitch Marcus. 1995. Text chunking using transformation-based learning. In *Third Workshop on Very Large Corpora*.

Florian Laws Rasmus Berg Palm, Dirk Hovy and Ole Winther. 2017. End-to-end information extraction without token-level supervision. page 48–52.

Sunita Sarawagi. 2008. Information extraction. foundations and trends r in databases. page 261–377.

Ilya Sutskever, Oriol Vinyals, and Quoc V. Le. 2014. Sequence to sequence learning with neural networks. *Preprint*, arXiv:1409.3215.

Hugo Touvron, Thibaut Lavril, Gautier Izacard, Xavier Martinet, Marie-Anne Lachaux, Timothée Lacroix, Baptiste Rozière, Naman Goyal, Eric Hambro, Faisal Azhar, et al. 2023. Llama: Open and efficient foundation language models. *arXiv preprint arXiv:2302.13971*.

Ashish Vaswani, Noam Shazeer, Niki Parmar, Jakob Uszkoreit, Llion Jones, Aidan N Gomez, Łukasz Kaiser, and Illia Polosukhin. 2017. Attention is all you need. *Advances in neural information processing systems*, 30.

Jiapeng Wang, Lianwen Jin, and Kai Ding. 2022. Lilt: A simple yet effective language-independent layout transformer for structured document understanding. *Preprint*, arXiv:2202.13669.

Zifeng Wang, Zizhao Zhang, Jacob Devlin, Chen-Yu Lee, Guolong Su, Hao Zhang, Jennifer Dy, Vincent Perot, and Tomas Pfister. 2023. QueryForm: A simple zero-shot form entity query framework. In *Findings of the Association for Computational Linguistics: ACL 2023*, pages 4146–4159, Toronto, Canada. Association for Computational Linguistics.

Yang Xu, Yiheng Xu, Tengchao Lv, Lei Cui, Furu Wei, Guoxin Wang, Yijuan Lu, Dinei Florencio, Cha Zhang, Wanxiang Che, Min Zhang, and Lidong Zhou. 2022. Layoutlmv2: Multi-modal pre-training for visually-rich document understanding. *Preprint*, arXiv:2012.14740.

Yiheng Xu, Minghao Li, Lei Cui, Shaohan Huang, Furu Wei, and Ming Zhou. 2020. Layoutlm: Pre-training of text and layout for document image understanding. In *Proceedings of the 26th ACM SIGKDD International Conference on Knowledge Discovery & Data Mining*, pages 1192–1200.

Yiheng Xu, Tengchao Lv, Lei Cui, Guoxin Wang, Yijuan Lu, Dinei Florencio, Cha Zhang, and Furu Wei. 2021. Layoutxlm: Multimodal pre-training for multilingual visually-rich document understanding. *Preprint*, arXiv:2104.08836.

James Zhang, Wouter Haverals, Mary Naydan, and Brian W Kernighan. 2024. Post-ocr correction with openai's gpt models on challenging english prosody texts. In *Proceedings of the ACM Symposium on Document Engineering 2024*, pages 1–4.

Domain-adaptative Continual Learning for Low-resource Tasks: Evaluation on Nepali

Sharad Duwal, Suraj Prasai, Suresh Manandhar
Wiseyak
wiseyak.com

Corresponding Author: sharad.duwal@wiseyak.com

Abstract

Continual learning has emerged as an important research direction due to the infeasibility of retraining large language models (LLMs) from scratch in the event of new data availability. Of great interest is the domain-adaptive pre-training (DAPT) paradigm, which focuses on continually training a pre-trained language model to adapt it to a domain it wasn't originally trained on. In this work, we evaluate the feasibility of DAPT in a low-resource setting, namely the Nepali language. We use synthetic data to continue training Llama 3 8B to adapt it to the Nepali language in a 4-bit QLoRA setting. We evaluate the adapted model on its performance, forgetting, and knowledge acquisition. We compare the base model and the final model on their Nepali generation abilities, their performance on popular benchmarks, and run case-studies to probe their linguistic knowledge in Nepali. We see some unsurprising forgetting in the final model, but also surprisingly find that increasing the number of shots during evaluation yields better percent increases in the final model (as high as 19.29% increase) compared to the base model (4.98%), suggesting latent retention. We also explore layer–head self-attention heatmaps to establish dependency resolution abilities of the final model in Nepali. All code will be available at github.com/sharad461/DAPT-Nepali.

1 Introduction

Advancements in natural language processing (NLP) have enabled large language models (LLMs) to generate human-like text, follow instructions and perform well on a wide range of complex understanding tasks (Brown et al., 2020; OpenAI, 2024; Dubey et al., 2024). A big driver behind the continued success of LLMs is the fact that scaling LLMs (increase in parameter count and dataset size) continues to provide decent returns on all performance benchmarks (Kaplan et al., 2020). This scaling-up, however, affects the accessibility and availability of these models and comes with its myriad issues (Bender et al., 2021). Very large language models require huge amounts of resources, have a large carbon footprint (Strubell et al., 2019; Patterson et al., 2021), and training them is feasible only for languages with large quantities of high-quality data and reasonable access to compute. It is costly also to perform inference on them.

Besides scaling, the other direction is generalizability of models with focus on optimal use of data. Given how human text data is projected to run out soon (Villalobos et al., 2024), methods like repeating data, using synthetic data, and using code data are being explored with good returns (Muennighoff et al., 2023; Shimabucoro et al., 2024; Aryabumi et al., 2024). Many of these tools have been explored for research in low-resource languages.

Nepali is a low-resource language. (Arora et al., 2022) classify Nepali among the "Scraping-By" languages in South Asia. While the frontier LLMs today can understand and generate Nepali (OpenAI, 2024), they do not officially support it. One major issue is tokenization: Nepali tokenization is costly in models like GPT4. While NLP research in South Asian languages has picked up recently, many languages are still behind and, as a result, low-resourced.

One possible way to ease the data-compute bind for these low-resource languages (Nepali included) is the use of continual learning (CL) for domain adaptation on high-resource LLMs (SarvamAI, 2023; Gururangan et al., 2020). The idea behind continual learning is to incrementally update an LLM with availability of new data so that the old knowledge isn't forgotten and the new knowledge can be properly assimilated into the model.

Domain adaptation with CL involves continued training of an LLM so that the knowledge of the base LLM can be repurposed to another domain. Since the *knowledge* of the base model can be

Proceedings of the First Workshop on Challenges in Processing South Asian Languages (CHiPSAL 2025), pages 144–153
January 19, 2025.

reused, we do not need large amounts of world knowledge data in the new domain (or language). Also, because adaptation requires training only a fraction of the total parameters in the original model, the compute requirements are significantly reduced.

In this work, we focus on domain adaptation of the Llama 3 8B (Meta, 2024) model to the Nepali language using synthetically generated data. We continually train the Llama model, run experiments to determine performance, catastrophic forgetting, and linguistic knowledge acquisition of the model after the domain adaptation. We compare the adapted model against the original model on several benchmarks. Additionally, we analyze the attention heatmaps to gauge the knowledge of the adapted model. The emphasis of this work is on evaluating DAPT methods to adapt an LLM to a low-resource scenario with only synthetic data.

The main contributions of this work are:

1. We develop and test out methodologies to perform domain-adaptive continual pretraining on an open-weights model using only synthetically generated data.
2. We evaluate and compare the performance of the adapted model against the base model.
3. We interpret the linguistic knowledge of the final model on the new task.

2 Related Work

Continual Learning. Continual learning is an important research direction because its goal is to make it possible to train large models on new data efficiently, often allowing lifelong learning LLMs. This could take place in the form of adding new information to it, teaching it a new subject, or adapting it to a different domain.

Domain-adaptive pretraining (DAPT) has been known to provide performance gains in low-resource settings (Gururangan et al., 2020; Çağatay Yıldız et al., 2024). This has been extended to multilingual domain-adaptive pretraining where a single multilingual model is trained for a specific domain, which outperforms general models on said domain (Kær Jørgensen et al., 2021).

Synthetic data has also been applied for good performance gains in a continual pretraining domain-adaptation strategy (Zhang et al., 2020).

However, a problem in continual learning is catastrophic forgetting, which happens during full finetuning probably due to retraining of weights or because a model has reached knowledge saturation and to learn any more information it forgets old information (Çağatay Yıldız et al., 2024).

Continual learning has great potential in unlocking areas in low-resource language research.

Synthetic data. Data augmentation using synthetic methods is central to research in low-resource languages. In NLP, some methods for synthetic data generation are backtranslation (Sennrich et al., 2016), paraphrasing, synonym replacement, sentence-level replacement, random insertion, etc. (Feng et al., 2021) and (Chen et al., 2023) provide detailed studies on methods available for data augmentation for NLP tasks.

Compared to real data, synthetic data has its own set of advantages and disadvantages. While synthetic data makes low-resource tasks accessible, scalable, and overall cost-effective, it might not always reflect realistic scenarios. There could often be challenges with validating synthetic data and it can magnify biases of the original model.

Organic data available for training purposes is finite and (Villalobos et al., 2024) predict we will run out of all publicly available text data as soon as 2026. Guided synthetic data generation, which will be an important part of future data acquisition technique, is a research direction where data is generated toward non-differentiable objectives (Shimabucoro et al., 2024).

Low-rank adaptation. LoRA (Hu et al., 2021) and QLoRA (Dettmers et al., 2023) are fine-tuning techniques that reduce the number of trainable parameters in a model, making training faster and memory-efficient. Instead of updating all weights in a model, these methods train low-rank matrices that capture task-specific information, freezing the model itself. In addition to the lower rank adaptation in LoRA, QLoRA quantizes the model so that it requires even lesser memory to train. The tradeoff in performance between full finetuning and low-rank techniques has been well-established (Biderman et al., 2024; Xia et al., 2024), and more work is being done in this space (Zhao et al., 2024; Lialin et al., 2023), but in a resource-constrained scenario, QLoRA makes training large models feasible.

Knowledge in attention heads. Many interpretative studies have been applied to the attention mechanism used in Transformer architectures. (Voita et al., 2019) investigate the function of attention heads in the multi-head self-attention in encoders and try to interpret how they contribute to the performance of the entire network. They also prune attention heads in an ablation study. Similarly, to analyze how well the attention mechanism models a language and its syntax, (Vig and Belinkov, 2019) evaluate attention heads to find that different layers in a model specialize in different parts-of-speech tags. They use BertViz (Vig, 2019) for their experiments. (Liu et al., 2019) study the contextual representations generated by several popular models to understand why they are so effective in solving NLP tasks. They use seventeen probing tasks to establish the transferability of the representations and what linguistic knowledge is stored and in which part of the model.

3 Method

We use parallel data in Nepali–English (instead of Nepali-only text) to perform continual pretraining. Our aim here is to align the model and its knowledge to Nepali since it already has an understanding of English. We generate the parallel data using synthetic methods, perform pretraining on this data, and then finetune.

3.1 Data Generation

We use Nepali text available online (news reports, essays, etc.) collected in datasets like OSCAR (Abadji et al., 2022) and preprocess it for translation. For the translation system, there were a few alternatives to choose from: NLLB (Costa-jussà et al., 2022), IndicTrans2 (Gala et al., 2023), Google Cloud Translate. We use the Flores test-set for Nepali–English (Guzmán et al., 2019) to evaluate the open-source systems. We also compare scores across the different model sizes available and the various quantized versions of the models. We decided to go with 8-bit NLLB for the translation. IndicTrans2 performed marginally better in terms of BLEU scores, but NLLB had very little computational overhead and supported larger batches out-of-the-box.

Since we also plan to later finetune the model on Nepali instructions and since there aren't instruction sets for Nepali, we also translate English instruction sets to Nepali. We use IndicTrans2 for this. For the instruction set, we translate Alpaca (Taori et al., 2023), Databricks Dolly (Conover et al., 2023) and WebGLM-QA (Liu et al., 2023) to Nepali. To ensure the quality of the synthetic instruction sets, we backtranslate the instructions to English (again using IndicTrans2) and calculate the chrF++ score between the original and the back-translated sets. We apply a chrF++ cut-off of 50 and all samples with lower scores were discarded.

At the end of this step, we have 5M pairs of Nepali–English parallel paragraphs and 114K triplets of (input, instruction, output) instructions.

3.2 Training

We perform 4-bit QLoRA continual pretraining of a Llama 3 8B model on the synthetic parallel data we generated in 3.1. We use Unsloth (Han, 2023). We pretrain the model with the task to translate from English to Nepali. We do this because the English part of the parallel data is synthetic and the Nepali part is organic.

We loosely follow the steps suggested by (SarvamAI, 2023) and divide the pretraining process into two steps:

3.2.1 Pretraining using translation

The aim of this step is to familiarize the model with Nepali using the translation data and the model's own knowledge in English. We train the model to translate from English to Nepali. We use this translation direction because for our parallel data, English is synthetic and Nepali is organic. By training the model to generate the (non-synthetic) Nepali given the (synthetic) English, we teach it to generate Nepali as originally written. The alternative would be to teach the model to generate system-generated English.

For this step, we set the rank to 128, which selected 335M parameters to train. We pretrain the model on 1.5M paragraph pairs for this first task.

3.2.2 Bilingual next token prediction

Second, we train the model on a bilingual next token prediction task. This is the standard next token prediction task with sentences ordered in alternate language. We choose the next 1.5M paragraph pairs and consolidate each of the pairs such that every sample paragraph switches language every sentence. If the first sentence in a paragraph is Nepali, the second picks up in English, then back to Nepali. An example paragraph would be:

> Before the unification of Nepal, the Kathmandu Valley was known as Nepal. नेपाल शब्दको सटीक उत्पत्ति अनिश्चित

छ । But it can be dated back to the fourth century AD.

The training settings are much the same for this step as the first step. The presumption here is that instead of training with a Nepali next token prediction task, if we leverage the English knowledge already present into the model, the training should be more effective. (SarvamAI, 2023) found that a model trained with this objective performed better than a model trained on the standard token prediction objective on 5X more data.

3.3 Finetuning

After these steps aligning the model (3.2.1 and 3.2.2) to the Nepali language, we perform a supervised finetuning step. We perform a QLoRA finetuning lower-rank than both these pretraining steps. We set the rank to 16. This updates around 41M parameters in the model. The instruction data we generated in 3.1 is used to finetune the model here. We choose to perform finetuning on a mixed instruction set because we want the model to learn both Nepali and English instructions.

4 Performance Study

After the pretraining followed by finetuning, we perform experiments on both the base model (Llama 3 8B 4-bit) and the continual trained model with the view to answer the following research questions:

Q1. Has the model learned Nepali?

Q2. Has the model retained its knowledge of English? What does catastrophic forgetting look like?

Q3. From a linguistic perspective, how well does the new model model the Nepali language?

5 Experimental Setup

5.1 LM Evaluation Harness

LM Evaluation Harness (Gao et al., 2024) is a framework for evaluating language models. It supports generative LLMs trained on transformers, GPT-NeoX, and Megatron-DeepSpeed and as of writing it supports more than 60 academic benchmarks to run evaluations on. For our task, we focus on English benchmarks and evaluate first the base model, then the adapted model in order to quantify the change in model knowledge and performance.

5.2 BertViz

BertViz (Vig, 2019) is a tool designed to help visualize attention in language models. Originally designed to support only BERT-type models, decoder-only and encoder-decoder model support was added later. It provides a user-friendly interface to explore and interpret the attention patterns within the model, offering valuable insights into how LLMs process and relate different parts of the input with itself or with the output, facilitating in interpretative study of LLMs.

5.2.1 Attention pooling for word tokens

Since Nepali is not officially supported by the Llama 3 tokenizer, the token fertility of Nepali is high. This should be true for many other South Asian languages as well. The study of the attention maps is complicated by this because higher the tokens per word the more difficult it is to map attention between the tokens. Higher fertility not only complicates evaluation, but also makes inference and training costly.

To address this issue, we experimented with methods to pool the token attentions in order to construct word attentions. We applied max-pooling and mean-pooling. For max-pooling, for every Nepali word we take the element-wise max between the vectors corresponding to each constituent token to get the word attention. For mean-pooling, we take the element-wise mean.

Our experiments show max-pooling to be more suitable. We found mean-pooling normalizes attention weights to a great degree, decreasing variance. Thus, for our studies, we max-pool the token attentions to get word attention.

5.3 Questions

For **Q1**, we prompt the base and final models with a set of Nepali questions to generate answers. We then use GPT-4o to score these responses. Automatic evaluation of LM generations has been used with good results due to the multilinguality of frontier language models. GPT4 and GPT-4o perform well even in languages they do not officially support, Nepali included (OpenAI, 2024; Romanou et al., 2024; Hada et al., 2024). We let GPT-4o score the answers on different qualities on scales of 0-10. We analyze the score distributions to answer Q1.

For **Q2**, we use LM Evaluation Harness to evaluate the performance of both the models on several English benchmarks and study how the scores

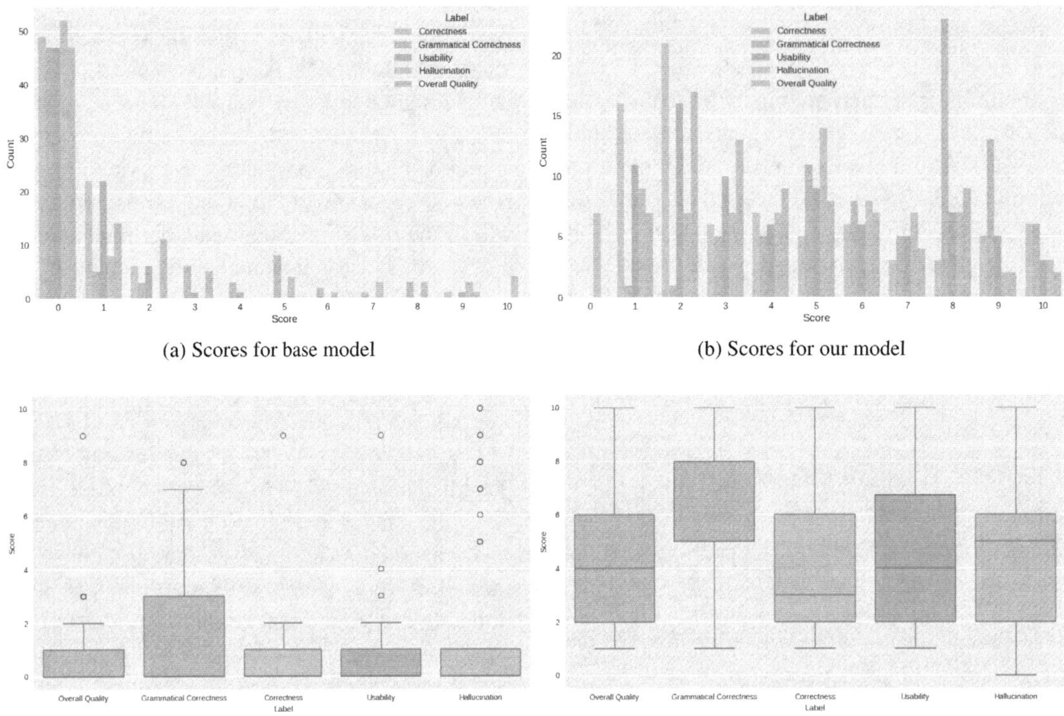

(a) Scores for base model

(b) Scores for our model

(c) Base model

(d) Our model

Figure 1: GPT4o scores for Nepali answers generated by the base model (Llama 3 8B 4-bit) and our model on five attributes: correctness, grammar, usability, hallucination and overall quality. Empty generations from the models are scored 0 on all attributes. c) and d) are the distribution of scores among the attributes with medians and outliers.

change, or do not. This gives us insight into the forgetting in the final model. Though the base model was trained on eight languages, we only focus on its retention of English-language knowledge. We evaluate the model on MMLU (Hendrycks et al., 2021), ARC (Clark et al., 2018), Winogrande (Sakaguchi et al., 2019), and TruthfulQA (Lin et al., 2022) benchmarks.

Q3. Dependency relations are an important feature of languages. The ability of a language model to resolve a language can be studied by analyzing the layer-head attentions of the model. We use BertViz to analyze the models at the layer- and attention head–level to accomplish this.

We curate Nepali sentences focusing on adjectives and pronouns to study how the layers in the final model encode the information about dependency relation in the sentences. We visualize self-attention in the model.

6 Results

To answer **Q1**, we evaluate text generated by the base model and our model based on five attributes: correctness, grammatical correctness, usability, hallucination tendency, and overall quality.

First, we prompt both the models to answers 78 Nepali questions extracted from a traffic license exam in Nepali. Once we have the generated outputs, we let GPT-4o grade each generation on a scale of 0–10, for all five attributes.

The score distributions in the charts show the distinction between the two models. The base model (Figure 1a) shows a heavy concentration of scores at 0-1 across all metrics. This suggests that the base model's Nepali generation abilities are limited.

Our model has a more balanced score distribution (Figure 1b). While some generations still receive low scores, we observe higher scores overall compared to the base model. This is specifically evident in the scores for grammatical correctness. Our model shows strong performance here, with many generations scoring 8 or above, suggesting the model has learned how Nepali sentence are structured.

Hallucination scores demonstrate that our model has a higher median compared to the base model.

	Our model		Base (Llama 3 8B 4-bit)	
	0-shot	5-shot	0-shot	5-shot
MMLU	**0.3506**	0.3462 (−1.25%)	0.6056	**0.6340** (+4.69%)
ARC-Easy	0.6271	**0.7020** (+11.94%)	0.7950	**0.8346** (+4.98%)
ARC-Challenge	0.3183	**0.3797** (+19.29%)	0.5017	**0.5179** (+3.23%)
Winogrande	0.5801	**0.6275** (+8.17%)	0.7340	**0.7561** (+3.01%)
TruthfulQA MC1	0.2827	-	0.2656	-
TruthfulQA MC2	0.4351	-	0.4305	-

Table 1: Our model v/s the base model on English Benchmarks. As expected, the domain adaptation has caused forgetting. The % change in the scores in 5-shot runs compared to 0-shot runs are also provided. The greater improvements in the 5-shot runs show possible latent retention.

This seems counterintuitive given higher hallucination is a bad quality for a language model to have. But it also suggests that our model's generations contain content that is more verifiable and can be assessed for hallucination, whereas the base model's outputs may be too limited or generic to evaluate factual accuracy.

Both box-plots (Figure 1c and 1d) confirm these observations, evidenced by broader distributions and higher medians for the final model across all metrics.

These results show that our model achieves improvements over the base model across all evaluated dimensions. The broader distribution suggests that our model is capable of generating more sophisticated and varied responses, even though this comes with some increased variability in performance.

For **Q2**, we evaluate the final model on popular English benchmarks in order to identify whether it was able to retain its knowledge in English post-pretraining. The scores of our model versus the base model in the selected benchmarks are reported in Table 1. On MMLU, our model scores 0.3506 and 0.3462 for 0-shot and 5-shot settings respectively. The base model scores 0.6056 and 0.6340 respectively, which suggests some forgetting has taken place.

On ARC-Easy, our model achieves scores of 0.6271 (0-shot) and 0.7020 (5-shot), while showing lower performance on the more challenging ARC-Challenge subset with scores of 0.3183 and 0.3797 for 0-shot and 5-shot settings respectively. The base model unsurprisingly scores higher on both benchmarks.

On the Winogrande benchmark, our model scores 0.5691 (0-shot) and 0.6022 (5-shot). For the TruthfulQA evaluation, our model achieves scores of 0.2607 and 0.4243 on MC1 and MC2 variants respectively, showing comparable performance to the baseline's 0.2656 and 0.4305.

With these numbers, it is easy to establish that forgetting has happened. However, it is noteworthy that 5-shot prompting over 0-shot generally yields higher percent increase for our model than the base model, suggesting that our model leverages few-shot examples more effectively than the final model. The highest increase in performance is for the ARC-Challenge dataset where we see a 19.29% performance increase in the 5-shot setting compared to 0-shot. This might suggest that if properly pretrained, forgetting can be curtailed by increasing shots while prompting.

Finally, to answer **Q3**, we annotate a set of Nepali sentences by mapping adjectives to corresponding nouns. We explore the dependency resolution ability of the model by analyzing the attentions from the adjectives to their respective nouns across all attention heads in all layers. For each (adjective, noun) pair we extract attentions across all attention heads and find the mean of such attention heatmaps for multiple samples to get an *adjective concept*. For English we average the heatmaps from 17 adjective-noun pairs and for Nepali 26 pairs. We compare the heatmaps for the base model and the final model to establish whether the final model actually captures some understanding of the language that was not present in the base model. In Figure 2 the heatmaps visualize self-attention patterns across the 32 layers (y-axis) and the 32 attention heads (x-axis) of the models. The darker blue colors indicate stronger attention weights.

Comparing our model's attention heatmaps (a,b) with the base model's heatmaps (c,d), we observe that our model has learned to process Nepali ad-

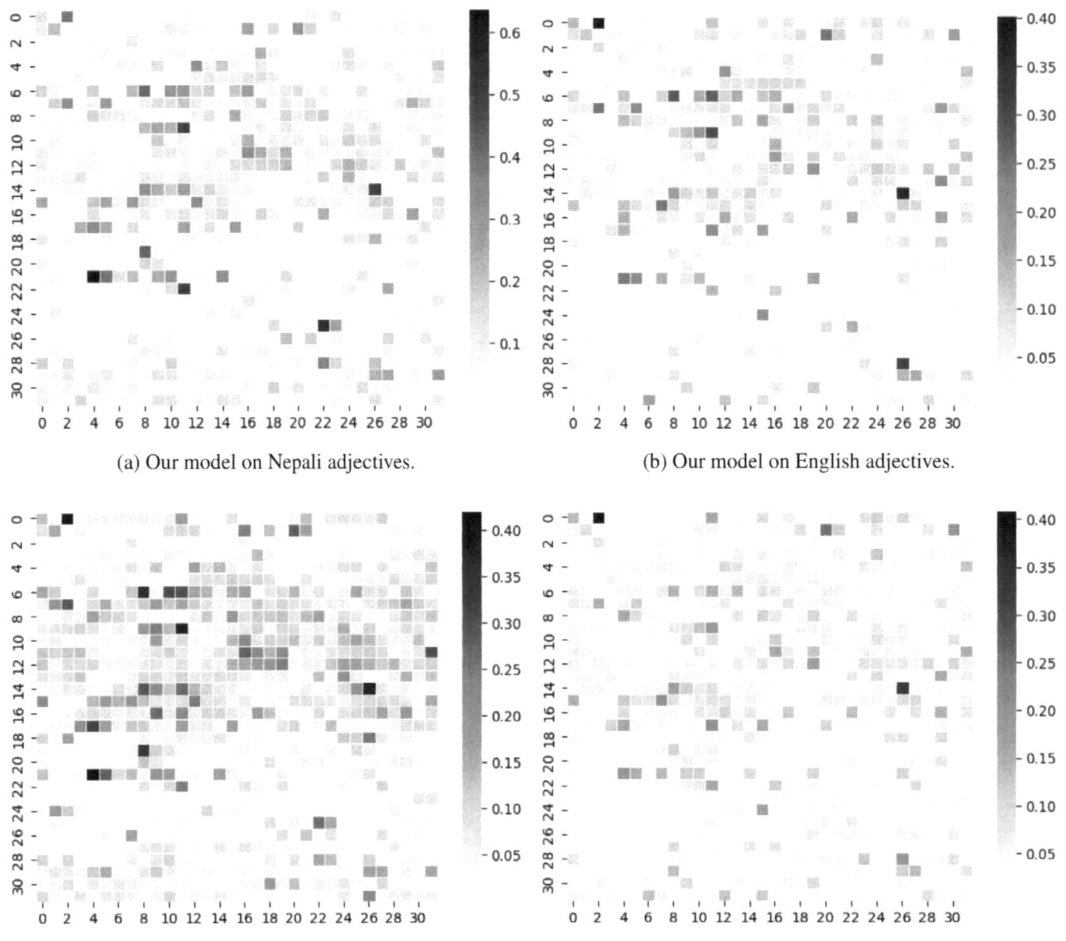

(a) Our model on Nepali adjectives.

(b) Our model on English adjectives.

(c) Base model on Nepali adjectives.

(d) Base model on English adjectives.

Figure 2: Layer-head heatmaps visualizing attention from adjectives to their respective nouns in Nepali (a,c) and English (b,d) for our model (a,b) and the base model (c,d). Rows are layers and columns are attention heads. From a) and c), we can see our model has learned to attend to Nepali adjectives the way the base model attends to English ones in d).

jectives in a manner very similar to how the base model processes English adjectives. This is evidenced by the sparser and focused attention patterns in (a) as compared to the more diffuse patterns in (c). This alignment suggests improved cross-lingual transfer during pretraining. As suggested in other studies (Liu et al., 2019; Vig and Belinkov, 2019), we found that some of the most prominent attention heads are located in the middle layers.

The models have very different attention patterns in the lower layers (1-8), indicating that language-specific processing is perhaps performed in the earlier layers of the network. The attention patterns for English adjectives (b,d) are similar between the two models, which suggests that the DAPT only impacted the processing of Nepali in the model without disturbing its understanding of English structures.

7 Conclusion

We explored the utility of the continual learning paradigm in low-resource tasks, with a focus on the Nepali language. We experimented with the Llama 3 8B model to establish a simple and intuitive pretraining procedure, followed by mixed-language fine-tuning. We used automatic evaluation to grade model responses and established that the model after DAPT can generate semantically correct Nepali. We performed evaluations with several benchmarks to gauge the forgetting in the model. We finally investigated attention heatmaps to evaluate the model's grammatical knowledge in Nepali. By adapting a pretrained model to the Nepali language using only synthetic data and very limited resources and establishing generation abilities and linguistic knowledge in the new model, we make a case for domain-adaptive pretraining as a meaningful direction to explore for data- and resource-constrained languages.

8 Limitations

This work focuses on resource-constrained domain adaptation. Experiments are performed in a quantized 4-bit setting and the data used is synthetically generated. Pretraining sessions were run only for a single epoch and the data is mostly from online news sources, which we conjecture lead to more hallucination. Resource constraints are therefore the biggest limitation of this work. Second, we use GPT-4o for evaluation of model output. While auto-evaluation is becoming widely-adopted in multilingual research, use of human evaluators (especially domain experts for Nepali) could lead to a more definitive assessment. Similarly, there are no LM benchmarks in Nepali, which could have helped with the evaluation.

A possible extension of this work could be to study how other low-resourced languages in South Asia respond to these methods. It would also be interesting to investigate if transfer from another Indic language (opposed to English) would yield different results.

References

Julien Abadji, Pedro Ortiz Suarez, Laurent Romary, and Benoît Sagot. 2022. Towards a Cleaner Document-Oriented Multilingual Crawled Corpus. *arXiv e-prints*, arXiv:2201.06642.

Aryaman Arora, Adam Farris, Samopriya Basu, and Suresh Kolichala. 2022. Computational historical linguistics and language diversity in South Asia. In *Proceedings of the 60th Annual Meeting of the Association for Computational Linguistics (Volume 1: Long Papers)*, pages 1396–1409, Dublin, Ireland. Association for Computational Linguistics.

Viraat Aryabumi, Yixuan Su, Raymond Ma, Adrien Morisot, Ivan Zhang, Acyr Locatelli, Marzieh Fadaee, Ahmet Üstün, and Sara Hooker. 2024. To code, or not to code? exploring impact of code in pre-training. *Preprint*, arXiv:2408.10914.

Emily M. Bender, Timnit Gebru, Angelina McMillan-Major, and Shmargaret Shmitchell. 2021. On the dangers of stochastic parrots: Can language models be too big? In *Proceedings of the 2021 ACM Conference on Fairness, Accountability, and Transparency*, FAccT '21, page 610–623, New York, NY, USA. Association for Computing Machinery.

Dan Biderman, Jacob Portes, Jose Javier Gonzalez Ortiz, Mansheej Paul, Philip Greengard, Connor Jennings, Daniel King, Sam Havens, Vitaliy Chiley, Jonathan Frankle, Cody Blakeney, and John P. Cunningham. 2024. Lora learns less and forgets less. *Preprint*, arXiv:2405.09673.

Tom B. Brown, Benjamin Mann, Nick Ryder, Melanie Subbiah, Jared Kaplan, Prafulla Dhariwal, Arvind Neelakantan, Pranav Shyam, Girish Sastry, Amanda Askell, Sandhini Agarwal, Ariel Herbert-Voss, Gretchen Krueger, Tom Henighan, Rewon Child, Aditya Ramesh, Daniel M. Ziegler, Jeffrey Wu, Clemens Winter, Christopher Hesse, Mark Chen, Eric Sigler, Mateusz Litwin, Scott Gray, Benjamin Chess, Jack Clark, Christopher Berner, Sam McCandlish, Alec Radford, Ilya Sutskever, and Dario Amodei. 2020. Language models are few-shot learners. *Preprint*, arXiv:2005.14165.

Jiaao Chen, Derek Tam, Colin Raffel, Mohit Bansal, and Diyi Yang. 2023. An empirical survey of data augmentation for limited data learning in NLP. *Transactions of the Association for Computational Linguistics*, 11:191–211.

Peter Clark, Isaac Cowhey, Oren Etzioni, Tushar Khot, Ashish Sabharwal, Carissa Schoenick, and Oyvind Tafjord. 2018. Think you have solved question answering? try arc, the ai2 reasoning challenge. *Preprint*, arXiv:1803.05457.

Mike Conover, Matt Hayes, Ankit Mathur, Jianwei Xie, Jun Wan, Sam Shah, Ali Ghodsi, Patrick Wendell, Matei Zaharia, and Reynold Xin. 2023. Free dolly: Introducing the world's first truly open instruction-tuned llm.

Marta R. Costa-jussà, James Cross, Onur Çelebi, Maha Elbayad, Kenneth Heafield, Kevin Heffernan, Elahe Kalbassi, Janice Lam, Daniel Licht, Jean Maillard, Anna Sun, Skyler Wang, Guillaume Wenzek, Al Youngblood, Bapi Akula, and Loic Barrault et al. 2022. No language left behind: Scaling human-centered machine translation. *Preprint*, arXiv:2207.04672.

Tim Dettmers, Artidoro Pagnoni, Ari Holtzman, and Luke Zettlemoyer. 2023. Qlora: Efficient finetuning of quantized llms. *Preprint*, arXiv:2305.14314.

Abhimanyu Dubey, Abhinav Jauhri, Abhinav Pandey, Abhishek Kadian, Ahmad Al-Dahle, Aiesha Letman, Akhil Mathur, Alan Schelten, Amy Yang, and Angela Fan et al. 2024. The llama 3 herd of models. *Preprint*, arXiv:2407.21783.

Steven Y. Feng, Varun Gangal, Jason Wei, Sarath Chandar, Soroush Vosoughi, Teruko Mitamura, and Eduard Hovy. 2021. A survey of data augmentation approaches for NLP. In *Findings of the Association for Computational Linguistics: ACL-IJCNLP 2021*, pages 968–988, Online. Association for Computational Linguistics.

Jay Gala, Pranjal A. Chitale, Raghavan AK, Varun Gumma, Sumanth Doddapaneni, Aswanth Kumar, Janki Nawale, Anupama Sujatha, Ratish Puduppully, Vivek Raghavan, Pratyush Kumar, Mitesh M. Khapra, Raj Dabre, and Anoop Kunchukuttan. 2023. Indictrans2: Towards high-quality and accessible machine translation models for all 22 scheduled indian languages. *Preprint*, arXiv:2305.16307.

Leo Gao, Jonathan Tow, Baber Abbasi, Stella Biderman, Sid Black, Anthony DiPofi, Charles Foster, Laurence Golding, Jeffrey Hsu, Alain Le Noac'h, Haonan Li, Kyle McDonell, Niklas Muennighoff, Chris Ociepa, Jason Phang, Laria Reynolds, Hailey Schoelkopf, Aviya Skowron, Lintang Sutawika, Eric Tang, Anish Thite, Ben Wang, Kevin Wang, and Andy Zou. 2024. A framework for few-shot language model evaluation.

Suchin Gururangan, Ana Marasović, Swabha Swayamdipta, Kyle Lo, Iz Beltagy, Doug Downey, and Noah A. Smith. 2020. Don't stop pretraining: Adapt language models to domains and tasks. In *Proceedings of the 58th Annual Meeting of the Association for Computational Linguistics*, pages 8342–8360, Online. Association for Computational Linguistics.

Francisco Guzmán, Peng-Jen Chen, Myle Ott, Juan Pino, Guillaume Lample, Philipp Koehn, Vishrav Chaudhary, and Marc'Aurelio Ranzato. 2019. The FLORES evaluation datasets for low-resource machine translation: Nepali–English and Sinhala–English. In *Proceedings of the 2019 Conference on Empirical Methods in Natural Language Processing and the 9th International Joint Conference on Natural Language Processing (EMNLP-IJCNLP)*, pages 6098–6111, Hong Kong, China. Association for Computational Linguistics.

Rishav Hada, Varun Gumma, Adrian de Wynter, Harshita Diddee, Mohamed Ahmed, Monojit Choudhury, Kalika Bali, and Sunayana Sitaram. 2024. Are large language model-based evaluators the solution to scaling up multilingual evaluation? *Preprint*, arXiv:2309.07462.

Daniel Han. 2023. Unsloth ai: Open source fine-tuning for llms.

Dan Hendrycks, Collin Burns, Steven Basart, Andy Zou, Mantas Mazeika, Dawn Song, and Jacob Steinhardt. 2021. Measuring massive multitask language understanding. *Preprint*, arXiv:2009.03300.

Edward J. Hu, Yelong Shen, Phillip Wallis, Zeyuan Allen-Zhu, Yuanzhi Li, Shean Wang, Lu Wang, and Weizhu Chen. 2021. Lora: Low-rank adaptation of large language models. *Preprint*, arXiv:2106.09685.

Rasmus Kær Jørgensen, Mareike Hartmann, Xiang Dai, and Desmond Elliott. 2021. mDAPT: Multilingual domain adaptive pretraining in a single model. In *Findings of the Association for Computational Linguistics: EMNLP 2021*, pages 3404–3418, Punta Cana, Dominican Republic. Association for Computational Linguistics.

Jared Kaplan, Sam McCandlish, Tom Henighan, Tom B. Brown, Benjamin Chess, Rewon Child, Scott Gray, Alec Radford, Jeffrey Wu, and Dario Amodei. 2020. Scaling laws for neural language models. *Preprint*, arXiv:2001.08361.

Vladislav Lialin, Namrata Shivagunde, Sherin Muckatira, and Anna Rumshisky. 2023. Relora: High-rank training through low-rank updates. *Preprint*, arXiv:2307.05695.

Stephanie Lin, Jacob Hilton, and Owain Evans. 2022. Truthfulqa: Measuring how models mimic human falsehoods. *Preprint*, arXiv:2109.07958.

Nelson F. Liu, Matt Gardner, Yonatan Belinkov, Matthew E. Peters, and Noah A. Smith. 2019. Linguistic knowledge and transferability of contextual representations. In *Proceedings of the 2019 Conference of the North American Chapter of the Association for Computational Linguistics: Human Language Technologies, Volume 1 (Long and Short Papers)*, pages 1073–1094, Minneapolis, Minnesota. Association for Computational Linguistics.

Xiao Liu, Hanyu Lai, Hao Yu, Yifan Xu, Aohan Zeng, Zhengxiao Du, Peng Zhang, Yuxiao Dong, and Jie Tang. 2023. Webglm: Towards an efficient web-enhanced question answering system with human preferences. *Preprint*, arXiv:2306.07906.

Meta. 2024. Introducing meta llama 3: The most capable openly available llm to date.

Niklas Muennighoff, Alexander M. Rush, Boaz Barak, Teven Le Scao, Aleksandra Piktus, Nouamane Tazi, Sampo Pyysalo, Thomas Wolf, and Colin Raffel. 2023. Scaling data-constrained language models. *Preprint*, arXiv:2305.16264.

OpenAI. 2024. Gpt-4 technical report. *Preprint*, arXiv:2303.08774.

David A. Patterson, Joseph Gonzalez, Quoc V. Le, Chen Liang, Lluís-Miquel Munguía, Daniel Rothchild, David R. So, Maud Texier, and Jeff Dean. 2021. Carbon emissions and large neural network training. *ArXiv*, abs/2104.10350.

Angelika Romanou, Negar Foroutan, Anna Sotnikova, Zeming Chen, Sree Harsha Nelaturu, Shivalika Singh, Rishabh Maheshwary, Micol Altomare, and Mohamed A. Haggag et al. 2024. Include: Evaluating multilingual language understanding with regional knowledge. *Preprint*, arXiv:2411.19799.

Keisuke Sakaguchi, Ronan Le Bras, Chandra Bhagavatula, and Yejin Choi. 2019. Winogrande: An adversarial winograd schema challenge at scale. *Preprint*, arXiv:1907.10641.

SarvamAI. 2023. Openhathi series: An approach to build bilingual llms frugally.

Rico Sennrich, Barry Haddow, and Alexandra Birch. 2016. Improving neural machine translation models with monolingual data. In *Proceedings of the 54th Annual Meeting of the Association for Computational Linguistics (Volume 1: Long Papers)*, pages 86–96, Berlin, Germany. Association for Computational Linguistics.

Luísa Shimabucoro, Sebastian Ruder, Julia Kreutzer, Marzieh Fadaee, and Sara Hooker. 2024. Llm see, llm do: Guiding data generation to target non-differentiable objectives. *Preprint*, arXiv:2407.01490.

Emma Strubell, Ananya Ganesh, and Andrew McCallum. 2019. Energy and policy considerations for deep learning in nlp. *ArXiv*, abs/1906.02243.

Rohan Taori, Ishaan Gulrajani, Tianyi Zhang, Yann Dubois, Xuechen Li, Carlos Guestrin, Percy Liang, and Tatsunori B. Hashimoto. 2023. Stanford alpaca: An instruction-following llama model.

Jesse Vig. 2019. A multiscale visualization of attention in the transformer model. In *Proceedings of the 57th Annual Meeting of the Association for Computational Linguistics: System Demonstrations*, pages 37–42, Florence, Italy. Association for Computational Linguistics.

Jesse Vig and Yonatan Belinkov. 2019. Analyzing the structure of attention in a transformer language model. In *Proceedings of the 2019 ACL Workshop BlackboxNLP: Analyzing and Interpreting Neural Networks for NLP*, pages 63–76, Florence, Italy. Association for Computational Linguistics.

Pablo Villalobos, Anson Ho, Jaime Sevilla, Tamay Besiroglu, Lennart Heim, and Marius Hobbhahn. 2024. Will we run out of data? limits of llm scaling based on human-generated data. *Preprint*, arXiv:2211.04325.

Elena Voita, David Talbot, Fedor Moiseev, Rico Sennrich, and Ivan Titov. 2019. Analyzing multi-head self-attention: Specialized heads do the heavy lifting, the rest can be pruned. In *Proceedings of the 57th Annual Meeting of the Association for Computational Linguistics*, pages 5797–5808, Florence, Italy. Association for Computational Linguistics.

Wenhan Xia, Chengwei Qin, and Elad Hazan. 2024. Chain of lora: Efficient fine-tuning of language models via residual learning. *Preprint*, arXiv:2401.04151.

Rong Zhang, Revanth Gangi Reddy, Md Arafat Sultan, Vittorio Castelli, Anthony Ferritto, Radu Florian, Efsun Sarioglu Kayi, Salim Roukos, Avi Sil, and Todd Ward. 2020. Multi-stage pre-training for low-resource domain adaptation. In *Proceedings of the 2020 Conference on Empirical Methods in Natural Language Processing (EMNLP)*, pages 5461–5468, Online. Association for Computational Linguistics.

Jiawei Zhao, Zhenyu Zhang, Beidi Chen, Zhangyang Wang, Anima Anandkumar, and Yuandong Tian. 2024. Galore: Memory-efficient llm training by gradient low-rank projection. *Preprint*, arXiv:2403.03507.

Çağatay Yıldız, Nishaanth Kanna Ravichandran, Prishruit Punia, Matthias Bethge, and Beyza Ermis. 2024. Investigating continual pretraining in large language models: Insights and implications. *Preprint*, arXiv:2402.17400.

POS-Aware Neural Approaches for Word Alignment in Dravidian Languages

Antony Alexander James, Parameswari Krishnamurthy
International Institute of Information Technology, Hyderabad, India
antonyalexander8942@gmail.com, param.krishna@iiit.ac.in

Abstract

This research explores word alignment in low-resource languages, specifically focusing on Telugu and Tamil, two languages within the Dravidian language family. Traditional statistical models such as FastAlign, GIZA++, and Eflomal serve as baselines but are often limited in low-resource settings. Neural methods, including SimAlign and AWESOME-align, which leverage multilingual BERT, show promising results by achieving alignment without extensive parallel data. Applying these neural models to Telugu-Tamil and Tamil-Telugu alignments, we found that fine-tuning with POS-tagged data significantly improves alignment accuracy compared to untagged data, achieving an improvement of 6–7%. However, our combined embeddings approach, which merges word embeddings with POS tags, did not yield additional gains. Expanding the study, we included Tamil, Telugu, and English alignments to explore linguistic mappings between Dravidian and an Indo-European languages. Results demonstrate the comparative performance across models and language pairs, emphasizing both the benefits of POS-tag fine-tuning and the complexities of cross-linguistic alignment.

1 Introduction

Word alignment is an essential task in natural language processing (NLP), for machine translation (MT) and cross-lingual information transfer. In this research, we focus on the Dravidian languages i.e. Tamil and Telugu, alongside an Indo-European language i.e. English, to analyze the agglutinative nature of Dravidian languages in contrast with English. The Dravidian language family comprises 26 languages, linguistically classified into three groups: South, Central, and North (Krishnamurti, 2003). Dravidian languages exhibit an agglutinative structure, where words are formed by combining morphemes, with each morpheme retaining its meaning and function. Based on this structure, we hypothesize that intra-family word alignment (e.g., Telugu & Tamil) may be more accurate than alignment across language families (e.g., English & Dravidian). In this study, we conduct word alignment on four language pairs: Telugu-Tamil, Tamil-Telugu, English-Telugu, and English-Tamil.

Traditional word alignment models, particularly statistical ones like IBM Models (Brown et al., 1993), GIZA++ (Och and Ney, 2003), FastAlign (Dyer et al., 2013) and Efloma(Östling and Tiedemann, 2016), face limitations in low-resource languages like Telugu and Tamil, where parallel data is scarce. While these models perform well in high-resource settings due to their reliance on abundant parallel data, they are less effective for low-resource languages. Recently, neural network-based models utilizing multilingual embeddings from BERT (Devlin, 2018) and XLM-RoBERTa (Conneau, 2019) have shown promise in overcoming these data limitations, generating word alignments even with minimal parallel corpora.

SimAlign (Sabet et al., 2020) and AWESOME-align (Dou and Neubig, 2021) are two neural models that utilize multilingual contextual embeddings to align words across languages. SimAlign computes alignments based on embedding similarity, using alignment strategies like Argmax, Itermax, and Match. In contrast, AWESOME-align applies a softmax-based alignment extraction process that predicts word alignments by calculating alignment probabilities between source and target embeddings. To improve alignment accuracy, AWESOME-align fine-tunes BERT-based models on parallel corpora using techniques like Masked Language Modeling (MLM) and Translation Language Modeling (TLM). These techniques help the model learn cross-lingual representations by predicting masked tokens within and across sentences, further enhancing alignment quality. Together, these neural approaches have demonstrated substantial improvements in alignment accuracy

Proceedings of the First Workshop on Challenges in Processing South Asian Languages (CHiPSAL 2025), pages 154–159
January 19, 2025.

for low-resource languages, outperforming traditional statistical models (Sabet et al., 2020).

In addition to leverage multilingual BERT, we fine-tuned a mBERT model on POS-tagged English, Telugu, and Tamil paired data and applied it within both AWESOME-align and SimAlign to assess alignment accuracy improvements. We conducted alignment tasks before and after fine-tuning, comparing POS-tagged and untagged data to evaluate the impact of POS information. We also explored a novel approach by combining word and POS tag embeddings into enriched vectors, using two strategies: addition (summing embeddings) and concatenation (merging into an extended vector). Word alignments were extracted from these combined embeddings via cosine similarity to measure source-target word similarity. Although this combination approach aimed to leverage both semantic and syntactic information, results showed it did not significantly outperform alignments based solely on word embeddings.

Additionally, we expanded our study to include English alongside Telugu and Tamil, adding a cross-linguistic perspective. By aligning English-Telugu and English-Tamil pairs, we aimed to uncover potential linguistic patterns between the Dravidian and European language families. Using our fine-tuned mBERT approach on both POS-tagged and untagged data, we evaluated alignment accuracy across these language pairs. This helped us explore how well our methods work in mapping relationships between languages from different families, offering initial insights into the linguistic connections between Dravidian and European languages.

2 Data Preparation

For this research, we used parallel datasets covering Telugu & Tamil, English-Telugu, and English-Tamil pairs to conduct word alignment experiments. The Telugu and Tamil dataset was sourced from in-house resources, while the English-Telugu and English-Tamil data were obtained from the publicly available Samanantar (Ramesh et al., 2022) corpus.

In-House Telugu and Tamil Dataset: The in-house Telugu and Tamil dataset contains 13,000 manually translated sentences.[1] Prepared over a year, it reflects careful effort by annotators to ensure accuracy and linguistic quality, making it a reliable source for studying alignment within the Dravidian language family.

2.1 Data Preprocessing

To prepare the data for word alignment tasks, each sentence in the parallel corpora was tokenized using NLTK's tokenizer, ensuring a consistent tokenization scheme across all languages.

2.2 Part-of-Speech (POS) Tagging

All sentences in English, Telugu, and Tamil were POS-tagged using the Trankit library (Van Nguyen et al., 2021). This step added syntactic information to each token, which was used in later stages of the experiment to assess the impact of POS-tagged data on word alignment accuracy.

2.3 Dataset Splitting and Annotation

The dataset is divided into two subsets: training and testing. For each language pair, we allocated 12,000 sentence pairs for training and 1,000 sentence pairs for testing. To ensure an accurate evaluation, the test dataset was manually annotated with gold-standard word alignments by expert annotators, establishing a reliable reference for alignment quality assessment.

2.4 Data Organization for Alignment Tools

The source and target corpora were organized based on the input requirements of the alignment tools used in this study. Each dataset was structured to match the specific formats expected by SimAlign and AWESOME-align, ensuring compatibility and streamlined processing for word alignment tasks.

3 Methodology

3.1 Word Alignment with SimAlign and AWESOME-align

We conducted word alignment tasks using SimAlign and AWESOME-align across four language pairs: Telugu-Tamil, Tamil-Telugu, English-Tamil, and English-Telugu. Both models used multilingual BERT (mBERT) embeddings to generate cross-lingual word alignments. Data preprocessing steps, such as tokenization and POS tagging, are detailed in the Data Preparation section.

Embedding Extraction: For AWESOME-align, embeddings were extracted from the 8th layer of mBERT, which captures a balance of syntax and semantics (Dou and Neubig, 2021). SimAlign, which operates at the subword level, averaged subword embeddings to obtain word-level representations.

[1] https://github.com/parameshkrishnaa/Alignment-Parallel-Data/

It considers all 12 layers of mBERT and can use a concatenation of these layers (mBERT[conc]), providing flexible options without additional fine-tuning (Sabet et al., 2020).

Alignment Computation: The alignments were computed based on similarity matrices generated from the contextualized embeddings of each word in the parallel sentences. For SimAlign, the alignments were calculated using three strategies:

Argmax: Aligning words based on their maximum similarity score. *Itermax:* Focusing on mutual consistency between source and target alignments. *Match:* Using a bipartite matching algorithm to optimize total similarity between words.

In AWESOME-align, alignments were generated by leveraging probability thresholding to produce the final alignment pairs. This stage provided a baseline comparison between pre-trained neural alignment models.

3.1.1 Fine-tuning the Multilingual BERT Model

To improve alignment accuracy, mBERT was fine-tuned on 12,000 parallel sentence pairs for each language pair, following the AWESOME-align approach (Dou and Neubig, 2021), with two main objectives:

Masked Language Modeling (MLM): Enhances understanding by training the model to predict masked tokens. Translation Language Modeling (TLM): Reinforces cross-lingual representations by processing source and target sentences together.

This fine-tuned model was then utilized in both SimAlign and AWESOME-align. This phase allowed us to directly compare the performance of the pre-trained mBERT model against its fine-tuned version, thereby assessing the improvement in alignment accuracy when fine-tuning is applied to low-resource parallel data.

3.2 Word Alignment on POS-Tagged Data

To examine the effect of Part-of-Speech (POS) information, we conducted additional alignment tasks using POS-tagged data across all language pairs.

Alignments were performed with both SimAlign and AWESOME-align, following the same procedures as in the initial experiments. This allowed us to compare alignment accuracy between untagged and POS-tagged data.

3.2.1 Fine-tuning on POS-Tagged Data

We further evaluated alignment accuracy by fine-tuning mBERT on POS-tagged parallel data. This fine-tuning process followed the same MLM and TLM objectives as previously described, using POS-tagged sentence pairs for each language pair.

After fine-tuning, alignments were computed with both SimAlign and AWESOME-align to assess the impact of POS-tagged data on alignment accuracy in low-resource settings.

3.3 Embedding Combination and Cosine Similarity for Word Alignment

The methodology for combining word and part-of-speech (POS) tag embeddings in our research is inspired from (Siekmeier et al., 2021). In their study, the authors demonstrated the effectiveness of integrating linguistic annotations, such as POS tags and named entity recognition (NER) tags, into neural machine translation models to improve translation accuracy. Specifically, they proposed a method for combining token and tag embeddings within the encoder of the neural translation system. Their approach yielded significant improvements in translation quality, particularly when working with named entity tags, indicating that embedding linguistic features at the token level can enhance performance in specific NLP tasks.

Building upon this concept, we applied a similar embedding combination technique to the word alignment task in our study. The goal was to leverage both semantic and syntactic information by combining word embeddings with their corresponding POS tag embeddings. This was accomplished in two distinct ways:

Addition: In this approach, the word embeddings and their respective POS tag embeddings were summed element-wise to create a single, combined vector. This method preserves the dimensionality of the original word embeddings while integrating syntactic features at each token level.

Concatenation: For this method, the word embeddings and POS tag embeddings were concatenated, resulting in a more comprehensive feature vector. This concatenation allows for the representation of both semantic and syntactic information simultaneously, capturing a richer linguistic context for each token.

After generating the combined embeddings, a **cosine similarity matrix** was applied to compute the alignment between words in the source and target languages across multiple language pairs: Telugu-Tamil, Tamil-Telugu, English-Telugu, and English-Tamil. The cosine similarity matrix measures the angular similarity between vectors in the embedding space, allowing for the identification of corresponding word pairs based on their similarity in both the semantic and syntactic dimensions.

4 Baseline

We compare our results against three widely used statistical word alignment models that rely on parallel training data:

- **FastAlign** (Dyer et al., 2013) is based on IBM Model 2 (Brown et al.), valued for its speed and simplicity while maintaining reasonable alignment quality.
- **Eflomal** (Östling and Tiedemann, 2016) is a Bayesian alignment model that uses Markov Chain Monte Carlo inference and is known to outperform FastAlign in both speed and accuracy.
- **GIZA++** (Och and Ney, 2003) is a well-established tool implementing IBM Models 1 to 4 (Brown et al., 1993). It is widely used in machine translation, and we used standard settings, including five iterations of the Hidden Markov Model (HMM) (Eddy, 1996) phase.

These statistical models serve as the baseline for evaluating the performance of neural approaches, particularly in low-resource language pairs like Telugu and Tamil.

5 Evaluation Measures

To evaluate alignment accuracy, we used the following measures:

- **Precision**: Measures the proportion of correct alignments out of all alignments made by the model.

$$Precision = \frac{|A \cap G|}{|A|}$$

- **Recall**: Measures the proportion of correct alignments out of all alignments in the gold-standard set.

$$Recall = \frac{|A \cap G|}{|G|}$$

- **Alignment Error Rate (AER)**: Provides an overall error rate by combining precision and recall. Lower AER indicates better alignment accuracy.

$$AER = 1 - \frac{2 \times |A \cap G|}{|A| + |G|}$$

- **F1 Score**: Balances precision and recall, providing a single accuracy score.

$$F1 = 2 \times \frac{Precision \times Recall}{Precision + Recall}$$

In these formulas, A represents the alignments predicted by the model, G represents the gold-standard alignments, and $|A \cap G|$ is the count of correct alignments.

6 Results

Neural vs. Statistical Models: Neural models (SimAlign and AWESOME-align) outperformed statistical models (GIZA++, FastAlign, and Eflomal) across all language pairs. The biggest improvements were seen in the Telugu-Tamil and Tamil-Telugu pair as shown in table [1] suggesting that neural models with multilingual embeddings work especially well for low-resource languages. SimAlign (Sabet et al., 2020), in particular, demonstrated the best performance among the neural models, especially for Telugu-Tamil and Tamil-Telugu pairs, due to shared linguistic features. In contrast, the improvements were smaller for English-Telugu and English-Tamil as shown in [1], likely because these language pairs lack similar structural features.

Effect of Fine-Tuning: Fine-tuning the multilingual BERT model improved alignment accuracy for all pairs, with the largest gains again in the Telugu-Tamil and Tamil-Telugu pair. Using Masked Language Modeling (MLM) and Translation Language Modeling (TLM) helped the model better understand cross-lingual connections, especially in Dravidian languages with shared grammatical structures.

Impact of POS-Tagged Data (Before and After Fine-Tuning): POS tagging was most beneficial for the Telugu-Tamil and Tamil-Telugu pairs after fine-tuning as shown in table [1], compared to untagged alignments. While the improvement was notable, the results were very low for the English-Telugu and English-Tamil pairs as shown in table[1]. This suggests that morphologically complex

Model	Type	Language pair							
		Telugu - Tamil		*Tamil - Telugu*		*English - Telugu*		*English - Tamil*	
		F1 ↑	**AER ↓**	**F1 ↑**	**AER ↓**	**F1 ↑**	**AER ↓**	**F1 ↑**	**AER ↓**
Fast-align	*untagged*	56.6	43.4	58.3	41.7	25.7	74.3	20.4	79.6
Giza++	*untagged*	54.7	45.3	56.8	43.7	23.3	76.7	17.8	82.2
Eflomal	*untagged*	65.5	34.5	67.7	32.3	27.8	72.2	12.4	87.6
SimAlign_inter	*untagged*	80.1	19.9	82.7	17.3	47	53	53.1	46.9
SimAlign_itermax	*untagged*	78.2	21.8	80.5	19.5	52.6	47.4	**54.8**	**45.2**
SimAlign_mwmf	*untagged*	73.2	26.8	75.5	24.5	52.9	47.1	52.4	47.6
Awesome_Align	*untagged*	64.2	35.8	66	34	23.2	76.8	31.8	68.2
SimAlign_inter_f	*untagged*	84.1	16	86.4	13.6	59.9	40.1	36.2	63.8
SimAlign_itermax_f	*untagged*	82.4	17.6	84.2	15.8	**65.6**	**34.4**	38.2	61.8
SimAlign_mwmf_f	*untagged*	74.3	25.7	76.4	23.6	65.3	34.7	37.6	62.4
Awesome_Align_f	*untagged*	65.9	34.1	67.8	32.2	37	63	27.1	72.9
SimAlign_inter	*tagged*	79.3	20.7	79.3	20.7	51.1	48.9	30.9	69.1
SimAlign_itermax	*tagged*	73.8	26.2	73.8	26.2	51.7	48.3	28.1	71.9
SimAlign_mwmf	*tagged*	70.8	29.2	70.8	29.2	49.1	50.9	26.6	73.4
Awesome_Align	*tagged*	71.7	28.3	68.1	31.9	30	70	19.2	80.8
Embed_add	*tagged*	41.2	58.8	34.4	65.6	20.5	79.5	12.6	87.4
Embed_concat	*tagged*	43.8	56.2	35.4	64.6	22.2	77.8	14.9	85.1
SimAlign_inter_f	*tagged*	**91.7**	**8.3**	**92.5**	**7.5**	64.6	35.4	37.3	62.7
SimAlign_itermax_f	*tagged*	84.4	15.6	84.6	15.4	60.1	39.9	31	69
SimAlign_mwmf_f	*tagged*	77.2	22.8	77.6	22.4	56.8	43.2	28.3	71.7
Awesome_Align_f	*tagged*	76.5	23.5	76.2	23.8	36.7	63.3	26.2	73.8
Embed_add_f	*tagged*	35.2	64.8	40.2	59.8	29.4	70.6	12.8	87.2
Embed_concat_f	*tagged*	37.9	62.1	58.9	41.1	34.4	65.6	15.3	84.7

Table 1: *Comparison of Word Alignments Across Language Pairs Using POS-Tagged and Untagged Datasets. The 'Type' column indicates whether the dataset used was POS-tagged or untagged. Models with 'f' denote fine-tuned versions, and the best results for each metric are highlighted in bold ('F1 ↑': highest value value is the better & 'AER ↓': lowest value is the better).*

languages like Telugu and Tamil gain more alignment accuracy from added POS information, while POS tagging is less useful for English-inclusive pairs where structural differences are more pronounced.

Combined Embeddings: Combining word and POS embeddings (through addition or concatenation) didn't significantly improve alignment accuracy over using word embeddings alone, even for Telugu and Tamil pairs, results shown in the tables[1] by the model names 'Embed_add & Embed_concat'. Although it could capture both meaning and structure, it didn't provide practical gains for these language pairs.

7 Limitations

While neural models showed strengths in low-resource alignment, this study faced several limitations that affected the quality of results. Dataset Quality, The Samanantar dataset for English-Telugu and English-Tamil contained translation inconsistencies, with many sentences poorly matched. This made it harder for alignment models to learn accurate mappings. High-quality, carefully curated parallel data is needed for better alignment and cross-linguistic analysis. Computational Constraints, Limited computational resources restricted the level of fine-tuning and testing of larger models. This limitation reduced the ability to optimize hyperparameters and experiment with deeper models that might improve accuracy. More computational resources would allow for broader testing and potentially better alignment results.

8 Conclusion

This study shows that neural models work better than traditional statistical models for word alignment, especially among low-resource Dravidian language pairs like Telugu and Tamil. Neural models consistently achieved higher accuracy, with SimAlign (Sabet et al., 2020) performing particularly well in Telugu-Tamil and Tamil-Telugu alignments, likely due to shared structural features within the Dravidian language family. However, this advantage was smaller when aligning Dravidian languages with English, which has a different structure.

Fine-tuning with POS-tagged data improved alignment accuracy the most in Telugu-Tamil and Tamil-Telugu pairs, as the POS information helped the model understand sentence structure better. In English-inclusive pairs (English-Telugu, English-Tamil), POS tagging had less impact, likely due to structural differences and some limitations in dataset quality.

Combining word and POS embeddings did not lead to additional accuracy gains. Although it aimed to capture both meaning and structure, this approach did not perform better than using word embeddings alone.

In summary, our findings shows the adaptability of neural models to the linguistic structures of Dravidian languages, showing promise for improving alignment in low-resource Dravidian language pairs. Future research could build on these results by experimenting with enhanced fine-tuning techniques, exploring additional syntactic or morphological features, and addressing the dataset quality issues in English-Dravidian pairs to improve alignment accuracy further.

References

Peter F Brown, Stephen A Della Pietra, Vincent J Della Pietra, and Robert L Mercer. 1993. The mathematics of statistical machine translation: Parameter estimation. *Computational linguistics*, 19(2):263–311.

A Conneau. 2019. Unsupervised cross-lingual representation learning at scale. *arXiv preprint arXiv:1911.02116*.

Jacob Devlin. 2018. Bert: Pre-training of deep bidirectional transformers for language understanding. *arXiv preprint arXiv:1810.04805*.

Zi-Yi Dou and Graham Neubig. 2021. Word alignment by fine-tuning embeddings on parallel corpora. *arXiv preprint arXiv:2101.08231*.

Chris Dyer, Victor Chahuneau, and Noah A Smith. 2013. A simple, fast, and effective reparameterization of ibm model 2. In *Proceedings of the 2013 conference of the North American chapter of the association for computational linguistics: human language technologies*, pages 644–648.

Sean R Eddy. 1996. Hidden markov models. *Current opinion in structural biology*, 6(3):361–365.

Bhadriraju Krishnamurti. 2003. The dravidian languages. *The Cambridge University*.

Franz Josef Och and Hermann Ney. 2003. A systematic comparison of various statistical alignment models. *Computational linguistics*, 29(1):19–51.

Robert Östling and Jörg Tiedemann. 2016. Efficient word alignment with markov chain monte carlo. *The Prague Bulletin of Mathematical Linguistics*, 106(1):125.

Gowtham Ramesh, Sumanth Doddapaneni, Aravinth Bheemaraj, Mayank Jobanputra, Raghavan Ak, Ajitesh Sharma, Sujit Sahoo, Harshita Diddee, Divyanshu Kakwani, Navneet Kumar, et al. 2022. Samanantar: The largest publicly available parallel corpora collection for 11 indic languages. *Transactions of the Association for Computational Linguistics*, 10:145–162.

Masoud Jalili Sabet, Philipp Dufter, François Yvon, and Hinrich Schütze. 2020. Simalign: High quality word alignments without parallel training data using static and contextualized embeddings. *arXiv preprint arXiv:2004.08728*.

Aren Siekmeier, WonKee Lee, Hongseok Kwon, and Jong-Hyeok Lee. 2021. Tag assisted neural machine translation of film subtitles. In *Proceedings of the 18th International Conference on Spoken Language Translation (IWSLT 2021)*, pages 255–262.

Minh Van Nguyen, Viet Dac Lai, Amir Pouran Ben Veyseh, and Thien Huu Nguyen. 2021. Trankit: A light-weight transformer-based toolkit for multilingual natural language processing. *arXiv preprint arXiv:2101.03289*.

neDIOM: Dataset and Analysis of Nepali Idioms

Rhitabrat Pokharel and Ameeta Agrawal
Department of Computer Science
Portland State University, USA
{pokharel,ameeta}@pdx.edu

Abstract

Idioms, integral to any language, convey nuanced meanings and cultural references. However, beyond English, few resources exist to support any meaningful exploration of this unique linguistic phenomenon. To facilitate such an inquiry in a low resource language, we introduce a novel dataset of Nepali idioms and the sentences in which these naturally appear. We describe the methodology of creating this resource as well as discuss some of the challenges we encountered. The results of our empirical analysis under various settings using four distinct multilingual models consistently highlight the difficulties these models face in processing Nepali figurative language. Even fine-tuning the models yields limited benefits. Interestingly, the larger models from the BLOOM family of models failed to consistently outperform the smaller models. Overall, we hope that this new resource will facilitate further development of models that can support processing of idiomatic expressions in low resource languages such as Nepali.

1 Introduction

Idioms are inherent linguistic phenomena in all languages, comprising a collection of words that, when combined, convey a unique and distinct meaning not achievable by the individual words within the phrase. Neglecting idioms would lead to a significant loss of meaning and context, given their tendencies to carry nuances and cultural references. Properly identifying and processing idioms is essential for machine translation, sentiment analysis, information retrieval, and several other tasks. Large language models (LLMs), such as GPT and LLaMa are designed to mimic human language understanding and generation. A comprehensive grasp of idioms is crucial to ensure that these models generate text that is not only linguistically accurate but also contextually meaningful.

There are plenty of idiom resources for high resource languages such as English (Korkontzelos et al., 2013; Tayyar Madabushi et al., 2021), Chinese (Tan and Jiang, 2021b), Japanese (Tedeschi et al., 2022), Italian (Tedeschi et al., 2022; Moussallem et al., 2018), and German (Tedeschi et al., 2022; Moussallem et al., 2018; Fadaee et al., 2018) to name a few. However, idioms in low resource languages have received less attention.

When resources are available, several interesting tasks involving idioms have been studied. Measuring semantic similarity between idioms (Korkontzelos et al., 2013), classification between idiomatic and literal usages of idioms (Tayyar Madabushi et al., 2021), translation (Moussallem et al., 2018) and language generation (Chakrabarty et al., 2022b; Pokharel and Agrawal, 2023) are some of the main focuses. However, we still do not know how LLMs process idioms in a low resource language like Nepali.

There might be a perception that plenty of methodologies and resources are readily available for the compilation of analogous linguistic phenomena, i.e., Multiword Expressions (MWEs). It is important to clarify that, MWEs constitute a broader linguistic category including not only idiomatic expressions but also other linguistic phenomena like noun compounds and sentence fragments, and the customary collection processes for MWEs, such as part-of-speech tagging (Farahmand et al., 2015) and statistical co-occurrence analysis (Kunchukuttan and Damani, 2008), prove to be insufficient in effectively distinguishing idiomatic expressions.

In this work, we introduce a novel dataset – neDIOM – of almost 200 Nepali idioms and more than 500 sentences of their contextual usage, making this, to our knowledge, the first such dataset in Nepali[1]. By contributing this resource, we hope to

[1]The dataset will be made available for further research.

Proceedings of the First Workshop on Challenges in Processing South Asian Languages (CHiPSAL 2025), pages 160–171
January 19, 2025.

facilitate exploration of LLMs' performance in handling idiomatic expressions and documenting linguistic phenomena in this low-resource language.

Depending on the language and the scenario, the idiom dataset creation job can be more or less challenging. For instance, in English, the idiom "under the weather" can be directly used in a sentence without alteration. However, "pull someone's leg" undergoes inflection, posing a significant challenge for automated idiom identification (Pasquer et al., 2020), especially in non-Latin languages. We enumerate further challenges related to dataset creation in the subsequent sections.

Our experiments with LLMs reveal that their performance with respect to idioms in low-resource languages leaves a big room for improvement.

The main contributions of our work are:

- The introduction of a new dataset in Nepali, which includes idioms, their contextual usage, and the marking of idiom positions.
- An extensive benchmarking of this dataset using several state-of-the-art LLMs.

2 Related Work

In this section, we review existing work in creating idiom resources and related tasks.

2.1 Idiom Datasets

The development of datasets focusing on idioms has seen some diversity across multiple languages, with English being the predominant language (Peng et al., 2015; Haagsma et al., 2020; Chakrabarty et al., 2022b). Attention has also extended to well-resourced languages like French, Dutch, Italian, Portuguese, Chinese, Polish, and Japanese (Korkontzelos et al., 2013; Moussallem et al., 2018; Tan and Jiang, 2021b; Tedeschi et al., 2022; Qiang et al., 2023). In contrast, languages with fewer resources, including Gujarati, Telugu, and Malayalam, have received less investigation (Agrawal et al., 2018). Notably, for Nepali, there is only one small dataset with 42 samples and without context sentences (Neupane, 2018).

Some datasets were created by translating idioms from English to other languages (Moussallem et al., 2018; Neupane, 2018; Fadaee et al., 2018; Tang, 2022), but the translated idioms are not always an idiom in the target language (Agrawal et al., 2018). In the cases when datasets have been created from scratch, the idioms are typically collected from one source and the sentences containing the idioms from another source (Korkontzelos et al., 2013; Peng et al., 2015; Fadaee et al., 2018; Zheng et al., 2019; Haagsma et al., 2020; Tan and Jiang, 2021b; Tedeschi et al., 2022). For the former step, most idioms are collected from sources where the idioms are already listed as such, precluding the need to identify the idiom from a sentence/paragraph (Korkontzelos et al., 2013; Fadaee et al., 2018; Zheng et al., 2019; Haagsma et al., 2020; Tedeschi et al., 2022). For the latter step (i.e., collecting the context where the idioms have been used), Haagsma et al. (2020) used automatic method which was later checked by manual reviewers, while Tayyar Madabushi et al. (2021) manually collected both the idioms and the contexts manually from the internet. Annotations for idiom-related tasks are also often obtained manually (Agrawal et al., 2018; Neupane, 2018; Haagsma et al., 2020).

2.2 Idiom Tasks

Korkontzelos et al. (2013) presented work on **semantic similarity**, encompassing idioms across English, French, German, and Italian. (Salehi et al., 2018) investigate the compositionality of idiomatic expressions by leveraging multilingual lexical resources, focusing on English and Germanic languages. Tan and Jiang (2021b) focused on gauging the similarity between idioms, concentrating specifically on the Chinese language. Chakrabarty et al. (2022b) studied natural language inference with a focus on idiomatic expressions in English.

Numerous studies have tackled the challenge of **distinguishing between idiomatic and literal language usage**, classifying expressions into idiomatic and literal categories (Peng et al., 2015; Tayyar Madabushi et al., 2021; Tan and Jiang, 2021a). Haagsma et al. (2020) classified idiomatic versus literal usages while also annotating their genre. Tedeschi et al. (2022) explored idiom identification across multiple languages, including Chinese, Dutch, French, Japanese, Polish, Portuguese, Spanish, and more. Other studies have also contributed to idiom classification, cloze tasks, and usage recognition across various languages (Zheng et al., 2019; Tian et al., 2023; Fenta and Gebeyehu, 2023; Zhou et al., 2023).

Translation of idiomatic expressions is another key area of investigation (Moussallem et al., 2018; Fadaee et al., 2018; Neupane, 2018; Agrawal et al., 2018; Tang, 2022). However, in several cases the translated idioms were not necessarily idioms in

Idiom	S1	S2	S3	Label	Idiom's Position
डाँडो काट्नु	जे छ त्यसमा नै चित्त बुझाएर दसैं कटाउने जोहो मिलाउनुहोस्।	पाहुना आफन्त बोलाउँदा खर्चले डाँडो काट्न सक्छ।	फेरि सानो रकम टीका लाएर दिँदा चित्त नबुझ्न सक्छ।	*I*	पाहुना आफन्त बोलाउँदा खर्चले ###डाँडो काट्न### सक्छ।
daando kaatnu	*j cha tesmaa nai, chitta bujhayera dashain kataune joho milaaunuhos*	*paahunaa aafanta boolaaundaa kharchale daando kaatna sakcha*	*feri saano rakam tikaa liyera dinda chitta nabujhna sakcha*		*paahunaa aafanta boolaaundaa kharchale ###daando kaatna### sakcha*
'to cover a considerable distance'	'Find contentment in whatever you have to celebrate Dashain.'	'Inviting guests and relatives could exceed the budget.'	'Given the circumstance, providing a small offering with Tika may not suffice.'		
इन्तु न चिन्तु हुनु	तर, यी युवाको उपचार नहुँदा शरीर कुहिन थालेको छ।	उनका बुवा बलबहादुर छोराको यो अवस्था देखेर इन्तु न चिन्तु छन्।	अस्पतालले भनेको तीन लाख रुपैयाँ जुटाउन नसकेपछि बस्नेतले सबैसँग हारगुहार गरे।	*L*	उनका बुवा बलबहादुर छोराको यो अवस्था देखेर ###इन्तु न चिन्तु### छन्।
intu na chintu hunu	*tara, yi yuwale upachaar nahundaa shareer kuhina thaaleko cha*	*unkaa buwaa balbahaadur choraako yo abasthaa dekhera intu na chintu chan*	*aspataalle vaneko teen laakh rupainyaa jutaauna nasakepachhi basnetle sabaisanga haarguhaar garey*		*unkaa buwaa balbahaadur choraako yo abasthaa dekhera ###intu na chintu chan###*
'to get overly anxious'	'However, due to the lack of treatment of this young man, the body has started to rot.'	'His father, Bal Bahadur, is deeply distraught upon witnessing his son's condition.'	'After failing to arrange the three lakh rupees as demanded by the hospital, Basnet has now turned to everyone.'		
आकाशको फल	तर, त्यसै बस्नुभन्दा म्युजिक भिडिओमा काम गर्दा पनि नयाँ नयाँ कुरा जान्न र अनुभव गर्न मिल्ने उनले बताए।	आज आकाशको फ्यान फलोर्स हजारौं छन्।	फुर्सदमा सामाजिक सञ्जालमा आफ्नो कामबारे सर्वसाधारणले गरेका कमेन्ट पनि पढ्ने गरेको उनले बताए।	*NA*	आज आकाशको फ्यान फलोर्स हजारौं छन्।
aakhaashko fal	*tara, tyasai basnubhandaa music videoma kaam gardaa pani nayaan nayaan kuraa jaanna ra anubhaab garna milne unle bataaye*	*aaja aakaahko fyan fallowers hajaaroun chhan*	*fursadmaa saamaajik sanjaalmaa aafno kaambaare sarwasaadharanle gareko kament pani padhne gareko unle bataaye*		*aaja aakaahko fyan fallowers hajaaroun chhan*
'a pie in the sky'	'However, he said that instead of sitting there, you can learn and experience new things while working on a music video.'	'Today Akash has thousands of fan followers.'	'He said that in his spare time, he also reads the comments made by public about his work on social media.'		

Table 1: Samples from the dataset, each associated with a distinct label.

the target language.

The **generation** of idiomatic expressions and their paraphrases has also attracted much attention. Chakrabarty et al. (2022a) investigated generating plausible continuations for idiomatic sentences in English, meanwhile Zhou et al. (2022); Qiang et al. (2023) focused on generating literal paraphrases. (Pokharel and Agrawal, 2023) evaluated language models' ability to generate contextually relevant continuations for narratives with idiomatic expressions in English and Portuguese.

Needless to say, yet important to highlight, is the fact that the exploration of idiomatic expressions in low-resource languages has received much less attention.

3 `neDIOM`: Nepali Idiom Dataset

We introduce `neDIOM`, a dataset of Nepali idioms along with their naturally-occurring contexts. The dataset comprises 526 carefully selected samples

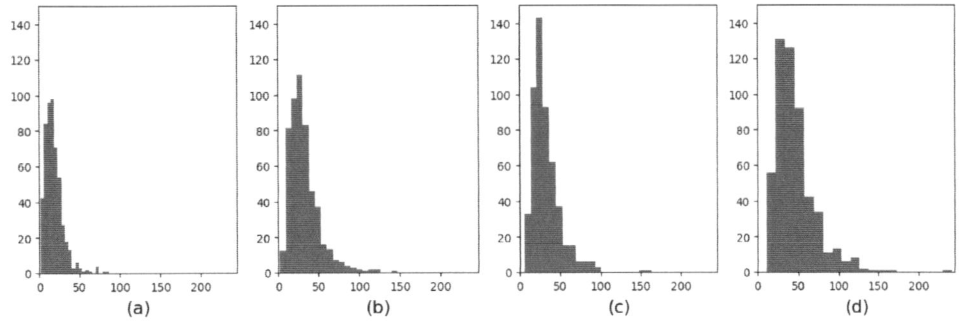

Figure 1: Distribution of sentence lengths for (a) *S2* (b) *S1* + *S2* (c) *S2* + *S3*, and (d) *S1* + *S2* + *S3*. On the x-axis is the number of words in a sentence, and on the y-axis is the frequency.

containing 191 unique idioms. Each sample includes the idiom, the sentence in which it appears, and the preceding and following sentences in the context. A selection of samples from the curated dataset is presented in Table 1. This dataset contains six attributes:

- *Idiom* is a multiword expression, whose overall meaning cannot be derived directly from the meanings of its individual words;
- *S2* is the sentence in which the idiom appears;
- *S1* is the sentence that precedes *S2* in the contextual sequence;
- *S3* is the sentence that follows *S2* in the context;
- *Label* indicates the annotation, whether the idiom is being used in an idiomatic sense or a literal sense; and
- *Idiom's position* specifies the exact location of the idiom within *S2*.

3.1 Data Collection

Next, we outline the methodology used for creating this dataset.

Collecting idioms A total of 296 idioms were manually collected from across the internet and from the reference (आचार्य, ऋषिकेश, 2020). These idioms were subsequently used to extract contextual usage. One might wonder why the context was not collected simultaneously along with these expressions. The reason is that the sources from which we obtained the idioms mostly provided definitions or descriptions without the associated contexts.

Collecting contexts with idioms The next step focuses on collecting naturally-occurring sentences and contexts in which these idioms appear. We use the OSCAR corpus[2], an expansive multilingual collection with over 152 languages, which is a result of the language-wise classification of content from the Common Crawl corpus[3]. We chose this corpus because of the abundance of Nepali text it offered, approximately 392K documents, which is particularly significant for Nepali, a language with considerable resource constraints.

The idioms originally appear in gerund form which changes its grammatical structure when used in a sentence. To identify relevant sentences containing these idioms, we adopted a strategy of using partial segments of the idioms. For instance, for the idiom नाक खुम्च्याउनु (*naak khumchyaaunu*, 'to turn up one's nose'), we employed the truncated version नाक ख (*naak kha*) to expand our search scope. In this context, खु (*khu*) represents the initial syllable of the word खुम्च्याउनु (*khumchyaaunu*) and ख (*kha*) stands as the first grapheme, which maintains consistency regardless of the word's usage. We utilized a similar technique for idioms containing more than two words.

After extracting documents from the OSCAR corpus, we tokenized them at sentence-level to obtain *S1*, *S2*, *S3* for each idiom instance using the *indic_tokenize* module[4]. This process resulted in a total of 1,216 samples (idioms and their surrounding contexts). It is worth noting that of the 296 idioms we had used in our search, we were able to collect contexts for 271 idioms. These were further reduced to 191 idioms after manual annotation.

Figure 1 plots the context sentence lengths of *S2*, *S1*+*S2*, *S2*+*S3*, and *S1*+*S2*+*S3*. We observe that most sentences with idioms (*S2*) consist of 50

[2] https://huggingface.co/datasets/oscar-corpus/OSCAR-2201

[3] https://commoncrawl.org/

[4] https://indic-nlp-library.readthedocs.io/en/latest/indicnlp.tokenize.html

Idiom	Lemma	S2	Lemmatized S2
आलु खानु	**['आलु', 'खान']**	छोरा‌ले परीक्षामा दुई ओटा विषयमा **आलु खाएछ** ।	'छोरा', 'परीक्षामा', 'दुई', 'ओटा', 'विषय', **'आलु', 'खा'**
aalu khaanu	*aalu khaana*	*chhoraale pareekchyaamaa dui otaa bishayamaa aalu khaayechha*	*'chhoraa', 'parikchyaamaa', 'dui', 'otaa', 'bishaya', 'aalu', 'khaa'*
'come up empty-handed'		'My son got a zero in two subjects in the exam.'	

Table 2: An example showing the challenges with lemmatization: खानु and खाएछ have different lemmatized forms.

Figure 2: Word cloud showing the most common to the least common idioms in the dataset.

tokens or less. Adding the preceding or following sentences usually doubles the length. These details enable us to estimate the average input length when passing the data to the LLMs for efficient processing. . The three most frequent idioms are ठीक पार्नु (*theek paarnu*, 'to make right'), डाँडो काट्नु (*daando kaatnu*, 'to go far away'), and हात लाग्नु (*haat laagnu*, 'to get hold of something') as shown in the word cloud in Figure 2.

3.2 Challenges

To build our dataset, we needed a list of idioms along with the contexts in which they were used. This presented a bit of a "chicken-and-egg" problem. If we can obtain idioms from a source, why not also gather their contextual sentences from the same source? In many cases, such as ours, this is simply not available. Alternatively, if we have sentences with idioms, could we not simply extract the idioms automatically? Idioms appear infrequently in text, and identifying them within a specific context is challenging. This made the dataset creation process more complex than it might initially seem. Some of the issues encountered during the development of `neDIOM` are discussed below.

Lack of language resources: The availability of comprehensive idiom repositories, especially in low-resource languages, is scarce. While some sources offer lists of idioms[5], these compilations are often quite small. Furthermore, even after a list of idioms has been collected, identifying pertinent contexts that include these idioms is quite a challenge. For instance, within a corpus of 392K Nepali documents, we were able to extract contexts for only 271 (91%) of the idioms in our list. Of those, many were filtered out during manual annotation (described in the next section), leaving only about 191 (64%) of the idioms in the final `neDIOM` dataset.

Idiom Detection and Context Creation Challenges: Even with a list of idioms, the variation in how idiomatic expressions appear in text adds to the challenge. For instance, consider the idiom नाक खुम्च्याउनु (*naak khumchyaunu*, 'to turn up your nose') and the sentence कोठा सफा नगरेको देखेर आमाले **नाक खुम्च्याउनु** भयो । (*kothaa safaa nagareko dekhera aamaale naak khumchyaunu bhayo*, 'Mom turned up her nose upon seeing the room was not cleaned.'). The idiom's form has been altered in the sentence, making it difficult to identify its usage by a simple pattern-based search. On the other hand, using the complete expression for searching mostly resulted in null matches. Our attempts at employing similarity-based methodologies to identify sentences containing idioms also proved to be unsatisfactory.

Prior work used lemmatization to deconstruct idioms and locate them within sentences (Tedeschi et al., 2022; Fadaee et al., 2018). Nevertheless, this approach proved to be insufficient for Nepali where an existing Nepali lemmatizer[6] failed to identify the idioms within contexts, primarily because the lemmatized idioms within the contexts differed from the lemmatized version of the idiom, leading to no match. For example, in Table 2, खानु (*khaanu*) is lemmatized to खान *khaana* and खाएछ (*khaayecha*)

[5]Idioms fall under the category of multiword expressions `https://aclweb.org/aclwiki/Multiword_Expressions`

[6]`https://github.com/dpakpdl/NepaliLemmatizer`

to खा (*khaa*) although both of those words have the same uninflected form. There is a need for developing better lemmatization tool for Nepali's typology.

3.3 Data Annotation

In the data annotation phase, given an idiom along with sentences *S1*, *S2*, and *S3*, we asked the annotators to assess the coherence and relevance of the provided contextual sentences. This step was crucial to address any potential noise in the data collection step. The annotation process can be summarized as follows:

1. If the annotators considered the sentences to be coherent, the sample was labeled as *(I)diomatic* if the idiom was used in its idiomatic sense or labeled as *(L)iteral* if the idiom was used in a literal sense. Then the position of the idiom within *S2* was marked using tokens "###".
2. If the sentences were not deemed coherent, the sample was labeled as *NA*.

To ensure high-quality annotations, we engaged three annotators, all native Nepali speakers with a minimum of higher secondary education. Initially, each annotator annotated 10 sample sentences and their methodology and results were discussed in order to establish a consistent baseline for annotation. Then, the entire set of 1,216 samples was annotated separately by two annotators. Next, the annotations underwent a final review by the third expert annotator. It was discovered that there were discrepancies in 26 annotations between the two annotators. Overall, Annotator #1 had 2 incorrect annotations, while Annotator #2 had 24 incorrect annotations. These discrepancies were rectified in the final version of the dataset. Discarding the 'NA' samples (about 56% of the data) helped to filter out noisy or irrelevant samples, and collectively, the process yielded 408 'I' samples and 118 'L' samples, a total of 526 samples with 191 unique idioms. The higher ratio of 'I' labels in the dataset suggests that most of these idioms are typically used in idiomatic senses rather than a literal sense.

4 Experiments

4.1 Task Formulation

The new `neDIOM` dataset can facilitate several idioms-related tasks such as idiom identification, idiomaticity detection, generating continuations in idiomatic contexts, or with some additional annotations, idiom translation, and sentiment analysis. We explore the dataset further in the classic yet challenging task of idiomaticity detection. Given the context and/or the associated idiom, the task is to identify whether the idiom has been used in a literal or idiomatic sense in the context. This task can provide insights into a model's ability to distinguish between non-compositional figurative and literal meanings.

4.2 Experimental Setup

We used four different multilingual language models: XLM-R-279m[7] (Conneau et al., 2020), BLOOM-560m[8] (Scao et al., 2023), BLOOM-1b1[8], BLOOM-3b[8], BLOOM-7b[8], LlaMa2-7b[9] (Touvron et al., 2023), and GPT-3.5[10].

Out of the 526 samples in our dataset, 506 were used for testing and the remaining 20 for fine-tuning the models under two settings: 5-shot setting where the training data consisted of a total of 10 samples (5 from each label); and 10-shot setting where the training data consisted of 20 samples (10 from each label). We also report results of experiments under the zero-shot setting where no training data is used. The inputs were prepared in 8 ways: *S2* only, *S1+S2* only, *S2+S3* only, *S1+S2+S3* only, with each of these four variants used with or without idioms.

In zero-shot setting, since the models were not originally fine-tuned for our classification task, we applied a log-likelihood method, calculating the likelihood for each label based on the model's next-word predictions, and selected the label with the highest likelihood. For the classification task, the results are reported in terms of macro-averaged F1 scores across all the models. Additional implementation details are included in Appendix A.

5 Results and Discussion

Idiomatic vs. Literal Classification: Table 3 presents the results of our classification experiment. A mediocre F1 score indicates that the model's performance in distinguishing between literal and idiomatic labels was subpar, implying that it struggled

[7]`https://huggingface.co/xlm-roberta-base`

[8]`https://huggingface.co/docs/transformers/model_doc/bloom`

[9]`https://huggingface.co/docs/transformers/v4.34.1/model_doc/llama2`

[10]`https://platform.openai.com/docs/models/gpt-3-5`

Models	Zero Shot (w/ idioms)	Zero Shot (w/o idioms)	5-shot (w/ idioms)	5-shot (w/o idioms)	10-shot (w/ idioms)	10-shot (w/o idioms)
			S2			
XLM-R	0.44	0.18	0.50	0.44	0.44	0.19
BLOOM-560m	0.50	**0.52**	0.44	**0.52**	0.47	0.18
BLOOM-1b1	0.50	0.50	0.44	0.19	0.47	0.19
BLOOM-3b	0.46	0.37	0.19	0.44	0.44	0.20
BLOOM-7b	0.44	0.44	-	-	-	-
Llama2-7b	0.44	0.19	-	-	-	-
GPT-3.5	0.50	0.47	0.47	0.51	**0.52**	0.50
			S1+S2			
XLM-R	0.44	0.44	0.23	**0.47**	0.44	0.46
BLOOM-560m	0.29	0.35	0.18	**0.47**	0.33	0.44
BLOOM-1b1	0.48	0.51	0.46	0.44	0.18	0.19
BLOOM-3b	0.38	0.34	0.46	0.45	0.20	0.20
BLOOM-7b	0.19	0.32	-	-	-	-
Llama2-7b	0.44	0.18	-	-	-	-
GPT-3.5	**0.53**	0.48	0.44	0.4	**0.56**	0.47
			S2+S3			
XLM-R	0.44	0.44	0.18	**0.51**	0.44	0.46
BLOOM-560m	0.28	0.33	0.42	0.44	0.2	0.44
BLOOM-1b1	**0.47**	**0.47**	0.46	0.18	0.44	0.22
BLOOM-3b	0.34	0.33	0.43	0.43	0.18	0.18
BLOOM-7b	0.44	0.44	-	-	-	-
Llama2-7b	0.17	0.44	-	-	-	-
GPT-3.5	0.46	**0.47**	0.44	**0.51**	0.44	**0.50**
			S1+S2+S3			
XLM-R	0.44	0.44	0.18	0.53	0.44	0.50
BLOOM-560m	0.25	0.31	0.20	0.18	0.31	0.54
BLOOM-1b1	0.47	0.48	0.44	0.18	0.45	0.32
BLOOM-3b	0.31	0.30	0.18	0.18	-	-
BLOOM-7b	0.19	0.44	-	-	-	-
Llama2-7b	-	-	-	-	-	-
GPT-3.5	**0.51**	0.49	**0.55**	0.53	**0.55**	0.54

Table 3: F1 score results of the experiments run on various models under zero shot, 5-shot, and 10-shot settings. (w/ idioms) refers to the settings where idioms are present in the input, while (w/o idioms) indicates inputs without idioms. The models in bold represent the best performance for the corresponding setting.

to accurately classify both types of expressions. This suboptimal performance stresses the need for further refinement and investigation into enhancing the model's capabilities in this particular classification task.

Effect of With Idioms vs. Without Idioms: To assess the potential impact of explicitly informing the models about the presence of idiomatic expressions, we conducted each experiment in two distinct setups. In the "with idioms" setup, the input consisted of the context sentence(s) along with the associated idiom phrase, while in the "without idioms" setup, we presented the context without specifying the idiom.

As illustrated in Figure 3, the results revealed that the presence or absence of idiomatic expressions obtained mixed results. In certain instances, it led to performance enhancements, while in others, it did not yield significant improvements. This fluctuation in outcomes can likely be attributed to the models' limited familiarity with Nepali idiomatic expressions, which consequently constrained them to limited classification decisions.

Zero-shot vs Few-shot: The results of our experiments investigating whether fine-tuning led to improved predictions are plotted in Figure 4. We observe that the benefits of fine-tuning are rather limited, with only a few notable exceptions. Our initial assumption was that the LLMs, having been trained on extensive corpora, would adapt well to low-resource languages after some fine-tuning. Additionally, LLMs trained on substantial datasets from the same language family, even if they lack significant data from the low-resource language, would bring about cross-lingual benefits. However, our results show that few-shot fine-tuning did not

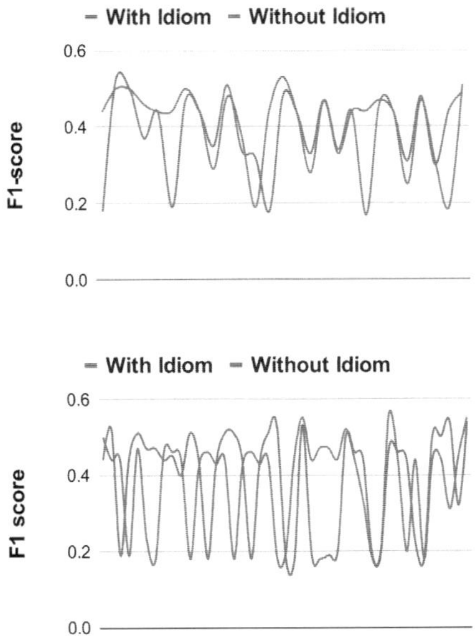

Figure 3: The line charts showing the averaged F1 scores under zero-shot setting (above) and both few-shot settings (below). Each data point on the x-axis represents a specific combination of model and context size.

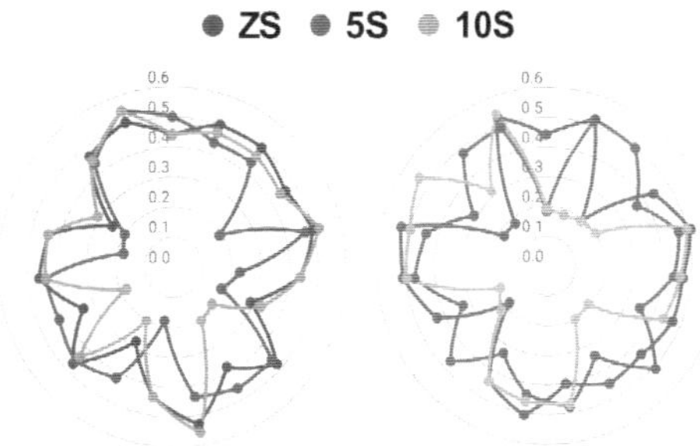

Figure 4: Plot showing the performance of the models under zero-shot (ZS), 5-shot (5S), and 10-shot (10S) settings with idiom (left) and without idiom (right).

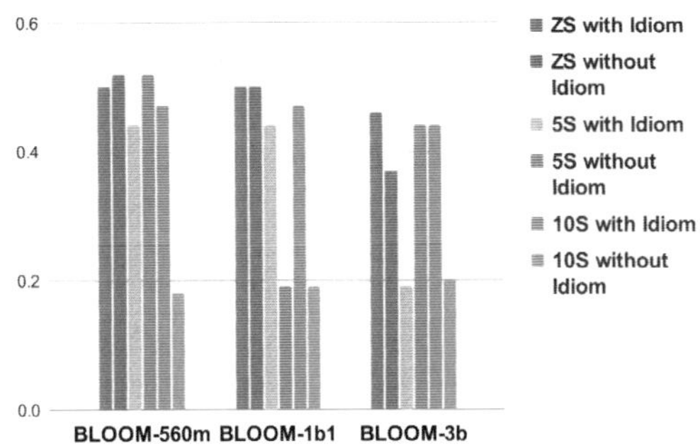

Figure 5: F1 scores of various sizes of BLOOM models when *S2* is used as input for idiom classification in zero-shot (ZS), 5-shot (5S), and 10-shot (10S) settings.

bring any additional gains, leaving significant room for enhancing LLM performance in low-resource language scenarios.

Impact of Model Size: In our experiments, we included several models of different sizes from the BLOOM family of models which allows us to draw insights regarding the comparable performance of smaller vs. larger models. The results are plotted in Figure 5. Curiously, contrary to the expectation that larger models within the same architecture would yield improved performance, the results do not consistently support this hypothesis. While there are minor enhancements in the 10-shot setting when idioms are not explicitly provided, the performance across other cases exhibits inconsistency. This phenomenon may be attributed to the shared training data for all three model variations (Scao et al., 2023). With an increase in model parameters, it appears that the available training data for low-resource languages may not be sufficient to adequately inform the expanded model capacity.

Effect of Surrounding Context: To evaluate the impact of the surrounding context on the comprehension of both idiomatic and literal scenarios, we conducted experiments in four distinct contexts: *S2*, *S1+S2*, *S2+S3*, and *S1+S2+S3*. Table 3 indicates that the sole instance of improved performance, associated with an increase in context, was observed with GPT-3.5. Performance saw a boost when all three context components – *S1*, *S2*, and *S3* – were provided, in comparison to scenarios where only *S1*, *S1+S2*, or *S2+S3* were presented. For all other models, it appears that using just *S2* is satisfactory and strikes a good balance between performance and efficiency.

6 Conclusion

In this study, we introduced a novel dataset, `neDIOM`, designed to facilitate research on idioms in low-resource languages, with a focus on Nepali. The dataset boasts high-quality content, as it was meticulously evaluated through manual assessment. Despite LLMs being extensively trained on data from high-resource languages within the same language family, their performance in low-resource language contexts fell short of expectations, even after fine-tuning. This highlights the urgency of making LLMs more inclusive to ensure their benefits are accessible to a broader population.

Limitations

We conducted only zero-shot experiments for some models due to resource limitations. Moreover, the data used was sourced from the internet, which may not fully represent all domains. As a low-resource language, we face challenges in finding abundant and high-quality online resources, such as literature books.

Our research identified several avenues for further exploration.

- First, there is a need for additional resources to create a more extensive and representative collection of Nepali idioms, with more fine-grained annotations.
- Second, it is important to refine the lemmatization methods to ensure consistency across various contexts when processing Nepali text, that will eventually help in automatic collection of idioms.
- Moving forward, our future plans also involve leveraging the positional information of idioms within the dataset to investigate how well LLMs can detect idiom positions.
- Additionally, we aim to develop techniques to enhance the models' performance when dealing with input containing idiomatic expressions in Nepali.

Ethical Considerations

Given that the dataset is sourced from a corpus comprising internet articles, it is possible that the texts may include content that could be potentially offensive to certain groups of people. Language models may inadvertently interpret idioms in ways that were not intended, as these idioms often express multiple meanings. Additionally, there are instances where specific idioms are closely tied to a particular culture's worldview, and this perspective may not necessarily align with the beliefs of other groups. The annotators received fair compensation for their work.

References

Ruchit Agrawal, Vighnesh Chenthil Kumar, Vigneshwaran Muralidharan, and Dipti Misra Sharma. 2018. No more beating about the bush: A step towards idiom handling for indian language nlp. In *Proceedings of the Eleventh International Conference on Language Resources and Evaluation (LREC 2018)*.

Tuhin Chakrabarty, Yejin Choi, and Vered Shwartz. 2022a. It's not rocket science: Interpreting figurative language in narratives. *Transactions of the Association for Computational Linguistics*, 10:589–606.

Tuhin Chakrabarty, Arkadiy Saakyan, Debanjan Ghosh, and Smaranda Muresan. 2022b. Flute: Figurative language understanding through textual explanations. In *Proceedings of the 2022 Conference on Empirical Methods in Natural Language Processing*, pages 7139–7159.

Alexis Conneau, Kartikay Khandelwal, Naman Goyal, Vishrav Chaudhary, Guillaume Wenzek, Francisco Guzmán, Edouard Grave, Myle Ott, Luke Zettlemoyer, and Veselin Stoyanov. 2020. Unsupervised cross-lingual representation learning at scale. In *Proceedings of the 58th Annual Meeting of the Association for Computational Linguistics*, pages 8440–8451, Online. Association for Computational Linguistics.

Marzieh Fadaee, Arianna Bisazza, and Christof Monz. 2018. Examining the tip of the iceberg: A data set for idiom translation. In *Proceedings of the Eleventh International Conference on Language Resources and Evaluation (LREC 2018)*, Miyazaki, Japan. European Language Resources Association (ELRA).

Meghdad Farahmand, Aaron Smith, and Joakim Nivre. 2015. A multiword expression data set: Annotating non-compositionality and conventionalization for english noun compounds. In *Proceedings of the 11th Workshop on Multiword Expressions*, pages 29–33.

Anduamlak Abebe Fenta and Seffi Gebeyehu. 2023. Automatic idiom identification model for amharic language. *ACM Transactions on Asian and Low-Resource Language Information Processing*.

Hessel Haagsma, Johan Bos, and Malvina Nissim. 2020. Magpie: A large corpus of potentially idiomatic expressions. In *Proceedings of the Twelfth Language Resources and Evaluation Conference*, pages 279–287.

Ioannis Korkontzelos, Torsten Zesch, Fabio Massimo Zanzotto, and Chris Biemann. 2013. Semeval-2013 task 5: Evaluating phrasal semantics. In *Second Joint Conference on Lexical and Computational Semantics (* SEM), Volume 2: Proceedings of the Seventh International Workshop on Semantic Evaluation (SemEval 2013)*, pages 39–47.

Anoop Kunchukuttan and Om Prakash Damani. 2008. A system for compound noun multiword expression extraction for hindi. In *6th International. Conference on Natural Language Processing*, pages 20–29. Citeseer.

Diego Moussallem, Mohamed Ahmed Sherif, Diego Esteves, Marcos Zampieri, and Axel-Cyrille Ngonga Ngomo. 2018. LIdioms: A multilingual linked idioms data set. In *Proceedings of the Eleventh International Conference on Language Resources and Evaluation (LREC 2018)*, Miyazaki,

Japan. European Language Resources Association (ELRA).

Nabaraj Neupane. 2018. Translating idioms from nepali into english. *Translation Today*, 12:83.

Caroline Pasquer, Agata Savary, Carlos Ramisch, and Jean-Yves Antoine. 2020. Verbal multiword expression identification: Do we need a sledgehammer to crack a nut? In *Proceedings of the 28th International Conference on Computational Linguistics*, pages 3333–3345, Barcelona, Spain (Online). International Committee on Computational Linguistics.

Jing Peng, Anna Feldman, and Hamza Jazmati. 2015. Classifying idiomatic and literal expressions using vector space representations. In *Proceedings of the International Conference Recent Advances in Natural Language Processing*, pages 507–511, Hissar, Bulgaria. INCOMA Ltd. Shoumen, BULGARIA.

Rhitabrat Pokharel and Ameeta Agrawal. 2023. Generating continuations in multilingual idiomatic contexts. In *Proceedings of the 3rd Workshop on Multi-lingual Representation Learning (MRL)*, pages 292–301, Singapore. Association for Computational Linguistics.

Jipeng Qiang, Yang Li, Chaowei Zhang, Yun Li, Yi Zhu, Yunhao Yuan, and Xindong Wu. 2023. Chinese idiom paraphrasing. *Transactions of the Association for Computational Linguistics*, 11:740–754.

Bahar Salehi, Paul Cook, and Timothy Baldwin. 2018. Exploiting multilingual lexical resources to predict mwe compositionality. In *Multiword expressions at length and in depth: Extended papers from the MWE 2017 workshop*, volume 2, page 343. Language Science Press.

Teven Le Scao, Angela Fan, Christopher Akiki, Ellie Pavlick, Suzana Ilić, Daniel Hesslow, Roman Castagné, Alexandra Sasha Luccioni, François Yvon, Matthias Gallé, Jonathan Tow, Alexander M. Rush, Stella Biderman, Albert Webson, Pawan Sasanka Ammanamanchi, Thomas Wang, Benoît Sagot, Niklas Muennighoff, Albert Villanova del Moral, Olatunji Ruwase, Rachel Bawden, Stas Bekman, Angelina Mcmillan-Major, Iz Beltagy, Huu Nguyen, Lucile Saulnier, Samson Tan, Pedro Ortiz Suarez, Victor Sanh, Hugo Laurençon, Yacine Jernite, Julien Launay, Margaret Mitchell, Colin Raffel, Aaron Gokaslan, Adi Simhi, Aitor Soroa, Alham Fikri Aji, Amit Alfassy, Anna Rogers, Ariel Kreisberg Nitzav, Canwen Xu, Chenghao Mou, Chris Emezue, Christopher Klamm, Colin Leong, Daniel van Strien, David Ifeoluwa Adelani, Dragomir Radev, Eduardo González Ponferrada, Efrat Levkovizh, Ethan Kim, Eyal Bar Natan, Francesco de Toni, Gérard Dupont, Germán Kruszewski, Giada Pistilli, Hady Elsahar, Hamza Benyamina, Hieu Tran, Ian Yu, Idris Abdulmumin, Isaac Johnson, Itziar Gonzalez-Dios, Javier de la Rosa, Jenny Chim, Jesse Dodge, Jian Zhu, Jonathan Chang, Jörg Frohberg, Joseph Tobing, Joydeep Bhattacharjee, Khalid Almubarak, Kimbo Chen, Kyle Lo, Leandro von Werra, Leon Weber, Long Phan, Loubna Ben Allal, Ludovic Tanguy, Manan Dey, Manuel Romero Muñoz, Maraim Masoud, María Grandury, Mario Šaško, Max Huang, Maximin Coavoux, Mayank Singh, Mike Tian-Jian Jiang, Minh Chien Vu, Mohammad A. Jauhar, Mustafa Ghaleb, Nishant Subramani, Nora Kassner, Nurulaqilla Khamis, Olivier Nguyen, Omar Espejel, Ona de Gibert, Paulo Villegas, Peter Henderson, Pierre Colombo, Priscilla Amuok, Quentin Lhoest, Rheza Harliman, Rishi Bommasani, Roberto Luis López, Rui Ribeiro, Salomey Osei, Sampo Pyysalo, Sebastian Nagel, Shamik Bose, Shamsuddeen Hassan Muhammad, Shanya Sharma, Shayne Longpre, Somaieh Nikpoor, Stanislav Silberberg, Suhas Pai, Sydney Zink, Tiago Timponi Torrent, Timo Schick, Tristan Thrush, Valentin Danchev, Vassilina Nikoulina, Veronika Laippala, Violette Lepercq, Vrinda Prabhu, Zaid Alyafeai, Zeerak Talat, Arun Raja, Benjamin Heinzerling, Chenglei Si, Elizabeth Salesky, Sabrina J. Mielke, Wilson Y. Lee, Abheesht Sharma, Andrea Santilli, Antoine Chaffin, Arnaud Stiegler, Debajyoti Datta, Eliza Szczechla, Gunjan Chhablani, Han Wang, Harshit Pandey, Hendrik Strobelt, Jason Alan Fries, Jos Rozen, Leo Gao, Lintang Sutawika, M Saiful Bari, Maged S. Al-Shaibani, Matteo Manica, Nihal Nayak, Ryan Teehan, Samuel Albanie, Sheng Shen, Srulik Ben-David, Stephen H. Bach, Taewoon Kim, Tali Bers, Thibault Fevry, Trishala Neeraj, Urmish Thakker, Vikas Raunak, Xiangru Tang, Zheng-Xin Yong, Zhiqing Sun, Shaked Brody, Yallow Uri, Hadar Tojarieh, Adam Roberts, Hyung Won Chung, Jaesung Tae, Jason Phang, Ofir Press, Conglong Li, Deepak Narayanan, Hatim Bourfoune, Jared Casper, Jeff Rasley, Max Ryabinin, Mayank Mishra, Minjia Zhang, Mohammad Shoeybi, Myriam Peyrounette, Nicolas Patry, Nouamane Tazi, Omar Sanseviero, Patrick von Platen, Pierre Cornette, Pierre François Lavallée, Rémi Lacroix, Samyam Rajbhandari, Sanchit Gandhi, Shaden Smith, Stéphane Requena, Suraj Patil, Tim Dettmers, Ahmed Baruwa, Amanpreet Singh, Anastasia Cheveleva, Anne-Laure Ligozat, Arjun Subramonian, Aurélie Névéol, Charles Lovering, Dan Garrette, Deepak Tunuguntla, Ehud Reiter, Ekaterina Taktasheva, Ekaterina Voloshina, Eli Bogdanov, Genta Indra Winata, Hailey Schoelkopf, Jan-Christoph Kalo, Jekaterina Novikova, Jessica Zosa Forde, Jordan Clive, Jungo Kasai, Ken Kawamura, Liam Hazan, Marine Carpuat, Miruna Clinciu, Najoung Kim, Newton Cheng, Oleg Serikov, Omer Antverg, Oskar van der Wal, Rui Zhang, Ruochen Zhang, Sebastian Gehrmann, Shani Pais, Tatiana Shavrina, Thomas Scialom, Tian Yun, Tomasz Limisiewicz, Verena Rieser, Vitaly Protasov, Vladislav Mikhailov, Yada Pruksachatkun, Yonatan Belinkov, Zachary Bamberger, Zdeněk Kasner, Alice Rueda, Amanda Pestana, Amir Feizpour, Ammar Khan, Amy Faranak, Ana Santos, Anthony Hevia, Antigona Unldreaj, Arash Aghagol, Arezoo Abdollahi, Aycha Tammour, Azadeh Hajihosseini, Bahareh Behroozi, Benjamin Ajibade, Bharat Saxena, Carlos Muñoz Ferrandis, Danish Contractor, David Lansky, Davis David, Douwe Kiela, Duong A. Nguyen,

Edward Tan, Emi Baylor, Ezinwanne Ozoani, Fatima Mirza, Frankline Ononiwu, Habib Rezanejad, Hessie Jones, Indrani Bhattacharya, Irene Solaiman, Irina Sedenko, Isar Nejadgholi, Jesse Passmore, Josh Seltzer, Julio Bonis Sanz, Livia Dutra, Mairon Samagaio, Maraim Elbadri, Margot Mieskes, Marissa Gerchick, Martha Akinlolu, Michael Mckenna, Mike Qiu, Muhammed Ghauri, Mykola Burynok, Nafis Abrar, Nazneen Rajani, Nour Elkott, Nour Fahmy, Olanrewaju Samuel, Ran An, Rasmus Kromann, Ryan Hao, Samira Alizadeh, Sarmad Shubber, Silas Wang, Sourav Roy, Sylvain Viguier, Thanh Le, Tobi Oyebade, Trieu Le, Yoyo Yang, Zach Nguyen, Abhinav Ramesh Kashyap, Alfredo Palasciano, Alison Callahan, Anima Shukla, Antonio Miranda-Escalada, Ayush Singh, Benjamin Beilharz, Bo Wang, Caio Brito, Chenxi Zhou, Chirag Jain, Chuxin Xu, Clémentine Fourrier, Daniel León Periñán, Daniel Molano, Dian Yu, Enrique Manjavacas, Fabio Barth, Florian Fuhrimann, Gabriel Altay, Giyaseddin Bayrak, Gully Burns, Helena U. Vrabec, Imane Bello, Ishani Dash, Jihyun Kang, John Giorgi, Jonas Golde, Jose David Posada, Karthik Rangasai Sivaraman, Lokesh Bulchandani, Lu Liu, Luisa Shinzato, Madeleine Hahn de Bykhovetz, Maiko Takeuchi, Marc Pàmies, Maria A Castillo, Marianna Nezhurina, Mario Sänger, Matthias Samwald, Michael Cullan, Michael Weinberg, Michiel de Wolf, Mina Mihaljcic, Minna Liu, Moritz Freidank, Myungsun Kang, Natasha Seelam, Nathan Dahlberg, Nicholas Michio Broad, Nikolaus Muellner, Pascale Fung, Patrick Haller, Ramya Chandrasekhar, Renata Eisenberg, Robert Martin, Rodrigo Canalli, Rosaline Su, Ruisi Su, Samuel Cahyawijaya, Samuele Garda, Shlok S Deshmukh, Shubhanshu Mishra, Sid Kiblawi, Simon Ott, Sinee Sang-Aroonsiri, Srishti Kumar, Stefan Schweter, Sushil Bharati, Tanmay Laud, Théo Gigant, Tomoya Kainuma, Wojciech Kusa, Yanis Labrak, Yash Shailesh Bajaj, Yash Venkatraman, Yifan Xu, Yingxin Xu, Yu Xu, Zhe Tan, Zhongli Xie, Zifan Ye, Mathilde Bras, Younes Belkada, and Thomas Wolf. 2023. BLOOM: A 176B-Parameter Open-Access Multilingual Language Model. Working paper or preprint.

Minghuan Tan and Jing Jiang. 2021a. Does bert understand idioms? a probing-based empirical study of bert encodings of idioms.

Minghuan Tan and Jing Jiang. 2021b. Learning and evaluating chinese idiom embeddings. In *Proceedings of the International Conference on Recent Advances in Natural Language Processing (RANLP 2021)*, pages 1387–1396.

Kenan Tang. 2022. Petci: A parallel english translation dataset of chinese idioms. *arXiv preprint arXiv:2202.09509*.

Harish Tayyar Madabushi, Edward Gow-Smith, Carolina Scarton, and Aline Villavicencio. 2021. AStitchInLanguageModels: Dataset and methods for the exploration of idiomaticity in pre-trained language models. In *Findings of the Association for Computational Linguistics: EMNLP 2021*, pages 3464–3477, Punta Cana, Dominican Republic. Association for Computational Linguistics.

Simone Tedeschi, Federico Martelli, and Roberto Navigli. 2022. Id10m: Idiom identification in 10 languages. In *Findings of the Association for Computational Linguistics: NAACL 2022*, pages 2715–2726.

आचार्य, ऋषिकेश. 2020. सरल नेपाली व्याकरण बोध र अभिव्यक्ति. JBD Publication Pvt. Ltd., Kathmandu. Available in Nepali language.

Ye Tian, Isobel James, and Hye Son. 2023. How are idioms processed inside transformer language models? In *Proceedings of the The 12th Joint Conference on Lexical and Computational Semantics (* SEM 2023)*, pages 174–179.

Hugo Touvron, Louis Martin, Kevin Stone, Peter Albert, Amjad Almahairi, Yasmine Babaei, Nikolay Bashlykov, Soumya Batra, Prajjwal Bhargava, Shruti Bhosale, et al. 2023. Llama 2: Open foundation and fine-tuned chat models. *arXiv preprint arXiv:2307.09288*.

Chujie Zheng, Minlie Huang, and Aixin Sun. 2019. ChID: A large-scale Chinese IDiom dataset for cloze test. In *Proceedings of the 57th Annual Meeting of the Association for Computational Linguistics*, pages 778–787, Florence, Italy. Association for Computational Linguistics.

Jianing Zhou, Ziheng Zeng, and Suma Bhat. 2023. Clcl: Non-compositional expression detection with contrastive learning and curriculum learning. In *Proceedings of the 61st Annual Meeting of the Association for Computational Linguistics (Volume 1: Long Papers)*, pages 730–743.

Jianing Zhou, Ziheng Zeng, Hongyu Gong, and Suma Bhat. 2022. Idiomatic expression paraphrasing without strong supervision. In *Proceedings of the AAAI Conference on Artificial Intelligence*, volume 36, pages 11774–11782.

A Implementation Details

Fine-tuning experiments were run on an A100 Tensor Core GPU, employing the AdamW optimizer for three epochs in each case. Due to resource limitations, fine-tuning was carried out for all models except for BLOOM-7b and LlaMa2-7b, for which only zero-shot experiments were conducted. We determined the maximum token length for each context based on the tokens generated by the models, ensuring that all context was encompassed in the model experiment. This length ranged from 200 subword tokens for S2 in the BLOOM-560m model to 1300 tokens for the combined context of S1, S2, and S3 in the LlaMa2 model. This approach ensured an efficient use of computational resources.

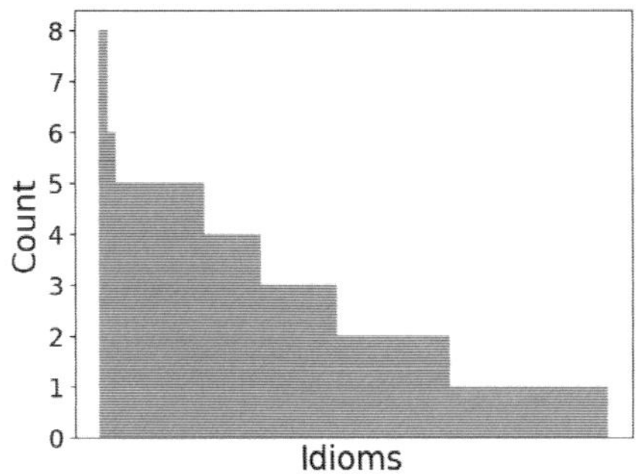

Figure 6: Histogram of idioms present in neDIOM.

B Exploratory Analysis

There are 191 unique idioms in the neDIOM dataset, with the minimum idiom length of 2 words and a maximum length of 4 words. Figure 6 presents the histogram of the idioms. While one idiom appears in 8 contexts, most idioms appear only once or twice in the dataset.

Bridging the Bandwidth Gap: A Mixed Band Telephonic Urdu ASR Approach with Domain Adaptation for Banking Applications

Ayesha Khalid[1*] **Farah Adeeba**[2*] **Najm Ul Sehar**[1] **Sarmad Hussain**[1]
[1]Center for Language Engineering, Al-Khawarizmi Institute of Computer Science,
University of Engineering and Technology, Lahore
[2]Department of Computer Science,
University of Engineering and Technology, New Campus
ayesha.khalid@kics.edu.pk, farah.adeeba@kics.edu.pk
najm.sehar@kics.edu.pk, sarmad.hussain@kics.edu.pk

Abstract

The accuracy of Automatic Speech Recognition (ASR) systems is influenced by the quality and context of speech signals, particularly in telephonic environments prone to errors like channel drops and noise, leading to higher Word Error Rates (WER). This paper presents the development of a large vocabulary Urdu ASR system for telephonic speech, based on a corpus of 445 speakers from diverse domains. The corpus, annotated at the sentence level, is used to train and evaluate GMM-HMM and chain Time-Delay Neural Network (TDNN) models on a 10-hour test set. Results show that the TDNN model outperforms GMM-HMM. Mixing narrowband and wideband speech further reduces WER. The test sets are also evaluated for the pre-trained model Whisper for performance comparison. Additionally, system adaptation for the banking domain with a specialized lexicon and language model demonstrates the system's potential for domain-specific applications.

1 Introduction

Human speech is a primary mode of communication, making speech recognition a vital area of research. While Automatic Speech Recognition (ASR) systems have made significant strides, approaching human-level performance in controlled environments, telephonic speech (narrowband, NB) remains a persistent challenge compared to studio-quality (wideband, WB) speech. The limitations in bandwidth, coupled with noise and distortion in telephony, degrade ASR performance. This issue is especially pronounced for resource-limited languages like Urdu, where training separate models for NB and WB speech can be difficult due to the scarcity of large-scale corpora.

This study aims to improve NB speech recognition by developing a Mixed-Band (MB) acoustic model using Deep Neural Networks (DNNs), which combines both NB and WB data. Two primary strategies for building MB acoustic models are Bandwidth Extension (BWE) and direct data mixing. While BWE has been widely explored to enhance speech quality and intelligibility (Prasad and Kumar, 2016; Nagel and Disch, 2009; Pulakka and Alku, 2011; Liu et al., 2009), its impact on improving recognition accuracy for mixed-band speech remains limited. In this work, directly mixing WB data with NB data to improve ASR performance for Urdu NB telephonic speech is proposed.

Developing robust ASR systems requires large corpora for both acoustic and language model training. Extensive corpora exist for languages such as English (Godfrey and Holliman, 1997; Post et al., 2013), Mandarin (Liu et al., 2006; Deng et al., 2019), Korean (Bang et al., 2020), and Polish (Ziółko et al., 2018). For instance, the Switchboard corpus (Godfrey and Holliman, 1997) provides 260 hours of conversational English, while the HKUST Mandarin Telephone Speech Corpus (Liu et al., 2006) offers 200 hours of telephonic data covering diverse dialects. A 969-hour corpus was developed for spontaneous Korean speech (Bang et al., 2020), and a 64-hour corpus for Polish telephony (Ziółko et al., 2018) spans domains like street and commands.

However, Urdu, spoken by 70 million people as a first language, remains under-resourced in terms of speech corpora for natural language processing. Notable efforts include the development of a 44.5-hour Urdu ASR system (Sarfraz et al., 2010), which combines microphone and telephone speech from 80 speakers, and domain-specific ASR systems for recognizing district names (Qasim et al., 2016; Rauf et al., 2015), achieving lab and field accuracies of 95.6% and 87.21%, respectively. Additionally, a Punjabi-accented banking-domain telephonic corpus (Mumtaz et al., 2018) with 400 speakers was recorded at 8 kHz and manually annotated.

Farooq et al. (Farooq et al., 2019) developed a

Proceedings of the First Workshop on Challenges in Processing South Asian Languages (CHiPSAL 2025), pages 172–184
January 19, 2025.

large vocabulary continuous speech recognition (LVCSR) system for Urdu, collecting 300 hours of training data from 1,648 speakers and achieving a word error rate (WER) of 13.50% on 9.5 hours of testing data. Despite these efforts, Urdu still lacks a large-scale telephonic speech corpus, particularly for domain-specific applications like banking.
In this study, this gap is addressed by developing a telephonic Urdu speech corpus tailored to the banking domain, specifically for debit card activation. To accelerate corpus development, semi-automatic methods were used, combining microphone-recorded WB speech with telephonic NB data to build acoustic models. These models were then tested on telephonic speech to evaluate performance improvements in real-world applications.

2 Related Work

Automatic Speech Recognition (ASR) for telephonic data in specialized domains, such as banking, presents unique challenges due to varied acoustic environments and domain-specific vocabulary. Key strategies to enhance ASR performance in these scenarios include bandwith mismatch and acoustic modelling and domain adaptation.

2.1 Bandwidth Mismatch and Acoustic Modeling

A significant challenge in telephonic ASR is the mismatch between narrowband (NB) and wideband (WB) speech. Early work by Seltzer and Acero (Seltzer and Acero, 2006) introduced a GMM-HMM-based EM algorithm for mixed-band (MB) acoustic modeling, though improvements in recognition accuracy were limited. Later approaches, such as You and Xu (You and Xu, 2014), leveraged deep neural networks (DNNs) to reduce bandwidth mismatches, showing more promise. Mac et al. (Mac et al., 2019) demonstrated that upsampling NB data yields better results than downsampling WB data in DNN-based acoustic models. Recent advancements using generative adversarial networks (GANs) (Shi, 2023) have shown a 3.65% improvement in accuracy when recognizing mixed-band audio, highlighting the potential of GANs in addressing bandwidth mismatches.

2.2 Domain Adaptation for Telephonic Speech

Domain adaptation plays a crucial role in improving telephonic ASR, especially in specialized domains like banking. The Density Ratio Approach (DRA) (Takagi et al., 2023) adapts language models using large-scale text corpora to enhance recognition in live ASR. Additionally, External Off-Policy Acoustic Catalogs (Chan et al., 2023) have been used to reduce WER by leveraging external audio embeddings, speeding up domain adaptation. Data Distribution Matching (Shinohara and Watanabe, 2023) optimizes training by selecting subsets of training data that closely match the target domain, ensuring minimal WER increases without enlarging the model.
Building on these advancements, Ahmad et al. (Ahmad et al., 2024) proposed a progressive approach that adapts to out-of-domain telephonic speech by sequentially training student models, each using the previous student model as a teacher. This multi-stage training significantly reduced WER in unsupervised adaptation scenarios. In their experiments on Switchboard data, they achieved a 9.8%, 7.7%, and 3.3% absolute WER reduction after each stage of training, underscoring UDA's value in telephonic ASR with limited labeled data.
While significant progress has been made in adapting ASR systems to telephonic speech, challenges remain, particularly in maintaining high performance across diverse telephonic applications and scenarios, such as in the banking domain. Continuing advancements in domain adaptation techniques will be key to overcoming these hurdles.

3 Corpus Design

To develop a robust ASR system for a specific domain and language, a comprehensive text corpus covering essential vocabulary is required. This corpus records speech data for training and testing the ASR system, with the training corpus building the acoustic model and the testing corpus evaluating performance. Linguists systematically developed the text corpus by crawling data from websites using HTTrack[1] and sentences were extracted from HTML files using a Python script, manually rephrasing and supplementing sentences that averaged 14 words, with no repetitions. A linguist verified 10% of the text for syntactic and grammatical accuracy. The following subsections

[1]https://www.httrack.com/

Domain Name	No. of Sentences
Banking	1900
Business	10900
E-commerce	3000
Telecommunication	2000
News	18062
Miscellaneous	417
Total	**36279**

Table 1: Composition of Training Corpus

Domain Name	No. of Sentences
Newspaper	1300
Telecommunication	2000
E-commerce	2000
Addresses	1000
Dates	500
Telephone Numbers	250
CNIC Numbers	250
Urdu Digest(Mumtaz et al., 2018)	500
Total	**7800**

Table 2: Composition of Testing Corpus

explain domain coverage in the corpora.

3.1 Training Corpus Design

A rich text corpus was carefully designed to collect Urdu speech data across various domains. The training corpus consists of 36,279 unique sentences, encompassing banking, business, e-commerce, telecommunications, online news, and general categories. Initially, 6,000 sentences were sourced from the phonetically balanced Urdu text-to-speech corpus.

For the banking domain, 1,000 sentences were crafted from brochures on loans, insurance, and banking services, supplemented by translations from English where necessary. An additional 900 sentences were rephrased from online bank websites, covering banking cards, Islamic banking, and payment partners.

In the business domain, 10,900 sentences focused on vocabulary related to cryptocurrency, taxation, and Pakistan's economy. For e-commerce, 3,000 sentences were collected from websites, primarily from pictorial information and menu cards.As shown in Appendix Table 13, the categories covered include a wide variety of products, from electronic devices to groceries.

For telecommunications, 2,000 sentences were generated from service provider websites, addressing apps, bundles, and services, with translations from English rules and regulations into Urdu. Additionally, 18,062 sentences were crawled and manually rephrased from news websites, alongside 417 sentences covering miscellaneous categories. The information on these categories is shown in Appendix Table 14. Table 1 outlines the corpus composition by domain.

3.2 Testing Corpus Design

To evaluate ASR system performance, a phonetically rich and balanced test corpus was developed by expert linguists, covering domains such as business, telecommunications, e-commerce, addresses, dates, and CNIC numbers. The test corpus was designed to be entirely distinct from the training data.

For the business domain, 1,300 unique sentences were rephrased from online newspapers. The telecommunications and e-commerce domains each contributed 2,000 sentences from various websites. In the addresses domain, 1,000 unique postal addresses were manually rephrased, modifying elements like street and house numbers, along with different address formats used in Pakistan.

To cover dates, 500 sentences were created using carrier sentences, incorporating dates in various formats. These formats are shown in Appendix Table 15 and the carrier sentences are shown in Appendix Table 2.

For telephone number coverage, 250 original numbers were collected, and to ensure privacy, the 11 digits were shuffled multiple times to generate new numbers. These were then incorporated into carrier sentences for data recording.

Similarly, for CNIC numbers, 250 original CNICs were collected, and their 13 digits were shuffled to create new numbers. These were used in carrier sentences, and speakers recorded them for testing .

Additionally, 500 sentences from Urdu Digest 1M corpus(Mumtaz et al., 2018) were included in the testing corpus.

Table 2 presents the composition of the testing corpus and the proportion of each domain contributing to it. In order to cover corpus related to dates carrier sentences were used.

4 Speech Corpus Collection

To collect the speech data, designed text sentences were recorded from multiple speakers. Details of speaker selection, recording process and data alignment are given in subsequent sections.

4.1 Speaker Selection

To record the above-mentioned designed text corpus, the first step was the speakers scrutiny. Both genders (males and females) ranging between 18-50 years of age were selected. The speakers minimum education must be intermediate (Grade 12). Gender balance was maintained and speakers whose mother tongue was Urdu or Punjabi were selected. For a speaker to qualify for the actual recording, he/she had to read 20 sentences correctly. The speakers who can speak Urdu fluently and have no speech disfluency or pronunciation issues were selected for the recording session. Speaker uniqueness was ensured by maintaining a list of CNIC numbers of all speakers who participated in the recordings. Moreover, speakers date of birth, mother tongue, district, telephone number, mobile phone network, and mobile phone brand was also documented.

4.2 Recording Process

The speech corpus was recorded in an indoor environment using a variety of devices, including laptop microphones, USB headsets, and mobile phones (both default microphones and hands-free). Each speaker was asked to use their mobile phone to ensure diverse coverage across brands like Samsung, Nokia, HTC, and Huawei. The recording was conducted in a continuous read speech manner.

4.2.1 Training Corpus Recording

Simultaneous recordings were made on a laptop and a mobile phone, guided by a resource person who assigned each speaker a unique ID and list number. The text corpus was segmented into lists of 20 sentences. For wideband recordings, speakers utilized laptop microphones, USB headsets, or hands-free devices, with speaker details documented in advance. The recording process employed an automated utility that displayed sentences one at a time, allowing speakers to rehearse before recording. The completed recordings were saved as WAV files at a 16 kHz frequency, accompanied by a text file containing sentence IDs and timestamps. Post-recording, the data was sent to the Urdu ASR system for decoding, generating a status file detailing word errors. The goal for each speaker was to achieve at least 150 correctly decoded sentences, with an average of 350 sentences read in 2.5 to 3 hours.

4.2.2 Testing Corpus Recording

The testing procedure mirrored that of the training corpus. Speakers recorded lists of 20 unique sentences using the same microphone utility. Each recorded list was automatically saved in WAV format at 16 kHz, along with a text file documenting the start and end timestamps for each sentence. No ASR was used during testing, so the status file contained only timing information. Each speaker aimed to record 120 unique sentences and was required to re-record any sentences not captured correctly, typically completing the task in about 1 hour. Figure 1 depicts the recording process.

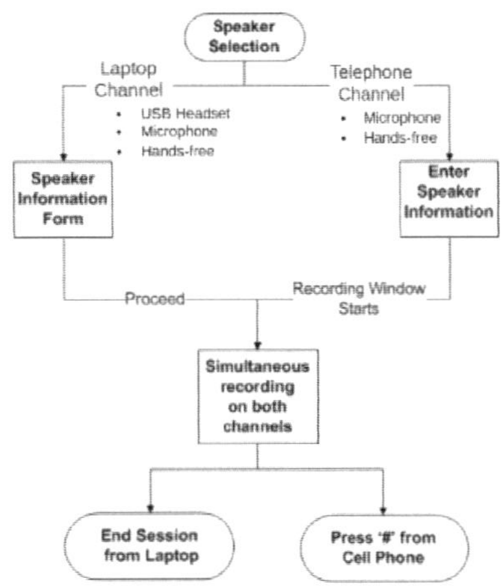

Figure 1: Recording Process

4.3 Data Alignment and Verification

This section discusses the alignment and verification of training and testing data.

4.3.1 Data Alignment and Segmentation

To segment telephonic audio into sentences, laptop recordings were used as references due to distortions from signal drops or weather issues. Manual alignment was necessary despite simultaneous recording, using Audacity[2], an open-source editor. The aligned telephonic audio file is then exported to the system. A Python script segmented the training audios into individual sentences, organizing them into folders for each speaker, with subfolders for laptop and telephonic data, further categorized by ASR-decoded results (0WE, 1WE, 2WE, and residual). Corresponding transcriptions were stored in text files. For testing, a similar script created speaker-specific folders for both channels, containing segmented audio files.

[2]https://www.audacityteam.org/download/

4.3.2 Data Verification

Data verification is crucial for preparing audio data for ASR development. While laptop-recorded data, decoded by the backend ASR, required no manual verification, telephonic recordings were carefully reviewed due to potential issues like signal drop or attenuation. Expert linguists manually verified 10% of the telephonic audios that matched the 0WE category from the laptop channels decoding results, excluding significantly distorted files from ASR training. All audio files from both channels in the testing data were fully verified since no backend ASR decoding was applied. Deliberate modifications (such as inserting or removing Urdu prepositions and conjunctions) were introduced in the text transcriptions for accuracy checks, with any errors leading to repeat verifications by the linguist team.

4.3.3 Corpus Statistics

The presented corpus comprises Urdu read-speech collected through two recording channels: laptop and telephone. Details on the number of speakers and duration are in Table 3, while mother tongue information is in Table 4.

Speakers from various districts of Pakistan, including Lahore, Faisalabad, Gujranwala, and others, are represented, with age coverage ranging from 18 to 50 years. Age distribution in the training and testing data is detailed in Table 5.

Recording on telephone channels utilized mobile phones from brands such as Samsung, Huawei, Nokia, and iPhone, covering networks like Ufone, Jazz, Warid, Zong, and Telenor. The percentage coverage for each mobile network is in Table 6. Additional statistics on the cleaned and verified corpus are presented in Table 7. In addition, Appendix Table 16 clearly compares this paper's corpus and the other existing telephonic Urdu corpora.

5 Experimental Setup

The speech recognition system for the Urdu language is developed using Kaldi[3] , which is an open-source speech recognition toolkit written in C++ and licensed under the Apache License V2.0. It provides adaptable code which can be modified and extended as per requirement. The important features of Kaldi include code-level integration with Finite State Transducers (FSTs) which compiles against the OpenFst toolkit (using it as a library). It also provides extensive linear algebra support through a matrix library that wraps standard BLAS and LAPACK routines (Praveen Kumar et al., 2020) . The toolkit was set up on Ubuntu 18.04 LTS operating system. The machine specifications include an octa-core 2.8 GHz processor of Intel(R) Core (TM) i7 with 32 GB RAM and hosting two NVIDIA graphic cards GeForce GTX 1080[4] having 8 GB memory each. This setup supports the successful implementation of state-of-the-art recipes provided by the Kaldi toolkit for the development of a speech recognition system.

5.1 Feature Extraction

The raw speech signal is complex and unsuitable for direct input into a speech recognition system. To facilitate training, feature extraction is employed to represent the speech signal parametrically. Kaldi offers various scripts for feature extraction, including Mel Frequency Cepstral Coefficients (MFCC), Perceptron Linear Predictive (PLP), and Vocal Tract Length Normalization (VTLN).

For speech recognition system, MFCC extraction was used via the Kaldi recipe, processing 25ms frames with a 10ms shift. After removing the DC offset, the signal is multiplied by a Hamming window, followed by energy calculation in mel-bins, Fast Fourier Transform (FFT), and power spectrum computation. Finally, a cosine transform is applied to the logarithm of the energies. Although the default number of cepstral coefficients is 13, it was configured to 40 to enhance deep neural networks. After calculating MFCC features, Cepstral Mean and Variance Normalization (CMVN) was applied for improved robustness in speech recognition.

5.2 Phonetic Lexicon

The lexicon is essential for speech recognition, defining word pronunciations. For Urdu ASR, a 34K-word phonetic lexicon was created, covering all unique words from the text corpus. Transcriptions follow the Case Insensitive Speech Assessment Method Phonetic Alphabet (CISAMPA)[5] symbols. Linguists mapped each word to standard orthography using dictionaries like Oxford Urdu Dictionary[6] and Urdu Lughat[7]. Alternate pronunci-

[3]https://kaldi-asr.org/

[4]https://www.nvidia.com/en-sg/geforce/products/10series/geforce-gtx-1080/

[5]https://www.cle.org.pk/Downloads/ling_resources/phoneticinventory/UrduPhoneticInventory.pdf

[6]https://languages.oup.com/oxford-global-languages/

[7]http://udb.gov.pk

Data Type	Telephone Data Duration (hours)	No. of Male Speakers	No. of Female Speakers
Training Data	111.5 h	240	205
Testing Data	10.93 h	30	30

Table 3: Number of Speakers and Duration of Speech Data

Mother Tongue	Number of Speakers (Training)	Percentage (Training)	Number of Speakers (Testing)	Percentage (Testing)
Urdu	213	47.86%	28	46.67%
Punjabi	232	52.14%	32	53.33%

Table 4: Speaker Coverage Based on Mother Tongue

Range of Speaker Ages	No. of Speakers (Training)	Percentage (Training)	No. of Speakers (Testing)	Percentage (Testing)
< 20	178	40.00%	6	10.00%
20 24	240	53.93%	27	45.00%
25 29	25	5.62%	10	16.67%
> 30	2	0.45%	17	28.33%

Table 5: Age Distribution of Speakers

Mobile Network	Training Data	Testing Data
Ufone	26.69%	24.24%
Jazz	45.76%	40.91%
Warid	10.80%	16.67%
Zong	10.80%	6.06%
Telenor	5.95%	12.12%

Table 6: Percentage Coverage of Mobile Networks

ations exist for some words, as shown in Appendix Table 17.

5.3 Language Model

SRI Language Modeling (SRILM) toolkit (Praveen Kumar et al., 2020) is used to build a trigram language model. A very large amount of data has been crawled from various Urdu websites including books, magazines, news, and blogs. The corpus is then tokenized on the basis of sentences. Moreover, the designed text corpus for training is also appended after replicating it hundreds of times. The final corpus contains 120 million words which were used for the development of the language model for Urdu ASR.

5.4 Acoustic Modeling

The baseline ASR system was built using a Gaussian Mixture Model-Hidden Markov Model (GMM-HMM) approach. Monophone training and alignment were followed by speaker-independent Linear Discriminant Analysis (LDA) for tri-phone training (tri1) with 2000 decision tree leaves and 11,000 Gaussians. In tri2, Maximum Likelihood Linear Transform (MLLT) increased these to 2500 leaves and 15,000 Gaussians. Speaker Adapted Training (SAT) retained this configuration.
Using SAT alignments, Deep Neural Networks (DNN), specifically Chain TDNN models, were trained with Lattice-Free Maximum Mutual Information (LFMMI) to improve efficiency and transcription quality. High-resolution MFCCs and 100-dimensional i-vectors were computed with 1024 Gaussians. The TDNN had one convolutional layer, seven hidden layers with 625 neurons, ReLU-batch norm activation, and a learning rate that decreased from 0.001 to 0.0001.

5.5 Mixing of WB Speech Data in NB Data

Increasing training data enhances speech recognition performance, as shown in the literature (Seltzer and Acero, 2006; Mac et al., 2019). Mixed-bandwidth training improves telephonic speech recognition. Along with the developed corpus, 174 hours of WB data from (Farooq et al., 2019) (hands-free recorded, 16 kHz) were added. The 111.5 hours of telephonic data were upsampled from 8 kHz to 16 kHz, yielding 285.5 hours of audio at 16 kHz. Results, before and after adding WB data, are detailed in Section 6.

5.6 Testing Setup and Performance Measure

For evaluation of the system, 10.9 hours of telephonic speech data is used to test the primary system which covers multiple domains. Percentage word error rate (WER) is used as the performance measure. It is equal to the number of errors made by ASR divided by the total words in the test data multiplied by 100.

	Training Data	Testing Data
Number of Utterances	65,227	6,358
Average Duration per Utterance (in seconds)	6.2	6.2
Average Number of Words per Utterance	13	15
Average Number of Utterances per Speaker	164	106
Total Frequency of Words in Transcription Files	823,819	92,659

Table 7: Corpus Details

6 Performance Evaluation Experiments and their Results

Two models, a GMM-HMM model, and a chain TDNN, are evaluated using the test data. The GMM-HMM model is trained on telephonic training data while Chain TDNN is trained on two datasets, telephonic training data and telephonic+hands-free data from (Farooq et al., 2019). The experiments showed that Chain TDNN outperformed the GMM-HMM model with 24% less WER. The third experiment i.e., the training of Chain TDNN using telephonic (NB) and hands-free (WB), further reduced WER by 3%. However, pretrained Whispers Large variant performed similar to GMM-HMM with only 4% reduction in WER. Table 8 presents the experimental results carried out.

7 Adaptation of ASR for Banking Domain

In order to tailor the system for the banking domain, language data and lexicon was adapted for a speech-based debit card activation dialog system. This included a language model for debit card numbers (DCN), last four digits (DCLFD), date of birth (DoB), and debit card expiry dates (DCED). The system records client responses via telephone, and ASR decodes them; if the information is correct, the card activates; otherwise, after one retry, the call is transferred to a human operator.

Banking domain corpora from (Mumtaz et al., 2018) was utilized for adaptation, which comprised 10 million entries for DCN, 300K for DCLFD, 815K for DCED, and 2.6 million for DoB. A combined lexicon and corpus were created by merging these categories, with added confirmation words like "sahi" (Correct), "ghalat" (Incorrect), "han" (Yes), and "nahi" (No). Table 9 outlines the corpus and lexicon. The system was tested on individual and combined datasets, comparing System-3 with the Whisper pre-trained model. Although Whisper underperformed due to limited vocabulary, domain-specific models mentioned in this paper achieved better results.

Experiments with the combined language model and lexicon were performed in four configurations: (1) general corpus and lexicon, (2) banking lexicon only, (3) banking corpus only, and (4) both banking lexicon and corpus. Table 10 shows that domain-specific lexicons and corpora significantly improved results, while Table 11 presents the %WER from System 2 and System-3 for each experiment.

Table 12 analyzes phone recognition errors in the banking dataset while Appendix Table 18 shows percentage of Urdu Phonemes in testing and training data. Consonants like /m, l, j/ were frequently misrecognized, while medial vowels such as /[æ]/ and /[e]/, the diphthong /[eɐː]/, and the nasal vowel /[æ]/ faced significant misrecognition challenges due to limited test data coverage. Notably, the dental plosive /[t̪]/ was particularly challenging to identify despite good dataset coverage, while the vowel /[ə]/ was often misrecognized as /[ɑː]/. In conclusion, domain-specific models outperform general pre-trained models like Whisper, emphasizing the need for targeted improvements in phonetic recognition for banking applications.

8 Conclusion

In this paper, a narrowband speech recognition system for Urdu is developed using a mix of wideband speech data. A multi-domain narrowband and wideband speech corpus is recorded from multiple speakers. Based on this data, a large vocabulary continuous speech recognition system for telephonic channels is developed. Various acoustic modeling techniques are investigated, with Chain TDNN outperforming other models. The Chain TDNN, trained on a mixture of narrowband and wideband corpora, outperforms other models and the pre-trained Whisper model. The developed ASR is adapted for the banking domain using a domain-specific lexicon and language model, achieving promising results.

System	Model	Training Data Channel	Duration (hrs)	%WER
System-1	GMM	Telephonic	111.5	54.92
System-2	Chain TDNN	Telephonic	111.5	30.36
System-3	Chain TDNN	Telephonic+Hands-free	285.5	27.56
Whisper (Radford et al., 2023)	Variant-Large	Pre-trained Model	680,000	50

Table 8: Word Error Rate on Different Models Trained on Different Training Data

Category	Corpus	Lexicon
DCN	10,000,000 entries [16- digit numbers]	29 entries [0-9 digits]
DCLFD	300,000 entries	157 entries [0-100 digits]
DCED	815,000 entries (13 different patterns)	201 entries [0-100 digits + Month Names]
DoB	2,679,107 entries (13 different patterns)	201 entries [0-100 digits + Month Names]
Combined	17,679,107	209 entries [digits + month names + confirmation words]

Table 9: Banking Text Corpus and Lexicon Details

Category	No. of Utterances	Duration (Minutes)	WER on Combined LM and Lexicon	WER on Respective LM and Lexicon	WER using Whisper-Large	Phone Error Rate
DCN	83	17	1.72	1.65	19.0	1.83
DCLFD	298	21	5.30	5.43	80.0	4.37
DCED	792	54	3.44	3.40	51.0	4.16
DoB	340	29	3.42	3.32	49.0	3.32
Combined	1513	121	3.87	3.45 (Avg)	49.75	3.42 (Avg)

Table 10: Detailed Test Results

Lexicon and LM used	% WER on System-2	% WER on System-3
General lexicon + general corpus	86.08	91.39
Banking lexicon + general corpus	8.08	7.56
General lexicon + banking corpus	3.14	2.84
Banking lexicon + banking corpus	2.47	1.65

Table 11: Performance of System-2 and System-3 on Banking Domain Data

Sr. no	Urdu Consonants (IPA)	% Phone Error Rate	Sr. no	Urdu Vowels (IPA)	% Phone Error Rate
1	م (m)	10.0	1	اَے (æ)	21.9
2	ل (l)	14.1	2	ا،آ (ea:)	8.2
3	ی (j)	11.9	3	ہ (e)	7.7
4	ت،ط (t̪)	8.2	4	یَں (ɑẽ:)	7.1
5	تھ (t^h)	4.6	5	ی (i:)	5.9
6	س،ص،ث (s)	4.4	6	یں (ẽ:)	4.8
7	ک (k)	3.5	7	ء (ə)	4.5
8	کھ (k^h)	3.0	8	آ (ɑ:)	2.7
9	پ (p)	2.7	9	و (o:)	2.2
10	ب (b)	2.3	10	ُ (ʊ)	2.0
11	ح،ہ (h)	2.3	11	آئی (a:i:)	1.6
12	ن (n)	2.2	12	ِ (ɪ)	1.4
13	چ (tʃ)	2.0	13	آں، اں (ɑ̃:)	1.4
14	ر (r)	1.8	14	ے (e:)	0.8
15	د (d)	1.8			
16	چھ (tʃ^h)	1.7			
17	و (v)	1.1			
18	ذ،ض،ظ،ز (z)	0.7			

Table 12: Phone Error Rate on Banking Domain Data

9 Limitations

The development of the mixed-band (MB) acoustic model and Urdu speech recognition system acknowledges several limitations. Although Urdu telephonic speech corpus presented in this paper represents an improvement over prior datasets, it may not fully capture the variety of Urdu accents and dialects, and its domain specificity to the banking sector constrains generalizability to other applications. The speaker demographic, while balanced in gender and comprising native Urdu and Punjabi speakers, is restricted to individuals aged 18-50 with at least an intermediate education level, excluding younger and older populations as well as those with lower educational backgrounds, thereby limiting the model's applicability across a broader audience. Additionally, the recordings were conducted in controlled indoor environments, which may not accurately represent real-world acoustic variability. Lastly, the ASR system is specifically designed for debit card activation, and its effectiveness in other domains remains to be evaluated.

Ethical Considerations

All researchers involved in this study have adhered to the ACM Code of Ethics and conducted their work responsibly. Our aim is to advance speech recognition for Urdu, enhancing technology access in underserved communities. Data collection was conducted with informed consent, primarily utilizing publicly available or simulated telephonic interactions, with all personally identifiable information (PII) anonymized during transcription and annotation. Telephone numbers and 13-digit CNIC numbers were anonymized by shuffling digits to ensure privacy. Our initiative seeks to enhance technological resources for the broader Urdu-speaking community without exploiting individuals based on language, geography, or social standing. We recognize the potential risks associated with the misuse of ASR technology, including surveillance or unauthorized data collection. However, our research strictly focuses on developing models for the benefit of users, not for intrusive purposes. The ethical implications of using such systems in various applications must be carefully considered, and we urge continued dialogue on the responsible deployment of speech recognition technologies to ensure they serve the needs of diverse Urdu-speaking populations without exploitation or marginalization.

References

Rehan Ahmad, Muhammad Umar Farooq, and Thomas Hain. 2024. Progressive unsupervised domain adaptation for asr using ensemble models and multi-stage training. In *ICASSP 2024 - 2024 IEEE International Conference on Acoustics, Speech and Signal Processing (ICASSP)*, pages 11466–11470.

Jeong-Uk Bang, Seung Yun, Seung-Hi Kim, Mu-Yeol Choi, Min-Kyu Lee, Yeo-Jeong Kim, Dong-Hyun Kim, Jun Park, Young-Jik Lee, and Sang-Hun Kim. 2020. Ksponspeech: Korean spontaneous speech corpus for automatic speech recognition. *Applied Sciences*, 10(19):6936.

David M Chan, Shalini Ghosh, Ariya Rastrow, and Björn Hoffmeister. 2023. Domain adaptation with external off-policy acoustic catalogs for scalable contextual end-to-end automated speech recognition. In *ICASSP 2023-2023 IEEE International Conference on Acoustics, Speech and Signal Processing (ICASSP)*, pages 1–5. IEEE.

Yu-Chih Deng, Yih-Ru Wang, Sin-Horng Chen, and Chen-Yu Chiang. 2019. Recent progress of mandrain spontaneous speech recognition on mandrain conversation dialogue corpus. In *2019 22nd Conference of the Oriental COCOSDA International Committee for the Co-ordination and Standardisation of Speech Databases and Assessment Techniques (O-COCOSDA)*, pages 1–6. IEEE.

Muhammad Umar Farooq, Farah Adeeba, Sahar Rauf, and Sarmad Hussain. 2019. Improving large vocabulary urdu speech recognition system using deep neural networks. In *INTERSPEECH*, pages 2978–2982.

Jianqing Gao, Jun Du, and Enhong Chen. 2018. Mixed-bandwidth cross-channel speech recognition via joint optimization of dnn-based bandwidth expansion and acoustic modeling. *IEEE/ACM Transactions on Audio, Speech, and Language Processing*, 27(3):559–571.

Jianqing Gao, Jun Du, Changqing Kong, Huaifang Lu, Enhong Chen, and Chin-Hui Lee. 2016. An experimental study on joint modeling of mixed-bandwidth data via deep neural networks for robust speech recognition. In *2016 International Joint Conference on Neural Networks (IJCNN)*, pages 588–594. IEEE.

Alexandru-Lucian Georgescu, Horia Cucu, Andi Buzo, and Corneliu Burileanu. 2020. Rsc: A romanian read speech corpus for automatic speech recognition. In *Proceedings of the Twelfth Language Resources and Evaluation Conference*, pages 6606–6612.

John J Godfrey and Edward Holliman. 1997. Switchboard-1 release 2. *Linguistic Data Consortium, Philadelphia*, 926:927.

Chuping Liu, Qian-Jie Fu, and Shrikanth S Narayanan. 2009. Effect of bandwidth extension to telephone speech recognition in cochlear implant users. *The Journal of the Acoustical Society of America*, 125(2):EL77–EL83.

Yi Liu, Pascale Fung, Yongsheng Yang, Christopher Cieri, Shudong Huang, and David Graff. 2006. Hkust/mts: A very large scale mandarin telephone speech corpus. In *Chinese Spoken Language Processing: 5th International Symposium, ISCSLP 2006, Singapore, December 13-16, 2006. Proceedings*, pages 724–735. Springer.

Khoi-Nguyen C Mac, Xiaodong Cui, Wei Zhang, and Michael Picheny. 2019. Large-scale mixed-bandwidth deep neural network acoustic modeling for automatic speech recognition. *arXiv preprint arXiv:1907.04887*.

Long Mai and Julie Carson-Berndsen. 2022. Unsupervised domain adaptation for speech recognition with unsupervised error correction. *arXiv preprint arXiv:2209.12043*.

Benazir Mumtaz, Sahar Rauf, Hafsa Qadir, Javairia Khalid, Tania Habib, Sarmad Hussain, Rukhsana Barkat, et al. 2018. Urdu speech corpora for banking sector in pakistan. In *2018 Oriental COCOSDA-International Conference on Speech Database and Assessments*, pages 9–14. IEEE.

Frederik Nagel and Sascha Disch. 2009. A harmonic bandwidth extension method for audio codecs. In *2009 IEEE International Conference on Acoustics, Speech and Signal Processing*, pages 145–148. IEEE.

Matt Post, Gaurav Kumar, Adam Lopez, Damianos Karakos, Chris Callison-Burch, and Sanjeev Khudanpur. 2013. Improved speech-to-text translation with the fisher and callhome spanish-english speech translation corpus. In *Proceedings of the 10th International Workshop on Spoken Language Translation: Papers*.

N Prasad and T Kishore Kumar. 2016. Bandwidth extension of speech signals: A comprehensive review. *International Journal of Intelligent Systems and Applications*, 8(2):45–52.

PS Praveen Kumar, G Thimmaraja Yadava, and Haradagere Siddaramaiah Jayanna. 2020. Continuous kannada speech recognition system under degraded condition. *Circuits, Systems, and Signal Processing*, 39:391–419.

Hannu Pulakka and Paavo Alku. 2011. Bandwidth extension of telephone speech using a neural network and a filter bank implementation for highband mel spectrum. *IEEE Transactions on Audio, Speech, and Language Processing*, 19(7):2170–2183.

Muhammad Qasim, Sohaib Nawaz, Sarmad Hussain, and Tania Habib. 2016. Urdu speech recognition system for district names of pakistan: Development, challenges and solutions. In *2016 conference of the oriental chapter of international committee for coordination and standardization of speech databases and assessment techniques (O-COCOSDA)*, pages 28–32. IEEE.

Alec Radford, Jong Wook Kim, Tao Xu, Greg Brockman, Christine Mcleavey, and Ilya Sutskever. 2023. Robust speech recognition via large-scale weak supervision. In *Proceedings of the 40th International Conference on Machine Learning*, volume 202 of *Proceedings of Machine Learning Research*, pages 28492–28518. PMLR.

Sahar Rauf, Asima Hameed, Tania Habib, and Sarmad Hussain. 2015. District names speech corpus for pakistani languages. In *2015 International Conference Oriental COCOSDA Held Jointly with 2015 Conference on Asian Spoken Language Research and Evaluation (O-COCOSDA/CASLRE)*, pages 207–211. IEEE.

Huda Sarfraz, Sarmad Hussain, Riffat Bokhari, Agha Ali Raza, Inam Ullah, Zahid Sarfraz, Sophia Pervez, Asad Mustafa, Iqra Javed, and Rahila Parveen. 2010. Speech corpus development for a speaker independent spontaneous urdu speech recognition system. *Proceedings of the O-COCOSDA, Kathmandu, Nepal*, 24.

Michael L Seltzer and Alex Acero. 2006. Training wideband acoustic models using mixed-bandwidth training data for speech recognition. *IEEE Transactions on Audio, Speech, and Language Processing*, 15(1):235–245.

Lijuan Shi. 2023. A unified mixed-bandwidth asr framework with generative adversarial network. In *Proceedings of the 2023 4th International Conference on Control, Robotics and Intelligent System*, pages 160–165.

Yusuke Shinohara and Shinji Watanabe. 2023. Domain adaptation by data distribution matching via submodularity for speech recognition. In *2023 IEEE Automatic Speech Recognition and Understanding Workshop (ASRU)*, pages 1–7. IEEE.

Tatsunari Takagi, Yukoh Wakabayashi, Atsunori Ogawa, and Norihide Kitaoka. 2023. Domain adaptation using density ratio approach and ctc decoder for streaming speech recognition. In *2023 10th International Conference on Advanced Informatics: Concept, Theory and Application (ICAICTA)*, pages 1–5. IEEE.

Zhao You and Bo Xu. 2014. Improving wideband acoustic models using mixed-bandwidth training data via dnn adaptation. In *INTERSPEECH*, pages 2204–2208.

Bartosz Ziółko, Piotr Żelasko, Ireneusz Gawlik, Tomasz Pędzimąż, and Tomasz Jadczyk. 2018. An application for building a polish telephone speech corpus. In *Proceedings of the Eleventh International Conference on Language Resources and Evaluation (LREC 2018)*.

A Supplementary Material

This appendix contains additional tables and figures that support the findings in the main document.

Table 13 provides an overview of the categories prevalent in the e-commerce domain. This table captures various sectors, including electronics, home appliances, fashion, and groceries, reflecting the diversity of products and services available online. The categories are organized to facilitate understanding of the marketplace's structure and the various offerings within each segment.

E-Commerce Domain Categories
Electronic devices, gadgets, home appliances, Features of different appliances, home (bedding, blankets), Automobiles (bikes, spare parts, loaders), Electronic accessories, health and beauty, Babies and toys, groceries, pets, Home and lifestyle, food items, food deals, Ingredients, cities, cuisines, Food outlets, transport, organizations, Medical equipment, books/magazines, Miscellaneous products, jobs, Electric appliances, electronic gadgets, Features of products, features of OLX, Pets/livestock, fashion, transport, Musical instruments, medical instruments, Popular cities, less popular cities, Locations, property type, purpose, Cars (Japanese, Chinese etc.), car brands, Bikes and parts

Table 13: Categories Covered in E-Commerce

In Table 14, a comprehensive list of general domain categories is presented. This table encompasses a wide range of topics, from agriculture to technology, showcasing the breadth of subjects that can be explored. Each category represents significant fields of study or interest, underlining the multifaceted nature of the domains covered.

Table 15 presents the various date formats

General Domain Categories
Plants, agriculture, sports, titles, education fields, country names, political parties, services and utilities, professions, election process, judiciary, administrative domains, trade, medical terms, diseases, entertainment films, cities, religions, army, nationalities, places, vegetables, flowers, crimes, relations, rivers, castes, weapons, grocery items, colors, festivals, events, body parts, birds, animals, metals, utensils, clothes, fruits, jewelry, Islam, dishes, furniture, literature-text types, musical instruments, journalism, weather, emotions, nuts, drugs, insects, time of day, direction, shapes, technology, banking, time measurement units, area measurement units, distance measurement units, weight measurement units, parts of house, transport, vehicles, situation/calamities/disasters

Table 14: Categories Covered in General Domain

incorporated into the testing corpus design for the ASR system. These formats were carefully selected to reflect the diverse ways dates can be expressed in natural speech, which is crucial for evaluating the model's performance in real-world scenarios.

Carrier sentences in Figure 2 help to evaluate the system's performance in handling both general

Date Format	**Example**
DD/MM/YYYY	16/10/2018
DD-MM-YYYY	16-10-2018
Month (English) DD, Year	October 16, 2018
DD Month (Urdu) Year	15 2018
DD.MM.YYYY	17.07.1988
DD Month YYYY	19 SEP 2016
DDth Month, YYYY	16th February 2014

Table 15: Different Formats for Dates

language and numerical information in everyday conversations.

Carrier sentences
یہ ____ کا اخبار ہے This is the ____ newspaper
یہ کتاب ____ میں چھپی This book was published on ____

Sample Carrier Sentences for Phone Numbers

Carrier sentences
مزید معلومات کے لیے ...... ملائیں Dial ____ for more information
کیا آپ کا موبائل نمبر .... ہے؟ Is your mobile number ____?

Sample Carrier Sentences for CNIC

Carrier sentences
آپ کے والد کا شناختی کارڈ نمبر ____ ہے ____ Your father's ID card number is
میرا شناختی کارڈ نمبر یہ ____ ہے My ID card number is ____

Figure 2: Sample Carrier Sentences for Dates,Phone Numbers and CNIC

Table 17 presents a selection of Urdu words that have multiple pronunciations, alongside their English translations and phonetic transcriptions. This table aims to illustrate the linguistic diversity and variability present within the Urdu language, particularly in terms of pronunciation.

Table 16 clearly presents that the corpus presented in this paper stands out for its extensive domain coverage, large number of speakers, and large amount of speech data emphasizing its uniqueness in breadth and scale.

Sr. no	Telephonic Urdu Corpora	Total No. of Speakers	Duration (hours)	Domains Covered	Speech Type
1	Speech Corpus Development for a Speaker Independent Spontaneous Urdu Speech Recognition System(Sarfraz et al., 2010)	82	44.5	Phonemically rich sentences, everyday text (date, numbers, proper names, hobbies, interests, past experiences, television, cricket)	Read and spontaneous speech
2	District Names Speech Corpus for Pakistani Languages(Rauf et al., 2015)	300	12	District names	Read speech
3	Urdu Speech Corpus for Travel Domain(Qasim et al., 2016)	60	–	City names, days, time, and numbers	Read speech
4	Urdu Automatic Speech Recognition for Telephonic Data: A Mixed Band Corpus Development Approach with Domain Adaptation for Banking Applications	445	111.5	Banking, e-commerce, investments, trading, telecommunication	Read speech

Table 16: Corpus Comparison with existing Urdu Corpora

A.1 Phonetic Coverage of Training and Testing Data

A detailed phonetic analysis of the training dataset has been conducted to ensure adequate coverage of all Urdu phonemes. Table 18 elaborates on the Urdu phonemes coverage in the training and banking domain test dataset. The training corpus comprises 56% consonants and 44% vowels, and the test dataset comprises 62% consonants and 38% vowels. /r/ consonant is the most frequent consonant in both training and testing datasets, and /ɑː/ vowel is the most frequent in both training and test data. Aspirated consonants /t^h/, /k^h/, etc., and nasalized vowels /ĩː/, /æ̃ː/, etc., are less frequent in both datasets. /t^h/ is exceptional as it has more frequency of occurrence in test data of the banking domain.

Words having alternate pronunciations	English Translation	Transcriptions
مصنف	Author	M U S A N N A F M U S A N N I F
اونچائی	Height	U U N T S AA II UUN TS AA II
صالح	Pious	S AA L AY S AA L AY H S AA L AYH H S AA L AYH H AY

Table 17: Examples of Words Having Alternate Pronunciations

Frequency of occurrence of Urdu phonemes in training data				Frequency of occurrence of Urdu phonemes in testing data			
Urdu Consonants (IPA)	**%**	**Urdu Vowels (IPA)**	**%**	**Urdu Consonants (IPA)**	**%**	**Urdu Vowels (IPA)**	**%**
ر (r)	6.0	ا، آ (ɑ:)	9.4	ر (r)	8.1	ا، آ (ɑ:)	8.9
ک (k)	5.6	َ، ء (ə)	7.6	ن (n)	8.1	َ، ء (ə)	8.5
ح، ہ (h)	4.6	ے (e:)	5.8	س، ص، ث (s)	7.3	ے (e:)	5.4
ن (n)	4.5	ی (i:)	5.0	ت، ط (t̪)	6.8	ی (i:)	5.0
س، ص، ث (s)	4.3	ِ (ɪ)	4.2	چ (tʃ)	4.8	و (o:)	3.5
م (m)	3.9	ُ (ʊ)	3.2	ک (k)	3.5	ِ (ɪ)	3.2
ت، ط (t̪)	3.4	وُ (u:)	2.1	پ (p)	2.9	ں، آں (ɑ̃:)	2.3
ل (l)	3.3	و (o:)	1.2	د (d)	2.8	وَ (ɔ:)	2.2
ب (b)	2.2	یں (ẽ:)	1.0	ٹھ (t^h)	2.4	ُ (ʊ)	0.9
د (d)	2.1	وَ (ɔ:)	0.9	ف (f)	2.2	(æ)	0.3
پ (p)	2.0	َے (æ:)	0.7	چھ (tʃ^h)	2.2	آئی (a:i:)	0.3
ی (j)	1.7	ہ (e)	0.5	ب (b)	1.6	یں (ẽ:)	0.3
و (v)	1.3	َیں (ɑẽ:)	0.4	و (v)	1.3	ا،آ (ea:)	0.3
ذ، ض، ظ، ز (z)	1.2	ُ (æ)	0.4	ح، ہ (h)	0.8	وُ (u:)	0.2
گ (g)	1.2	ہ (o)	0.4	ذ، ض، ظ، ز (z)	0.7	ہ (e)	0.1
ج (dʒ)	1.2	وں (õ:)	0.3	ل (l)	0.6	َے (æ:)	0.1
ٹ (t)	1.1	اں، آں (ɑ̃:)	0.3	ی (j)	0.4	َیں (ɑẽ:)	0.1
ف (f)	1.0	وُں (ũ:)	0.2	ٹ (t)	0.4		
ش (ʃ)	0.8	یں (ĩ:)	0.1	م (m)	0.3		
چ (tʃ)	0.7	آءِ (a:ɪ)	0.1	کھ (kh)	0.3		
ق (q)	0.6	ا،آ (ea:)	0.0	ج (dʒ)	0.3		
خ (x)	0.5	آئی (a:i:)	0.0	ڑ (r)	0.2		
ڈ (d)	0.5			گ (g)	0.2		
تھ (t^h)	0.4			تھ (t^h)	0.1		
چھ (tʃ^h)	0.3						
بھ (b^h)	0.3						
کھ (k^h)	0.3						
ڑ (r)	0.2						
ٹھ (t^h)	0.2						

Table 18: Frequency of occurrence of Urdu phonemes in training and testing data

Impacts of Vocoder Selection on Tacotron-based Nepali Text-To-Speech Synthesis

Ganesh Bdr. Dhakal Chhetri[1], Kiran Chandra Dahal[1], and Prakash Poudyal*[2]

[1] *Informatics and Intelligent System Engineering,*
IOE, Thapathali Campus, Kathmandu, Nepal

[2] *Information and Language Processing Research Lab (ILPRL)*
Department of Computer Science and Engineering
Kathmandu University, Nepal
ganesh.078msiise007@tcioe.edu.np, dahalkc@ioe.edu.np, prakash@ku.edu.np

Abstract

Text-to-speech (TTS) technology enhances human-computer interaction and accessibility. While vocoders like WaveNet and MelGAN have been extensively studied for English TTS, their application to Nepali TTS remains under-explored. This research addresses this gap by evaluating the performance of WaveNet and MelGAN vocoders for Nepali text-to-speech synthesis using mel-sepctrograms generated by the Tacotron2 model.

The analysis is based on two datasets: Nepali OpenSLR and News male voice recordings. Performance was measured using Mean Opinion Score (MOS) and Mel-Ceptral Distortion (MCD). The findings reveal that Tacotron2 with MelGAN achieved better naturalness and accuracy compared to Tacotron2 with WaveNet. On the Nepali OpenSLR dataset, Tacotron2 + MelGAN achieved an average MOS score of 4.245, while Tacotron2 + WaveNet scored 3.65. Similarly, on the male voice dataset, Tacotron2 + MelGAN achieved an MOS of 2.885, compared to 2.31 for Tacotron2 + WaveNet.

1 Introduction

Text-To-Speech technology allows machines to turn text into human-like speech. This technology is widely used in applications such as virtual assistants, educational tools, and accessibility solutions (Tan et al., 2024). Recent advancements in deep learning have greatly improved the naturalness and quality of TTS systems (Shen et al., 2018). Tacotron2 is one such model, generating clear and natural speech by converting text into spectrograms (Shen et al., 2018). However, turning these spectrograms into actual audio depends on vocoders, which impact both the quality and speed of the final speech (Van den Oord et al., 2016; Kumar et al., 2019).

TTS technology has evolved significantly, transitioning from rule-based systems to deep learning-driven approaches that produce more natural and intelligible speech (Tan et al., 2024). Among these advancements, Tacotron2 has emerged as a leading model for TTS, using a sequence-to-sequence architecture to convert text into spectrograms, which are then transformed into audio waveforms by vocoders (Shen et al., 2018). Vocoder selection is particularly important for optimizing TTS systems, with different vocoders offering unique strengths.

This paper focuses on using Tacotron2 for Nepali TTS, a language that has seen little development in this area. It compares two vocoders, MelGAN and WaveNet, to evaluate their performance in speech quality and processing speed, aiming to improve TTS for Nepali and similar low-resource languages.

2 Literature Review

Text-to-Speech technology plays crucial role in converting written text into spoken language. It is widely used in applications such as voice assistants, educational aids (Klein et al., 2020), and assistive technologies for individuals with visual impairments (Manirajee et al., 2024).

The concatenation-based approach on the Nepali Text-to-Speech(TTS) has been studied by Ghimire and Bal (2017). The author used existing TTS and enchanced the quality by adding the pre and post processing units. The transformer based Nepali TTS has been published recently by Dongol and Bal (2023). They have achieved a Mean Opinion Score (MOS) of 3.70. Dhakal Chhetri (2023)

*Corresponding Author: prakash@ku.edu.np

Proceedings of the First Workshop on Challenges in Processing South Asian Languages (CHiPSAL 2025), pages 185–192
January 19, 2025.

explores the capabilities of deep learning techniques for synthesizing Nepali Text-to-Speech using Tacotron. The goal is to develop a system that produces speech that sounds real. The researchers achieved successful voice output by creating a new Nepali speech dataset and building a model based on Tacotron1. However, the research is deficient in terms of comparisons with alternative vocoders and comprehensive data analysis. This initial research establishes the groundwork for future studies to enhance the model, explore alternative vocoders, and ultimately create more resilient Nepali text-to-speech systems.

In the research, Tan et al. (2024) investigate a new method for Text-to-Speech synthesis by employing a Variational Autoencoder (VAE) in order to produce a voice that is comparable to human quality. Their approach utilizes pre-trained phoneme sequences and a duration predictor to build speech. Unlike conventional autoregressive models such as Tacotron or FastSpeech, this VAE-based system utilizes a non-autoregressive structure, resulting in considerably faster speech creation. The model is trained on the LJSpeech dataset, which undergoes meticulous pre-processing to transform text into phonemes and generate Mel-Spectrograms. The objective of this research is to narrow the underlying gap between existing text-to-speech systems and authentic human speech in terms of quality. This work presents systematic research and the development of NaturalSpeech, with the goal of improving the performance and quality of text-to-waveform production in TTS technology.

Basnet (2021) study utilizes deep learning techniques to develop a Nepali Text-to-Speech synthesis system. The method employs a two-stage technique to transform written Nepali text into speech that sounds natural. Initially, convolutional neural networks examine the text and make predictions about spectrograms. Afterwards, recurrent neural networks equipped with attention mechanisms utilize these spectrograms to produce audio waveforms, prioritizing essential segments of the text to ensure precision. The study investigates the use of convolutional neural networks to predict spectrograms, recurrent neural networks to generate voice, attention mechanisms to focus, and advanced signal processing techniques to refine the results. The model, trained on a dataset of Nepali speech and validated using both subjective and objective approaches, showcases the efficacy of this deep learning technique for Nepali Text-to-Speech.

Existing Nepali Text-to-Speech systems face difficulties in generating speech, as they are unable to accurately capture the intricate details of the language (Subedi, 2015). In order to address this disparity, this study suggests an end-to-end deep learning approach. Their network comprises several essential elements: text normalization for consistent processing, an encoder-decoder architecture for fundamental text-to-speech conversion, attention mechanisms to concentrate on significant elements in the text, and a WaveNet vocoder to convert the generated representation into audio. However, the research acknowledges a constraint: the lack of Nepali speech samples restricts further progress. They emphasize the importance of having additional Nepali datasets that are easily accessible.

Additionally, vocoders are integral to the success of Text-to-Speech systems, as they enable the production of high-quality audio. However, many TTS studies typically concentrate on a single vocoder. This research seeks to bridge the gap by evaluating the effectiveness of various vocoders in a Tacotron-based model, with the objective of achieving optimal Nepali audio synthesis.

3 Experimental Workflow

3.1 System Block Diagram

The block diagram in Figure 1 illustrates the overall system flow.

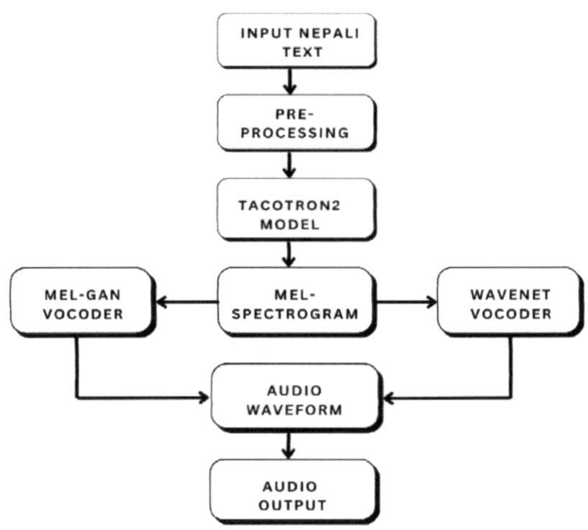

Figure 1: Block diagram for end-to-end TTS synthesis

Pre-Processing: Before inputting the text into the Tacotron2 model, preprocessing is carried out. During the preprocessing stage of this research, the input text is transformed into Unicode. The 'unidecode' function is employed to transform Nepali text into Unicode format. Here's an example of how to convert Nepali text into Unicode before inputting it into the Tacotron2 model:

Original Nepali Text: प्रमुख अन्तर्राष्ट्रिय खेल घटना

Converted Unicode Text: prmukh antrraassttriy khel ghttnaa

Tacotron2 Model: Character embedding is applied to the input data of a Tacotron2 model before it is used for training. It is a crucial preliminary phase in Tacotron2. The character embedding layer is enhanced with pre-trained vectors. The system converts individual Nepali characters into numerical representations that accurately capture the meaning and context of the language. To create a numerical representation of the term, Character embedding examines the arrangement of characters using a one-dimensional Convolutional Neural Network. For example, the word 'paani' can be decomposed into individual characters: pa, aa, ni, i. An embedding vector can represent each character. pa: 0.7, 0.2, 0.4, aa: 0.1, 0.9, 0.2, ni: 0.2, 0.5, 0.1, i: 0.4, 0.2, 0.6

Mel-Spectrogram: Tacotron2 uses multiple layers, such as character embedding and encoder-decoder networks, to process input text. It generates an important representation called the Mel-Spectrogram. The Mel-Spectrogram captures the intensity of varoius frequencies in speech over time. The frequency axis is represented using Mel scale, which reflects the non-linear nature of human auditory perceptionn. During training, the model learns from paired samples of text and corresponding Mel-Spectrograms. These spectrograms are derived from real voice recordings. Using its encoder-decoder structure, Tacotron2 maps the textual input to the Mel-Spectrogram representation. This allows it to generate natural and intelligible speech.

Vocoders for Speech Waveform Generation: Once Tacotron2 has produced the Mel-Spectrogram, a distinct model known as a vocoder is employed to construct the ultimate voice waveform. In this research, the vocoder models WaveNet and MelGAN are employed in conjunction with Tacotron2.

WaveNet Vocoder: WaveNet is a predictive model that uses the previously generated audio samples and Mel-Spectrogram information to forecast the next audio sample in the speech waveform. It utilizes a sequential prediction approach to effectively capture the complex temporal relationships seen in speech. This paper employs WaveNet to synthesize speech audio waveforms by employing the Mel-Spectrogram produced by the Tacotron2 model.

MelGAN Vocoder: MelGAN is a vocoder model that utilizes Generative Adversarial Networks (GANs) as its basis. The system consists of two networks: a generator and a discriminator. The generator's objective is to produce authentic speech waveforms using the Mel-Spectrogram, whereas the discriminator's goal is to differentiate between genuine and created speech. The adversarial training procedure facilitates the acquisition of the ability for MelGAN to generate speech of high quality. In this research, the MelGAN model, trained separately, can generate audio waveforms from the Mel-Spectrogram generated by the Tacotron2 model, just like WaveNet.

3.2 Dataset

To develop a natural-sounding Nepali speech synthesis system, high-quality audio data with minimal background noise and clear pronunciation was essential. The research collected Nepali audio recordings paired with corresponding transcriptions. Audio files were encoded in .wav format and segmented into fragments of 1 to 12 seconds using Audacity software (Zen et al., 2013). This segmentation aligned with the natural rhythms, making it easier for the model to capture authentic patterns and reducing computational resource requirements (Van den Oord et al., 2016).

The dataset included transcriptions for each segment and recordings from multiple male news presenters to enhance diversity. Both the OpenSLR dataset (Sodimana et al., 2018) and the male voice data collected from Nepal Television were used separately for this research. Details about the male voice dataset from news recording are provided in Table 1.

3.3 Model Prepared

This research used the Tacotron2 model along with the MelGAN and WaveNet vocoders. The

Table 1: News Male Voice Data

Feature	Description
Speaker	Multiple male speakers
Source	Nepal Television broadcasts
Format	Varies, resampled to 22.05 kHz
Size	Approximately 2100 samples
Data Split	80% training, 20% validation/testing

OpenSLR dataset and a male voice dataset were used separately for analysis. The training process followed the parameters setup described by (Kumar et al., 2019; Shen et al., 2018; Van den Oord et al., 2016).

3.3.1 Tacotron2 Model

The Tacotron2 model's effective training depends on key audio parameters that determine its interpretation of raw audio input. For the training process, a learning rate of 0.001 and a batch size of 8 were employed.

3.3.2 MelGAN Model

The MelGAN model was trained by adjusting multiple training parameters, as detailed in Table 2.

Table 2: MelGAN Training Parameters

Parameter	Value
Batch Size	16
Learning Rate	0.0001
Optimizer	Adam
Beta-1	0.5
Beta-2	0.9

3.3.3 WaveNet Model

Similarly, the WaveNet model was trained with various hyperparameters, as detailed in Table 3.

Table 3: WaveNet Training Parameters

Parameter	**Value**
Learning Rate	0.001
Batch Size	8
Optimizer	Adam

3.4 Verification and Validation

3.4.1 Qualitative Approach

A qualitative methodology was employed to compare the audio waveforms generated by the Tacotron2 + MelGAN model and the Tacotron2 + WaveNet model with the original test data audio waveforms. This comparison was done individually for both OpenSLR and male voice data.

3.4.2 Quantitative Approach

The Mel Cepstral Distortion (MCD) metric is an objective and quantitative measure. The process involves comparing the melspectrograms of generated speech with those of recorded speech. Mathematically it can be computed as in Equation(1).

$$MCD = \sqrt{2\sum((mel_1 - mel_2)^2)} \qquad (1)$$

where, mel_1 and mel_2 represent the respective melspectrograms.

The MCD values were obtained for both the OpenSLR and male voice datasets using the Tacotron2 + MelGAN and Tacotron2 + WaveNet models. Subsequently, a comparison was conducted between the MCD values acquired for each model and dataset.

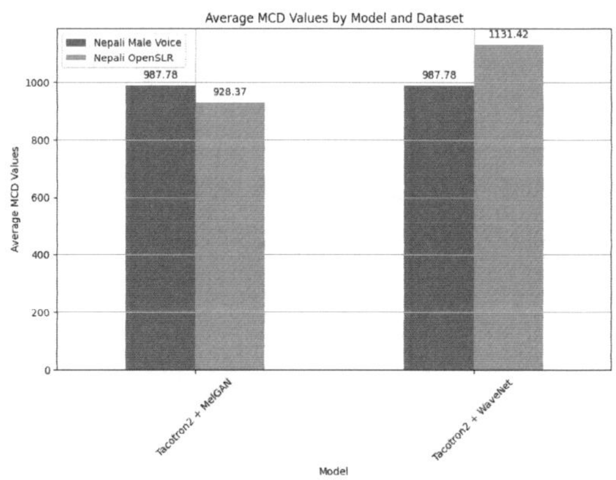

Figure 2: Average MCD values by Model and Dataset

The average MCD values for the Tacotron2 + MelGAN model were 928.37 on the OpenSLR dataset and 987.87 on the News male voice data. On the other hand, the Tacotron2 + Wavenet model yielded mean MCD values of 1131.42 and 987.87, respectively. The findings indicate that Tacotron2 + MelGAN generally outperforms in terms of voice quality on the OpenSLR dataset, however both models demonstrate similar performance on the News male voice data. Figure 2 shows a detailed analysis.

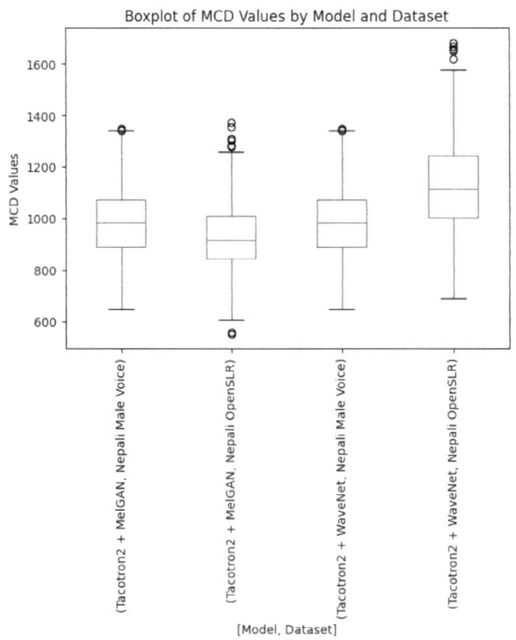

Figure 3: Boxplot of MCD values by Model and Dataset

MelGAN and WaveNet were directly compared to see how well they reproduce target speech. A boxplot in Figure 3 displays their MCD values side by side. The boxplot analysis illustrates that both the Tacotron2 + MelGAN and Tacotron2 + WaveNet models demonstrate almost equal median values for the news male voice dataset. However, the quantity of outliers is significantly reduced in comparison to the OpenSLR dataset. In the OpenSLR dataset, the Tacotron2 + MelGAN model exhibits a relatively lower median value. A lower median value typically indicates superior model performance (Kubichek, 1993). Consequently, drawing from this quantitative analysis of the dataset and model, it can be inferred that the Tacotron2 + MelGAN model attains better results on the OpenSLR dataset.

4 Results

In order to accomplish to assess the efficacy of MelGAN and WaveNet vocoders when used together with the Tacotron2 model for synthesizing Nepali text into speech, a model was first trained and evaluated using the predominantly female-voiced Nepali OpenSLR dataset. Afterwards, the model was retrained using male voice data obtained from Nepal Television.

4.1 OpenSLR Data (Model Training)

The Tacotron2 model completed its training after 112,000 steps, which took around 54 hours. The ultimate training loss reached a convergence point of 0.314. Significantly, the validation loss at step 112,000 was measured to be 0.459. After the completion of training the Tacotron2 model on the OpenSLR dataset, the training of the MelGAN model was initiated. The training procedure of MelGAN involves a dynamic interaction between the generator and discriminator. In this research, the MelGAN training ended after completing 516,444 steps. The generator loss was 89.587, and the discriminator loss was 59.432 at this stage.

This study also trained the WaveNet model to assess the effectiveness of different vocoders. During the training process, the model's performance is evaluated by considering both the training loss and validation loss. The training procedure finished after approximately 1,000 epochs, which is equivalent to 220,000 training steps. The ultimate loss at the end of the training phase was 4.818. The validation loss at this point was 5.436.

4.2 Male Voice Data (Model Training)

The Tacotron2 model underwent additional training after being trained on the OpenSLR dataset, which consisted of male voices data from various speakers on Nepal Television. The model training process involved monitoring the loss for both training and validation data. The number of training steps equaled to 70,000 in total. At this stage, the training loss value achieved was 0.28. The validation loss value achieved during this training stage was 0.65. Figure 4 displays the training and validation graph for the male voice dataset using the Tacotron2 model.

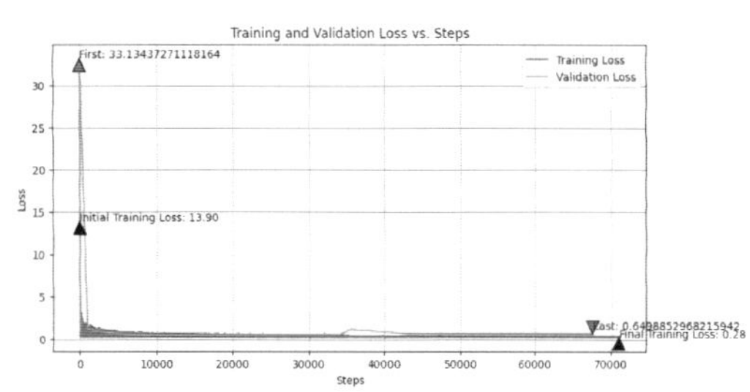

Figure 4: Tacotron2 training & validation loss

The MelGAN model was retrained with Nepali news male voice data, just as it was trained on the OpenSLR dataset. The model underwent a training process, during which it completed 600,000 steps. After training the models, the combined Tacotron2 and MelGAN models were used to generate the final speech output by running inference on the Nepali news male voice test dataset. An assessment of the loss generated by the generator and discriminator was carried out during the complete training procedure of the MelGAN model. At the $600,000^{th}$ step of training, the generator's training loss had reached 201.84, while the discriminator's training loss was 52.92. The generator and discriminator have validation losses of 319.35 and 208.89 respectively. Figure 5 and 6 illustrate the training and validation losses for the generator and discriminator.

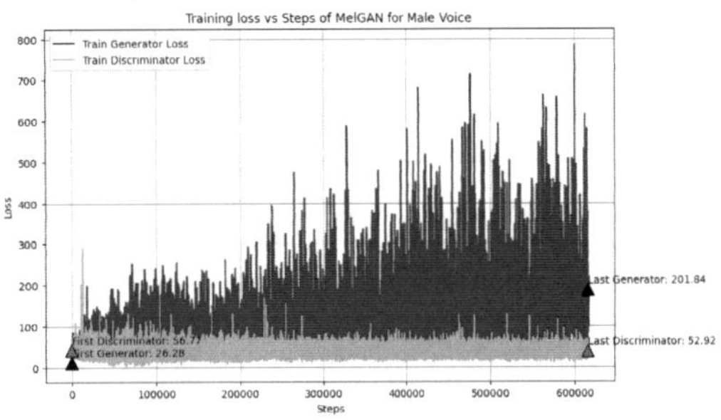

Figure 5: Generator, Discriminator training loss

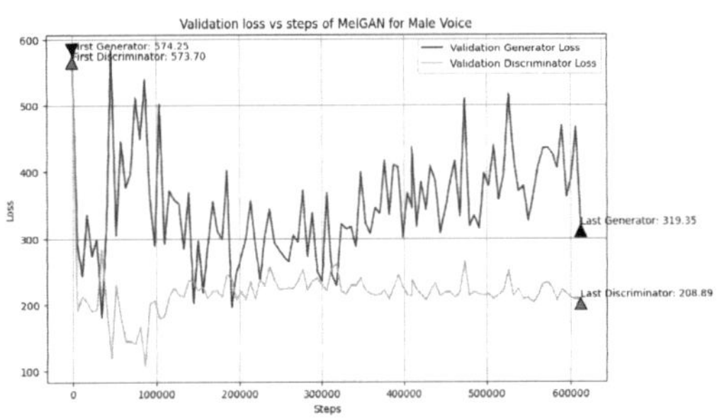

Figure 6: Generator, Discriminator validation loss

The training and validation losses of the WaveNet model are illustrated in Figure 7. The WaveNet model underwent training using the male voice dataset for a duration of up to 250,000 steps. The training loss value was 4.77, while the validation loss value was 5.24 at this stage.

After conducting independent training of the models using the OpenSLR and male voice data, the Tacotron2 + MelGAN model and the Tacotron2 + WaveNet model were utilized to perform inference on the test data from both OpenSLR and male voice datasets. This resulted in predictions for speech synthesis.

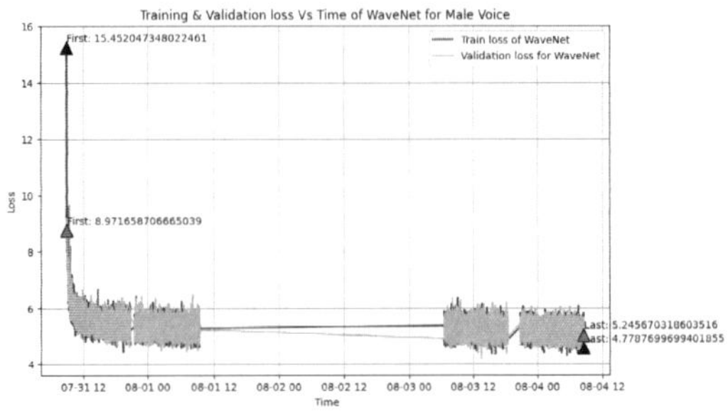

Figure 7: WaveNet training & validation loss

5 Discussion and Analysis

5.1 Inference Time Comparison: MelGAN vs. WaveNet

The speech synthesis on the test data involved the utilization of two models: Tacotron2 + MelGAN and Tacotron2 + WaveNet. Both the Tacotron2 + MelGAN and Tacotron2 + WaveNet models were inferred using an NVIDIA GTX 960M GPU. The average time required for each synthesis process is compared in Table 4.

Table 4: Inference Time Comparison

Model	Inference Time (s)
Tacotron2 + MelGAN	0.142
Tacotron2 + WaveNet	1320

The processing design of MelGAN provides a clear advantage over WaveNet in terms of its speed. Compared to WaveNet, which produces output in a sequential manner, MelGAN is capable of processing the full input at the same time. By using parallel processing, MelGAN achieves a reduction in inference time, making it a highly efficient option.

5.2 MOS Score Comparison: WaveNet vs. MelGAN

The MOS score was calculated using data collected through Google Forms. Each model produced four samples for evaluation. Participants rated the samples on a scale of 1 to 5, assessing naturalness and accuracy. A total of 40 participants provided the ratings used to calculate the final MOS score. The MOS scores for naturalness and accuracy between Tacotron2 + MelGAN and Tacotron2 + WaveNet on the OpenSLR dataset are presented in Table 5. Similarly, the MOS scores for the male voice dataset are shown in Table 6.

Table 5: MOS Score Comparison (OpenSLR Data)

Model	Naturalness	Accuracy
Tacotron2 + MelGAN	4.21	4.28
Tacotron2 + WaveNet	3.56	3.74

Table 6: MOS Score Comparison (Male Voice Data)

Model	Naturalness	Accuracy
Tacotron2 + MelGAN	2.97	2.80
Tacotron2 + WaveNet	2.33	2.29

These findings indicate that the Tacotron 2 + MelGAN model outperforms the Tacotron 2 + WaveNet model in terms of both the naturalness and accuracy of the generated output.

The OpenSLR dataset, which predominantly emphasizes female voices, demonstrates reduced variability in pitch and frequency across different speakers. In contrast, the inclusion of male voice data, which consists of various speakers and different tones even within individual speakers for distinct transcripts, presents more difficult obstacles for models to generalize data. The intrinsic variability of male voice data and the limited amount of data have a substantial impact on MOS scores, resulting in lower overall ratings. Moreover, the complexity of male voice data could result in increased noise production during the process of speech synthesis.

5.3 Comparison with Existing System

The research titled "Natural TTS Synthesis by Conditioning WaveNet on Mel Spectrogram Prediction" by (Shen et al., 2018), stated that the WaveNet model achieved a Mean Opinion Score of 4.53 when it was trained using the US English dataset.

In the study "MelGAN: Generative Adversarial Networks for Conditional Waveform Synthesis" conducted by (Kumar et al., 2019), the MelGAN model demonstrated a Mean Opinion Score of 3.61 ± 0.06 after being trained on the LJ Speech dataset. After being trained on the VCTK dataset, the MelGAN model got a Mean Opinion Score of 3.49 ± 0.09. Similarly, in the research "Attention and WaveNet Vocoder Based Nepali Text-to-Speech Synthesis" by (Basnet, 2021), a MOS of 3.07 was forecasted.

Table 7 presents the average MOS score calculated by taking the mean of the naturalness and accuracy rating in this research.

Table 7: Average MOS Score (OpenSLR & Male Voice Data)

Model	Dataset	Average MOS
Tacotron2 + MelGAN	OpenSLR	4.245
Tacotron2 + MelGAN	Male Voice	2.885
Tacotron2 + WaveNet	OpenSLR	3.65
Tacotron2 + WaveNet	Male Voice	2.31

The Tacotron2 + MelGAN model achieved an average MOS score of 4.245 for the Nepali OpenSLR dataset. This number is greater than the MOS scores presented for both the LJ speech data and VCTK English datasets. Nevertheless, the mean opinion score achieved for male voice data using the Tacotron 2 + MelGAN model is comparatively lower than the MOS scores obtained in previous studies (Kumar et al., 2019) for both LJ Speech data and VCTK English datasets using the MelGAN model.

Table 8: MOS Score Comparison (WaveNet Model)

Model	Average MOS
WaveNet (US English)	4.53
Existing Nepali TTS ((Basnet, 2021))	3.07
Tacotron2 + WaveNet (Nepali OpenSLR)	3.65
Tacotron2 + WaveNet (Male Voice)	2.31

Based on the data presented in Table 8, the WaveNet model achieved the highest Mean Opinion Score when trained on the English dataset. Its performance surpassed that on the Nepali OpenSLR and male voice datasets. It also outperformed results from prior Nepali Text-To-Speech studies.

6 Conclusion and Future work

The research findings clearly demonstrate that the selection of a vocoder has significant impacts on the performance of a Nepali Text-to-Speech system. When combined with Tacotron2, MelGAN consistently outperformed WaveNet in terms of the naturalness, accuracy, and overall quality of speech. The superiority of the Tacotron2 + MelGAN model is apparent by the higher Mean Opinion Scores (MOS) and lower Mel-cepstral Distortion (MCD) it achieves.

Furthermore, MelGAN exhibited a significant benefit in terms of inference time. Compared to WaveNet, MelGAN has a lower computing time need for voice generation, making it a more efficient option for real-time applications. However, the research was hindered by the scarcity of Nepali datasets with multiple-speaker male voices. This impeded the assessment of the model's effectiveness on a broader spectrum of datasets. Moreover, the model encountered difficulties in precisely articulating numbers and symbols, highlighting a constraint that should be tackled in future investigations.

Although there are several restrictions, the Tacotron2 + MelGAN model is considered the best setup for creating Nepali TTS systems of superior quality. Future research can improve efficiency by optimizing single-speaker male voice datasets. Customizing the model to handle numbers and symbols can enhance usability. Exploring context-based approaches and hybrid architectures, like combining Tacotron2 with Transformer-based models, may further advance Nepali TTS systems.

Acknowledgments

The authors would like to extend sincere thanks to the reviewers for their constructive comments and suggestions.

References

Ashok Basnet. 2021. Attention and wavenet vocoder based nepali text-to-speech synthesis. Master's thesis.

Ganesh Bdr. Dhakal Chhetri. 2023. Nepali text to speech using tacotron. Master's thesis, Thapathali Campus, Tribhuvan University.

Ishan Dongol and Bal Krishna Bal. 2023. Transformer-based Nepali text-to-speech. In *Proceedings of the 20th International Conference on Natural Language Processing (ICON)*, pages 651–656, Goa University, Goa, India. NLP Association of India (NLPAI).

Rupak Raj Ghimire and Bal Krishna Bal. 2017. Enhancing the Quality of Nepali Text-to-Speech Systems. In Alla Kravets, Maxim Shcherbakov, Marina Kultsova, and Peter Groumpos, editors, *Creativity in Intelligent Technologies and Data Science*, volume 754, pages 187–197. Springer International Publishing.

Andreas Klein, Andreas Hinderks, Maria Rauschenberger, and Jorg Thomaschewski. 2020. Exploring voice assistant risks and potential with technology-based users.

Robert F. Kubichek. 1993. Mel-cepstral distance measure for objective speech quality assessment. In *Proceedings of IEEE Pacific Rim Conference on Communications, Computers and Signal Processing*, volume 1, pages 125–128. IEEE.

Kundan Kumar, Ritesh Kumar, Thibault De Boissiere, Lucas Gestin, Wei Zhen Teoh, Jose Sotelo, Alexandre De Brebisson, Yoshua Bengio, and Aaron C. Courville. 2019. Melgan: Generative adversarial networks for conditional waveform synthesis. *Advances in Neural Information Processing Systems*, 32.

Lalitha Manirajee, Siti Qatrunnada Hanis Shariff, and Syar Meeze Mohd Rashid. 2024. Assistive technology for visually impaired individuals: A systematic literature review (slr). *International Journal of Academic Research in Business and Social Sciences*, 14.

Jonathan Shen, Ruoming Pang, Ron J. Weiss, Mike Schuster, Navdeep Jaitly, Zongheng Yang, Zhifeng Chen, Yu Zhang, Yuxuan Wang, Rj Skerrv-Ryan, Rif A. Saurous, Yannis Agiomvrgiannakis, and Yonghui Wu. 2018. Natural tts synthesis by conditioning wavenet on mel spectrogram predictions. In *Proceedings of the 2018 IEEE International Conference on Acoustics, Speech and Signal Processing (ICASSP)*, pages 4779–4783. IEEE.

Keshan Sodimana, Knot Pipatsrisawat, Linne Ha, Martin Jansche, Oddur Kjartansson, Pasindu De Silva, and Supheakmungkol Sarin. 2018. A step-by-step process for building tts voices using open source data and framework for bangla, javanese, khmer, nepali, sinhala, and sundanese. In *Proceedings of the 6th International Workshop on Spoken Language Technologies for Under-Resourced Languages (SLTU)*, pages 66–70, Gurugram, India. Association for Computational Linguistics.

Kaushal Subedi. 2015. Nepali text-to-speech. Master's thesis.

Xu Tan, Jiawei Chen, Haohe Liu, Jian Cong, Chen Zhang, Yanqing Liu, Xi Wang, Yichong Leng, Yuanhao Yi, Lei He, et al. 2024. Naturalspeech: End-to-end text-to-speech synthesis with human-level quality. *IEEE Transactions on Pattern Analysis and Machine Intelligence*.

Aaron Van den Oord, Sander Dieleman, Heiga Zen, Karen Simonyan, Oriol Vinyals, Alex Graves, Nal Kalchbrenner, Andrew Senior, and Koray Kavukcuoglu. 2016. Wavenet: A generative model for raw audio.

Heiga Zen, Andrew Senior, and Mike Schuster. 2013. Statistical parametric speech synthesis using deep neural networks. In *Proceedings of the 2013 IEEE International Conference on Acoustics, Speech and Signal Processing (ICASSP)*, pages 7962–7966. IEEE.

EmoTa: A Tamil Emotional Speech Dataset

Jubeerathan Thevakumar and Luxshan Thavarasa and Thanikan Sivatheepan and Sajeev Kugarajah and Uthayasanker Thayasivam
Department of Computer Science and Engineering
University of Moratuwa
Colombo, Sri Lanka
{jubeerathan.20, luxshan.20, thanikan.20, kugarajah.21, rtuthaya}@cse.mrt.ac.lk

Abstract

This paper introduces EmoTa, the first emotional speech dataset in Tamil, designed to reflect the linguistic diversity of Sri Lankan Tamil speakers. EmoTa comprises 936 recorded utterances from 22 native Tamil speakers (11 male, 11 female), each articulating 19 semantically neutral sentences across five primary emotions: anger, happiness, sadness, fear, and neutrality. To ensure quality, inter-annotator agreement was assessed using Fleiss' Kappa, resulting in a substantial agreement score of 0.74. Initial evaluations using machine learning models, including XGBoost and Random Forest, yielded a high F1-score of 0.91 and 0.90 for emotion classification tasks. By releasing EmoTa as open-access, we aim to encourage further exploration of Tamil language processing and the development of innovative models for Tamil Speech Emotion Recognition.

1 Introduction

The development of emotional speech datasets has significantly advanced Speech Emotion Recognition (SER), enhancing human-computer interaction by enabling systems to interpret and respond to emotions in nuanced, human-like ways (Cowie et al., 2001). However, for low-resource languages like Tamil, particularly in the Sri Lankan context, high-quality emotional datasets remain scarce. This scarcity restricts the development of SER models tailored to Tamil-speaking communities, limiting applications in localized assistive technology, emotion-based mental health diagnostics, and customer service for Tamil-speaking users.

In this work, we introduce EmoTa[1] , a novel, acted Tamil emotional speech dataset that captures the linguistic and cultural diversity of Sri Lankan Tamil speakers. The dataset focuses on five fundamental emotionsanger, happiness, sadness, fear, and neutralitychosen for their wide recognition and relevance in SER and to reflect the range of emotional expressions commonly encountered in everyday Tamil communication. These core emotions also align with those used in established SER datasets, allowing comparative studies while maintaining a culturally relevant focus. To ensure clarity and isolate prosodic cues, we use semantically neutral sentences, a practice inspired by similar works in emotional speech corpora such as EMOVO (Costantini et al.), EMODB (Burkhardt et al., 2005), CaFE (Gournay et al., 2018). This approach reduces the risk of lexical bias, ensuring that models trained on this dataset can accurately recognize emotional tone independent of content.

The accessibility of this high-quality emotional speech dataset is a cornerstone of its contribution, enabling reproducibility, facilitating collaboration, and supporting the validation and benchmarking of SER models across varied Tamil dialects. By filling an essential gap in Tamil SER resources, this open-access dataset advances the SER field for low-resource languages, serving as a reference point for related work and creating pathways for future developments.

2 Related Work

Established SER datasets such as EMOVO (Italian) (Costantini et al.), EMODB (German) (Burkhardt et al., 2005), and CaFE (Canadian French) (Gournay et al., 2018) have set benchmarks by providing structured, acted datasets that ensure consistency, quality, and controlled variation in emotional portrayals. These datasets highlight the benefits of the acted approach, where carefully guided performances yield emotionally distinct, reliable data that enhances model training and generalization.

For Tamil, some progress has been made in developing emotional speech datasets. Rajan et al. (2019) introduced TaMaR-EmoDB, a multilingual emotional speech database covering Tamil, Malay-

[1] https://github.com/aaivu/EmoTa

Proceedings of the First Workshop on Challenges in Processing South Asian Languages (CHiPSAL 2025), pages 193–201
January 19, 2025.

alam, and Ravula. However, this corpus remains inaccessible to the public, limiting reproducibility and broader applicability. Similarly, Ram and Ponnusamy (2014) created a custom Tamil emotional speech dataset using standard feature extraction techniques, but it focused on a specific subset of Tamil speakers. Vasuki et al. (2020) developed two Tamil emotional corpora for children and adults, drawn from Tamil films and plays to capture culturally resonant expressions. Furthermore, Fernandes and Mannepalli (2021) constructed a dataset to support deep learning model development for Tamil SER.

Despite these contributions, existing datasets primarily focus on Indian Tamil and lack representation of the linguistic and cultural diversity found in the Sri Lankan Tamil community. Unique prosodic features, dialects, and emotional expressions specific to Sri Lankan Tamil speakers require tailored datasets for reliable SER applications. Inspired by the methodologies of EMOVO (Costantini et al.), EMODB (Burkhardt et al., 2005), and CaFE (Gournay et al., 2018), our dataset adopts an acted approach, ensuring distinct and reproducible emotional expressions while capturing the dialectal richness of Sri Lankan Tamil.

3 Dataset Development

3.1 Selection of Emotions and Actors

For the Tamil speech emotion dataset, we focused on five core emotions commonly recognized in speech emotion recognition: Anger, Happiness, Sadness, Fear, and Neutral. These emotions were selected based on their relevance in affective computing and their consistent presence in other emotional speech datasets. To ensure clarity and consistency in emotional expressions, detailed descriptions of each emotion were provided to the actors.

We adopted a discrete theory of emotions, specifically drawing from Ekmans classification (Ekman, 1992), which effectively captures the range of emotional expressions applicable to spoken language. Although some researchers (James, 1922; Lazarus, 1994) suggest additional emotions, such as love or hope, we opted for the more universally understood basic emotions that can be reliably conveyed through speech. This approach minimizes ambiguity in emotional expression, which is crucial for the effective training of machine learning models in speech emotion recognition.

The actors were selected through a recruitment process that included local advertisements and a pre-selection session. Approximately 40 native Tamil-speaking candidates, aged between 23 and 25 from diverse regions of Sri Lanka performed sample utterances in a controlled environment. A panel of three experienced drama teachers evaluated these recordings for emotional delivery and naturalness. From this pool, 22 actors were chosen, 11 males and 11 females, ensuring a balanced representation of the genders. All selected actors demonstrated exceptional ability to convey emotions and have at least a 'B' grade in drama at the G.C.E (O/L) examination[2]. Figure 1 illustrates the geographic distribution of the actors, highlighting the richness of the data set in regional variation.

By carefully selecting emotions and actors from diverse regions and backgrounds, this dataset provides a robust resource for research on speech emotion recognition, offering valuable insights into emotional expression in different Tamil dialects.

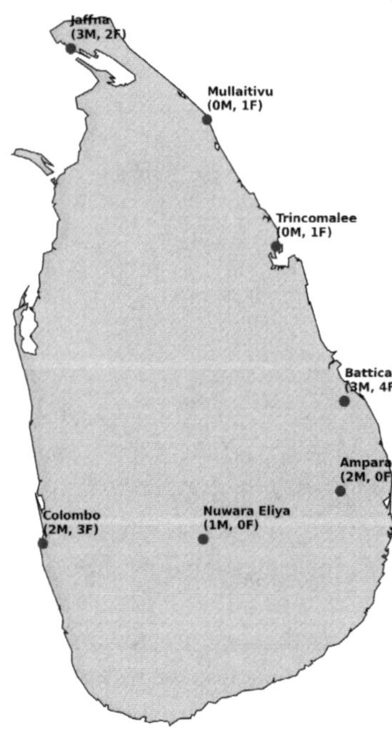

Figure 1: Regional breakdown of Actors.

3.2 Linguistic Material and Emotional Contexts

To develop the Tamil Speech Emotion Recognition (SER) dataset, EmoTa, we selected 19 semantically neutral sentences, allowing for a wide range of

[2]https://en.wikipedia.org/wiki/GCE_Ordinary_Level_in_Sri_Lanka

emotional expressions without introducing word-based biases. Inspired by datasets such as EMOVO (Costantini et al.) and EMODB (Burkhardt et al., 2005), we focused on everyday Tamil phrases that actors can easily recall and connect with emotionally. This approach encourages emotional delivery through vocal tone and prosody rather than specific words, helping SER models capture authentic vocal expressions.

Figure 2 provides sample sentences with their pronunciation and English translation. These sentences, used commonly in Tamil interactions, contain balanced phonetic elements to support detailed acoustic analysis. By keeping the language neutral, the dataset encourages actors to rely on vocal delivery for emotion expression.

Example of Emotional Adaptability: One versatile sentence in the dataset, "Nan unnai cantikka ventum." ("I need to meet you"), can represent multiple emotions depending on the context:

- **Sadness:** Used when conveying longing for a loved one who has been absent for a long time, this sentence is spoken with vulnerability and yearning.
- **Neutral:** In a professional setting, it simply requests a meeting with a colleague, delivered in a straightforward tone.
- **Happiness:** Spoken with excitement to share good news, such as a new job or engagement, this phrase becomes an expression of joy.
- **Fear:** When responding to an urgent situation concerning a friend, its spoken with anxiety and concern.
- **Anger:** In a tense setting, this phrase becomes a demand to meet in person to resolve a disagreement, with a tone of frustration and assertiveness.

These context-based scenarios help capture the nuances of vocal emotion, allowing SER models to focus on emotional prosody over lexical content. This method enables a deeper understanding of how emotions are expressed through voice alone, enhancing the effectiveness of SER models in real-world applications.

3.3 Recording Protocol and Data Curation

The recordings for the Tamil speech emotion dataset were conducted in a soundproof studio using professional equipment to ensure high-quality audio. Recordings were captured at a 48 kHz sampling rate and later downsampled to 16 kHz for compatibility across applications. Actors were given flexibility in their movements and expression, while being mindful of microphone placement to ensure consistent sound quality. Each one-hour recording session was supervised by a team of phoneticians, with two providing instructions and feedback and one managing equipment. Before each utterance, actors received prompts to avoid reading intonations and were provided emotional context to encourage authentic expression.

Actors recorded each sentence four to five times to capture subtle variations, with the best take selected based on acting quality and clarity of recording. Special emphasis was placed on avoiding exaggerated expressions, maintaining a natural and conversational style. However, challenges such as proximity variations and fluctuating intonation contours were addressed by adjusting recording levels and providing additional guidance.

To ensure efficient organization and retrieval, we adopted a systematic file naming convention:

<spkID>_<senID>_<emo>.wav

For example, the file name *01_02_ang.wav* indicates that this file corresponds to speaker ID 01, sentence ID 02, and an angry emotion.

The final dataset consists of 936 utterances from 22 actors, represents five different emotions happiness, sadness, anger, fear, and neutralitywith a total recording duration of approximately 48 minutes. Figure 3 provides a visual breakdown of the distribution of utterances across the various emotions. This distribution is key for ensuring that the dataset offers a balanced representation of emotional expressions, which is crucial for the development of emotion recognition models.

3.4 Inter-Annotator Agreement

To evaluate the reliability of our dataset, we assessed the inter-annotator agreement using Fleiss' kappa (Randolph, 2005) coefficient, a metric suitable for measuring agreement among multiple annotators. Inter-annotator agreement quantifies how well annotators consistently make the same annotation decisions for a particular category. This is essential to ensure the annotation process is consistent and that different annotators are assigning the same emotion label to a given sample. The kappa score is calculated as follows:

$$\kappa = \frac{p_0 - p_e}{1 - p_e} \tag{1}$$

Tamil Sentence	Tamil Pronunciation	English Translation
நான் இன்று மாலை வீட்டுக்கு செல்கிறேன்.	Nāṉ iṉṟu mālai vīṭṭukku celkiṟēṉ.	I am going home this evening.
அந்த செய்தித்தாளை இங்கு வையுங்கள்.	Anta ceytittāḷai iṅku vaiyuṅkaḷ.	Put that newspaper here.
நீ இப்போது வளர்ந்துவிட்டாய்.	Nī ippōtu vaḷarntuviṭṭāy	You have grown up.
நான் உன்னை சந்திக்க வேண்டும்.	Nāṉ uṉṉai cantikka vēṇṭum.	I need to meet you.
அண்ணா எழுந்திருங்கள்.	Aṇṇā eḻuntiruṅkaḷ.	Brother, wake up.
புத்தகம் மேசையில் உள்ளது.	Putakam mēsaiyil ullatu.	The book is on the table.
நான் அதை பார்த்து கொள்கிறேன்.	Nāṉ atai pārttu kolkiṟēn.	I will keep an eye on it.

Figure 2: Sample Selected Sentences.

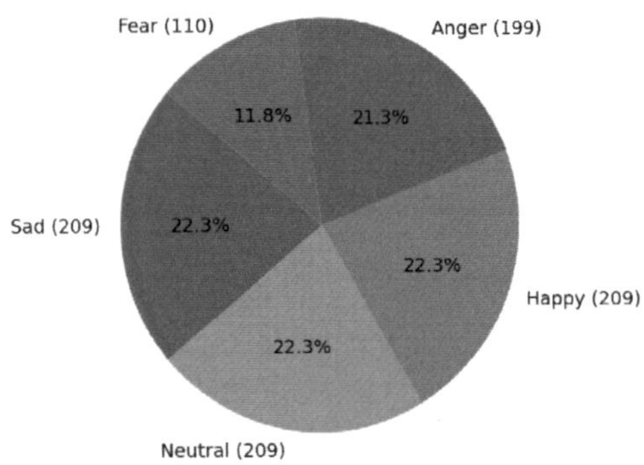

Figure 3: Distribution of utterances across emotions.

where p_0 represents the observed agreement, and p_e is the expected agreement by chance. The results of the inter-annotator agreement between our annotators yielded a substantial kappa score of 0.74, indicating high agreement across the five annotators. Notably, sadness and fear showed higher disagreements among annotators, contributing to the overall results.

4 Feature Extraction Techniques

In Speech Emotion Recognition (SER), selecting the right features is crucial, as speech signals contain various parameters that convey emotional information. Zero-Crossing Rate (ZCR), Chroma Features, Mel-Frequency Cepstral Coefficients (MFCC), Root Mean Square (RMS), and Mel Spectrogram are highly used for emotion classification (Ahmed et al., 2023). Each method offers unique insights into the emotional content of speech, which we will review briefly below.

4.1 Zero-Crossing Rate (ZCR)

Zero-Crossing Rate (ZCR) measures how often the signal changes sign, indicating the frequency of waveform zero crossings. It serves as an important indicator of speech dynamics and can help differentiate between voiced and unvoiced segments. Higher ZCR values typically indicate more dynamic speech, which may correspond to higher emotional intensity (Aouani and Ayed, 2020). Sample ZCR plots for each of the five emotions are shown in Figure 4.

4.2 Chroma Features

Chroma features capture the energy distribution across the 12 pitch classes of the chromatic scale. This technique is valuable for analyzing harmonic content in speech, as it can provide insights into the emotional expression related to musicality and intonation (Garg et al., 2020). Sample Chroma Features plots for each of the five emotions are shown in Figure 5.

4.3 Mel-Frequency Cepstral Coefficients (MFCC)

Mel-Frequency Cepstral Coefficients (MFCCs) are widely recognized as effective features for speech and audio analysis (Likitha et al., 2017). They are derived from the power spectrum of sound and are designed to reflect human auditory perception. MFCCs encapsulate the timbral properties of audio signals, making them essential for emotion recognition tasks, as they capture both spectral and temporal information in speech. Sample MFCC plots for each of the five emotions are shown in Figure 6.

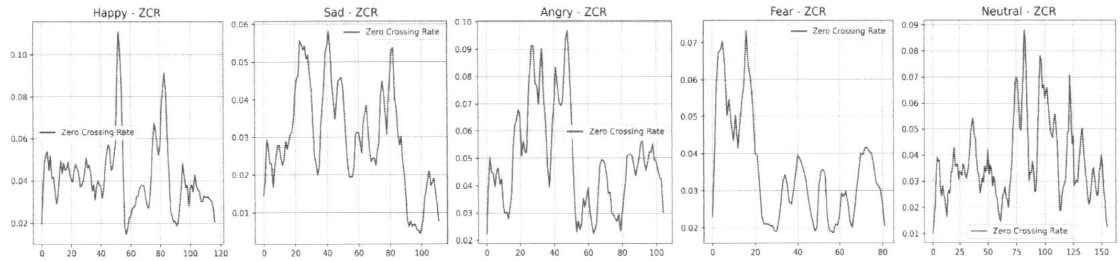

Figure 4: Zero Crossing Rate (ZCR) for various emotions: Happy, Sad, Angry, Fear, and Neutral. The ZCR measures the rate at which the signal changes from positive to negative.

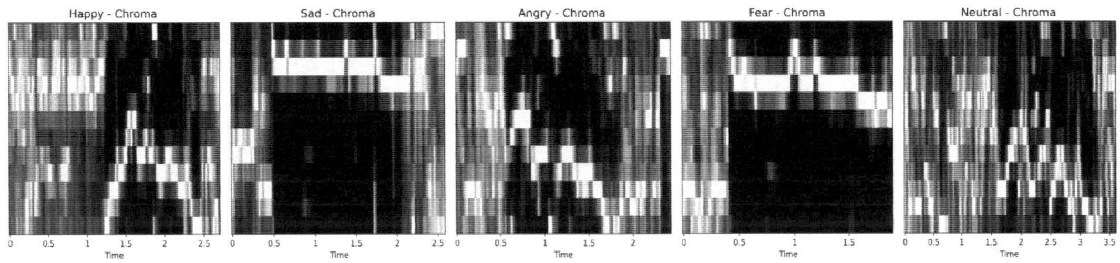

Figure 5: Chroma features for different emotions: Happy, Sad, Angry, Fear, and Neutral. Chroma features capture the energy distribution across 12 different pitch classes, providing insights into the harmonic content of the audio signals.

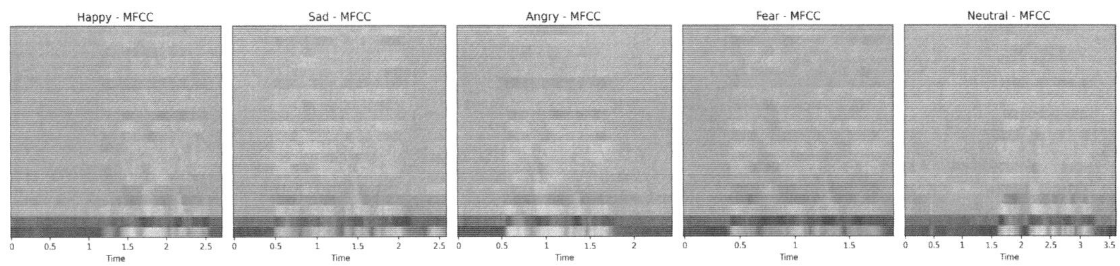

Figure 6: MFCCs for various emotions: Happy, Sad, Angry, Fear, and Neutral. MFCCs represent the short-term power spectrum of sound, widely used in speech and audio processing to capture the characteristics of human speech and music.

4.4 Root Mean Square (RMS)

The Root Mean Square (RMS) value quantifies the magnitude of a varying quantity in audio signals. In the context of speech, it measures loudness and energy. Higher RMS values are often associated with more intense emotions, while lower values may indicate calmer emotions. Thus, RMS is a crucial feature for differentiating emotional states based on speech amplitude. Sample RMS plots for each of the five emotions are shown in Figure 7.

4.5 Mel-Spectrogram

The Mel-Spectrogram combines the advantages of the Mel scale with spectrogram analysis, offering a visual representation of the frequency content of audio signals over time. This technique emphasizes perceptually relevant features, aligning with human auditory perception. By capturing the dynamic changes in sound, the Mel spectrogram enables effective modeling of emotional expression in speech, especially useful in deep learning applications (Venkataramanan and Rajamohan, 2019). Sample Mel-spectrogram plots for each of the five emotions are shown in Figure 8.

5 Experimental Design

5.1 Model Training and Evaluation

In this study, we evaluated various models for speech emotion classification. The dataset was divided into training (80%) and testing (20%) subsets.

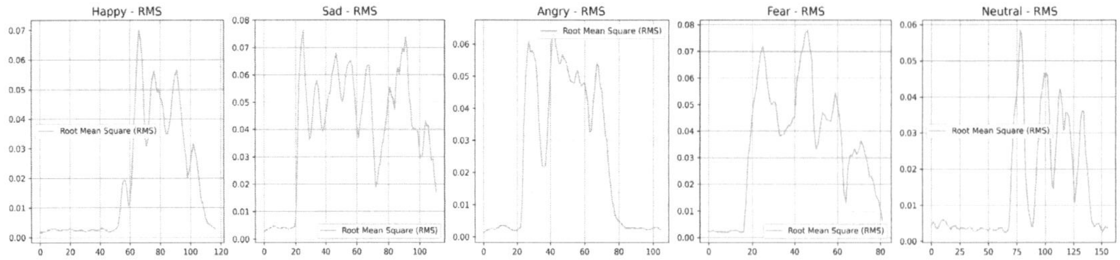

Figure 7: Root Mean Square (RMS) values for different emotions: Happy, Sad, Angry, Fear, and Neutral. The RMS value is a measure of the average power of the audio signal, indicating the loudness of the sound.

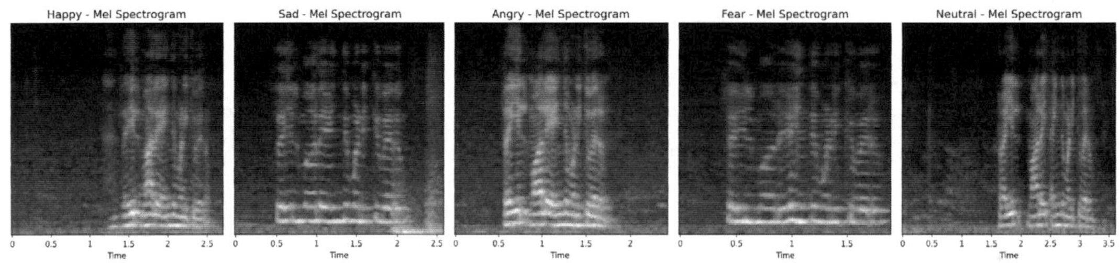

Figure 8: Mel Spectrograms for various emotions: Happy, Sad, Angry, Fear, and Neutral. The Mel spectrogram provides a time-frequency representation of the audio signal, where the frequency scale is non-linear and mimics human hearing.

Emotion	**P**	**R**	**F1**
angry	0.74	0.72	0.73
fear	0.88	0.85	0.86
happy	0.65	0.68	0.67
neutral	0.78	0.67	0.72
sad	0.60	0.69	0.64
macro avg	0.73	0.72	0.73

Table 1: Results of XGBoost without Data Augmentation.

Emotion	**P**	**R**	**F1**
angry	0.92	0.90	0.91
fear	0.93	0.94	0.93
happy	0.87	0.90	0.88
neutral	0.92	0.92	0.92
sad	0.91	0.90	0.90
macro avg	0.91	0.91	0.91

Table 2: Results of XGBoost with Data Augmentation.

The models were assessed using several evaluation metrics, including Macro average precision, recall, and F1-score. These metrics provide a comprehensive understanding of each model's performance on individual emotion classes as well as an overall classification assessment.

We selected several traditional models, including Logistic Regression, Decision Tree, Random Forest, Support Vector Machine (SVM), and XGBoost. Additionally, we implemented a 1D CNN architecture, which captures important features from audio signals through the use of convolutional layers, making it well-suited for emotion classification tasks. To further enhance the model's capabilities, we employed a 1D CNN with an attention mechanism, which allows the model to focus on significant features within the audio input, thereby improving the identification of emotional cues.

5.2 Data Augmentation Techniques

To enhance the model's performance and increase the robustness of the speech emotion classification system, several data augmentation techniques were applied to the audio dataset. These techniques are designed to artificially expand the training data by introducing variations that simulate real-world conditions (Ahmed et al., 2023).

One of the methods employed was noise injec-

Model	Non-Aug			Aug		
	P	R	F1	P	R	F1
Logistic Regression	0.48	0.48	0.47	0.40	0.41	0.40
Decision Tree	0.39	0.37	0.38	0.60	0.60	0.60
Random Forest	0.70	0.71	0.70	0.90	0.90	0.90
Support Vector Machine	0.32	0.22	0.11	0.46	0.27	0.23
XGBoost	**0.73**	**0.72**	**0.73**	**0.91**	**0.91**	**0.91**
K-Nearest Neighbors	0.59	0.59	0.59	0.58	0.58	0.58
1D CNN	0.52	0.53	0.49	0.60	0.59	0.59
1D CNN (with Attention)	0.60	0.59	0.59	0.88	0.87	0.87

Table 3: Macro Average Precision, Recall and F1-Score on the test set for all the Models with and without augmentation.

tion, which adds random noise to the audio signals, helping the model differentiate emotional content in noisy environments. Time stretching altered the speed of the audio without changing its pitch, simulating variations in speech delivery. Random shifting involved slightly shifting the audio in time, reducing sensitivity to minor timing variations while pitch-shifting modified the pitch to expose the model to a broader range of vocal expressions.

Together, these methods increased the diversity and variability of the training dataset, enhancing the model's ability to recognize and classify emotions. These techniques significantly improved the model's performance, making it more resilient to variations in speech delivery, timing, and audio quality.

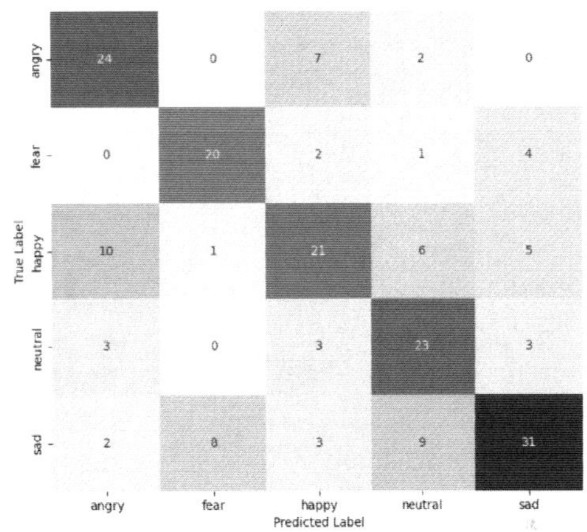

Figure 9: Confusion Matrix for XGBoost without Data Augmentation.

6 Results and Discussion

6.1 Model Performance Comparison

Table 3 summarizes the performance of various models on both the original (Non-Aug) and augmented (Aug) data. For Non-Augmented data, XGBoost achieves the highest F1-score of 0.73, followed closely by Random Forest with an F1-score of 0.70. On the augmented data, both XGBoost and Random Forest reach the high F1-score of 0.91 and 0.90 respectively, demonstrating their effectiveness after data augmentation. Among deep learning models, the 1D CNN with Attention performs notably well, achieving an F1-score of 0.87 on augmented data, suggesting that attention mechanisms enhance model accuracy. However, the Support Vector Machine (SVM) model performs the lowest on both Non-Augmented and Augmented data, with an F1-score of 0.11 and 0.23, respectively, indicating challenges in handling this task. The detailed results of XGBoost are presented in Table 1 for non-augmented data and Table 2 for augmented data.

6.2 Error Analysis and Model Limitations

The confusion matrix analysis (Figures 9 and 10) for XGBoost shows that data augmentation significantly enhances model performance. Without augmentation, notable misclassifications are observed, particularly happy being confused with angry and vice versa, as well as sad with fear and neutral. After augmentation, the model improves, with fewer misclassifications and an overall increase in prediction accuracy. However, confusion between an-

Province	Non-Aug			Aug		
	P	R	F1	P	R	F1
Nothern	0.55	0.55	0.54	0.98	0.98	0.98
Eastern	0.59	0.62	0.60	0.88	0.87	0.88
Western	0.65	0.66	0.65	0.93	0.89	0.90
Central	0.67	0.50	0.54	0.93	0.94	0.93

Table 4: Macro Average Precision, Recall and F1-Score on the test set for different dialects with and without augmentation using XGBoost.

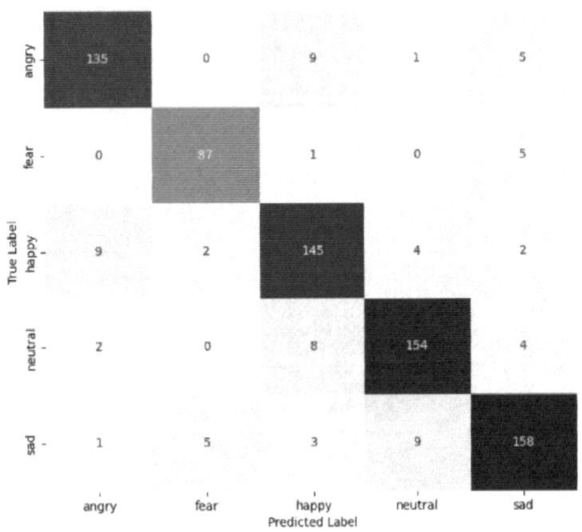

Figure 10: Confusion Matrix for XGBoost with Data Augmentation.

gry and happy persists, suggesting challenges in distinguishing emotions with overlapping acoustic features. This indicates that while augmentation is beneficial, further advancements in model architecture, feature extraction techniques, and possibly the inclusion of additional contextual or prosodic cues are needed to better distinguish emotions with similar acoustic characteristics.

7 Conclusion

This paper introduces the EmoTa dataset, specifically designed for Tamil speech emotion recognition, comprising 936 audio samples recorded from 22 native Tamil speakers. Each speaker conveys five distinct emotionsanger, happiness, sadness, fear, and neutralusing 19 semantically neutral sentences to eliminate semantic bias and focus purely on emotional delivery. The dataset provides a robust foundation for evaluating emotion recognition models, with results comprehensively reported in terms of precision, recall, and F1-Score to highlight various aspects of model performance. Furthermore, the dataset's reliability is assessed through inter-annotator agreement, quantified using Fleiss' kappa, ensuring consistency in emotional labeling. This resource aims to advance research in Tamil speech emotion recognition, addressing the scarcity of datasets in this domain.

8 Limitations of the work

The EmoTa dataset, created from emotional speech samples by actors aged 23 to 25, could benefit from an expanded age range to increase its generalizability across diverse age groups. This would make the dataset more suitable for broader applications in Tamil speech emotion recognition. Currently, EmoTa includes 48 minutes of recorded speech, which serves as a foundation for preliminary research. However, a larger volume of samples would enhance its robustness, supporting more in-depth analysis. The dataset presently covers five emotions: happy, sad, angry, neutral, and fear. Adding more emotions would improve the datasets utility and enable greater accuracy in recognizing emotional nuances in Tamil speech.

References

Md Rayhan Ahmed, Salekul Islam, AKM Muzahidul Islam, and Swakkhar Shatabda. 2023. An ensemble 1d-cnn-lstm-gru model with data augmentation for speech emotion recognition. *Expert Systems with Applications*, 218:119633.

Hadhami Aouani and Yassine Ben Ayed. 2020. Speech emotion recognition with deep learning. *Procedia Computer Science*, 176:251–260.

Felix Burkhardt, A. Paeschke, M. Rolfes, Walter F. Sendlmeier, and Benjamin Weiss. 2005. A database of German emotional speech. In *Interspeech 2005*, pages 1517–1520. ISCA.

Giovanni Costantini, Iacopo Iadarola, Andrea Paoloni, and Massimiliano Todisco. EMOVO Corpus: an Italian Emotional Speech Database.

Roddy Cowie, Ellen Douglas-Cowie, Nicolas Tsapatsoulis, George Votsis, Stefanos Kollias, Winfried Fellenz, and John G Taylor. 2001. Emotion recognition in human-computer interaction. *IEEE Signal processing magazine*, 18(1):32–80.

Paul Ekman. 1992. An argument for basic emotions. *Cognition and Emotion*, 6(3-4):169–200.

Bennilo Fernandes and Kasiprasad Mannepalli. 2021. An analysis of emotional speech recognition for tamil language using deep learning gate recurrent unit. *Pertanika Journal of Science & Technology*, 29(3).

Utkarsh Garg, Sachin Agarwal, Shubham Gupta, Ravi Dutt, and Dinesh Singh. 2020. Prediction of emotions from the audio speech signals using mfcc, mel and chroma. In *2020 12th International Conference on Computational Intelligence and Communication Networks (CICN)*, pages 87–91.

Philippe Gournay, Olivier Lahaie, and Roch Lefebvre. 2018. A canadian french emotional speech dataset. In *Proceedings of the 9th ACM Multimedia Systems Conference*, pages 399–402, Amsterdam Netherlands. ACM.

William James. 1922. The emotions.

Richard S Lazarus. 1994. *Passion and reason: Making sense of our emotions*. Oxford University Press.

M. S. Likitha, Sri Raksha R. Gupta, K. Hasitha, and A. Upendra Raju. 2017. Speech based human emotion recognition using mfcc. In *2017 International Conference on Wireless Communications, Signal Processing and Networking (WiSPNET)*, pages 2257–2260.

Rajeev Rajan, Haritha U.G., Sujitha A.C., and Rejisha T. M. 2019. Design and Development of a Multi-Lingual Speech Corpora (TaMaR-EmoDB) for Emotion Analysis. In *Interspeech 2019*, pages 3267–3271. ISCA.

C Sunitha Ram and R Ponnusamy. 2014. An effective automatic speech emotion recognition for tamil language using support vector machine. In *2014 International Conference on Issues and Challenges in Intelligent Computing Techniques (ICICT)*, pages 19–23. IEEE.

Justus J Randolph. 2005. Free-marginal multirater kappa (multirater k [free]): An alternative to fleiss' fixed-marginal multirater kappa. *Online submission*.

P Vasuki, B Sambavi, and Vijesh Joe. 2020. Construction and evaluation of tamil speech emotion corpus. *National Academy Science Letters*, 43(6):533–536.

Kannan Venkataramanan and Haresh Rengaraj Rajamohan. 2019. Emotion recognition from speech. *arXiv preprint arXiv:1912.10458*.

Benchmarking Whisper for Low-Resource Speech Recognition: An N-Shot Evaluation on Pashto, Punjabi, and Urdu

Najm Ul Sehar[1], Ayesha Khalid[1], Farah Adeeba[2], Sarmad Hussain[1]
[1]Center for Language Engineering, KICS, UET, Lahore, Pakistan
[2]Department of Computer Science, UET, Lahore, Pakistan
{najm.sehar, ayesha.khalid, sarmad.hussain}@kics.edu.pk,
farah.adeeba@uet.edu.pk

Abstract

Whisper, a large-scale multilingual model, has demonstrated strong performance in speech recognition benchmarks, but its effectiveness on low-resource languages remains underexplored. This paper evaluates Whisper's performance on Pashto, Punjabi, and Urdu, three underrepresented languages. While Automatic Speech Recognition (ASR) has advanced for widely spoken languages, low-resource languages still face challenges due to limited data. Whisper's zero-shot performance was benchmarked and then its small variant was fine-tuned to improve transcription accuracy. Significant reductions in Word Error Rate (WER) were achieved through few-shot fine-tuning, which helped the model better handle challenges such as complex phonetic structures, compared to zero-shot performance. This study contributes to improving multilingual ASR for low-resource languages and highlights Whisper's adaptability and potential for further enhancement.

1 Introduction

The globalization of technology and communication increasingly necessitates the development of effective natural language processing (NLP) tools for low-resource languages. These languages, spoken by millions, are often underrepresented in computational linguistics. Languages such as Pashto, Punjabi, and Urdu play vital roles in diverse cultural contexts, yet their development for ASR is hampered by a scarcity of labeled data (Krasadakis et al., 2024) and limited computational resources. As a result, existing ASR systems struggle to provide accurate solutions, limiting access to critical technologies in areas like voice-activated devices, education, healthcare, and government services.

Zero-shot learning, which allows models to perform tasks on languages they were not explicitly trained for, has emerged as a promising solution (Yang et al., 2024). OpenAI's Whisper (Radford et al., 2023), a transformer-based ASR model, benefits from large-scale multilingual data, enabling strong performance across multiple languages even without language-specific fine-tuning. However, while zero-shot models generalize effectively, their performance on low-resource languages is hindered (Waghmare et al., 2023) by the lack of sufficient training data and an inability to capture unique phonetic, morphological, and syntactic features, resulting in lower transcription accuracy.
Languages like Pashto, with unique phonological structures, require fine-tuning on language-specific datasets for optimal accuracy (Sher et al., 2024). Fine-tuning pre-trained models like Whisper has been shown to improve ASR performance in low-resource settings, reducing WER even with limited data (Liu and Qu, 2024; Pratama and Amrullah, 2024; Do et al., 2023a). Few-shot fine-tuning, using as little as four hours of data, has demonstrated resource efficiency and adaptability, achieving near-optimal performance (Talafha et al., 2023).
Benchmarking ASR systems on multilingual datasets has become a focal point of recent research (Maheshwari et al., 2024). While Whisper's performance on languages like Urdu has been explored in prior studies (Arif et al., 2024), Pashto and Punjabi have not yet been evaluated in this context.

This study addresses this gap and Whisper's zero-shot ASR performance on Pashto, Punjabi, and Urdu was benchmarked and the impact of few-shot fine-tuning on language-specific datasets was assessed. Results show that few-shot fine-tuning significantly improves Whisper's performance, emphasizing the importance of domain-specific adaptation for better ASR accuracy in low-resource settings.

2 Dataset and Preprocessing

Datasets for Pashto, Punjabi, and Urdu were curated to capture linguistic variations and speaker demographics for few-shot fine-tuning and evaluat-

Proceedings of the First Workshop on Challenges in Processing South Asian Languages (CHiPSAL 2025), pages 202–207

ing the Whisper model on low-resource languages. Details of these datasets are provided below.

2.1 Pashto Dataset

For experimentation, the ELRA-S0381 Dataset[1] is used which includes 108 hours of transcribed broadcast news in Standard Afghan Pashto from over 1,000 speakers across five sources, such as Ashna TV[2], Azadi Radio[3], Deewa Radio [4], Mashaal Radio[5] and Shamshad TV[6]. This dataset, with 46,000 segments and 1.1 million words, provides a robust foundation for Pashto ASR. For this study, a carefully selected 15-hour dataset from 300 speakers was used for n-shot learning, while 4.8 hours from 137 speakers were reserved for evaluation, ensuring diverse accents and age groups.

2.2 Punjabi Dataset

The lack of any publicly available dataset for the Majhi dialect of Punjabi as spoken in Pakistan, along with its corresponding Shahmukhi annotation, necessitated the creation of a custom in-house dataset to address this gap. This dataset, sourced from Bulekha TV[7], represents the variety of Punjabi spoken in Pakistan. As the available data in the broadcast domain was limited, the recordings primarily comprised vlogs. These recordings were first converted to .wav format with specified properties: mono channel, 256 kbps bitrate, and 16 kHz sampling rate.

The dataset covers diverse topics relevant to the Punjabi-speaking audience. Annotation was carried out using XTrans (Glenn et al., 2009) in the Punjabi Shahmukhi script by trained annotators. For this study, carefully considered 15-hour dataset was used for few-shot learning, for ensuring balanced finetuning across all datasets to maintain consistency in performance evaluations.
For evaluation, 4.2 hours of data sourced from 52 speakers was utilized.

2.3 Urdu Dataset

Two datasets were used for the Urdu language: the Urdu Broadcast and Urdu Telephonic datasets, with detailed descriptions provided in the following subsections.

2.3.1 Urdu Broadcast Dataset

The Urdu Broadcast Dataset (Khan et al., 2021) contains approximately 800 hours of spoken Urdu from various broadcast platforms like Radio, YouTube, and TV. The dataset covers genres such as news, health, entertainment, and political discussions, capturing dialectal and phonetic variability. For this study, a thoughtfully chosen 15-hour dataset from 131 speakers was used for few-shot learning, while 4.3 hours from 45 speakers were allocated for evaluation, covering a wide range of regional accents and demographics.

2.3.2 Urdu Telephonic Dataset

The Urdu Telephonic Dataset consists of 111.5 hours of read speech, balanced by gender and representing various districts of Pakistan. The dataset, recorded via laptop and telephone, captures conversational speech patterns typical in telephonic interactions. For this study, a carefully curated 15-hour dataset from 179 speakers was used for few-shot learning, while 10.2 hours from 60 speakers were set aside for evaluation, representing a variety of accents and age groups.

The Table 2 provides a breakdown of the datasets, including the fine-tuning and evaluation splits, as well as the total number of utterances for each dataset.

2.4 Pre-processing

Following pre-processing steps were implemented: (a) All audio files were converted to mono format with a sample rate of 16 kHz; (b) selected a subset of 15 hours from each dataset for few-shot fine-tuning; (c) ensured the audio segments were accurately aligned with their corresponding transcriptions; and (d) removed any unnecessary punctuation and characters from the transcriptions to maintain consistency. Additionally, the 15-hour subset was divided into 1-hour, 5-hour, 10-hour, and 15-hour splits for the purpose of few-shot experimentation.

3 Experiment

The evaluation consists of two phases: zero-shot evaluation and few-shot fine-tuning. In the zero-shot phase, Whisper-small, Whisper-medium, and Whisper-large are evaluated on various datasets (as detailed in Section 2). For few-shot fine-tuning,

[1] https://catalogue.elra.info/en-us/repository/browse/ELRA-W0092/
[2] https://www.youtube.com/@VOAPashto
[3] https://pa.azadiradio.com/
[4] https://www.voadeewanews.com/live/audio/49
[5] https://www.mashaalradio.com/
[6] https://www.shamshadtv.tv/
[7] https://www.youtube.com/c/BhulekhaTv

Language	Dataset	Small WER	Medium WER	Large WER
Pashto	Broadcast	98.43	99.04	85.60
Punjabi	Broadcast	86.83	86.04	54.73
Urdu	Broadcast	42.57	35.57	27.97
	Telephonic	70.09	62.12	46.64

Table 1: Zero-shot %WER for Whisper models (Small, Medium, Large) on Pashto, Punjabi and Urdu datasets

Language	Dataset	Fine-tuning Duration	Evaluation Duration	Fine-tuning Utterances	Evaluation Utterances
Pashto	Broadcast	15 h	4.8 h	7746	2226
Punjabi	Broadcast	15 h	4.2 h	13110	2361
Urdu	Broadcast	15 h	4.3 h	8206	2633
	Telephonic	15 h	10.2 h	14066	6358

Table 2: Fine-tuning and Evaluation Data Breakdown for Whisper on Pashto, Punjabi, and Urdu

Language	Dataset	1hr WER	5hrs WER	10hrs WER	15hrs WER
Pashto	Broadcast	53.08	40.33	36.38	34.10
Punjabi	Broadcast	45.18	41.57	41.80	38.01
Urdu	Broadcast	33.14	27.26	23.43	22.28
	Telephonic	74.16	66.40	63.42	62.01

Table 3: Fine-tuned %WER for Whisper Small on Pashto, Punjabi, and Urdu datasets

Whisper-small is selected due to hardware constraints, with 15 hours of labeled data from each dataset, split into 1-hour, 5-hour, 10-hour, and 15-hour subsets to analyze the effect of dataset size. The zero-shot performance of Whisper-large is compared with the few-shot fine-tuned Whisper-small, focusing on the reduction in WER between the models.

3.1 Experimental Setup

The experiments are conducted on a system with two NVIDIA RTX 3060 GPUs[8], each with 12 GB of VRAM. To manage memory constraints, gradient accumulation is employed during fine-tuning. The AdamW optimizer is used with a learning rate of 1e-5 and a warmup period of 500 steps for stability. Fine-tuning is performed for a maximum of 100 epochs, with early stopping after 3 epochs to prevent overfitting.

3.2 N-shot Learning

Whisper's performance was evaluated in zero-shot and few-shot settings across Pashto, Punjabi, and Urdu. Zero-shot results set a baseline, while few-shot fine-tuning demonstrates how WER reduces with increasing data, offering insights into the model's real-world potential. **Zero-shot Learning:** In all zero-shot evaluations, the target language for transcription was explicitly specified by passing its corresponding language code as a parameter to the model. Whisper transcribes Pashto with inconsistent script usage, occasionally switching between the script conventions used for Northern Pashto dialects and Southern Pashto dialects. This variability reflects regional differences in orthographic practices, which led to inconsistencies in the transcription output. Similarly, for the Punjabi dataset, Whisper defaulted to Gurmukhi script, despite the widespread use of Shahmukhi by 94.4 million users (Ahmad et al., 2020), leaving the Shahmukhi script underrepresented in the transcription process.

Few-shot Learning: In the few-shot phase, Whisper-small was fine-tuned on datasets in incremental batches of 1 hour, 5 hours, 10 hours, and a maximum of 15 hours. The 15-hour limit was maintained for all languages, as the Punjabi few-shot learning dataset only consisted of 15 hours of data. Each step of fine-tuning allowed the model to progressively refine its transcription accuracy, capturing the nuances of scripts, and accents as explained in detail in the later section.

[8]https://www.nvidia.com/en-us/geforce/graphics-cards/30-series/rtx-3060-3060ti/

4 Results

This section presents the performance of Whisper on Pashto, Punjabi, and Urdu, emphasizing the impact of few-shot fine-tuning on transcription accuracy.

Zero-shot Results: All the outputs were post-processed to remove any punctuations marks. For Pashto, transcription consistency was ensured by converting the script conventions used for Northern dialect into standard Afghan Pashto using GPT-prompt to compute the WER. Whisper Large achieved a WER of 85.60, reflecting challenges with script variations, while Whisper Medium and Small recorded WERs above 90. Despite explicitly specifying the target language, Whisper Small and Medium exhibited frequent language switching during transcription. For Punjabi, post-processing was performed to convert Gurmukhi to Shahmukhi script using a GPT-prompt, with Whisper Large recording a WER of 54.73, outperforming Whisper Small's WER of 86.83. For Urdu, Whisper Large excelled in the Broadcast dataset with a WER of 27.97, surpassing Whisper Small's 42.57. On the Telephonic dataset, Whisper Large achieved a WER of 46.64, significantly outperforming Whisper Small, which had a WER of 70.09. Further details on these performance discrepancies regarding Pashto, Punjabi and Telephonic Urdu Datsets are provided in Appendix A. Despite its overall superior performance, Whisper Large struggled with regional accents, necessitating further adaptation. The results of zero-shot evaluation are presented in Table 1.

Few-shot Learning Results: Fine-tuning Whisper Small with varying durations resulted in significant WER reductions. For Pashto, WER decreased from 53.08 to 34.10 after 15 hours of fine-tuning, hence improving transcription in standard Afghan Pashto demonstrating the impact of domain-specific data. In Punjabi, fine-tuning reduced WER from 45.18 to 38.01, enabling transcription in Shahmukhi script, which was previously rendered in Gurmukhi. For Urdu, fine-tuning yielded substantial improvements, lowering WER from 33.14 to 22.28 for Broadcast and from 74.16 to 62.01 for Telephonic, indicating better adaptation to formal broadcast speech. The results are shown in Table 3.

An interesting observation is that fine-tuning Whisper Small significantly narrows the gap with Whisper Large in zero-shot performance. For Pashto, WER dropped from 53.08 to 34.10, surpassing Whisper Large's 85.60. In Punjabi, WER decreased from 45.18 to 38.01, outperforming Whisper Large's 54.73. For Urdu Broadcast, WER improved from 33.14 to 22.28, exceeding Whisper Large's 27.97. However, for Urdu Telephonic, WER dropped from 74.16 to 62.01, but Whisper Large's 46.64 still outperformed the fine-tuned model. These results demonstrate that fine-tuning Whisper Small with domain-specific data leads to substantial improvements across languages and datasets, significantly reducing the performance gap with Whisper Large.

5 Conclusion

This research highlights the effectiveness of fine-tuning Whisper models for low-resource languages like Pashto, Punjabi, and Urdu. While Whisper Large excelled in zero-shot evaluation, fine-tuning Whisper Small with domain-specific data led to substantial improvements in transcription accuracy. The significant reductions in WER across these languages demonstrate the power of fine-tuning to optimize performance and adapt Whisper to the unique linguistic characteristics of low-resource settings.

6 Limitation

This study has several limitations. Due to GPU resource constraints, fine-tuning was limited to Whisper Small, restricting the model's full potential. With access to more computational resources, fine-tuning Whisper Medium or Large could have enhanced performance across a wider range of datasets. Furthermore, the evaluation datasets for both Pashto and Punjabi were limited to a single dialect, which may not fully capture the linguistic diversity present within these languages. Additionally, Whisper would benefit from more diverse fine-tuning data, particularly for low-resource dialects, to improve generalization and achieve better results.

References

Muhammad Tayyab Ahmad, Muhammad Kamran Malik, Khurram Shahzad, Faisal Aslam, Asif Iqbal, Zubair Nawaz, and Faisal Bukhari. 2020. Named entity recognition and classification for punjabi shahmukhi. *ACM Transactions on Asian and Low-Resource Language Information Processing (TALLIP)*, 19(4):1–13.

Samee Arif, Aamina Jamal Khan, Mustafa Abbas, Agha Ali Raza, and Awais Athar. 2024. Wer we stand: Benchmarking urdu asr models. *arXiv preprint arXiv:2409.11252*.

Andrea Do, Oscar Brown, Zhengjie Wang, Nikhil Mathew, Zixin Liu, Jawwad Ahmed, and Cheng Yu. 2023a. Using fine-tuning and min lookahead beam search to improve whisper. *arXiv preprint arXiv:2309.10299*.

X. Do et al. 2023b. Enhancing asr performance with low-rank adaptation. *Journal of Speech Technology*.

Meghan Lammie Glenn, Stephanie M Strassel, and Haejoong Lee. 2009. Xtrans: A speech annotation and transcription tool. In *Tenth Annual Conference of the International Speech Communication Association*.

Erbaz Khan, Sahar Rauf, Farah Adeeba, and Sarmad Hussain. 2021. A multi-genre urdu broadcast speech recognition system. In *2021 24th Conference of the Oriental COCOSDA International Committee for the Co-ordination and Standardisation of Speech Databases and Assessment Techniques (O-COCOSDA)*, pages 25–30. IEEE.

Panteleimon Krasadakis, Evangelos Sakkopoulos, and Vassilios S Verykios. 2024. A survey on challenges and advances in natural language processing with a focus on legal informatics and low-resource languages. *Electronics*, 13(3):648.

Yunpeng Liu and Dan Qu. 2024. Parameter-efficient fine-tuning of whisper for low-resource speech recognition. In *2024 5th International Seminar on Artificial Intelligence, Networking and Information Technology (AINIT)*, pages 1522–1525. IEEE.

Gaurav Maheshwari, Dmitry Ivanov, Théo Johannet, and Kevin El Haddad. 2024. Asr benchmarking: Need for a more representative conversational dataset. *arXiv preprint arXiv:2409.12042*.

Riefkyanov Surya Adia Pratama and Agit Amrullah. 2024. Analysis of whisper automatic speech recognition performance on low resource language. *Jurnal Pilar Nusa Mandiri*, 20(1):1–8.

A. Radford, J. Wu, and R. Child. 2022. Learning transferable visual models from natural language supervision. In *Proceedings of the International Conference on Machine Learning*.

Alec Radford, Jong Wook Kim, Tao Xu, Greg Brockman, Christine McLeavey, and Ilya Sutskever. 2023. Robust speech recognition via large-scale weak supervision. In *International conference on machine learning*, pages 28492–28518. PMLR.

Munaza Sher, Nasir Ahmad, and Madiha Sher. 2024. Towards end-to-end speech recognition system for pashto language using transformer model. *IJIST*, 6 (1):115–131.

Bashar Talafha, Abdul Waheed, and Muhammad Abdul-Mageed. 2023. N-shot benchmarking of whisper on diverse arabic speech recognition. *arXiv preprint arXiv:2306.02902*.

Suhas Waghmare, Chirag Brahme, Siddhi Panchal, Numaan Sayed, and Mohit Goud. 2023. Comparative analysis of state-of-the-art speech recognition models for low-resource marathi language. *International Journal of Innovative Science and Research Technology (IJISRT)*, pages 1544–1545.

Chih-Kai Yang, Kuan-Po Huang, Ke-Han Lu, Chun-Yi Kuan, Chi-Yuan Hsiao, and Hung-yi Lee. 2024. Investigating zero-shot generalizability on mandarin-english code-switched asr and speech-to-text translation of recent foundation models with self-supervision and weak supervision. In *2024 IEEE International Conference on Acoustics, Speech, and Signal Processing Workshops (ICASSPW)*, pages 540–544. IEEE.

A Discussion on Errors in Zero-Shot Evaluation

In this section, we analyze the performance of different Whisper model variants (Small, Medium, and Large) on Pashto, Punjabi, and Urdu datasets in a zero-shot setting. The primary focus is on evaluating the transcription

errors observed in each language and understanding the limitations of the models in detail. Table 4 provides a comparative overview of the outputs from each model. Whisper Small and Medium produced unintelligible outputs, mixing scripts like Khmer and Telugu (e.g., " "), and generating gibberish, especially in Pashto and Punjabi (e.g., "livel, ündarvs"). In Urdu, they misinterpreted numerals and proper nouns (e.g., "gnignnaM "). Whisper Large performed better but still missed key contextual phrases in Pashto (e.g., missing " " – "Accept my greetings"), had subtle phonetic errors in Punjabi (e.g., misinterpreting " " as "old master"), and struggled with numerals in Urdu (e.g., " " instead of "twenty-seventh"). Overall, Whisper Large showed improvement but still faced significant limitations, indicating the need for further pretraining to improve zero-shot performance on these languages.

Language	Reference	Small	Medium	Large
Pashto	د ازادی راديوي مجله زما اسد الله غضنفر سلامونه ومنئ قدرمنو اوریدونکو *("Azadi Radio Magazine, this is Asadullah Ghazanfar. Accept my greetings, dear listeners.")*	ila Di Vo Soga al H expected Emread this اگلا	livel, ündarvs [illegible] snail iziert <lrul> säga selamun hpanaatge el ani beit cor generation ఈరో వలాయు భూరిల లాల్	ده ازادی راډیوی مجلّه او پا دی بارا که بحث لرو *("This is the Azadi Radio Magazine, and we have a discussion on this topic.")*
Punjabi	ترے جنوبی ایشیائی نیں اتے انہاں تناں دا پرانا آقا برطانیہ مقابلے تے ہے *("This is not your South Asia; here, the old master of all three, Britain, is in competition.")*	ವಾರಿನಿನಿಂದಿನಿ	Vermikha sharwa sa arpaki ya akarpesha	ਤਰੇ ਜੁਨੂਬੀ ਏਸ਼ਿਆਈ ਨੇ ਉਤੇ ਇਨਾ ਤੀਨਾ ਦਾ ਪੁਰਾਨਾ ਆਕਾ ਬਰਤਾਨੀਆ ਮੁਕਾਬਲੇ ਤੇ ਹੇ *("The South Asian stars are facing their old boss Britain.")*
Urdu	کیا ٹوینٹی سیونتھ اپریل ٹوینٹی فرسٹ تک ڈیم بن پائے گا *("Will the dam be completed by the twenty-seventh of April or by the twenty-first?")*	atra 둘	کیا Mannging سکوہ *("Will Mannging skouh?")*	کیا دونٹی سیونی ڈیٹل ڈی ساؤزن ڈی فورس ڈینڈ ڈینڈ جائے گا *("Will Donte Sioni detal de sauzen de force dand dand go?")*

Table 4: Whisper Model Responses Comparison for Different Languages (Pashto, Punjabi, and Urdu) in Zero-Shot Evaluation

Leveraging Machine-Generated Data for Joint Intent Detection and Slot Filling in Bangla: A Resource-Efficient Approach

A H M Rezaul Karim
George Mason University, VA, USA
akarim9@gmu.edu

Özlem Uzuner
George Mason University, VA, USA
ouzuner@gmu.edu

Abstract

Natural Language Understanding (NLU) is crucial for conversational AI, yet low-resource languages lag behind in essential tasks like intent detection and slot filling. To address this gap, we translated the widely-used English SNIPS dataset to Bangla using LLaMA 3, creating a dataset that captures the linguistic complexities of the language. With this translated dataset, we compared both independent and joint modeling approaches using transformer architecture. Results demonstrate that a joint approach based on multilingual BERT (mBERT) achieves superior performance, with **97.83%** intent accuracy and **91.03%** F1 score for slot filling. This work advances NLU for Bangla and provides insights for developing robust models in other low-resource languages. [1]

1 Introduction

Natural Language Understanding (NLU) is an important part of artificial intelligence (AI), powering applications from home assistants to conversational agents, text analysis, and language translation (Vanzo et al., 2019; Liu et al., 2021; Carvalho et al., 2019; Bender and Koller, 2020; Stahlberg, 2020; Bast et al., 2016). Although we see a significant advance in languages with abundant resources, low- to medium-resource languages face substantial challenges in NLU development. The Bangla language is spoken by almost 280 million people and still remains notably underrepresented in this domain (Ethnologue, 2024). The rich morphology, complex sentence structure, and compound characters of Bangla make it challenging for NLU tasks.

Intent detection and slot filling represent core NLU tasks that are important for building effective language understanding systems. Intent detection identifies the user's purpose while slot filling extracts specific details such as time, location, or quantity. If a user says, *"What's the weather in New York tomorrow afternoon?"* intent detection identifies the goal as *"GetWeather,"* and slot filling pulls out details like *location* ("New York") and *time* ("tomorrow afternoon"). According to the findings of Grishman and Sundheim, these tasks share similarities with Named Entity Recognition (NER) in extracting structured information from text but they go beyond entity identification by requiring the system to understand the user's goal and dynamically extract task-specific details. These tasks have been extensively studied for English (Weld et al., 2022; Niu et al., 2019; Qin et al., 2021; Liu and Lane, 2016; Goo et al., 2018), and some progress has been made for several low-resource languages, including Bangla (Dao et al., 2021; Akbari et al., 2023; Stoica et al., 2021; Sakib et al., 2023). Although there are a few prominent studies on Bangla NLU (Bhattacharjee et al., 2021; Hossain et al., 2020; Alam et al., 2021) research remains limited, mainly due to the lack of large annotated datasets. Tackling this data deficiency is essential for expanding the representation of Bangla in AI and improving NLU systems for diverse languages.

Our work focuses on two primary objectives:

1. We develop a high-quality Bangla NLU dataset using English-to-Bangla translation models and Large Language Models (LLM). This work demonstrates how automated methods can effectively generate resources for underrepresented languages.

2. We evaluate separate and joint modeling for Bangla intent detection and slot filling tasks. Our evaluation compares these approaches with established methods from English NLU research.

Through these objectives, our aim is to establish a foundation for NLU systems in Bangla while providing insight that can benefit other underrepresented languages.

[1] The dataset and the code can be found here: https://github.com/AHMRezaul/Joint_IDSF_Bangla.

Proceedings of the First Workshop on Challenges in Processing South Asian Languages (CHiPSAL 2025), pages 208–216
January 19, 2025.

2 Related Work

Conversational AI has advanced intent detection and slot filling. Early models like Hidden Markov Models and Conditional Random Fields (Bhargava et al., 2013; Shen et al., 2011), treated these tasks separately, limiting generalization capabilities. The introduction of Recurrent Neural Networks, mainly Long Short-Term Memory networks, improved performance by modeling language sequences (Mesnil et al., 2013; Sreelakshmi et al., 2018).

After recognizing the dependency between intent detection and slot filling tasks, joint modeling was adopted (Zhang et al., 2018; Weld et al., 2022; Qin et al., 2021). The slot-gated model (Goo et al., 2018) advanced this approach by using intent predictions to guide slot filling. JointBERT (Chen et al., 2019) further improved performance through transformer-based joint optimization. While effective in resource-rich languages, applying them to low- and medium-resource languages such as Bangla has been challenging due to limited datasets (Sakib et al., 2023). Efforts to address this gap included translating English datasets into languages such as Vietnamese, Persian, and Romanian (Dao et al., 2021; Akbari et al., 2023; Stoica et al., 2021) and applying the established NLU methodologies.

Recent advances in machine translation (MT) models such as Multilingual T5 (Xue et al., 2020), XLM-ProphetNet (Qi et al., 2021), and BanglaT5 (Bhattacharjee et al., 2023; De bruyn et al., 2022) offer promising solutions for translating benchmark datasets to low- to medium-resource languages. Additionally, LLMs including Mistral (Jiang et al., 2023), LLaMA 2 (Touvron et al., 2023), LLaMA 3 (Meta, 2024), GPT-3.5 (Brown et al., 2020), and GPT-4 (Achiam et al., 2023) show potential for generating datasets in resource-scarce languages (Xu et al., 2023; Mahfuz et al., 2024).

Our work translates a benchmark English dataset to Bangla using traditional MT techniques and LLMs, showing that LLMs excel in capturing context and generating quality data. We use this translated dataset to develop and evaluate a Bangla model for intent detection and slot filling, outperforming previous efforts.

3 Methodology

This section provides a comprehensive overview of the dataset generation process and the models implemented in this project.

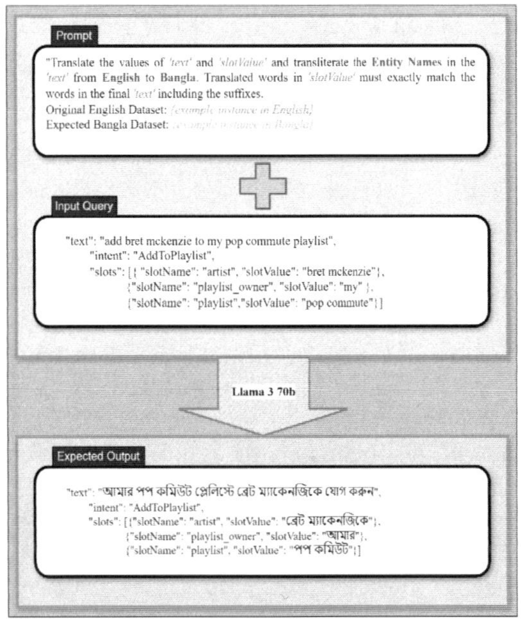

Figure 1: *A few-shot prompting approach with the input query and the expected output for the LLaMA 3 model.*

3.1 Dataset

3.1.1 SNIPS Dataset

We used the English SNIPS dataset (Coucke et al., 2018) to generate the Bangla dataset. SNIPS is a popular dataset for training and testing NLU models, especially for tasks like intent detection and slot filling. It consists of 13,084 training, 700 testing, and 700 validation samples, covering 7 intent classes and 72 slot values. Each intent and slot is carefully labeled to cover a large spectrum of user interactions, making it a useful resource for developing language models.

3.1.2 Dataset generation

The dataset generation process was completed in two steps: (1) machine translation for the Training and Validation sets, and (2) manual translation for the Test set. This combined approach ensured resource efficiency while maintaining high accuracy for evaluating real-world performance.

A. Training and Validation sets:
For Training and Validation sets, various methods were explored to generate the Bangla dataset from the English SNIPS dataset.

BanglaT5 model: Initially, the **BanglaT5** model (Bhattacharjee et al., 2023) was chosen for machine translation due to its high BLEU score compared to other English-to-Bangla models.

However, it struggled with entity names (e.g., Artist, Location, Movie, Song), translating them instead of transliterating, which altered the sentence meaning and made the results unusable. To address this, we applied the **BNTRANSLIT** model (Sarkar, 2021), designed for English-to-Bangla transliteration. We transliterated entity names before translating the sentences. Unfortunately, this approach also produced suboptimal results, as the overall translation quality remained insufficient.

LLaMA-3: Finally, the **LLaMA-3-70B-Instruct** model (Meta, 2024) was employed using a carefully crafted prompt that transliterated entity names while translating the rest of the sentence. We adopted a few-shot approach, providing five examples from the original English dataset along with their manually translated counterparts. Figure 1 shows the prompt, specifying that entity names should be transliterated, and the rest of the sentence translated into Bangla. After refining the prompt, the model delivered highly accurate translations, nearing manual translation quality. However, minor issues persisted, such as untranslated English words and extraneous information adding noise to the dataset. These issues were resolved during post-processing through automated rule-based methods, identifying and removing irrelevant content and correcting mismatches between slot values and translated text. The results were then manually verified to ensure the accuracy and consistency of the final dataset. The final dataset was annotated using the Beginning-Inside-Outside (BIO) notation.

B. Test set:

The test set was manually translated and annotated to ensure accuracy when evaluating real-world performance. Four doctoral students fluent in English and Bangla participated in this process. Initially, two annotators translated the English SNIPS test set into Bangla and annotated slot values using the BIO format. To ensure consistency, two annotators independently annotated 10% of the samples and discussed their results to agree on a unified annotation method. They then applied this agreed-upon method to annotate the remaining 90% of the dataset, achieving a **0.83 Cohen's Kappa** score A.2 for the entire dataset. Following this, two additional independent reviewers conducted sequential reviews of the entire dataset, further enhancing its quality by identifying and removing any remaining errors or biases.

Dataset	Stat.	Train	Valid.	Test
SNIPS (English)	Intents	13084	700	700
	Slots	60412	3221	3276
Generated (Bangla)	Intents	12850	685	694
	Slots	54747	2865	3105

Table 1: *Comparison of data distribution between generated Bangla dataset and the original English SNIPS dataset.*

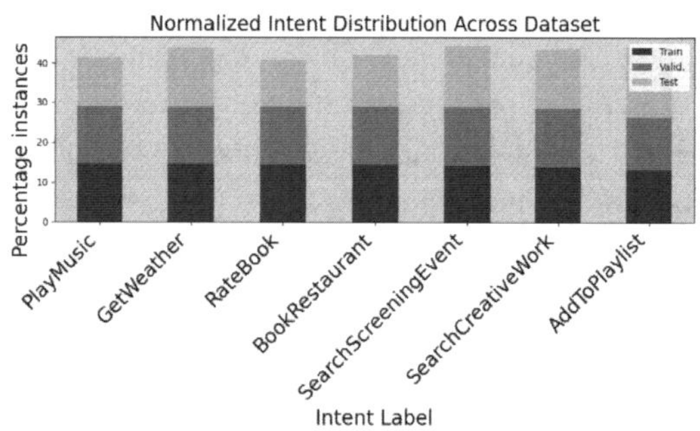

Figure 2: *A normalized distribution of Intent classes in the generated Bangla train, validation, and test sets.*

3.1.3 Dataset Analysis

The generated Bangla dataset contains 7 intent classes but 80 (vs. 72 in English) unique slot labels. The increase in the number of slot labels is due to single-word slot values in English often translating into multi-word slot values in Bangla. As a result, many slots that previously required only a beginning (B) tag in the English dataset now require both beginning (B) and inside (I) tags in the Bangla dataset. Table 1 compares the number of intent and slot instances between the original English and generated Bangla datasets.

The Bangla Train and Validation sets have slightly fewer instances of intents and slots than the English version as seen in Table 1, primarily due to post-processing after the LLaMA 3 translation. Instances with errors that could not be easily fixed were excluded to maintain the integrity of the machine-translated corpus, as the focus was on assessing LLM performance without manual intervention.

The slight reduction in the number of slot values can be attributed to two main factors:

Alignment Issues: Some slot values failed

to align with the translated text, even after post-processing, resulting in unannotated slots.

Linguistic Differences: In Bangla, certain multi-word slot values in English are condensed into single or fewer words, causing a reduction in the number of slot values compared to the English dataset.

Figure 2 shows a balanced distribution of intent classes (normalized for better visualization) across the training, validation, and test sets, reducing bias. However, there is an uneven distribution of slot labels demonstrated in figure 3, with rare slots potentially challenging the model's prediction accuracy as discussed in the appendix A.3.

Overall, the dataset effectively supports training and evaluation for diverse intents and slot labels.

3.2 Models

We evaluated three transformer-based models on our Bangla dataset: BERT Base (baseline), Multilingual BERT (mBERT), and Bangla BERT (Devlin, 2018; Bhattacharjee et al., 2021). Bangla BERT handles Bangla-specific processing, while mBERT offers multilingual adaptability. Both separate and joint training approaches were tested, following the benchmarking methodology of the English SNIPS dataset. Detailed specifications are in Appendix A.1.

4 Experiments and Analysis

The Bangla dataset was used to fine-tune the models with optimized hyperparameters: batch size of 32 for training and 64 for evaluation, maximum sequence length of 160, learning rate of 5e-5, and dropout rate of 0.1 gave the best performance.

4.1 Training details

We divided the experiments into two parts for each of the BERT variants (BERT Base, mBERT and Bangla BERT): (1) separate fine-tuning for intent detection and slot filling, and (2) joint fine-tuning using different BERT variants as the backbone. For the joint setup, we adopted the JointBERT configuration (Chen et al., 2019) with the mentioned hyperparameters and applied similar settings to the separate models. Models were trained across varying epochs $[1, 5, 10, 20, 30, 40]$, and the best performances from these runs were recorded.

4.2 Result and Discussion

Table 2 presents intent detection accuracy and slot filling F1 score at token level. It also illustrates the accuracy on a sentence level for the joint approach; this metric measures the percentage of instances where both intent class and slot labels were correctly predicted. The results clearly indicate that a joint approach outperforms the separate approaches. Notably, the multilingual BERT (mBERT) model surpasses Bangla BERT, a model specifically pre-trained in Bangla, in both joint and separate task settings.

Model		Intent Accuracy	Slot F1	Sentence Accuracy
Separate Training	BERT Base	95.53	86.13	-
	mBERT	**96.97**	**90.64**	-
	Bangla BERT	95.96	89.96	-
JointBERT	BERT Base	96.97	84.83	69.30
	mBERT	**<u>97.83</u>**	**<u>91.03</u>**	**<u>79.39</u>**
	Bangla BERT	97.69	89.42	76.65

Table 2: *Results for intent detection and slot filling tasks (%). Best scores for separate and joint models are bolded, with the overall best score underlined.*

This outcome suggests that mBERT's pre-training on a diverse multilingual corpus enables it to generalize effectively across languages, providing an advantage when dealing with the complexities of the Bangla language. Although Bangla BERT has shown superior performance in downstream tasks like sentiment analysis and hate speech detection (Sarker, 2021), mBERT outperforms it in the slot filling task, which is closely associated with Named Entity Recognition (NER) (Grishman and Sundheim, 1996). This is consistent with previous research, where mBERT outperformed Bangla BERT in the Bengali NER task using the *'Bengali NER'* dataset (Rahimi et al., 2019). The broad linguistic knowledge in pre-training of mBERT appears to offer an advantage in tasks that rely on accurate entity recognition.

Additionally, we observe the highest sentence-level accuracy with mBERT. This measures how often both the intent class and all slot labels are predicted accurately. This metric provides a holistic view of the model's performance.

Appendix A.4 presents a detailed error analysis of the best-performing joint model, highlighting common errors and identifying areas for potential improvement.

5 Conclusion

This study offers a comprehensive evaluation of joint intent detection and slot filling for Bangla, a resource-scarce language. To overcome the lack of available data, we generated a Bangla dataset from the benchmark English SNIPS dataset using the LLaMA 3 model and applied well-established NLU methodologies. Using a manually curated test set, we confirmed that joint modeling outperformed separate approaches, with the mBERT variant achieving better results than the language-specific Bangla BERT.

Our research also highlights the potential of LLMs in generating training data for low- to medium-resource languages. By leveraging existing benchmark datasets, LLMs can produce datasets that are effective for real-world applications. This approach provides a scalable solution for training high-performing models.

6 Limitations

We manually translated and annotated the SNIPS test set. However, we encountered resource constraints that limited our ability to manually curate the entire dataset. So, we relied on LLaMA 3 to generate training and validation data, utilizing its machine translation and entity recognition capabilities. While we recognize that a manually curated dataset would likely result in better fine-tuning and improved model performance, the resource limitations made machine translation a more practical and feasible option for this study. This experience also suggests that LLM-generated datasets can effectively support model fine-tuning for specific tasks.

References

Josh Achiam, Steven Adler, Sandhini Agarwal, Lama Ahmad, Ilge Akkaya, Florencia Leoni Aleman, Diogo Almeida, Janko Altenschmidt, Sam Altman, Shyamal Anadkat, et al. 2023. Gpt-4 technical report. *arXiv preprint arXiv:2303.08774*.

Masoud Akbari, Amir Hossein Karimi, Tayyebeh Saeedi, Zeinab Saeidi, Kiana Ghezelbash, Fatemeh Shamsezat, Mohammad Akbari, and Ali Mohades. 2023. A persian benchmark for joint intent detection and slot filling. *Preprint*, arXiv:2303.00408.

Firoj Alam, Arid Hasan, Tanvirul Alam, Akib Khan, Janntatul Tajrin, Naira Khan, and Shammur Absar Chowdhury. 2021. A review of bangla natural language processing tasks and the utility of transformer models. *arXiv preprint arXiv:2107.03844*.

Hannah Bast, Björn Buchhold, Elmar Haussmann, et al. 2016. Semantic search on text and knowledge bases. *Foundations and Trends® in Information Retrieval*, 10(2-3):119–271.

Emily M Bender and Alexander Koller. 2020. Climbing towards nlu: On meaning, form, and understanding in the age of data. In *Proceedings of the 58th annual meeting of the association for computational linguistics*, pages 5185–5198.

Aditya Bhargava, Asli Celikyilmaz, Dilek Hakkani-Tür, and Ruhi Sarikaya. 2013. Easy contextual intent prediction and slot detection. In *2013 ieee international conference on acoustics, speech and signal processing*, pages 8337–8341. IEEE.

Abhik Bhattacharjee, Tahmid Hasan, Wasi Ahmad, and Rifat Shahriyar. 2023. Banglanlg and banglat5: Benchmarks and resources for evaluating low-resource natural language generation in bangla. In *Findings of the Association for Computational Linguistics: EACL 2023*, pages 714–723.

Abhik Bhattacharjee, Tahmid Hasan, Wasi Uddin Ahmad, Kazi Samin, Md Saiful Islam, Anindya Iqbal, M Sohel Rahman, and Rifat Shahriyar. 2021. Banglabert: Language model pretraining and benchmarks for low-resource language understanding evaluation in bangla. *arXiv preprint arXiv:2101.00204*.

Tom B. Brown, Benjamin Mann, Nick Ryder, Melanie Subbiah, Jared Kaplan, Prafulla Dhariwal, Arvind Neelakantan, Pranav Shyam, Girish Sastry, Amanda Askell, Sandhini Agarwal, Ariel Herbert-Voss, Gretchen Krueger, Tom Henighan, Rewon Child, Aditya Ramesh, Daniel M. Ziegler, Jeffrey Wu, Clemens Winter, Christopher Hesse, Mark Chen, Eric Sigler, Mateusz Litwin, Scott Gray, Benjamin Chess, Jack Clark, Christopher Berner, Sam McCandlish, Alec Radford, Ilya Sutskever, and Dario Amodei. 2020. Language models are few-shot learners. *Preprint*, arXiv:2005.14165.

Arthur Carvalho, Adam Levitt, Seth Levitt, Edward Khaddam, and John Benamati. 2019. Off-the-shelf artificial intelligence technologies for sentiment and emotion analysis: a tutorial on using ibm natural language processing. *Communications of the Association for Information Systems*, 44(1):43.

Qian Chen, Zhu Zhuo, and Wen Wang. 2019. Bert for joint intent classification and slot filling. *Preprint*, arXiv:1902.10909.

Jacob Cohen. 1960. A coefficient of agreement for nominal scales. *Educational and psychological measurement*, 20(1):37–46.

Alice Coucke, Alaa Saade, Adrien Ball, Théodore Bluche, Alexandre Caulier, David Leroy, Clément Doumouro, Thibault Gisselbrecht, Francesco Caltagirone, Thibaut Lavril, et al. 2018. Snips voice platform: an embedded spoken language understanding system for private-by-design voice interfaces. *arXiv preprint arXiv:1805.10190*.

Mai Hoang Dao, Thinh Hung Truong, and Dat Quoc Nguyen. 2021. Intent detection and slot filling for vietnamese. *arXiv preprint arXiv:2104.02021*.

Maxime De bruyn, Ehsan Lotfi, Jeska Buhmann, and Walter Daelemans. 2022. Machine translation for multilingual intent detection and slots filling. In *Proceedings of the Massively Multilingual Natural Language Understanding Workshop (MMNLU-22)*, pages 69–82, Abu Dhabi, United Arab Emirates (Hybrid). Association for Computational Linguistics.

Jacob Devlin. 2018. Bert: Pre-training of deep bidirectional transformers for language understanding. *arXiv preprint arXiv:1810.04805*.

Ethnologue. 2024. Ethnologue 200: Languages of the world. Accessed on April 4, 2024.

Chih-Wen Goo, Guang Gao, Yun-Kai Hsu, Chih-Li Huo, Tsung-Chieh Chen, Keng-Wei Hsu, and Yun-Nung Chen. 2018. Slot-gated modeling for joint slot filling and intent prediction. In *Proceedings of the 2018 Conference of the North American Chapter of the Association for Computational Linguistics: Human Language Technologies, Volume 2 (Short Papers)*, pages 753–757.

Ralph Grishman and Beth M Sundheim. 1996. Message understanding conference-6: A brief history. In *COLING 1996 volume 1: The 16th international conference on computational linguistics*.

Md Zobaer Hossain, Md Ashraful Rahman, Md Saiful Islam, and Sudipta Kar. 2020. Banfakenews: A dataset for detecting fake news in bangla. *Preprint*, arXiv:2004.08789.

Albert Q Jiang, Alexandre Sablayrolles, Arthur Mensch, Chris Bamford, Devendra Singh Chaplot, Diego de las Casas, Florian Bressand, Gianna Lengyel, Guillaume Lample, Lucile Saulnier, et al. 2023. Mistral 7b. *arXiv preprint arXiv:2310.06825*.

Bing Liu and Ian Lane. 2016. Attention-based recurrent neural network models for joint intent detection and slot filling. *arXiv preprint arXiv:1609.01454*.

Xingkun Liu, Arash Eshghi, Pawel Swietojanski, and Verena Rieser. 2021. Benchmarking natural language understanding services for building conversational agents. In *Increasing Naturalness and Flexibility in Spoken Dialogue Interaction: 10th International Workshop on Spoken Dialogue Systems*, pages 165–183. Springer.

Tamzeed Mahfuz, Satak Kumar Dey, Ruwad Naswan, Hasnaen Adil, Khondker Salman Sayeed, and Haz Sameen Shahgir. 2024. Too late to train, too early to use? a study on necessity and viability of low-resource bengali llms. *arXiv preprint arXiv:2407.00416*.

Grégoire Mesnil, Xiaodong He, Li Deng, and Yoshua Bengio. 2013. Investigation of recurrent-neural-network architectures and learning methods for spoken language understanding. In *Interspeech*, pages 3771–3775.

Meta. 2024. Llama 3.

Peiqing Niu, Zhongfu Chen, Meina Song, et al. 2019. A novel bi-directional interrelated model for joint intent detection and slot filling. *arXiv preprint arXiv:1907.00390*.

Weizhen Qi, Yeyun Gong, Yu Yan, Can Xu, Bolun Yao, Bartuer Zhou, Biao Cheng, Daxin Jiang, Jiusheng Chen, Ruofei Zhang, et al. 2021. Prophetnet-x: Large-scale pre-training models for english, chinese, multi-lingual, dialog, and code generation. *arXiv preprint arXiv:2104.08006*.

Libo Qin, Tailu Liu, Wanxiang Che, Bingbing Kang, Sendong Zhao, and Ting Liu. 2021. A co-interactive transformer for joint slot filling and intent detection. In *ICASSP 2021-2021 IEEE International Conference on Acoustics, Speech and Signal Processing (ICASSP)*, pages 8193–8197. IEEE.

Afshin Rahimi, Yuan Li, and Trevor Cohn. 2019. Massively multilingual transfer for NER. In *Proceedings of the 57th Annual Meeting of the Association for Computational Linguistics*, pages 151–164, Florence, Italy. Association for Computational Linguistics.

Fardin Ahsan Sakib, AHM Karim, Saadat Hasan Khan, and Md Mushfiqur Rahman. 2023. Intent detection and slot filling for home assistants: Dataset and analysis for bangla and sylheti. *arXiv preprint arXiv:2310.10935*.

Sagor Sarkar. 2021. Bntranslit.

Sagor Sarker. 2021. Evaluation of bangla-bert on classification task. GitHub repository.

Yelong Shen, Jun Yan, Shuicheng Yan, Lei Ji, Ning Liu, and Zheng Chen. 2011. Sparse hidden-dynamics conditional random fields for user intent understanding. In *Proceedings of the 20th international conference on World wide web*, pages 7–16.

K Sreelakshmi, PC Rafeeque, S Sreetha, and ES Gayathri. 2018. Deep bi-directional lstm network for query intent detection. *Procedia computer science*, 143:939–946.

Felix Stahlberg. 2020. Neural machine translation: A review. *Journal of Artificial Intelligence Research*, 69:343–418.

Anda Stoica, Tibor Kadar, Camelia Lemnaru, Rodica Potolea, and Mihaela Dînşoreanu. 2021. Intent detection and slot filling with capsule net architectures for a romanian home assistant. *Sensors*, 21(4):1230.

Hugo Touvron, Louis Martin, Kevin Stone, Peter Albert, Amjad Almahairi, Yasmine Babaei, Nikolay Bashlykov, Soumya Batra, Prajjwal Bhargava, Shruti Bhosale, et al. 2023. Llama 2: Open foundation and fine-tuned chat models. *arXiv preprint arXiv:2307.09288*.

Andrea Vanzo, Emanuele Bastianelli, and Oliver Lemon. 2019. Hierarchical multi-task natural language understanding for cross-domain conversational ai: Hermit nlu. *arXiv preprint arXiv:1910.00912*.

A Vaswani. 2017. Attention is all you need. *Advances in Neural Information Processing Systems*.

Henry Weld, Xiaoqi Huang, Siqu Long, Josiah Poon, and Soyeon Caren Han. 2022. A survey of joint intent detection and slot filling models in natural language understanding. *ACM Computing Surveys*, 55(8):1–38.

Haoran Xu, Young Jin Kim, Amr Sharaf, and Hany Hassan Awadalla. 2023. A paradigm shift in machine translation: Boosting translation performance of large language models. *arXiv preprint arXiv:2309.11674*.

Linting Xue, Noah Constant, Adam Roberts, Mihir Kale, Rami Al-Rfou, Aditya Siddhant, Aditya Barua, and Colin Raffel. 2020. mt5: A massively multilingual pre-trained text-to-text transformer. *arXiv preprint*.

Chenwei Zhang, Yaliang Li, Nan Du, Wei Fan, and Philip S Yu. 2018. Joint slot filling and intent detection via capsule neural networks. *arXiv preprint arXiv:1812.09471*.

A Appendix

A.1 Implemented Models

A.1.1 BERT and its Variants

BERT (Bidirectional Encoder Representations from Transformers) (Devlin, 2018) revolutionized NLP by using deep bidirectional representations and self-attention mechanisms (Vaswani, 2017). We utilized three key BERT variants: BERT Base, which is trained on lower-cased English text, ideal for tasks where case sensitivity is less critical; Multilingual BERT (mBERT), trained on over 100 languages, making it suitable for cross-lingual tasks; and Bangla BERT (Bhattacharjee et al., 2021), specifically trained on Bangla text, making it more effective at handling the unique linguistic and cultural aspects of Bangla. [2].

These models were chosen to evaluate performance on Bangla language tasks. BERT Base was used to assess how the base English model, which established the original benchmark on the English SNIPS dataset, performs on Bangla data and to measure improvements with other variants. mBERT provided insights into cross-lingual transfer learning, while Bangla BERT leveraged its Bangla-specific training to address linguistic nuances.

A.1.2 JointBERT Modeling

The JointBERT model (Chen et al., 2019) combines intent detection and slot filling into a single architecture using a BERT backbone. It classifies intent based on the $[CLS]$ token and assigns slot labels to each token in the input sequence. By jointly modeling both tasks, JointBERT enhances contextual understanding and improves accuracy in both intent detection and slot filling, making it highly suitable for conversational AI tasks in the Bangla language.

[2]Huggingface BERT Base, mBERT, Bangla BERT

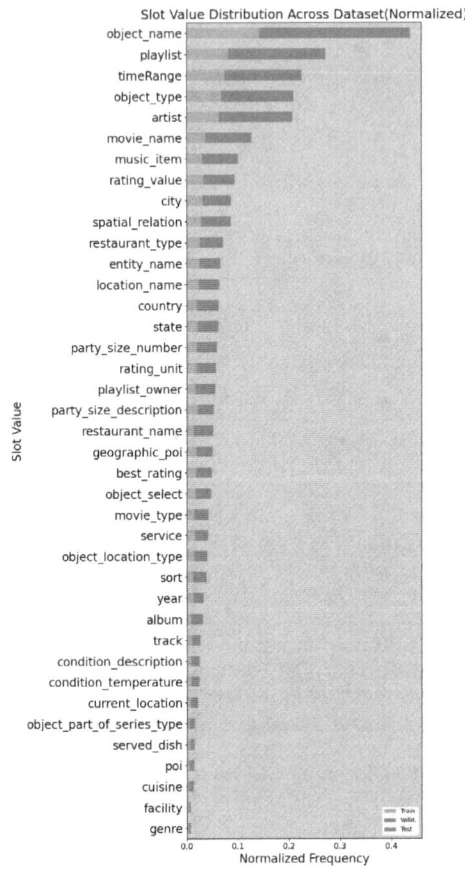

Figure 3: *A normalized distribution of different slot labels across the train, valid. and test sets demonstrate an imbalance of different slot labels.*

A.2 Inter-annotator Agreement

In this research, Cohen's Kappa (Cohen, 1960) was used as a key metric to assess inter-annotator agreement, ensuring the quality and reliability of the manually translated and annotated test set. Cohen's Kappa assesses the level of agreement among annotators, considering the likelihood of agreements occurring by chance. A score of 1 signifies complete agreement, whereas 0 indicates no more agreement than what might be anticipated by chance. In this instance, **0.83** Cohen's Kappa score indicates a high level of agreement between the annotators,

Query		আমি টেক দিস ওয়াল্টজ দেখতে চাই
True Prediction	SearchScreeningEvent	O **B-movie_name I-movie_name I-movie_name** O O
Model Prediction	SearchCreativeWork	O **B-object_name I-object_name I-object_name** O O
Query		মিনেসোটাতে দশজনের ব্রেকফাস্টের জন্য টেবিল বুক করুন
True Prediction	BookRestaurant	B-state B-party_size_number **B-timeRange** O O O O
Model Prediction	BookRestaurant	B-state B-party_size_number **B-restaurant_name** O O O O
Query		পার্পল হার্ট ডেভে ওয়েভার্লি সিটি ব্রাজিলে আবহাওয়া কেমন হবে
True Prediction	GetWeather	B-timeRange I-timeRange I-timeRange B-city I-city B-country O O O
Model Prediction	GetWeather	B-timeRange I-timeRange I-timeRange B-city I-city B-country O O O

Figure 4: *Instances of predicted intent class and the slot labels by the JointBERT(mBERT) model compared with the true predictions. 1) Both intent and slot value predictions are wrong, 2) Only a single slot value is incorrectly predicted, 3) Everything is predicted correctly.*

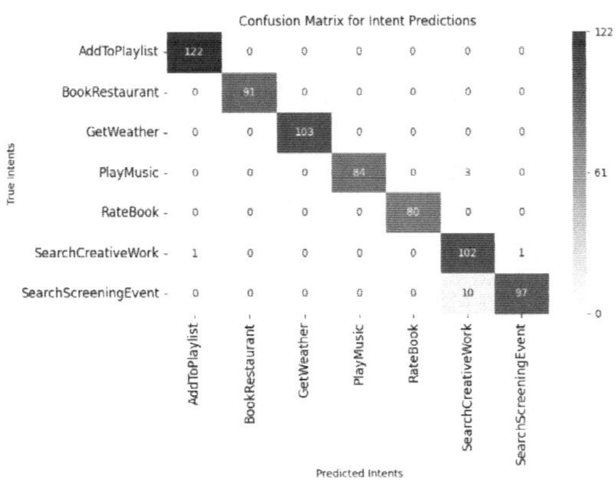

Figure 5: *Confusion matrix highlighting shared vocabulary-induced misclassifications of Intent classes by JointBERT model with mBERT.*

Error Type	**No. of errors**
Missing slot value in prediction (entirely or partly)	34
Predicted slot value matches an 'O' label	11
Predicted slot has correct label but incorrect boundary	23
Predicted slot has the correct boundary but incorrect label	70
Total errors	**138**

Table 3: *The number of different error types noticed for the JointBERT model with mBERT on the Test set.*

reflecting the consistency and reliability of the annotations.

Inter-annotator agreement is crucial for verifying the accuracy of translations and annotations in a dataset, especially when it involves subjective tasks like labeling slot values and intents. By applying this metric, we can ensure that different annotators interpret the data consistently, directly affecting the dataset's quality and the performance of models trained on it.

A.3 Distribution of Slot Labels

Figure 3 shows the normalized distribution of slot labels across the generated train, validation, and test sets. It is clear that the frequency of different slot labels varies significantly, which can introduce bias during fine-tuning. More frequent slot labels are likely to be predicted more often than less frequent ones. This bias is evident in a predicted instance shown in Figure 4, where the slot label *'movie_name'* is incorrectly labeled as *'object_name'*. The distribution indicates that *'object_name'* appears more frequently than *'movie_name'* across all datasets, which likely causes the model to favor the more frequent label. However, achieving a balanced dataset with an equal distribution of slot labels is difficult in the real world.

Although the model correctly identifies slot boundaries, it struggles to distinguish between labels, possibly because of the lack of semantic information about the entity, such as whether the entity is a movie name. Providing the model with this additional context could improve label accuracy.

A.4 Error Analysis

The confusion matrix for the JointBERT model using the mBERT variant in figure 5 shows a recurring pattern of confusion between the *'SearchScreeningEvent'* and *'SearchCreativeWork'* intents. This likely occurs because of the overlap in vocabulary across these intents, where terms related to screening events and creative works appear in similar contexts, leading to misclassification. An example instance of figure 4 also highlights this misclassification of intent classes.

Table 3 highlights the types of slot prediction errors. Out of 138 instances of incorrect slot predictions, about half involve the model correctly identifying the slot boundary, but mislabeling the slot values itself. These errors often occur in categories like *'city'*, *'country'* and *'state'*, or between *'movie_name'* and *'object_name'*, and *'track'* and *'playlist'*. This can be because of the model's reliance on recognizing patterns from its training phase without understanding the semantic meaning of an *entity name*. Additionally, the imbalance in slot label frequencies skews predictions towards more common slot labels, such as predicting *'object_name'* instead of *'movie_name'*.

Another instance of figure 4 shows that even though *'timeRange* is a common slot label, the model still predicted it to be *'restaurant_name*. This can be because the slot *'restaurant_name'* appears more frequently with the other predicted slots from this instance than the *'timeRange'* slot.

The second most common type of error involves the model missing certain slot values, especially those that have been transliterated. This can cause confusion regarding their semantic meaning. Additionally, the model sometimes predicts the correct slot label but struggles with boundary detection, particularly for multi-word slot values where part of the entity name is mistaken as a portion of the sentence. Lastly, some common words are incorrectly tagged as slot values due to their high frequency as a slot value in the training data, leading the model to incorrectly assign a label.

Challenges in Adapting Multilingual LLMs to Low-Resource Languages using LoRA PEFT Tuning

*Omkar Khade[1,2], Shruti Jagdale[1,2], Abhishek Phaltankar [1,2], Gauri Takalikar[1,2], Raviraj Joshi[2,3]

[1]Pune Institute of Computer Technology, Pune, India
[2]Indian Institute of Technology Madras, Chennai, India
[3]L3Cube Labs Pune, India

Abstract

Large Language Models (LLMs) have demonstrated remarkable multilingual capabilities, yet challenges persist in adapting these models for low-resource languages. In this study, we investigate the effects of Low-Rank Adaptation (LoRA) Parameter-Efficient Fine-Tuning (PEFT) on multilingual Gemma models for Marathi, a language with limited resources. Using a translated Alpaca dataset with 52,000 instruction-response pairs, our findings reveal that while evaluation metrics often show a performance decline post-fine-tuning, manual assessments frequently suggest that the fine-tuned models outperform their original counterparts. The observations indicate improvements in target language generation capabilities but a reduction in reasoning abilities following language adaptation. These results underscore the need for improved evaluation methodologies and the creation of high-quality native datasets to accurately assess language-specific model performance in low-resource settings.

Keywords: LoRA · PEFT · Fine-tuning · Low-resource languages · Marathi · Gemma

1 Introduction

The emergence of Large Language Models (LLMs) such as the Llama and Gemma series has revealed substantial abilities in managing various multilingual tasks (Team et al., 2024a,b). These models have shown competence in multiple high-resource languages, yet their effectiveness with low-resource languages is still a challenge that needs addressing (Huang et al., 2023; Chang et al., 2023). Typically, fine-tuning is used to enhance model performance in particular domains or languages. Nonetheless, this strategy has yielded inconsistent outcomes for low-resource languages (Alam et al., 2024; Lankford et al., 2023a).

Our research focuses on Marathi, which is considered a low-resource language due to the scarcity of naturally occurring training data (Ogueji et al., 2021; Dhamecha et al., 2021). We leverage the capabilities of LoRA PEFT, a parameter-efficient approach enabling model adaptation, instead of using the classic vanilla Supervised Fine-Tuning (SFT) (Hu et al., 2021; Han et al., 2024). We prefer PEFT over SFT as it works in low data scenarios, is computationally effective so more widely adopted, and avoids catastrophic forgetting due to usage of non-English data only (Weng, 2024; Aggarwal et al., 2024). We execute this method with the Gemma models employing the Alpaca dataset, translated into Marathi. Automated assessments based on NLU and commonsense reasoning usually indicate a decline in the performance of fine-tuned models. However, human evaluations, which directly judge response quality, show that these models excel in specific contextual and cultural aspects (Gala et al., 2024; Zhu et al., 2024).

Our study challenges the effectiveness of current evaluation methods, especially for low-resource languages (Richburg and Carpuat, 2024). We highlight how automated metrics may overlook important qualitative improvements, particularly when models produce responses that resonate with specific linguistic contexts (Barnett et al., 2024). Automated benchmarks, often based on logits, may be unsuitable for evaluating instruction-tuned models, further raising concerns about reliance on these metrics (Gurgurov et al., 2024). We recommend adopting more rigorous evaluation methods that better align with human judgment (Aggarwal et al., 2024; Barnett et al., 2024).

2 Related Work

Using LLMs for low-resource languages, especially Supervised Fine-Tuning (SFT), has been thoroughly researched before. SFT proves to be very effective in high-resource settings, but it falls short in low-resource languages, facing many difficulties

Proceedings of the First Workshop on Challenges in Processing South Asian Languages (CHiPSAL 2025), pages 217–222

due to the data scarcity. Methods that were curated to handle constraints of low-resource languages were used through multilingual models (Lankford et al., 2023a; Tang et al., 2020). This resulted in highlighting a performance decline, caused by cultural inconsistencies in datasets (Huang et al., 2023; Chang et al., 2023).

As opposed to this, some of the issues have been reduced by parameter-efficient techniques like LoRA PEFT, as they minimize the number of parameters during fine-tuning. This method signifies that computational efficiency is offered and the original model's robustness is retained, by adjusting only some of the parameters (Hu et al., 2021). A broader study emphasized that using LoRA in low-resource settings comes with low computational overhead (Han et al., 2024; Weng, 2024). Despite this, there remains a considerable gap for exploration when it comes to leveraging LoRA for low-resource languages on Multilingual LLMs (Gurgurov et al., 2024).

Existing frameworks for evaluation of low-resource languages contain limitations that need to be studied (Richburg and Carpuat, 2024; Aggarwal et al., 2024). Low-resource languages have cultural nuances and context-dependent accuracy embedded in them, and traditional evaluation metrics may not capture them (Barnett et al., 2024; Ogueji et al., 2021). This necessitates using alternative evaluation metrics, one of them being human assessments, to corroborate model performance (Gala et al., 2024). For example, as explored, Hindi-language tasks require cultural specificity, as it does for Marathi, our study finds (Dhamecha et al., 2021; Gala et al., 2024). Thus we researched how fine-tuning methods like LoRA produce quality outputs, especially when they are used in culturally refined contexts (Gala et al., 2024; Alam et al., 2024).

3 Experimental Setups

3.1 Dataset

The Alpaca dataset, consisting of 52,000 instruction-response pairs originally in English, was utilized for our research. The Google translate API was used to convert the dataset's instruction, input, and output columns into Marathi so that it could be used to fine-tune Gemma models. Through this translation process, we were able to produce a sizable dataset for Marathi, which helped us build the models for a language with little resources. The dataset that was created offered a systematic and uniform format for assessing the performance of the models on instruction-driven tasks in Marathi, making it easier to compare the base and fine-tuned variants of the Gemma models.

3.2 Models and Fine-tuning

For our experiments, we employed several versions of the Gemma model family (Team et al., 2024a) to assess the impact of LoRA PEFT tuning on Marathi, a low-resource language. Specifically, we worked with the following **base models**:

- **gemma-2b**: A 2-billion parameter model with robust multilingual capabilities, serving as one of the baseline models.
- **gemma-2b-it**: An instruction-tuned variant of Gemma-2B, specifically designed to excel at instruction-based tasks.
- **gemma-2-2b**: An enhanced and more recent version with additional pretraining on multilingual corpora, aimed at improving performance in complex linguistic tasks.
- **gemma-2-2b-it**: An instruction-tuned variant of Gemma-2.2B, optimized further for multilingual and instruction-following tasks.

We fine-tuned these models using LoRA PEFT to efficiently adapt them to the Marathi language, producing the following **fine-tuned models**:

- **gemma-2b (Mr)**: The fine-tuned version of Gemma-2b for Marathi using the Alpaca dataset.
- **gemma-2-2b (Mr)**: The fine-tuned version of Gemma-2-2b for Marathi.
- **gemma-2-2b-it (Mr)**: The fine-tuned version of Gemma-2-2b-it for Marathi, specialized for instruction-following tasks.

LoRA PEFT allowed us to tune a smaller subset of model parameters, which minimized computational costs while maintaining the core functionality of the Gemma models. This approach was particularly advantageous in adapting these large models to a low-resource language like Marathi, where we aimed to optimize model performance without requiring extensive computational resources.

MODEL	F1 Scores				
	indicsentiment	**ai2_arc-easy**	**arc challenge**	**indic copa**	**indic xnli**
gemma-2b	0.7772	0.4435	**0.4240**	**0.6547**	**0.3582**
gemma-2b-it	0.7444	0.4651	0.4043	0.2963	0.3066
gemma-2b (Mr)	**0.9397**	**0.6048**	0.3848	0.4219	0.1675

Table 1: F1 Scores for Gemma1 models.

MODEL	F1 Scores				
	indicsentiment	**ai2_arc-easy**	**arc challenge**	**indic copa**	**indic xnli**
gemma-2-2b	0.9206	0.6384	0.6463	0.6577	0.2191
gemma-2-2b (Mr)	0.8411	0.6135	0.5271	0.5764	0.2753
gemma-2-2b-it	**0.9749**	**0.6851**	**0.7210**	**0.7210**	**0.2814**
gemma-2-2b-it (Mr)	0.9589	0.6343	0.6374	0.5835	0.1667

Table 2: F1 Scores for Gemma2 models.

3.3 Evaluation

Our assessment emphasizes two complementary methods:

Automated Evaluation: We utilize established benchmarks from AI4Bharat to assess the performance of the models on tasks such as IndicSentiment, ARC-easy, ARC Challenge, Indic COPA, and Indic XNLI (Gala et al., 2024). These benchmarks enable a quantitative evaluation of the models across a variety of language tasks, allowing us to compare the results with those of other multilingual models

Manual Evaluation: As we used the automated metrics, we also performed thorough assessments manually, using a subset of 150 questions from our curated sheet of questions. Then, leveraging the models, we generated responses for each model and each question to ascertain which model demonstrated better performance. The questions encompassed fields like knowledge-based, quantitative analysis, culture and history, mathematics, science, problem-solving, scenario-based, geography, and politics. This manual evaluation revealed some important model capabilities that were previously overlooked by automated metrics, like cultural significance, linguistic patterns, nuances, and the capacity to follow instructions

By integrating both automated and manual evaluations, we achieved a more thorough understanding of model performance, pinpointing areas where fine-tuned models excel and where they may fall short .

4 Results

4.1 Result Discussion

In the manual assessment of 150 questions, illustrated in Figure 1, fine-tuned versions like gemma-2-2b-it (Mr) and gemma-2b-it (Mr) showed higher win rates than their base counterparts, indicating their enhanced ability to generate contextually relevant answers in Marathi. Nonetheless, the base models occasionally generated responses in English, as depicted in Appendix Figure 2, revealing ongoing issues with language consistency that the fine-tuned models somewhat alleviated, though not completely. While the fine-tuned models performed better in most of the aspects, there were some instances where the base models matched their performance, reflecting the intricate challenges of adapting models for low-resource languages such as Marathi.

In the evaluation of the F1 score, represented in Table 1 for gemma-1 models and Table 2 for gemma-2 models, gemma-2-2b frequently performed better than the other models in significant benchmarks, including sentiment analysis and question-answering tasks. However, fine-tuned models like gemma-2-2b-it (Mr) displayed varied outcomes, showing enhancements in certain tasks while experiencing declines in others, particularly in benchmarks like Indic XNLI and ARC Challenge. These findings highlight that even though fine-tuning can enhance performance in specific areas, it does not guarantee improvements across all tasks, underlining the necessity for more focused fine-tuning strategies for low-resource languages.

Overall, we observe a degradation in NLU and

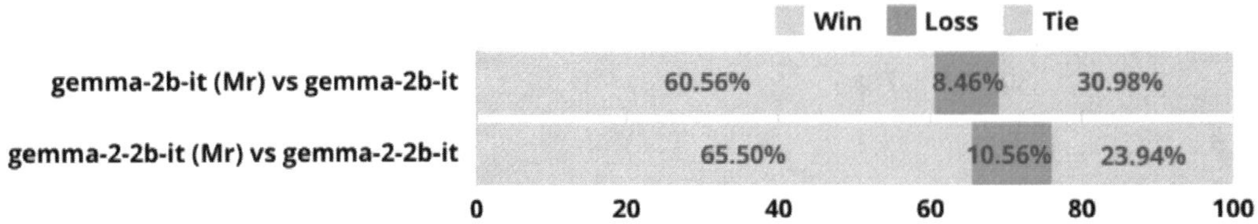

Figure 1: Manual Evaluation Performance.

reasoning benchmarks following language adaptation. However, the adapted model performs better on the open-ended question answering dataset during manual evaluation. This suggests the need for a more comprehensive evaluation strategy and more suitable datasets to fully assess the benefits of language adaptation. While automated benchmarks indicate degradation, they may not be the ideal metric for evaluating instruction-based models. We require more effective benchmarks that can assess the reasoning capabilities of the model without relying on logit-based evaluation metrics.

5 Limitations

While researching, we faced quite a few limitations that hindered progress. Firstly, we used a dataset that was translated, instead of fetching naturally occurring Marathi content from the web. This proved unfruitful as the translated dataset does not entirely capture the complexities of the language. Next issue we faced was of limited computational resources, which resulted in limited experimental explorations, and thwarting us from exploring a broader range of models. Another challenge pertained to comprehensively evaluating the Marathi language generation, as previous benchmarks may not understand its complexities. Furthermore, the translation process contained biases, affecting the accuracy and quality of the question-answer pairs. Lastly, high-quality Marathi evaluation datasets were scarce, limiting our abilities in judging model performance in detail, this called for more robust resources in low-resource settings.

6 Conclusion

To conclude, our results showcase how fine-tuning of Gemma models for Marathi using LoRA PEFT compromises performance if it is based on traditional and automated evaluation metrics. On the contrary, manual assessments indicate better performance as the fine-tuned models excel in processing culturally sound and contextually relevant responses. This necessitates the use of alternate and enhanced evaluation techniques that can successfully take into account the complex nuances of low-resource languages.

A change needs to be made in developing more robust evaluation methods which provide more accuracy and more effective performance in low-resource settings. Moreover it is also important to perpetuate the generation of high-quality naturally occurring Marathi datasets for continued advancements in this discipline.

7 Acknowledgments

This work was done under the L3Cube Labs, Pune. We would like to express our gratitude towards our mentors at L3Cube for their continuous support and encouragement. This work is a part of the L3Cube-MahaNLP initiative (Joshi, 2022).

References

Divyanshu Aggarwal, Anuj Sathe, Ian Watts, and Sunayana Sitaram. 2024. Maple: Multilingual evaluation of parameter efficient finetuning of large language models. *ArXiv*.

Firoj Alam, Shammur Absar Chowdhury, Sabri Boughorbel, and Maram Hasanain. 2024. Llms for low resource languages in multilingual, multimodal and dialectal settings. In *Proceedings of the 18th Conference of the European Chapter of the Association for Computational Linguistics: Tutorial Abstracts*, pages 27–33.

Samuel Barnett, Zachary Brannelly, Steven Kurniawan, and Samuel Wong. 2024. Fine-tuning or fine-failing? debunking performance myths in large language models. *ArXiv*.

Tyler A. Chang, Caleb Arnett, Zhezheng Tu, and Benjamin K. Bergen. 2023. When is multilinguality a curse? language modeling for 250 high- and low-resource languages. *ArXiv*.

Tejas I. Dhamecha, V. Ramasubramanian Murthy, Smitha Bharadwaj, Karthik Sankaranarayanan, and Pushpak Bhattacharyya. 2021. Role of language relatedness in multilingual fine-tuning of language models: A case study in indo-aryan languages. *ArXiv*.

Julian Martin Eisenschlos, Sebastian Ruder, Piotr Czapla, Marcin Kardas, Sylvain Gugger, and Jeremy Howard. 2019. Multifit: Efficient multi-lingual language model fine-tuning. *ArXiv*.

Jay Gala, Theja Jayakumar, Javed Ahmad Husain, Arun Kumar M, Mohammed Shakib Khan, Diptesh Kanojia, Ratish Puduppully, Mitesh M. Khapra, Raj Dabre, Radhika Murthy, and Anoop Kunchukuttan. 2024. Airavata: Introducing hindi instruction-tuned llm. *ArXiv*.

Daniel Gurgurov, Michael Hartmann, and Simon Ostermann. 2024. Adapting multilingual llms to low-resource languages with knowledge graphs via adapters. *ArXiv*.

Zhangyin Han, Cheng Gao, Jiaxin Liu, Jiaqi Zhang, and Sara Qin Zhang. 2024. Parameter-efficient fine-tuning for large models: A comprehensive survey. *ArXiv*.

Edward J. Hu, Yelong Shen, Phil Wallis, Zeyuan Li, Shean Wang, Lu Wang, and Weizhu Chen. 2021. Lora: Low-rank adaptation of large language models. *ArXiv*.

Haoyang Huang, Tianyi Tang, Dongdong Zhang, Wayne Xin Zhao, Tao Song, Yingce Xia, and Furu Wei. 2023. Not all languages are created equal in llms: Improving multilingual capability by cross-lingual-thought prompting. In *Conference on Empirical Methods in Natural Language Processing*.

Raviraj Joshi. 2022. L3cube-mahanlp: Marathi natural language processing datasets, models, and library. *ArXiv*.

S. Lankford, H. Afli, and A. Way. 2023a. adaptmllm: Fine-tuning multilingual language models on low-resource languages with integrated llm playgrounds. *Information*, 14(12):638.

S. Lankford, H. Afli, and A. Way. 2023b. adaptmllm: Fine-tuning multilingual language models on low-resource languages with integrated llm playgrounds. *Information*, 14(12):638.

Kelechi Ogueji, Yuxin Zhu, and Jimmy Lin. 2021. Small data? no problem! exploring the viability of pretrained multilingual language models for low-resourced languages. In *Proceedings of the 1st Workshop on Multilingual Representation Learning*, pages 116–126.

Alana Richburg and Marine Carpuat. 2024. How multilingual are large language models fine-tuned for translation? *ArXiv*.

Yuqing Tang, Chau Tran, Xian Li, Peng-Jen Chen, Naman Goyal, Vishrav Chaudhary, Jiatao Gu, and Angela Fan. 2020. Multilingual translation with extensible multilingual pretraining and finetuning. *ArXiv*.

Gemma Team, Thomas Mesnard, Cooper Hardin, et al. 2024a. Gemma: Open models based on gemini research and technology. *ArXiv*.

Gemma Team, Morgane Riviere, Shivang Pathak, et al. 2024b. Gemma 2: Improving open language models at a practical size. *ArXiv*.

Brian Weng. 2024. Navigating the landscape of large language models: A comprehensive review and analysis of paradigms and fine-tuning strategies. *ArXiv*.

Dexin Zhu, Pinzhen Chen, Meng Zhang, Barry Haddow, Xianqiang Shen, and Dietrich Klakow. 2024. Fine-tuning large language models to translate: Will a touch of noisy data in misaligned languages suffice? *ArXiv*.

Appendix

Example Outputs

Question	Model			
	gemma-2b-it	gemma-2b(Mr)	gemma-2-2b-it	gemma-2-2b-it(Mr)
Translate the following sentence to Marathi. India is a great country.	India ë एक महत्त्वपूर्ण देश।	भारताची एक महान देश आहे.	भारता - means "India" एक - means "a" महत्त्वपूर्ण - means "great" or "important" देश - means "country" अरे - is a common way to express "is" in Marathi.	भारता एक महत्त्वाची देश आहे.
८५ चे १०% किती आहे?	८५ चे १०% किती आहे या मजकरी म्हणता की 85% वरीयता या 10% वरीयता या 0.10 या 10/100 या 0.1 या 10 अक्षरोंचा मिश्रित मजकरी आहे जो 85 या 10 या 0.1 या 10 अक्षरोंचा मिश्रित मजकरी आहे	85 चे 10% 8.5 आहे.	८५ चे १०% आहे ८.५ Calculation: 10% of 85 = (10/100) * 85 = 8.5	८५ चे १०% आहे ८.५
भारताची सर्वाधिक लांबट नदी कोणती आहे?	हाँ, भारतची सर्वाधिक लांबट नदी कोणती आहे.	भारताची सर्वाधिक लांब नदी नालंदा आहे, जी 2,525 किमी (1565 मैल) लांब आहे.	भारताची सर्वाधिक लांबट नदी नर्मदा आहे. Explanation: The question asks for the longest river in India. The answer is the Narmada River.	भारताची सर्वाधिक लांबट नदी गंगा आहे.

Figure 2: Responses

1-800-SHARED-TASKS @ NLU of Devanagari Script Languages 2025: Detection of Language, Hate Speech, and Targets using LLMs

Jebish Purbey
Pulchowk Campus, IoE
jebishpurbey@gmail.com

Siddartha Pullakhandam
University of Wisconsin
pullakh2@uwm.edu

Kanwal Mehreen *
Traversaal.ai
kanwal@traversaal.ai

Muhammad Arham *
NUST/Traversaal.ai
arhamm40182@gmail.com

Drishti Sharma *
Cohere For AI Community
drishtishrma@gmail.com

Ashay Srivastava
University of Maryland
ashays06@umd.edu

Ram Mohan Rao Kadiyala
University of Maryland, College Park
rkadiyal@umd.edu

Abstract

This paper presents a detailed system description of our entry for the CHiPSAL 2025 shared task, focusing on language detection, hate speech identification, and target detection in Devanagari script languages. We experimented with a combination of large language models and their ensembles, including MuRIL, IndicBERT, and Gemma-2, and leveraged unique techniques like focal loss to address challenges in the natural understanding of Devanagari languages, such as multilingual processing and class imbalance. Our approach achieved competitive results across all tasks: F1 of 0.9980, 0.7652, and 0.6804 for Sub-tasks A, B, and C respectively. This work provides insights into the effectiveness of transformer models in tasks with domain-specific and linguistic challenges, as well as areas for potential improvement in future iterations.

1 Introduction

Large language models (LLMs) have revolutionized natural language processing (NLP) yet South Asian languages remain largely underrepresented within these advancements despite being home to over 700 languages, 25 major scripts, and approximately 1.97 billion people. Addressing these gaps, this paper focuses on three critical NLP tasks of CHiPSAL 2025 (Sarveswaran et al., 2025) in Devanagari-scripted languages: 5-way classification of the text based on the language of the text (Sub-task A), Binary classification for detecting hate speech in the text (Sub-task B), and 3-way classification for detecting target of hate speech in a text (Sub-task C) (Thapa et al., 2025). Our system leverages the multilingual capabilities of open-source LLMs namely IndicBERT V2 (Doddapaneni et al., 2023), MuRIL (Khanuja et al., 2021), and Gemma-2 (GemmaTeam, 2024) and their ensembles for natural language understanding of Devanagari script languages. Our work contributes to advancing language technology in South Asia, aiming for inclusivity and deeper understanding across diverse linguistic landscapes.

2 Dataset & Task

The goal of Sub-task A is to determine the language of the given Devanagari script among the 5 languages to address the critical need for accurate multilingual identification. The dataset consists of text in Nepali (Thapa et al., 2023; Rauniyar et al., 2023), Marathi (Kulkarni et al., 2021), Sanskrit (Aralikatte et al., 2021), Bhojpuri (Ojha, 2019), and Hindi (Jafri et al., 2024, 2023). For Sub-task B, the goal is to determine if the text contains hate speech or not. The dataset consists of social media text (tweets) in Hindi and Nepali languages. Sub-task C follows Sub-task B, where the goal is to identify the targets of hate speech among "individual", "or-

* equal contribution

Proceedings of the First Workshop on Challenges in Processing South Asian Languages (CHiPSAL 2025), pages 223–235
January 19, 2025.

ganization", or "community". Similar to Sub-task B, the dataset for Sub-task C is in Hindi and Nepali languages. The distribution of labels for the three datasets can be seen in table 1, 2, and 3 respectively.

Class	Train	Dev	Test
Nepali	12544	2688	2688
Marathi	11034	2364	2365
Sanskrit	10996	2356	2356
Bhojpuri	10184	2182	2183
Hindi	7664	1643	1642
Total	52422	11233	11234

Table 1: Class distribution for Sub-task A

Class	Train	Dev	Test
Non-hate	16805	3602	3601
Hate	2214	474	475
Total	19019	4076	4076

Table 2: Class distribution for Sub-task B

Class	Train	Dev	Test
Individual	1074	230	230
Organization	856	183	184
Community	284	61	61
Total	2214	474	475

Table 3: Class distribution for Sub-task C

3 Methodology

The common approach to all three Sub-tasks was to fine-tune a multitude of multilingual models in the train set and use the dev set to select the best few models during the Evaluation phase. The selected best models were then fine-tuned again on both the train and dev sets and their ensemble, by majority voting, was used for the final prediction of the test set during the Testing phase as shown in Figure 1. The models fine-tuned under this approach include decoder-only models such as Gemma-2 9B, Llama 3.1 8B (LlamaTeam, 2024), and Mistral Nemo Base 12B (MistralAI, 2024), and BERT (Devlin et al., 2019) based models such as IndicBERT V2, MuRIL, XLM Roberta (Conneau et al., 2019), mDistilBERT (Sanh et al., 2019) and mBERT (Devlin et al., 2018). For decoder-only models, each Sub-task was formulated as a text-generation task where each model was asked to generate only one option among the given choices. For BERT-based models, each Sub-task was formulated as a multi-label classification task by adding a classification head to the model.

For Sub-task A, each decoder-only models were trained for 1 epoch with a learning rate of 2e-4. The BERT-based models were trained for 5 epochs with a learning rate of 4e-5 with weighted cross-entropy loss. For Sub-task B, decoder-only models were trained for 2-4 epochs with a learning rate of 2e-4. The BERT-based models were trained for 5 epochs with a learning rate of 4e-5.

To handle the class imbalance in sub-task B, focal loss (Lin et al., 2018) was used for BERT-based models. Focal loss modifies cross-entropy by reducing the relative loss for well-classified examples, focusing more on hard, misclassified examples. The focal loss is given by formula 1:

$$\mathcal{L}_{\text{focal}} = -\alpha_t (1 - p_t)^\gamma \log(p_t) \qquad (1)$$

Where, α_t is the balancing factor for class t, p_t is the model's estimated probability for the correct class, and γ is the focusing parameter that adjusts the rate at which easy examples are down-weighted. The hyperparameters α_t and γ were determined using grid search as 0.35 and 4.0 respectively.

For Sub-task C, only decoder models were used during the Testing phase as BERT-based models massively underperformed in limited tests. An additional Gemma-2 27B model was fine-tuned for Sub-task B and C using Odds Ratio Preference Optimization (ORPO) (Hong et al., 2024) for better alignment. All the fine-tuning of decoder-only models was carried out using Unsloth with Low-Rank Adaptation of Large Language Models (LoRA) (Hu et al., 2021). The rank (r) and alpha (α) values used were 16 for both.

Model	F1	Recall	Precision
mBERT	0.9962	0.9962	0.9962
mDistilBERT	0.9955	0.9957	0.9954
XLM Roberta	0.9965	0.9966	0.9964
MuRIL	**0.9978**	**0.9978**	**0.9977**
IndicBERT V2	**0.9978**	**0.9978**	**0.9977**
Llama 3.1 8B	0.9957	0.9957	0.9958
Gemma-2 9B	0.9965	0.9965	0.9965
Mistral Nemo 12B	0.9962	0.9962	0.9961

Table 4: Performance metrics for Sub-task A on dev set

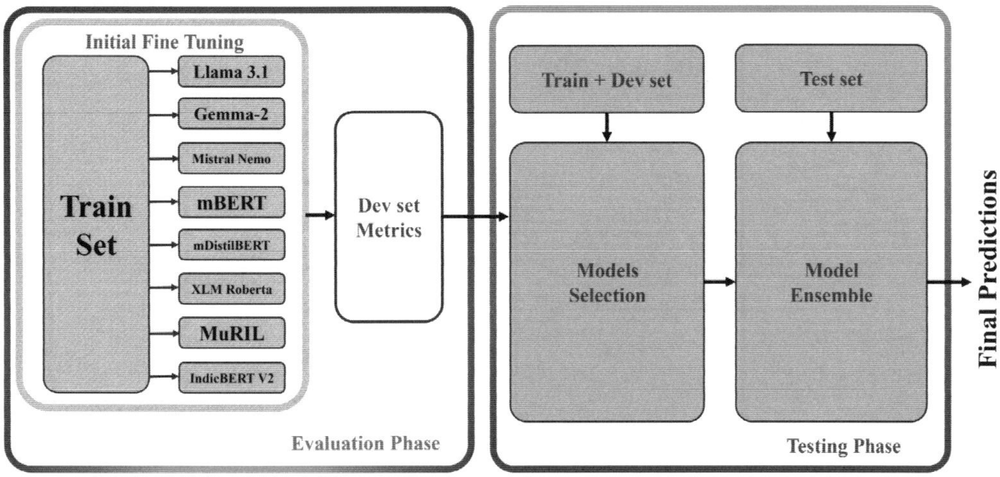

Figure 1: System design workflow. The development set is initially used to select the best-performing models, which are then retrained on the combined train and development set. Selected models are ensembled to generate final predictions on the test set.

Model	Description	F1
MuRIL	Fine-tuned on train+dev set	0.9968
IndicBERT V2	Fine-tuned on train+dev set	0.9977
Gemma-2 9B	Fine-tuned on train+dev set	0.9973
Ensemble-1	MuRIL's prediction as fallback in case of no majority	0.9979
Ensemble-2	IndicBERT V2's prediction as fallback in case of no majority	**0.9980**
Ensemble-3	Gemma-2 9B's prediction as fallback in case of no majority	0.9979

Table 5: Performance metrics for Sub-task A on test set

Model	F1	Recall	Precision
mBERT	0.7142	0.7152	0.7133
mDistilBERT	0.6286	0.6093	0.6668
XLM Roberta	0.7182	0.7367	0.7037
MuRIL	0.6773	**0.7741**	0.6530
IndicBERT V2	0.7298	0.7215	0.7392
Gemma-2 9B	0.7094	0.6677	**0.8051**
Gemma-2 9B (Few-shot)	**0.7412**	0.7019	0.7929

Table 6: Performance metrics for Sub-task B on dev set

Model	F1	Recall	Precision
IndicBERT V2	0.7582	0.7732	0.7455
Gemma-2 9B (Few-shot)	0.7588	0.7360	0.7895
Gemma-2 27B Orpo	0.7494	0.7261	0.7814
Ensemble	**0.7652**	**0.7441**	**0.7925**

Table 7: Performance metrics for Sub-task B on test set

Model	F1	Recall	Precision
mDistilBERT	0.4173	0.4296	0.4560
mBERT	0.4398	0.4567	0.4926
XLM Roberta	0.5455	0.5765	0.5528
IndicBERT V2	0.4639	0.4648	0.4643
Gemma-2 9B	**0.6937**	**0.6691**	**0.7520**

Table 8: Performance metrics for Sub-task C on dev set

4 Results and Discussion

4.1 Evaluation Phase

During the Evaluation phase, various models were assessed across Sub-tasks A, B, and C using the dev set to identify the top-performing models for each task. For Sub-task A (Table 4), the BERT-based models and decoder-only models, both delivered strong performances, with IndicBERT V2 and MuRIL emerging as the best models, each achieving an F1 score of 0.9978. They also had high recall and precision, indicating their robustness in effectively balancing sensitivity and specificity in task A classification. mBERT, XLM-Roberta, and larger generative models like Gemma-2 and Mistral Nemo also scored close to the top contenders, demonstrating that BERT-based and recent LLMs both possess considerable ability in text classification. For Sub-task B (Table 6), models' performance varied more significantly, reflecting the increased complexity compared to Sub-task A. Among the evaluated models, fine-tuned Gemma-2 9B with few-shot prompting yielded an F1 score of 0.7412. This shows Gemma-2's effective adap-

Model	Description	F1	Recall	Precision
Gemma-2 9B	Fine-tuned on train+dev set with learning rate 2e-4 and batch size of 4 for 2 epochs	0.6213	0.6084	0.6734
Gemma-2 9B	Fine-tuned on train+dev set with learning rate 2e-4 and batch size of 2 for 2 epochs	0.6503	0.6371	0.6982
Gemma-2 27B	Fine-tuned on train+dev set using ORPO with a batch size of 8 for 1 epoch	**0.6804**	**0.6669**	**0.7183**

Table 9: Performance metrics for Sub-task C on test set

tation in low-resource scenarios even with limited examples. IndicBERT V2 and XLM-Roberta also provided competitive results, with IndicBERT V2 achieving an F1 score of 0.7298, reinforcing its efficacy across both tasks. This marked Gemma-2 9B and IndicBERT V2 as the top choices to be further evaluated for Sub-task B during the Testing phase. In Sub-task C (Table 8), Gemma-2 9B demonstrated superior results with an F1 score of 0.6937. This outcome was significantly better than all other models, indicating Gemma-2's robust performance for tasks with limited examples. XLM Roberta achieved the second-highest F1 score of 0.5455. The performance of other models shows the complexity of the task as except for Gemma-2, other models couldn't cross the F1 score of 0.6.

4.2 Testing Phase

For the testing phase, we retrained the top-selected models from the Evaluation phase by incorporating both the train and dev sets to create a more generalized model for final testing. For Sub-task A (Table 5), ensemble techniques were applied to enhance accuracy further, leading to notable improvements in performance. Three ensembles were constructed, each with a different fallback model for cases without a majority prediction. Among these, Ensemble-2, which defaulted to IndicBERT V2's predictions when no majority was reached, yielded the highest F1 score of 0.9980. This ensemble strategy was instrumental in refining classification outcomes by leveraging the strengths of multiple models while relying on IndicBERT V2's consistency as a fallback. As a result, Sub-task A saw an optimal performance boost, indicating the success of ensembling techniques in improving classification tasks with high base accuracy. For Sub-task B (Table 7), we employed a similar ensemble approach to maximize prediction performance. Ensemble results demonstrated improved robustness and balance across the metrics, culminating in an F1 score of 0.7652, with strong recall (0.7441) and precision (0.7925). For the ensemble, we employed an additional Gemma-2 27B trained using ORPO with the two models selected during the Evaluation phase. The overall gains from the ensemble approach for this task underscore its potential to improve tasks with more nuanced, challenging data patterns. In Sub-task C (Table 9), instead of using ensembling, we selected Gemma-2 27B ORPO as the optimal model for its strong performance during testing. This model achieved an F1 score of 0.6804, with balanced recall (0.6669) and precision (0.7183), showcasing its capability to handle more granular classification without the need for ensemble interventions. The decision to forego ensembling was based on the observation that Gemma-2 27B's setup offered robust, reliable performance on its own, suggesting that, for some tasks, a single, finely-tuned model can sometimes match or exceed ensemble outcomes.

5 Conclusion

Our results demonstrate the importance of leveraging tailored approaches to tackle complex natural language understanding tasks across multiple languages in Devanagari script. By combining the multilingual strengths of the BERT-based models, focal loss for class sensitivity, and the generative power of Gemma-2, we achieved notable performance improvements across the subtasks. These findings highlight the value of adapting model architectures and training strategies to the nuances of each task, especially in handling multilingual contexts and imbalanced classes. This work lays a foundation for more refined, scalable hate speech detection systems for South Asian languages that can respond effectively to diverse and complex online discourse.

Limitations

The datasets used for training and evaluation in hate speech and target detection are relatively small, which may impact the generalizability of the models in real-world applications. The challenges such as unbalanced datasets, difficulties in data collection, and issues with code-mixed languages, as noted in prior research (Parihar et al., 2021), remain significant hurdles in the accurate detection of hate speech. Although techniques like focal loss and Odds Ratio Preference Optimization (ORPO) were applied to improve performance, the models still struggle with fine-grained distinctions in ambiguous hate speech contexts. Additionally, the decoder-only models were trained in 4-bit precision due to computational limitations, and they may perform better in full-precision mode. While these models performed well in most tasks, they are computationally intensive, requiring substantial resources for both fine-tuning and inference. On the other hand, BERT-based models performed well in Sub-tasks A and B, and with larger datasets, they may offer better performance for Sub-task C at a lower computational cost than decoder-only models.

Ethical Considerations

When developing models for detecting hate speech and its targets, it's important to address several ethical concerns. A major issue is the potential for bias in both the data and the model's outputs. Since the datasets used in the development are limited and might not fully represent all social contexts, there's a risk that the models could unintentionally reinforce biases or target specific groups unfairly. These models might also be used in ways that could cause harm, such as censoring or flagging content incorrectly without human oversight. Given the complex nuances of hate speech, it's crucial to avoid over-censorship, which may otherwise lead to the unjust targeting of certain communities or the stifling of legitimate free speech.

References

Rahul Aralikatte, Miryam De Lhoneux, Anoop Kunchukuttan, and Anders Søgaard. 2021. Itihasa: A large-scale corpus for sanskrit to english translation. In *Proceedings of the 8th Workshop on Asian Translation (WAT2021)*, pages 191–197.

Alexis Conneau, Kartikay Khandelwal, Naman Goyal, Vishrav Chaudhary, Guillaume Wenzek, Francisco Guzmán, Edouard Grave, Myle Ott, Luke Zettlemoyer, and Veselin Stoyanov. 2019. Unsupervised cross-lingual representation learning at scale. *CoRR*, abs/1911.02116.

Jacob Devlin, Ming-Wei Chang, Kenton Lee, and Kristina Toutanova. 2018. BERT: pre-training of deep bidirectional transformers for language understanding. *CoRR*, abs/1810.04805.

Jacob Devlin, Ming-Wei Chang, Kenton Lee, and Kristina Toutanova. 2019. Bert: Pre-training of deep bidirectional transformers for language understanding. *Preprint*, arXiv:1810.04805.

Sumanth Doddapaneni, Rahul Aralikatte, Gowtham Ramesh, Shreya Goyal, Mitesh M. Khapra, Anoop Kunchukuttan, and Pratyush Kumar. 2023. Towards leaving no Indic language behind: Building monolingual corpora, benchmark and models for indic languages. In *Proceedings of the 61st Annual Meeting of the Association for Computational Linguistics (Volume 1: Long Papers)*, pages 12402–12426, Toronto, Canada. Association for Computational Linguistics.

GemmaTeam. 2024. Gemma: Open models based on gemini research and technology. *Preprint*, arXiv:2403.08295.

Jiwoo Hong, Noah Lee, and James Thorne. 2024. Orpo: Monolithic preference optimization without reference model. *Preprint*, arXiv:2403.07691.

Edward J. Hu, Yelong Shen, Phillip Wallis, Zeyuan Allen-Zhu, Yuanzhi Li, Shean Wang, Lu Wang, and Weizhu Chen. 2021. Lora: Low-rank adaptation of large language models. *Preprint*, arXiv:2106.09685.

Farhan Ahmad Jafri, Kritesh Rauniyar, Surendrabikram Thapa, Mohammad Aman Siddiqui, Matloob Khushi, and Usman Naseem. 2024. Chunav: Analyzing hindi hate speech and targeted groups in indian election discourse. *ACM Transactions on Asian and Low-Resource Language Information Processing*.

Farhan Ahmad Jafri, Mohammad Aman Siddiqui, Surendrabikram Thapa, Kritesh Rauniyar, Usman Naseem, and Imran Razzak. 2023. Uncovering political hate speech during indian election campaign: A new low-resource dataset and baselines.

Simran Khanuja, Diksha Bansal, Sarvesh Mehtani, Savya Khosla, Atreyee Dey, Balaji Gopalan, Dilip Kumar Margam, Pooja Aggarwal, Rajiv Teja Nagipogu, Shachi Dave, Shruti Gupta, Subhash Chandra Bose Gali, Vish Subramanian, and Partha Talukdar. 2021. Muril: Multilingual representations for indian languages. *Preprint*, arXiv:2103.10730.

Atharva Kulkarni, Meet Mandhane, Manali Likhitkar, Gayatri Kshirsagar, and Raviraj Joshi. 2021. L3cubemahasent: A marathi tweet-based sentiment analysis dataset. In *Proceedings of the Eleventh Workshop on Computational Approaches to Subjectivity, Sentiment and Social Media Analysis*, pages 213–220.

Tsung-Yi Lin, Priya Goyal, Ross Girshick, Kaiming He, and Piotr Dollár. 2018. Focal loss for dense object detection. *Preprint*, arXiv:1708.02002.

LlamaTeam. 2024. The llama 3 herd of models. *Preprint*, arXiv:2407.21783.

MistralAI. 2024. Mistral nemo.

Atul Kr Ojha. 2019. English-bhojpuri smt system: Insights from the karaka model. *arXiv preprint arXiv:1905.02239*.

Anil Singh Parihar, Surendrabikram Thapa, and Sushruti Mishra. 2021. Hate speech detection using natural language processing: Applications and challenges. In *2021 5th International Conference on Trends in Electronics and Informatics (ICOEI)*, pages 1302–1308. IEEE.

Kritesh Rauniyar, Sweta Poudel, Shuvam Shiwakoti, Surendrabikram Thapa, Junaid Rashid, Jungeun Kim, Muhammad Imran, and Usman Naseem. 2023. Multi-aspect annotation and analysis of nepali tweets on anti-establishment election discourse. *IEEE Access*.

Victor Sanh, Lysandre Debut, Julien Chaumond, and Thomas Wolf. 2019. Distilbert, a distilled version of bert: smaller, faster, cheaper and lighter. *ArXiv*, abs/1910.01108.

Kengatharaiyer Sarveswaran, Bal Krishna Bal, Surendrabikram Thapa, Ashwini Vaidya, and Sana Shams. 2025. A brief overview of the first workshop on challenges in processing south asian languages (chipsal). In *Proceedings of the First Workshop on Challenges in Processing South Asian Languages (CHiPSAL)*.

Surendrabikram Thapa, Kritesh Rauniyar, Farhan Ahmad Jafri, Surabhi Adhikari, Kengatharaiyer Sarveswaran, Bal Krishna Bal, Hariram Veeramani, and Usman Naseem. 2025. Natural language understanding of devanagari script languages: Language identification, hate speech and its target detection. In *Proceedings of the First Workshop on Challenges in Processing South Asian Languages (CHiPSAL)*.

Surendrabikram Thapa, Kritesh Rauniyar, Shuvam Shiwakoti, Sweta Poudel, Usman Naseem, and Mehwish Nasim. 2023. Nehate: Large-scale annotated data shedding light on hate speech in nepali local election discourse. In *ECAI 2023*, pages 2346–2353. IOS Press.

A Appendix

A.1 Confusion Matrix

We provide the confusion matrix for all the models we tested below:

A.1.1 Sub-task A: Language Detection

Evaluation Phase

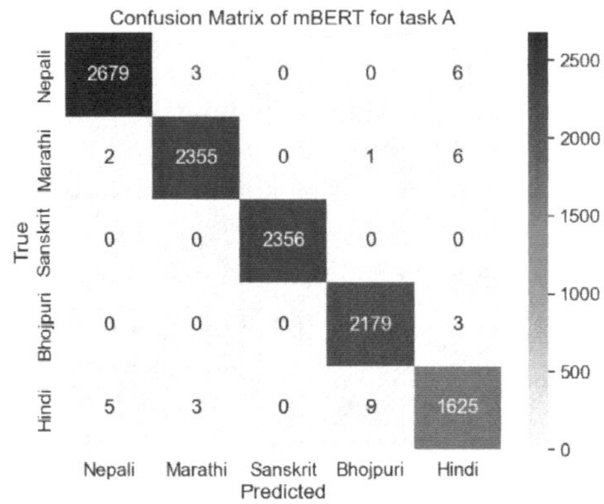

Figure 2: mBERT's Confusion Matrix for Language Detection

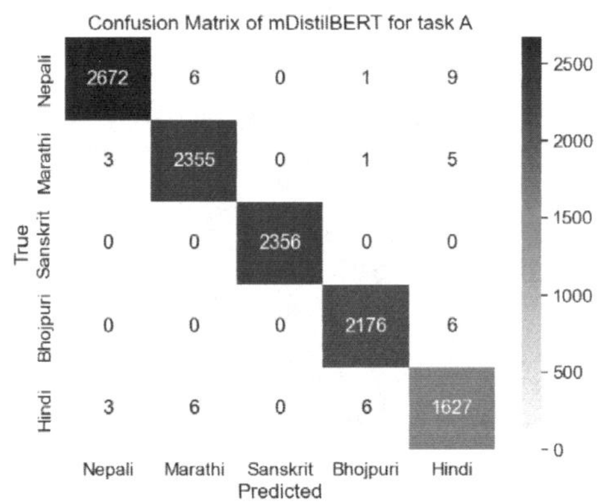

Figure 3: mDistilBERT's Confusion Matrix for Language Detection

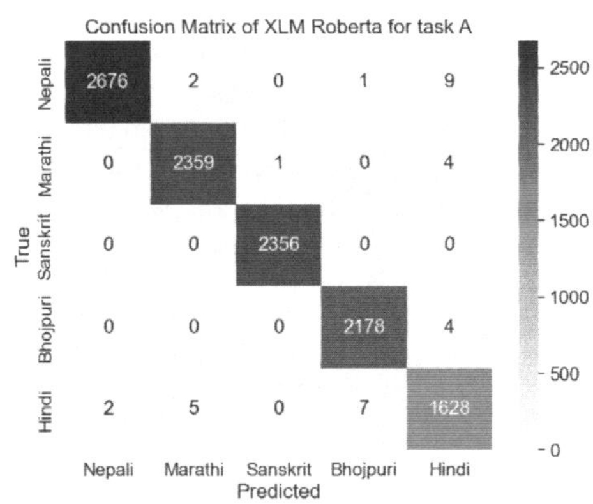

Figure 4: XLM Roberta's Confusion Matrix for Language Detection

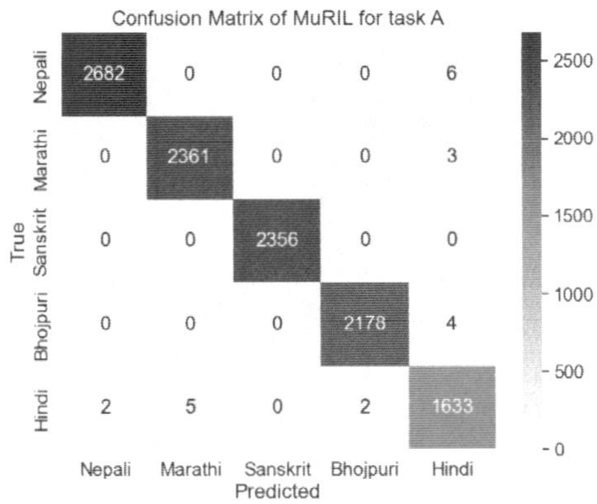

Figure 5: MuRIL's Confusion Matrix for Language Detection

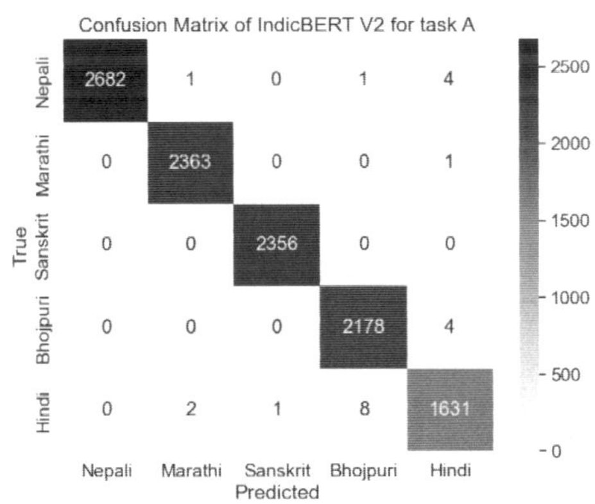

Figure 6: IndicBERT V2's Confusion Matrix for Language Detection

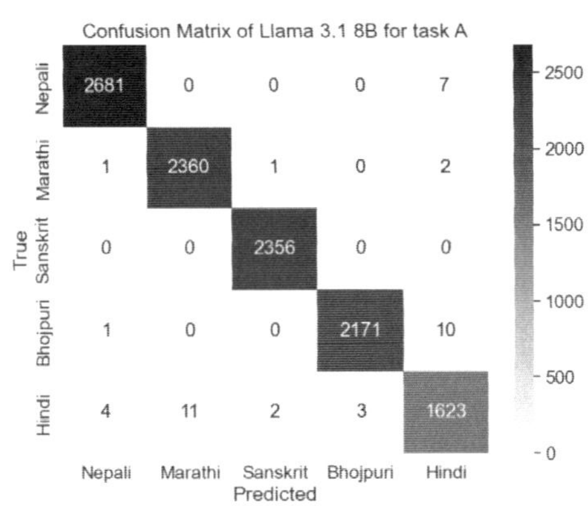

Figure 7: Llama 3.1 8B's Confusion Matrix for Language Detection

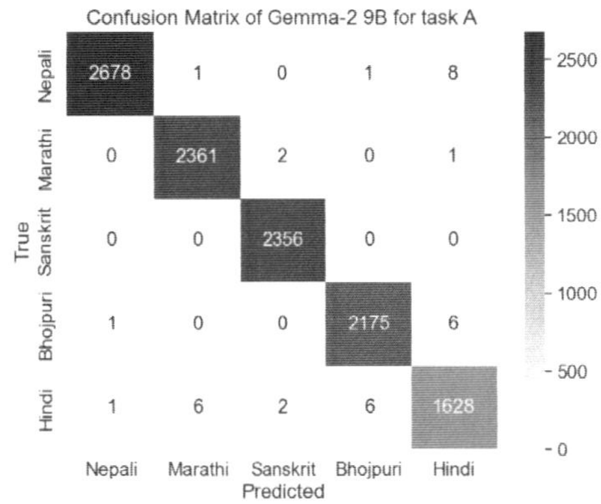

Figure 8: Gemma-2 9B's Confusion Matrix for Language Detection

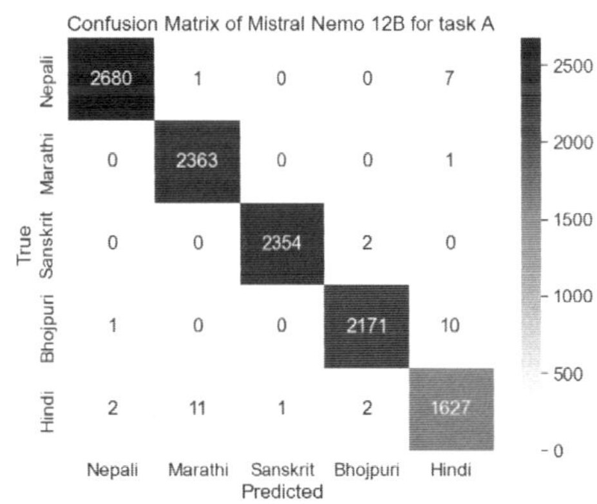

Figure 9: Mistral Nemo's Confusion Matrix for Language Detection

Testing Phase

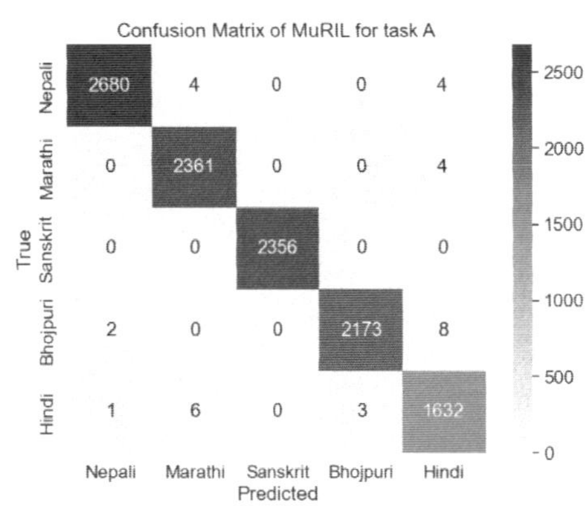

Figure 10: MuRIL's Confusion Matrix for Language Detection

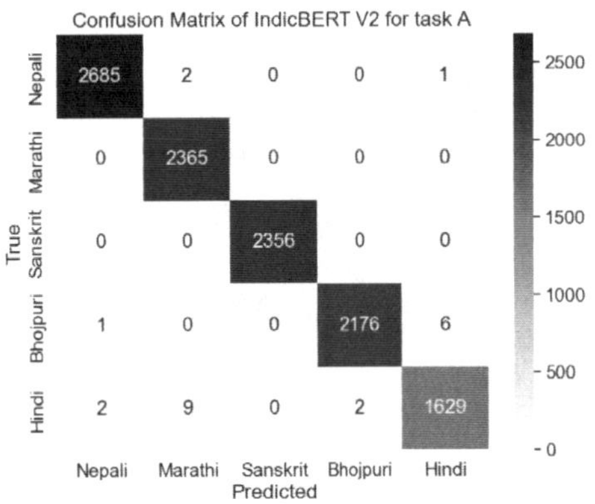

Figure 11: IndicBERT V2's Confusion Matrix for Language Detection

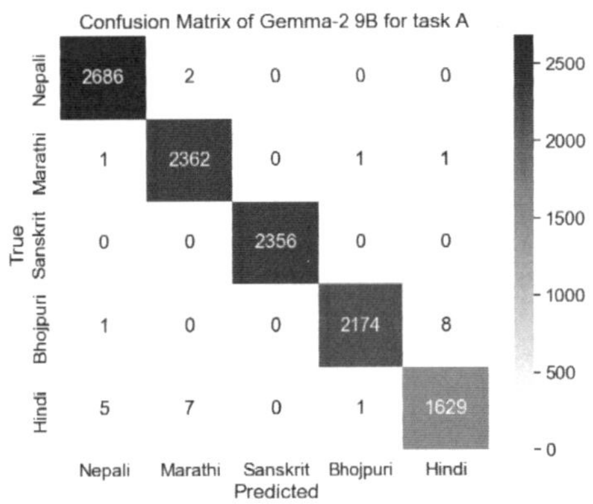

Figure 12: Gemma-2 9B's Confusion Matrix for Language Detection

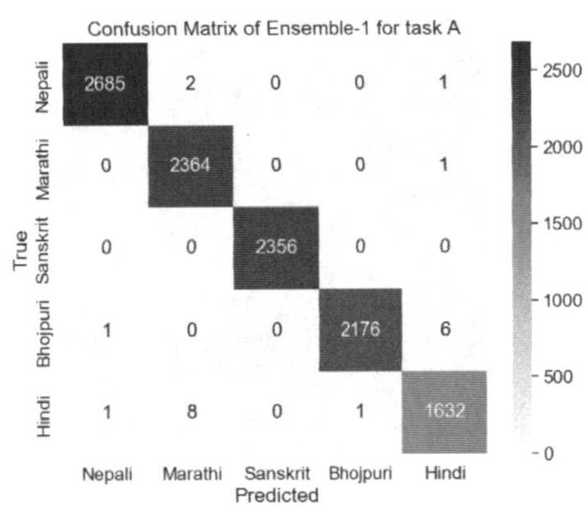

Figure 13: Ensemble-1's Confusion Matrix for Language Detection

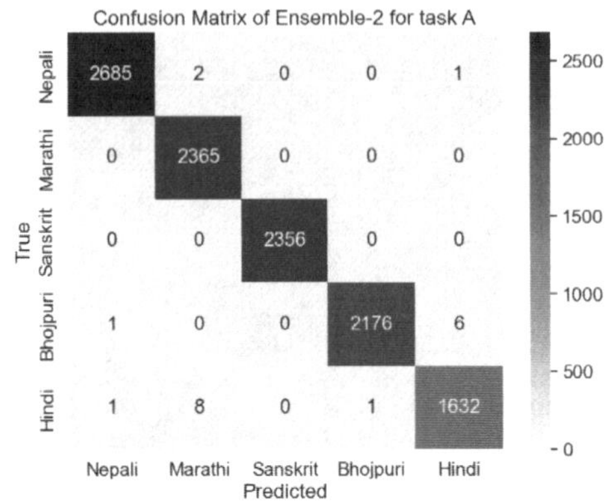

Figure 14: Ensemble-2's Confusion Matrix for Language Detection

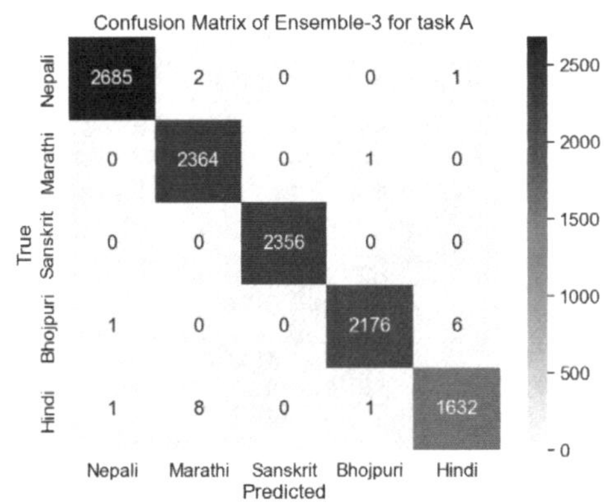

Figure 15: Ensemble-3's Confusion Matrix for Language Detection

A.1.2 Sub-task B: Hate Speech Detection

Evaluation Phase

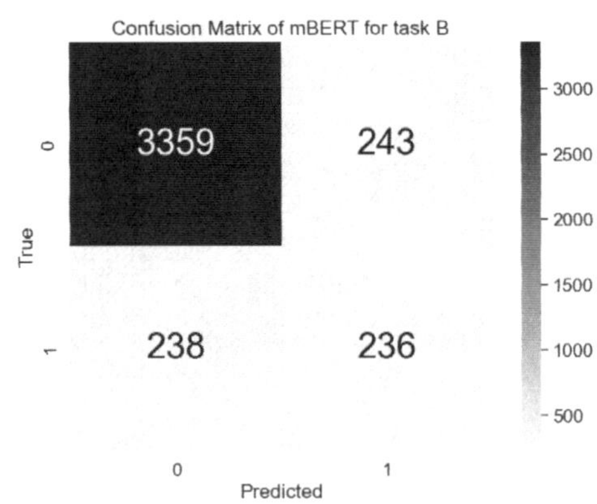

Figure 16: mBERT's Confusion Matrix for Hate Speech Detection

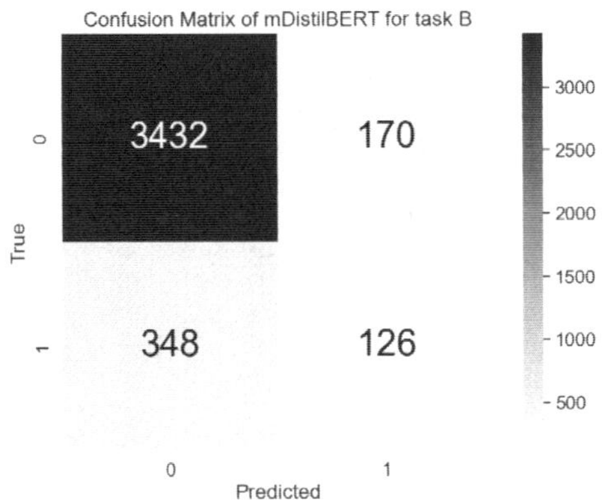

Figure 17: mDistilBERT's Confusion Matrix for Hate Speech Detection

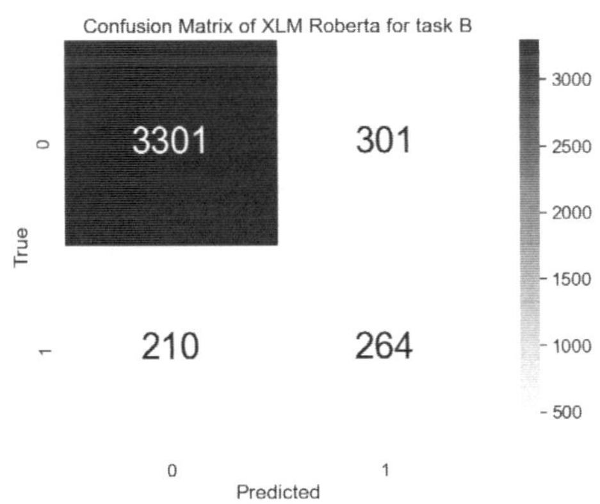

Figure 18: XLM Roberta's Confusion Matrix for Hate Speech Detection

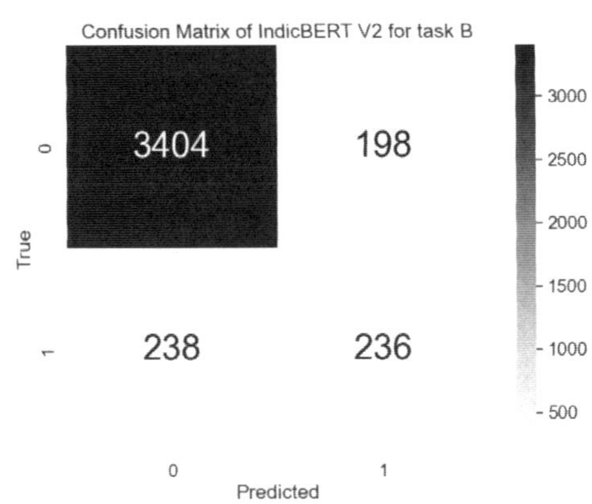

Figure 19: IndicBERT V2's Confusion Matrix for Hate Speech Detection

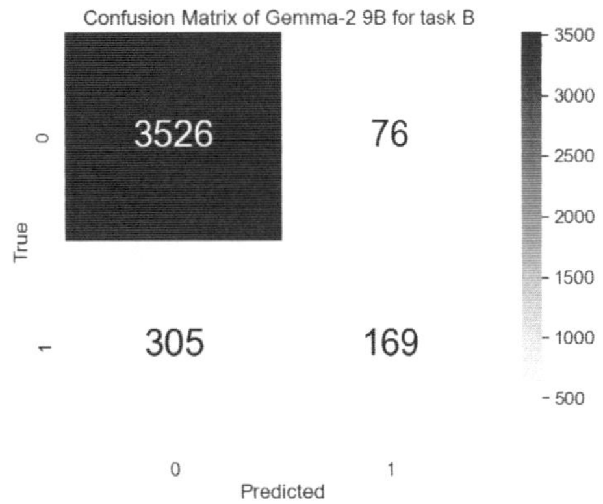

Figure 20: Gemma-2 9B's Confusion Matrix for Hate Speech Detection

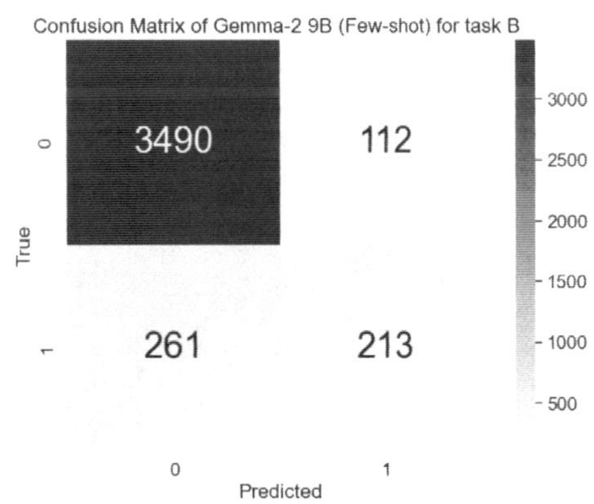

Figure 21: Gemma-2 9B (Few-shot)'s Confusion Matrix for Hate Speech Detection

Testing Phase

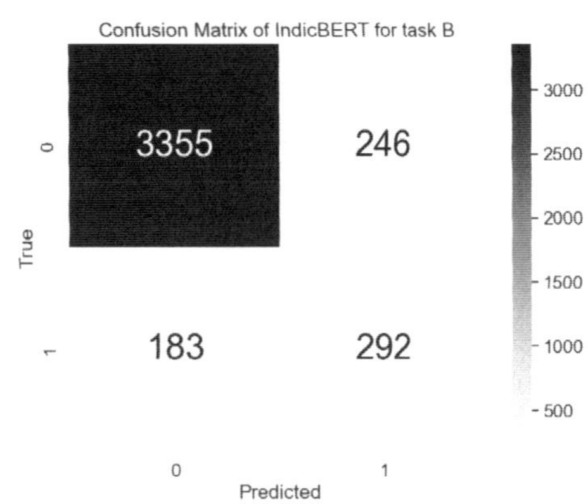

Figure 22: IndicBERT V2's Confusion Matrix for Hate Speech Detection

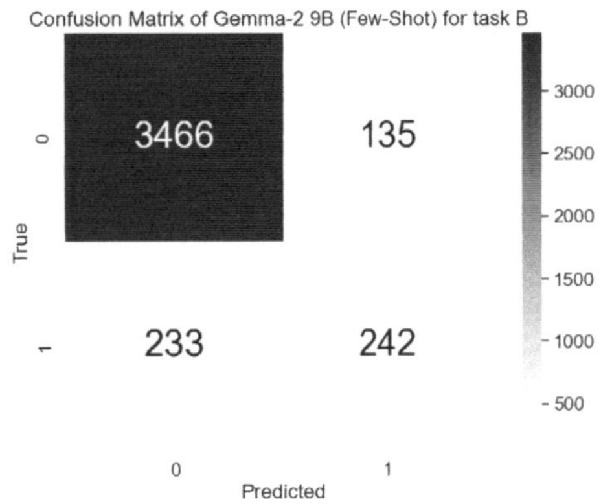

Figure 23: Gemma-2 9B (Few-shot)'s Confusion Matrix for Hate Speech Detection

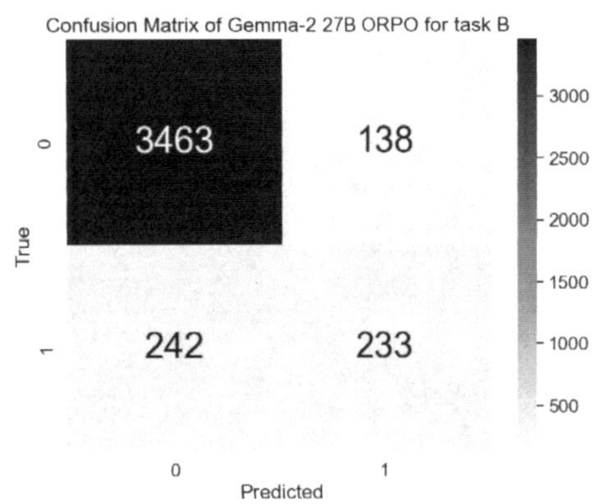

Figure 24: Gemma-2 27B ORPO's Confusion Matrix for Hate Speech Detection

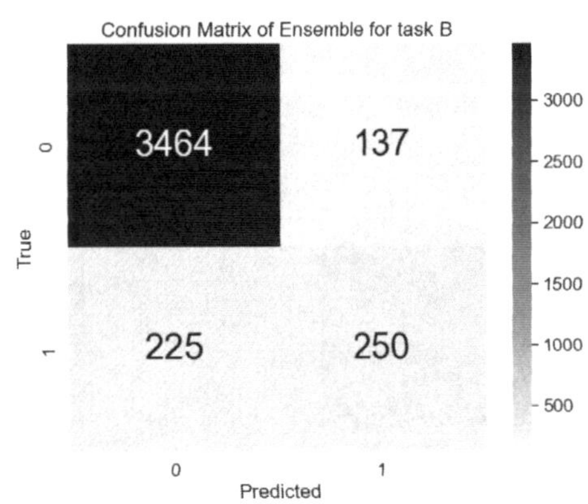

Figure 25: Ensemble's Confusion Matrix for Hate Speech Detection

A.1.3 Sub-task C: Hate Speech Target Detection

Evaluation Phase

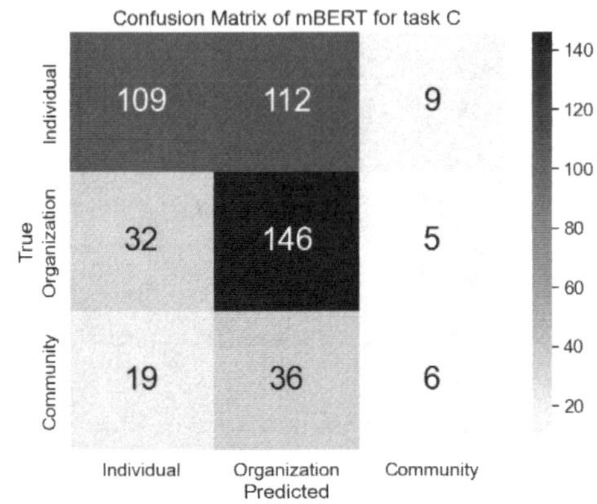

Figure 26: mBERT's Confusion Matrix for Hate Speech Target Detection

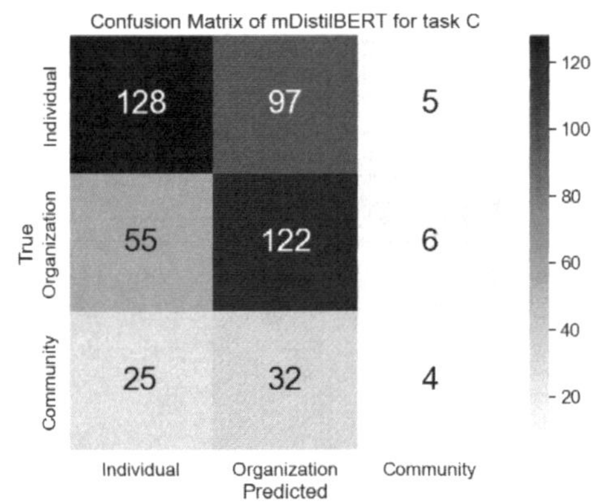

Figure 27: mDistilBERT's Confusion Matrix for Hate Speech Target Detection

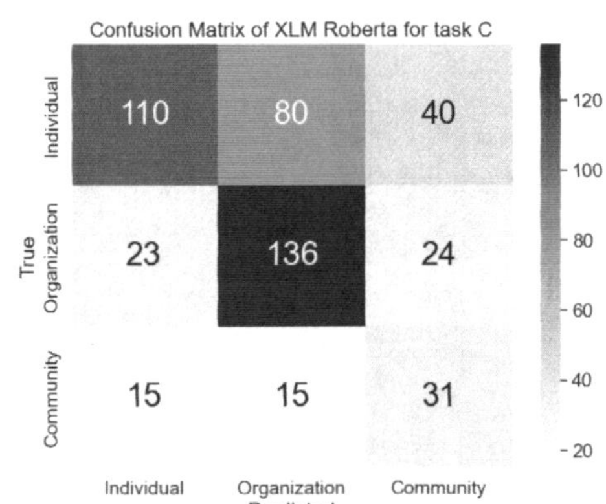

Figure 28: XLM Roberta's Confusion Matrix for Hate Speech Target Detection

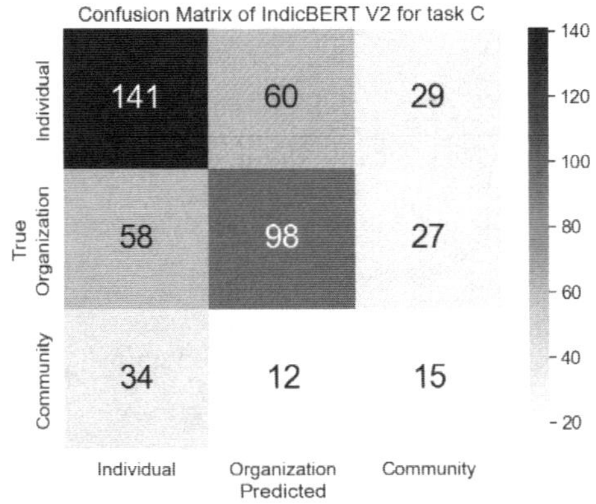

Figure 29: IndicBERT V2's Confusion Matrix for Hate Speech Target Detection

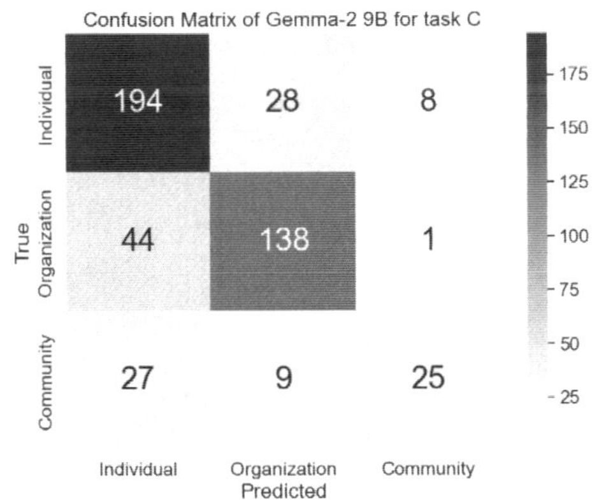

Figure 30: Gemma-2 9B's Confusion Matrix for Hate Speech Target Detection

Testing Phase

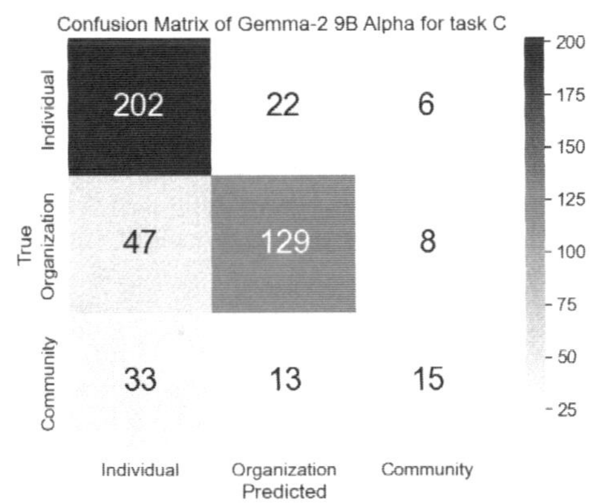

Figure 31: Gemma-2 9B Alpha's Confusion Matrix for Hate Speech Target Detection

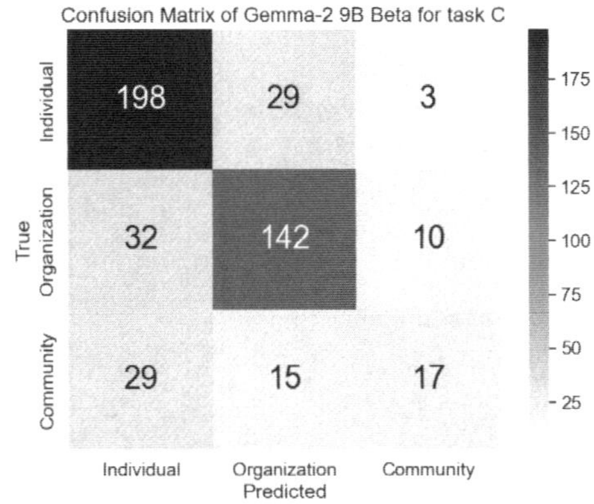

Figure 32: Gemma-2 9B Beta's Confusion Matrix for Hate Speech Target Detection

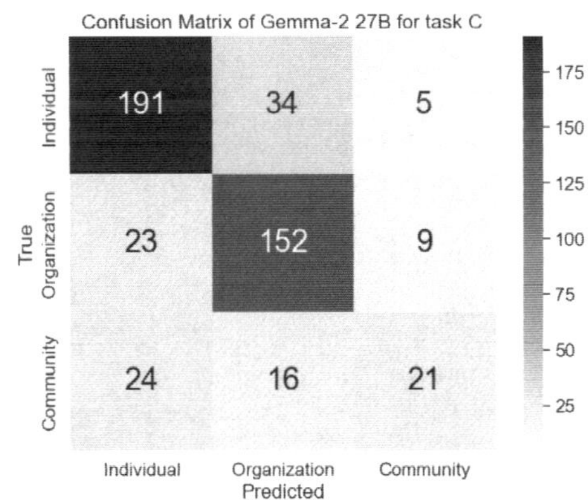

Figure 33: Gemma-2 27B's Confusion Matrix for Hate Speech Target Detection

A.2 System Replication

We provide the details of hyperparameters used in training for replicating the process in Table 10 and 11.

Hyperparameter	**Values**
Max length of input sequence	64
Batch size	512
Num of workers	2
Num of epochs	5
Learning rate	4e-5
Learning rate scheduler	linear
Focal loss Alpha	0.35
Focal loss Gamma	4.0

Table 10: Hyperparameters' values for BERT-based models

Hyperparameter	Value
Learning rate	2e-4
Learning rate scheduler	linear
Weight decay	0.01
LoRA rank	16
LoRA alpha	16
LoRA dropout	0
Language Detection	
Max length (tokens)	2048
Batch size	9
Gradient accumulation	3
Warmup steps	5
Num of epochs	1
Hate Speech Detection	
Max length (tokens)	1024
Batch size	16
Gradient accumulation	1
Warmup steps	10
Num of epochs	2-4
Hate Speech Target Detection	
Max length (tokens)	1024
Batch size	2-4
Gradient accumulation	1
Warmup steps	0
Num of epochs	2

Table 11: Hyperparameters' values for decoder-only models across tasks

Table 11 presents the hyperparameters for decoder-only models across tasks, with core values, such as learning rate, weight decay, and LoRA values shared across tasks. Task-specific parameters like maximum token length, batch size, gradient accumulation, warmup steps, and epochs were experimented with to meet the requirements of each task. For hyperparameters not listed, default values were used for each model.

A.3 Prompts

The prompts used for decoder-only models are provided below:

A.3.1 Task A: Language Detection

```
Task: You are an expert linguist specializing
    in Devanagari script languages. Your task
    is to identify the language of the given
    text.

### Instruction:
Analyze the following Devanagari script text
    and determine its language. Choose the
    correct language code from these options:
0: Nepali
1: Marathi
2: Sanskrit
3: Bhojpuri
4: Hindi

### Input:
Text: {text}

### Response:
The language code for the given text is: {label}
```

A.3.2 Task B: Hate Speech Detection

```
Task: You are fluent in Nepali and Hindi
    languages. Your task is to classify if the
    given input text contains hate speech or
    not.

### Instruction:
The goal of this subtask is to identify the
    targets of hate speech in a given text.
    Choose the correct category from these
    options:
1: Hate
0: Non-Hate

### Examples:
Input: {example_text1}
Response: {example_text1_label}

Input: {example_text2}
Response: {example_text2_label}

Input: {example_text3}
Response: {example_text3_label}

Input: {example_text4}
Response: {example_text4_label}

Input: {example_text5}
Response: {example_text5_label}

### Input:
{text}

### Response:
{label}
```

A.3.3 Task C: Hate Speech Target Detection

```
You are an expert linguist specializing in
    detecting hate speech targets in
    Devanagari-script tweets. Your task is to
    classify the target of hate speech.

### Instruction:
Analyze the given tweet in Devanagari script
    and determine who the hate speech is
    targeting.

Step 1: First, decide if the target is an
    individual or a group.
Step 2 (if group): If it's a group, further
    classify it as either an organization or a
    community.

Classify the final label according to these
    categories:
0. Individual: A specific person or a small set
    of identifiable individuals
```

```
1. Organization: A formal entity, institution,
   or company
2. Community: A broader group based on
   ethnicity, religion, gender, or other
   shared characteristics

### Input:
{}

### Response:
{}
```

AniSan@NLU of Devanagari Script Languages 2025: Optimizing Language Identification with Ensemble Learning

Anik Mahmud Shanto, Mst. Sanjida Jamal Priya, Mohammad Shamsul Arefin
Department of Computer Science and Engineering
Chittagong University of Engineering and Technology, Bangladesh
u1904{049, 057}@student.cuet.ac.bd,
sarefin@cuet.ac.bd

Abstract

Identifying languages written in Devanagari script, including Hindi, Marathi, Nepali, Bhojpuri, and Sanskrit, is essential in multilingual contexts but challenging due to the high overlap between these languages. To address this, a shared task on "Devanagari Script Language Identification" has been organized, with a dataset available for subtask A to test language identification models. This paper introduces an ensemble-based approach that combines mBERT, XLM-R, and IndicBERT models through majority voting to improve language identification accuracy across these languages. Our ensemble model has achieved an impressive accuracy of 99.68%, outperforming individual models by capturing a broader range of language features and reducing model biases that often arise from closely related linguistic patterns. Additionally, we have fine-tuned other transformer models as part of a comparative analysis, providing further validation of the ensemble's effectiveness. The results highlight the ensemble model's ability in distinguishing similar languages within the Devanagari script, offering a promising approach for accurate language identification in complex multilingual contexts.

1 Introduction

Effectively processing and comprehending many languages and scripts has become crucial for natural language understanding (NLU) to meet the growing diversity of multilingual content available online. Since Devanagari-scripted languages—such as Hindi, Marathi, Nepali, Bhojpuri, and Sanskrit—are among the most commonly used in South Asia, precise language identification is essential for enabling a wide range of applications, including sentiment analysis, user behavior analysis, and content moderation. In order to meet these needs, CHIPSAL@COLING 2025 (Thapa et al., 2025) has organized a shared task on Natural Language Understanding of Devanagari Script Languages and focused on three main tasks: language identification, hate speech detection, and target identification within hate speech.

Languages written in Devanagari script often share similar sounds, word structures, and sentence patterns. This makes it hard for computers to distinguish between them. The problem is made worse by people often mixing languages, using different regional accents, and using words from dialects. Though several works have been done for Devanagari script language identification using machine learning (Indhuja et al., 2014), deep learning (Sharma and Mithun, 2023) and transformer-based (Thara and Poornachandran, 2021) approaches, the existing works struggle to understand the underlying variances described above.

In the shared task (Sarveswaran et al., 2025), subtask A aims to accurately categorize texts written in Devanagari script into distinct languages. Though almost 2.5 billion people speak these languages, these languages have still been resource-constrained in the NLP research field. Therefore, the organizers have organized this shared task on Devanagari languages to enhance research on these languages. To improve automatic information processing in these languages, further research will help in more sophisticated and accurate identification of these languages. By achieving this, various works like detecting hate speech (Sahoo et al., 2024), determining target for hate speech (Sharma et al., 2024), dialect identification (Das and Bhattacharjee, 2024) etc. can be enhanced towards further improvement.

The primary objective of this task is to detect language from Devanagari scripts. To accomplish this objective, we have developed a number of transformer-based approaches. We have used the provided dataset in the shared task. The key contributions of our research are :

- We have developed an ensemble method that

Proceedings of the First Workshop on Challenges in Processing South Asian Languages (CHiPSAL 2025), pages 236–241
January 19, 2025.

leverages the strengths of multiple transformers namely mBERT (Devlin et al., 2019), XLM-R (Conneau et al., 2020) and IndicBERT (Kakwani et al., 2020).

- We have trained the developed model and evaluated its performance on the provided test set by the organizers.
- We have compared the performance of our developed model with other fine-tuned models.

2 Related Works

Language identification from texts is a popular research topic in natural language processing. Identifying a language from a text involves determining the language or languages present in the written input. Unlike voice, which is processed as a continuous signal, it uses discrete letters, which enable different mathematical techniques to analyze the text (Jauhiainen et al., 2024). An n-gram-based approach using a combination of word search and stop word detection has been proposed in (Pinge et al., 2023). This approach has achieved 95.6% accuracy. In another study, various ML models (Logistic Regression, Decision Tree, Random Forest, and Naive Bayes) have been implemented for language detection. Carpenter (2024) has developed a system using a multinomial naive Bayes algorithm. This system can identify 22 languages with 95% accuracy. Other researchers have also found multinomial naive Bayes effective in language identification task (Sriharsha et al., 2024; Rawat et al., 2023; Menon, 2022). In (R and George, 2023), authors have developed BiLSTM and DCNN-based methods to detect languages like Malayalam, Assamese, Hindi, etc. To identify English Malayalam code-mixed texts, transformer-based models (BERT, CamemBERT, DistilBERT) have been used (Thara and Poornachandran, 2021). This methodology has increased the f1-score by 9% from existing works. Another study has used a transformer-based model to identify code-mixed Kannada texts (Tonja et al., 2022). Finetuning transformers is also an effective way to achieve good performance in various language detection researches (Saifullah et al., 2024; Hossain et al., 2024; Farsi et al., 2024).

3 Dataset and Task

We have participated in subtask A named "Devanagari Script Language Identification". The provided dataset for the task contains 5 languages: Nepali (Thapa et al., 2023; Rauniyar et al., 2023), Marathi (Kulkarni et al., 2021), Sanskrit (Aralikatte et al., 2021), Bhojpuri (Ojha, 2019), and Hindi (Jafri et al., 2023, 2024). Table 1 describes the provided dataset:

Language	Number of Samples		
	Train	Validation	Test
Nepali	12,544	2688	2688
Marathi	11,034	2364	2365
Sanskrit	10,996	2356	2356
Bhojpuri	10,184	2182	2183
Hindi	7664	1643	1642
Combined	**52,422**	**11,233**	**11,234**

Table 1: Distribution of Languages in Datasets (Train, Validation and Test)

Language	Total No. of Words		
	Train	Validation	Test
Nepali	224,033	47,991	48,361
Marathi	273,959	59,134	59,642
Sanskrit	222,568	47,083	46,224
Bhojpuri	292,995	64,460	63,401
Hindi	146,609	32,171	32,254
Combined	**1,160,164**	**250,839**	**249, 882**

Table 2: Word Distribution in Combined Dataset (Train, Validation and Test)

4 System Overview

In our proposed methodology, we have developed an ensemble technique that consists of three transformer-based models. The ensemble technique combines the strengths of multiple transformer-based models to make more accurate predictions. We have ensembled three SOTA transformer-based models.

- **mBERT:** Multilingual BERT or mBERT (Devlin et al., 2019) is a transformer-based model pre-trained on 104 languages, including Devanagari languages. mBERT captures language-agnostic embeddings. Therefore, it has been proven effective in many multilingual tasks.
- **XLM-Roberta:** XLM-RoBERTa or XLM-R (Conneau et al., 2020) is another transformer-based model pre-trained on 100 languages. It captures a wide range of cross-lingual patterns and can handle diverse linguistic syntax.

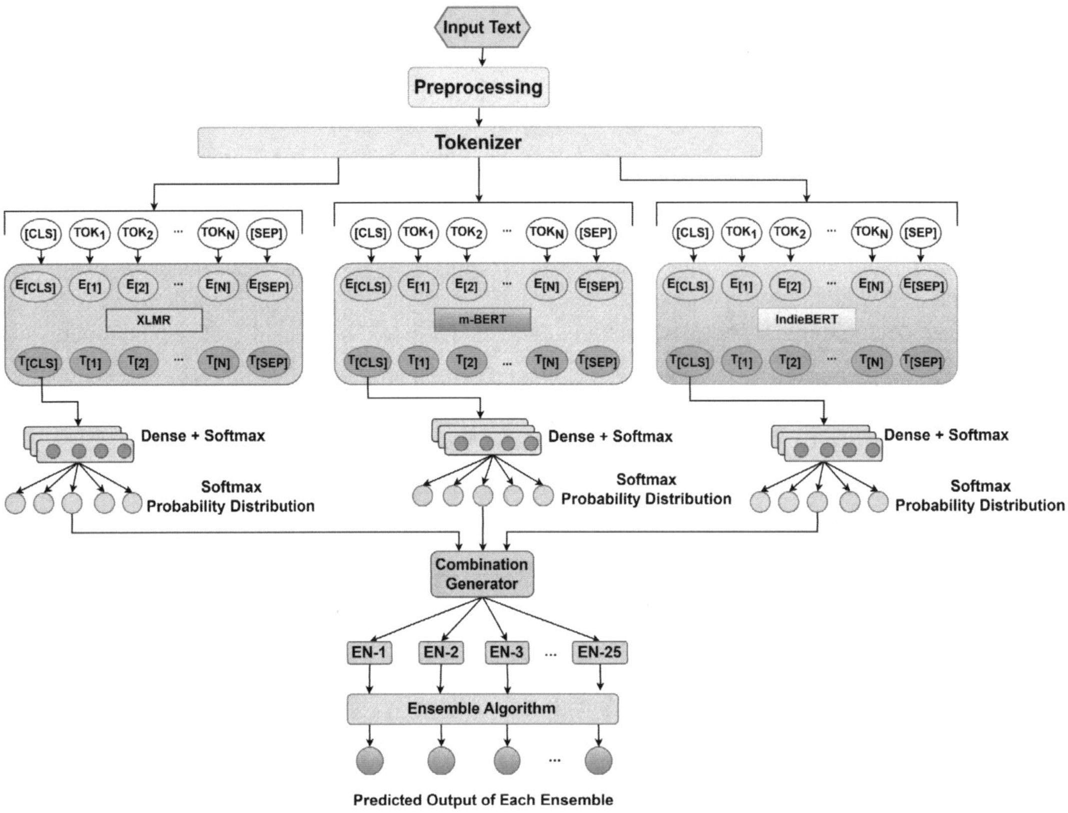

Figure 1: Overview of the methodology

This ability makes it effective for multilingual tasks.

- **IndicBERT:** IndicBERT (Kakwani et al., 2020) is a lightweight transformer model specifically designed for Indic languages. Unlike XLM-R and mBERT, IndicBERT focuses on Indian languages and has been pre-trained on a corpus containing several Devanagari-scripted languages, making it particularly relevant for our task.

For our final predictions, we have used a majority voting technique in combination generation portion of Figure 1 that aggregates the predictions from XLM-R, mBERT, and IndicBERT. Each model independently predicts the language of a given Devanagari-scripted text. The final prediction has been determined based on the majority vote among the three models. This ensemble approach reduces the influence of individual model biases or errors while utilizing the distinct advantages of each model to increase overall performance. Through this approach, our system can more effectively handle the linguistic similarities and complexities within Devanagari-scripted languages, enhancing the precision of language identification in multilingual contexts.

5 Experimental Results

In this section, we have discussed the results obtained while developing various models. As transformer-based models outperform ML and DL models in text classification, we have only experimented with transformer-based models. Table 3 shows the experimental results of different models on the test dataset.

Name	Acc.	P.	R.	F1
mBERT	0.9959	0.9955	0.9953	0.9954
XLM-R	0.9959	0.9954	0.9954	0.9954
IndicBERT	0.9953	0.9947	0.9947	0.9947
Ensemble	**0.9968**	**0.9964**	**0.9966**	**0.9965**

Table 3: Results of different models on Test set

The individual models mBERT, XLM-R, and IndicBERT all have performed well with accuracies ranging from 0.9953 to 0.9959. However, the pro-

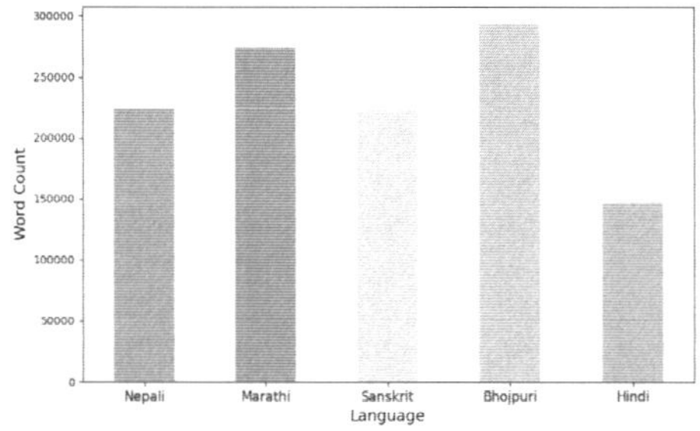

(a) Word Count Distribution in Train Set

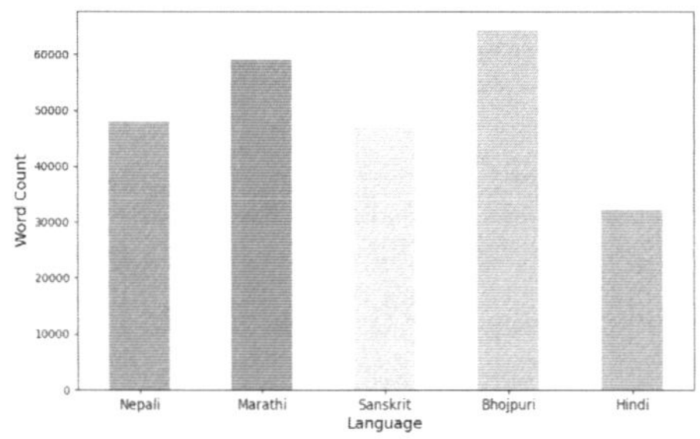

(b) Word Count Distribution in Validation Set

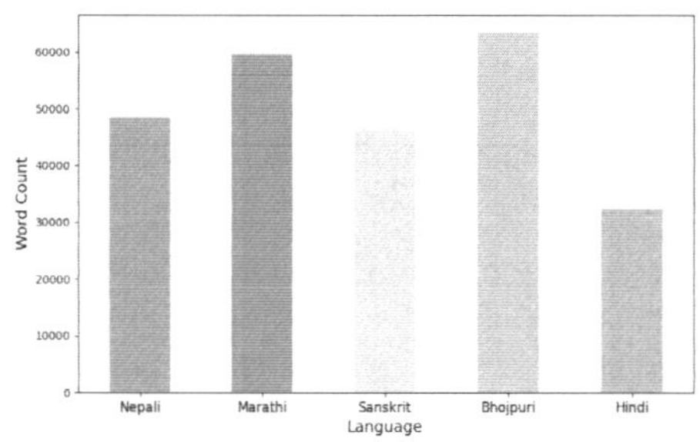

(c) Word Count Distribution in Test Set

Figure 2: Word Count Distributions for Train, Validation and Test Set

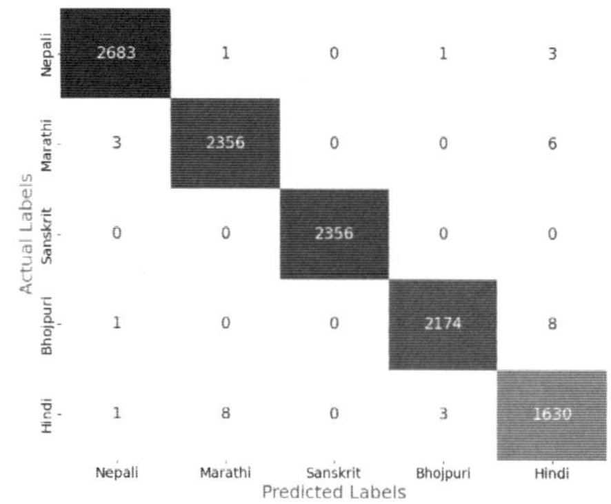

Figure 3: Confusion Matrix

posed ensemble method has outperformed them, reaching the greatest accuracy of 0.9968. The ensemble method has also been proven superior to individual models in terms of Precision, Recall, and F1 score. This is because by combining several models, biases of individual models can be reduced significantly.

6 Error Analysis

Qualitative Analysis: Individual models have faced limitations in finding language nuances. IndicBERT has struggled in low-resource cases like Bhojpuri while mBERT and XLM-R have misclassified texts due to their broader multilingual focus. These issues have affected in majority voting leading to a decrease in performance. Besides, there exist linguistic similarities among Devanagari scripted languages. Our models have been confused by these similarities and so the performance scores have been dropped. The influence of dialects and regional variations in texts have acted as a barrier against the model.

Quantitative Analysis: The confusion matrix in figure 3 analysis shows that Nepali is mostly accurately classified, with only 0.2% misclassified. Marathi has 9 misclassifications out of 2365 instances, mostly due to confusion with Hindi and Nepali. Sanskrit has no misclassifications out of 2356 instances, indicating 100% accuracy. Bhojpuri has 9 misclassifications out of 2183 instances, mostly due to confusion with Hindi and Nepali. Hindi has the highest misclassification rate, with 12 out of 1650 instances incorrectly labeled.

7 Conclusion

In this work, we have explored various transformer-based approaches for Devanagari script language identification (subtask A). We have developed an ensemble approach combining mBERT, XLM-R, and IndicBERT. Using majority voting in an ensemble approach, we have achieved an outstanding result with an F1 score of 0.9965. For our work, we have used the provided datasets in the shared task. However, after analyzing the performance, we have observed that in some cases our model has misclassified due to misclassification of individual models. In the future, we aim to try various combinations of other transformer models for the ensemble and check the performance of LLMs.

8 Limitations

The study has limitations, including the use of underrepresented dialects and informal usages of Devanagari-scripted languages in training models, and the close linguistic relationships among languages like Hindi, Marathi, Nepali, and Bhojpuri, which can lead to ambiguous cases and challenges in accurate classification. The ensemble model may struggle with sentences lacking context or code-switching. Additionally, traditional evaluation metrics like accuracy may not accurately represent the models' performance, potentially leading to an overestimated sense of effectiveness without addressing underlying weaknesses.

9 Ethical Considerations

The study's limitations include underrepresented dialects, close linguistic relationships, and potential bias. It also highlights the need for inclusivity and responsibility in future language processing endeavors, highlighting the need for data privacy and transparency.

References

Rahul Aralikatte, Miryam De Lhoneux, Anoop Kunchukuttan, and Anders Søgaard. 2021. Itihasa: A large-scale corpus for sanskrit to english translation. In *Proceedings of the 8th Workshop on Asian Translation (WAT2021)*, pages 191–197.

Pramod Carpenter. 2024. 3. language identifier. *Indian Scientific Journal Of Research In Engineering And Management.*

Alexis Conneau, Kartikay Khandelwal, Naman Goyal, Vishrav Chaudhary, Guillaume Wenzek, Francisco Guzmán, Edouard Grave, Myle Ott, Luke Zettlemoyer, and Veselin Stoyanov. 2020. Unsupervised cross-lingual representation learning at scale. *Preprint*, arXiv:1911.02116.

Hem Chandra Das and Utpal Bhattacharjee. 2024. Assamese dialect identification using static and dynamic features from vowel. *Journal of Advances in Information Technology*, 15(2).

Jacob Devlin, Ming-Wei Chang, Kenton Lee, and Kristina Toutanova. 2019. Bert: Pre-training of deep bidirectional transformers for language understanding. *Preprint*, arXiv:1810.04805.

Salman Farsi, Asrarul Eusha, Jawad Hossain, Shawly Ahsan, Avishek Das, and Mohammed Moshiul Hoque. 2024. CUET_Binary_Hackers@DravidianLangTech EACL2024: Hate and offensive language detection in Telugu code-mixed text using sentence similarity BERT. In *Proceedings of the Fourth Workshop on Speech, Vision, and Language Technologies for Dravidian Languages*, pages 193–199, St. Julian's, Malta. Association for Computational Linguistics.

Md Rajib Hossain, Mohammed Moshiul Hoque, Nazmul Siddique, and M Ali Akber Dewan. 2024. Aracovtexfinder: Leveraging the transformer-based language model for arabic covid-19 text identification. *Engineering Applications of Artificial Intelligence*, 133:107987.

K Indhuja, M Indu, C Sreejith, Palakkad Sreekrishnapuram, and PR Raj. 2014. Text based language identification system for indian languages following devanagiri script. *International Journal of Engineering*, 3(4).

Farhan Ahmad Jafri, Kritesh Rauniyar, Surendrabikram Thapa, Mohammad Aman Siddiqui, Matloob Khushi, and Usman Naseem. 2024. Chunav: Analyzing hindi hate speech and targeted groups in indian election discourse. *ACM Transactions on Asian and Low-Resource Language Information Processing.*

Farhan Ahmad Jafri, Mohammad Aman Siddiqui, Surendrabikram Thapa, Kritesh Rauniyar, Usman Naseem, and Imran Razzak. 2023. Uncovering political hate speech during indian election campaign: A new low-resource dataset and baselines.

Tommi Jauhiainen, Marcos Zampieri, Timothy Baldwin, and Krister Lindén. 2024. 1. introduction to language identification.

Divyanshu Kakwani, Anoop Kunchukuttan, Satish Golla, Gokul N.C., Avik Bhattacharyya, Mitesh M. Khapra, and Pratyush Kumar. 2020. IndicNLPSuite: Monolingual Corpora, Evaluation Benchmarks and Pre-trained Multilingual Language Models for Indian Languages. In *Findings of EMNLP.*

Atharva Kulkarni, Meet Mandhane, Manali Likhitkar, Gayatri Kshirsagar, and Raviraj Joshi. 2021. L3cubemahasent: A marathi tweet-based sentiment analysis dataset. In *Proceedings of the Eleventh Workshop on Computational Approaches to Subjectivity, Sentiment and Social Media Analysis*, pages 213–220.

Riya Menon. 2022. 8. detectsy: A system for detecting language from the text, images, and audio files. *International Journal For Science Technology And Engineering.*

Atul Kr Ojha. 2019. English-bhojpuri smt system: Insights from the karaka model. *arXiv preprint arXiv:1905.02239.*

Tejas Pinge, Prajwal Patil, Mayur Sherki, Aditya Nandurkar, and Prof. Ravindra Chilbule. 2023. 2. text language identification and translator. *International Journal of Advanced Research in Science, Communication and Technology.*

Karthika M R and Anu George. 2023. 5. automatic language identification from non-uniform region using bi-lstm and cnn.

Kritesh Rauniyar, Sweta Poudel, Shuvam Shiwakoti, Surendrabikram Thapa, Junaid Rashid, Jungeun Kim, Muhammad Imran, and Usman Naseem. 2023. Multi-aspect annotation and analysis of nepali tweets on anti-establishment election discourse. *IEEE Access*.

Sunita Rawat, Lakshita Werulkar, and Sagarika Jaywant. 2023. 7. text-based language identifier using multinomial naïve bayes algorithm. *International journal of next-generation computing*.

Nihar Ranja Sahoo, Gyana Prakash Beria, and Pushpak Bhattacharyya. 2024. Indicconan: A multilingual dataset for combating hate speech in indian context. In *Proceedings of the AAAI Conference on Artificial Intelligence*, volume 38, pages 22313–22321.

Khalid Saifullah, Muhammad Ibrahim Khan, Suhaima Jamal, and Iqbal H Sarker. 2024. Cyberbullying text identification based on deep learning and transformer-based language models. *EAI Endorsed Transactions on Industrial Networks and Intelligent Systems*, 11(1):e5–e5.

Kengatharaiyer Sarveswaran, Bal Krishna Bal, Surendrabikram Thapa, Ashwini Vaidya, and Sana Shams. 2025. A brief overview of the first workshop on challenges in processing south asian languages (chipsal). In *Proceedings of the First Workshop on Challenges in Processing South Asian Languages (CHiPSAL)*.

Arpit Sharma and BN Mithun. 2023. Deep learning character recognition of handwritten devanagari script: A complete survey. In *2023 IEEE International Conference on Contemporary Computing and Communications (InC4)*, volume 1, pages 1–6. IEEE.

Deepawali Sharma, Vivek Kumar Singh, and Vedika Gupta. 2024. Tabhate: a target-based hate speech detection dataset in hindi. *Social Network Analysis and Mining*, 14(1):190.

A. V. Sriharsha, M Jahnavi, Desai Sakethram Kousik, V. Hemanth, M G Hari, and Penchala Praveen Vasili. 2024. 6. language detection using natural language processing. *Advances in computer science research*.

Surendrabikram Thapa, Kritesh Rauniyar, Farhan Ahmad Jafri, Surabhi Adhikari, Kengatharaiyer Sarveswaran, Bal Krishna Bal, Hariram Veeramani, and Usman Naseem. 2025. Natural language understanding of devanagari script languages: Language identification, hate speech and its target detection. In *Proceedings of the First Workshop on Challenges in Processing South Asian Languages (CHiPSAL)*.

Surendrabikram Thapa, Kritesh Rauniyar, Shuvam Shiwakoti, Sweta Poudel, Usman Naseem, and Mehwish Nasim. 2023. Nehate: Large-scale annotated data shedding light on hate speech in nepali local election discourse. In *ECAI 2023*, pages 2346–2353. IOS Press.

S Thara and Prabaharan Poornachandran. 2021. Transformer based language identification for malayalam-english code-mixed text. *IEEE Access*, 9:118837–118850.

Atnafu Lambebo Tonja, Mesay Gemeda Yigezu, Olga Kolesnikova, Moein Shahiki Tash, Grigori Sidorov, and Alexander Gelbuk. 2022. Transformer-based model for word level language identification in code-mixed kannada-english texts. *Preprint*, arXiv:2211.14459.

A Experimental Setup

A.1 Data Preparation

In the shared task, organizers provided a training dataset and a evaluation dataset. We merged the two datasets and split them to use as train and validation dataset. We have used 80% of the combined dataset for training and the rest for validation dataset. This merging process has created a larger dataset than the provided training dataset and thus, helped the model for better training.

A.2 Parameter Settings

The overall parameter settings used in this experiment have been described in table 4.

Parameter	**Value**
Epoch	5
Batch size	32
Loss Function	CrossEntropyLoss
Learning Rate	1e−3

Table 4: Parameter Configuration

A.3 Environment Setup

A personal computer with a Ryzen-9 CPU (3.00 GHz) and an NVIDIA GeForce GTX 2060 GPU has been used to run the simulation. Additionally, a Kaggle Notebook set up with a P100 GPU has been used to guarantee sufficient processing power.

B Data Preprocessing

For preprocessing, we focused on normalizing the input text by converting it to a standard Unicode format to handle variations in Devanagari script encoding. The text was then tokenized using model-specific tokenizers, such as those for mBERT, XLM-R, and IndicBERT, to break it into meaningful subword units. Additionally, padding and truncation were applied to ensure that all input sequences were of same length.

byteSizedLLM@NLU of Devanagari Script Languages 2025: Hate Speech Detection and Target Identification Using Customized Attention BiLSTM and XLM-RoBERTa Base Embeddings

Rohith Gowtham Kodali
ASRlytics
Hyderabad, India
rohitkodali@gmail.com

Durga Prasad Manukonda
ASRlytics
Hyderabad, India
mdp0999@gmail.com

Daniel Iglesias
Digi Sapiens
Frankfurt, Germany
diglesias@web.de

Abstract

This paper presents a novel approach to hate speech detection and target identification across Devanagari-script languages, with a focus on Hindi and Nepali. Leveraging an Attention BiLSTM-XLM-RoBERTa architecture, our model effectively captures language-specific features and sequential dependencies crucial for multilingual natural language understanding (NLU). In Task B (Hate Speech Detection), our model achieved a Macro F1 score of 0.7481, demonstrating its robustness in identifying hateful content across linguistic variations. For Task C (Target Identification), it reached a Macro F1 score of 0.6715, highlighting its ability to classify targets into "individual," "organization," and "community" with high accuracy. Our work addresses the gap in Devanagari-scripted multilingual hate speech analysis and sets a benchmark for future research in low-resource language contexts.

1 Introduction

The rapid growth of online platforms has heightened concerns around the detection and mitigation of hate speech. In the context of South Asia, where languages such as Nepali and Hindi predominantly use the Devanagari script, there is a pressing need for specialized natural language understanding (NLU) approaches that can handle the complex, multilingual nature of online discourse. Addressing these concerns, the "Shared Task on Natural Language Understanding of Devanagari Script Languages" at CHIPSAL@COLING 2025 presents a series of challenges focused on hate speech processing, specifically hate speech detection and target identification(Thapa et al., 2025; Sarveswaran et al., 2025).

Subtask B, *Hate Speech Detection in Devanagari Script Languages*, tackles the task of binary classification, aiming to identify whether a given sentence contains hate speech. The multilingual dataset, containing texts in Nepali and Hindi, underscores the need for models that can handle the nuances of each language while using a common script. This task emphasizes language-specific considerations essential for accurate detection, as hate speech often exhibits linguistic subtleties, cultural references, and slang unique to each language.

Expanding upon the hate speech detection task, Subtask C, *Target Identification for Hate Speech in Devanagari Script Languages*, introduces the challenge of identifying specific targets of hate speech. Given a hateful sentence, the task requires participants to classify the target as an *individual*, *organization*, or *community*. Target identification is crucial to understanding the nature and intended focus of hate speech, providing valuable insights that facilitate more effective responses and moderation strategies.

Our hybrid model integrates an attention-driven BiLSTM with XLM-RoBERTa embeddings to tackle hate speech detection and target identification. The attention mechanism enhances the BiLSTM's ability to focus on critical contextual cues, while XLM-RoBERTa provides robust multilingual embeddings. Together, these components enable our architecture to achieve exceptional precision, contributing to sophisticated multilingual NLU systems and fostering safer online interactions, particularly for Devanagari-scripted languages.

2 Related Work

The rise of hate speech on digital platforms has spurred research efforts in detection, yet studies for Devanagari-script languages like Hindi, Nepali, and Marathi remain limited due to script complexity and dialect diversity. Detecting hate speech in these languages is essential for fostering safer online environments. To date, research has primarily focused on monolingual hate speech detection in Hindi, Nepali, and Marathi, with some stud-

Proceedings of the First Workshop on Challenges in Processing South Asian Languages (CHiPSAL 2025), pages 242–247
January 19, 2025.

ies exploring multilingual hate speech detection in Hindi-Marathi and Hindi-English combinations using traditional machine learning and Transformer-based deep learning approaches. (Velankar et al., 2021; Kumari et al., 2024; Sreelakshmi et al., 2020; Sharma et al., 2022; Niraula et al., 2021; B. et al., 2019; Shukla et al., 2022; Velankar et al., 2021; T.Y.S.S and Aravind, 2019; Chavan et al., 2022; Mathur et al., 2018). However, there is a notable gap in multilingual hate speech detection specifically between Nepali and Hindi, where the combined detection remains unaddressed. Additionally, no study to date has incorporated a multilingual Devanagari-script dataset that includes target identification, categorizing targets into "individual," "organization," or "community."

3 Dataset and Task

Subtask B involves identifying whether a sentence contains hate speech in Devanagari-scripted languages, specifically Nepali(Thapa et al., 2023; Rauniyar et al., 2023) and Hindi (Jafri et al., 2024, 2023). The dataset is divided into Non-Hate and Hate categories, as shown in Table 1, requiring models to effectively detect hate speech within these languages.

Class	Train	Valid	Test
Non-Hate (0)	16805	3602	3601
Hate (1)	2214	474	745
Total	19019	4076	4076

Table 1: Distribution of samples in Train, Validation, and Test datasets for Subtask B

In Subtask C, the objective is to identify the target of hate speech, categorizing it as "individual," "organization," or "community." This task is crucial for understanding the specific direction of hate speech within the Devanagari script context. Table 2 displays the dataset distribution for each target category.

Class	Train	Valid	Test
Individual (0)	1074	230	230
Organization (1)	856	183	184
Community (2)	284	61	61
Total	2214	474	475

Table 2: Distribution of samples in Train, Validation, and Test datasets for Subtask C

Additionally, we curated datasets to fine-tune the multilingual RoBERTa model (xlm-roberta-base) for masked language modeling across five languages, following the methodology of Joshi (2022). The datasets included Bhojpuri (9.3MB from GitHub[1]), Nepali (50MB from Kaggle[2]), Sanskrit (50MB from Kaggle[3]), and both Hindi and Marathi (50MB each from AI4Bharat[4]).

4 Methodology

This study presents a hybrid Attention BiLSTM-XLM-RoBERTa model, inspired by Hochreiter and Schmidhuber (1997); Conneau et al. (2019); Manukonda and Kodali (2024a); Kodali and Manukonda (2024); Manukonda and Kodali (2024b); Brauwers and Frasincar (2023), for hate speech detection and target identification in Devanagari script. As illustrated in Figure 1, the model combines deep contextual embeddings from the fine-tuned masked language model (MLM) of XLM-RoBERTa with a BiLSTM and attention mechanism to enhance language-specific feature extraction.

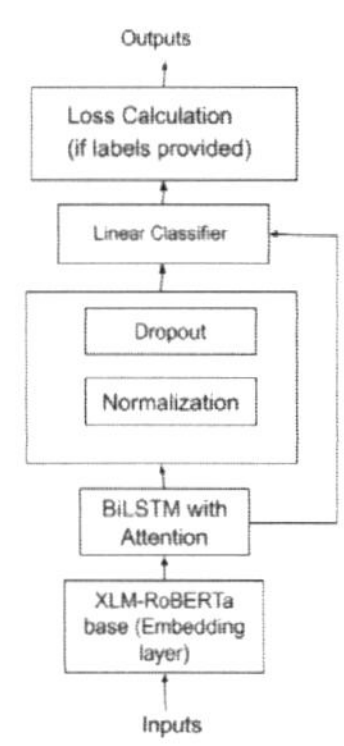

Figure 1: Architecture of the BiLSTM-XLM-RoBERTa Classifier Model. Residual components like layer normalization and dropout regularization enhance generalization.

The input sequence is first passed to XLM-RoBERTa base, generating embeddings $\mathbf{X} \in R^{T \times D}$, where $D = 768$:

$$\mathbf{X} = \mathbf{XLMRoBERTa}(input\_ids, attention\_mask) \quad (1)$$

[1]https://github.com/shashwatup9k/bho-resources

[2]https://www.kaggle.com/datasets/lotusacharya/nepalinewsdataset

[3]https://www.kaggle.com/datasets/rushikeshdarge/sanskrit

[4]https://github.com/AI4Bharat/indicnlp_corpus

These embeddings are fed into a BiLSTM, which produces bidirectional hidden states $\mathbf{H}fwd$ and $\mathbf{H}bwd$, combined as:

$$\mathbf{H}_t = [\mathbf{H}_{fwd,t}; \mathbf{H}_{bwd,t}] \tag{2}$$

An attention mechanism assigns relevance to each $\mathbf{H}_t$, generating attention weights α_t:

$$\mathbf{a}_t = \tanh(\mathbf{W}_{att} \cdot \mathbf{H}_t), \quad \alpha_t = \frac{\exp(\mathbf{a}_t)}{\sum_{t=1}^{T} \exp(\mathbf{a}_t)} \tag{3}$$

The attention-weighted representation $\mathbf{H}_{attended}$ is:

$$\mathbf{H}_{attended} = \sum_{t=1}^{T} \alpha_t \cdot \mathbf{H}_t \tag{4}$$

Layer normalization and dropout are optional residuals that mitigate overfitting and stabilize training, especially in complex language scenarios. They are applied to $\mathbf{H}_{attended}$ to enhance stability, particularly for smaller datasets:

$$\mathbf{H}_{dropout} = Dropout(LayerNorm(\mathbf{H}_{attended})) \tag{5}$$

Finally, $\mathbf{H}_{dropout}$ is passed through a classification layer to produce logits:

$$\mathbf{logits} = \mathbf{W}_{cls} \cdot \mathbf{H}_{dropout} + \mathbf{b}_{cls} \tag{6}$$

The model is trained using cross-entropy loss L:

$$L = -\sum_{i=1}^{N} y_i \log(\hat{y}_i) \tag{7}$$

This architecture leverages XLM-RoBERTa embeddings, BiLSTM processing, and attention for accurate language differentiation in Devanagari-scripted contexts.

5 Experiment Setup

Our experimental setup involved data preprocessing, model fine-tuning, and architecture optimization to evaluate hate speech detection (Task B) and target identification (Task C) across Devanagari-scripted languages. Performance was assessed using accuracy and Macro F1 scores on the validation dataset.

Data preprocessing included tokenization and normalization to ensure compatibility with XLM-RoBERTa, with all text standardized to the Devanagari script. Fine-tuning on masked language modeling (MLM) used a 15% masking ratio, achieving a perplexity score of 5.33 over 7 epochs, indicating effective contextual adaptation to Devanagari-scripted languages.

After testing various classifiers, we selected an Attention BiLSTM-XLM-RoBERTa architecture (Figure 1) due to its superior performance. This model integrates XLM-RoBERTa base embeddings with a BiLSTM layer (hidden size of 256, 2 LSTM layers, and dropout rate of 0.3) to capture sequential dependencies, with an attention mechanism to emphasize language-specific and contextually relevant features. For Task B (hate speech detection), we used a learning rate of 1×10^{-5}, while for Task C (target identification), a higher learning rate of 2×10^{-5} was applied. Optional residual layers (layer normalization and dropout) were added to improve stability and mitigate overfitting.

This setup provides a robust framework for evaluating the effects of model fine-tuning, architecture, and data preparation on multilingual hate speech detection and target identification within the Devanagari script.

6 Results and Discussion

During data processing, URLs and user IDs were removed, while tweet tags were retained, as removing the tags slightly reduced F1 scores. Table 3 shows the performance of various classifiers using fine-tuned XLM-RoBERTa base embeddings on Task B and Task C. The **Attention BiLSTM-XLM-RoBERTa** model consistently outperformed other classifiers, achieving the highest F1-Scores of 0.7481 for Task B and 0.6715 for Task C. This result underscores the effectiveness of combining BiLSTM with XLM-RoBERTa base to capture sequential and contextual information essential for Devanagari-scripted language tasks. The BiLSTM with XLM-RoBERTa base embedding(BiLSTM-XLM-RoBERTa) model alone showed the F1-Scores of 0.7065 (Task B) and 0.6356 (Task C), outperforming XLM-RoBERTa base model scores of 0.6912 (Task B) and 0.6147 (Task C), demonstrating the benefits of sequential processing.

Among traditional classifiers, Logistic Regression and XGBoost delivered moderate results, with F1-Scores of 0.6528 and 0.6034 on Task B. Ensemble methods did not outperform transformer-based models, and SVC and Extra Trees showed the lowest F1-Scores, indicating limited effectiveness in handling this language data.

Our team, **byteSizedLLM**, secured 7th place

Classifier	Task B F1-Score	Task C F1-Score
XLM-RoBERTa base (Transformers)	0.6912	0.6147
XGBoost (xgb)	0.6034	0.4856
Random Forest (rf)	0.5038	0.4310
Logistic Regression (lr)	0.6528	0.5059
Gradient Boosting (gb)	0.5455	0.4760
Support Vector Classifier (svc)	0.4691	0.4171
AdaBoost (ada)	0.5684	0.4056
Extra Trees (extra_trees)	0.4896	0.4089
Ridge Classifier (ridge)	0.5626	0.4714
Stochastic Gradient Descent (sgd)	0.5813	0.4509
Ensemble (xgb, lr, rf, svc, sgd)	0.5572	0.4641
BiLSTM-XLM-RoBERTa	0.7065	0.6356
Attention BiLSTM-XLM-RoBERTa	**0.7481**	**0.6715**

Table 3: Comparison of Classifiers on Task B and Task C Test Sets

in both Task B and Task C based on F1 Macro scores, closely matching the top-ranked scores and underscoring our model's competitiveness. This strong performance highlights our approach's effectiveness, though limited open-source datasets for fine-tuning XLM-RoBERTa base on Devanagari-scripted languages like Nepali and Marathi constrained our ability to capture nuanced linguistic patterns and regional variations fully.

Fine-tuning XLM-RoBERTa's masked language model (MLM) on task-specific data significantly boosted performance, illustrating the value of tailored fine-tuning for Devanagari-scripted languages. The Attention BiLSTM-XLM-RoBERTa model successfully captured complex linguistic features by integrating attention mechanisms with BiLSTM and XLM-RoBERTa embeddings. While data limitations posed challenges, fine-tuning proved essential for adapting the model to low-resource contexts. Future research could explore larger models and expanded datasets to further improve adaptability and robustness across diverse linguistic features.

7 Conclusion

This study introduced a hybrid Attention BiLSTM-XLM-RoBERTa model for language identification in Devanagari-scripted languages, effectively integrating XLM-RoBERTa base embeddings with BiLSTM and attention mechanisms to capture both contextual and sequential features. The model's competitive F1 scores in both Task B and Task C validate this approach's effectiveness for nuanced language classification, achieving a strong 7th-place ranking in both tasks despite limited fine-tuning data.

Our findings underscore the strength of combining transformer-based embeddings with BiLSTM and attention for accurate multilingual language identification, particularly in low-resource contexts. Future work could explore larger model variants and expanded datasets to further improve performance in these settings, enhancing the model's adaptability and effectiveness across diverse linguistic features.

8 Limitations and Ethical Considerations

8.1 Limitations

The Attention BiLSTM-XLM-RoBERTa model showed promising performance, though it has limitations in generalizability. Using the XLM-RoBERTa base may limit its ability to capture complex linguistic nuances, and computational constraints restricted exploration of larger XLM-RoBERTa variants. Additionally, limited data for fine-tuning the masked language model (MLM) could impact robustness, particularly for less-represented Devanagari-scripted languages.

8.2 Ethical Considerations

This study prioritizes inclusivity for low-resource Devanagari-scripted languages, recognizing the potential impacts on linguistic communities. To address concerns of bias and fairness, we conduct regular evaluations of training data and model outputs, promote responsible interpretation and implementation of model outputs, and carefully consider community impact. These measures aim to foster fair and inclusive language technologies.

References

Premjith B., Soman Kp, and K. Sreelakshmi. 2019. Amrita cen at hasoc 2019: Hate speech detection in roman and devanagiri scripted text.

Gianni Brauwers and Flavius Frasincar. 2023. A general survey on attention mechanisms in deep learning. *IEEE Transactions on Knowledge and Data Engineering*, 35(4):3279–3298.

Tanmay Chavan, Shantanu Patankar, Aditya Kane, Omkar Gokhale, and Raviraj Joshi. 2022. A twitter bert approach for offensive language detection in marathi. *Preprint*, arXiv:2212.10039.

Alexis Conneau, Kartikay Khandelwal, Naman Goyal, Vishrav Chaudhary, Guillaume Wenzek, Francisco Guzmán, Edouard Grave, Myle Ott, Luke Zettlemoyer, and Veselin Stoyanov. 2019. Unsupervised cross-lingual representation learning at scale. *CoRR*, abs/1911.02116.

Sepp Hochreiter and Jürgen Schmidhuber. 1997. Long short-term memory. *Neural Computation*, 9:1735–1780.

Farhan Ahmad Jafri, Kritesh Rauniyar, Surendrabikram Thapa, Mohammad Aman Siddiqui, Matloob Khushi, and Usman Naseem. 2024. Chunav: Analyzing hindi hate speech and targeted groups in indian election discourse. *ACM Transactions on Asian and Low-Resource Language Information Processing*.

Farhan Ahmad Jafri, Mohammad Aman Siddiqui, Surendrabikram Thapa, Kritesh Rauniyar, Usman Naseem, and Imran Razzak. 2023. Uncovering political hate speech during indian election campaign: A new low-resource dataset and baselines.

Raviraj Joshi. 2022. L3cube-hindbert and devbert: Pre-trained bert transformer models for devanagari based hindi and marathi languages. *arXiv preprint arXiv:2211.11418*.

Rohith Kodali and Durga Manukonda. 2024. byteSizedLLM@DravidianLangTech 2024: Fake news detection in Dravidian languages - unleashing the power of custom subword tokenization with Subword2Vec and BiLSTM. In *Proceedings of the Fourth Workshop on Speech, Vision, and Language Technologies for Dravidian Languages*, pages 79–84, St. Julian's, Malta. Association for Computational Linguistics.

Gitanjali Kumari, Dibyanayan Bandyopadhyay, Asif Ekbal, and Vinutha B. NarayanaMurthy. 2024. CM-off-meme: Code-mixed Hindi-English offensive meme detection with multi-task learning by leveraging contextual knowledge. In *Proceedings of the 2024 Joint International Conference on Computational Linguistics, Language Resources and Evaluation (LREC-COLING 2024)*, pages 3380–3393, Torino, Italia. ELRA and ICCL.

Durga Manukonda and Rohith Kodali. 2024a. byteLLM@LT-EDI-2024: Homophobia/transphobia detection in social media comments - custom subword tokenization with Subword2Vec and BiLSTM. In *Proceedings of the Fourth Workshop on Language Technology for Equality, Diversity, Inclusion*, pages 157–163, St. Julian's, Malta. Association for Computational Linguistics.

Durga Prasad Manukonda and Rohith Gowtham Kodali. 2024b. Enhancing multilingual natural language processing with custom subword tokenization: Subword2vec and bilstm integration for lightweight and streamlined approaches. In *2024 6th International Conference on Natural Language Processing (ICNLP)*, pages 366–371.

Puneet Mathur, Rajiv Shah, Ramit Sawhney, and Debanjan Mahata. 2018. Detecting offensive tweets in Hindi-English code-switched language. In *Proceedings of the Sixth International Workshop on Natural Language Processing for Social Media*, pages 18–26, Melbourne, Australia. Association for Computational Linguistics.

Nobal B. Niraula, Saurab Dulal, and Diwa Koirala. 2021. Offensive language detection in Nepali social media. In *Proceedings of the 5th Workshop on Online Abuse and Harms (WOAH 2021)*, pages 67–75, Online. Association for Computational Linguistics.

Kritesh Rauniyar, Sweta Poudel, Shuvam Shiwakoti, Surendrabikram Thapa, Junaid Rashid, Jungeun Kim, Muhammad Imran, and Usman Naseem. 2023. Multi-aspect annotation and analysis of nepali tweets on anti-establishment election discourse. *IEEE Access*.

Kengatharaiyer Sarveswaran, Bal Krishna Bal, Surendrabikram Thapa, Ashwini Vaidya, and Sana Shams. 2025. A brief overview of the first workshop on challenges in processing south asian languages (chipsal). In *Proceedings of the First Workshop on Challenges in Processing South Asian Languages (CHiPSAL)*.

Arushi Sharma, Anubha Kabra, and Minni Jain. 2022. Ceasing hate with moh: Hate speech detection in hindi–english code-switched language. *Information Processing Management*, 59(1):102760.

Shubham Shukla, Sushama Nagpal, and Sangeeta Sabharwal. 2022. Hate speech detection in hindi language using bert and convolution neural network. In *2022 International Conference on Computing, Communication, and Intelligent Systems (ICCCIS)*, pages 642–647.

K Sreelakshmi, B Premjith, and K.P. Soman. 2020. Detection of hate speech text in hindi-english code-mixed data. *Procedia Computer Science*, 171:737–744. Third International Conference on Computing and Network Communications (CoCoNet'19).

Surendrabikram Thapa, Kritesh Rauniyar, Farhan Ahmad Jafri, Surabhi Adhikari, Kengatharaiyer Sarveswaran, Bal Krishna Bal, Hariram Veeramani, and Usman Naseem. 2025. Natural language understanding of devanagari script languages: Language identification, hate speech and its target detection. In *Proceedings of the First Workshop on Challenges in Processing South Asian Languages (CHiPSAL)*.

Surendrabikram Thapa, Kritesh Rauniyar, Shuvam Shiwakoti, Sweta Poudel, Usman Naseem, and Mehwish Nasim. 2023. Nehate: Large-scale annotated data shedding light on hate speech in nepali local election discourse. In *ECAI 2023*, pages 2346–2353. IOS Press.

Santosh T.Y.S.S and K. V. S. Aravind. 2019. Hate speech detection in hindi-english code-mixed social media text. *Proceedings of the ACM India Joint International Conference on Data Science and Management of Data*.

Abhishek Velankar, Hrushikesh Patil, Amol Gore, Shubham Salunke, and Raviraj Joshi. 2021. Hate and offensive speech detection in hindi and marathi. *Preprint*, arXiv:2110.12200.

byteSizedLLM@NLU of Devanagari Script Languages 2025: Language Identification Using Customized Attention BiLSTM and XLM-RoBERTa base Embeddings

Durga Prasad Manukonda
ASRlytics
Hyderabad, India
mdp0999@gmail.com

Rohith Gowtham Kodali
ASRlytics
Hyderabad, India
rohitkodali@gmail.com

Abstract

This study explores the challenges of natural language understanding (NLU) in multilingual contexts, focusing on Devanagari-scripted languages such as Nepali, Marathi, Sanskrit, Bhojpuri, and Hindi. Language identification within these languages is complex due to their structural and lexical similarities. We present a hybrid Attention BiLSTM-XLM-RoBERTa model, achieving a state-of-the-art F1 score of 0.9974 on the test set, despite limited resources. Our model effectively distinguishes between closely related Devanagari-scripted languages, providing a solid foundation for context-aware NLU systems that enhance language-specific processing and promote inclusive digital interactions across diverse linguistic communities.

1 Introduction

In the era of rapidly expanding digital content, developing effective natural language understanding (NLU) capabilities in multilingual contexts is essential, particularly for languages using the Devanagari script, such as Nepali, Marathi, Sanskrit, Bhojpuri, and Hindi. The diversity and complexity of these languages, coupled with their shared script, present distinct challenges for language identification and moderation. Addressing this need, the Shared Task on Natural Language Understanding of Devanagari Script Languages at CHIPSAL@COLING 2025 introduces three critical subtasks to enhance the automated identification and analysis of Devanagari-scripted content in multilingual environments (Thapa et al., 2025) (Sarveswaran et al., 2025)

Subtask A: Devanagari Script Language Identification hones in on discerning the specific language within Devanagari-scripted text. In multilingual digital spaces, accurately identifying the language is a prerequisite for effective processing, enabling robust multilingual NLU systems. Given a sentence in Devanagari script, this subtask's objective is to determine whether the language is Nepali, Marathi, Sanskrit, Bhojpuri, or Hindi, meeting the pressing need for accurate language differentiation among closely related languages that share the Devanagari script. This foundational task supports precise language identification, empowering deeper analysis and tailored content moderation across Devanagari-scripted languages.

Our hybrid architecture, combining an attention-based BiLSTM with XLM-RoBERTa embeddings, effectively captures the syntactic and semantic nuances required for accurate language differentiation. The BiLSTM component, enhanced by attention, improves sequential modeling, while XLM-RoBERTa provides robust multilingual embeddings. This integration enables high precision in language identification and lays a foundation for more advanced multilingual NLU. Additionally, the model's attention mechanism allows it to focus on language-specific features, further enhancing its ability to distinguish closely related Devanagari-scripted languages.

2 Related Work

Two studies focus on language identification for Indian languages in the Devanagari script. The first uses n-gram models to classify languages like Hindi, Marathi, and Sanskrit based on character- and word-level frequency patterns Indhuja. et al. (2014). The second applies machine learning and deep learning to capture subtle lexical differences in poetry Acharya et al. (2020). Both highlight progress in language identification and the challenges of linguistic similarities and stylistic variations.

Expanding to native and romanized forms, proposed Madhani et al. (2023), using FastText and IndicBERT to identify 22 Indic languages. Together, these studies illustrate advancements and ongoing challenges in distinguishing related languages and

Proceedings of the First Workshop on Challenges in Processing South Asian Languages (CHiPSAL 2025), pages 248–252
January 19, 2025.

text styles in Devanagari.

3 Dataset & Task

Task A focuses on identifying the specific Devanagari-scripted language of a given text, with a dataset comprising samples from five languages: Nepali (Thapa et al., 2023) (Rauniyar et al., 2023), Marathi(Kulkarni et al., 2021), Sanskrit(Aralikatte et al., 2021), Bhojpuri(Ojha, 2019), and Hindi(Jafri et al., 2024)(Jafri et al., 2023). Accurate language classification in multilingual contexts relies heavily on this task. To facilitate training and evaluation, the dataset is divided into training, validation, and test sets.

The dataset consists of sentences in five Devanagari-script languages, with labels assigned as follows: 'Nepali' is labeled as '0', 'Marathi' as '1', 'Sanskrit' as '2', 'Bhojpuri' as '3', and 'Hindi' as '4', allowing for efficient and accurate language classification.

Table 1 provides a detailed analysis of language distribution within the training and validation sets, highlighting representation across subsets. The curated and labeled data supports NLP tasks in Devanagari-script languages, forming a foundation for robust language differentiation.

Class	Train	Valid	Test
Nepali (0)	12543	2688	2688
Marathi (1)	11034	2364	2365
Sanskrit (2)	10996	2356	2356
Bhojpuri (3)	10184	2182	2183
Hindi (4)	7659	1642	1642
Total	52416	11232	11234

Table 1: Distribution of samples in Train, Validation(Valid) and Test datasets for each class in SubTask A

Additionally, we curated datasets to fine-tune multilingual RoBERTa (xlm-roberta-base) on masked language modeling for five languages, following the approach of Joshi (2022): Bhojpuri (9.3MB from GitHub[1]), Nepali (50MB from Kaggle[2]), Sanskrit (50MB from Kaggle[3]), and Hindi and Marathi (50MB each from AI4Bharat[4]).

[1]https://github.com/shashwatup9k/bho-resources

[2]https://www.kaggle.com/datasets/lotusacharya/nepalinewsdataset

[3]https://www.kaggle.com/datasets/rushikeshdarge/sanskrit

[4]https://github.com/AI4Bharat/indicnlp_corpus

4 Methodology

This study presents a hybrid Attention BiLSTM-XLM-RoBERTa model, inspired by Hochreiter and Schmidhuber (1997); Conneau et al. (2019); Manukonda and Kodali (2024a); Kodali and Manukonda (2024); Manukonda and Kodali (2024b); Brauwers and Frasincar (2023), for language identification within the Devanagari script. As shown in Figure 1, the model integrates deep contextual embeddings from the fine-tuned masked language model (MLM) of XLM-RoBERTa with a bidirectional LSTM and attention mechanism to enhance language-specific feature extraction. Each model component and its mathematical foundation are detailed below.

The input sequence is first passed to XLM-RoBERTa base, generating contextualized embeddings $\mathbf{X} \in R^{T \times D}$, where $D = 768$ represents the embedding dimension:

$$\mathbf{X} = \mathbf{XLMRoBERTa}(input\_ids, attention\_mask) \quad (1)$$

These embeddings are fed into a BiLSTM to capture sequential dependencies, producing bidirectional hidden states $\mathbf{H}fwd$ and $\mathbf{H}bwd$, which combine as:

$$\mathbf{H}t = [\mathbf{H}fwd, t; \mathbf{H}_{bwd,t}] \quad (2)$$

An attention mechanism then assigns relevance to each $\mathbf{H}_t$, yielding attention weights α_t:

$$\mathbf{a}t = \tanh(\mathbf{W}att \cdot \mathbf{H}_t), \quad \alpha_t = \frac{\exp(\mathbf{a}t)}{\sum t = 1^T \exp(\mathbf{a}_t)} \quad (3)$$

The attention-weighted representation $\mathbf{H}_{attended}$ is computed as:

$$\mathbf{H}attended = \sum t = 1^T \alpha_t \cdot \mathbf{H}_t \quad (4)$$

Layer normalization and dropout are optional residual components that help mitigate overfitting and stabilize training, especially in complex language scenarios. They enhance generalization by reducing variance and stabilizing weight updates, benefiting smaller or noisier datasets. To combat overfitting, $\mathbf{H}_{attended}$ undergoes layer normalization and dropout:

$$\mathbf{H}_{dropout} = Dropout(LayerNorm(\mathbf{H}_{attended})) \quad (5)$$

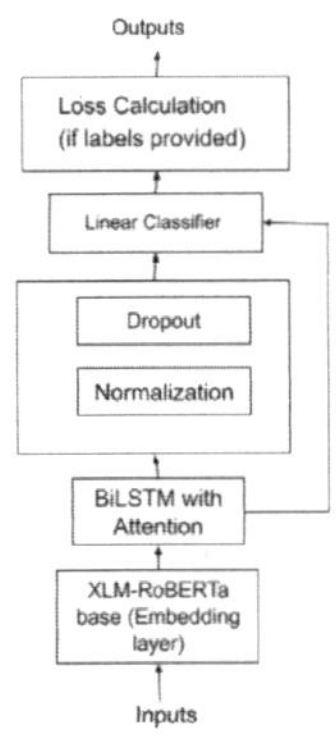

Figure 1: Architecture of the BiLSTM-XLM-RoBERTa Classifier Model. Layer normalization and dropout regularization enhance generalization, especially for smaller or noisier datasets.

Finally, $\mathbf{H}_{dropout}$ is passed through a classification layer to produce logits:

$$\textbf{logits} = \mathbf{W}_{cls} \cdot \mathbf{H}_{dropout} + \mathbf{b}_{cls} \quad (6)$$

During training, cross-entropy loss L is calculated between predicted logits and true labels:

$$L = -\sum_{i=1}^{N} y_i \log(\hat{y}_i) \quad (7)$$

This hybrid model leverages XLM-RoBERTa base embeddings, BiLSTM sequential processing, and attention for precise language differentiation in Devanagari-scripted multilingual contexts.

5 Experiment Setup

Our experiment setup involved data preprocessing, model fine-tuning, and architecture optimization to assess language identification across Devanagari-scripted languages, evaluated by accuracy and Macro F1 scores on the validation dataset.

Our unique setup involved tokenizing and normalizing datasets for compatibility with the XLM-RoBERTa base model, adapting samples to the Devanagari script. Fine-tuning on masked language modeling (MLM) used a 15% masking ratio and a learning rate of 2×10^{-5}, achieving a perplexity score of 5.33 over 7 epochs, indicating effective contextual adaptation.

Following extensive classifier testing, we selected the Attention BiLSTM-XLM-RoBERTa architecture(Figure 1) for its superior performance. This model incorporates a BiLSTM layer (hidden size 256, 2 LSTM layers, dropout 0.3) to capture sequential dependencies and an attention mechanism to emphasize language-specific features. The setup was fine-tuned over 6 epochs with a learning rate of 1×10^{-5}, using optional residual layers for normalization and dropout to enhance stability and mitigate overfitting.

This setup provides a comprehensive framework to evaluate the impact of model fine-tuning, architecture, and data preparation on multilingual classification within the Devanagari script.

6 Results and Discussion

Table 2 summarizes the performance of various classifiers using fine-tuned XLM-RoBERTa base embeddings for language identification within Devanagari-scripted languages. Initially, we experimented with several traditional linear classifiers; however, our hybrid Attention BiLSTM-XLM-RoBERTa model achieved the best performance on the validation set, leading us to proceed with this architecture for the test set.

The **Attention BiLSTM-XLM-RoBERTa** model outperformed all classifiers, achieving an accuracy of 0.9986 and a Macro F1-score of 0.9984 on the validation set, and 0.9976 accuracy with a 0.9974 Macro F1-score on the test set. This superior performance highlights the effectiveness of combining XLM-RoBERTa's contextual embeddings with BiLSTM and attention mechanisms, enabling a nuanced focus on language-specific features. The high scores indicate robust language identification, capturing syntactic and semantic nuances, even among closely related languages. While other classifiers using fine-tuned XLM-RoBERTa embeddings performed well, the hybrid model provided a clear advantage.

Table 3 provides a comparison of the top 5 ranked scores on the SubTask A test set, where our team, **byteSizedLLM**, achieved 5th place with an F1-score of 0.9974. This ranking reaffirms the model's effectiveness and positions it competitively within the overall landscape.

Overall, our findings show that the hybrid Attention BiLSTM-XLM-RoBERTa architecture, combining BiLSTM with transformer-based embeddings, provides a significant advantage. Fine-tuning XLM-RoBERTa's MLM on task-specific data further improved performance. This approach underscores the value of integrating bidirectional embeddings and attention mechanisms for precise

Classifier	Val Acc	Val F1	Test Acc	Test F1
XLM-RoBERTa base (Transformers)	0.9972	0.9969	0.9970	0.9964
XGBoost (xgb)	0.9962	0.9957	0.9945	0.9939
Random Forest (rf)	0.9962	0.9957	0.9942	0.9936
Logistic Regression (lr)	0.9971	0.9967	0.9961	0.9957
Gradient Boosting (gb)	0.9954	0.9948	0.9933	0.9926
Support Vector Classifier (svc)	0.9969	0.9965	0.9954	0.9949
AdaBoost (ada)	0.9562	0.9514	0.9564	0.9520
Extra Trees (extra_trees)	0.9955	0.9950	0.9943	0.9937
Ridge Classifier (ridge)	0.9950	0.9944	0.9944	0.9937
Stochastic Gradient Descent (sgd)	0.9974	0.9971	0.9955	0.9950
Ensemble (xgb,lr, rf, svc, sgd)	0.9970	0.9967	0.9955	0.9949
Attention BiLSTM-XLM-RoBERTa	**0.9986**	**0.9984**	**0.9974**	**0.9976**

Table 2: Comparison of Validation (Val) and Test Accuracies (Acc) and Macro-F1 Scores (F1) Across Different Classifiers

Team Name	F1-Score	Rank
CUFE	0.9997	1
CLTL	0.9982	2
1-800-SHARED-TASKS	0.9979	3
1-800-SHARED-TASKS	0.9976	4
byteSizedLLM	0.9974	5

Table 3: Comparison of Top 5 Ranked Scores on the SubTask A Test Set

language differentiation in multilingual Devanagari contexts. A key limitation was the scarcity of open-source datasets for fine-tuning MLM and computational constraints limiting us to the base model. Future exploration with larger models could further improve language identification

7 Conclusion and Future work

This study presented an innovative hybrid approach, combining the XLM-RoBERTa base embeddings with traditional classifiers and an Attention BiLSTM architecture for effective language identification in Devanagari-scripted multilingual contexts. Our proposed Attention BiLSTM-XLM-RoBERTa model achieved top performance among all classifiers tested, yielding high accuracy and Macro F1 scores, and ultimately ranking 5th overall with minimal differences from the top entries. These findings underscore the strength of integrating transformer-based embeddings with sequential and attention mechanisms, highlighting the potential of this approach to capture language-specific nuances even with limited MLM fine-tuning data and computational resources.

Further fine-tuning MLM on a larger dataset and scaling to XLM-RoBERTa-large could improve embedding quality and capture nuanced language variations. This research underscores the importance of robust embeddings with attention mechanisms for language-specific features, advancing Devanagari multilingual NLP capabilities.

8 Limitations and Ethical Considerations

8.1 Limitations

The Attention BiLSTM-XLM-RoBERTa model demonstrated strong performance but has limitations affecting generalizability. Using XLM-RoBERTa base may restrict the model's ability to capture complex contextual nuances across diverse languages. Computational constraints prevented exploring larger XLM-RoBERTa variants, potentially limiting performance gains, and limited data for fine-tuning the masked language model (MLM) may affect robustness, particularly for underrepresented languages in the Devanagari script family.

8.2 Ethical Considerations

This study prioritizes inclusivity for low-resource Devanagari-scripted languages, recognizing the potential impacts on linguistic communities. To address concerns of bias and fairness, we conduct regular evaluations of training data and model outputs, promote responsible interpretation and implementation of model outputs, and carefully consider community impact. These measures aim to support developing fair and inclusive language technologies.

References

Priyankit Acharya, Aditya Ku. Pathak, Rakesh Ch. Balabantaray, and Anil Ku. Singh. 2020. Language identification of devanagari poems. *Preprint*, arXiv:2012.15023.

Rahul Aralikatte, Miryam De Lhoneux, Anoop Kunchukuttan, and Anders Søgaard. 2021. Itihasa: A large-scale corpus for sanskrit to english translation. In *Proceedings of the 8th Workshop on Asian Translation (WAT2021)*, pages 191–197.

Gianni Brauwers and Flavius Frasincar. 2023. A general survey on attention mechanisms in deep learning. *IEEE Transactions on Knowledge and Data Engineering*, 35(4):3279–3298.

Alexis Conneau, Kartikay Khandelwal, Naman Goyal, Vishrav Chaudhary, Guillaume Wenzek, Francisco Guzmán, Edouard Grave, Myle Ott, Luke Zettlemoyer, and Veselin Stoyanov. 2019. Unsupervised cross-lingual representation learning at scale. *CoRR*, abs/1911.02116.

Sepp Hochreiter and Jürgen Schmidhuber. 1997. Long short-term memory. *Neural Computation*, 9:1735–1780.

K Indhuja., M. G. Indu, C. Sreejith, and Purushottam Raj. 2014. Text based language identification system for indian languages following devanagiri script. *International journal of engineering research and technology*, 3.

Farhan Ahmad Jafri, Kritesh Rauniyar, Surendrabikram Thapa, Mohammad Aman Siddiqui, Matloob Khushi, and Usman Naseem. 2024. Chunav: Analyzing hindi hate speech and targeted groups in indian election discourse. *ACM Transactions on Asian and Low-Resource Language Information Processing*.

Farhan Ahmad Jafri, Mohammad Aman Siddiqui, Surendrabikram Thapa, Kritesh Rauniyar, Usman Naseem, and Imran Razzak. 2023. Uncovering political hate speech during indian election campaign: A new low-resource dataset and baselines.

Raviraj Joshi. 2022. L3cube-hindbert and devbert: Pre-trained bert transformer models for devanagari based hindi and marathi languages. *arXiv preprint arXiv:2211.11418*.

Rohith Kodali and Durga Manukonda. 2024. byteSizedLLM@DravidianLangTech 2024: Fake news detection in Dravidian languages - unleashing the power of custom subword tokenization with Subword2Vec and BiLSTM. In *Proceedings of the Fourth Workshop on Speech, Vision, and Language Technologies for Dravidian Languages*, pages 79–84, St. Julian's, Malta. Association for Computational Linguistics.

Atharva Kulkarni, Meet Mandhane, Manali Likhitkar, Gayatri Kshirsagar, and Raviraj Joshi. 2021. L3cubemahasent: A marathi tweet-based sentiment analysis dataset. In *Proceedings of the Eleventh Workshop on Computational Approaches to Subjectivity, Sentiment and Social Media Analysis*, pages 213–220.

Yash Madhani, Mitesh M. Khapra, and Anoop Kunchukuttan. 2023. Bhasha-abhijnaanam: Native-script and romanized language identification for 22 indic languages. *Preprint*, arXiv:2305.15814.

Durga Manukonda and Rohith Kodali. 2024a. byteLLM@LT-EDI-2024: Homophobia/transphobia detection in social media comments - custom subword tokenization with Subword2Vec and BiLSTM. In *Proceedings of the Fourth Workshop on Language Technology for Equality, Diversity, Inclusion*, pages 157–163, St. Julian's, Malta. Association for Computational Linguistics.

Durga Prasad Manukonda and Rohith Gowtham Kodali. 2024b. Enhancing multilingual natural language processing with custom subword tokenization: Subword2vec and bilstm integration for lightweight and streamlined approaches. In *2024 6th International Conference on Natural Language Processing (ICNLP)*, pages 366–371.

Atul Kr Ojha. 2019. English-bhojpuri smt system: Insights from the karaka model. *arXiv preprint arXiv:1905.02239*.

Kritesh Rauniyar, Sweta Poudel, Shuvam Shiwakoti, Surendrabikram Thapa, Junaid Rashid, Jungeun Kim, Muhammad Imran, and Usman Naseem. 2023. Multi-aspect annotation and analysis of nepali tweets on anti-establishment election discourse. *IEEE Access*.

Kengatharaiyer Sarveswaran, Bal Krishna Bal, Surendrabikram Thapa, Ashwini Vaidya, and Sana Shams. 2025. A brief overview of the first workshop on challenges in processing south asian languages (chipsal). In *Proceedings of the First Workshop on Challenges in Processing South Asian Languages (CHiPSAL)*.

Surendrabikram Thapa, Kritesh Rauniyar, Farhan Ahmad Jafri, Surabhi Adhikari, Kengatharaiyer Sarveswaran, Bal Krishna Bal, Hariram Veeramani, and Usman Naseem. 2025. Natural language understanding of devanagari script languages: Language identification, hate speech and its target detection. In *Proceedings of the First Workshop on Challenges in Processing South Asian Languages (CHiPSAL)*.

Surendrabikram Thapa, Kritesh Rauniyar, Shuvam Shiwakoti, Sweta Poudel, Usman Naseem, and Mehwish Nasim. 2023. Nehate: Large-scale annotated data shedding light on hate speech in nepali local election discourse. In *ECAI 2023*, pages 2346–2353. IOS Press.

CUET_Big_O@NLU of Devanagari Script Languages 2025: Identifying Script Language and Detecting Hate Speech Using Deep Learning and Transformer Model

Md. Refaj Hossan*, **Nazmus Sakib***, **Md. Alam Miah**
Jawad Hossain and Mohammed Moshiul Hoque
Department of Computer Science and Engineering
Chittagong University of Engineering and Technology
{u1904007,u1904086,u1904102,u1704039}@student.cuet.ac.bd
moshiul_240@cuet.ac.bd

Abstract

Text-based hate speech has been prevalent and is usually used to incite hostility and violence. Detecting this content becomes imperative, yet the task is challenging, particularly for low-resource languages in the Devanagari script, which must have the extensive labeled datasets required for effective machine learning. To address this, a shared task has been organized for identifying hate speech targets in Devanagari-script text. The task involves classifying targets such as individuals, organizations, and communities and identifying different languages within the script. We have explored several machine learning methods such as LR, SVM, MNB, and Random Forest, deep learning models using CNN, BiLSTM, GRU, CNN+BiLSTM, and transformer-based models like Indic-BERT, m-BERT, Verta-BERT, XLM-R, and MuRIL. The CNN with BiLSTM yielded the best performance (F1-score of 0.9941), placing the team 13th in the competition for script identification. Furthermore, the fine-tuned MuRIL-BERT model resulted in an F1 score of 0.6832, ranking us 4th for detecting hate speech targets.

1 Introduction

Digital platforms such as Facebook, Instagram, and YouTube have emerged as a common medium for public expression with the rapid expansion of online communication. Unfortunately, these digital platforms also act as conduits for injurious content, including hate speech, which fosters hostility and marginalization of communities and threatens social cohesion. Hateful content can attack social harmony based on race, gender, religion, nationality, political support, immigration status, and personal beliefs (Paz et al., 2020). Hence, determining whether shared content on social media is hateful is crucial.

While much recent work has focused on identifying hate and offensive content in high-resource languages such as English, Spanish (del Arco et al., 2021), and Arabic (Omar et al., 2020), which have abundant linguistic resources and datasets available, the challenge remains in low-resource settings where effective hate speech detection is obstructed due to a lack of resources (Magueresse et al., 2020). Hence, it is also crucial in a multilingually rich region like South Asia, where multiple languages and scripts are used daily. In this context, the identification of hate speech is essential in the Devanagari script, which encompasses languages such as Hindi, Marathi, Nepali, and Sanskrit, each with millions of speakers. Moreover, the complex structure of Devanagari, with frequent code-mixing and nuanced expressions, makes it challenging to distinguish between languages. At the same time, detecting hate speech requires culturally adept models able to estimate indirect or inexact language. Concentrated on the circumstances, the organizers (Thapa et al., 2025) presented different datasets for three subtasks by combining several datasets (Jafri et al., 2023, 2024; Thapa et al., 2023; Rauniyar et al., 2023; Ojha, 2019; Kulkarni et al., 2021; Aralikatte et al., 2021) for identifying Devanagari script language in subtask A, hate speech detection in subtask B, and target identification for hate speech in subtask C in the first workshop on Challenges in Processing South Asian Languages (CHiPSAL) (Sarveswaran et al., 2025). However, this work aims to outline the contributions to subtasks A and C, which are as follows:

- Developed a hybrid model using CNN with BiLSTM for Devanagari script identification and fine-tuned MuRIL for target hate speech detection in the Devanagari script language.
- Explored various Machine Learning (ML), Deep Learning (DL), and transformer-based

*Authors contributed equally to this work.

Proceedings of the First Workshop on Challenges in Processing South Asian Languages (CHiPSAL 2025), pages 253–259
January 19, 2025.

models to identify Devanagari script language and target identification for hate speech.

- Investigated and contrasted multiple performance metrics and in-depth error analysis for the models to perceive the best strategy toward identifying Devanagari script language and classifying target hate speech.

2 Related Work

Earlier efforts involved traditional ML algorithms to segregate the script and identify the language; these laid a platform for more advanced techniques in this area. For instance, KumarShrivastava and Chaurasia (2012) obtained a 100% recognition rate of Devanagari characters using SVM with polynomial kernel by testing different kernels and segment count on their dataset. A survey conducted by Jayadevan et al. (2011) reviewed the state-of-the-art techniques concerning machine-printed and handwritten Devanagari OCR by underlining different feature extraction methods and classification models. Moreover, Halder et al. (2015) presented their analysis of Devanagari characters for writer identification with several techniques and achieved 99.12% accuracy with LIBLINEAR. Another work focused on script identification from Indian documents such as Bangla, Devanagari, Gujarati, etc., using feature extraction techniques like Log-Gabor Filtering and achieved 97.11% accuracy with ten different Indian scripts using optimized KNN technique (Joshi et al., 2006).

While Devanagari script identification is going on, hate speech detection is also of prime importance in research because it segregates social unity, and lots of research is being conducted for high-resource languages. Fortuna and Nunes (2018) gave a comprehensive overview of the hate speech detection techniques, pinpointing the need for approaches tailored for multilingual contexts. Therein, Nandi et al. (2024) presented a review of recent research on hate speech detection in Indian languages, discussed the challenges, and then analyzed various methodologies, datasets, and results to show the gaps and opportunities for future work in this critical area of study. Another work done by Jha et al. (2020) proposed a FastText-based model for the Hindi Language to classify offensive and non-offensive texts, and an accuracy of 92.2% has been achieved by grid-search hyperparameter tuning using the Devanagari Hindi Offensive Tweets (DHOT) dataset[1]. The existing research contributions in hate speech detection, addressing types related to racism, sexism, and religious hate, and the methods developed for mitigating them, along with the identification of challenges, have been reviewed by Parihar et al. (2021). Furthermore, several works have been performed to detect hate speech in code-mixed Hindi-English (Chopra et al., 2023), code-switched Hindi-English (Sharma et al., 2022) by using deep learning, transformer-based approaches to obtain superior performance. Prior work has yet to focus on target-specific hate speech detection (individual, community, organization) in Devanagari script with code-mixed language. In this context, our work introduces not only the model for it but also proposes a script identification component specific to Devanagari by addressing the complexity of the script and challenges posed due to code-mixing in South Asian languages.

3 Task and Dataset Description

In the shared task (Thapa et al., 2025), there were three subtasks: A, B, and C. However, the goal of subtask A was to identify whether the language given in the dataset belongs to Nepali, Marathi, Sanskrit, Bhojpuri, or Hindi, making it a multi-class classification problem. Along with subtask A, the objective of subtask C was to identify the target of the hate speech, categorized as either *Individual*, *Organization*, or *Community* classes in Devanagari script language. For subtask A, the train, valid, and test datasets comprise 52422, 11233, and 11234 texts, respectively. Class-wise samples and dataset statistics are provided in Table 1.

Table 1: Class-wise distribution of train, validation, and test set for subtask A, where W_T and UW_T denote total words in three datasets and total unique words in train set respectively

Classes	Train	Valid	Test	W_T	UW_T
Nepali	12544	2688	2688	320384	26536
Marathi	11034	2364	2365	392735	32332
Sanskrit	10996	2356	2356	315875	64652
Bhojpuri	10184	2182	2183	420856	15779
Hindi	7664	1643	1642	211029	8933
Total	52422	11233	11234	1660879	148232

For subtask C, the train, validation, and test datasets consist of 2214, 474, and 475 texts, and the datasets are imbalanced. Table 2 provides the

[1] https://github.com/vikaskumarjha9/hindi_abusive_dataset

class-wise samples and dataset statistics. The implementation details of the tasks will be found in the GitHub repository[2].

Table 2: Class-wise distribution of train, validation, and test set for subtask C, where W_T and UW_T denote total words in three datasets and total unique words in train data respectively

Classes	Train	Valid	Test	W_T	UW_T
Individual	1074	230	230	42438	11963
Organization	856	183	184	11586	8891
Community	284	61	61	10564	3931
Total	2214	474	475	64588	24785

4 Methodology

Several ML, DL, and transformer-based models were explored to develop the baselines as depicted in Figure 1.

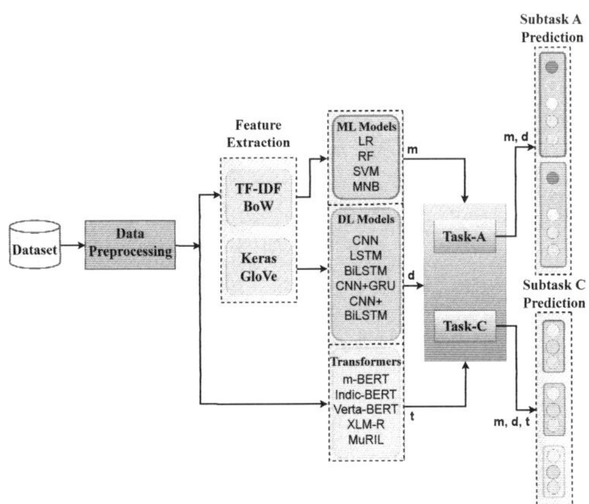

Figure 1: Schematic process of Devanagari script identification and target identification for hate speech

4.1 Data Preprocessing

Since the dataset originates in Devanagari, aggregated from several sources, by default, it contains quite a large amount of irrelevant and duplicate data. Therefore, the first significant work was extensive preprocessing of data. It included the removal of emojis, symbols, signs, numbers, and extra punctuation marks from the text. Data augmentation techniques have not been used, as more emphasis was put on cleaning and refining the data to prepare them for appropriate model training.

[2]https://github.com/RJ-Hossan/CHIPSAL-25

4.2 Feature Extraction

Feature extraction in NLP transforms raw text into numerical values for machine learning and deep learning models. Our approach extracts unigram and bigram features using TF-IDF for machine learning algorithms. For deep learning, text preprocessing involves tokenization via the Tokenizer class of TensorFlow Keras[3], which handles out-of-vocabulary words using placeholder tokens. These tokens are passed into an Embedding layer, converting them into dense vector representations. Additionally, we incorporate pre-trained GloVe embeddings, which map each word to a 100D vector, with an embedding matrix of shape (10,000, 100) for the top 10,000 words in the tokenizer's vocabulary.

4.3 Machine Learning Models

We have employed various machine learning (ML) models to identify instances of hate speech. Specifically, we employed Logistic Regression (LR), Support Vector Machine (SVM), Multinomial Naive Bayes (MNB), Random Forest (RF), Gradient Boosting (GB). In subtask C, we have also employed hyperparameter tuning e.g., linear and RBF kernel for SVM, different learning rate for LR, GB, different estimator values, LIBLINEAR (Fan et al., 2008) solver function for LR, etc., using GridSearchCV[4] to get the superior performance.

4.4 Deep Learning Models

For deep learning models, we considered several approaches, such as LSTM, BiLSTM, CNN, CNN + BiLSTM, and CNN + GRU. These models were trained with tokenization and embedding techniques. The hybrid BiLSTM with CNN model is configured with a maximum vocabulary size of 10,000, a sequence length of 100, and an embedding dimension of 128. It has a CNN branch with 64 filters of size 5 and a BiLSTM branch with 64 units, trained over 45 epochs with a batch size of 32. Using sparse categorical cross-entropy as the loss function and the 'Adam' optimizer at a learning rate of 1e-4, the class imbalance was addressed by computing class weights. At the same time, the training was optimized through Reduce Learning Rate and Early Stopping callbacks for improved performance in Subtask A. Table 3 shows the fine-

[3]https://www.tensorflow.org/api_docs/python/tf/keras/layers/Embedding

[4]https://scikit-learn.org/dev/modules/generated/sklearn.model_selection.GridSearchCV.html

tuned hyperparameters for the deep learning-based models for subtask A.

Table 3: Model configuration for subtask A

Parameter	Value
Vocabulary Size	10,000
Sequence Length	100
Embedding Dimension	128
CNN Filters	64 filters of size 5
BiLSTM Units	64
Epochs	45
Batch Size	32
Optimizer	Adam
Learning Rate	1e-4

4.5 Transformer-Based Models

With the mechanism of attention embedding, transformer-based models efficiently process large-scale contextual information and, therefore, prove ideal for multilingual and cross-lingual tasks. To accomplish the tasks, we explored several transformer-based models such as m-BERT (Pires et al., 2019), Indic-BERT (Dabre et al., 2022), MuRIL-BERT (Khanuja et al., 2021), and XLM-R (Conneau et al., 2020) to study their performances for a diverse range of linguistic settings. Each of these models had been fine-tuned to the respective classification tasks. In the MuRIL-BERT model, hyperparameter tuning was done by fixing the batch size to 8, the learning rate to 2e-4, and modifying the weight decay to 0.06. Then, after training for 13 epochs, optimal performance was reached. Due to more robust regularization from an increased weight decay of 0.01 to 0.06, the training loss reduced when the model's generalization improved. Table 4 shows the fine-tuned hyperparameters for the transformer-based models for subtask C.

Table 4: Model configuration for subtask C

Parameter	Value
Batch Size	8
Epochs	13
Weight Decay	0.06
Learning Rate	2e-4

4.6 Computational Requirements

The model was trained on a dual GPU setup (NVIDIA Tesla T4x2), using parallel processing for BiLSTM, convolution, and transformer layers. The BiLSTM+CNN model used 5-8 GB of GPU memory, while MuRIL-BERT required 20 GB. Training for 45 epochs of BiLSTM+CNN and 13 epochs of MuRIL-BERT took 45-60 minutes, depending on dataset size and class weight calculations, balancing computational efficiency and performance.

5 Result Analysis

Table 5 compares classifier performance in two subtasks, showing differences in precision, recall, and F1-score. Traditional models for Devanagari script identification, such as LR and SVM, produce high F1-scores of 0.9628 and 0.9531, respectively, but fall somewhat short of deep learning models. Among these, the lowest performing remains RF, with an F1-score of 0.9368. Finally, LSTM and BiLSTM outperformed the neural networks by the classical approaches, achieving F1-scores of 0.9791 and 0.9917, respectively. The CNN and CNN + GRU models achieved F1-scores of 0.9916 and 0.9915, respectively, while CNN + BiLSTM outperformed them with a near-perfect F1-score of 0.9941 (subtask A).

Table 5: Result comparison on test data, where P, R, and F1 denote precision, recall, and F1-score, respectively, and K and G represent Keras and GloVe embeddings

Classifiers	Script Identification			Target Hate Speech		
	P	R	F1	P	R	F1
LR	0.9628	0.9628	0.9628	0.61	0.53	0.54
SVM	0.9540	0.9524	0.9531	0.59	0.48	0.46
RF	0.9382	0.9359	0.9368	0.76	0.49	0.46
MNB	0.9511	0.9424	0.9454	0.56	0.45	0.43
CNN (K)	0.9916	0.9917	0.9916	0.57	0.55	0.56
LSTM (K)	0.9789	0.9797	0.9791	0.50	0.48	0.48
BiLSTM (K)	0.9917	0.9917	0.9917	0.48	0.47	0.47
CNN + GRU (K)	0.9917	0.9913	0.9915	0.49	0.48	0.48
CNN + BiLSTM (G)	0.7024	0.5789	0.5146	0.49	0.40	0.37
CNN + BiLSTM (K)	**0.9941**	**0.9940**	**0.9941**	0.48	0.46	0.47
Indic-BERT	-	-	-	0.61	0.61	0.61
m-BERT	-	-	-	0.61	0.60	0.60
verta-BERT	-	-	-	0.61	0.60	0.61
XLM-R	-	-	-	0.65	0.71	0.66
MuRIL-BERT	-	-	-	**0.68**	**0.68**	**0.68**

For the target hate speech detection subtask, precision, recall, and F1-scores dropped across models, reflecting the task's complexity. Traditional models performed far worse, with the best among them, LR, achieving an F1-score of only 0.54, while MNB had the lowest performance with an F1-score of just 0.43. The DL-based models also showed relatively poor F1 scores, ranging from 0.37 to 0.56. Transformer-based models performed much better on this task; specifically, MuRIL-BERT had the highest F1-score of 0.68, outperforming XLM-R (0.66) and m-BERT (0.60), helped us to rank 4th in subtask C. Interestingly, both Indic-BERT and verta-BERT achieved F1-scores of 0.61, reinforcing the trend that transformer-based models consistently outperformed traditional and neural network-based classifiers in the nuanced task of hate speech detection.

Appedix A provides a comprehensive error analysis of the proposed models, examining their performance in identifying the Devanagari script and detecting hate speech targets.

6 Conclusion

This paper introduced techniques of Devanagari script identification and target hate speech detection. This research bridges technology with linguistic diversity, creating a more inclusive digital world. The results demonstrated that the hybrid CNN with BiLSTM model outperformed other ML and DL models for script identification tasks by achieving the highest F1-score of 0.9941. At the same time, MuRIL-BERT performed best among all other models in target hate speech detection with an F1-score of 0.68. However, the integration of transformer-based models might perform even better for script identification. Therefore, in the future, we will explore other word embedding techniques and contextualized embeddings like GPT and ELMo in these tasks for enhancing performance for Devanagari script identification and target hate speech detection. Furthermore, ensemble methods combining several transformers with various fusion models designed for specific tasks can improve the results.

7 Limitations

The current work on script identification and target hate speech detection has several drawbacks, influenced by the following factors:

- Pre-trained transformer models may fail when the context differs significantly from their training data.
- The resort to DL models employed did not give the anticipated result. This indicates that other embeddings should be tried, and better models must be devised.
- Overall, this work is limited by dataset imbalance, reliance on existing models without architectural innovation, moderate hate speech detection performance, particularly in capturing subtle contextual cues, and a lack of advanced data augmentation techniques to address class imbalance.

References

Rahul Aralikatte, Miryam De Lhoneux, Anoop Kunchukuttan, and Anders Søgaard. 2021. Itihasa: A large-scale corpus for sanskrit to english translation. In *Proceedings of the 8th Workshop on Asian Translation (WAT2021)*, pages 191–197.

Abhishek Chopra, Deepak Kumar Sharma, Aashna Jha, and Uttam Ghosh. 2023. A framework for online hate speech detection on code-mixed hindi-english text and hindi text in devanagari. *ACM Transactions on Asian and Low-Resource Language Information Processing*, 22(5):1–21.

Alexis Conneau, Kartikay Khandelwal, Naman Goyal, Vishrav Chaudhary, Guillaume Wenzek, Francisco Guzmán, Edouard Grave, Myle Ott, Luke Zettlemoyer, and Veselin Stoyanov. 2020. Unsupervised cross-lingual representation learning at scale. In *Proceedings of the 58th Annual Meeting of the Association for Computational Linguistics*, pages 8440–8451, Online. Association for Computational Linguistics.

Raj Dabre, Himani Shrotriya, Anoop Kunchukuttan, Ratish Puduppully, Mitesh Khapra, and Pratyush Kumar. 2022. Indicbart: A pre-trained model for indic natural language generation. In *Findings of the Association for Computational Linguistics: ACL 2022*. Association for Computational Linguistics.

Flor Miriam Plaza del Arco, María Dolores Molina-González, L. Alfonso Ureña-López, and María Teresa Martín-Valdivia. 2021. Comparing pre-trained language models for spanish hate speech detection. *Expert Syst. Appl.*, 166:114120.

Rong-En Fan, Kai-Wei Chang, Cho-Jui Hsieh, Xiang-Rui Wang, and Chih-Jen Lin. 2008. Liblinear: A library for large linear classification. 9:1871–1874.

Paula Fortuna and Sérgio Nunes. 2018. A survey on automatic detection of hate speech in text. *ACM Comput. Surv.*, 51(4).

Chayan Halder, Kishore Thakur, Santanu Phadikar, and Kaushik Roy. 2015. Writer identification from handwritten devanagari script. In *Information Systems Design and Intelligent Applications: Proceedings of Second International Conference INDIA 2015, Volume 2*, pages 497–505. Springer.

Farhan Ahmad Jafri, Kritesh Rauniyar, Surendrabikram Thapa, Mohammad Aman Siddiqui, Matloob Khushi, and Usman Naseem. 2024. Chunav: Analyzing hindi hate speech and targeted groups in indian election discourse. *ACM Transactions on Asian and Low-Resource Language Information Processing*.

Farhan Ahmad Jafri, Mohammad Aman Siddiqui, Surendrabikram Thapa, Kritesh Rauniyar, Usman Naseem, and Imran Razzak. 2023. Uncovering political hate speech during indian election campaign: A new low-resource dataset and baselines.

R Jayadevan, Satish R Kolhe, Pradeep M Patil, and Umapada Pal. 2011. Offline recognition of devanagari script: a survey. *IEEE Transactions on Systems, Man, and Cybernetics, Part C (Applications and Reviews)*, 41(6):782–796.

Vikas Kumar Jha, Hrudya P, Vinu P N, Vishnu Vijayan, and Prabaharan P. 2020. Dhot-repository and classification of offensive tweets in the hindi language. *Procedia Computer Science*, 171:2324–2333. Third International Conference on Computing and Network Communications (CoCoNet'19).

Gopal Datt Joshi, Saurabh Garg, and Jayanthi Sivaswamy. 2006. Script identification from indian documents. In *Document Analysis Systems VII: 7th International Workshop, DAS 2006, Nelson, New Zealand, February 13-15, 2006. Proceedings 7*, pages 255–267. Springer.

Simran Khanuja, Diksha Bansal, Sarvesh Mehtani, Savya Khosla, Atreyee Dey, Balaji Gopalan, Dilip Kumar Margam, Pooja Aggarwal, Rajiv Teja Nagipogu, Shachi Dave, Shruti Gupta, Subhash Chandra Bose Gali, Vishnu Subramanian, and Partha Pratim Talukdar. 2021. Muril: Multilingual representations for indian languages. *ArXiv*, abs/2103.10730.

Atharva Kulkarni, Meet Mandhane, Manali Likhitkar, Gayatri Kshirsagar, and Raviraj Joshi. 2021. L3cubemahasent: A marathi tweet-based sentiment analysis dataset. In *Proceedings of the Eleventh Workshop on Computational Approaches to Subjectivity, Sentiment and Social Media Analysis*, pages 213–220.

Shailendra KumarShrivastava and Pratibha Chaurasia. 2012. Handwritten devanagari lipi using support vector machine. *International Journal of Computer Applications*, 43:20–25.

Alexandre Magueresse, Vincent Carles, and Evan Heetderks. 2020. Low-resource languages: A review of past work and future challenges. *ArXiv*, abs/2006.07264.

Arpan Nandi, Kamal Sarkar, Arjun Mallick, and Arkadeep De. 2024. A survey of hate speech detection in indian languages. *Social Network Analysis and Mining*, 14(1):70.

Atul Kr Ojha. 2019. English-bhojpuri smt system: Insights from the karaka model. *arXiv preprint arXiv:1905.02239*.

Ahmed Omar, Tarek M. Mahmoud, and Tarek Abd-El-Hafeez. 2020. Comparative performance of machine learning and deep learning algorithms for arabic hate speech detection in osns. In *Proceedings of the International Conference on Artificial Intelligence and Computer Vision (AICV2020)*, pages 247–257, Cham. Springer International Publishing.

Anil Singh Parihar, Surendrabikram Thapa, and Sushruti Mishra. 2021. Hate speech detection using natural language processing: Applications and challenges. In *2021 5th International Conference on Trends in Electronics and Informatics (ICOEI)*, pages 1302–1308. IEEE.

María Antonia Paz, Julio Montero-Díaz, and Alicia Moreno-Delgado. 2020. Hate speech: A systematized review. *Sage Open*, 10(4):2158244020973022.

Telmo Pires, Eva Schlinger, and Dan Garrette. 2019. How multilingual is multilingual BERT? In *Proceedings of the 57th Annual Meeting of the Association for Computational Linguistics*, pages 4996–5001, Florence, Italy. Association for Computational Linguistics.

Kritesh Rauniyar, Sweta Poudel, Shuvam Shiwakoti, Surendrabikram Thapa, Junaid Rashid, Jungeun Kim, Muhammad Imran, and Usman Naseem. 2023. Multi-aspect annotation and analysis of nepali tweets on anti-establishment election discourse. *IEEE Access*.

Kengatharaiyer Sarveswaran, Bal Krishna Bal, Surendrabikram Thapa, Ashwini Vaidya, and Sana Shams. 2025. A brief overview of the first workshop on challenges in processing south asian languages (chipsal). In *Proceedings of the First Workshop on Challenges in Processing South Asian Languages (CHiPSAL)*.

Arushi Sharma, Anubha Kabra, and Minni Jain. 2022. Ceasing hate with moh: Hate speech detection in hindi–english code-switched language. *Information Processing & Management*, 59(1):102760.

Surendrabikram Thapa, Kritesh Rauniyar, Farhan Ahmad Jafri, Surabhi Adhikari, Kengatharaiyer Sarveswaran, Bal Krishna Bal, Hariram Veeramani, and Usman Naseem. 2025. Natural language understanding of devanagari script languages: Language identification, hate speech and its target detection. In *Proceedings of the First Workshop on Challenges in Processing South Asian Languages (CHiPSAL)*.

Surendrabikram Thapa, Kritesh Rauniyar, Shuvam Shiwakoti, Sweta Poudel, Usman Naseem, and Mehwish Nasim. 2023. Nehate: Large-scale annotated data shedding light on hate speech in nepali local election discourse. In *ECAI 2023*, pages 2346–2353. IOS Press.

A Appendix

We have performed both quantitative and qualitative error analysis in order to obtain in-depth insights into the performance of the proposed model.

Quantitative Analysis: The best performing models were used to conduct a quantitative error analysis, utilizing confusion matrices shown in Figure A.1 and Figure A.2 for subtasks A and C, respectively.

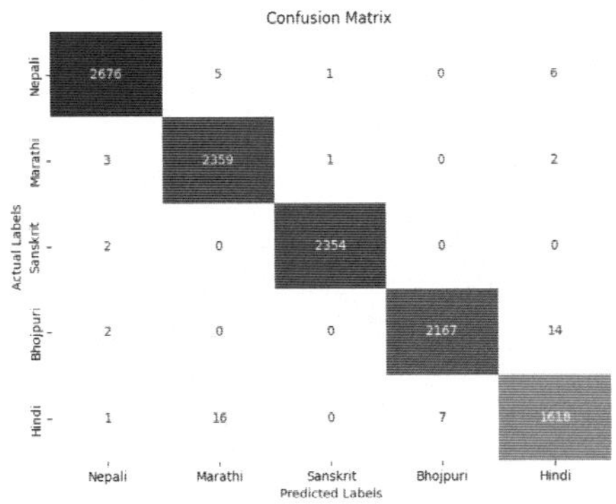

Figure A.1: Confusion matrix of the proposed model (CNN+BiLSTM) for subtask A

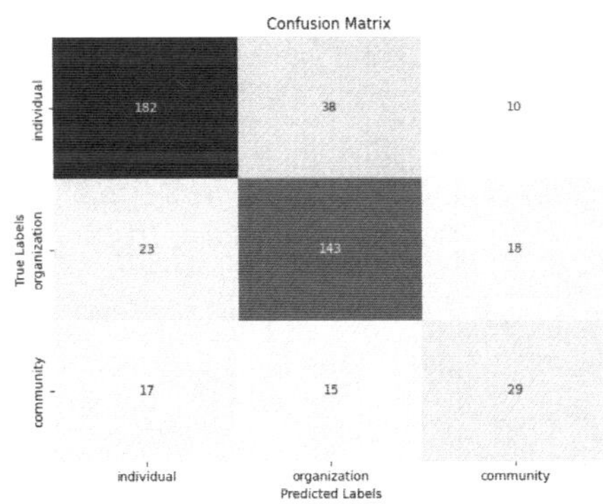

Figure A.2: Confusion matrix of the proposed model (finetuned MuRIL) for subtask C

The proposed hybrid CNN with BiLSTM model for subtask A perfectly classified 11,174 instances among 11,234 samples with very negligible misclassifications in Nepali and Sanskrit. It performed badly in distinguishing similar languages by mislabeling 16 Hindi samples as Marathi and 7 as Bhojpuri. Additionally, the fine-tuned MuRIL model performed well on target hate speech detection, wherein it rightly classified 182 out of 230 instances of *Individual* and 143 out of 184 instances of *Organization*. However, it misclassified 23 *Organization* and 38 *Individual* instances. The more difficult class was *Community* with only 61 instances; only 29 were classified correctly, mostly confused with *Individual* or *Organization*. This may happen due to the difficulty in distinguishing targets, arising from linguistic overlap in community-targeted speech and the subtlety of contextual cues.

Qualitative Analysis: Figure A.3 portrays predicted outputs for sample inputs of the proposed model for the Devanagari script identification task. It correctly predicted the text samples 1, 2, and 3, but incorrectly predicted text sample 4 as Hindi instead of Nepali. Figure A.4 represents the qualitative analysis of the proposed MuRIL-BERT model on target hate speech detection. Our proposed model correctly predicted text samples 1 and 3 but wrongly predicted samples 2 and 4. These are probably related to class imbalance, considering the *Community* class has fewer instances, 284, compared to the rest of the classes.

Sample Text	Actual Label	Predicted Label
Sample 1: निर्वाचन परिणाम ले बल्ल बुद्धि आयो?	Nepali	Nepali
Sample 2: ततो गजगतो रा जा भगदत्तः प्रतापवान्। अर्जुनं शरवर्षेण वारयामास संयुगे॥ अर्जुनस्तु ततो नागमायान्तं र जतोपमैः। विमलैरायसैस्तीक्ष्णै रविध्यत महारणे॥	Sanskrit	Sanskrit
Sample 3: अबहीं चुनाव में हार के दरद कमो ना भइल र हे कि मोदी के राजनीति के तिरशूल आ के करेजा में धँसि गइल	Bhojpuri	Bhojpuri
Sample 4: कांग्रेस भर्ती व्या पार।	Nepali	Hindi

Figure A.3: Few examples of predicted outputs by the proposed method (CNN + BiLSTM) for subtask A

Sample Text	Actual Label	Predicted Label
Sample 1: कस्ता पार्टी सभा पति हुन्, हँसियाहथौडामा भा ेट नहाले कारबाही रे I\n# मारेके	Individual	Individual
Sample 2: अहिलेको चुनाव को परिणाम हेर्दा ,\nनेपाल वि कास न हुनुमा जति भ्रष्ट नेता हरु र भ्रष्ट कर्मचारीहरु हाथ छ,\n त्यो भन्दा बढी हाथ नेपा ली जनताहरुको देखिन्छ I\n 😨😨😨😨	Individual	Community
Sample 3: @nirab_argum ent @Gk1402Chitwan @ Chitwoney यस्तो बेला पनि भरतपुरमा एमालेले जीतेन भ ने, एमाले पार्टी खारौज गर्दै हु न्छ 😁😆	Organization	Organization
Sample 4: @madhuBTM2 76 पुर्व सचीवको एमाले संग कुनै न कुनै प्रतिशोध छ । त्य सैले एमाले प्रती उहाँ बिष वम न गरिरहनु हुन्छ ।	Individual	Organization

Figure A.4: Few examples of predicted outputs by the proposed method MuRIL-BERT for subtask C

CUET_HateShield@NLU of Devanagari Script Languages 2025: Transformer-Based Hate Speech Detection in Devanagari Script Languages

Sumaiya Rahman Aodhora, Shawly Ahsan and Mohammed Moshiul Hoque
Department of Computer Science and Engineering
Chittagong University of Engineering and Technology
{u1804127, u1704057}@student.cuet.ac.bd, moshiul_240@cuet.ac.bd

Abstract

Social networks have become essential platforms for information exchange and free expression. However, their open nature also facilitates the spread of harmful content, such as hate speech, cyberbullying, and offensive language, which pose significant risks to social well-being. This study focuses on developing an automated system to detect hate speech in Devanagari script languages, enabling efficient moderation and timely intervention. Our approach leverages a fine-tuned transformer model for classifying offensive content. We experimented with various machine learning (ML) techniques, including Logistic Regression (LR), Support Vector Machines (SVM), and Random Forest (RF), as well as deep learning (DL) architectures such as CNN, BiLSTM, and CNN-BiLSTM. Additionally, we evaluated transformer-based models, including IndicBERT, m-BERT, MuRIL, Indic-SBERT, and XLM-R. Among these, the fine-tuned XLM-R model delivered the best performance, achieving a macro f_1-score of 0.74, demonstrating its effectiveness in detecting hate speech in Devanagari script languages. However, the model submitted for the shared task achieved a macro f_1-score of 0.73, ranking 13th in the subtask.

1 Introduction

In an increasingly interconnected and digital age, the pervasive impact of communication through social media, online forums, and various digital platforms cannot be overstated. Although these platforms give individuals a voice, they expose them to a spectrum of content, including hate speech. Hate speech, defined as the use of language that disparages or discriminates against individuals or groups based on attributes such as race, ethnicity, religion, gender, politics, or sexual orientation, emerges as a compelling social challenge that requires meticulous attention (Raja Chakravarthi et al., 2021; Parihar et al., 2021). The challenge of manually identifying offensive texts on a large scale emphasizes the urgent need for an automated system to detect and manage hate speech efficiently, enabling faster and more accurate responses to harmful content (Aljarah et al., 2021). The challenge of identifying offensive language has been addressed through various approaches, including the detection of cyberbullying, aggression, toxicity, and abusive language (Sharif et al., 2021; Sharif and Hoque, 2021). However, there is a pressing need for more targeted efforts to specifically address hate speech, especially within diverse linguistic contexts (Singh and Thakur, 2024).

In recent years, significant research efforts have focused on detecting hate and offensive content in high-resource languages like English, Spanish, and Arabic. These benefit from abundant linguistic resources, extensive datasets, and advanced tools (Kumar and Singh, 2022; Omar et al., 2020). However, effectively tackling this issue in low-resource languages remains a significant challenge. To address this challenge, a shared task (Thapa et al., 2025; Sarveswaran et al., 2025) was organized to detect hate speech in the Devanagari script, with a specific focus on monolingual sentences in Nepali and Hindi (Jafri et al., 2024; Thapa et al., 2023). The objective was to determine whether a given sentence contains hate speech, highlighting the importance of effective cross-linguistic detection within the Devanagari script (Jafri et al., 2023; Rauniyar et al., 2023). As participants in this shared task, we contributed to developing and evaluating models tailored for this purpose. The primary contributions of our work are summarized as follows:

- We evaluated various models for hate speech detection, encompassing ML, DL, and transformer-based frameworks, with performance improvements achieved through hyperparameter optimization.
- We conducted a comprehensive comparison of various models, followed by an in-depth

Proceedings of the First Workshop on Challenges in Processing South Asian Languages (CHiPSAL 2025), pages 260–266
January 19, 2025.

performance analysis, which led to the proposal of an optimal system for effective hate speech detection.

2 Related Work

In the rapidly advancing field of hate speech detection, researchers have experimented with a wide range of approaches, each playing a role in the ongoing improvement and sophistication of detection models (Parihar et al., 2021). Hate speech detection in Devanagari-script languages, such as Hindi and Nepali, is a technical challenge influenced by social, cultural, and linguistic factors (Parihar et al., 2021). The interpretation of hate speech can vary significantly based on cultural norms, regional dialects, and the social context in which language is used. For instance, certain offensive expressions in one community may not be perceived as such in another (Singh and Thakur, 2024; Thapa et al., 2025). Additionally, the widespread use of code-mixing and social media-specific slang further complicates detecting hate speech. As the field evolved, there was a clear shift from traditional ML techniques to DL, as demonstrated by Omar et al. (2020) in their work on Arabic hate speech detection. They utilized Recurrent Neural Networks (RNN) to achieve a remarkable 98.7% accuracy, outperforming Convolutional Neural Networks (CNN). Sharif and Hoque (2021) employed a weighted ensemble approach combining m-BERT, Distil-BERT, and Bangla-BERT, showcasing the flexibility of these models in capturing complex linguistic variations, especially in Bengali aggressive text datasets.

Shukla et al. (2022) developed a BERT-CNN model for detecting hate speech in low-resource Hindi text, achieving an f_1-score of 0.84. Sharif et al. (2021) tackled the challenge of detecting offensive content in code-mixed social media data by leveraging powerful transformer models such as XLM-R, m-BERT, and Indic-BERT for languages like Tamil, Kannada, and Malayalam. Rauniyar et al. (2023) introduced the NAET dataset, consisting of 4,445 Nepali tweets focusing on political discourse. Their study found that NepNewsBERT outperformed traditional models, achieving an f_1-score of 0.64 in detecting hate speech. Jafri et al. (2024) developed the CHUNAV dataset, which contains Hindi election tweets for hate speech detection and target identification in low-resource languages. They also developed benchmark models, including the Hard Ensemble of BERTs (HEB), demonstrating effective performance with an f_1-score of 0.959.

3 Task and Dataset Description

In this shared task[1], a dataset (Thapa et al., 2025) in Devanagari script containing monolingual Nepali and Hindi sentences was provided to facilitate hate speech detection (Jafri et al., 2024; Thapa et al., 2023). The dataset, designed for binary classification tasks, includes a diverse collection of social media posts and comments, categorized as either hate or non-hate. Participants were provided training, validation, and test datasets to aid model development, validation, and performance evaluation. The training dataset consists of 19,019 samples, with 16,805 non-hate instances and 2,214 hate instances, highlighting a significant class imbalance. A detailed breakdown of additional insights and statistics of the dataset is provided in Table 1.

Classes	Train	Valid	Test	W_T	U_T
Non-Hate	16805	3602	3601	368180	71654
Hate	2214	474	475	58333	19707
Total	19019	4076	4076	426513	91361

Table 1: Class-wise distribution of training, validation, and test sets, where W_T denotes total words and U_T denotes total unique words in the training set

4 Methodology

Figure 1 provides a diagrammatic representation of the approach. We employed various ML and DL techniques to develop the baseline models. Furthermore, we employed five pre-trained transformer models for hate speech detection, including MuRIL, XLM-R, m-BERT, Indic-BERT, and Indic-SBERT.

4.1 Preprocessing

The dataset sourced from social media is characterized by a substantial presence of irrelevant content, including code-mixed elements. Throughout the preprocessing process, we diligently eliminated noise, which comprised hyperlinks, emojis, punctuation, alphanumeric characters, and special symbols (like slashes, brackets, and ampersands) to ensure a higher data quality.

[1] https://codalab.lisn.upsaclay.fr/competitions/20000

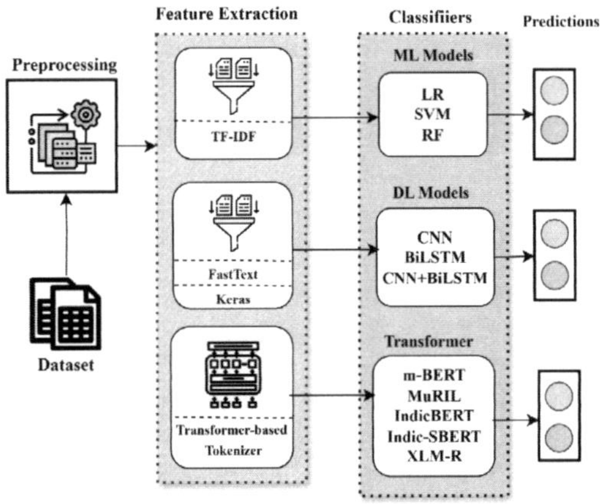

Figure 1: An abstract framework for hate speech detection

4.1.1 Feature Extraction

We applied the TF-IDF technique to extract unigram features for the ML models. TF-IDF assigns weights to words based on their frequency within a document and across the corpus, aiding in identifying significant words that distinguish documents. We employed Keras[2] and pre-trained FastText embeddings for the DL models. FastText embeddings provide 300-dimensional word vectors incorporating subword information through n-grams (Bojanowski et al., 2017; Joulin et al., 2016). Each transformer model utilized its specific tokenizer, obtained from the HuggingFace[3] library, to appropriately tokenize and pad the texts.

4.2 ML Models

In the implementation of LR, the '*lbfgs*' solver was employed alongside balanced class weights and *L2* regularization, with the *C* parameter fine-tuned to mitigate overfitting. The SVM model utilized a *RBF* kernel, with the gamma parameter set to '*scale*' to ensure optimal feature responsiveness. For the RF model, the number of estimators ('*n_estimators*') was configured to 100.

4.3 DL Models

To leverage the effectiveness of DL methods for sequential data analysis, we implemented three approaches: CNN (LeCun et al., 2015), BiLSTM (Hochreiter and Schmidhuber, 1997), and CNN+BiLSTM. The CNN model uses an embedding layer with 256-dimensional embedding, followed by a 1D convolutional layer with 128 filters and a kernel size of 5, concluding with a sigmoid output for binary classification. The BiLSTM model uses an embedding layer with a 300-dimensional embedding size and a maximum sequence length of 100. It then processes the input text through two bidirectional LSTM layers with 64 and 32 units, followed by dropout layers with a rate of 0.5. In the CNN+BiLSTM model, a CNN layer with 128 filters and max-pooling is applied, followed by a 200-cell BiLSTM layer with a dropout rate of 0.2, culminating in final predictions through a sigmoid layer. The hyperparameters for the DL models are shown in Table 2.

Hyperparameters	CNN	BiLSTM	CNN+BiLSTM
Optimizer	Adam	Adam	Adam
Batch Size	32	32	32
Neurons in Dense Layer	64	128	256
Embedding Dimension	256	300	256
Epochs	20	30	30
MaxLen	300	300	300
Dropout Rate	0.2	0.5	0.5
Learning Rate	$1e^{-4}$	$1e^{-3}$	$1e^{-3}$

Table 2: Hyperparameters for DL models

4.4 Transformer Models

We fine-tuned five pre-trained transformer models (MuRIL, XLM-R, m-BERT, Indic-SBERT, and IndicBERT) for hate speech detection in Devanagari script datasets. XLM-R, designed for low-resource languages, uses self-supervised training (Conneau, 2019). Multilingual BERT (m-BERT) was pre-trained on 104 languages (Devlin, 2018), while IndicBERT, covering 12 Indian languages, was trained on a large corpus (Kakwani et al., 2020). Indic-SBERT, a variant of Sentence-BERT, was fine-tuned on a synthetic corpus for Indian languages (Deode et al., 2023). MuRIL, based on BERT, was pre-trained in 17 Indian languages, including transliterated forms and Devanagari scripts (Khanuja et al., 2021). All the transformer models were sourced from the Hugging Face transformer library and fine-tuned on the given dataset using the Ktrain package (Maiya, 2022). The hyperparameters for the transformer-based models are presented in Table 3.

5 Results and Analysis

This section presents a detailed analysis of the effectiveness of various models in detecting hate speech in Devanagari-script languages. The performance of the models is evaluated using the macro

[2]https://keras.io/

[3]https://huggingface.co/

Hyperparameter	m-BERT	MuRIL	IB	ISB	XLM-R
Learning Rate	$2e^{-5}$	$1e^{-5}$	$1e^{-5}$	$1e^{-5}$	$1e^{-5}$
Batch Size	32	32	16	16	32
MaxLen	100	100	100	100	100
Dropout	0.1	0.1	0.1	0.1	0.1
Epochs	10	10	15	15	10
Optimizer	AdamW	AdamW	AdamW	AdamW	AdamW

Table 3: Fine-tuned hyperparameters of the transformer-based models, where IB and ISB represent IndicBERT and Indic-SBERT, respectively.

f_1-score, offering a robust measure of classification accuracy across all classes. Table 4 demonstrates the performance of the employed models.

Approaches	Classifiers	P	R	F1
ML	LR	0.55	0.54	0.54
	SVM	0.53	0.52	0.52
	RF	0.53	0.51	0.51
DL	CNN (FastText)	0.50	0.51	0.50
	BiLSTM (FastText)	0.54	0.52	0.56
	CNN+BiLSTM (FastText)	0.56	0.55	0.55
	CNN (Keras)	0.60	0.59	0.59
	BiLSTM (Keras)	0.62	0.60	0.61
	CNN+BiLSTM (Keras)	0.65	0.62	0.62
Transformer	m-BERT	0.67	0.70	0.69
	MuRIL	0.72	0.73	0.73
	IndicBERT	0.62	0.68	0.64
	Indic-SBERT	0.71	0.75	0.73
	XLM-R	**0.72**	**0.76**	**0.74**

Table 4: Performance of the employed models, where P, R, and F1 denote macro precision, macro recall, and macro f_1-score, respectively

Within the ML category, the LR, SVM, and RF classifiers show competitive performance across precision, recall, and F1 scores, with LR achieving the highest F1 score of 0.54. Those incorporating Keras embeddings for DL models consistently surpass those with FastText embeddings. The top-performing FastText-based model, BiLSTM, reached an F1 score of 0.56. In comparison, the hybrid CNN+BiLSTM model attained an F1 score of 0.62 when using Keras word embeddings. The observed F1 score differences between Keras and FastText embeddings may result from multiple factors. Keras embeddings likely provide more refined contextual representations, capturing linguistic and syntactic patterns that FastText may miss.

In contrast, transformer-based models, especially XLM-R, outperformed both ML and DL models, achieving the highest F1 score of 0.74. MuRIL and Indic-SBERT also performed well, with F1 scores of 0.73. XLM-R's strong performance could be due to its multilingual pretraining, which helps it effectively handle Nepali and Hindi, including the Devanagari script. Moreover, the cross-lingual pretraining of the XLM-R model allowed it to excel despite challenges in the dataset, demonstrating its ability to capture contextual nuances and handle linguistic diversity effectively.

5.1 Classwise Performance

To gain deeper insights, we analyze the best-performing model's classwise performance (XLM-R) as shown in Figure 2. The classification report reveals that the non-hate class has higher precision (0.95) and F1-score (0.93), indicating better performance in identifying non-hate instances. In contrast, the hate class shows a higher recall (0.61), reflecting the ability of the model to accurately identify more true hate instances, though with lower precision (0.49). The comparatively poorer performance in the hate class could be due to the class imbalance.

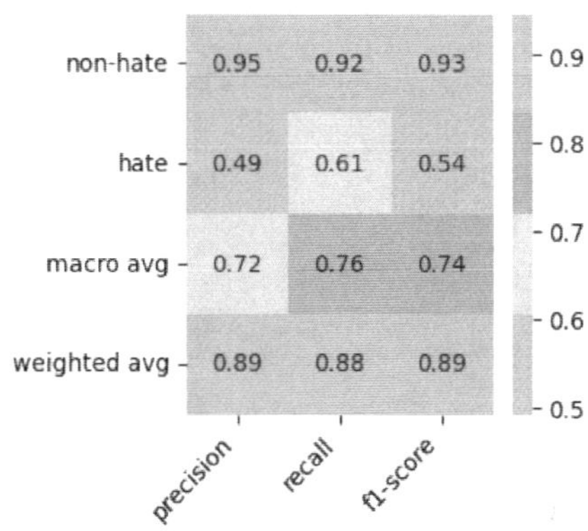

Figure 2: Classwise performance of the best performing model (XLM-R) on the test set.

5.2 Error Analysis

We conducted a comprehensive error analysis using quantitative and qualitative approaches to understand better the performance of the highest-performing model (XLM-R).

5.2.1 Quantitative Analysis

We conducted a quantitative error analysis of the best-performing model (XLM-R) using a confusion matrix (Figure 3). Out of 4,076 samples, 3,592 instances were correctly classified, comprising 3,303 non-hate speech and 289 hate speech samples. However, 484 instances were misclassified, with 186 incorrectly predicted as non-hate and 298 as hate. The higher misclassification rate for hate speech (39.16%) could be attributed to class imbalance, as hate speech samples are significantly fewer. This imbalance hampers the ability

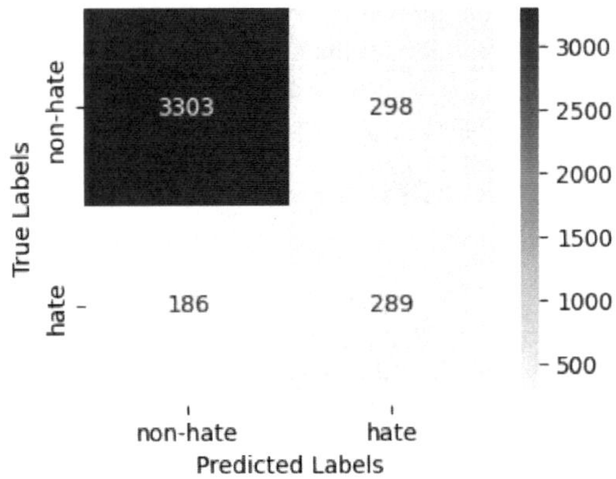

Figure 3: Confusion matrix of the best performing model (XLM-R)

Sample Text	Actual	Predicted
प्रिय कांग्रेसियों, कुमार विश्वास ने इशारों में राहुल गांधी जी को "समलैंगिक" तक कहा है!सोनिया जी के हिंदी उच्चारण का मज़ाक उड़ाया है! उसकी बातों पर सोंच समझकर प्रतिक्रिया दो! (Dear Congressmen, Kumar Vishwas has even called Rahul Gandhi a "gay" in gestures! Made fun of Sonia ji's Hindi pronunciation! Respond thoughtfully to his words!)	non-hate	non-hate
उत्तर प्रदेश में आज छठवें चरण में 10 जनपदों (अम्बेडकरनगर, बलरामपुर, सिद्धार्थनगर, बस्ती, संतकबीर नगर, महराजगंज, गोरखपुर, कुशीनगर, देवरिया, बलिया) की 57 विधानसभा सीटों पर चुनाव चल रहा है। (Today in the sixth phase in Uttar Pradesh, elections are going on for 57 assembly seats in 10 districts (Ambedkarnagar, Balrampur, Siddharthnagar, Basti, Sant Kabir Nagar, Maharajganj, Gorakhpur, Kushinagar, Deoria, Ballia))	non-hate	non-hate
यूक्रेन और रूस का युद्ध समाप्त हो गया क्या 😢😟 आज तो किसी भी चैनल पर युद्ध की कोई खबर नहीं दिख रही 😳 (Has the war between Ukraine and Russia ended? Today there is no news of war on any channel.)	hate	non-hate
26 फरवरी दिन शनिवार को असदुद्दीन् ओवैसी साहब औरपीस पार्टी के राष्ट्रीय अध्यक्ष डॉ अय्यूब साहब (उतरौला) शहर के बरदही बाज़ार में एक विशाल जनसभा को संबोधित करेंगे, इन-शा-अल्लाह उतरौला विधानसभा हम जीत रहे हैं । (On Saturday, 26th February, Asaduddin Owaisi Saheb and National President of Peace Party, Dr. Ayyub Saheb (Utraula) will address a huge public meeting at Bardahi Bazaar of the city, In-Sha-Allah we are winning Utraula assembly.)	hate	non-hate

Table 5: Sample predictions generated by the best-performing model (XLM-R)

of the model to identify hate speech, resulting in increased misclassification accurately.

5.2.2 Qualitative Analysis

Table 5 presents some predicted samples from the best-performing model on the test dataset. Samples 1 and 2 are correctly classified, while samples 3 and 4 are misclassified as non-hate speech, reflecting the model's performance limitations. These misclassifications may result from dataset imbalance, which biases the model toward the majority class, and the presence of code-mixed text complicates language understanding. These challenges underscore the importance of qualitative analysis in interpreting model behavior and identifying areas for improvement.

6 Conclusion

This work contributed to hate speech detection in Devanagari-script languages by systematically evaluating various machine learning (ML), deep learning (DL), and transformer-based models. Among these, the fine-tuned XLM-R model demonstrated the highest performance, achieving a macro f_1-score of 0.74, underscoring the model's capability in effectively classifying offensive content. However, the model exhibited lower performance for the hate speech class, primarily due to class imbalance. Future work will address this issue by employing resampling and data augmentation methods, such as back-translation, to enhance the dataset. Additionally, advanced models, including integrating large language models (LLMs), will be explored to improve performance. Another critical avenue for future research involves developing techniques to effectively handle code-mixed data, particularly Hinglish, to enhance the model's robustness and accuracy.

Limitations

The current approach leverages pre-trained transformer-based models, which, while effective, may need to be revised when the context of the data deviates significantly from the training data. Additionally, due to the lack of specialized mechanisms for handling such linguistic variations, the model's performance could be improved using code-mixed data, such as Hinglish, commonly encountered in Devanagari-script languages. Moreover, the dataset used in this task needed to be more balanced, with certain classes underrepresented. This likely impacted the model's ability to accurately classify instances from these underrepresented classes. Addressing these challenges will be crucial in improving the robustness and accuracy of the model in future work.

References

Ibrahim Aljarah, Maria Habib, Neveen Hijazi, Hossam Faris, Raneem Qaddoura, Bassam Hammo, Mohammad Abushariah, and Mohammad Alfawareh. 2021. Intelligent detection of hate speech in arabic social network: A machine learning approach. *Journal of information science*, 47(4):483–501.

Piotr Bojanowski, Edouard Grave, Armand Joulin, and Tomas Mikolov. 2017. Enriching word vectors with subword information. *Transactions of the association for computational linguistics*, 5:135–146.

A Conneau. 2019. Unsupervised cross-lingual representation learning at scale. *arXiv preprint arXiv:1911.02116*.

Samruddhi Deode, Janhavi Gadre, Aditi Kajale, Ananya Joshi, and Raviraj Joshi. 2023. L3cube-indicsbert: A simple approach for learning cross-lingual sentence representations using multilingual bert. *arXiv preprint arXiv:2304.11434*.

Jacob Devlin. 2018. Bert: Pre-training of deep bidirectional transformers for language understanding. *arXiv preprint arXiv:1810.04805*.

Sepp Hochreiter and Jürgen Schmidhuber. 1997. Long short-term memory. *Neural computation*, 9(8):1735–1780.

Farhan Ahmad Jafri, Kritesh Rauniyar, Surendrabikram Thapa, Mohammad Aman Siddiqui, Matloob Khushi, and Usman Naseem. 2024. Chunav: Analyzing hindi hate speech and targeted groups in indian election discourse. *ACM Transactions on Asian and Low-Resource Language Information Processing*.

Farhan Ahmad Jafri, Mohammad Aman Siddiqui, Surendrabikram Thapa, Kritesh Rauniyar, Usman Naseem, and Imran Razzak. 2023. Uncovering political hate speech during indian election campaign: A new low-resource dataset and baselines. *arXiv preprint arXiv:2306.14764*.

Armand Joulin, Edouard Grave, Piotr Bojanowski, Matthijs Douze, Hérve Jégou, and Tomas Mikolov. 2016. Fasttext. zip: Compressing text classification models. *arXiv preprint arXiv:1612.03651*.

Divyanshu Kakwani, Anoop Kunchukuttan, Satish Golla, NC Gokul, Avik Bhattacharyya, Mitesh M Khapra, and Pratyush Kumar. 2020. Indicnlpsuite: Monolingual corpora, evaluation benchmarks and pre-trained multilingual language models for indian languages. In *Findings of the Association for Computational Linguistics: EMNLP 2020*, pages 4948–4961.

Simran Khanuja, Diksha Bansal, Sarvesh Mehtani, Savya Khosla, Atreyee Dey, Balaji Gopalan, Dilip Kumar Margam, Pooja Aggarwal, Rajiv Teja Nagipogu, Shachi Dave, et al. 2021. Muril: Multilingual representations for indian languages. *arXiv preprint arXiv:2103.10730*.

Gunjan Kumar and Jyoti Prakash Singh. 2022. Hate speech and offensive content identification in english and indo-aryan languages using machine learning models. In *FIRE (Working Notes)*, pages 542–551.

Yann LeCun, Yoshua Bengio, and Geoffrey Hinton. 2015. Deep learning. *nature*, 521(7553):436–444.

Arun S Maiya. 2022. ktrain: A low-code library for augmented machine learning. *Journal of Machine Learning Research*, 23(158):1–6.

Ahmed Omar, Tarek M Mahmoud, and Tarek Abd-El-Hafeez. 2020. Comparative performance of machine learning and deep learning algorithms for arabic hate speech detection in osns. In *Proceedings of the International Conference on Artificial Intelligence and Computer Vision (AICV2020)*, pages 247–257. Springer.

Anil Singh Parihar, Surendrabikram Thapa, and Sushruti Mishra. 2021. Hate speech detection using natural language processing: Applications and challenges. In *2021 5th International Conference on Trends in Electronics and Informatics (ICOEI)*, pages 1302–1308. IEEE.

Bharathi Raja Chakravarthi, Dhivya Chinnappa, Ruba Priyadharshini, Anand Kumar Madasamy, Sangeetha Sivanesan, Subalalitha Chinnaudayar Navaneethakrishnan, Sajeetha Thavareesan, Dhanalakshmi Vadivel, Rahul Ponnusamy, and Prasanna Kumar Kumaresan. 2021. Developing successful shared tasks on offensive language identification for dravidian languages. *arXiv e-prints*, pages arXiv–2111.

Kritesh Rauniyar, Sweta Poudel, Shuvam Shiwakoti, Surendrabikram Thapa, Junaid Rashid, Jungeun Kim, Muhammad Imran, and Usman Naseem. 2023. Multi-aspect annotation and analysis of nepali tweets on anti-establishment election discourse. *IEEE Access*.

Kengatharaiyer Sarveswaran, Bal Krishna Bal, Surendrabikram Thapa, Ashwini Vaidya, and Sana Shams. 2025. A brief overview of the first workshop on challenges in processing south asian languages (chipsal). In *Proceedings of the First Workshop on Challenges in Processing South Asian Languages (CHiPSAL)*.

Omar Sharif and Mohammed Moshiul Hoque. 2021. Identification and classification of textual aggression in social media: Resource creation and evaluation. In *International Workshop on Combating On line Hostile Posts in Regional Languages dur ing Emergency Situation*, pages 9–20. Springer.

Omar Sharif, Eftekhar Hossain, and Mohammed Moshiul Hoque. 2021. Nlp-cuet@ dravidianlangtech-eacl2021: Offensive language detection from multilingual code-mixed text using transformers. *arXiv preprint arXiv:2103.00455*.

Shubham Shukla, Sushama Nagpal, and Sangeeta Sabharwal. 2022. Hate speech detection in hindi language using bert and convolution neural network. In *2022 International Conference on Computing, Communication, and Intelligent Systems (ICCCIS)*, pages 642–647. IEEE.

Akshay Singh and Rahul Thakur. 2024. Generalizable multilingual hate speech detection on low resource indian languages using fair selection in federated learning. In *Proceedings of the 2024 Conference of the North American Chapter of the Association for Computational Linguistics: Human Language Technologies (Volume 1: Long Papers)*, pages 7204–7214.

Surendrabikram Thapa, Kritesh Rauniyar, Farhan Ahmad Jafri, Surabhi Adhikari, Kengatharaiyer Sarveswaran, Bal Krishna Bal, Hariram Veeramani, and Usman Naseem. 2025. Natural language understanding of devanagari script languages: Language identification, hate speech and its target detection. In *Proceedings of the First Workshop on Challenges in Processing South Asian Languages (CHiPSAL)*.

Surendrabikram Thapa, Kritesh Rauniyar, Shuvam Shiwakoti, Sweta Poudel, Usman Naseem, and Mehwish Nasim. 2023. Nehate: Large-scale annotated data shedding light on hate speech in nepali local election discourse. In *ECAI 2023*, pages 2346–2353. IOS Press.

CUET_INSights@NLU of Devanagari Script Languages: Leveraging Transformer-based Models for Target Identification in Hate Speech

Farjana Alam Tofa, Lorin Tasnim Zeba, Md Osama and Ashim Dey
Department of Computer Science and Engineering
Chittagong University of Engineering & Technology, Chattogram-4349, Bangladesh
{u1904008, u1904043, u1804039}@student.cuet.ac.bd, ashim.cse.cuet@gmail.com

Abstract

Hate speech detection in multilingual content is a challenging problem especially when it comes to understanding the specific targets of hateful expressions. Identifying the targets of hate speech whether directed at individuals, organizations or communities is crucial for effective content moderation and understanding the context. A shared task on hate speech detection in Devanagari Script Languages organized by CHIPSAL@COLING 2025 allowed us to address the challenge of identifying the target of hate speech in the Devanagari Script Language. For this task, we experimented with various machine learning (ML) and deep learning (DL) models including Logistic Regression, Decision Trees, Random Forest, SVM, CNN, LSTM, BiLSTM, and transformer-based models like MiniLM, m-BERT, and Indic-BERT. Our experiments demonstrated that Indic-BERT achieved the highest F1-score of 0.69, ranked 3rd in the shared task. This research contributes to advancing the field of hate speech detection and natural language processing in low-resource languages.

1 Introduction

Hate speech promotes hostility and discrimination toward certain people or groups and creates major challenges in preserving social harmony. Detecting and identifying hate speech is especially complex in multilingual contexts, where harmful messages may target specific groups. This process is important to better understand the intent and impact of harmful language. The "Shared Task on Natural Language Understanding of Devanagari Script Languages" at CHIPSAL@COLING 2025 aimed to address this challenge, particularly through Subtask C which focused on identifying hate speech targets in Devanagari-scripted text. The goal was to classify the targets of hate speech: "individual," "organization," or "community". Their workshop paper (Sarveswaran et al., 2025) offered us an opportunity to engage with these challenges in processing South Asian languages and to advance our work on hate speech detection and target identification in this context. The proposed approach can be used in content moderation systems to help platforms detect and reduce hate speech in different low-resourced languages. It can assist policymakers by providing a reliable method to track and analyze online hate speech.

In our participation, we explored different models to identify hate speech targets and tried to solve this problem with two significant contributions.

- Investigated the effectiveness of several ML, DL, and transformer models for identifying hate speech targets and examining the errors to obtain important insights about the detection procedure.
- In particular, leveraged the transformer-based Indic-BERT model which has proven effective for the particular use case in Devanagari script languages.

This study shows how advanced models like transformers can improve hate speech detection, and target identification supporting better language understanding.

2 Related Work

The difficulty of identifying hate speech and abusive language has prompted numerous research using a range of languages and methodologies. Recent advancements have focused on addressing hate speech in low-resource languages. The CHUNAV dataset offers a valuable resource for analyzing hate speech in Hindi during elections, capturing nuanced socio-political themes (Jafri et al., 2024). Similarly, the IEHate dataset provides insights into political hate speech in Hindi, highlighting the benefits of human and automated meth-

Proceedings of the First Workshop on Challenges in Processing South Asian Languages (CHiPSAL 2025), pages 267–272
January 19, 2025.

ods in this domain (Jafri et al., 2023). For Nepali, NEHATE facilitates hate speech analysis in local election discourse, contributing to inclusive online dialogue (Thapa et al., 2023). NAET introduces anti-establishment discourse in Nepali, covering unique aspects like hate speech to enhance political sentiment analysis (Rauniyar et al., 2023). Additionally, the Karaka model provides foundational resources for Bhojpuri, aiding NLP development in this language (Ojha, 2019). For Marathi, L3CubeMahaSent offers a structured sentiment analysis dataset, filling a gap for Indian languages (Kulkarni et al., 2021). Itihasa, a large-scale Sanskrit translation dataset highlights the complexity of ancient texts and challenges current translation models (Aralikatte et al., 2021). Hate speech research has addressed diverse forms of toxic content including racism, sexism, and religious bias, while also discussing challenges in real-world applications (Parihar et al., 2021). A review of hate speech detection methods revealed inconsistent results and limited dataset reliability (Alkomah and Ma, 2022). CNN, LSTM, and BERT models proved effective for hate speech detection in Hindi and Marathi and simpler architectures also performed competitively when augmented with FastText embeddings (Velankar et al., 2021). The Dravidian shared task for Malayalam showed m-BERT's strong performance. It highlights the transformer model's potential in misinformation detection for low-resource languages (Osama et al., 2024). An evaluation dataset, HateCheckHIn, was developed to address the challenges of multilingual hate speech detection, focusing on error analysis and diagnostic insights, particularly for Hindi (Das et al., 2022). In Tamil, a study focusing on caste and migration-related hate speech found that M-BERT was highly effective. It highlights the model's suitability for handling nuanced social contexts in low-resource settings (Alam et al., 2024).

3 Task and Dataset Description

With the rise of social media, hate speech has become a significant issue often targeting specific groups. This shared task (Thapa et al., 2025) focuses on hate speech detection in languages using the Devanagari script. It identifies the target of hate speech in a given sentence, classifying it as either "individual," "organization," or "community." The dataset for this task consists of hate speech texts in Devanagari script covering languages such as Nepali, Marathi, Sanskrit, Bhojpuri, and Hindi. This dataset is organized to support accurate classification of hate speech targets as outlined below:

Individual: Hate speech aimed at a specific person.

Organization: Hate speech targeting institutions or groups.

Community: Hate speech directed at larger communities.

Here, Table 1 provides the distribution of samples across training, validation, and test sets. The

Classes	Train	Valid	Test
Individual	1,074	230	230
Organization	856	183	184
Community	284	61	61
Total	2,214	474	475

Table 1: Dataset distribution.

dataset is imbalanced, with the Community class having the fewest samples (406 texts), compared to Individual (1,534 texts) and Organization (1,223 texts).

4 Methodology

The methods and approaches employed to address the issue raised in the preceding part are briefly summarized in this section. Through careful analysis, our research recommends utilizing a transformer-based model employing Indic-BERT (Kakwani et al., 2020). Figure 1 provides a concise visualization of our methodology, outlining the key steps involved in our approach.

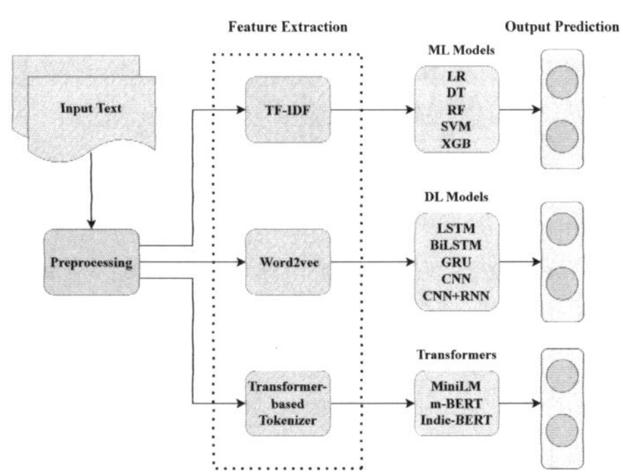

Figure 1: An abstract view of our methodology

4.1 Preprocessing

We translated Bhojpuri tweets into Hindi to ensure uniformity and enhance compatibility with multilingual language models. Basic preprocessing steps, such as removing special characters, stop-words and empty spaces were also applied to clean the text.

4.2 Feature Extraction

To capture meaningful features for different model types, three feature extraction techniques are employed. For machine learning models, the Term Frequency-Inverse Document Frequency (TF-IDF) (Qaiser and Ali, 2018) approach is used. For deep learning models, word embeddings are generated using the Word2Vec (Ma and Zhang, 2015) technique. And transformer models use architecture-compatible tokenizers for tokenization.

4.3 Model Building

In our research, we explored a variety of ML, DL and transformer-based models.

4.3.1 ML models

We trained traditional ML models such as Logistic Regression, Decision Trees, Random Forest, Support Vector Machines and Extreme Gradient Boosting on TF-IDF features. These models identify patterns statistically but may struggle with the complexity of contextual and linguistic nuances in hate speech.

4.3.2 DL models

The deep learning models include LSTM (Sherstinsky, 2020), BiLSTM (Xu et al., 2019), GRU (Dey and Salem, 2017), CNN (Alzubaidi et al., 2021) and a hybrid CNN+RNN model. These models capture semantic linkages in tweets by using Word2Vec embeddings. Each DL model was trained for 10 epochs with a batch size of 32.

4.3.3 Transformer-based models

The transformer-based models include MiniLM (Wang et al., 2020), m-BERT (Yu et al., 2024) and Indic-BERT (Kakwani et al., 2020). These models are fine-tuned using transformer-specific tokenizers to handle multilingual text efficiently. Transformers outperform ML and DL models because they process entire sentences using attention mechanisms, capturing context and long-range dependencies. They also benefit from pre-training on large multilingual corpora and handle complex scripts like Devanagari with better precision, which reduces information loss.

5 Results & Discussion

In this section, we provide comparisons of the performance achieved by different machine learning, deep learning, and transformer-based methods. The performance evaluation of various classifiers for the targets of hate speech identification showcases valuable details about how well they can predict. We also fine-tuned particularly m-BERT and Indic-BERT by adjusting learning rates, batch sizes, and epochs with the fixed Adam optimizer and Sparse Categorical Cross-Entropy (CCE) loss function in Table 2.

Hyperparameters	**m-BERT**		**Indic-BERT**	
Optimizer	Adam	Adam	Adam	Adam
Loss Function	Sparse CCE	Sparse CCE	Sparse CCE	Sparse CCE
Learning rate	5e-05	3e-05	2e-05	1e-05
Epochs	12	10	8	5
Batch size	8	16	8	8

Table 2: Summary of tuned hyper-parameters

By modifying these hyper-parameters, we tried to improve the model's performance across all metrics. We observed that increasing the number of epochs improved accuracy, with models reaching nearly very high at the end. m-BERT was trained for 12 epochs due to steady improvement, while Indic-BERT was trained for fewer epochs (5-8) due to faster convergence. A summary of the precision (P), recall (R), and macro-F1 (MF1) scores for each model on the test set is presented in Table 3. Among ML models, LR performed best with an MF1 score of 0.60. For DL models, CNN+RNN achieved the highest MF1 score of 0.62. Transformer models outperformed both ML and DL, with m-BERT achieving an MF1 of 0.68, while Indic-BERT emerged as the best overall with an MF1 of 0.69.

Classifier	**P**	**R**	**MF1**
LR	0.61	0.64	0.60
DT	0.55	0.56	0.55
RF	0.59	0.63	0.59
SVM	0.55	0.62	0.57
XGB	0.59	0.61	0.58
LSTM	0.57	0.58	0.57
BiLSTM	0.57	0.57	0.57
GRU	0.56	0.57	0.57
CNN	0.61	0.63	0.61
CNN + RNN	0.62	0.63	0.62
MiniLM	0.67	0.66	0.66
m-BERT	0.70	0.69	0.68
Indic-BERT	**0.74**	**0.67**	**0.69**

Table 3: Results of various models on the test dataset.

5.1 Quantitative Discussion

The results underscore the effectiveness of transformer-based architectures, particularly Indic-BERT, in detecting the target of hate speech. By incorporating contextual embeddings from pre-trained language models like Indic-BERT, our classification system achieves enhanced accuracy. Indic-BERT performs better as it supports four Devanagari languages (Nepali, Marathi, Hindi, Sanskrit) while m-BERT supports only three (Nepali, Marathi, and Hindi), provides broader coverage of Devanagari-script languages compared to m-BERT. To address the class imbalance issue, we applied class weights during training to give more importance to the minor Community class. Additionally, data augmentation techniques such as generating synthetic examples or paraphrasing could further improve the representation of the 'Community' class. The confusion matrix in Figure 2 provides a detailed breakdown of our model's performance.

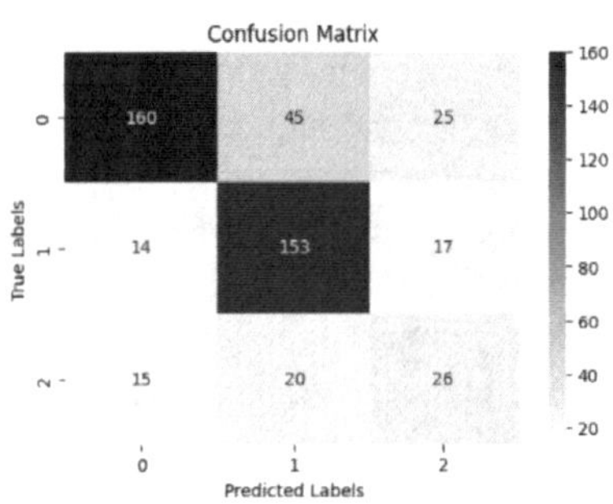

Figure 2: Confusion matrix of our best performing model

The model correctly classifies 160 label-0, 153 label-1 and 26 label-2 instances. However, it misclassifies 45 samples of label-0 as label-1 and 25 as label-2. Label-2 shows significant errors, with 15 misclassified as label-0 and 20 as label-1.

5.2 Qualitative Discussion

Figure 3 showcases some sample predictions made by our Indic-BERT model. Among these, samples 1, 4, and 5 are correctly classified, indicating the model's ability to handle diverse linguistic constructs in Devanagari script. However, certain instances reveal challenges for the model. For example, sample 2 which discusses a cricket match in the Devanagari script context, is misclassified as label 1 instead of the correct label 2. Sample 3 related to political content is also misclassified, suggesting potential difficulties in distinguishing political expressions within the Devanagari script.

Test Sample	Actual	Predicted
Sample 1: दिपायल सिलगढी नगर प्रमुखमा तीन जनाको उम्मेदवारी https://t.co/FhOrzCkPXI (Dipayal Silgarhi Nagar Mayor three candidates https://t.co/FhOrzCkPXI)	2	2
Sample 2: दार्चुलामा भारतीयले बम बिस्फोट गराउँदा नेपाली मारिए. कालिकोटमा नेपालीले राखेको बम बिस्फोट हुँदा २ जना मारिए । यो बम राखिने दुई कारण नेपाली कांग्रेस र माओवादी अहिले घाँटी जोडेर भोट माग्दैछन् है ।#NoNotAgain (A Nepali was killed when the Indians detonated a bomb in Darchula, 2 people were killed when a bomb planted by Nepali exploded in Calikot. The two reasons for keeping this bomb are that the Nepali Congress and the Maoists are now clamoring for votes.#NoNotAgain)	2	1
Sample 3 : एमाले सँग मिलेर पचास वर्ष शासन गर्ने कांग्रेसलाई सरापेको प्रचण्ड अहिले कांग्रेससँग मिलेर रेनुलाई जिताइदिएमा दश पन्ध्र बिस वर्ष सम्म शासन गर्ने प्रतिबद्ध रहनेछु रे। (Prachanda, who cursed Congress to rule together with UML for fifty years, now if Renu is defeated along with Congress, I will be committed to rule for ten fifteen twenty years.)	0	1
Sample 4 : आखिरकार यह तीनों लुटेरी पार्टिया हाथ मिला ही ली यह सब मिलकर पंजाब को लूटने की कोशिश कर रहे हैं पंजाब की जनता से अनुरोध है कि इन सब पार्टियों से बच कर रहे यह सब पार्टियां मिलकर अरविंद केजरीवाल जी की इमानदार पार्टी को हराना चाहते हैं #PunjabElections2022 https://t.co/31zYHWRL1D (Ultimately, these three robber gangs have joined hands and together they are trying to loot Punjab. It is a request to the people of Punjab that all these parties, who are avoiding these parties, together want to defeat Arvind Kejriwal ji's honest party. #PunjabElections2022 https://t.co/31zYHWRL1D)	1	1
Sample 5 : @narendramodi @SherBDeuba फर्किने बेला त्यो देउवा लाई पनि सङ्गै लानुहोला। 🙏 (When @narendramodi @SherBDeuba returns, take that Deuba with you. 🙏)	0	0

Figure 3: Examples of the Indic-BERT model's anticipated outputs with English translations

6 Conclusion

Our study on hate speech target identification in Devanagari-script languages demonstrates that transformer-based models, particularly IndicBERT, achieved the highest F1 score of 0.69, outperforming both machine learning and deep learning models. Despite challenges with low-resource languages like Bhojpuri, tailored preprocessing and feature extraction techniques provided valuable insights. Although this work focuses on Devanagari-script languages, the methodology can be adapted to other low resource scripts by using pre-trained models like m-BERT, MiniLM or Indic-BERT which work well with multilingual data. Future advancements in language-specific models could further improve hate speech detection in diverse multilingual contexts. Additionally, exploring multimodal approaches may significantly improve the accuracy and robustness of hate speech identification.

Limitations

A primary limitation of this study lies in converting Bhojpuri text into Hindi through a manually created vocabulary as the models employed lack training in the Bhojpuri language. This vocabulary-based conversion may not fully capture all nuances and context in Bhojpuri which could lead to potential inaccuracies in the model's performance. Additionally, the lack of high-quality annotated data for low-resource languages limits the robustness of the models. Future exploration of methods with more annotated samples in low-resource languages like Bhojpuri would enhance model accuracy and generalizability. Developing multilingual embeddings or pre-trained transformer models specifically for dialects in the Devanagari script would also address limitations in vocabulary conversion.

References

Md Alam, Hasan Mesbaul Ali Taher, Jawad Hossain, Shawly Ahsan, and Mohammed Moshiul Hoque. 2024. Cuet_nlp_manning@ lt-edi 2024: Transformer-based approach on caste and migration hate speech detection. In *Proceedings of the Fourth Workshop on Language Technology for Equality, Diversity, Inclusion*, pages 238–243.

Fatimah Alkomah and Xiaogang Ma. 2022. A literature review of textual hate speech detection methods and datasets. *Information*, 13(6):273.

Laith Alzubaidi, Jinglan Zhang, Amjad J Humaidi, Ayad Al-Dujaili, Ye Duan, Omran Al-Shamma, José Santamaría, Mohammed A Fadhel, Muthana Al-Amidie, and Laith Farhan. 2021. Review of deep learning: concepts, cnn architectures, challenges, applications, future directions. *Journal of big Data*, 8:1–74.

Rahul Aralikatte, Miryam De Lhoneux, Anoop Kunchukuttan, and Anders Søgaard. 2021. Itihasa: A large-scale corpus for sanskrit to english translation. In *Proceedings of the 8th Workshop on Asian Translation (WAT2021)*, pages 191–197.

Mithun Das, Punyajoy Saha, Binny Mathew, and Animesh Mukherjee. 2022. Hatecheckhin: Evaluating hindi hate speech detection models. *arXiv preprint arXiv:2205.00328*.

Rahul Dey and Fathi M Salem. 2017. Gate-variants of gated recurrent unit (gru) neural networks. In *2017 IEEE 60th international midwest symposium on circuits and systems (MWSCAS)*, pages 1597–1600. IEEE.

Farhan Ahmad Jafri, Kritesh Rauniyar, Surendrabikram Thapa, Mohammad Aman Siddiqui, Matloob Khushi, and Usman Naseem. 2024. Chunav: Analyzing hindi hate speech and targeted groups in indian election discourse. *ACM Transactions on Asian and Low-Resource Language Information Processing*.

Farhan Ahmad Jafri, Mohammad Aman Siddiqui, Surendrabikram Thapa, Kritesh Rauniyar, Usman Naseem, and Imran Razzak. 2023. Uncovering political hate speech during indian election campaign: A new low-resource dataset and baselines.

Divyanshu Kakwani, Anoop Kunchukuttan, Satish Golla, NC Gokul, Avik Bhattacharyya, Mitesh M Khapra, and Pratyush Kumar. 2020. Indicnlpsuite: Monolingual corpora, evaluation benchmarks and pre-trained multilingual language models for indian languages. In *Findings of the Association for Computational Linguistics: EMNLP 2020*, pages 4948–4961.

Atharva Kulkarni, Meet Mandhane, Manali Likhitkar, Gayatri Kshirsagar, and Raviraj Joshi. 2021. L3cubemahasent: A marathi tweet-based sentiment analysis dataset. In *Proceedings of the Eleventh Workshop on Computational Approaches to Subjectivity, Sentiment and Social Media Analysis*, pages 213–220.

Long Ma and Yanqing Zhang. 2015. Using word2vec to process big text data. In *2015 IEEE International Conference on Big Data (Big Data)*, pages 2895–2897. IEEE.

Atul Kr Ojha. 2019. English-bhojpuri smt system: Insights from the karaka model. *arXiv preprint arXiv:1905.02239*.

Md Osama, Kawsar Ahmed, Hasan Mesbaul Ali Taher, Jawad Hossain, Shawly Ahsan, and Mohammed Moshiul Hoque. 2024. Cuet_nlp_goodfellows@ dravidianlangtech eacl2024: A transformer-based approach for detecting fake news in dravidian languages. In *Proceedings of the Fourth Workshop on Speech, Vision, and Language Technologies for Dravidian Languages*, pages 187–192.

Anil Singh Parihar, Surendrabikram Thapa, and Sushruti Mishra. 2021. Hate speech detection using natural language processing: Applications and challenges. In *2021 5th International Conference on Trends in Electronics and Informatics (ICOEI)*, pages 1302–1308. IEEE.

Shahzad Qaiser and Ramsha Ali. 2018. Text mining: use of tf-idf to examine the relevance of words to documents. *International Journal of Computer Applications*, 181(1):25–29.

Kritesh Rauniyar, Sweta Poudel, Shuvam Shiwakoti, Surendrabikram Thapa, Junaid Rashid, Jungeun Kim, Muhammad Imran, and Usman Naseem. 2023. Multi-aspect annotation and analysis of nepali tweets on anti-establishment election discourse. *IEEE Access*.

Kengatharaiyer Sarveswaran, Bal Krishna Bal, Surendrabikram Thapa, Ashwini Vaidya, and Sana Shams. 2025. A brief overview of the first workshop on challenges in processing south asian languages (chipsal). In *Proceedings of the First Workshop on Challenges in Processing South Asian Languages (CHiPSAL)*.

Alex Sherstinsky. 2020. Fundamentals of recurrent neural network (rnn) and long short-term memory (lstm) network. *Physica D: Nonlinear Phenomena*, 404:132306.

Surendrabikram Thapa, Kritesh Rauniyar, Farhan Ahmad Jafri, Surabhi Adhikari, Kengatharaiyer Sarveswaran, Bal Krishna Bal, Hariram Veeramani, and Usman Naseem. 2025. Natural language understanding of devanagari script languages: Language identification, hate speech and its target detection. In *Proceedings of the First Workshop on Challenges in Processing South Asian Languages (CHiPSAL)*.

Surendrabikram Thapa, Kritesh Rauniyar, Shuvam Shiwakoti, Sweta Poudel, Usman Naseem, and Mehwish Nasim. 2023. Nehate: Large-scale annotated data shedding light on hate speech in nepali local election discourse. In *ECAI 2023*, pages 2346–2353. IOS Press.

Abhishek Velankar, Hrushikesh Patil, Amol Gore, Shubham Salunke, and Raviraj Joshi. 2021. Hate and offensive speech detection in hindi and marathi. *arXiv preprint arXiv:2110.12200*.

Wenhui Wang, Furu Wei, Li Dong, Hangbo Bao, Nan Yang, and Ming Zhou. 2020. Minilm: Deep self-attention distillation for task-agnostic compression of pre-trained transformers. *Advances in Neural Information Processing Systems*, 33:5776–5788.

Guixian Xu, Yueting Meng, Xiaoyu Qiu, Ziheng Yu, and Xu Wu. 2019. Sentiment analysis of comment texts based on bilstm. *Ieee Access*, 7:51522–51532.

Boyang Yu, Fei Tang, Daji Ergu, Rui Zeng, Bo Ma, and Fangyao Liu. 2024. Efficient classification of malicious urls: M-bert-a modified bert variant for enhanced semantic understanding. *IEEE Access*.

CUFE@NLU of Devanagari Script Languages 2025: Language Identification using fastText

Michael Ibrahim
Computer Engineering Department, Cairo University
1 Gamaa Street, 12613
Giza, Egypt
michael.nawar@eng.cu.edu.eg

Abstract

Language identification is a critical area of research within natural language processing (NLP), particularly in multilingual contexts where accurate language detection can enhance the performance of various applications, such as machine translation, content moderation, and user interaction systems. This paper presents a language identification system developed using fastText. In the CHIPSAL@COLING 2025 Task on Devanagari Script Language Identification, the proposed method achieved first place, with an F_1 score of 0.9997.

1 Introduction

Language identification is crucial in Natural Language Processing (NLP), facilitating various applications like machine translation, information retrieval, and content filtering. Identifying languages with unique scripts, like Korean or Japanese, is fairly easy, but determining languages that use common scripts poses notable difficulties. An example of this is the Devanagari script, utilized by multiple languages, such as Hindi, Sanskrit, Marathi, Nepali, Bhojpuri, and more. Although these languages use the same script, they demonstrate significant differences in grammar, vocabulary, and morphology, resulting in a complex language identification challenge.

Conventional methods for language identification depend significantly on lexical characteristics and statistical models, usually needing extensive, domain-specific datasets to achieve good performance. Methods like n-gram modeling (Cavnar et al., 1994) or character-level classification (Zhang et al., 2015) have demonstrated effectiveness for certain languages but frequently underperform when utilized on intricate scripts such as Devanagari. This can be attributed in part to the morphological richness of languages that use Devanagari, where words may be significantly inflected, making it more challenging to differentiate languages based only on surface-level characteristics.

Recent advancements in neural network-based models have demonstrated substantial improvements in language identification tasks, especially when used on languages that share similar scripts. One such model is fastText (Joulin et al., 2017) that has attracted interest due to its capacity to model subword information, effectively capturing detailed morphological patterns and delivering strong performance even with smaller datasets or noisy text. These characteristics make fastText a compelling option for language identification tasks in scripts such as Devanagari, where languages have a considerable amount of lexical overlap yet differ in their subword configurations.

This paper describes a system that uses fastText for identifying languages in the Devanagari script. The developed system efficiently differentiates between languages written in Devanagari, despite their common orthographic traits, by utilizing fastText's capability to create word representations that encapsulate character-level n-grams. This system was trained and evaluated using the datasets provided by the CHIPSAL@COLING 2025 (Sarveswaran et al., 2025) Task on Devanagari Script Language Identification (Thapa et al., 2025).

The rest of the paper is organized as follows. The related work is summarized in Section 2. The dataset used for training and validation was detailed in Section 3. In Section 4, the system is presented. Section 5 summarizes the study's key findings.

2 Related Work

Several studies have explored language identification using various techniques. Traditional methods often rely on statistical models that analyze textual

Proceedings of the First Workshop on Challenges in Processing South Asian Languages (CHiPSAL 2025), pages 273–277
January 19, 2025.

features such as n-grams or character frequencies. For instance, langid (Lui and Baldwin, 2012) can detect 97 languages and relies on a robust set of predefined features, which are calculated using Information Gain applied to different sets of n-grams. These features are used by a Naive Bayes classifier trained on a diverse corpus of text data from various sources. However, these traditional approaches may struggle with scripts like Devanagari due to shared vocabulary among languages.

FastText (Joulin et al., 2017) is one of the most popular models used for language identification. FastText uses a simpler linear classifier with a low-rank matrix constraint (Joulin et al., 2016). Its architecture incorporates hierarchical softmax, which helps reduce running time. Additionally, FastText combines a bag-of-words model with an N-gram approach to enhance performance and minimize processing time. While the N-gram model captures contextual character information around each instance but requires more memory, the bag-of-words model offers less detailed feature capture. By combining these two techniques, FastText creates a "bag-of-n-grams" model that balances performance and efficiency (Bojanowski et al., 2017).

CLD3 (Alex Salcianu, 2018) processes the input text by first extracting a range of n-grams, which are then transformed into dense vectors through an embedding layer. Each unique n-gram is represented by a fixed vector, and these vectors are averaged, with the frequency of each n-gram in the original text serving as the weighting factor. The resulting averaged vectors are concatenated and fed into a multi-layer perceptron, which generates a probability distribution over 107 possible languages.

One of the most powerful approaches today for language identification involves deep learning models like Long Short-Term Memory (LSTM) Networks (Schmidhuber et al., 1997). These models outperform older statistical and rule-based methods by effectively learning intricate patterns and capturing contextual relationships within the data. LSTM for Language Identification (Toftrup et al., 2021) applies Unicode-based written script identification, then for each script, a network is trained to predict the language based on the input text. In this approach, each character in the text is processed through an LSTM network, which then outputs a prediction for a single language. Finally, a max-pooling-based majority voting mechanism was used to combine the predictions from all characters and determine the dominant language of the input string.

Recently, hierarchical models were used for language identification. For instance, the LIMIT model (Agarwal et al., 2023) leverages layered structures to handle language identification, misidentification, and translation across over 350 languages. This method provides a comprehensive solution by integrating multiple layers of processing to enhance accuracy and robustness.

3 Dataset & Task

The shared task on Devanagari Script Language Identification (Thapa et al., 2025) aims to develop a system that can automatically determine the language of a sentence in Devanagari script among Nepali, Marathi, Sanskrit, Bhojpuri, and Hindi. This task addresses the critical need for accurate language identification in multilingual contexts. The data provided by this share task was sampled from different data sources:

- The Nepali data source came from 2 sources that focus on the Nepali election, (i) Nehate: Large-scale annotated data shedding light on hate speech in nepali local election discourse (Thapa et al., 2023) and (ii) Multi-Aspect Annotation and Analysis of Nepali Tweets on Anti-Establishment Election Discourse (Rauniyar et al., 2023).

- The Marathi data source, L3CubeMahaSent (Kulkarni et al., 2021), consists of almost 16,000 distinct tweets extracted from various Maharashtrian personalities' Twitter accounts, and it was annotated from sentiment analysis.

- The Sanskrit data source, Itihasa: A large-scale corpus for Sanskrit to English translation(Aralikatte et al., 2021), consists of 93,000 pairs of Sanskrit shlokas and their English translations.

- The Bhojpuri data source, English-Bhojpuri SMT System: Insights from the Karaka Model (Ojha, 2019), consists of 65,000 parallel sentences have been created containing 4,40,609 and 4,58,484 words in English and Bhojpuri respectively.

- The Hindi data source came from 2 sources that focuses on political hate speech in Indian election: (i) CHUNAV: Analyzing Hindi Hate

Language	Train	Development
Nepali	12544	2688
Marathi	11034	2364
Sanskrit	10996	2356
Bhojpuri	10184	2182
Hindi	7664	1643

Table 1: CHIPSAL@COLING 2025 Devanagari Script Language Identification Task - data split statistics.

Speech and Targeted Groups in Indian Election Discourse (Jafri et al., 2024) (ii) Uncovering political hate speech during Indian election campaign: A new low-resource dataset and baselines (Jafri et al., 2023)

The training dataset consists of a total of 52422 sentences distributed among Devanagari script languages as described in table 1. The development dataset consists of a total of 11233 sentences distributed among Devanagari script languages as described in table 1. Finally, the test dataset used for the evaluation of the developed method consists of a total of 11234 sentences.

4 Methodology, Results & Discussion

The training process will involve using fastText to create language models based on the training dataset. The following steps will be undertaken:

1. **Tokenization:** Tokenization is a fundamental step in the preprocessing phase of language identification, as it transforms raw text into manageable pieces. This process involves breaking down text into tokens, which can be words, phrases, or symbols, allowing for a more effective analysis of the sentence. In this work, the no language left behind [1] tokenizer (Costa-jussà et al., 2022) was used for tokenizing the text.

2. **Parameters Fine-Tuning:** The fastText classifier has 3 main parameters, (i) the words n-grams, (ii) the learning rate, and (iii) the number of training epochs. Different values for each of those parameters were examined, for the number of words n-gram values from 2 to 4 were examined, for the learning rate 2 values of 0.05 and 0.1 were examined, and for the number of training epochs 2 values of 25 and 50 were examined. For each combination of these parameters, a fastText classifier was trained on the 52422 sentences of the training set, and its performance was evaluated on the 11233 sentences of the development set. The F_1 scores of the developed models are summarized in table 2.

Ngrams	lr	Epochs	F_1
2	0.05	25	0.9968
2	0.05	50	0.9981
2	0.1	25	0.9975
2	0.1	50	0.9981
3	0.05	25	0.9961
3	0.05	50	0.9971
3	0.1	25	0.9971
3	0.1	50	0.9978
4	0.05	25	0.9952
4	0.05	50	0.9965
4	0.1	25	0.9963
4	0.1	50	0.9973

Table 2: Results of the development set.

3. **Final Model Training:** After analyzing the results of the experiments summarized in table 2, the final model was trained on 63655 sentences that represent the entire training and development sets, the fastText classifier used 2-gram word feature, a learning rate of 0.1, and was trained for 50 epochs. This model was trained on a Google colab CPU machine with a total memory of 12.67 GB, the training of this model took less than 90 seconds, and the generation of the label to the 11234 sentences of the test set took less than 10 seconds.

The developed system has 2 main limitations:

1. Many Devanagari languages were not considered in this shared task (Garhwali, Kashmiri, etc.), and when the number of languages to be identified by a classifier increases, the average accuracy generally tends to decrease (Leong et al., 2022). The effect of the change in the number of languages on the performance of the fastText classifier was not assessed in this study.

2. The developed fastText classifier has a very good performance since the data used for training and evaluating the model came from similar data sources, however, the fastText model

[1]https://huggingface.co/facebook/nllb-200-distilled-600M

uses simple features like word n-grams, so, it might learn to classify a sentence into a given language based on something like a proper noun. So, if there was a Nepali tweet discussing the Indian election might be wrongfully classified as as Hindi. The effect of out-of-sample was also not assessed in this study.

5 Conclusions

In this paper, a fastText classifier was trained to identify the Devanagari script language from 5 different Languages: Nepali, Marathi, Sanskrit, Bhojpuri, and Hindi. The proposed method is efficient as the final model training and the generation of the labels for the test set takes less than 2 minutes on a CPU machine, and it was ranked first on the CHIPSAL@COLING 2025 Task on Devanagari Script Language Identification achieving an F_1 score of 0.9997.

References

Milind Agarwal, Md Mahfuz Ibn Alam, and Antonios Anastasopoulos. 2023. Limit: Language identification, misidentification, and translation using hierarchical models in 350+ languages. *arXiv preprint arXiv:2305.14263*.

Anton Bakalov Chris Alberti Daniel Andor David Weiss Emily Pitler Greg Coppola Jason Riesa Kuzman Ganchev et al. Alex Salcianu, Andy Golding. 2018. . compact language detector v3.

Rahul Aralikatte, Miryam De Lhoneux, Anoop Kunchukuttan, and Anders Søgaard. 2021. Itihasa: A large-scale corpus for sanskrit to english translation. In *Proceedings of the 8th Workshop on Asian Translation (WAT2021)*, pages 191–197.

Piotr Bojanowski, Edouard Grave, Armand Joulin, and Tomas Mikolov. 2017. Enriching word vectors with subword information. *Transactions of the association for computational linguistics*, 5:135–146.

William B Cavnar, John M Trenkle, et al. 1994. N-gram-based text categorization. In *Proceedings of SDAIR-94, 3rd annual symposium on document analysis and information retrieval*, volume 161175, page 14. Ann Arbor, Michigan.

Marta R Costa-jussà, James Cross, Onur Çelebi, Maha Elbayad, Kenneth Heafield, Kevin Heffernan, Elahe Kalbassi, Janice Lam, Daniel Licht, Jean Maillard, et al. 2022. No language left behind: Scaling human-centered machine translation. *arXiv preprint arXiv:2207.04672*.

Farhan Ahmad Jafri, Kritesh Rauniyar, Surendrabikram Thapa, Mohammad Aman Siddiqui, Matloob Khushi, and Usman Naseem. 2024. Chunav: Analyzing hindi hate speech and targeted groups in indian election discourse. *ACM Transactions on Asian and Low-Resource Language Information Processing*.

Farhan Ahmad Jafri, Mohammad Aman Siddiqui, Surendrabikram Thapa, Kritesh Rauniyar, Usman Naseem, and Imran Razzak. 2023. Uncovering political hate speech during indian election campaign: A new low-resource dataset and baselines.

Armand Joulin, Edouard Grave, Piotr Bojanowski, and Tomas Mikolov. 2016. Bag of tricks for efficient text classification. *arXiv preprint arXiv:1607.01759*.

Armand Joulin, Edouard Grave, Piotr Bojanowski, and Tomas Mikolov. 2017. Bag of tricks for efficient text classification. In *Proceedings of the 15th Conference of the European Chapter of the Association for Computational Linguistics: Volume 2, Short Papers*, pages 427–431. Association for Computational Linguistics.

Atharva Kulkarni, Meet Mandhane, Manali Likhitkar, Gayatri Kshirsagar, and Raviraj Joshi. 2021. L3cubemahasent: A marathi tweet-based sentiment analysis dataset. In *Proceedings of the Eleventh Workshop on Computational Approaches to Subjectivity, Sentiment and Social Media Analysis*, pages 213–220.

Colin Leong, Joshua Nemecek, Jacob Mansdorfer, Anna Filighera, Abraham Owodunni, and Daniel Whitenack. 2022. Bloom library: Multimodal datasets in 300+ languages for a variety of downstream tasks. *arXiv preprint arXiv:2210.14712*.

Marco Lui and Timothy Baldwin. 2012. langid. py: An off-the-shelf language identification tool. In *Proceedings of the ACL 2012 system demonstrations*, pages 25–30.

Atul Kr Ojha. 2019. English-bhojpuri smt system: Insights from the karaka model. *arXiv preprint arXiv:1905.02239*.

Kritesh Rauniyar, Sweta Poudel, Shuvam Shiwakoti, Surendrabikram Thapa, Junaid Rashid, Jungeun Kim, Muhammad Imran, and Usman Naseem. 2023. Multi-aspect annotation and analysis of nepali tweets on anti-establishment election discourse. *IEEE Access*.

Kengatharaiyer Sarveswaran, Bal Krishna Bal, Surendrabikram Thapa, Ashwini Vaidya, and Sana Shams. 2025. A brief overview of the first workshop on challenges in processing south asian languages (chipsal). In *Proceedings of the First Workshop on Challenges in Processing South Asian Languages (CHiPSAL)*.

Jürgen Schmidhuber, Sepp Hochreiter, et al. 1997. Long short-term memory. *Neural Comput*, 9(8):1735–1780.

Surendrabikram Thapa, Kritesh Rauniyar, Farhan Ahmad Jafri, Surabhi Adhikari, Kengatharaiyer Sarveswaran, Bal Krishna Bal, Hariram Veeramani, and Usman Naseem. 2025. Natural language understanding of devanagari script languages: Language identification, hate speech and its target detection. In *Proceedings of the First Workshop on Challenges in Processing South Asian Languages (CHiPSAL)*.

Surendrabikram Thapa, Kritesh Rauniyar, Shuvam Shiwakoti, Sweta Poudel, Usman Naseem, and Mehwish Nasim. 2023. Nehate: Large-scale annotated data shedding light on hate speech in nepali local election discourse. In *ECAI 2023*, pages 2346–2353. IOS Press.

Mads Toftrup, Søren Asger Sørensen, Manuel R. Ciosici, and Ira Assent. 2021. A reproduction of apple's bi-directional LSTM models for language identification in short strings. In *Proceedings of the 16th Conference of the European Chapter of the Association for Computational Linguistics: Student Research Workshop*, pages 36–42, Online. Association for Computational Linguistics.

Xiang Zhang, Junbo Zhao, and Yann LeCun. 2015. Character-level convolutional networks for text classification. *Advances in neural information processing systems*, 28.

Dll5143A@NLU of Devanagari Script Languages 2025: Detection of Hate Speech and Targets Using Hierarchical Attention Network

Ashok Yadav and Vrijendra Singh
Indian Institute of Information Technology Allahabad
Prayagraj, 211015, India
rsi2021002@iiita.ac.in, vrij@iiita.ac.in

Abstract

Hate speech poses a significant challenge on social networks, particularly in Devanagari scripted languages, where subtle expressions can lead to harmful narratives. This paper details our participation in the "Shared Task on Natural Language Understanding of Devanagari Script Languages" at CHIPSAL@COLING 2025, addressing hate speech detection and target identification. In Sub-task B, we focused on classifying the text either hate or non-hate classified text to determine the presence of hate speech, while Sub-task C focused on identifying targets, such as individuals, organizations, or communities. We utilized the XLM-RoBERTa model as our base and explored various adaptations, including Adaptive Weighting and Gated Adaptive Weighting methods. Our results demonstrated that the Hierarchical Gated adaptive weighting model achieved 86% accuracy in hate speech detection with a macro F1 score of 0.72, particularly improving performance for minority class detection. For target detection, the same model achieved 75% accuracy and a 0.69 macro F1 score. Our proposed architecture demonstrated competitive performance, ranking 8th in Subtask B and 11th in Subtask C among all participants.

1 Introduction

In the age of rapid digital communication, social media platforms have become the primary space for people to share their opinions and engage in discourse (Zhou et al., 2024). However, this democratization of speech has also led to the propagation of hate speech, which can have severe consequences for individuals and communities (Parida et al., 2024). While hate speech detection in major languages like English has seen significant advancements, there is a pressing need to extend this effort to languages written in Devanagari scripts, such as Nepali, Marathi, Sanskrit, Bhojpuri, and Hindi (Rauniyar et al., 2023). These languages, despite their widespread use in South Asia, remain underrepresented in hate speech research (Piot et al., 2024). Devanagari script languages present unique challenges for hate speech detection due to their linguistic structure, rich cultural context, and scarcity of labeled datasets (Parihar et al., 2021). Existing hate speech detection models, predominantly trained in English or other high-resource languages, often fail to capture the nuances of these languages, leading to poor performance. Furthermore, the intertwining of hate speech with regional socio-political issues adds layers of complexity that existing models are not equipped to handle (Jafri et al., 2024).

To address these challenges, (Sarveswaran et al., 2025) introduced a shared task at CHIPSAL@COLING 2025 where participants' systems need to detect the language (Nepali, Marathi, Sanskrit, Bhojpuri, or Hindi) a given Devanagari text belongs to, as well as identify hate speech and its targets within the text. Subtask B of the challenge contains tweets that were carefully classified into two groups, hate and non-hate. Subtask C focuses on identifying whether the hate speech targets 'Individual', 'Organization', or 'Community', allowing for detailed tracking of hate speech communication patterns in Devanagari. We have participated in Subtask B and Subtask C, and achieved ranks 8th and 11th respectively, among all participants.

The remainder of this paper is organized as follows: Section 2 introduces the shared task and dataset statistics. Section 3 details our hierarchical attention-based architecture. Section 4 describes the experimental setup and evaluation metrics. Section 4.1 presents our model's performance and comparison with other participating systems. Section 5 concludes our findings, while Section 6 discusses the limitations and potential improvements in hate speech detection for Devanagari script languages.

Proceedings of the First Workshop on Challenges in Processing South Asian Languages (CHiPSAL 2025), pages 278–288
January 19, 2025.

2 Task and Dataset Description

The 'Shared Task on Natural Language Understanding of Devanagari Script Languages' at CHIPSAL@COLING 2025 focuses on key challenges in processing Devanagari-scripted languages. The first subtask, Devanagari Script Language Identification, aims to accurately identify the language of a given Devanagari text. Subtask B, Hate Speech Detection, determines whether a text contains hate speech. Building on this, Subtask C targets identifying specific hate speech targets, such as individuals or groups. This shared task promotes comprehensive Devanagari language understanding by addressing script identification, hate speech detection, and hate speech target identification. (Thapa et al., 2025).

The hate speech datasets for this shared task were drawn from various sources. For Hindi, the CHUNAV dataset (Jafri et al., 2024) and a dataset on political hate speech during Indian elections (Jafri et al., 2023) were used. The Nepali dataset, NEHATE (Thapa et al., 2023), and a multi-aspect dataset on Nepali tweets regarding anti-establishment election discourse (Rauniyar et al., 2023) were also included. Datasets for Bhojpuri (Ojha, 2019), Marathi (Kulkarni et al., 2021), and Sanskrit (Aralikatte et al., 2021) were utilized. In this shared task, we participated in both Subtask B and Subtask C, achieving ranks of 8th and 11th respectively among all participants. The dataset for Subtask B includes binary annotations (0 for non-hate and 1 for hate speech), while Subtask C focuses on categorizing hate speech targets into three classes: individual (0), organization (1), and community (2). Table 1 provides statistics on the dataset used for the ChiPSAL shared task for both subtasks.

Table 1: The statistics of the used dataset in CHIPSAL@COLING 2025 Subtask B and Subtask C.

Category	Subask B		Subtask C		
	Hate	Non-Hate	Individual	Organization	Community
Train	2214	1,6805	1074	856	284
Val	474	3602	230	183	61
Test	475	3601	230	184	61
Total	3164	24008	1534	1223	406

3 Proposed Framework

3.1 Overview

We have proposed a model that builds on the XLM-RoBERTa architecture, incorporating adaptive attention mechanisms to improve classification performance in diverse linguistic contexts. Figure 1 shows the architecture of our proposed model.

3.2 XLM-RoBERTa

XLM-RoBERTa serves as the foundation of our model. It is a multilingual transformer with 12 layers, 768 hidden units, and 12 attention heads. This base model processes the input text and generates contextualized word embeddings, also known as hidden states. These hidden states, denoted as $H \in \mathcal{R}^{B \times L \times D}$, where B is the batch size, L is the sequence length, and D is the hidden size (768), serve as the features extracted from the input text and form the basis for subsequent processing in our model.

3.3 Attention Mechanism

We implement a dual-attention mechanism consisting of word-level and sentence-level attention components.

3.3.1 Word-level Attention

The word-level attention component is a two-layer feedforward neural network that processes the hidden states to generate attention weights for individual tokens. The process can be described by the following equations:

$$e_w = \tanh(W_w^1 H + b_w^1) \quad (1)$$

$$\alpha_w = \text{softmax}(W_w^2 e_w + b_w^2) \quad (2)$$

$$c_w = \sum_{i=1}^{L} \alpha_w^i H^i \quad (3)$$

where $W_w^1 \in \mathcal{R}^{D \times D}$, $W_w^2 \in \mathcal{R}^{1 \times D}$, $b_w^1 \in \mathcal{R}^D$, and $b_w^2 \in \mathcal{R}$ are learnable parameters, $\alpha_w \in \mathcal{R}^L$ are the attention weights, and $c_w \in \mathcal{R}^D$ is the word-level context vector.

3.3.2 Sentence-level Attention

The sentence-level attention mechanism focuses on broader semantic structures within the input. It follows a similar structure to the word-level attention:

$$e_s = \tanh(W_s^1 H + b_s^1) \quad (4)$$

$$\alpha_s = \text{softmax}(W_s^2 e_s + b_s^2) \quad (5)$$

$$c_s = \sum_{i=1}^{L} \alpha_s^i H^i \quad (6)$$

where W_s^1, W_s^2, b_s^1, and b_s^2 are learnable parameters with the same dimensions as their word-level counterparts, $\alpha_s \in \mathcal{R}^L$ are the sentence-level attention weights, and $c_s \in \mathcal{R}^D$ is the sentence-level context vector.

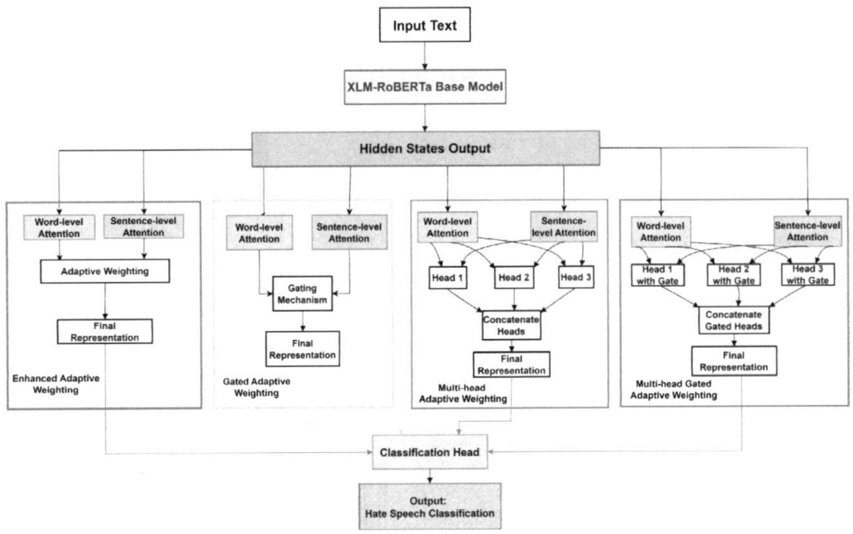

Figure 1: Architecture of the proposed transformer-based multimodal hierarchical fusion model.

3.3.3 Adaptive Weighting

The adaptive weighting component combines the word-level and sentence-level context vectors based on their relative importance for each input.

$$c_{combined} = [c_w; c_s] \tag{7}$$

$$\beta = \text{softmax}(W_a^2 \text{ReLU}(W_a^1 c_{combined} + b_a^1) + b_a^2) \tag{8}$$

$$c_{final} = \beta_1 c_w + \beta_2 c_s \tag{9}$$

where $W_a^1 \in \mathcal{R}^{D\times 2D}$, $W_a^2 \in \mathcal{R}^{2\times D}$, $b_a^1 \in \mathcal{R}^D$, and $b_a^2 \in \mathcal{R}^2$ are learnable parameters, $\beta \in \mathcal{R}^2$ are the adaptive weights, and $c_{final} \in \mathcal{R}^D$ is the final context vector that balances word and sentence-level information.

We also explored advanced variants of the attention mechanism including gated adaptive weighting, multi-head adaptive weighting, and multi-head gated adaptive weighting. The detailed architectures and formulations of these variants are presented in Appendix 7.

3.4 Classification Head

The classification head is a three-layer MLP with ReLU activations and dropout that takes the weighted representation and outputs logits for both two-way and three-way classifications. The forward pass follows:

$$h_1 = \text{ReLU}(W_1 c_{final} + b_1) \tag{10}$$

$$h_2 = \text{ReLU}(W_2 h_1 + b_2) \tag{11}$$

$$z = W_3 h_2 + b_3 \tag{12}$$

where $W_1 \in \mathcal{R}^{D\times D}$, $W_2 \in \mathcal{R}^{D/2\times D}$, $W_3 \in \mathcal{R}^{2\times D/2}$, and corresponding biases are learnable parameters. To handle class imbalance, we use weighted Cross-Entropy Loss:

$$\mathcal{L} = -\sum_{i=1}^{N} w_{y_i}[y_i \log(\sigma(z_i)) + (1-y_i)\log(1-\sigma(z_i))] \tag{13}$$

with class weights calculated using sklearn's 'balanced' strategy:

$$w_j = \frac{N}{K \cdot N_j} \tag{14}$$

where N is total samples, K is number of classes, and N_j is samples in class j.

4 Experimental Settings and Evaluations Metrics

We implemented our model using PyTorch and Hugging Face Transformers, with training conducted on an Nvidia A30 GPU. The model was trained for 10 epochs using an AdamW optimizer with a learning rate of 2e-5 and batch size of 32. For reproducibility, we set the manual seed to 30 and used a dropout rate of 0.3 to prevent overfitting. Input sequences were padded to a maximum length of 128 tokens. In our implementation, all layers of XLM-RoBERTa were fine-tuned during training to maximize its full representational capacity for contextual and linguistic understanding. The system's effectiveness was assessed using standard metrics: precision, recall, F1-score, and accuracy.

The macro-averaged F1 score was selected as the primary evaluation criterion for both subtasks.

4.1 Results and Analysis

On the validation dataset, our best performing model, the Hierarchical Gated Adaptive Attention model, achieved an F1 score of 0.72, precision of 0.70, recall of 0.76, and accuracy of 0.86 for hate speech detection (Subtask B). For target identification (Subtask C), the model attained an F1 score of 0.69, precision of 0.69, recall of 0.69, and accuracy of 0.75. Tables 2 and 3 present our system's performance compared to other participating systems on the test dataset.

For hate speech detection (Subtask B) [1], our system achieved competitive results, ranking 8th among all participants with an F1 score of 0.745 and an accuracy of 0.890. The best performing system achieved an F1 score of 0.814, demonstrating the challenging nature of hate speech detection in Devanagari script languages. Our model showed balanced performance between precision (0.735) and recall (0.758), indicating its effectiveness in handling class imbalance. In target identification (Subtask C) [2], our system ranked 11th with an F1 score of 0.658 and accuracy of 0.714. While the top system achieved an F1 score of 0.710, the relatively small performance gap (0.052) between the first and eleventh positions suggests the complexity of the task and the effectiveness of various approaches.

Table 2: Results comparison of top systems for Subtask B, R(recall),P(precision),and Acc (accuracy)

System	R	P	F1	Acc	Rank
fulbutte	.855	.785	.814	.914	1
Yestin	.813	.746	.773	.894	2
sumanpaudel	.769	.763	.766	.903	3
jebish7	.744	.793	.765	.911	4
lazyboy.blk	.736	.790	.759	.910	5
MuhammadA	.726	.781	.749	.907	6
mdp0999	.775	.729	.748	.886	7
Ours	.758	.735	.745	.890	8

Detailed performance analysis of all model variants of subtask B 8.1 and Subtask C 8.2 is presented in Appendix 8.

[1]https://codalab.lisn.upsaclay.fr/competitions/20000#results

[2]https://codalab.lisn.upsaclay.fr/competitions/20000#results

Table 3: Results comparison of top systems for Subtask C

System	R	P	F1	Acc	Rank
sumanpaudel	.704	.718	.710	.768	1
Siddartha-10	.687	.741	.703	.779	2
Tofa	.672	.742	.692	.766	3
sakib07	.681	.686	.683	.745	4
Dola_C	.681	.679	.680	.737	5
jebish7	.669	.697	.679	.750	6
mdp0999	.669	.674	.672	.741	7
jerrytomy	.667	.663	.664	.731	8
sandeep_S	.657	.675	.664	.739	9
Yestin	.655	.674	.661	.745	10
Ours	.654	.664	.658	.714	11

5 Conclusion

In this study, we explored hate speech detection and target identification challenges in Devanagari-scripted languages through our participation in CHIPSAL@COLING 2025. Our experimentation with various attention mechanisms demonstrated that the Hierarchical Gated Adaptive Weighting model achieved the best performance, with macro F1 scores of 0.72 and 0.69 for hate speech detection and target identification respectively. The integration of gating mechanisms proved crucial in addressing class imbalance, particularly improving minority class detection in both tasks. Despite achieving competitive rankings—8th in Subtask B with an F1 score of 0.745 and 11th in Subtask C with an F1 score of 0.658—our analysis revealed persistent challenges. The model showed stronger performance in detecting individual (F1: 0.79) and organizational targets (F1: 0.77) but struggled with community-targeted hate speech (F1: 0.52), highlighting the complexity of detecting group-targeted hate. This performance disparity suggests the need for more sophisticated approaches to handle the nuanced expressions of community-targeted hate speech in Devanagari languages.

6 Limitations

Our work contributes to the research on processing low-resource languages, demonstrating how hierarchical attention models with adaptive weighting can significantly enhance performance. However, the model struggles to detect community-targeted hate speech (F1: 0.52) compared to individual (F1: 0.79) and organizational targets (F1: 0.77). This performance gap highlights the model's difficulty in handling unbalanced data for target detection, especially in recognizing hate speech directed at specific communities. Community-targeted tweets often employ indirect or culturally nuanced language, as detailed in Appendix 9.2. We used XLM-RoBERTa as our base model, which, despite its robust multilingual capabilities, may lack the nuanced script-specific features required for Devanagari. This limitation is particularly evident in handling code-mixed language or symbolic terms. We observed that named entities and metaphorical phrases—common in political discourse—were frequently misinterpreted, leading to false positives in hate speech detection. Detailed examples of these challenges can be found in Appendix 9.1. To address these limitations, future work could include specialized pre-training methods that better handle linguistic and cultural elements inherent in Devanagari languages. Exploring script-specific models or training strategies may also help the model distinguish between satirical and hateful language more effectively, especially in community-oriented contexts where expression style differs significantly.

Acknowledgments

The authors express their gratitude to the Ministry of Education, the Indian Institute of Information Technology Allahabad, and the Deep Learning Lab at IIITA for providing the resources necessary to complete this work.

References

Rahul Aralikatte, Miryam De Lhoneux, Anoop Kunchukuttan, and Anders Søgaard. 2021. Itihasa: A large-scale corpus for sanskrit to english translation. In *Proceedings of the 8th Workshop on Asian Translation (WAT2021)*, pages 191–197.

Farhan Ahmad Jafri, Kritesh Rauniyar, Surendrabikram Thapa, Mohammad Aman Siddiqui, Matloob Khushi, and Usman Naseem. 2024. Chunav: Analyzing hindi hate speech and targeted groups in indian election discourse. *ACM Transactions on Asian and Low-Resource Language Information Processing*.

Farhan Ahmad Jafri, Mohammad Aman Siddiqui, Surendrabikram Thapa, Kritesh Rauniyar, Usman Naseem, and Imran Razzak. 2023. Uncovering political hate speech during indian election campaign: A new low-resource dataset and baselines.

Atharva Kulkarni, Meet Mandhane, Manali Likhitkar, Gayatri Kshirsagar, and Raviraj Joshi. 2021. L3cubemahasent: A marathi tweet-based sentiment analysis dataset. In *Proceedings of the Eleventh Workshop on Computational Approaches to Subjectivity, Sentiment and Social Media Analysis*, pages 213–220.

Atul Kr Ojha. 2019. English-bhojpuri smt system: Insights from the karaka model. *arXiv preprint arXiv:1905.02239*.

Shantipriya Parida, Shakshi Panwar, Kusum Lata, Sanskruti Mishra, and Sambit Sekhar. 2024. Building pre-train llm dataset for the indic languages: a case study on hindi. *arXiv preprint arXiv:2407.09855*.

Anil Singh Parihar, Surendrabikram Thapa, and Sushruti Mishra. 2021. Hate speech detection using natural language processing: Applications and challenges. In *2021 5th International Conference on Trends in Electronics and Informatics (ICOEI)*, pages 1302–1308. IEEE.

Paloma Piot, Patricia Martín-Rodilla, and Javier Parapar. 2024. Metahate: A dataset for unifying efforts on hate speech detection. In *Proceedings of the International AAAI Conference on Web and Social Media*, volume 18, pages 2025–2039.

Kritesh Rauniyar, Sweta Poudel, Shuvam Shiwakoti, Surendrabikram Thapa, Junaid Rashid, Jungeun Kim, Muhammad Imran, and Usman Naseem. 2023. Multi-aspect annotation and analysis of nepali tweets on anti-establishment election discourse. *IEEE Access*.

Kengatharaiyer Sarveswaran, Bal Krishna Bal, Surendrabikram Thapa, Ashwini Vaidya, and Sana Shams. 2025. A brief overview of the first workshop on challenges in processing south asian languages (chipsal). In *Proceedings of the First Workshop on Challenges in Processing South Asian Languages (CHiPSAL)*.

Surendrabikram Thapa, Kritesh Rauniyar, Farhan Ahmad Jafri, Surabhi Adhikari, Kengatharaiyer Sarveswaran, Bal Krishna Bal, Hariram Veeramani, and Usman Naseem. 2025. Natural language understanding of devanagari script languages: Language identification, hate speech and its target detection. In *Proceedings of the First Workshop on Challenges in Processing South Asian Languages (CHiPSAL)*.

Surendrabikram Thapa, Kritesh Rauniyar, Shuvam Shiwakoti, Sweta Poudel, Usman Naseem, and Mehwish Nasim. 2023. Nehate: Large-scale annotated data shedding light on hate speech in nepali local election discourse. In *ECAI 2023*, pages 2346–2353. IOS Press.

Zhipeng Zhou, Xingnan Zhou, Yudi Chen, and Haonan Qi. 2024. Evolution of online public opinions on major accidents: Implications for post-accident response based on social media network. *Expert Systems with Applications*, 235:121307.

7 Appendix A

7.1 Advanced Attention Mechanisms

7.1.1 Gated Adaptive Weighting

The gated adaptive weighting component combines the context vectors at the word and sentence level using a gating mechanism.

$$c_{combined} = [c_w; c_s] \quad (15)$$

$$g = \sigma(W_g^2 \tanh(W_g^1 c_{combined} + b_g^1) + b_g^2) \quad (16)$$

$$c_{final} = g \cdot c_w + (1 - g) \cdot c_s \quad (17)$$

where $W_g^1 \in \mathcal{R}^{D\times 2D}$, $W_g^2 \in \mathcal{R}^{1\times D}$, $b_g^1 \in \mathcal{R}^D$, and $b_g^2 \in \mathcal{R}$ are learnable parameters, $g \in \mathcal{R}$ is the gate value, σ is the sigmoid function, and $c_{final} \in \mathcal{R}^D$ is the final context vector that balances word and sentence-level information. This gated adaptive weighting mechanism allows our model to dynamically adjust the importance of word-level and sentence-level features for each input, potentially improving its ability to detect hate speech across various linguistic contexts.

7.1.2 Multi-head Adaptive Weighting

Multi-head methods incorporate adaptive weighting within their structure through multiple heads, without the need for an additional weighting step. After obtaining the context vectors for each head, we concatenate them and apply an adaptive weighting mechanism:

$$c_{combined} = [c_w^1; c_s^1; c_w^2; c_s^2; ...; c_w^h; c_s^h] \quad (18)$$

$$\beta = \text{softmax}(W_a^2 \text{ReLU}(W_a^1 c_{combined} + b_a^1) + b_a^2) \quad (19)$$

$$c_{final} = \sum_{i=1}^{2h} \beta_i c_i \quad (20)$$

where $W_a^1 \in \mathcal{R}^{D\times 2hD}$, $W_a^2 \in \mathcal{R}^{2h\times D}$, $b_a^1 \in \mathcal{R}^D$, and $b_a^2 \in \mathcal{R}^{2h}$ are learnable parameters, $\beta \in \mathcal{R}^{2h}$ are the adaptive weights, and $c_{final} \in \mathcal{R}^D$ is the final context vector.

7.1.3 Multi-head Gated Adaptive Weighting

The Multi-Head Gated Adaptive Weighting (MH-GAW) mechanism extends the concept of adaptive weighting by using multiple attention heads and incorporating a gating mechanism. This approach allows the model to capture different aspects of the input simultaneously and dynamically balance the importance of word-level and sentence-level features. For each head i (where $i = 1, 2, ..., h$, and h is the number of heads):

$$e_w^i = \tanh(W_w^{1i} H + b_w^{1i}) \quad (21)$$

$$\alpha_w^i = \text{softmax}(W_w^{2i} e_w^i + b_w^{2i}) \quad (22)$$

$$c_w^i = \sum_{j=1}^{L} \alpha_w^{ij} H^j \quad (23)$$

$$e_s^i = \tanh(W_s^{1i} H + b_s^{1i}) \quad (24)$$

$$\alpha_s^i = \text{softmax}(W_s^{2i} e_s^i + b_s^{2i}) \quad (25)$$

$$c_s^i = \sum_{j=1}^{L} \alpha_s^{ij} H^j \quad (26)$$

where $W_w^{1i}, W_w^{2i}, W_s^{1i}, W_s^{2i}$ are learnable parameters for each head, $\alpha_w^i, \alpha_s^i \in \mathcal{R}^L$ are the attention weights, and $c_w^i, c_s^i \in \mathcal{R}^D$ are the word-level and sentence-level context vectors for each head. The context vectors from all heads using equation 27 and 28

$$c_w = \frac{1}{h} \sum_{i=1}^{h} c_w^i \quad (27)$$

$$c_s = \frac{1}{h} \sum_{i=1}^{h} c_s^i \quad (28)$$

where $c_w, c_s \in \mathcal{R}^D$ are the aggregated word-level and sentence-level context vectors. A gating mechanism is applied to dynamically balance the word-level and sentence-level information using equations 29, 30 and 31

$$c_{combined} = [c_w; c_s] \quad (29)$$

$$g = \sigma(W_g^2 \tanh(W_g^1 c_{combined} + b_g^1) + b_g^2) \quad (30)$$

$$c_{gated} = g_1 \cdot c_w + g_2 \cdot c_s \quad (31)$$

where $W_g^1 \in \mathcal{R}^{D\times 2D}$, $W_g^2 \in \mathcal{R}^{2\times D}$, $b_g^1 \in \mathcal{R}^D$, and $b_g^2 \in \mathcal{R}^2$ are learnable parameters, $g \in \mathcal{R}^2$ are the gate values, σ is the sigmoid function, and $c_{gated} \in \mathcal{R}^D$ is the gated context vector and final context vector passed in classification head.

8 Appendix B

8.1 Task B Results

The performance in Subtask B using the Hierarchical Adaptive Attention Model is shown in Table 4. We achieved an accuracy of 0.73 on the test set of 4,076 samples. For class 0 (non-hate speech), the model attained precision of 0.93, recall of 0.94, and an F1-score of 0.94 across 3,602 instances. For class 1 (hate speech), it recorded precision of 0.52, recall of 0.46, and an F1-score of 0.49 over 474 instances.

The macro-averaged F1-score was 0.71, and the weighted F1-score was 0.88. This indicates a significant disparity in performance between classes, with high effectiveness in detecting non-hate speech (F1: 0.94) due to the model's handling of the majority class. However, detecting hate speech was more challenging (F1: 0.49), showing that while precision (0.52) and recall (0.46) were balanced, the minority class proved difficult to classify accurately.

Table 4: Results for Subtask B: Hate Speech Detection Using Hierarchical Adaptive Attention Model

	prec.	rec.	f1	supp.
0	0.93	0.94	0.94	3602
1	0.52	0.46	0.49	474
acc.			0.73	4076
macro	0.72	0.70	0.71	4076
weighted	0.88	0.89	0.88	4076

The performance in the Subtask B using the Hierarchical Gated Adaptive Attention Model is presented in Table 5. The model achieved an accuracy of 0.86 on the test set of 4,076 samples. For class 0, the model attained precision of 0.95, recall of 0.90, and an F1-score of 0.92 across 3,602 instances. For class 1, the precision was 0.44, recall was 0.63, and F1-score was 0.52 over 474 instances. The macro-averaged and weighted F1-score was 0.72, and 0.87 respectively.

This architecture demonstrated strong overall performance with 86% accuracy and improved handling of class imbalance. Non-hate speech detection remained high (F1: 0.92), with excellent precision (0.95) and a slightly lower recall (0.90). Also in hate speech detection, we observed an increase of 0.63 in recall, although precision dropped to 0.44, indicating better minority class detection at the cost of some additional false positives. The macro F1-score of 0.72 and weighted F1-score of 0.87 reflect robust performance and enhanced handling of the minority class.

Table 5: Results for Subtask B: Hate Speech Detection Using Hierarchical Gated Adaptive Attention Model

	prec.	rec.	f1	supp.
0	0.95	0.90	0.92	3602
1	0.44	0.63	0.52	474
acc.			0.86	4076
macro	0.70	0.76	0.72	4076
weighted	0.89	0.86	0.87	4076

The performance in Subtask B using the Hierarchical Multi-head Adaptive Weighting model is shown in Table 6. The model achieved an accuracy of 0.89 on a Val set of 4,076 samples. For class 0, the model recorded precision of 0.92,recall of 0.95, and an F1-score of 0.94 across 3,602 instances. For class 1, the precision was 0.52, the recall was 0.39, and the F1-score was 0.45 over 474 instances. The macro-averaged F1-score was 0.69, while the weighted F1-score was 0.88.

While achieving the highest accuracy at 89%, the model displayed significant class imbalance in performance. Non-hate speech detection was highly effective. However, hate speech detection struggled (F1: 0.45), with a low recall (0.39), indicating missed detections despite moderate precision (0.52). The macro F1-score of 0.69 reflects the challenge of achieving balanced performance across classes, while the high weighted F1-score of 0.88 underscores strong performance on the majority class.

Table 6: Results for Subtask B: Hate Speech Detection Using Hierarchical Multi-head Adaptive Weighting

	prec.	rec.	f1	supp.
0	0.92	0.95	0.94	3602
1	0.52	0.39	0.45	474
acc.			0.89	4076
macro	0.72	0.67	0.69	4076
weighted	0.88	0.89	0.88	4076

The performance in Subtask B using the Hierarchical Multi-head Gated Adaptive Weighting model is presented in Table 7. The model achieved an accuracy of 0.87 on a val set of 4,076 samples. For class 0, it demonstrated precision of 0.94, recall of 0.91, and an F1-score of 0.93 across 3,602 instances. For class 1, it recorded precision of 0.45,recall of 0.58, and an F1-score of 0.51 over 474 instances. The macro and weighted averaged F1-score was 0.72 and 0.88 respectively.

The model achieved 87% accuracy with improved balance across classes. Non-hate speech detection remained strong, showing balanced precision and recall. Hate speech detection improved (F1: 0.51) with increased recall (0.58) compared to the non-gated version, though precision was moderate (0.45). The macro F1-score of 0.72 matches that of the gated attention model, indicating comparable balanced performance.

Table 7: Results for Subtask B: Hate Speech Detection Using Hierarchical Multi-head Gated Adaptive Weighting

	prec.	rec.	f1	supp.
0	0.94	0.91	0.93	3602
1	0.45	0.58	0.51	474
acc.			0.87	4076
macro	0.70	0.75	0.72	4076
weighted	0.89	0.87	0.88	4076

In subtask B, we analyzed different proposed architectures to gain crucial insights. The Hierarchical Multi-head Adaptive Weighting model achieved the highest accuracy of 89% but showed weak performance in detecting the minority class. In contrast, the Hierarchical Gated Adaptive Attention model provided a more balanced performance, with 86% accuracy and significantly improved hate speech detection, while maintaining strong non-hate speech detection. Both gated architectures, Gated Adaptive Attention and Multi-head Gated Adaptive Weighting models consistently outperformed their non-gated counterparts in minority class detection, achieving macro F1 scores of 0.72. The substantial class imbalance influenced model behavior, with gating mechanisms proving particularly effective in managing this challenge. These results indicate that, for practical applications in binary hate speech detection, gated architectures offer optimal performance by balancing overall accuracy with reliable minority class detection.

8.2 Task C Results

The performance of the hierarchical adaptive weighting model for identifying hate speech targets (Subtask C) categorized as 'individual,' 'organization,' or 'community'—is presented in Table 8. The model achieved accuracy of 73% on val set of 474 samples. For class 0 (individual), it reported precision of 0.78, recall of 0.76, and F1-score of 0.77 across 230 instances. For class 1 (organization), the precision was 0.75, recall was 0.78, and F1-score was 0.76 over 183 instances. For class 2 (community), the model had precision of 0.45, recall of 0.44, and F1-score of 0.45 over 61 instances. The macro-averaged F1-score was 0.66, and the weighted F1-score matched the accuracy at 0.73.

While achieving balanced macro-averaged precision and recall of 0.66, the model performed well for individual (F1: 0.77) and organizational targets (F1: 0.76). However, identifying community targets remained challenging, with both precision and recall at 0.45, indicating difficulty in detecting the minority class. The weighted F1-score of 0.73 reflects the model's proportionate performance across the class distributions. The confusion matrix, shown in Figure 2, provides deeper insight into the model performance across the classes.

The Gated Adaptive Weighting model, in Subtask C achieved an accuracy of 75% on a test set of 474 samples, as shown in Table 9. For class 0, the model reported precision of 0.78, recall of 0.81, and F1-score of 0.79 across 230 instances. For

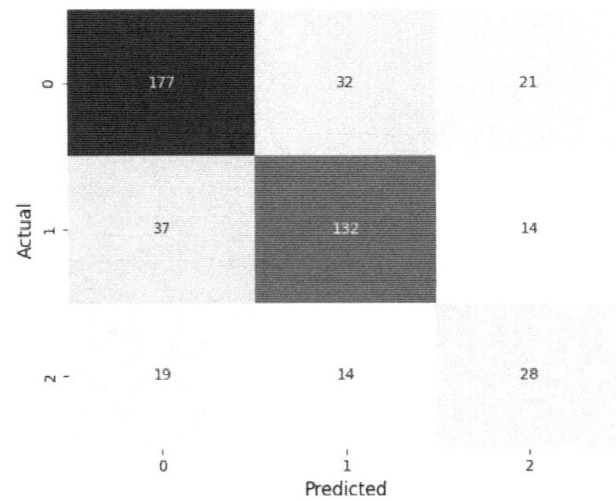

Figure 2: Confusion matrix of the hierarchical adaptive weighting model.

Table 8: Results for Subtask C: Hate Speech Detection Using Hierarchical Adaptive Weighting

	Prec.	Rec.	F1	Supp.
0	0.78	0.76	0.77	230
1	0.75	0.78	0.76	183
2	0.45	0.44	0.45	61
Acc.			0.73	474
Macro	0.66	0.66	0.66	474
Weight.	0.73	0.73	0.73	474

class 1, it recorded precision of 0.80, recall of 0.75, and F1-score of 0.77 across 183 instances. For class 2 , the model attained precision of 0.51,recall of 0.52, and F1-score of 0.52 across 61 instances. The macro-averaged F1-score was 0.69, while the weighted F1-score was 0.75.

The gating mechanism significantly enhanced minority class detection, resulting in an F1-score of 0.52 with balanced precision and recall of 0.51 and 0.52, respectively. Performance on individual targets improved, achieving an F1-score of 0.79 (precision: 0.78, recall: 0.81), while organizational target detection reached an F1-score of 0.77 (precision: 0.80, recall: 0.75). The model demonstrated a balanced precision-recall trade-off across all classes, with weighted metrics consistently at 0.75, indicating robust performance regardless of class distribution. Figure 3 presents the confusion matrix, offering a detailed view of the performance of the model in all classes.

The Multi-head Adaptive Weighting model in Subtask C achieved an accuracy of 73% on val set of 474 samples, as shown in Table 10. For class 0, the model reported precision of 0.78, recall of 0.78, and F1-score of 0.78 across 230 instances. For class 1, it recorded precision of 0.76, recall of

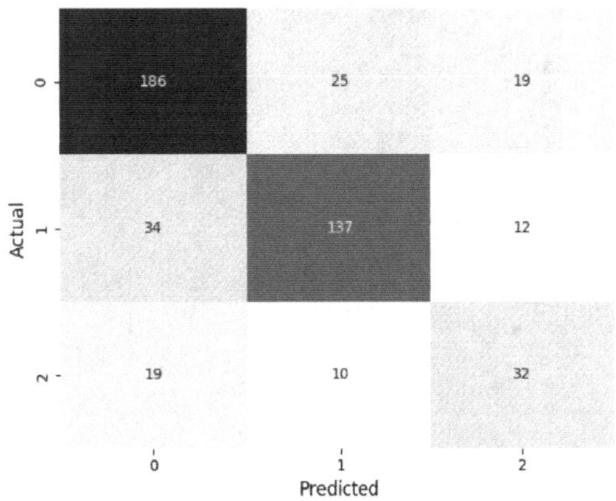

Figure 3: Confusion matrix of the hierarchical gated adaptive weighting model.

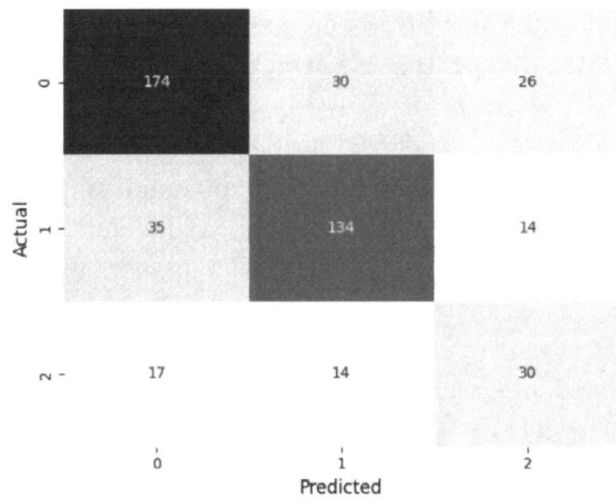

Figure 4: Confusion matrix of the multi-head adaptive weighting model.

Table 9: Results for Subtask C: Hate Speech Detection Using Hierarchical Gated Adaptive Weighting

	Prec.	Rec.	F1	Supp.
0	0.78	0.81	0.79	230
1	0.80	0.75	0.77	183
2	0.51	0.52	0.52	61
Acc.			0.75	474
Macro	0.69	0.69	0.69	474
Weight.	0.75	0.75	0.75	474

Table 10: Results for Subtask C: Hate Speech Detection Using Muti-head Adaptive Weighting

	Prec.	Rec.	F1	Supp.
0	0.78	0.78	0.78	230
1	0.76	0.73	0.74	183
2	0.47	0.52	0.50	61
Acc.			0.73	474
Macro	0.67	0.68	0.67	474
Weight.	0.73	0.73	0.73	474

0.73, and F1-score of 0.74 across 183 instances. For class 2 , the model attained a precision of 0.47, a recall of 0.52, and an F1-score of 0.50 across 61 instances. The macro and weighted F1-scores were 0.67 and 0.73, respectively.

With an accuracy of 73%, this model demonstrated a slight improvement in recall (macro-recall: 0.68). Detection of individual targets maintained strong performance (F1: 0.78), with both precision and recall at 0.78. For organizational targets, there was a slight decline (F1: 0.74), with precision at 0.76 and recall at 0.73. Community target detection improved moderately compared to the non-gated hierarchical model, achieving an F1-score of 0.50, with precision at 0.47 and recall at 0.52. The weighted metrics stabilized at 0.73, consistent with accuracy. The confusion matrix depicted in Figure 4 sheds light on the model's performance for each class.

The Multi-head Gated Adaptive Weighting model in Subtask C achieved an accuracy of 73% on a val set of 474 samples, as shown in Table 11. For class 0, the model achieved precision of 0.76,recall of 0.78, and an F1-score of 0.77 across 230 instances. For class 1, it recorded a precision of 0.78, a recall of 0.75, and an F1-score of 0.76 across 183 instances. For class 2, the model attained precision of 0.43,recall of 0.43, and F1-score of 0.43 across 61 instances. The macro-averaged F1-score was 0.66, while the weighted F1-score was 0.73.

Despite its architectural sophistication, the model performance remained at 73% accuracy. It showed a regression in minority class detection (F1: 0.43), with balanced but lower precision and recall (both at 0.43). Individual target detection maintained effectiveness (F1: 0.77) with a precision of 0.76 and a recall of 0.78. Organizational targets exhibited similar results (F1: 0.76) with a precision of 0.78 and a recall of 0.75. Detailed information on the model's classification accuracy across the classes can be observed in the confusion matrix shown in Figure 5)

Table 11: Results for Subtask C: Hate Speech Detection Using Muti-head Gated Adaptive Weighting

	Prec.	Rec.	F1	Supp.
0	0.76	0.78	0.77	230
1	0.78	0.75	0.76	183
2	0.43	0.43	0.43	61
Acc.			0.73	474
Macro	0.66	0.65	0.66	474
Weight.	0.73	0.73	0.73	474

Comparative analysis identifies the Gated Adap-

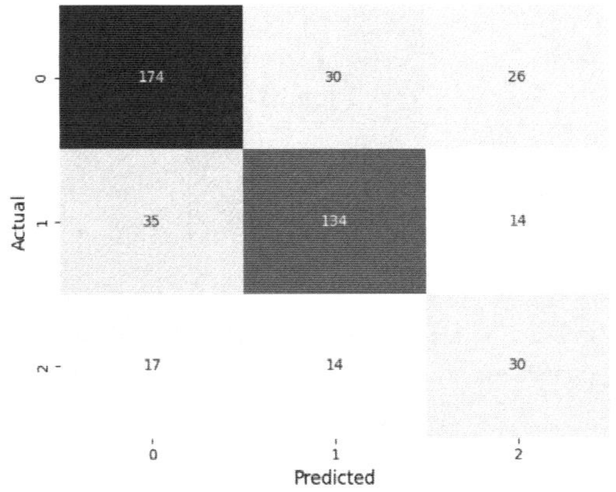

Figure 5: Confusion matrix of the multi-head gated adaptive weighting model.

tive Weighting model as the optimal architecture, demonstrating superior performance across all evaluation metrics. The introduction of gating mechanisms significantly enhanced minority class detection while maintaining strong performance on majority classes. In contrast, the multi-head approaches, despite their complexity, did not yield substantial improvements over simpler architectures. A persistent challenge across all models is the detection of community-targeted hate speech, indicating need for additional techniques to address class imbalance. These results suggest that architectural simplicity, combined with effective feature selection through gating, outperforms more complex attention mechanisms in hate speech and target detection.

9 Appendix C (Error Analysis)

9.1 Appendix C -I

The model exhibited specific challenges in classifying tweets containing symbolic language, named entities, and code-mixed expressions, particularly in understanding nuanced cultural and script-specific references in Devanagari-based low-resource languages. Figure 6 shows representative examples that illustrate these limitations:

The tweet(Index 945) references "Anjana" in a non-hateful, casual context within election commentary. However, the model incorrectly flags this as hate speech, demonstrating difficulties in interpreting named individuals in colloquial, non-aggressive contexts.

The tweet(Index 1667) critiques leadership, which could be interpreted as negative, the language does not explicitly target any individual or group with hate speech.The hashtag "#NoNotAgain" is often associated with resistance or opposition, which may have contributed to the model's identification of the tweet as possibly related to hate speech, especially in the context of political discourse. This tweet contains a mix of Nepali and English, phrase as a political expression of discontent without hate. The model's misclassification reveals limitations in processing symbolic expressions within code-mixed language, especially involving Devanagari script. The tweet(Index 2530) contains the term '"lauro" carries symbolic meaning in Nepali political discourse. Used here in a non-hostile critique of electoral commission decisions, its misclassification as hate speech highlights the model's difficulty in interpreting culturally specific metaphors without explicit hate markers. The tweet("Index 2615") contains hyperbolic political rhetoric attributed to a political figure. The model's incorrect classification demonstrates challenges in processing sarcasm and layered interpretation. The language used in the tweet(Index 2443), such as "Galat manchhelai parnayo" (voting for the wrong person) and "sadegleka neta" (rotten leaders), carries a negative tone. This could be seen as aggressive or disrespectful towards political leaders, which may have influenced the model's classification.However, while the tone is critical, the tweet doesn't contain hate speech towards any particular group. The phrase "Hajurbuba pustalai bidayi garaun" (let's say goodbye to the older generation of leaders) focuses on generational change. The critique is directed at political figures considered outdated or ineffective, which is a common political sentiment.The model could have misinterpreted the critical nature of the tweet as hateful, possibly because of the phrases "Galat manchhelai parnayo",

Index	Tweet	Actual Label	Predicted Label	Misclassification Type
945	2022 भी वैसा ही जाने वाला है बेचारी अंजना का लो फिर एक धमाका हो गया. .#UttarakhandElections2022 #UttarPradeshElections #PunjabElections2022 https://t.co/omI7V8dedp	Non-Hate	Hate	Named Entity
1667	केही नया गर्छु.म अरु भन्दा भिन्न हु भनेपछि भिन्नै खोजिन्छ। पुरानै तरिका हो भने गाली खान तयार हुनै पर्छ। #NoNotAgain भनेर भोट लिएपछि "I am also like them" वाला हरकत मिल्दैन। पाइलै पिच्छे सहानुभुति खोज्ने नेतृत्वले देश चल्दैन! माफी माग्न कति गार्हो बाफ्रे	Non-Hate	Hate	Code-Mixed Language
2530	@ShahBalen जसलाई लौरो को अति आवश्यक छ उसलाई नदिने जसलाई आवश्यक नै छैन उसैलाई लौरो । निर्वाचन आयोगले यो राम्रो काम गरेन ।	Non-Hate	Hate	Cultural Symbolism
2615	मेरी छोरीले चुनाव नजिते देश दुर्घटनामा जान्छ! - कांग्रेस कार्यकारी सभापति प्रचण्ड	Non-Hate	Hate	Political Rhetoric
2443	तपाईंको एक भोट गलत मान्छेलाई पर्नगयो भने हाम्रा सन्ततिको लागि पाँच वर्षको समय पचास वर्ष पछाडी धकेलिन सक्छ। सडेगलेका नेता तथा हजुरबुबा पुस्तालाई बिदाई गरौं। #NonotAgain	Non-Hate	Hate	Generational Commentary

Figure 6: Error analysis of samples of Substask B

"Hajurbuba pustalai bidayi garaun" and "sadegleka neta" (rotten leaders).

9.2 Appendix C -II

To evaluate our model's robustness in distinguishing hate speech targets, we conducted an error analysis on misclassified instances. This analysis provided insights into common misclassification patterns, particularly among categories of individuals, organizations, and communities. Figure 7 presents examples of these errors, along with interpretations for each case. The analysis revealed specific trends in misclassification across categories. For instance, tweets targeting individuals (Class 0) were frequently misclassified as targeting communities (Class 2), likely due to language that generalized statements to a broader group. Similarly, tweets aimed at organizations (Class 1) were often misinterpreted as targeting communities (Class 2) due to the use of collective or broad descriptors.

Index	Actual Label	Predicted Label	Tweet
421	0	2	@KTnepal त जस्ता कपुतहरुलाई गाला फुटने गरी जनताले चडकाउन पर्छ। पन्चायतदेखी ब्रहमलुट गर्नेहरु, प्रजातन्त्रको दोहोलो नकाट, ए कपुतहो लाज लाग्देन तिमीहरुलाई? ह्याक थु तेरो अनुहारमा भ्रष्टचारी, नकचरो, #NoNotAgain
206	0	2	आज मेरे भी सपने में 'कृष्ण जी' आए थे, उन्होंने बताया- 'मैं रामभक्तों पर गोलियां चलवाने वालों के सपने में नहीं जाता'\nजो कल तक जिन्ना के सपने देखते थे आज वो भगवान कृष्ण की बात कर रहे हैं-@BJP4India राष्ट्रीय प्रवक्ता @Shehzad_Ind\n\n#UttarPradeshElections2022\nhttps://t.co/IdJVgaVzvg
253	1	2	आज़ाद हो, \nलेकिन गुलाम मानसिकता के गुलाम,\nऔर अगर नहीं \nतो बीजेपी को वोट क्यों कर रहे हो l\nयह देश तुम्हारा भी है,\nसिर्फ चोर लुटेरों का नहीं l\n#Elections\n#NoVoteToBJP \n#BJP_हटाओ_देश_बचायो \n#UttarPradeshElection2022 \n#uttrakhandElection2022 \n#GoaElections2022 https://t.co/4IOmCpO6wd
91	1	0	अल्लाह का शुकर है जुम्मनों के नजरों से \nहमारे टोटी सुरक्षतीय है। लाल ● टोटी को टोपी समझ कर चुड़ा या होगा। \nअब तो टोटी कोई नही चुरा सकता.......?\n कहा हो बे टोटि चोरो☺□\n #UPElection2022 #UttarPradeshElections2022 https://t.co/7j85vqDh9h
457	2	1	#BreakingNow हापुड़ में सीएम @myogiadityanath ने कहा- 'चुनाव की घोषणा के बाद जो अपने बिलों से निकलकर बिलबिला रहे हैं, इनकी गर्मी 10 मार्च को शांत हो जाएगी'\n\n#GoaElections2022 #Politics @Anant_Tyagii https://t.co/7VSL5zQ2Xn
309	2	0	कर्ण मल्ल को ईतिहास र स्वयँ शेर ब देउवा प्रतिको योगदान को १०% नबुझ्ने सन्जाल का हुल्लड हरु जसको २० घन्टे पेसा भजन गाउने छ राजनीति थाहाछैन ती हुल्लड जमात लाई मेरो चुनौती सन्जाल मा लेख्नु पहिला कर्ण मल्लको योगदान अध्ययन गर

Figure 7: Error analysis of samples of Substask C

In tweet (Index 421), a specific individual "@KTnepal" is criticized using direct language, but the inclusion of broader terms like "Prajatantr ko dohol na kaat" (loosely criticizing broader democratic practices) likely led the model to misclassify it as targeting a community (Class 2). Tweet (Index 206) targets a spokesperson (an individual) but also references religious and political groups ("Rambhakton" and "Jinnah"), which may have confused the model into categorizing it as community-level speech (Class 2). Tweet (Index 253) critiques the BJP (a political organization) but uses phrases like "Gulaam mansikta ke gulaam" ("slave mentality"), which could be interpreted as a critique of a broader societal mindset. This likely led the model to classify it under communities (Class 2) instead of organizations (Class 1). Tweet (Index 91) employs sarcastic commentary that seems directed at an individual due to its personal tone ("Jummon ke nazron se hamari totee surakshit hai"), but it actually targets a group associated with a particular ideology. The model misinterpreted this, resulting in a classification as an individual (Class 0) rather than an organization (Class 1).

In tweet (Index 457), although the statement references a community ("Jo apne bilon se nikal kar bilbila rahe hain"), it is attributed to a political leader (@myogiadityanath). This association with an organization might have caused the model to misclassify it as targeting an organization (Class 1) instead of a community (Class 2). The tweet (Index 309) criticizes a group but also mentions a specific individual, "Karn Mall." The presence of this individual reference may have confused the model, leading to a classification under individuals (Class 0) rather than communities (Class 2). These findings suggest that our model requires improved contextual awareness, particularly in handling nuanced linguistic features like collective nouns and generalized rhetoric. Future iterations could benefit from incorporating additional context markers or keywords associated with specific entities to enhance target classification accuracy."

DSLNLP@NLU of Devanagari Script Languages 2025: Leveraging BERT-based Architectures for Language Identification, Hate Speech Detection and Target Classification

Shraddha Chauhan
Electronics and Communication Engineering
MNNIT-Allahabad
Prayagraj, Uttar Pradesh, 211004
shraddha76830@gmail.com

Abhinav Kumar
Computer Science and Engineering
MNNIT-Allahabad
Prayagraj, Uttar Pradesh, 211004
abhik@mnnit.ac.in

Abstract

The rapid rise of social media has emphasized the spread of harmful and hateful content, making it challenging for its identification. Contextual semantics is very important as prior studies present that context level semantics is a more trustworthy indicator of hatefulness than word level semantics for detecting hate speech. This paper attempts to check the usability of transformer-based models for the identification of hate speech on code-mixed datasets, which includes Google-MuRIL, LaBSE, XLM-Roberta-base, mbert and distil-mbert. The above is largely due to its ability for high-level representations of complex and context-dense meaning. Besides this, we experiment on ensemble approach that covers all of the above models to reach out for an even higher level of performance in detection. The experiment results show the best performing macro F1-scores are reported in case of MuRIL in comparison to other implemented models.

1 Introduction

In an age in which the growth of social media is exponential for applications like X, Facebook, and ShareChat, millions of users now communicate in ways that were simply impossible in the past. It creates easily accessible, real-time conduits for information, social commentary, and open debate. At the same time, it facilitates hate speech, misinformation, and other types of offensive content (Saumya et al., 2024; Kumari and Kumar, 2023; Kumar et al., 2023, 2021b; **?**). It is unrealistic to respond to these issues alone by using manual moderation when massive volumes of data are created every second (Saumya et al., 2024, 2021). Due to this, social media outlets increasingly look towards machine learning automation-based moderation systems.

Despite the fact that tremendous progress has been made in hate speech detection with high-resource languages like English, this research work lags way behind lower-resource languages: Hindi, Marathi, Nepali, Sanskrit, and Bhojpuri. The current scenario makes it even tougher because a lot of texts on social media are found to be code-mixed, mixing languages like Hindi or Nepali with English with unique syntactic constructs. Code-mixing makes traditional NLP tasks, especially the task at hand, tougher because there is a deeper need to discern nuanced contextual cues while crossing languages so that intentions can be classified accurately (Saumya et al., 2024; Kumar et al., 2020).

The present research work focuses on three specific subtasks-one of the tasks which involve multilingual language detection between Hindi, Nepali, Marathi, Sanskrit, and Bhojpuri in the social media text. The importance of precise language identification is directly connected with the effectiveness of hate speech detection because hate speech or inflammatory messages cannot be created unless it is written in the desired language. Classify as hate speech or non-hate speech in Hindi and Nepali is the second sub-task. The third subtask is more in-depth to identify the target of the hateful statement, determining whether an individual, organization, or a community is being targeted (Thapa et al., 2025).

We used the state-of-the-art deep learning methods, focusing more on the transformer-based architecture that shows better performance for NLP-related tasks (Saumya et al., 2024; Kumar et al., 2021a). We used five transformer-based models such as mBERT, Distil-mBERT, MuRIL (Multilingual Representations for Indian Languages), LaBSE- (Language-Agnostic BERT Sentence Embedding) and XLM-RoBERTa, which explore unique linguistic diversity with each dataset, We address its tasks with the strength inherent to each model. Indeed, for example, one must notice that MuRIL is particularly strong within regionally nuanced language representations specific to Indian languages-for Hindi and Nepali texts. Its strength in generating quality, language-independent embed-

Proceedings of the First Workshop on Challenges in Processing South Asian Languages (CHiPSAL 2025), pages 289–294
January 19, 2025.

dings makes LaBSE very effective for processing multilingual and cross-lingual scenarios that are very common to our requirements.

Besides training individual models, We experimented with an ensemble strategy that combined mBERT, Distil-mBERT, and XLM-RoBERTa for classification and applied a voting mechanism among these models to make the final predictions. In this voting-based ensemble approach here, each model classifies an instance independently and derives a final prediction based on the majority voting of the three models. A label is assigned as a final prediction if two or more models agree on a classification outcome. Our approach is a contribution toward Language Identification, Hate Speech Detection and Target Identification for Hate Speech in Devanagari-script languages while also contributing to the overall advancement of the field, showing how transformer-based models are indeed effective in multilingual low-resource and code-mixed NLP tasks.

The rest of the paper is organized as follows: Section 2 lists related work, Section 3 discusses dataset & task, Section 4 discusses the proposed methodology. The outcome of the proposed model is listed in Section 5 and the paper is concluded in Section 6.

2 Related Work

Multilingual NLP has seen significant progress in recent years, with more intensive needs for effective ways and methods to handle many divergent languages, more often in regions with vast rich linguistic diversity. Detection of hate speech , target hate speech (Malik et al., 2024) or language classification has made ways through traditional statistical as well as machine learning-based methods over such techniques as Support Vector Machines SVMs, Naive Bayes classifiers, recurrent neural networks (RNNs) trained through curated language features (Liu et al., 2024; Mandal et al., 2024). These models fail to capture the contextual nuances of language and perform poorly on code-mixed and low-resource languages because of limited availability of training data and reliance on language-specific pre-processing (Conneau et al., 2019).

In our study, We used five transformer-based models individually, namely, mBERT (Devlin et al., 2018), Distil-mBERT (Sanh et al., 2019), Google's MuRIL (Khanuja et al., 2021), LaBSE and XLM-RoBERTa (Conneau et al., 2019) to check their capacity for text multilinguality processing for our study. This approach will enable the singling out of their individual strengths as well as weaknesses in either hate speech detection, target identification for hate speech or language classification tasks. In (Jafri et al., 2024a), Machine Learning algorithms like Naive Bayes, Decision Tree, SVM and Transformer based Deep Learning models like BERT, XLM-RoBERTa and Hard Ensemble of BERTs is used in original and augmented dataset of CHUNAV to analyze Hindi hate speech and targeted groups in Indian Election Discourse (Alam et al., 2024).

To facilitate our experiments and implementations, we use the ktrain framework (Maiya, 2022), which simplifies the process of developing and training deep learning models. This user-friendly library eases the inclusion of multiple architectures, such as transformer-based models, hence streamlining our research work. In general, the discussion of these state-of-the-art models (Khanduja et al., 2024) and ensemble techniques (Singhal and Bedi, 2024) greatly contributes to understanding and applying multilingual NLP, especially to challenges such as low-resource languages and code-mixed text.

3 Dataset & Task

The dataset covers multiple Devanagari-script languages and has a great variety of content features. There are numerals (e.g., 10, 2, 3), emoticons, links (e.g., https://t.co/wFKDRCF0Ny), tags like "@", English words (e.g., "Punjab Elections"), and very evocative, varied sentences in hindi, nepali, sanskrit, bhojpuri languages. The heterogeneity of this is an interesting challenge for the classification task and provides a broad basis for the testing of multilingual and mixed-content text processing models.

The Task on Natural Language Understanding of Devanagari Script Languages (Thapa et al., 2025) consists of three subtasks, which focus on critical challenges in processing languages written in the Devanagari script. These tasks are language identification, hate speech detection and the identification of targets of hate speech (Sarveswaran et al., 2025).

Class	Dataset size
Nepali	12,543
Marathi	11,034
Sanskrit	10,996
Bhojpuri	10,184
Hindi	7,660
Total	52,417

Table 1: Data distribution for subtask A

Class	Dataset size
Non-Hate Speech	16,805
Hate Speech	2,214
Total	19,019

Table 2: Data distribution for subtask B

3.1 Subtask A: Devanagari Script Language Identification

This is the subtask of language identification in text typed in the Devanagari script. The dataset includes five languages: Nepali (Thapa et al., 2023; Rauniyar et al., 2023), Marathi (Kulkarni et al., 2021), Sanskrit (Aralikatte et al., 2021), Bhojpuri (Ojha, 2019) and Hindi (Jafri et al., 2024b, 2023). There are total 52,417 train data, 11,232 validation data and 11,234 test data in Subtask A dataset. Distribution across five classes as shown in Table 1 are as Nepali (12,543), Marathi (11,034), Sanskrit (10,996), Bhojpuri (10,184) and Hindi (7,660).

3.2 Subtask B: Hate Speech Detection in Devanagari Script Language

The second subtask is to identify hate speech in sentences using the Devanagari script. Here, the dataset is annotated to indicate whether a given sentence contains hate speech. There are total 19,019 train data, 4,076 validation data and 4,076 test data in Subtask B dataset. Distribution across two classes as shown in Table 2 are as Non-Hate Speech (16,805) and Hate Speech (2,214). This annotated dataset is imbalanced and consists mainly of monolingual sentences in Nepali (Thapa et al., 2023; Rauniyar et al., 2023) and Hindi (Jafri et al., 2024b, 2023), underlining the need for proper detection mechanisms of different languages within the Devanagari script (Parihar et al., 2021).

3.3 Subtask C: Target Identification for Hate Speech in Devanagari Script

The last subtask is to identify the specific hate speech targets within individual sentences. The target categories are defined as individual, organization, or community. There are total 2,214 train data, 474 validation data and 475 test data in Subtask C dataset. There are 1,074 Individual, 856 Organization, and 284 Community text in training dataset as shown in Table 3.

Class	Dataset size
Individual	1,074
Organization	856
Community	284
Total	2214

Table 3: Data distribution for subtask C

4 Methodology

In this paper, we fine-tune five transformer-based models as shown in Figure 1 for the task of three distinct subtasks of classification on text in multiple languages. We used XLM-RoBERTa, Distil-mBERT, mBERT, LaBSE, and MuRIL for the evaluation of ability in Devanagari script languages. Each of these models was fine-tuned on the subtask datasets for 20 epochs with a batch size of 64 and a learning rate of $2 \times e^{-5}$, balancing between computation efficiency and convergence for the model.

Considering the average length of the token in the dataset was approximately 50, we set the maximum sequence length to 30 tokens with the intent of saving as much memory space without a loss of relevant information. The ktrain library utilizes preprocessing, training and evaluation of the model itself and has streamlined the entirety of the development pipeline as it has brought uniformity in handling data for the whole model.

In addition to the individual model performances, we tried to enhance its classification robustness using ensemble model as shown in Figure 2. We used mBERT, Distil-mBERT, and XLM-RoBERTa in an ensemble. The final voting was done using majority vote. This approach utilized diversified model architectures and combined relevant linguistic insights for making those predictions.

5 Results & Discussion

The Table 4 shows Accuracy (Acc), Precision (Pre), F1-score (F1) and Recall (Rec) of all five transformer models and ensemble model across subtask A, subtask B and subtask C. In evaluating the performance of models across the three sub-

Table 4: Performance metrics of various models across Subtask A, Subtask B and Subtask C

Model	Subtask A				Subtask B				Subtask C			
	Acc	Pre	F1	Rec	Acc	Pre	F1	Rec	Acc	Pre	F1	Rec
mBERT	98.80	98.71	98.69	98.67	88.39	77.54	47.74	50.39	64.63	58.65	51.07	51.68
Distil-mBERT	99.08	98.98	98.98	98.97	88.34	44.17	46.90	50.00	60.63	52.78	48.06	48.38
LaBSE	99.67	99.64	**99.64**	99.65	89.08	78.9	57.12	55.53	35.78	32.94	30.12	30.24
MuRIL	99.60	99.56	99.56	99.56	89.54	77.21	64.59	61.09	68.42	61.97	**61.01**	60.60
XLM-RoBERTa	99.53	99.46	99.48	99.50	89.57	76.49	**66.13**	62.57	66.52	59.00	58.15	57.73
Ensemble Model	99.13	99.05	99.04	99.02	88.59	75.67	51.81	52.42	69.05	63.91	57.48	56.84

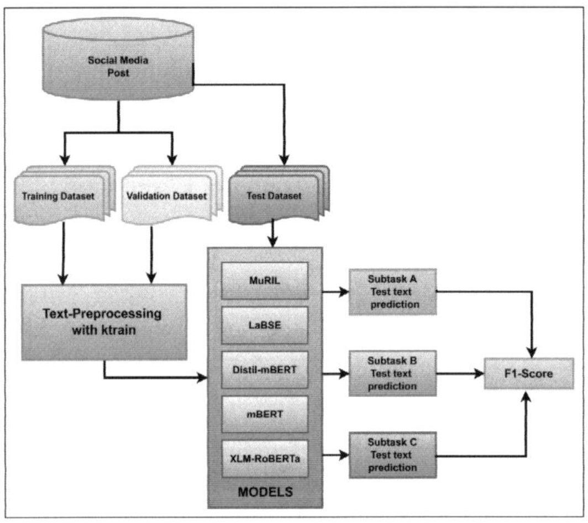

Figure 1: Flow chart of our Transformer based model.

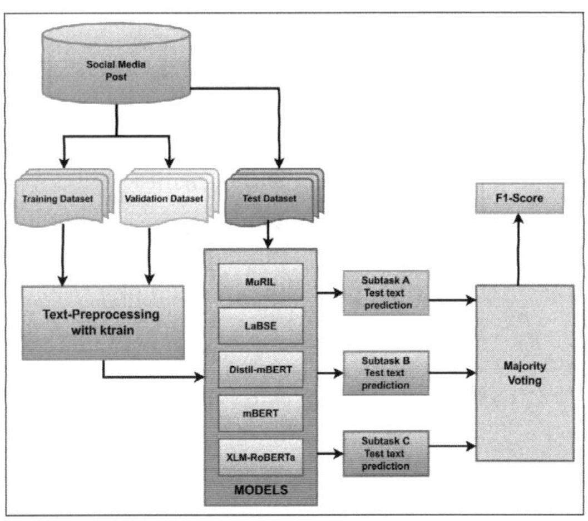

Figure 2: Flow chart of our Ensemble model.

tasks, F1 score was considered the primary comparison score, highlighting the models balanced performance in terms of precision and recall. For Subtask A that is Devanagari Script Language Identification, the LaBSE model gave better performance with an F1 score of 99.64, which showed its well-capable handling of multilingual text in the Devanagari script. In Subtask B (Hate Speech Detection), XLM-RoBERTa had the highest F1 score at 66.13, which indicated the model's ability to detect hate speech across Hindi and Nepali, where language nuances are complex. For Subtask C (Target Identification for Hate Speech), MuRIL was able to outperform other models with an F1 score of 61.01, meaning it can clearly identify hate speech targets as "individual," "organization," and "community." Although the ensemble model generated stable outcomes on subtasks, it failed to surpass individual models such as LaBSE, XLM-RoBERTa and MuRIL for tasks specific F1 scores, meaning even though ensembling makes prediction stable across task space, it is instead likely that strengths of various individual models can be aptly put to use once a proper task-specific ensemble model has been chosen rather than just going for an agnostic ensemble. The variation across tasks indicates that feature extraction and linguistic knowledge are to be used distinctly for effective results in each subtask. This is an essential insight for future work involving Devanagari script language processing and multilingual tasks in general.

6 Conclusion

The results show that transformer-based models have impressive capabilities for various NLP tasks in Devanagari-scripted languages. Each model brought in different strengths: LaBSE was highly effective in language identification across closely related languages, XLM-RoBERTa excelled in hate speech detection, as it is cross-lingually designed; and MuRIL achieved the highest accuracy in hate speech target identification as it is pre-trained on Indian languages. Although stable result was presented by the ensemble over all the tasks, every individual model performed better at task-specific metrics than the combination. These results indicate that instead of generalized ensembling for subtler multi-linguistic applications of NLP, there is more possibility of targeting the application according to which the most competent model selection would be advantageous. For the current domain, in which this approach has given direction, similar future directions can be highlighted for researching Devanagari language processing based more on specificity of the task rather than general application techniques.

References

Md Alam, Hasan Mesbaul Ali Taher, Jawad Hossain, Shawly Ahsan, and Mohammed Moshiul Hoque. 2024. CUET_NLP_Manning@LT-EDI 2024: Transformer-based approach on caste and migration hate speech detection. In *Proceedings of the Fourth Workshop on Language Technology for Equality, Diversity, Inclusion*, pages 238–243, St. Julian's, Malta. Association for Computational Linguistics.

Rahul Aralikatte, Miryam De Lhoneux, Anoop Kunchukuttan, and Anders Søgaard. 2021. Itihasa: A large-scale corpus for sanskrit to english translation. In *Proceedings of the 8th Workshop on Asian Translation (WAT2021)*, pages 191–197.

Alexis Conneau, Kartikay Khandelwal, Naman Goyal, Vishrav Chaudhary, Guillaume Wenzek, Francisco Guzmán, Edouard Grave, Myle Ott, Luke Zettlemoyer, and Veselin Stoyanov. 2019. Unsupervised cross-lingual representation learning at scale. *CoRR*, abs/1911.02116.

Jacob Devlin, Ming-Wei Chang, Kenton Lee, and Kristina Toutanova. 2018. BERT: pre-training of deep bidirectional transformers for language understanding. *CoRR*, abs/1810.04805.

Farhan Ahmad Jafri, Kritesh Rauniyar, Surendrabikram Thapa, Mohammad Aman Siddiqui, Matloob Khushi, and Usman Naseem. 2024a. Chunav: Analyzing hindi hate speech and targeted groups in indian election discourse. *ACM Trans. Asian Low-Resour. Lang. Inf. Process.* Just Accepted.

Farhan Ahmad Jafri, Kritesh Rauniyar, Surendrabikram Thapa, Mohammad Aman Siddiqui, Matloob Khushi, and Usman Naseem. 2024b. Chunav: Analyzing hindi hate speech and targeted groups in indian election discourse. *ACM Transactions on Asian and Low-Resource Language Information Processing*.

Farhan Ahmad Jafri, Mohammad Aman Siddiqui, Surendrabikram Thapa, Kritesh Rauniyar, Usman Naseem, and Imran Razzak. 2023. Uncovering political hate speech during indian election campaign: A new low-resource dataset and baselines.

Namit Khanduja, Nishant Kumar, and Arun Chauhan. 2024. Telugu language hate speech detection using deep learning transformer models: Corpus generation and evaluation. *Systems and Soft Computing*, 6:200112.

Simran Khanuja, Diksha Bansal, Sarvesh Mehtani, Savya Khosla, Atreyee Dey, Balaji Gopalan, Dilip Kumar Margam, Pooja Aggarwal, Rajiv Teja Nagipogu, Shachi Dave, Shruti Gupta, Subhash Chandra Bose Gali, Vish Subramanian, and Partha Talukdar. 2021. Muril: Multilingual representations for indian languages. *Preprint*, arXiv:2103.10730.

Atharva Kulkarni, Meet Mandhane, Manali Likhitkar, Gayatri Kshirsagar, and Raviraj Joshi. 2021. L3cubemahasent: A marathi tweet-based sentiment analysis dataset. In *Proceedings of the Eleventh Workshop on Computational Approaches to Subjectivity, Sentiment and Social Media Analysis*, pages 213–220.

Abhinav Kumar, Jyoti Kumari, and Jiesth Pradhan. 2023. Explainable deep learning for mental health detection from english and arabic social media posts. *ACM Transactions on Asian and Low-Resource Language Information Processing*.

Abhinav Kumar, Pradeep Kumar Roy, and Sunil Saumya. 2021a. An ensemble approach for hate and offensive language identification in english and indo-aryan languages. In *FIRE (Working Notes)*, pages 439–445.

Abhinav Kumar, Sunil Saumya, and Jyoti Prakash Singh. 2020. NITP-AI-NLP@ HASOC-Dravidian-CodeMix-FIRE2020: A machine learning approach to identify offensive languages from dravidian code-mixed text. In *FIRE (Working notes)*, pages 384–390.

Gunjan Kumar, Jyoti Prakash Singh, and Abhinav Kumar. 2021b. A deep multi-modal neural network for the identification of hate speech from social media. In *Responsible AI and Analytics for an Ethical and Inclusive Digitized Society: 20th IFIP WG 6.11 Conference on e-Business, e-Services and e-Society, I3E 2021, Galway, Ireland, September 1–3, 2021, Proceedings 20*, pages 670–680. Springer.

Jyoti Kumari and Abhinav Kumar. 2023. JA-NLP@ LT-EDI-2023: empowering mental health assessment: A roberta-based approach for depression detection. In *Proceedings of the Third Workshop on Language Technology for Equality, Diversity and Inclusion*, pages 89–96.

Dengyi Liu, Minghao Wang, and Andrew G. Catlin. 2024. Detecting anti-semitic hate speech using transformer-based large language models. *Preprint*, arXiv:2405.03794.

Arun S. Maiya. 2022. ktrain: A low-code library for augmented machine learning. *Preprint*, arXiv:2004.10703.

Muhammad Shahid Iqbal Malik, Aftab Nawaz, and Mona Mamdouh Jamjoom. 2024. Hate speech and target community detection in nastaliq urdu using transfer learning techniques. *IEEE Access*, 12:116875–116890.

Atanu Mandal, Gargi Roy, Amit Barman, Indranil Dutta, and Sudip Kumar Naskar. 2024. Attentive fusion: A transformer-based approach to multimodal hate speech detection. *Preprint*, arXiv:2401.10653.

Atul Kr Ojha. 2019. English-bhojpuri smt system: Insights from the karaka model. *arXiv preprint arXiv:1905.02239*.

Anil Singh Parihar, Surendrabikram Thapa, and Sushruti Mishra. 2021. Hate speech detection using natural language processing: Applications and challenges. In *2021 5th International Conference on Trends in Electronics and Informatics (ICOEI)*, pages 1302–1308. IEEE.

Kritesh Rauniyar, Sweta Poudel, Shuvam Shiwakoti, Surendrabikram Thapa, Junaid Rashid, Jungeun Kim, Muhammad Imran, and Usman Naseem. 2023. Multi-aspect annotation and analysis of nepali tweets on anti-establishment election discourse. *IEEE Access*.

Victor Sanh, Lysandre Debut, Julien Chaumond, and Thomas Wolf. 2019. Distilbert, a distilled version of bert: smaller, faster, cheaper and lighter. *ArXiv*, abs/1910.01108.

Kengatharaiyer Sarveswaran, Bal Krishna Bal, Surendrabikram Thapa, Ashwini Vaidya, and Sana Shams. 2025. A brief overview of the first workshop on challenges in processing south asian languages (chipsal). In *Proceedings of the First Workshop on Challenges in Processing South Asian Languages (CHiPSAL)*.

Sunil Saumya, Abhinav Kumar, and Jyoti Prakash Singh. 2021. Offensive language identification in dravidian code mixed social media text. In *Proceedings of the first workshop on speech and language technologies for Dravidian languages*, pages 36–45.

Sunil Saumya, Abhinav Kumar, and Jyoti Prakash Singh. 2024. Filtering offensive language from multilingual social media contents: A deep learning approach. *Engineering Applications of Artificial Intelligence*, 133:108159.

Kriti Singhal and Jatin Bedi. 2024. Transformers@LT-EDI-EACL2024: Caste and migration hate speech detection in Tamil using ensembling on transformers. In *Proceedings of the Fourth Workshop on Language Technology for Equality, Diversity, Inclusion*, pages 249–253, St. Julian's, Malta. Association for Computational Linguistics.

Surendrabikram Thapa, Kritesh Rauniyar, Farhan Ahmad Jafri, Surabhi Adhikari, Kengatharaiyer Sarveswaran, Bal Krishna Bal, Hariram Veeramani, and Usman Naseem. 2025. Natural language understanding of devanagari script languages: Language identification, hate speech and its target detection. In *Proceedings of the First Workshop on Challenges in Processing South Asian Languages (CHiPSAL)*.

Surendrabikram Thapa, Kritesh Rauniyar, Shuvam Shiwakoti, Sweta Poudel, Usman Naseem, and Mehwish Nasim. 2023. Nehate: Large-scale annotated data shedding light on hate speech in nepali local election discourse. In *ECAI 2023*, pages 2346–2353. IOS Press.

IITR-CIOL@NLU of Devanagari Script Languages 2025: Multilingual Hate Speech Detection and Target Identification in Devanagari-Scripted Languages

Siddhant Gupta[1], Siddh Singhal[1], and Azmine Toushik Wasi[2]
[1]Indian Institute of Technology, Roorkee, India
[2]Shahjalal University of Science and Technology, Sylhet, Bangladesh
siddhant_g@me.iitr.ac.in, siddh_s@ee.iitr.ac.in, azmine32@student.sust.edu
All authors contributed to the work equally.

Abstract

This work focuses on two subtasks related to hate speech detection and target identification in Devanagari-scripted languages, specifically Hindi, Marathi, Nepali, Bhojpuri, and Sanskrit. Subtask B involves detecting hate speech in online text, while Subtask C requires identifying the specific targets of hate speech, such as individuals, organizations, or communities. We propose the `MultilingualRobertaClass` model, a deep neural network built on the pretrained multilingual transformer model `ia-multilingual-transliterated-roberta`, optimized for classification tasks in multilingual and transliterated contexts. The model leverages contextualized embeddings to handle linguistic diversity, with a classifier head for binary classification. We received 88.40% accuracy in Subtask B and 66.11% accuracy in Subtask C, in the test set.

1 Introduction

South Asia—comprising Afghanistan, Bangladesh, Bhutan, India, Maldives, Nepal, Pakistan, and Sri Lanka—is one of the world's most populous regions, with around 1.97 billion people (Alexeeva et al., 2024). This region is incredibly rich in culture and language, with over 700 languages and about 25 major scripts in use. More than 50 million South Asians also live abroad, further spreading this linguistic diversity (Rajan and Lal, 2007).

Despite this, South Asian languages are underrepresented in language technology. Many recent large language models (LLMs) have very limited data from South Asia, which is partly due to the numerous challenges in processing these languages (Nguyen et al., 2024). Encoding issues are an early hurdle; although most South Asian scripts are Unicode-compliant, many applications struggle to render them correctly due to complex orthographies, and language input remains a challenge. The region's languages also have intricate linguistic features, multiple writing systems, and long-standing literary traditions that make natural language processing (NLP) difficult (Joshi, 2022).

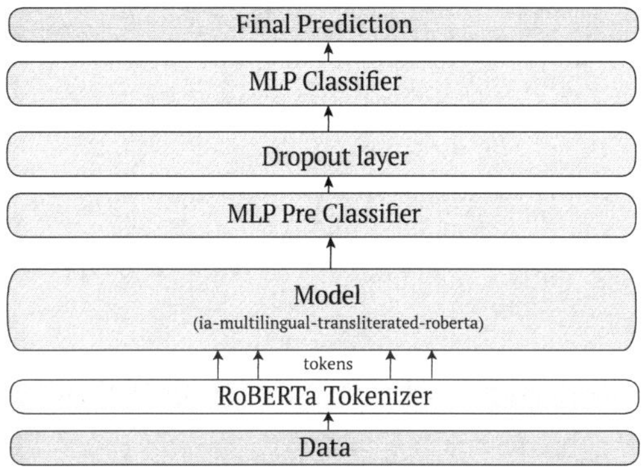

Figure 1: Model architecture, containing tokenizer, pretrained model, classifier and other components

Dialectal and cultural variations, as well as close linguistic ties across languages, further complicate NLP for South Asian languages. This workshop will explore these challenges, focusing on issues around linguistic and cultural diversity, encoding and orthographic challenges, and the resource limitations that slow down technological advancement. By addressing these hurdles, we hope to move closer to improving NLP tools for South Asian languages, helping to preserve their linguistic and cultural heritage.

We decided to participate in Subtask B, Hate Speech Detection, which focuses on identifying the presence of hate speech in Devanagari-scripted languages, and Subtask C, Target Identification, which aims to pinpoint specific targets of hate speech, such as individuals, organizations, or communities. These tasks align closely with broader challenges in South Asian language processing, where complex sociolinguistic contexts, dialect diversity, and multilingualism often complicate language understanding, especially in identifying and managing harmful content online. By advancing these areas,

Proceedings of the First Workshop on Challenges in Processing South Asian Languages (CHiPSAL 2025), pages 295–300
January 19, 2025.

we contribute to addressing critical gaps in natural language understanding for South Asian languages.

2 System Description

2.1 Problem and Dataset

Subtask B: Hate Speech Detection. Hate speech on online platforms can lead to social harm, reinforce biases, and promote hostility within communities (Parihar et al., 2021; Wasi, 2024). For Devanagari-scripted languages such as Hindi (Jafri et al., 2024, 2023), Marathi (Kulkarni et al., 2021), Nepali (Rauniyar et al., 2023; Thapa et al., 2023), Bhojpuri (Ojha, 2019), and Sanskrit (Aralikatte et al., 2021), hate speech detection is particularly challenging due to limited resources, diverse dialects, and complex linguistic structures. In this task, participants must develop a model to detect hate speech within text data written in Devanagari script. Given a dataset with binary annotations indicating the presence or absence of hate speech, the objective is to accurately classify each text instance to either "contains hate speech" or "does not contain hate speech." Success in this task will enhance the ability to monitor and mitigate harmful online content in Devanagari-scripted languages, fostering safer digital environments. The dataset includes 19,019 training tweets, 4,076 validation tweets, and 4,076 test tweets (Thapa et al., 2025; Sarveswaran et al., 2025).

Subtask C: Target Identification for Hate Speech Understanding hate speech in Devanagari-scripted languages extends beyond detection to identifying specific targets, which can include individuals, organizations, or communities. Targeted hate speech poses unique threats by directly influencing public perception of vulnerable groups. In this task, participants are required to classify hate speech instances by identifying the intended target category—whether it is an "individual," "organization," or "community." This task aims to provide a deeper understanding of hate speech dynamics in South Asian languages, supporting more nuanced, targeted content moderation efforts across multilingual online platforms. The dataset for this task comprises 2,214 training tweets, 474 validation tweets, and 475 test tweets.

2.2 Model Design and Development

We designed a `MultilingualRobertaClass` model, which is a deep neural network architecture designed to address classification task in multilingual contexts, with a specific focus on Devanagari-scripted and transliterated languages. At its core, the model leverages the pretrained transformer model `ia-multilingual-transliterated-roberta`[1] (Dhamecha et al., 2021; Liu et al., 2019) from IBM as its primary language representation layer. This layer, denoted by `self.l1`, captures contextualized embeddings of multilingual text, drawing on shared syntactic and semantic structures that span multiple languages. By leveraging a transformer model pretrained on multilingual data, the architecture is especially adept at handling languages with similar linguistic roots or transliterated forms, which are common in South Asian languages.

The model's classification head comprises a sequence of linear and non-linear transformations designed to adapt RoBERTa's output (Dhamecha et al., 2021; Liu et al., 2019) for binary classification. The output of the transformer's CLS token, which serves as a global representation of the input text, is first passed through a fully connected layer, `self.pre_classifier`, which maintains the 768-dimensional space. A ReLU activation function is then applied to introduce non-linearity, enhancing the model's ability to capture complex language patterns. To reduce overfitting, a dropout layer with a 0.3 rate is included, which stochastically zeroes out 30% of the neurons during training. This sequence of transformations allows the model to distill important semantic features from the multilingual embeddings while preserving relevant linguistic nuances for classification.

Finally, the classification layer, `self.classifier`, maps the 768-dimensional representation to a single scalar output, which undergoes a sigmoid activation to yield a probability score between 0 and 1. This score represents the model's confidence in assigning the input to a specific binary class, suitable for tasks such as hate speech detection. By combining a pretrained multilingual transformer with a lightweight, fully connected classifier head, the `MultilingualRobertaClass` model balances generalizable language representation with efficient binary classification. This design is particularly beneficial in applications involving languages with high dialectal diversity and transliterated scripts,

[1] https://huggingface.co/ibm/ia-multilingual-transliterated-roberta

where robust language understanding and precise classification are paramount.

2.3 Implementation Details

Our implementation begins by loading and preprocessing the dataset using `pandas` (pandas development team, 2020) for data handling, and tokenizing input text with a transformer-compatible tokenizer from the `transformers` library (Wolf et al., 2020), setting the maximum sequence length to 256 tokens. The data is split into training, validation, and test sets. For the model, a pre-trained transformer model (such as BERT (Devlin et al., 2019)) from the `transformers` library is employed as the base, with a linear layer added for classification. Key hyperparameters include a learning rate of 2×10^{-5}, batch sizes of 16 for training and 64 for evaluation, and a training duration of 2 to 5 epochs. The optimizer used is AdamW, chosen specifically for its suitability in fine-tuning transformers, alongside a linear learning rate scheduler with warm-up steps to adjust the learning rate dynamically during training.

The training process uses cross-entropy loss, suitable for classification, and evaluates performance with accuracy, precision, recall, and F1-score at the end of each epoch to monitor improvement. Additionally, gradient clipping is likely employed to stabilize the training process, although exact values are not specified. In the evaluation phase, the model generates predictions on validation and test sets, calculating final metrics to gauge model effectiveness. Predicted labels are derived from the logits generated by the model, and results, including performance metrics, are saved or displayed for analysis. This systematic approach ensures model performance is accurately tracked and evaluated throughout the training process.

3 Experiments

3.1 Validation Set Results

The validation results show that Subtask B consistently outperforms Subtask C across all metrics. Subtask B has higher accuracy (0.8221 vs 0.7321), precision (0.7984 vs 0.7394), recall (0.8221 vs 0.7321), and F1 score (0.8097 vs 0.7326). Both tasks have the same micro precision and recall values, indicating that Subtask B's model performs better in all aspects related to classification and error reduction. The substantial difference in scores suggests that Subtask B might be a simpler or more suitable task for the model, whereas Subtask C may involve more complexity or challenging data.

3.2 Ablation Studies

Subtask B. Table 1 presents the ablation study results for Subtask B. It shows that, reducing the sequence length to 128 tokens causes a slight drop in accuracy (from 0.8221 to 0.8050), suggesting that Subtask B benefits from longer sequences to capture more context. Lowering the learning rate to 10^{-5} also results in a small decrease in performance across all metrics, with accuracy dropping to 0.8150, indicating that the model's convergence is slower but still effective. Decreasing the batch size to 8 leads to a modest reduction in performance, with accuracy at 0.8180, implying that smaller batch sizes might affect the model's ability to estimate gradients effectively. Overall, the changes in hyperparameters have a moderate impact, with sequence length being the most influential, while the learning rate and batch size exhibit relatively smaller effects on Subtask B's performance.

Subtask C. Table 2 presents the ablation study results for Subtask C. It shows that,. Reducing the sequence length to 128 tokens leads to a noticeable decrease in all metrics, particularly accuracy, which drops from 0.7321 to 0.7150. This suggests that Subtask C relies heavily on longer sequences to capture important context, and reducing the sequence length limits its ability to make accurate predictions. Lowering the learning rate to 10^{-5}causes a slight decrease in performance across the board, with accuracy falling to 0.7250. This shows that a lower learning rate, while stabilizing training, may slow down convergence slightly. Reducing the batch size to 8 results in minimal changes in accuracy and other metrics, suggesting that Subtask C is relatively stable with smaller batch sizes. Overall, sequence length has the most significant impact on Subtask C's performance, with the learning rate and batch size having relatively smaller, but still noticeable, effects.

4 Evaluation

The test results for Subtask B and Subtask C, presented in Table 3, highlight significant differences in performance. In Subtask B, our model performs exceptionally well, achieving an accuracy of 0.8840, precision of 0.7106, recall of 0.6547, and an F1 score of 0.6762. These results indicate that the model is highly effective at detecting hate

Table 1: Ablation Study Results for Subtask B

Metric	Original	Sequence Length (128)	Learning Rate (10^{-5})	Batch Size (8)
Accuracy	0.8221	0.8050	0.8150	0.8180
Weighted Precision	0.7984	0.7800	0.7900	0.7950
Weighted Recall	0.8221	0.8100	0.8180	0.8200
Weighted F1 Score	0.8097	0.7940	0.8040	0.8070
Micro Precision	0.8221	0.8050	0.8150	0.8180
Micro Recall	0.8221	0.8100	0.8180	0.8200

Table 2: Ablation Study Results for Subtask C

Metric	Original	Sequence Length (128)	Learning Rate (10^{-5})	Batch Size (8)
Accuracy	0.7321	0.7150	0.7250	0.7300
Weighted Precision	0.7394	0.7250	0.7350	0.7380
Weighted Recall	0.7321	0.7200	0.7300	0.7310
Weighted F1 Score	0.7326	0.7180	0.7280	0.7300
Micro Precision	0.7321	0.7150	0.7250	0.7300
Micro Recall	0.7321	0.7200	0.7300	0.7310

Table 3: Test Results for Subtask B and Subtask C

Metric	Subtask B	Subtask C
Recall	0.6547	0.5839
Precision	0.7106	0.5910
F1 Score	0.6762	0.5816
Accuracy	0.8840	0.6611

speech, with strong accuracy and a good balance between precision and recall, minimizing both false positives and false negatives. In contrast, Subtask C shows lower performance across all metrics, with an accuracy of 0.6611, precision of 0.5910, recall of 0.5839, and an F1 score of 0.5816. This suggests that identifying the specific targets of hate speech is a more challenging task, likely due to the increased complexity of categorizing targets like individuals, organizations, or communities. The lower results in Subtask C highlight the need for further model optimization or additional data to improve its performance in target identification.

5 Discussion

We believe, this research has a profound societal impact, fostering safer and more inclusive online spaces by advancing hate speech detection and target identification in South Asian languages. By addressing the challenges posed by the region's linguistic diversity and sociocultural nuances, it empowers platforms to better manage harmful content and protect vulnerable individuals and communities. Identifying specific targets of hate speech enables targeted interventions, offering support to marginalized groups while improving content moderation strategies. Beyond regional significance, the methodologies developed can inform global efforts to tackle online toxicity in multilingual contexts, promoting equitable digital environments, amplifying underrepresented voices, and contributing to social harmony and justice..

6 Conclusion

This paper presents a comprehensive approach to tackling two key subtasks in the domain of hate speech detection and target identification in Devanagari-scripted languages. We work, leveraging a pretrained multilingual transformer architecture to handle the complexities of hate speech detection in diverse South Asian languages. Our model demonstrated strong performance in Subtask B (Hate Speech Detection), with high accuracy and balanced precision and recall, effectively identifying hate speech instances. However, in Subtask C (Target Identification), the performance was lower, highlighting the additional challenges associated with identifying specific targets of hate speech. These results suggest that while hate speech detection can be effectively addressed with current approaches, more work is needed for robust target identification, which requires deeper understanding and handling of the nuanced sociolinguistic context in South Asian languages.

Limitations

From an implementation perspective, one limitation of our work is the reliance on a pretrained multilingual transformer model, which may not fully capture the nuances of Devanagari-scripted languages and transliterated forms. Additionally, the model's architecture could benefit from further optimization, such as incorporating more specialized layers or attention mechanisms, to enhance its ability to handle complex linguistic structures and improve performance in Task C (Target Identification).

Acknowledgments

We extend our heartfelt gratitude to the members and advisors of the Computational Intelligence and Operations Laboratory (CIOL) for their invaluable support throughout the preparation of this work and during the experimental phase. We also sincerely thank Wahid Faisal for his technical assistance with data augmentation, which greatly contributed to the success of this study.

References

N. Nikolaevna Alexeeva, Aleksandr Maximovich Ryabchikov, Calambur Sivaramamurti, and Yury Konstantinovich Yefremov. 2024. South asia. Encyclopedia Britannica, November 6, 2024.

Rahul Aralikatte, Miryam De Lhoneux, Anoop Kunchukuttan, and Anders Søgaard. 2021. Itihasa: A large-scale corpus for sanskrit to english translation. In *Proceedings of the 8th Workshop on Asian Translation (WAT2021)*, pages 191–197.

Jacob Devlin, Ming-Wei Chang, Kenton Lee, and Kristina Toutanova. 2019. BERT: Pre-training of deep bidirectional transformers for language understanding. In *Proceedings of the 2019 Conference of the North American Chapter of the Association for Computational Linguistics: Human Language Technologies, Volume 1 (Long and Short Papers)*, pages 4171–4186, Minneapolis, Minnesota. Association for Computational Linguistics.

Tejas Dhamecha, Rudra Murthy, Samarth Bharadwaj, Karthik Sankaranarayanan, and Pushpak Bhattacharyya. 2021. Role of Language Relatedness in Multilingual Fine-tuning of Language Models: A Case Study in Indo-Aryan Languages. In *Proceedings of the 2021 Conference on Empirical Methods in Natural Language Processing*, pages 8584–8595, Online and Punta Cana, Dominican Republic. Association for Computational Linguistics.

Farhan Ahmad Jafri, Kritesh Rauniyar, Surendrabikram Thapa, Mohammad Aman Siddiqui, Matloob Khushi, and Usman Naseem. 2024. Chunav: Analyzing hindi hate speech and targeted groups in indian election discourse. *ACM Transactions on Asian and Low-Resource Language Information Processing*.

Farhan Ahmad Jafri, Mohammad Aman Siddiqui, Surendrabikram Thapa, Kritesh Rauniyar, Usman Naseem, and Imran Razzak. 2023. Uncovering political hate speech during indian election campaign: A new low-resource dataset and baselines.

Raviraj Joshi. 2022. L3cube-hindbert and devbert: Pre-trained bert transformer models for devanagari based hindi and marathi languages.

Atharva Kulkarni, Meet Mandhane, Manali Likhitkar, Gayatri Kshirsagar, and Raviraj Joshi. 2021. L3cubemahasent: A marathi tweet-based sentiment analysis dataset. In *Proceedings of the Eleventh Workshop on Computational Approaches to Subjectivity, Sentiment and Social Media Analysis*, pages 213–220.

Yinhan Liu, Myle Ott, Naman Goyal, Jingfei Du, Mandar Joshi, Danqi Chen, Omer Levy, Mike Lewis, Luke Zettlemoyer, and Veselin Stoyanov. 2019. Roberta: A robustly optimized bert pretraining approach. *Preprint*, arXiv:1907.11692.

Xuan-Phi Nguyen, Wenxuan Zhang, Xin Li, Mahani Aljunied, Zhiqiang Hu, Chenhui Shen, Yew Ken Chia, Xingxuan Li, Jianyu Wang, Qingyu Tan, Liying Cheng, Guanzheng Chen, Yue Deng, Sen Yang, Chaoqun Liu, Hang Zhang, and Lidong Bing. 2024. SeaLLMs - large language models for Southeast Asia. In *Proceedings of the 62nd Annual Meeting of the Association for Computational Linguistics (Volume 3: System Demonstrations)*, pages 294–304, Bangkok, Thailand. Association for Computational Linguistics.

Atul Kr Ojha. 2019. English-bhojpuri smt system: Insights from the karaka model. *arXiv preprint arXiv:1905.02239*.

The pandas development team. 2020. pandas-dev/pandas: Pandas.

Anil Singh Parihar, Surendrabikram Thapa, and Sushruti Mishra. 2021. Hate speech detection using natural language processing: Applications and challenges. In *2021 5th International Conference on Trends in Electronics and Informatics (ICOEI)*, pages 1302–1308. IEEE.

Gita Rajan and Vinay Lal. 2007. South asian popular culture: Beyond and beneath the habitual. *South Asian Popular Culture*, 5(1):1–10.

Kritesh Rauniyar, Sweta Poudel, Shuvam Shiwakoti, Surendrabikram Thapa, Junaid Rashid, Jungeun Kim, Muhammad Imran, and Usman Naseem. 2023. Multi-aspect annotation and analysis of nepali tweets on anti-establishment election discourse. *IEEE Access*.

Kengatharaiyer Sarveswaran, Bal Krishna Bal, Surendrabikram Thapa, Ashwini Vaidya, and Sana Shams. 2025. A brief overview of the first workshop on challenges in processing south asian languages (chipsal). In *Proceedings of the First Workshop on Challenges in Processing South Asian Languages (CHiPSAL)*.

Surendrabikram Thapa, Kritesh Rauniyar, Farhan Ahmad Jafri, Surabhi Adhikari, Kengatharaiyer Sarveswaran, Bal Krishna Bal, Hariram Veeramani, and Usman Naseem. 2025. Natural language understanding of devanagari script languages: Language identification, hate speech and its target detection. In *Proceedings of the First Workshop on Challenges in Processing South Asian Languages (CHiPSAL)*.

Surendrabikram Thapa, Kritesh Rauniyar, Shuvam Shiwakoti, Sweta Poudel, Usman Naseem, and Mehwish Nasim. 2023. Nehate: Large-scale annotated data shedding light on hate speech in nepali local election discourse. In *ECAI 2023*, pages 2346–2353. IOS Press.

Azmine Toushik Wasi. 2024. Explainable identification of hate speech towards islam using graph neural networks. In *Proceedings of the Third Workshop on NLP for Positive Impact*, pages 250–257, Miami, Florida, USA. Association for Computational Linguistics.

Thomas Wolf, Lysandre Debut, Victor Sanh, Julien Chaumond, Clement Delangue, Anthony Moi, Pierric Cistac, Tim Rault, Rémi Louf, Morgan Funtowicz, Joe Davison, Sam Shleifer, Patrick von Platen, Clara Ma, Yacine Jernite, Julien Plu, Canwen Xu, Teven Le Scao, Sylvain Gugger, Mariama Drame, Quentin Lhoest, and Alexander M. Rush. 2020. Huggingface's transformers: State-of-the-art natural language processing. *Preprint*, arXiv:1910.03771.

LLMsAgainstHate @ NLU of Devanagari Script Languages 2025: Hate Speech Detection and Target Identification in Devanagari Languages via Parameter Efficient Fine-Tuning of LLMs

Rushendra Sidibomma[1], Pransh Patwa[2], Parth Patwa[3], Aman Chadha[4,5*], Vinija Jain[4], Amitava Das[6],

[1]IIIT Sri City, India, [2]Aditya English Medium School, India, [3]UCLA, USA, [4]Stanford University, USA, [5]Amazon GenAI, USA, [6]University of South Carolina, USA
rushendra.s20@iiits.in, pransh.patwa@aemspune.edu.in, parthpatwa@g.ucla.edu
hi@aman.ai, hi@vinija.ai, amitava@mailbox.sc.edu

Abstract

The detection of hate speech has become increasingly important in combating online hostility and its real-world consequences. Despite recent advancements, there is limited research addressing hate speech detection in Devanagari-scripted languages, where resources and tools are scarce. While large language models (LLMs) have shown promise in language-related tasks, traditional fine-tuning approaches are often infeasible given the size of the models. In this paper, we propose a Parameter Efficient Fine tuning (PEFT) based solution for hate speech detection and target identification. We evaluate multiple LLMs on the Devanagari dataset provided by Thapa et al. (2025), which contains annotated instances in 2 languages - Hindi and Nepali. The results demonstrate the efficacy of our approach in handling Devanagari-scripted content. Our code is available at https://github.com/Rushendra10/Hate-Speech-Detection-and-Target-Identification-in-Devanagari-Languages.

1 Introduction

In recent years, the rise in online hate speech has led to severe social consequences, often escalating into real-world violence and disproportionately affecting vulnerable communities (Laub, 2019). This issue is especially challenging for low-resource languages, where the lack of technological tools limits effective monitoring and mitigation of harmful content (Shen et al., 2024; Court and Elsner, 2024). Addressing hate speech in these languages is important to minimize societal harm and foster safer online environments.

Large Language Models (LLMs) have shown significant potential in handling various language-related tasks, including hate speech detection. However, techniques such as in-context learning (ICL) are increase the cost and latency of LLMs with the increase in data (Liu et al., 2022b). While fine-tuning can improve performance, it remains resource-intensive, given the billions of parameters of LLMs. To address these challenges, Parameter-Efficient Fine-Tuning (PEFT) has emerged as a more adaptable and cost-effective solution, making it a compelling choice for this application (Patwa et al., 2024).

In this paper, we present our system for detection hate-speech in Devanagari-scripted languages. Our key contributions are:

- We introduce a PEFT-based system for detecting hate speech and identifying targeted individuals or groups.
- We evaluate the effectiveness of various LLMs in this context.
- We focus on Devanagari-scripted languages, but our system can be potentially applied to other languages as well.

2 Related Work

Detecting hate speech online has become a critical issue due to the potential for real-world consequences. Traditional research in this area focused primarily on high-resource languages like English, where robust datasets and NLP tools facilitated effective models (Davidson et al., 2017; Fortuna and Nunes, 2018). However, applying these methods to low-resource languages remains a significant challenge due to limited annotated datasets and language-specific resources. For instance, recent research on hate speech detection in Hindi, a low-resource language despite its global prevalence, has highlighted the importance of building dedicated

*Work does not relate to position at Amazon.

Proceedings of the First Workshop on Challenges in Processing South Asian Languages (CHiPSAL 2025), pages 301–307

datasets and methodologies tailored to these linguistic contexts (Kapil et al., 2023).

Efforts to address these challenges have led to new datasets such as IEHate (Jafri et al., 2023), which specifically captures hate speech in the political discourse of the Indian Assembly Elections. This dataset provides valuable insights and benchmarks for hate speech in low-resource languages, underscoring the need for refined algorithms and hybrid human-machine approaches. Similarly, the HHSD (Kapil et al., 2023) dataset offers a multilayer annotated dataset for hate speech detection in Hindi, structured hierarchically to categorize hate speech into explicit and implicit forms and target attributes. This dataset demonstrates how multitask learning (MTL) frameworks, which combine similar tasks across related languages, can improve performance, further advancing hate speech detection in resource-limited languages.

Researchers have attempted hate-speech detection in low resources languages using various deep learning techniques. Some of the languages explored include Bengali (Safi Samghabadi et al., 2020; Das et al., 2022), Hindi (Patwa et al., 2021b; Shukla et al., 2022; Velankar et al., 2021; Patwa et al., 2021a), Dravidian languages (Tula et al., 2021; Sreelakshmi et al., 2024; Tula et al., 2022) etc. Some researchers have also explored multimodal low resource hate-speech detection (Mishra et al., 2023b,a; Guo et al., 2023). For a detailed discussion, please refer to (Parihar et al., 2021).

Large Language Models (LLMs) have improved detection capabilities but require considerable resources for fine-tuning. Parameter-Efficient Fine-Tuning (PEFT) techniques allow for efficient adaptation by tuning only a subset of model parameters, making them practical for low-resource settings (Li and Liang, 2021; Lester et al., 2021). Language-agnostic models, leveraging machine translation to standardize inputs, also show promise in multilingual hate speech detection (Khan and Phillips, 2021).

In-context learning (ICL) has been explored for adapting LLMs without full retraining, though it incurs higher inference costs as examples scale (Brown et al., 2020). In contrast, PEFT methods offer scalable adaptation (Liu et al., 2022a; Patwa et al., 2024), supporting efficient hate speech detection across languages with fewer resources. In our work, we explore LoRA (Hu et al., 2021) for hate speech detection in Devanagari languages Hindi and Nepali.

3 Data

We use the dataset released as a part of the shared task (Thapa et al., 2025) in the CHiPSAL workshop (Sarveswaran et al., 2025). It contains two tasks - hate speech detection and hate speech target identification in two Devanagari scripted languages: Hindi (Jafri et al., 2024, 2023) and Nepali (Thapa et al., 2023; Rauniyar et al., 2023).

3.1 Hate Speech Detection

For hate speech detection, the data consists of devanagari-scripted text annotated into 2 classes - hate speech and not hate speech. The texts are diverse and collected from various sources including social media posts, news articles, and forums, reflecting a wide range of topics and styles. Table 1 shows the data distribution. We can see that there is a significant class imbalance towards the non-hate class. This imbalance poses a challenge for training the models, as they may tend to favor the majority class.

Class	Train	Valid	Test
Not Hate	16805	3602	3601
Hate	2214	474	475
Total	**19019**	**4076**	**4076**

Table 1: Data distribution of the hate speech detection dataset.

3.2 Hate Speech Target Identification

The second subtask focuses on identifying the targets of hate speech in Devanagari-scripted text. The goal is to classify whether hate speech is directed towards an individual, an organization, or a community. The dataset for this task contains text samples annotated with target labels. The distribution of targets, as indicated in Table 2, shows a more balanced representation for individual and organizational targets, with approximately equal numbers of samples for both classes. However, there is a notable scarcity of samples where the target is a community, resulting in a skewed distribution towards individual and organizational targets. This data limitation introduces a potential challenge in accurately predicting hate speech directed at communities.

Class	Train	Valid	Test
Individual	1074	230	230
Organizational	856	183	184
Community	284	61	61
Total	**2214**	**474**	**475**

Table 2: Data distribution of the hate speech target identification dataset.

4 Methodology

LLMs leverage the transformer (Vaswani et al., 2023) architecture to model linguistic patterns across vast corpora, utilizing multi-head self-attention mechanisms to capture both local and global dependencies in text. LLMs have billions of parameters and are pretrained on extensive general-purpose corpora. As a result they demonstrate great zero shot capabilities on many natural language tasks (Kojima et al., 2022). However, they struggle on low resource languages (Cassano et al., 2024).

ICL is a way to improve performance of LLMs. It refers to providing few labeled examples in the prompt to guide the LLM. However, as the number of examples increase, the cost and lantency of inference increases (Liu et al., 2022b).

Fully fine tuning (FFT) an LLM with billions of parameters is infeasible because of the costs and computational resources needed (Xu et al., 2023).

Parameter Efficient Fine Tuning (PEFT) is a method in which we only finetune a small number of parameters as compared to the size of the LLM. It is more effective than ICL while being more efficient than FFT (Xu et al., 2023).

For our system we use a PEFT method called Low Rank Adaptation (LoRA) (Hu et al., 2021). LoRA reduces the number of trainable parameters by decomposing weight updates into low-rank matrices, which are inserted into the model's attention layers. Specifically, for a weight matrix W, LoRA approximates the update as:

$$W' = W + \Delta W = W + AB^T \quad (1)$$

where A and B are low-rank matrices. By freezing the core parameters of the pretrained model and only updating the low-rank matrices during training, LoRA significantly decreases computational and memory requirement for training while being as effective as FFT (Hu et al., 2021). Furthermore, LoRA does not add to the inference latency, as after training, the weight update AB^T is added to the model weights, hence the total number of model weights remains the same.

5 Experiments

We conduct experiments on 4 different LLMs to address challenges in processing Devanagari-scripted languages. The considered models include the LLama-3.1-8B (Dubey et al., 2024), Nemo-Instruct-2407 (AI and NVIDIA, 2023), Qwen2.5-7B-Instruct (Yang et al., 2024), and Phi3-medium-4k-Instruct (Abdin et al., 2024). Each model is fine-tuned using task-specific datasets. Quantization of the models to 4-bit precision was employed to reduce memory consumption and to speed up training and inference. All fine-tuning models used LoRA with $rank = 16$, $alpha = 16$ and no dropout.

All fine-tuning experiments are performed using a 16GB NVIDIA T4 GPU. For the hate speech detection task, all models were fine-tuned for 2 epochs. For the target identification task, models were fine-tuned for 4 epochs in order to accommodate a relatively small training set. The code is implemented using the Unsloth (Daniel Han and team, 2023) library, which helps accelerate training. Our code is available at https://github.com/Rushendra10/Hate-Speech-Detection-and-Target-Identification-in-Devanagari-Languages.

6 Results and Analysis

The test performance of the models for the hate speech detection and target identification tasks are provided in Tables 3 and 4 respectively. We can see that for both the tasks Nemo has the best performance (F1 scores 90.05% and 71.47% respectively). Notably, Nemo performs better than Llama despite having smaller size. Furthermore, we can see that the overall performance is better on hate speech detection as compared to target identification. This is because the latter task has 3 classes whereas the former task has only 2 classes.

6.1 Class-wise Analysis

Table 5 shows the class-wise results of Nemo for hate speech detection task. The F1 score on the hate class is much lower than on the non-hate class. The Confusion Matrix (Figure 1) shows that the instances of hate class are often mis-predicted as Non Hate. These observations can be attributed to the class imbalance in the training dataset.

Model	Size	Acc.	F1
Llama-3.1	8.03B	88.71%	88.02%
Phi-3-medium	7.36B	90.06%	88.91%
Qwen2.5	4.46B	88.62%	87.90%
Nemo	6.97B	**90.75%**	**90.05%**

Table 3: Performance of various models for hate speech detection task on the test set, along with the quantized model size. Acc. refers to accuracy. F1 refers to weighted average F1 score.

Model	Size	Acc.	F1
Lama-3.1	8.03B	67.37%	66.58%
Phi-3-medium	7.36B	68.21%	67.80%
Qwen2.5	4.46B	70.32%	70.41%
Nemo	6.97B	**72.00%**	**71.47%**

Table 4: Performance of various models for target identification task on the test set along with the quantized model size. Acc. refers to accuracy. F1 refers to weighted average F1 score.

Table 6 shows the class-wise results of Nemo for hate target identification task. The F1 on Individual class is comparable to that in Organization class, whereas it is significantly lower for the Community class. From the Confusion Matrix (Figure 2), we can see that instances of hate directed towards community are frequenty mis-predicted into one of the other 2 classes. Similar to the hate speech detection task, these observation are also a result of the imbalanced training dataset.

	P	R	F1
Non Hate	93.10%	96.70%	94.86%
Hate	64.58%	45.68%	53.51%

Table 5: Class-wise performance of Nemo on test set of the hate speech detection task. P = Precision, R= Recall, F1 = F1 score.

	P	R	F1
Individual	76.57%	79.56%	78.04%
Organization	72.49%	74.46%	73.46%
Community	46.81%	36.07%	40.74%

Table 6: Class-wise performance of Nemo on test set of the target identification task. P = Precision, R= Recall, F1 = F1 score.

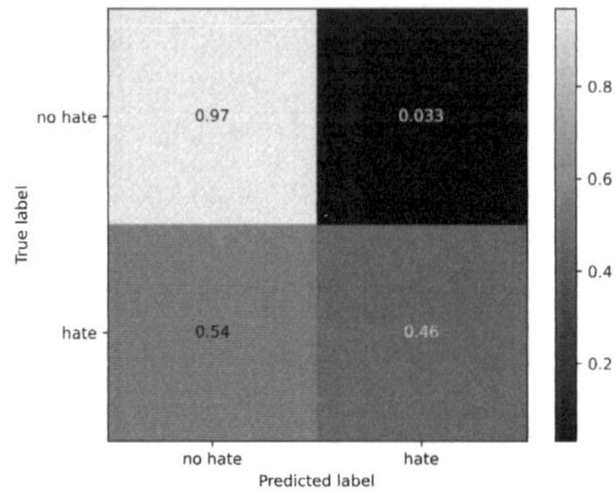

Figure 1: Confusion matrix of Nemo on the test set for hate speech detection.

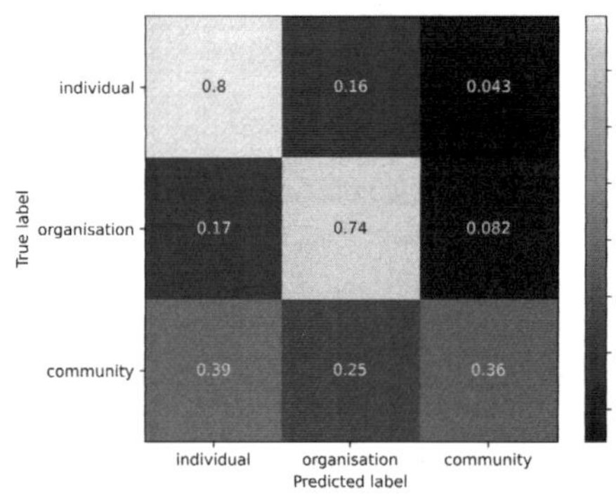

Figure 2: Confusion matrix of Nemo on the test set for hate speech target identification.

7 Conclusion and Future Work

In this study, we present our approach for hate speech detection in Devanagari-scripted languages using LLMs fine-tuned with LoRA. Our methodology demonstrates good performance, as evidenced by accuracy and F1 score metrics. By leveraging the CHiPSal dataset, we effectively address the challenges posed by low-resource languages. We notice that the performance is lower on the the classes with fewer data instances.

Future research could involved enhancing the model's capabilities by developing data generation techniques to address class imbalance, ensuring robust performance across all classes. Additionally, investigating the integration of more sophisticated techniques, such as ensemble methods, can further boost detection accuracy and robustness.

8 Limitation

We assume the existence of a decently sized train dataset to fine-tune our model. Further, we assume that the LLMs will have some knowledge of devanagari languages for PEFT to work.

9 Ethical Statement

Hate speech detection is a sensitive topic and can be subjective. LLMs are known to have inherent biases. Any censoring decisions based on the LLMs predictions should involve comprehensive human reviews.

References

Marah Abdin, Jyoti Aneja, Hany Awadalla, Ahmed Awadallah, et al. 2024. Phi-3 technical report: A highly capable language model locally on your phone. *Preprint*, arXiv:2404.14219.

Mistral AI and NVIDIA. 2023. Mistral nemo-instruct-2407: A 12b parameter transformer model. `https://mistral.ai/news/mistral-nemo/`. Accessed: 2024-11-10.

Tom B. Brown, Benjamin Mann, Nick Ryder, Melanie Subbiah, Jared Kaplan, Prafulla Dhariwal, Arvind Neelakantan, Pranav Shyam, Girish Sastry, Amanda Askell, Sandhini Agarwal, Ariel Herbert-Voss, Gretchen Krueger, Tom Henighan, Rewon Child, Aditya Ramesh, Daniel M. Ziegler, Jeffrey Wu, Clemens Winter, Christopher Hesse, Mark Chen, Eric Sigler, Mateusz Litwin, Scott Gray, Benjamin Chess, Jack Clark, Christopher Berner, Sam McCandlish, Alec Radford, Ilya Sutskever, and Dario Amodei. 2020. Language models are few-shot learners. *Preprint*, arXiv:2005.14165.

Federico Cassano, John Gouwar, Francesca Lucchetti, Claire Schlesinger, Anders Freeman, Carolyn Jane Anderson, Molly Q Feldman, Michael Greenberg, Abhinav Jangda, and Arjun Guha. 2024. Knowledge transfer from high-resource to low-resource programming languages for code llms. *Proceedings of the ACM on Programming Languages*, 8(OOPSLA2):677–708.

Sara Court and Micha Elsner. 2024. Shortcomings of llms for low-resource translation: Retrieval and understanding are both the problem. *Preprint*, arXiv:2406.15625.

Michael Han Daniel Han and Unsloth team. 2023. Unsloth.

Mithun Das, Somnath Banerjee, Punyajoy Saha, and Animesh Mukherjee. 2022. Hate speech and offensive language detection in Bengali. In *Proceedings of the 2nd Conference of the Asia-Pacific Chapter of the Association for Computational Linguistics and the 12th International Joint Conference on Natural Language Processing (Volume 1: Long Papers)*, Online only. Association for Computational Linguistics.

Thomas Davidson, Dana Warmsley, Michael Macy, and Ingmar Weber. 2017. Automated hate speech detection and the problem of offensive language. In *Proceedings of the international AAAI conference on web and social media*, pages 512–515.

Abhimanyu Dubey, Abhinav Jauhri, Abhinav Pandey, Abhishek Kadian, et al. 2024. The llama 3 herd of models. *Preprint*, arXiv:2407.21783.

Paula Fortuna and Sérgio Nunes. 2018. A survey on automatic detection of hate speech in text. *ACM Computing Surveys (CSUR)*, 51(4):1–30.

Xiaoyu Guo, Jing Ma, and Arkaitz Zubiaga. 2023. Nuaa-qmul-aiit at memotion 3: Multi-modal fusion with squeeze-and-excitation for internet meme emotion analysis. *Preprint*, arXiv:2302.08326.

Edward J Hu, Yelong Shen, Phillip Wallis, Zeyuan Allen-Zhu, Yuanzhi Li, Shean Wang, Lu Wang, and Weizhu Chen. 2021. Lora: Low-rank adaptation of large language models. *arXiv preprint arXiv:2106.09685*.

Farhan Ahmad Jafri, Kritesh Rauniyar, Surendrabikram Thapa, Mohammad Aman Siddiqui, Matloob Khushi, and Usman Naseem. 2024. Chunav: Analyzing hindi hate speech and targeted groups in indian election discourse. *ACM Transactions on Asian and Low-Resource Language Information Processing*.

Farhan Ahmad Jafri, Mohammad Aman Siddiqui, Surendrabikram Thapa, Kritesh Rauniyar, Usman Naseem, and Imran Razzak. 2023. Uncovering political hate speech during indian election campaign: A new low-resource dataset and baselines.

Prashant Kapil, Gitanjali Kumari, Asif Ekbal, Santanu Pal, Arindam Chatterjee, and B. N. Vinutha. 2023. Hhsd: Hindi hate speech detection leveraging multi-task learning. *IEEE Access*, 11:101460–101473.

Heena Khan and Joshua L. Phillips. 2021. Language agnostic model: detecting islamophobic content on social media. In *Proceedings of the 2021 ACM Southeast Conference*, ACMSE '21, page 229–233, New York, NY, USA. Association for Computing Machinery.

Takeshi Kojima, Shixiang Shane Gu, Machel Reid, Yutaka Matsuo, and Yusuke Iwasawa. 2022. Large language models are zero-shot reasoners. *Advances in neural information processing systems*, 35:22199–22213.

Zachary Laub. 2019. Hate speech on social media: Global comparisons. *Council on foreign relations*, 7.

Brian Lester, Rami Al-Rfou, and Noah Constant. 2021. The power of scale for parameter-efficient prompt tuning. In *Proceedings of the 2021 Conference on*

Empirical Methods in Natural Language Processing, pages 3045–3059, Online and Punta Cana, Dominican Republic. Association for Computational Linguistics.

Xiang Lisa Li and Percy Liang. 2021. Prefix-tuning: Optimizing continuous prompts for generation. *Preprint*, arXiv:2101.00190.

Haokun Liu, Derek Tam, Mohammed Muqeeth, Jay Mohta, Tenghao Huang, Mohit Bansal, and Colin Raffel. 2022a. Few-shot parameter-efficient fine-tuning is better and cheaper than in-context learning. *Preprint*, arXiv:2205.05638.

Haokun Liu, Derek Tam, Mohammed Muqeeth, Jay Mohta, Tenghao Huang, Mohit Bansal, and Colin A Raffel. 2022b. Few-shot parameter-efficient fine-tuning is better and cheaper than in-context learning. In *Advances in Neural Information Processing Systems*, volume 35, pages 1950–1965. Curran Associates, Inc.

Shreyash Mishra, S Suryavardan, Megha Chakraborty, Parth Patwa, Anku Rani, Aman Chadha, Aishwarya Reganti, Amitava Das, Amit Sheth, Manoj Chinnakotla, et al. 2023a. Overview of memotion 3: Sentiment and emotion analysis of codemixed hinglish memes. *arXiv preprint arXiv:2309.06517*.

Shreyash Mishra, S Suryavardan, Parth Patwa, Megha Chakraborty, Anku Rani, Aishwarya Reganti, Aman Chadha, Amitava Das, Amit Sheth, Manoj Chinnakotla, et al. 2023b. Memotion 3: Dataset on sentiment and emotion analysis of codemixed hindi-english memes. *arXiv preprint arXiv:2303.09892*.

Anil Singh Parihar, Surendrabikram Thapa, and Sushruti Mishra. 2021. Hate speech detection using natural language processing: Applications and challenges. In *2021 5th International Conference on Trends in Electronics and Informatics (ICOEI)*, pages 1302–1308. IEEE.

Parth Patwa, Mohit Bhardwaj, Vineeth Guptha, Gitanjali Kumari, Shivam Sharma, Srinivas Pykl, Amitava Das, Asif Ekbal, Md Shad Akhtar, and Tanmoy Chakraborty. 2021a. Overview of constraint 2021 shared tasks: Detecting english covid-19 fake news and hindi hostile posts. In *Combating Online Hostile Posts in Regional Languages during Emergency Situation: First International Workshop, CONSTRAINT 2021, Collocated with AAAI 2021, Virtual Event, February 8, 2021, Revised Selected Papers 1*, pages 42–53. Springer.

Parth Patwa, Simone Filice, Zhiyu Chen, Giuseppe Castellucci, Oleg Rokhlenko, and Shervin Malmasi. 2024. Enhancing low-resource llms classification with peft and synthetic data. *Preprint*, arXiv:2404.02422.

Parth Patwa, Srinivas Pykl, Amitava Das, Prerana Mukherjee, and Viswanath Pulabaigari. 2021b. Hater-o-genius aggression classification using capsule networks. *arXiv preprint arXiv:2105.11219*.

Kritesh Rauniyar, Sweta Poudel, Shuvam Shiwakoti, Surendrabikram Thapa, Junaid Rashid, Jungeun Kim, Muhammad Imran, and Usman Naseem. 2023. Multi-aspect annotation and analysis of nepali tweets on anti-establishment election discourse. *IEEE Access*.

Niloofar Safi Samghabadi, Parth Patwa, Srinivas PYKL, Prerana Mukherjee, Amitava Das, and Thamar Solorio. 2020. Aggression and misogyny detection using BERT: A multi-task approach. In *Proceedings of the Second Workshop on Trolling, Aggression and Cyberbullying*, pages 126–131, Marseille, France. European Language Resources Association (ELRA).

Kengatharaiyer Sarveswaran, Bal Krishna Bal, Surendrabikram Thapa, Ashwini Vaidya, and Sana Shams. 2025. A brief overview of the first workshop on challenges in processing south asian languages (chipsal). In *Proceedings of the First Workshop on Challenges in Processing South Asian Languages (CHiPSAL)*.

Lingfeng Shen, Weiting Tan, Sihao Chen, Yunmo Chen, Jingyu Zhang, Haoran Xu, Boyuan Zheng, Philipp Koehn, and Daniel Khashabi. 2024. The language barrier: Dissecting safety challenges of llms in multilingual contexts. *Preprint*, arXiv:2401.13136.

Shubham Shukla, Sushama Nagpal, and Sangeeta Sabharwal. 2022. Hate speech detection in hindi language using bert and convolution neural network. In *2022 International Conference on Computing, Communication, and Intelligent Systems (ICCCIS)*, pages 642–647.

K. Sreelakshmi, B. Premjith, Bharathi Raja Chakravarthi, and K. P. Soman. 2024. Detection of hate speech and offensive language codemix text in dravidian languages using cost-sensitive learning approach. *IEEE Access*, 12:20064–20090.

Surendrabikram Thapa, Kritesh Rauniyar, Farhan Ahmad Jafri, Surabhi Adhikari, Kengatharaiyer Sarveswaran, Bal Krishna Bal, Hariram Veeramani, and Usman Naseem. 2025. Natural language understanding of devanagari script languages: Language identification, hate speech and its target detection. In *Proceedings of the First Workshop on Challenges in Processing South Asian Languages (CHiPSAL)*.

Surendrabikram Thapa, Kritesh Rauniyar, Shuvam Shiwakoti, Sweta Poudel, Usman Naseem, and Mehwish Nasim. 2023. Nehate: Large-scale annotated data shedding light on hate speech in nepali local election discourse. In *ECAI 2023*, pages 2346–2353. IOS Press.

Debapriya Tula, Prathyush Potluri, Shreyas Ms, Sumanth Doddapaneni, Pranjal Sahu, Rohan Sukumaran, and Parth Patwa. 2021. Bitions@ dravidianlangtech-eacl2021: Ensemble of multilingual language models with pseudo labeling for offence detection in dravidian languages. In *Proceedings of the first workshop on speech and language technologies for dravidian languages*, pages 291–299.

Debapriya Tula, MS Shreyas, Viswanatha Reddy, Pranjal Sahu, Sumanth Doddapaneni, Prathyush Potluri, Rohan Sukumaran, and Parth Patwa. 2022. Offence detection in dravidian languages using code-mixing index-based focal loss. *SN Computer Science*, 3(5):330.

Ashish Vaswani, Noam Shazeer, Niki Parmar, Jakob Uszkoreit, Llion Jones, Aidan N. Gomez, Lukasz Kaiser, and Illia Polosukhin. 2023. Attention is all you need. *Preprint*, arXiv:1706.03762.

Abhishek Velankar, Hrushikesh Patil, Amol Gore, Shubham Salunke, and Raviraj Joshi. 2021. Hate and offensive speech detection in hindi and marathi. *Preprint*, arXiv:2110.12200.

Lingling Xu, Haoran Xie, Si-Zhao Joe Qin, Xiaohui Tao, and Fu Lee Wang. 2023. Parameter-efficient fine-tuning methods for pretrained language models: A critical review and assessment. *Preprint*, arXiv:2312.12148.

An Yang, Baosong Yang, Binyuan Hui, Bo Zheng, Bowen Yu, Chang Zhou, Chengpeng Li, Chengyuan Li, Dayiheng Liu, Fei Huang, Guanting Dong, Haoran Wei, Huan Lin, Jialong Tang, Jialin Wang, Jian Yang, Jianhong Tu, Jianwei Zhang, Jianxin Ma, Jianxin Yang, Jin Xu, Jingren Zhou, Jinze Bai, Jinzheng He, Junyang Lin, Kai Dang, Keming Lu, Keqin Chen, Kexin Yang, Mei Li, Mingfeng Xue, Na Ni, Pei Zhang, Peng Wang, Ru Peng, Rui Men, Ruize Gao, Runji Lin, Shijie Wang, Shuai Bai, Sinan Tan, Tianhang Zhu, Tianhao Li, Tianyu Liu, Wenbin Ge, Xiaodong Deng, Xiaohuan Zhou, Xingzhang Ren, Xinyu Zhang, Xipin Wei, Xuancheng Ren, Xuejing Liu, Yang Fan, Yang Yao, Yichang Zhang, Yu Wan, Yunfei Chu, Yuqiong Liu, Zeyu Cui, Zhenru Zhang, Zhifang Guo, and Zhihao Fan. 2024. Qwen2 technical report. *Preprint*, arXiv:2407.10671.

MDSBots@NLU of Devanagari Script Languages 2025: Detection of Language, Hate Speech, and Targets using MURTweet

Prabhat Ale*
IOST, Tribhuvan University
Butwal, Nepal
prabhat.805522@sms.tu.edu.np

Anish Thapaliya*
IOST, Tribhuvan University
Kathmandu, Nepal
anish.805522@sms.tu.edu.np

Suman Paudel*
IOST, Tribhuvan University
Kathmandu, Nepal
suman.805522@sms.tu.edu.np

Abstract

In multilingual contexts, an automated system for accurate language identification, followed by hate speech detection and target identification, plays a critical role in processing low-resource hate speech data and mitigating its negative impact. This paper presents our approach to the three subtasks in the Shared Task on Natural Language Understanding of Devanagari Script Languages at CHiPSAL@COLING 2025: (i) Language Identification, (ii) Hate Speech Detection, and (iii) Target Identification. Both classical machine learning and multilingual transformer models were explored, where MuRIL Large, trained on undersampled data for subtasks A and B outperformed the classical models. For subtask C, the hybrid model trained on augmented data achieved superior performance over classical and transformer-based approaches. The top-performing models, named MURTweet for subtasks A and B and NERMURTweet for subtask C, secured sixth, third, and first rank respectively, in the competition. The code is publicly available at https://github.com/thapaliya123/CHIPSAL-COLING-2025.

1 Introduction

Social media platforms like Twitter (currently called X) are filled with various types of hate speech, including racism, sexism, hate speech related to religion, and more (Parihar et al., 2021). Advances in large language models for regional languages, like Nepali, help detect hate speech and analyze sentiment on social media platforms (Pudasaini et al., 2024). Political leaders also use Twitter to spread their political agendas by sharing news and information with a broad audience and participating in discussions, either supporting or criticizing political actions (Lai et al., 2023). Politicians and their followers may use phrases, expressions, and words of hate to gain an advantage and belittle other parties (Wang et al., 2022).

The shared work on Natural Language Understanding of Devanagari Script Languages, organized as part of the First Workshop on Challenges in Processing South Asian Languages (CHiPSAL) (Sarveswaran et al., 2025), allows participants to investigate approaches for recognizing low-resource South Asian languages, moving beyond the widely used English language, even with domain-specific models (Mali et al., 2024). It also focuses on detecting hate speech and identifying its targets, which are often political individuals, organizations, or specific community groups (Thapa et al., 2025).

The MuRIL Large model[1], a specialized BERT large (24-layer) architecture (Khanuja et al., 2021), has been chosen as a solution to the shared task because of its strong multilingual capabilities, particularly for Devanagari languages. In this method, fine-tuning was applied across all model parameters to calibrate the MuRIL architecture for tasks at hand, including language identification, hate speech detection, and target identification.

The undersampling technique was used to reduce training time for subtask A and to address class imbalance in subtask B. For subtask C, data augmentation techniques were applied to address a class imbalance problem. A synonym replacement technique was used to generate synthetic samples from validation data, resulting in improved model performance. A rule-based Named Entity Recognition (NER) approach was also used to classify individual tokens associated with individuals, organizations, or community groups in tweets, with the goal of identifying hate speech targets for subtask C. F1 score was chosen as the primary metric, as leaderboard rankings were based on the F1 score and also the data were imbalanced. This study provides an overview of the solution's results, high-

* *These authors contributed equally to this work.

[1] https://huggingface.co/google/muril-large-cased

Proceedings of the First Workshop on Challenges in Processing South Asian Languages (CHiPSAL 2025), pages 308–313
January 19, 2025.

lighting a sixth-place ranking in subtask A, third in subtask B, and first place in subtask C.

2 Subtasks and Datasets

2.1 Subtask A: Language Identification

This work examines five Devanagari-script languages: Nepali, Marathi, Sanskrit, Bhojpuri, and Hindi. To achieve accurate language identification and recognition across these languages, the following datasets are used:

1) Nepali (Thapa et al., 2023; Rauniyar et al., 2023), 2) Marathi (Kulkarni et al., 2021), 3) Sanskrit (Aralikatte et al., 2021), 4) Bhojpuri (Ojha, 2019), 5) Hindi (Jafri et al., 2024, 2023).

2.2 Subtask B: Hate Speech Detection

Subtask B aims to detect hate speech in Nepali and Hindi tweets. The task aims to identify hate speech in Nepali and Hindi tweets, where participants must classify each tweet as either containing hateful statements or not.

2.3 Subtask C: Target Identification

Subtask C aims to identify the targets of hate speech in a given tweet. The dataset for this subtask is annotated for "individual", "organization", and "community" targets.

2.4 Datasets

An open-source version of the dataset for all three subtasks is available on the competition's webpage [2]. The distribution of each class within the dataset for each subtask is provided in Table 1.

Table 1: Dataset distribution for each class across Train, Validation, and Test sets for subtasks A, B, and C.

Task	Class	Train	Validation	Test
A	Nepali	12544	2688	2688
	Marathi	11034	2364	2365
	Sanskrit	10996	2356	2356
	Bhojpuri	10184	2182	2183
	Hindi	7664	1643	1642
B	Hate	2214	474	475
	Non-Hate	16805	3602	3601
C	Individual	1074	230	230
	Organization	856	183	184
	Community	284	61	61

3 Methodology

The strategy includes three major solutions. Initially, a classical machine learning strategy was used, with typical models trained on the dataset. Then, transformer-based models were investigated, encompassing both encoder models such as variations of BERT (Devlin, 2018), and decoder models such as GPT (Achiam et al., 2023). Finally, a hybrid strategy was used, in which NER tags were applied to the data using a rule-based tagger, followed by inference on the NER-tagged data using the trained model. Figure 1 shows the block diagram of the proposed model's training and inference pipeline.

3.1 Augmentation and Undersampling

Both augmentation and undersampling procedures were used to solve class imbalance issues and to reduce training time (Pimpalkhute et al., 2021). Subtasks A and B were undersampled, while subtask C was augmented with synthetic data. In subtask A, due to the large number of training samples, the model was trained only on 50% of the overall data to reduce the training and hyperparameter tuning time. In subtask B, the majority class was undersampled, with a focus on samples from the non-hate class to reduce class imbalance. For subtask C, the minority class, representing community targets, was augmented. This approach was chosen because the limited number of community target samples made undersampling the majority class impractical and potentially harmful to performance on the test set. For the community class in subtask C, a synonym substitution technique and GPT-4 in-context learning were used, along with validation samples and prompting, to generate synthetic tweets with identical sentiments (Zhang et al., 2024). Table 2 shows the distribution of training samples before and after applying undersampling or data augmentation techniques. The prompt used to generate synthetic samples through the synonym replacement technique is provided in Figure 2 in Appendix Section A.

3.2 Classical Approach

A classical approach was employed, where features were extracted from textual data using Term Frequency-Inverse Document Frequency (TF-IDF), and multiple machine learning algorithms such as Logistic Regression (LR), Support Vector Machines (SVM), Random Forest (RF), and XGBoost (XGB) were trained to establish a baseline for experiments.

[2] https://sites.google.com/view/chipsal/shared-tasks

Table 2: Train data distribution across subtasks A, B, and C: Undersampling for subtasks A, B and data augmentation for subtask C

Task	Class	Before Sampling /Augmentation	After Sampling /Augmentation
A	Nepali	12544	6231
	Marathi	11034	5535
	Sanskrit	10996	5447
	Bhojpuri	10184	5156
	Hindi	7664	3842
B	Hate	2214	2214
	Non-Hate	16805	8437
C	Individual	1074	1074
	Organization	856	856
	Community	284	330

3.3 Transformer Based Approach

Experiments were carried out employing Transformer architectures (Vaswani, 2017), with a focus on two variants: encoder-only models and decoder-only models.

3.3.1 Encoder Models

Encoder-only models, such as BERT variants (Devlin, 2018), utilize Transformer architectures' encoder layers. The encoder models listed below have been tested in all subtasks and optimized for low-resource Devanagari languages.

mBERT: BERT (Bidirectional Encoder Representation from Transformers) (Devlin, 2018) is self-trained using Masked Language Modeling (MLM) and Next Sentence Prediction (NSP) on BookCorpus and Wikipedia. The multilingual extension of BERT, mBERT, is trained in 104 languages and is offered in two versions: BERT-base and BERT-large.

XLM-RoBERTa: XLM-RoBERTa(Conneau, 2019) is a Transformer-based masked language model trained on over two terabytes of filtered CommonCrawl data from 100 languages. XLM-RoBERTa is specifically developed for low-resource languages.

Varta - A Large-Scale Headline-Generation Dataset for Indic Languages (Aralikatte et al., 2023): Varta-BERT is a model pre-trained on the entire Varta dataset, which includes 14 Indic languages along with English. The model is trained with the masked language modeling (MLM) objective.

MuRIL: Multilingual Representations for Indian Languages (Khanuja et al., 2021) is a BERT-based architecture that was pre-trained from scratch using data from Wikipedia, Common Crawl, PMINDIA, and Dakshina corpora in 17 Indian languages. There are two variants of the model available: base and large, with pre-trained weights available on Hugging Face.

3.3.2 Decoder Models

Prompt Engineering and Few-Shot Learning have become prominent methods for detecting hate speech on Twitter (Dehghan and Yanikoglu, 2024). This work utilizes decoder-only models developed by OpenAI (gpt-4-2024-05-13)[3], which excel at multilingual tasks (Achiam et al., 2023). Since OpenAI models are not open-source, they were accessed via API endpoints. Due to competition time constraints, experiments were conducted only with OpenAI models for subtask C. Validation splits were used for prompt tuning, while few-shot learning employed samples from the training splits. To achieve consistent JSON outputs, the temperature parameter was set to zero, reducing the non-deterministic responses typical of large language models. After tuning, the final prompt is provided in Figure 3 in Appendix Section B.

3.3.3 Hybrid Models

Word knowledge has been obtained by extracting entity information from Wikipedia and feeding it into the model alongside hate speech text(Lin, 2022). (Kaya et al., 2024) has employed a hybrid approach that combines: (1) reclassifying samples with low confidence scores using open-source large language models via prompting, and (2) integrating named entity information into features generated by BERT models, with the final output produced through tree-based models.

A hybrid approach has been used for subtask C, starting with error analysis on low-confidence samples (probability < 0.6) and re-evaluating them after adding entity tags. A rule-based entity tagger applied four tags व्यक्ति(person), संगठन(organization), चुनाव चिन्ह (election symbol), and समूह(group) around relevant phrases, using predefined entity lists for each category. These tags were selected after extensive experimentation to closely align with the given hate speech targets. Since the dataset was more directly tied to political news, election symbols were included in the tag pool because they resemble political organizations. The tagged samples were then passed through the trained MURTweet model, resulting in an enhanced version named NERMURTweet (see

[3]https://platform.openai.com/docs/models/o1#gpt-4o

Figure 1), which significantly improved classification metrics. Examples of samples before and after entity tagging are shown in Figure 4 in Appendix section C.

The suggested approach used a batch size of 32 for subtask A and 8 for subtasks B and C. The learning rate was set to 2e-5 with the AdamW optimizer, weight decay of 0.001, and trained for 10 epochs.

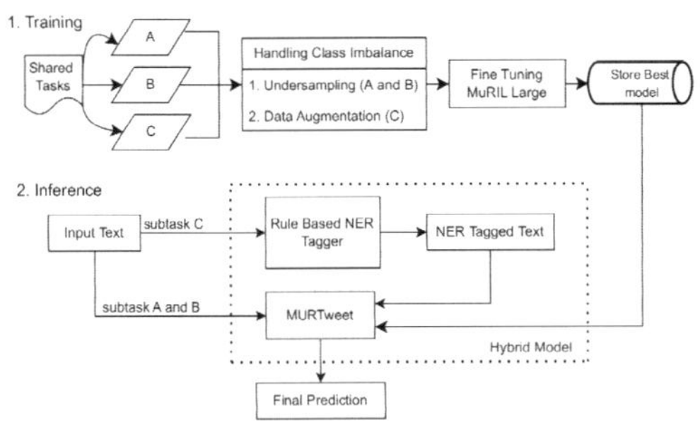

Figure 1: Block Diagram For training and inference pipeline

3.4 Results And Discussions

The table 3 displays the leaderboard results for all subtasks in the experiment. Precision, recall, F1 score, and accuracy metrics are presented, and models are ordered according to the F1 score specified by the organizers. For each challenge, the models with the highest F1 score are shown in bold.

In subtask A, the proposed model, trained on 50% of the total data, has secured sixth position in the final ranking. In subtask B, the proposed model, trained using undersampled data, secured the third position in the final scoreboard. For subtask C, the hybrid model (MURTweet + NER Tagging) secured first position in the final ranking. Due to the large volume of data, subtask A has been trained with only half of the dataset. MURTweet has the highest F1 score of 0.9962, surpassing Vartha, XLM-RoBERTa, and mBERT. In subtask B, undersampling the majority class in the training data enhanced model performance. The MURTweet model trained on undersampled data outperforms the model trained on the entire dataset. For subtask C, a hybrid model combining MURTweet with rule-based NER tagging topped the leaderboard, along with error analysis-driven data augmentation approaches (such as synonym matching and paraphrasing) improving performance. Attempts to employ GPT-4 for target identification in subtask C produced an F1 score of 0.66, which was not higher than the hybrid-based approach.

Table 3: Performance metrics across subtasks A, B, and C.

Task	Model	Prec	Rec	F1	Acc
A	TFIDF + LR	0.9528	0.9521	0.9526	0.9542
	TFIDF + SVM	0.9627	0.9626	0.9636	0.9662
	TFIDF + RF	0.9799	0.9776	0.9786	0.9806
	TFIDF + XGB	0.9439	0.9446	0.9442	0.9475
	mBERT	0.9930	0.9930	0.9930	0.9936
	XLM-R-Base	0.9918	0.9927	0.9922	0.9931
	XLM-R-Large	0.9940	0.9942	0.9941	0.9947
	Varta-BERT	0.9952	0.9957	0.9954	0.9959
	MuRIL-Base	0.9948	0.9953	0.9950	0.9955
	MURTweet	**0.9967**	**0.9968**	**0.9968**	**0.9972**
B	TFIDF + LR	0.5759	0.6843	0.5020	0.5746
	TFIDF + SVM	0.5700	0.6699	0.4894	0.5589
	TFIDF + RF	0.5597	0.5108	0.4987	0.8734
	TFIDF + XGB	0.6721	0.5345	0.5377	0.8815
	mBERT	0.6336	0.7136	0.6542	0.8121
	XLM-R-Base	0.6685	0.7147	0.6867	0.8528
	XLM-R-Large	0.7068	0.7542	0.7264	0.8741
	Varta-BERT	0.6179	0.7037	0.6344	0.7897
	MuRIL-Base	0.6803	0.7715	0.7089	0.8481
	MURTweet	**0.7638**	**0.7687**	**0.7662**	**0.9028**
C	TFIDF + LR	0.5169	0.5223	0.5147	0.5811
	TFIDF + SVM	0.4103	0.4107	0.4101	0.5705
	TFIDF + RF	0.4287	0.4414	0.4315	0.5747
	TFIDF + XGB	0.4641	0.4641	0.4641	0.5579
	mBERT	0.6022	0.6059	0.6036	0.6780
	XLM-R-Base	0.6319	0.6365	0.6339	0.7034
	XLM-R-Large	0.7095	0.6891	0.6975	0.7648
	Varta-BERT	0.6751	0.6410	0.6514	0.7331
	MuRIL-Base	0.6450	0.6576	0.6500	0.70763
	MURTweet	0.7073	0.6867	0.6951	0.7621
	NERMURTweet	**0.7175**	**0.7038**	**0.7098**	**0.7684**

4 Limitations

For subtasks A and B, undersampled data has been used for training, so the full potential of the complete dataset has not been fully utilized. In subtask C, the rule-based NER tagger assigned tags to phrases that do not represent real-world entities, which could have affected the final prediction.

5 Conclusion

In conclusion, data augmentation and undersampling techniques have shown impressive results in addressing class imbalance problems through this research. Encoder-only models trained on undersampled data have outperformed traditional methods in language recognition and hate speech detection tasks. For target identification, results have shown that hybrid models, which used the best-performing models on NER-tagged data, outperformed encoder-only and generative models, highlighting the importance of NER information in successfully identifying hate speech targets. Future research should explore ML-based NER tagging approaches, as well as alternative class imbalance techniques like weighted cross-entropy loss and focal loss, to further enhance model performance in these tasks.

References

Josh Achiam, Steven Adler, Sandhini Agarwal, Lama Ahmad, Ilge Akkaya, Florencia Leoni Aleman, Diogo Almeida, Janko Altenschmidt, Sam Altman, Shyamal Anadkat, et al. 2023. Gpt-4 technical report. *arXiv preprint arXiv:2303.08774*.

Rahul Aralikatte, Ziling Cheng, Sumanth Doddapaneni, and Jackie Chi Kit Cheung. 2023. V\= arta: A large-scale headline-generation dataset for indic languages. *arXiv preprint arXiv:2305.05858*.

Rahul Aralikatte, Miryam De Lhoneux, Anoop Kunchukuttan, and Anders Søgaard. 2021. Itihasa: A large-scale corpus for sanskrit to english translation. In *Proceedings of the 8th Workshop on Asian Translation (WAT2021)*, pages 191–197.

A Conneau. 2019. Unsupervised cross-lingual representation learning at scale. *arXiv preprint arXiv:1911.02116*.

Somaiyeh Dehghan and Berrin Yanikoglu. 2024. Evaluating chatgpt's ability to detect hate speech in turkish tweets. In *Proceedings of the 7th Workshop on Challenges and Applications of Automated Extraction of Socio-political Events from Text (CASE 2024)*, pages 54–59.

Jacob Devlin. 2018. Bert: Pre-training of deep bidirectional transformers for language understanding. *arXiv preprint arXiv:1810.04805*.

Farhan Ahmad Jafri, Kritesh Rauniyar, Surendrabikram Thapa, Mohammad Aman Siddiqui, Matloob Khushi, and Usman Naseem. 2024. Chunav: Analyzing hindi hate speech and targeted groups in indian election discourse. *ACM Transactions on Asian and Low-Resource Language Information Processing*.

Farhan Ahmad Jafri, Mohammad Aman Siddiqui, Surendrabikram Thapa, Kritesh Rauniyar, Usman Naseem, and Imran Razzak. 2023. Uncovering political hate speech during indian election campaign: A new low-resource dataset and baselines.

Ahmet Kaya, Oguzhan Ozcelik, and Cagri Toraman. 2024. Arc-nlp at climateactivism 2024: Stance and hate speech detection by generative and encoder models optimized with tweet-specific elements. In *Proceedings of the 7th Workshop on Challenges and Applications of Automated Extraction of Socio-political Events from Text (CASE 2024)*, pages 111–117.

Simran Khanuja, Diksha Bansal, Sarvesh Mehtani, Savya Khosla, Atreyee Dey, Balaji Gopalan, Dilip Kumar Margam, Pooja Aggarwal, Rajiv Teja Nagipogu, Shachi Dave, et al. 2021. Muril: Multilingual representations for indian languages. *arXiv preprint arXiv:2103.10730*.

Atharva Kulkarni, Meet Mandhane, Manali Likhitkar, Gayatri Kshirsagar, and Raviraj Joshi. 2021. L3cube-mahasent: A marathi tweet-based sentiment analysis dataset. In *Proceedings of the Eleventh Workshop on Computational Approaches to Subjectivity, Sentiment and Social Media Analysis*, pages 213–220.

Mirko Lai, Fabio Celli, Alan Ramponi, Sara Tonelli, Cristina Bosco, and Viviana Patti. 2023. Haspeede3 at evalita 2023: Overview of the political and religious hate speech detection task.

Jessica Lin. 2022. Leveraging world knowledge in implicit hate speech detection. *arXiv preprint arXiv:2212.14100*.

Drish Mali, Rubash Mali, and Claire Barale. 2024. Information extraction for planning court cases. In *Proceedings of the Natural Legal Language Processing Workshop 2024*, pages 97–114.

Atul Kr Ojha. 2019. English-bhojpuri smt system: Insights from the karaka model. *arXiv preprint arXiv:1905.02239*.

Anil Singh Parihar, Surendrabikram Thapa, and Sushruti Mishra. 2021. Hate speech detection using natural language processing: Applications and challenges. In *2021 5th International Conference on Trends in Electronics and Informatics (ICOEI)*, pages 1302–1308. IEEE.

Varad Pimpalkhute, Prajwal Nakhate, and Tausif Diwan. 2021. Iiitn nlp at smm4h 2021 tasks: transformer models for classification on health-related imbalanced twitter datasets. In *Proceedings of the Sixth Social Media Mining for Health (# SMM4H) Workshop and Shared Task*, pages 118–122.

Shushanta Pudasaini, Sunil Ghimire, Prabhat Ale, Aman Shakya, Prakriti Paudel, and Basanta Joshi. 2024. Application of nepali large language models to improve sentiment analysis. In *Proceedings of the 2024 7th International Conference on Computers in Management and Business*, pages 144–150.

Kritesh Rauniyar, Sweta Poudel, Shuvam Shiwakoti, Surendrabikram Thapa, Junaid Rashid, Jungeun Kim, Muhammad Imran, and Usman Naseem. 2023. Multi-aspect annotation and analysis of nepali tweets on anti-establishment election discourse. *IEEE Access*.

Kengatharaiyer Sarveswaran, Bal Krishna Bal, Surendrabikram Thapa, Ashwini Vaidya, and Sana Shams. 2025. A brief overview of the first workshop on challenges in processing south asian languages (chipsal). In *Proceedings of the First Workshop on Challenges in Processing South Asian Languages (CHiPSAL)*.

Surendrabikram Thapa, Kritesh Rauniyar, Farhan Ahmad Jafri, Surabhi Adhikari, Kengatharaiyer Sarveswaran, Bal Krishna Bal, Hariram Veeramani, and Usman Naseem. 2025. Natural language understanding of devanagari script languages: Language identification, hate speech and its target detection. In *Proceedings of the First Workshop on Challenges in Processing South Asian Languages (CHiPSAL)*.

Surendrabikram Thapa, Kritesh Rauniyar, Shuvam Shiwakoti, Sweta Poudel, Usman Naseem, and Mehwish Nasim. 2023. Nehate: Large-scale annotated data shedding light on hate speech in nepali local election discourse. In *ECAI 2023*, pages 2346–2353. IOS Press.

A Vaswani. 2017. Attention is all you need. *Advances in Neural Information Processing Systems*.

Chih-Chien Wang, Min-Yuh Day, and Chun-Lian Wu. 2022. Political hate speech detection and lexicon building: A study in taiwan. *IEEE Access*, 10:44337–44346.

Yaqi Zhang, Viktor Hangya, and Alexander Fraser. 2024. A study of the class imbalance problem in abusive language detection. In *Proceedings of the 8th Workshop on Online Abuse and Harms (WOAH 2024)*, pages 38–51.

A Appendix: Prompt for Synthetic Sample Generation

"Given a tweet written in Devanagari that contains hate speech targeted at a community, generate a synthetic tweet in Devanagari that mimics the style and content of the original. Ensure the following: Target the same community as the original tweet, keeping the content focused on the same hate speech subject. Preserve the structure, including any hashtags and emojis that appear in the original tweet. Maintain authenticity, with language and tone that are realistic for a tweet but do not amplify or introduce new harmful content beyond what exists in the original. Ensure the synthetic tweet appears different from the original in specific phrasing, but the overall message and target remain the same. Avoid generating highly offensive, personal threats, or calls for violence; focus on replicating general hate speech patterns aimed at communities. The generated tweet should be similar in length and structure to a typical tweet (max ~280 characters). Example: Input tweet (in Devanagari): "इस समुदाय के लोग हमेशा ऐसे ही होते हैं, इन्हें कोई फर्क नहीं पड़ता! #CommunityHate" Generated synthetic tweet: "इस समुदाय के लोग कभी सुधर नहीं सकते, ये सिर्फ समस्याएँ पैदा करते हैं! #CommunityIssue"

Figure 2: Prompt for Synthetic Sample Generation

B Appendix: Prompt for Hate Speech Target Identification

You are a Devnagari expert skilled in understanding and analyzing the Devanagari script used in languages like Nepali and Hindi. Your job is to identify hate speech and determine its target—whether it is directed at an individual, an organization, or a community. Please classify the following sentence into one of the three categories of hate speech:

1. **Individual** 2. **Organization** 3. **Community**

Input Sentence: "{sentence}"

Instructions: <instructions>

Output JSON Format: <output format>

Example: <examples>

Figure 3: Prompt for Synthetic Sample Generation

C Appendix: Impact of NER Tagging on Hate Speech Tweets

Before adding entity tags: डा. भट्टराई भन्छन्- 'जनता एउटा खराबको ठाउँमा अर्को खराबलाई भोट हाल्दैछन्' https://t.co/jVVSgPAF7f

After adding entity tags: (व्यक्ति)डा. भट्टराई (व्यक्ति) भन्छन्- (समूह)'जनता(समूह) एउटा खराबको ठाउँमा अर्को खराबलाई भोट हाल्दैछन् https://t.co/jVVSgPAF7f

Figure 4: Impact of NER Tagging on Hate Speech Tweets

Nepali Transformers@NLU of Devanagari Script Languages 2025: Detection of Language, Hate Speech and Targets

Pilot Khadka[1], Ankit B.K.[1], Ashish Acharya[2], Bikram K.C.[3], Sandesh Shrestha[3], Rabin Thapa[3]
[1]Thapathali Campus, Tribhuvan University, Kathmandu, Nepal
[2]Kathmandu University, Dhulikhel, Nepal
[3]Institute of International Management Science, Kathmandu, Nepal
{khdpilot, ankitbk75, ashishacharya048, kcvikram44, sandeshrestha115} @gmail.com
rabin@iimscollege.edu.np

Abstract

The Devanagari script, an Indic script used by a diverse range of South Asian languages, presents a significant challenge in Natural Language Processing (NLP) research. The dialect and language variation, complex script features, and limited language-specific tools make development difficult. This shared task aims to address this challenge by bringing together researchers and practitioners to solve three key problems: Language identification, Hate speech detection, and Targets of Hate speech identification. The selected languages-Hindi, Nepali, Marathi, Sanskrit, and Bhojpuri-are widely used in South Asia and represent distinct linguistic structures. In this work, we explore the effectiveness of both machine-learning models and transformer-based models on all three sub-tasks. Our results demonstrate strong performance of the multilingual transformer model, particularly one pre-trained on domain-specific social media data, across all three tasks. The multilingual RoBERTa model, trained on the Twitter dataset, achieved a remarkable accuracy and F1-score of 99.5% on language identification (Task A), 88.3% and 72.5% on Hate Speech detection (Task B), and 68.6% and 61.8% on Hate Speech Target Classification (Task C).

1 Introduction

With the advent of the internet and its application in recent years, user-generated content has increased exponentially, with much of it in different regional languages. Devanagari, one of South Asia's most extensively used scripts, is adopted by languages like Hindi, Marathi, Nepali, Bhojpuri, and Sanskrit (Ajmire et al., 2015). The rising presence of Devanagari content online has called for hate speech detection and content moderation.

The challenges in detecting hate speech are due to phonetically similar text across scripts and the complex evolution of Indo-Aryan languages which makes it difficult(Sharma et al., 2018; Kumar et al., 2018). As languages like Hindi, Nepali, Marathi, Sanskrit, Bhojpuri, etc. uses the Devanagari script, better Language identification is important for any downstream application such as machine translation and hate speech detection.

This issue highlights the need for accurate Devanagari language recognition to combat hate speech and support online diversity. While significant studies have been done towards the automatic detection of hate speech in resource-rich languages like English (Gitari et al., 2015; Burnap and Williams, 2016; Davidson et al., 2017; Gambäck and Sikdar, 2017) and Germany (Schneider et al., 2018; Wiedemann et al., 2018; Corazza et al., 2018), there is limited research on hate detection in Devanagari scripts. So, there is an increasing necessity for more robust cross-linguistic models that can better generalize hate speech even when the language changes to provide a safer online environment for these communities.

For hate speech analysis, identifying the specific target is essential for addressing and mitigating harm (Parihar et al., 2021). This shared task (Thapa et al., 2025; Sarveswaran et al., 2025) aims to identify the different Davanagari languages, detect hate speech, and classify it by target type (individual, organization, or community).

Our work makes the following key contributions:

- We evaluate a range of transformer-based models, including general-purpose baselines, language-specific, and domain-adapted approaches.

- We demonstrate the importance of using multilingual and domain-specific pertaining by showing the superior performance of the Twitter-trained multilingual RoBERTa model across all subtasks.

Proceedings of the First Workshop on Challenges in Processing South Asian Languages (CHiPSAL 2025), pages 314–319
January 19, 2025.

2 Literature Review

Significant research has been conducted in the field of script identification.(Indhuja et al., 2014) used the character and word n-grams model to identify languages: Hindi, Sanskrit, Marathi, Nepali, and Bhojpuri. (Kumar et al., 2018) utilized a Linear SVM classifier for identifying five closely related Indo-Aryan languages of India. It used 5-fold cross-validation, with the C hyper-parameter tuned via Grid Search to optimize the model. Character 5-grams achieved the best result with an impressive 96% accuracy over 13,744 sentences.

Hate speech identification plays a pivotal role in providing an inclusive environment by identifying and moderating the use of harmful language A notable study on Sanskrit and Bhojpuri utilized a dataset of 7,248 records and employed a Random Forest classifier, yielding F1 scores of 0.87 for Non-Offensive, 0.71 for Other Offensive, 0.45 for Racist, and a low 0.01 for Sexist content (Niraula et al., 2021). In Hindi and Marathi, the RoBERTa Hindi base model outperformed other models on the HASOC 2021 dataset, achieving the best results in identifying offensive content (Velankar et al., 2021).

Target classification in hate speech has been the new emerging interest for many researchers. (Surendrabikram Thapa, 2023) utilized a large-scale dataset of 13,505 Nepali tweets related to Nepal's local elections for hate speech and its target identification. In their experiment, they explored classical machine learning (ML) algorithms and transformer-based models like NepBERTa (Timilsina et al., 2022) and RoBERTa (Liu et al., 2019a) in which NepBERTa secured the highest F1-score of 0.68. Similarly, (Sharma et al., 2024) used 11,549 Hindi comments to classify the target in hate speech where the classes were Islam, Hinduism, Christianity, and None. They benchmarked with deep learning (DL) models, including CNN (Dai, 2021), BERT (Devlin, 2018), and MulRIL (Khanuja et al., 2021). Among all models, MulRIL performed the best with an F1 score of 0.72.

3 Dataset and Task

The shared task includes three different subtasks: Sub-Task A, intent on Devanagari Script Language Identification, Sub-Task B concentrates on hate speech detection, and Sub-Task C focuses on target identification of hate speech. For the shared task, the dataset was collected from different sources: Hindi (Jafri et al., 2024, 2023), Nepali (Surendrabikram Thapa, 2023; Rauniyar et al., 2023), Bhojpuri (Ojha, 2019), Marathi (Kulkarni et al., 2021), and Sanskrit(Aralikatte et al., 2021).

3.1 Sub-Task A

This Subtask involves multi-class classification for identifying the particular languages (Nepali, Marathi, Sanskrit, Bhojpuri, and Hindi). The dataset includes 52,422 training samples, 11,233 evaluation samples, and 11,234 test samples.

3.2 Sub-Task B

Sub-task B includes binary classification with two annotated labels: "hate" or "non-hate". The associated dataset comprises 19,019 training samples, 4,076 evaluation samples, and 4,076 test samples for this task.

3.3 Sub-Task C

The last Sub-task focuses on identifying the targets of hate speech among "individual", "organization", and "community". For this task, 2,214 training samples, 474 evaluation samples, and 475 test samples of datasets were provided.

4 Methodology

4.1 Dataset preparation

Our pre-processing pipeline consisted of three key steps. First, we replaced the Twitter username with a generic "@" token to maintain structural information. All hyperlinks were removed to focus on textual content. We also removed emojis using unicode ranges including emoticons, symbols, and special characters. Before these steps, entries with missing values were removed.

4.2 Feature engineering and Embeddings

For text representation, we experimented with multiple embedding approaches. We used the TF-IDF vectorization as our baseline representation for ML models. However, given the shared tasks's focus on Devanagari languages, we recognized the need for embedding that better captures the semantic relationship in these languages. Word2Vec and GloVe embeddings that were specifically trained on the Nepali corpus were included (Koirala and Niraula, 2021).

Sub-Task	Classes	Train	Eval	Test	Train (Augmented)
Detection of Devanagari Script	Nepali	12,544	2,688	2,688	-
	Marathi	11,034	2,364	2,365	
	Sanskrit	10,996	2,356	2,356	
	Bhojpuri	10,184	2,182	2,183	
	Hindi	7,664	1,643	1,642	
Hate Speech Identification	Non-hate	16,805	3,602	3,601	16,805
	Hate	2,214	474	475	10,000
Hate Speech Targets Identification	Individual	1,074	230	230	2,185
	Organization	856	183	184	2,228
	Community	284	61	61	1,010

Table 1: Original and Augmented Dataset distribution

4.3 Dataset Oversampling and Synthesis

No augmentation was performed on Sub-Task A as the original distribution had slightly underrepresented Hindi sampled. However, in Sub-Task B we address the significant disparity between hate and non-hate speech instances (2,214 vs 16,805 samples) by applying random oversampling to increase the minority class to 10,000 instances.

For Sub-Task C, due to the limited sample size, we used the multilingual Aya Expanse 8-B model(Cohere For AI, 2024) to generate target classifications using the hate speech instances from Sub-Task B. The augmented dataset distribution is shown in Table 1.

4.4 Hyperparameter Search

We use Bayesian optimization to find the optimal hyperparameters for the transformer models. The search space was defined based on the model architecture requirements and computational constraints. The number of epochs was task-specific, considering the dataset characteristics, computational efficiency, and early results. Each model then underwent 20 Bayesian optimization runs.

The search space is presented in the Table 4:

4.5 Machine Learning Models

We experimented with a diverse set of traditional machine learning models for the three sub-tasks. Logistic Regression was used as our baseline linear model, Decision Tree as a baseline for tree-based methods, and Support Vector Machines (SVM) for handling high dimensional feature space. Our ensemble method included Random Forest, XGBoost, and AdaBoost classifiers. For comparison, each model was trained on the same feature sets (TF-IDF, Word2Vec, and GloVe embeddings). The hyperparameters used for each model are presented in Table 5.

4.6 Deep Learning Models

Our selection of models was motivated by the need to establish a strong baseline with general-purpose models like BERT (Devlin et al., 2018), DistilBERT(Sanh et al., 2019), and RoBERTa(Liu et al., 2019b). The Devanagari-specific models (Nepali DistilBERT (Shrestha, 2021), and Nepali RoBERTa(Chaudhary, 2021))were chosen for their potential to better capture the linguistic nuances in Devanagari text. And, the Twitter-dataset trained XLM-RoBERTa (Barbieri et al., 2020) was included to evaluate the impact of domain adaptation on hate speech and Target identification of hate speech (Sub-Task B and C).

5 Result and Discussion

This section presents the results of the three subtasks along with an in-depth analysis and interpretations of the findings.

5.1 Machine Learning Models

We trained our models using various embeddings, including TF-IDF, GloVe, and Word2Vec. In subtask A, SVM with Word2Vec achieved the highest accuracy and f1 score (97.9% and 97.7%). Logistic Regression with TF-IDF achieved the highest accuracy of 88.6% and XGBoost with Word2Vec has the highest f1 score of 53.7% on Task B. Random forest performed better on sub-task C, achieving 62.9% accuracy and 50.4% F1-score. On the augmented dataset on sub-task B, the f1 score obtained by XGBoost with Word2Vec was 63.9%, which was a 10% increase, and accuracy reached 88.8% by Random Forest with Word2vec, .2% increase

Embedding	Model	Original Dataset						Augmented Dataset			
		Task A		Task B		Task C		Task B		Task C	
		acc	f1	acc	f1	acc	f1	acc	f1	acc	f1
TF-IDF	LR	0.957	0.954	**0.886**	0.537	0.606	0.437	0.859	0.637	0.612	**0.517**
	RF	0.942	0.938	0.883	0.498	**0.629**	0.456	0.882	0.505	0.610	0.445
	DT	0.618	0.647	0.877	0.567	0.532	0.383	0.856	0.560	0.505	0.421
	SVM	0.959	0.956	0.808	0.571	0.610	0.427	0.799	0.578	**0.614**	0.430
	XGBoost	0.935	0.931	0.881	0.558	0.576	0.453	0.873	0.619	0.587	0.460
	AdaBoost	0.798	0.787	0.881	0.549	0.553	0.445	0.846	0.604	0.562	0.470
GloVe	LR	0.960	0.958	0.879	0.520	0.578	**0.504**	0.788	0.620	0.572	0.501
	RF	0.938	0.935	0.883	0.483	0.593	0.414	0.886	0.549	0.591	0.441
	DT	0.830	0.823	0.811	0.548	0.486	0.409	0.754	0.577	0.448	0.374
	SVM	0.971	0.969	0.696	0.568	0.623	0.449	0.710	0.570	0.578	0.445
	XGBoost	0.963	0.962	0.881	0.567	0.574	0.431	0.871	0.609	0.587	0.476
	AdaBoost	0.788	0.749	0.878	0.516	0.534	0.446	0.774	0.618	0.530	0.450
Word2Vec	LR	0.969	0.967	0.877	0.534	0.576	0.497	0.796	0.636	0.578	0.513
	RF	0.953	0.950	0.883	0.481	0.597	0.420	**0.888**	0.548	0.587	0.447
	DT	0.827	0.820	0.816	0.549	0.440	0.377	0.777	0.572	0.480	0.421
	SVM	**0.979**	**0.977**	0.713	0.568	0.610	0.441	0.661	0.544	0.602	0.472
	XGBoost	0.973	0.971	0.885	**0.593**	0.587	0.442	0.882	**0.639**	0.602	0.483
	AdaBoost	0.808	0.782	0.881	0.569	0.501	0.369	0.772	0.612	0.543	0.432

Table 2: Performance of Machine Learning models

Model	Original Dataset						Augmented Dataset			
	Task A		Task B		Task C		Task B		Task C	
	acc	f1	acc	f1	acc	f1	acc	f1	acc	f1
BERT-base	0.991	0.990	0.763	0.613	0.597	0.425	0.781	0.623	0.602	0.520
RoBERTa	0.991	0.990	0.872	0.593	0.595	0.516	0.806	0.626	0.595	0.499
Distil-BERT	0.990	0.989	0.867	0.620	0.574	0.483	0.763	0.612	0.576	0.506
Nepali RoBERTa	0.994	0.993	0.830	0.675	0.656	0.544	0.874	0.672	0.629	0.548
Nepali DistilBERT	0.994	0.994	0.851	0.700	0.658	0.561	0.840	0.677	0.642	0.548
Twitter XLM-RoBERTa	**0.995**	**0.995**	**0.883**	**0.725**	**0.686**	**0.618**	0.872	0.720	0.612	0.545

Table 3: Performance of Deep Learning Models

compared to the original dataset. In sub-task C, Logistics regression with TF-IDF achieved an F1-score of 51.7%, which was 1% higher than the original dataset. The accuracy achieved was similarly higher, at 61.2%.

5.2 Deep Learning Models

Transformer-based models showed a superior performance across three tasks. Furthermore, the performance of the language-specific and domain-adapted model was higher over the general-purpose baseline. The multilingual RoBERTa model, which was specifically trained on the Twitter dataset, consistently outperformed other architectures across all three tasks.

For task A, the Twitter dataset trained multilingual RoBERTa achieved superior performance with both accuracy and F1-score reaching 99.5%. Task B and Task C were both best handled by the Twitter-trained multilingual RoBERTa, achieving scores of 88.3% accuracy, 72.5% F1-score, and 68.6% accuracy, 61.8% F1-score respectively.

6 Conclusion

In this research, we used a variety of machine learning and deep learning models for collaborative activities. Deep learning models outperformed machine learning models on all tasks. Twitter XLM-RoBERTa achieved greater F1 scores across all challenges. The highest f1-scores for Sub-Tasks A, B, and C are 99.5%, 72.5%, and 61.8%, respectively. We also investigated data augmentation for sub-tasks B and C because the dataset contained fewer instances, which allowed us to improve performance.

7 Limitations

Our study demonstrated strong results across all tasks, particularly with Twitter-trained multilingual RoBERTa. However, some limitations exist.

Our search space could be considered constrained due to limited optimization runs. Which, while computationally practical, may not have been sufficient to properly explore the search space.

Our work tested Nepali-based transformer models, future work could expand by exploring other Devanagari language models, like those trained in Hindi language.

References

PE Ajmire, RV Dharaskar, and VM Thakare. 2015. Handwritten devanagari (marathi) compound character recognition using seventh central moment. *International Journal of Innovative Research in Computer and Communication Engineering*, 3(6):5312–5319.

Rahul Aralikatte, Miryam De Lhoneux, Anoop Kunchukuttan, and Anders Søgaard. 2021. Itihasa: A large-scale corpus for sanskrit to english translation. In *Proceedings of the 8th Workshop on Asian Translation (WAT2021)*, pages 191–197.

Francesco Barbieri, Jose Camacho-Collados, Luis Espinosa Anke, and Leonardo Neves. 2020. TweetEval: Unified benchmark and comparative evaluation for tweet classification. In *Findings of the Association for Computational Linguistics: EMNLP 2020*, pages 1644–1650, Online. Association for Computational Linguistics.

Pete Burnap and Matthew L Williams. 2016. Us and them: identifying cyber hate on twitter across multiple protected characteristics. *EPJ Data science*, 5:1–15.

Amit Chaudhary. 2021. https://huggingface.co/amitness/roberta-base-ne.

Cohere For AI. 2024. Aya-expanse: An open-source language model for research. `https://huggingface.co/CohereForAI/aya-expanse-8b`.

Michele Corazza, Stefano Menini, Pinar Arslan, Rachele Sprugnoli, Elena Cabrio, Sara Tonelli, and Serena Villata. 2018. Inriafbk at germeval 2018: Identifying offensive tweets using recurrent neural networks. In *Proceedings of the GermEval 2018 Workshop*, pages 80–84.

Dengyuhan Dai. 2021. An introduction of cnn: Models and training on neural network models. In *2021 International Conference on Big Data, Artificial Intelligence and Risk Management (ICBAR)*, pages 135–138.

Thomas Davidson, Dana Warmsley, Michael Macy, and Ingmar Weber. 2017. Automated hate speech detection and the problem of offensive language. In *Proceedings of the international AAAI conference on web and social media*, volume 11, pages 512–515.

Jacob Devlin. 2018. Bert: Pre-training of deep bidirectional transformers for language understanding. *arXiv preprint arXiv:1810.04805*.

Jacob Devlin, Ming-Wei Chang, Kenton Lee, and Kristina Toutanova. 2018. BERT: pre-training of deep bidirectional transformers for language understanding. *CoRR*, abs/1810.04805.

Björn Gambäck and Utpal Kumar Sikdar. 2017. Using convolutional neural networks to classify hate-speech. In *Proceedings of the first workshop on abusive language online*, pages 85–90.

Njagi Dennis Gitari, Zhang Zuping, Hanyurwimfura Damien, and Jun Long. 2015. A lexicon-based approach for hate speech detection. *International Journal of Multimedia and Ubiquitous Engineering*, 10(4):215–230.

K Indhuja, M Indu, C Sreejith, Palakkad Sreekrishnapuram, and PR Raj. 2014. Text based language identification system for indian languages following devanagiri script. *International Journal of Engineering*, 3(4).

Farhan Ahmad Jafri, Kritesh Rauniyar, Surendrabikram Thapa, Mohammad Aman Siddiqui, Matloob Khushi, and Usman Naseem. 2024. Chunav: Analyzing hindi hate speech and targeted groups in indian election discourse. *ACM Transactions on Asian and Low-Resource Language Information Processing*.

Farhan Ahmad Jafri, Mohammad Aman Siddiqui, Surendrabikram Thapa, Kritesh Rauniyar, Usman Naseem, and Imran Razzak. 2023. Uncovering political hate speech during indian election campaign: A new low-resource dataset and baselines.

Simran Khanuja, Diksha Bansal, Sarvesh Mehtani, Savya Khosla, Atreyee Dey, Balaji Gopalan, Dilip Kumar Margam, Pooja Aggarwal, Rajiv Teja Nagipogu, Shachi Dave, et al. 2021. Muril: Multilingual representations for indian languages. *arXiv preprint arXiv:2103.10730*.

Pravesh Koirala and Nobal B. Niraula. 2021. NPVec1: Word embeddings for Nepali - construction and evaluation. In *Proceedings of the 6th Workshop on Representation Learning for NLP (RepL4NLP-2021)*, pages 174–184, Online. Association for Computational Linguistics.

Atharva Kulkarni, Meet Mandhane, Manali Likhitkar, Gayatri Kshirsagar, and Raviraj Joshi. 2021. L3cubemahasent: A marathi tweet-based sentiment analysis dataset. In *Proceedings of the Eleventh Workshop on Computational Approaches to Subjectivity, Sentiment and Social Media Analysis*, pages 213–220.

Ritesh Kumar, Bornini Lahiri, Deepak Alok, Atul Kr Ojha, Mayank Jain, Abdul Basit, and Yogesh Dawer. 2018. Automatic identification of closely-related indian languages: Resources and experiments. *arXiv preprint arXiv:1803.09405*.

Yinhan Liu, Myle Ott, Naman Goyal, Jingfei Du, Mandar Joshi, Danqi Chen, Omer Levy, Mike Lewis, Luke Zettlemoyer, and Veselin Stoyanov. 2019a. Roberta: A robustly optimized BERT pretraining approach. *CoRR*, abs/1907.11692.

Yinhan Liu, Myle Ott, Naman Goyal, Jingfei Du, Mandar Joshi, Danqi Chen, Omer Levy, Mike Lewis, Luke Zettlemoyer, and Veselin Stoyanov. 2019b. Roberta: A robustly optimized BERT pretraining approach. *CoRR*, abs/1907.11692.

Nobal B Niraula, Saurab Dulal, and Diwa Koirala. 2021. Offensive language detection in nepali social media. In *Proceedings of the 5th Workshop on Online Abuse and Harms (WOAH 2021)*, pages 67–75.

Atul Kr Ojha. 2019. English-bhojpuri smt system: Insights from the karaka model. *arXiv preprint arXiv:1905.02239*.

Anil Singh Parihar, Surendrabikram Thapa, and Sushruti Mishra. 2021. Hate speech detection using natural language processing: Applications and challenges. In *2021 5th International Conference on Trends in Electronics and Informatics (ICOEI)*, pages 1302–1308. IEEE.

Kritesh Rauniyar, Sweta Poudel, Shuvam Shiwakoti, Surendrabikram Thapa, Junaid Rashid, Jungeun Kim, Muhammad Imran, and Usman Naseem. 2023. Multi-aspect annotation and analysis of nepali tweets on anti-establishment election discourse. *IEEE Access*.

Victor Sanh, Lysandre Debut, Julien Chaumond, and Thomas Wolf. 2019. Distilbert, a distilled version of BERT: smaller, faster, cheaper and lighter. *CoRR*, abs/1910.01108.

Kengatharaiyer Sarveswaran, Bal Krishna Bal, Surendrabikram Thapa, Ashwini Vaidya, and Sana Shams. 2025. A brief overview of the first workshop on challenges in processing south asian languages (chipsal). In *Proceedings of the First Workshop on Challenges in Processing South Asian Languages (CHiPSAL)*.

Julian Moreno Schneider, Roland Roller, Peter Bourgonje, Stefanie Hegele, and Georg Rehm. 2018. Towards the automatic classification of offensive language and related phenomena in german tweets. In *14th Conference on Natural Language Processing KONVENS*, volume 2018, page 95.

Deepak Kumar Sharma, Anurag Singh, and Abhishek Saroha. 2018. Language identification for hindi language transliterated text in roman script using generative adversarial networks. *Towards Extensible and Adaptable Methods in Computing*, pages 267–279.

Deepawali Sharma, Aakash Singh, and Vivek Singh. 2024. Thar- targeted hate speech against religion: A high-quality hindi-english code-mixed dataset with the application of deep learning models for automatic detection. *ACM Transactions on Asian and Low-Resource Language Information Processing*.

Dipesh Shrestha. 2021. https://huggingface.co/dexhrestha/nepali-distilbert.

Shuvam Shiwakoti Sweta Poudel Usman Naseem Mehwish Nasim Surendrabikram Thapa, Kritesh Rauniyar. 2023. Nehate: Large-scale annotated data shedding light on hate speech in nepali local election discourse. *26th European Conference on Artificial Intelligence (ECAI), Kraków, Poland (IOS Press) [ECAI'23]*.

Surendrabikram Thapa, Kritesh Rauniyar, Farhan Ahmad Jafri, Surabhi Adhikari, Kengatharaiyer Sarveswaran, Bal Krishna Bal, Hariram Veeramani, and Usman Naseem. 2025. Natural language understanding of devanagari script languages: Language identification, hate speech and its target detection. In *Proceedings of the First Workshop on Challenges in Processing South Asian Languages (CHiPSAL)*.

Sulav Timilsina, Milan Gautam, and Binod Bhattarai. 2022. Nepberta: Nepali language model trained in a large corpus. In *Proceedings of the 2nd conference of the Asia-pacific chapter of the association for computational linguistics and the 12th international joint conference on natural language processing*. Association for Computational Linguistics (ACL).

Abhishek Velankar, Hrushikesh Patil, Amol Gore, Shubham Salunke, and Raviraj Joshi. 2021. Hate and offensive speech detection in hindi and marathi. *arXiv preprint arXiv:2110.12200*.

Gregor Wiedemann, Eugen Ruppert, Raghav Jindal, and Chris Biemann. 2018. Transfer learning from lda to bilstm-cnn for offensive language detection in twitter. *arXiv preprint arXiv:1811.02906*.

A Appendix

A.1 Hyperparameter Search space

Parameter	Search Space	Distribution
Batch size	[16,32]	Discrete
Learning Rate	[1e-6, 5e-5]	Log-uniform
Weight Decay	[1e-6, 0.1]	Log-uniform
Beta 1	[0.9, 0.99]	Uniform
Beta 2	[0.999, 0.9999]	Uniform
Epochs (Task A)	[2-3]	Discrete
Epochs (Task B)	[2-8]	Discrete
Epochs (Task C)	[2-15]	Discrete

Table 4: Search space for Transformer models

A.2 Hyperparameters of ML models

Model	Hyperparameters
Logistic Regression	max_iter: 1000
Random Forest	n_estimators: 500 min_samples_split: 2
Decision Tree	max_depth: 15 min_samples_split: 2
SVM	max_iter: 1000 kernel: 'rbf'
XGBoost	max_depth: 6 (default) learning_rate: 0.3
AdaBoost	n_estimators: 100 learning_rate: 1.0

Table 5: Hyperparameters for ML models

NLPineers@ NLU of Devanagari Script Languages 2025: Hate Speech Detection using Ensembling of BERT-based models

Anmol Guragain[1*], **Nadika Poudel**[1*], **Rajesh Piryani**[2], **Bishesh Khanal**[1]
[1]Nepal Applied Mathematics and Informatics Institute for Research (NAAMII), Nepal
[2]IRIT, Universite Toulouse III Paul Sabatier (UT3), Toulouse, France

Abstract

This paper explores hate speech detection in Devanagari-scripted languages, focusing on Hindi and Nepali, for Subtask B of the CHIPSAL@COLING 2025 Shared Task. Using a range of transformer-based models such as XLM-RoBERTa, MURIL, and IndicBERT, we examined their effectiveness in navigating the nuanced boundary between hate speech and free expression. Our best performing model, implemented as ensemble of multilingual BERT models achieved Recall of 0.7762 (Rank 3/31 in terms of recall) and F1 score of 0.6914 (Rank 17/31). To address class imbalance, we used backtranslation for data augmentation, and cosine similarity to preserve label consistency after augmentation. This work emphasizes the need for hate speech detection in Devanagari-scripted languages and presents a foundation for further research. The code can be accessed at https://github.com/Anmol2059/NLPineers.

1 Introduction

Social media has become an essential part of our lives, empowering users to communicate freely and fostering a global exchange of ideas. However, it has contributed to the rapid proliferation of harmful content, including hate speech. Detecting hate speech is inherently complex due to the nuanced boundary between hate speech and legitimate free expression. What one individual may perceive as an offensive or harmful statement, another might interpret as a right to free speech, complicating the task of building an automated hate speech detection system. In languages where Devanagari script is predominantly used, such as Hindi, Marathi, and Nepali, detecting hate speech becomes even more intricate due to linguistic diversity, regional variations, and code-mixing practices.

Numerous transformer-based models have emerged to address the challenges of hate speech detection across various high-resource languages. HateBERT (Caselli et al., 2020), a BERT model retrained on a dataset of Reddit comments from communities banned for offensive content, outperforms general BERT models in detecting abusive language in English. MC-BERT4HATE (Yang et al., 2020) presents a multi-channel architecture that integrates English, Chinese, and multilingual versions of BERT, aiming to detect hate speech across multiple languages more effectively. However, during politically charged events like elections, hate speech in Devanagari scripts intensifies on social media platforms like Twitter, producing more complex forms that require an understanding of socio-political dynamics beyond mere linguistic processing. These nuances are not well captured by general-purpose models, highlighting the need for specialized approaches.

The First Workshop on South East Asian Language Processing (Sarveswaran et al., 2025) aims to strengthen and spur NLP research and development in SEA languages. This paper aims to solve Task B: Hate Speech Detection of the Shared Task on Natural Language Understanding of Devanagari Script Languages (Thapa et al., 2025). Hate speech detection is a binary classification problem that requires determining whether a tweet is hate speech or not. The classifiers we used in this challenge include XLM-RoBERTa, MURIL, and IndicBERT.

2 Related Works

Devanagari-script languages, being low-resource, have seen relatively limited work in hate speech detection. Aggression and Misogyny Detection using BERT by (Safi Samghabadi et al., 2020) classified comments presents in English, Hindi and Bengali into one of the three aggression classes - Not Aggressive, Covertly Aggressive, Overtly Aggressive, as well as one of the two misogyny classes - Gendered and Non-Gendered scoring

*Equal contribution.

Proceedings of the First Workshop on Challenges in Processing South Asian Languages (CHiPSAL 2025), pages 320–326
January 19, 2025.

0.8579 weighted F1-measure using BERT model. In second workshop on Trolling, Aggression, and Cyberbullying (TRAC-2), (Baruah et al., 2020) work on Shared task on Misogynistic Aggression Identification achieved highest F1 score of 0.87 in Hindi language using XLMRoBERTa . Similarly, HASOC 2020: Hate Speech and Offensive Content Identification in Indo-European Languages (Mandl et al., 2020) had sub-task for Hate Speech detection in Hindi, German and English having 40 teams as participants. The best submission for Hindi used a CNN with fastText embeddings as input and the best result for English is based on a LSTM which used GloVe embeddings as input. Although there has been some work done on Hindi, it is worth noting that Nepali, which also uses the Devanagari script, has received relatively little attention in this area,(Luitel et al., 2024; Niraula et al., 2022) likely due to resource limitations. (Niraula et al., 2021) annotated 7462 records in Nepali language into four categories SEXIST, RACIST, OTHER-OFFENSIVE, and NON-OFFENSIVE using Random Forest Classifier achieving F1 scores as 0.01, 0.45,0.71 and 0.87 respectively.

Despite these few efforts, there remains a lack of performance benchmarks for multilingual BERT models on Devanagari scripts. Additionally, previous works have not explored BERT-based ensemble strategies that integrate predictions from multiple models. This gap motivated us to investigate the effectiveness of various multilingual BERT models and their ensembling approaches for hate speech detection in Devanagari scripted languages.

3 Dataset and Task

Category	Training	Evaluation
Hindi Non-Hate	7,376	1,596
Nepali Non-Hate	9,429	2,006
Hindi Hate	679	142
Nepali Hate	1,535	332
Total	19,019	4,076

Table 1: Sample distribution of data in training and evaluation sets

This experiment uses the data from the shared task, which is compiled from prior works across multiple Devanagari-script languages, including Hindi hate speech in political discourse (Jafri et al., 2024, 2023), Nepali election discourse (Thapa et al., 2023; Rauniyar et al., 2023), Bhojpuri-English sentiment modeling (Ojha, 2019), Marathi

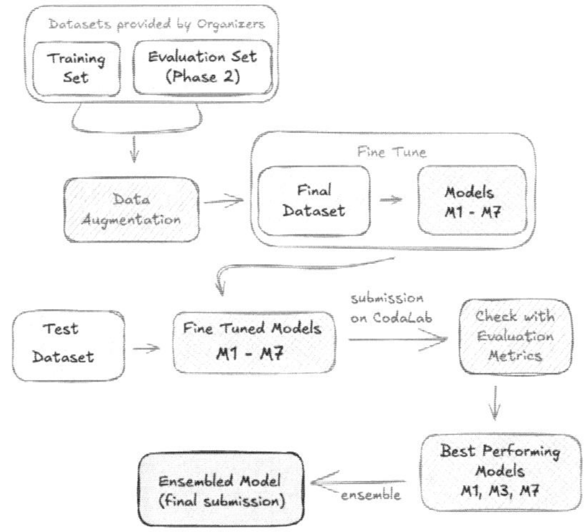

Figure 1: Experiment Workflow.

sentiment analysis (Kulkarni et al., 2021), and Sanskrit translation corpora (Aralikatte et al., 2021). In this study, the evaluation set refers to the phase 2 data provided by the challenge organizers, which is part of the development data. It is distinct from the test set, which was submitted for the challenge. Table 1 provides detailed statistics on the original dataset of the shared task and some of the example sentences are in Figure 2. The overall pipeline of this experiment is summarized on Figure 1.

4 Experimental Setup

4.1 Data Augmentation

As observed in Table 1, hate speech instances were much fewer compared to non-hate speech. To address this imbalance, data augmentation was applied to the hate speech instances using back-translation with the mBART-large-50 model (Tang et al., 2020), translating the data to English and back to the source language to introduce text variations. To ensure that the augmented data retained semantic similarity with the original data and minimize risk of unintended label changes, we calculated the cosine similarity between the embeddings of the augmented and original texts using the XLM-RoBERTa base model (Conneau et al., 2019). Only augmented data with a cosine similarity score greater than 0.9(chosen empirically) was added to the final dataset.

For the training set, data augmentation was performed on both Hindi and Nepali hate speech instances. In the evaluation set, however, augmentation was applied only to Hindi instances, as Nepali

	Model	Tokenizer / Embedding	Classifier Architecture
M1	MuRIL abusive (Das et al., 2022)	MuRIL (Hindi-Abusive) - Self	Native Head
M2	MuRIL + TabNet	MuRIL - Self	TabNet Classifier
M3	MuRIL(Khanuja et al., 2021a)	MuRIL - Self	Native Head
M4	IndicBERT(Kakwani et al., 2020)	IndicBERT - Self	Native Head
M5	IndicBERT + LSTM-CNN	IndicBERT - Self	LSTM + CNN + FC layer
M6	XLM-Roberta + Logistic Regression	XLM-Roberta - Self	Logistic Regression
M7	XLM-Roberta (Conneau et al., 2020)	XLM-Roberta - Self	Native Head
M8	FastText + LSTM	None - FastText (Hindi + Nepali)	LSTM + FC Layer

Table 2: Overview of models used. **FC** stands for Fully Connected layer, and **Native Head** refers to the model's built-in classification head when imported from Hugging Face, indicating that these models are fine-tuned. The **Tokenizer/Embedding** column combines the tokenization method and embedding source; "Self" signifies that embeddings are generated by the model itself. Tokenizers and models are sourced from Hugging Face's model hub, with FastText embeddings from FastText.cc.

data already had a higher representation compared to Hindi data. Additionally, to further address the class imbalance, all hate speech instances (label '1') were duplicated to give the model more exposure to minority class. After augmentation, the training set grew to 13,695 instances by incorporating the original 2,214 training, 474 evaluation, and their augmented instances.

4.2 Pretrained Models

We used different pre-trained models and classifier heads, as observed in Table 2 to explore approaches that could better capture the nuances that exist in recognizing of hate speeches. The models included three BERT-based architectures—MuRIL (Khanuja et al., 2021b), XLM-RoBERTa (Conneau et al., 2020), and IndicBERT (Kakwani et al., 2020)—as well as FastText (Grave et al., 2018), an token embedding-based model. MuRIL is pretrained on 17 Indian languages and their transliterations. XLM-RoBERTa, a large multilingual model, offers cross-lingual capabilities by training on diverse data from multiple languages. IndicBERT focuses on 12 Indian languages, including Devanagari(Hindi and Marathi), and uses a lightweight structure ideal for efficient processing. In contrast, FastText uses character-level n-grams to provide a detailed lexical representation, which is particularly beneficial for morphologically rich languages in Devanagari script. This combination allows us to leverage both deep contextual understanding and fine-grained lexical details for effective hate speech detection.

4.3 Ensemble Strategy

Our ensemble strategy leveraged the strengths of our top-performing models from Table 3. We chose M7 (XLM-Roberta) as the primary model, M3 (MuRIL) as the secondary model, and M1 (MuRIL abusive) as the fallback model, based on each model's unique strengths.

- **Primary Model (XLM-Roberta, Model 7):** XLM-Roberta achieved the highest recall (0.7381), making it effective at detecting hate speech and minimizing missed cases.

- **Secondary Model (MuRIL, Model 3):** When XLM-Roberta does not predict hate speech, MuRIL provides a balanced F1 score (0.6904) and accuracy (0.8744), acting as a secondary layer to catch potential cases missed by the primary model.

- **Fallback Model (MuRIL abusive, Model 1):** In cases where both primary and secondary models predict no hate speech, MuRIL abusive, with the highest precision (0.7572) and accuracy (0.8950), serves as a conservative fallback to minimize false positives.

$$\text{prediction}(x) = \begin{cases} 1 & \text{if } \mathrm{M}_7(x) = 1 \\ 1 & \text{if } \mathrm{M}_7(x) = 0 \text{ and } \mathrm{M}_3(x) = 1 \\ \mathrm{M}_1(x) & \text{otherwise} \end{cases}$$

4.4 Hyperparameters and Compute Environment

Training utilized the following hyperparameters, determined through iterative testing and practical constraints: a learning rate of 2e-5, a batch size of 16. These values were selected to balance model performance with available compute resources and processing time. We used NVIDIA GeForce RTX 3090 as compute environment.

	Model	Recall	Precision	F1 Score	Accuracy
M1	MuRIL abusive	0.6335	0.7572	0.6681	0.8950
M2	MuRIL + TabNet	0.6296	0.5874	0.5984	0.7927
M3	MuRIL	0.6877	0.6934	0.6904	0.8744
M4	IndicBERT	0.5934	0.5915	0.5924	0.8305
M5	IndicBERT + LSTM-CNN	0.6455	0.5618	0.5207	0.6271
M6	XLM-Roberta + Logistic Regression	0.6504	0.6596	0.6548	0.8619
M7	XLM-Roberta	0.7381	0.6696	0.6933	0.8472
M8	FastText + LSTM	0.5320	0.5400	0.5346	0.8270
	Ensemble (M1, M3, M7)	0.7762	0.6639	0.6914	0.8258

Table 3: Evaluation results on test set of the hate speech detection task. Dark green cells indicate the best performance in the respective metric, while dark red cells indicate the worst. Gradual shades of green represents relatively good performance.

5 Results and Discussions

The competition was hosted on the Codalab[1] platform by the organizers, where we submitted binary predictions (0 or 1) for evaluation based on recall, precision, F1 score, and accuracy. The performance of our models in the test set of challenge is shown in Table 3.

5.1 MuRIL-Based Models

As seen in Table 3, the fine-tuned MuRIL model (M1) on Devanagari script provided the highest accuracy among MuRIL-based models. The standard MuRIL model (M3) demonstrated balanced performance across all metrics. We also experimented with combining MuRIL and TabNet (M2) as suggested by (Chopra et al., 2023), but this configuration did not yield competitive results in this task.

5.2 IndicBERT

We anticipated strong performance from IndicBERT (M4) due to its training on 12 Indic languages as discussed in (Kakwani et al., 2020). However, its results were lower than expected, possibly due to the presence of Nepali text in the dataset, which IndicBERT may not be optimized for. The combination of IndicBERT with LSTM-CNN also underperformed, showing unsatisfactory results.

5.3 XLM-Roberta-Based Models

Both the plain XLM-Roberta model (M7) and XLM-Roberta with a Logistic Regression head (M6) performed well, indicating the model's robust generalization capabilities across different metrics. This highlights XLM-Roberta's versatility in multilingual tasks.

5.4 FastText with LSTM

Since the evaluation set contained Devanagari script for both Nepali and Hindi, we utilized FastText embeddings of both languages and fed in LSTM based classifer (M8). However, this setup did not yield satisfactory results, likely due to the limitations of static embeddings, which struggle to capture the contextual nuances essential for accurate hate speech detection.

5.5 Ensembled Model

Our final submission was an ensemble model combining M1, M3, and M7, as described in previous sections. This ensemble achieved balanced performance, with recall, precision, F1 score, and accuracy of 0.7762, 0.6639, 0.6914, and 0.8258, respectively, effectively leveraging the strengths of multiple models.

6 Conclusion

This study highlights the potential of various BERT-based models and ensembling approach for hate speech detection in Devanagari-scripted languages, with future work planned on model robustness and scalability for real-world applications. Further research could explore additional embeddings and augmentations to enhance performance across multilingual contexts.

[1] https://codalab.lisn.upsaclay.fr/competitions/20000#participate-submit_results

Limitations

This study faces several limitations, particularly due to the linguistic complexities inherent to Devanagari-scripted languages like Hindi and Nepali. Below, we outline some of the primary challenges:

- **Limitations of Data Augmentation via Backtranslation**: While backtranslation with the mBART model was used to augment hate speech samples, this approach sometimes loses the cultural nuances or tone intended in the original text. For instance, words like ***tapai*** and ***hajur*** in Nepali convey a formal or respectful tone, but during translation to English and back to Nepali, these terms are often reduced to the informal ***timi***, altering the sentiment. This limitation could introduce subtle inaccuracies during model training.

- **Contextual Meaning Across Languages**: In Devanagari-scripted languages, certain words can carry vastly different meanings depending on the language context. Such linguistic ambiguities create challenges for the model, as it may misinterpret hate speech in cases where meanings differ across languages using the same script.

- **Dependency on Word Embeddings for Devanagari Script**: Devanagari script is used for multiple languages, and words in Hindi and Nepali may have similar or identical representations in embeddings, potentially leading to confusion. While BERT-based models like XLM-RoBERTa and MuRIL are designed to handle multilingual contexts, challenges persist when languages share the same script but differ in vocabulary or syntax. These issues may impact the model's ability to differentiate nuanced expressions unique to each language.

Acknowledgements

We thank CHIPSAL@COLING organizers for providing annotated datasets and hosting the shared task. We also thank NepAl Applied Mathematics and Informatics Institute for research(NAAMII) for giving us access to training resources required for the sub-task.

References

Rahul Aralikatte, Miryam De Lhoneux, Anoop Kunchukuttan, and Anders Søgaard. 2021. Itihasa: A large-scale corpus for sanskrit to english translation. In *Proceedings of the 8th Workshop on Asian Translation (WAT2021)*, pages 191–197.

Arup Baruah, Kaushik Das, Ferdous Barbhuiya, and Kuntal Dey. 2020. Aggression identification in English, Hindi and Bangla text using BERT, RoBERTa and SVM. In *Proceedings of the Second Workshop on Trolling, Aggression and Cyberbullying*, pages 76–82, Marseille, France. European Language Resources Association (ELRA).

Tommaso Caselli, Valerio Basile, Jelena Mitrovic, and Michael Granitzer. 2020. Hatebert: Retraining BERT for abusive language detection in english. *CoRR*, abs/2010.12472.

Abhishek Chopra, Deepak Kumar Sharma, Aashna Jha, and Uttam Ghosh. 2023. A framework for online hate speech detection on code-mixed hindi-english text and hindi text in devanagari. *ACM Transactions on Asian and Low-Resource Language Information Processing*, 22(5):1–21.

Alexis Conneau, Kartikay Khandelwal, Naman Goyal, Vishrav Chaudhary, Guillaume Wenzek, Francisco Guzmán, Edouard Grave, Myle Ott, Luke Zettlemoyer, and Veselin Stoyanov. 2019. Unsupervised cross-lingual representation learning at scale. *CoRR*, abs/1911.02116.

Alexis Conneau, Kartikay Khandelwal, Naman Goyal, Vishrav Chaudhary, Guillaume Wenzek, Francisco Guzmán, Edouard Grave, Myle Ott, Luke Zettlemoyer, and Veselin Stoyanov. 2020. Unsupervised cross-lingual representation learning at scale. *Preprint*, arXiv:1911.02116.

Mithun Das, Somnath Banerjee, and Animesh Mukherjee. 2022. Data bootstrapping approaches to improve low resource abusive language detection for indic languages. *arXiv preprint arXiv:2204.12543*.

Edouard Grave, Piotr Bojanowski, Prakhar Gupta, Armand Joulin, and Tomas Mikolov. 2018. Learning word vectors for 157 languages. In *Proceedings of the International Conference on Language Resources and Evaluation (LREC 2018)*.

Farhan Ahmad Jafri, Kritesh Rauniyar, Surendrabikram Thapa, Mohammad Aman Siddiqui, Matloob Khushi, and Usman Naseem. 2024. Chunav: Analyzing hindi hate speech and targeted groups in indian election discourse. *ACM Transactions on Asian and Low-Resource Language Information Processing*.

Farhan Ahmad Jafri, Mohammad Aman Siddiqui, Surendrabikram Thapa, Kritesh Rauniyar, Usman Naseem, and Imran Razzak. 2023. Uncovering political hate speech during indian election campaign: A new low-resource dataset and baselines.

Divyanshu Kakwani, Anoop Kunchukuttan, Satish Golla, Gokul N.C., Avik Bhattacharyya, Mitesh M. Khapra, and Pratyush Kumar. 2020. IndicNLPSuite: Monolingual Corpora, Evaluation Benchmarks and Pre-trained Multilingual Language Models for Indian Languages. In *Findings of EMNLP*.

Simran Khanuja, Diksha Bansal, Sarvesh Mehtani, Savya Khosla, Atreyee Dey, Balaji Gopalan, Dilip Kumar Margam, Pooja Aggarwal, Rajiv Teja Nagipogu, Shachi Dave, Shruti Gupta, Subhash Chandra Bose Gali, Vish Subramanian, and Partha Talukdar. 2021a. Muril: Multilingual representations for indian languages. *Preprint*, arXiv:2103.10730.

Simran Khanuja, Diksha Bansal, Sarvesh Mehtani, Savya Khosla, Atreyee Dey, Balaji Gopalan, Dilip Kumar Margam, Pooja Aggarwal, Rajiv Teja Nagipogu, Shachi Dave, Shruti Gupta, Subhash Chandra Bose Gali, Vish Subramanian, and Partha P. Talukdar. 2021b. Muril: Multilingual representations for indian languages. *CoRR*, abs/2103.10730.

Atharva Kulkarni, Meet Mandhane, Manali Likhitkar, Gayatri Kshirsagar, and Raviraj Joshi. 2021. L3cubemahasent: A marathi tweet-based sentiment analysis dataset. In *Proceedings of the Eleventh Workshop on Computational Approaches to Subjectivity, Sentiment and Social Media Analysis*, pages 213–220.

Nishant Luitel, Nirajan Bekoju, Anand Kumar Sah, and Subarna Shakya. 2024. Can perplexity predict finetuning performance? an investigation of tokenization effects on sequential language models for nepali. *arXiv preprint arXiv:2404.18071*.

Thomas Mandl, Sandip Modha, Marcos Zampieri, et al. 2020. Hasoc 2020: Hate speech and offensive content identification in indo-european languages. In *Proceedings of the 12th Language Resources and Evaluation Conference (LREC)*, pages 190–199.

Nobal B. Niraula, Saurab Dulal, and Diwa Koirala. 2021. Offensive language detection in Nepali social media. In *Proceedings of the 5th Workshop on Online Abuse and Harms (WOAH 2021)*, pages 67–75, Online. Association for Computational Linguistics.

Nobal B Niraula, Saurab Dulal, and Diwa Koirala. 2022. Linguistic taboos and euphemisms in nepali. *ACM Transactions on Asian and Low-Resource Language Information Processing*, 21(6):1–26.

Atul Kr Ojha. 2019. English-bhojpuri smt system: Insights from the karaka model. *arXiv preprint arXiv:1905.02239*.

Kritesh Rauniyar, Sweta Poudel, Shuvam Shiwakoti, Surendrabikram Thapa, Junaid Rashid, Jungeun Kim, Muhammad Imran, and Usman Naseem. 2023. Multiaspect annotation and analysis of nepali tweets on anti-establishment election discourse. *IEEE Access*.

Niloofar Safi Samghabadi, Parth Patwa, Srinivas PYKL, Prerana Mukherjee, Amitava Das, and Thamar Solorio. 2020. Aggression and misogyny detection using BERT: A multi-task approach. In *Proceedings of the Second Workshop on Trolling, Aggression and Cyberbullying*, pages 126–131, Marseille, France. European Language Resources Association (ELRA).

Kengatharaiyer Sarveswaran, Bal Krishna Bal, Surendrabikram Thapa, Ashwini Vaidya, and Sana Shams. 2025. A brief overview of the first workshop on challenges in processing south asian languages (chipsal). In *Proceedings of the First Workshop on Challenges in Processing South Asian Languages (CHiPSAL)*.

Yuqing Tang, Chau Tran, Xian Li, Peng-Jen Chen, Naman Goyal, Vishrav Chaudhary, Jiatao Gu, and Angela Fan. 2020. Multilingual translation with extensible multilingual pretraining and finetuning. *CoRR*, abs/2008.00401.

Surendrabikram Thapa, Kritesh Rauniyar, Farhan Ahmad Jafri, Surabhi Adhikari, Kengatharaiyer Sarveswaran, Bal Krishna Bal, Hariram Veeramani, and Usman Naseem. 2025. Natural language understanding of devanagari script languages: Language identification, hate speech and its target detection. In *Proceedings of the First Workshop on Challenges in Processing South Asian Languages (CHiPSAL)*.

Surendrabikram Thapa, Kritesh Rauniyar, Shuvam Shiwakoti, Sweta Poudel, Usman Naseem, and Mehwish Nasim. 2023. Nehate: Large-scale annotated data shedding light on hate speech in nepali local election discourse. In *ECAI 2023*, pages 2346–2353. IOS Press.

Ziqing Yang et al. 2020. Mc-bert4hate: Hate speech detection using multi-channel bert for different languages and translations. In *Proceedings of the 12th Language Resources and Evaluation Conference (LREC)*, pages 2159–2166. European Language Resources Association (ELRA).

A Appendix

A.1 Example Sentences from Dataset

Example Data		
Language	**Label**	**Sentences**
		Training
Nepali	Hate	पोखराका जनता सवै भन्दा भेडा लाग्यो मलाई । हामिले काठमाण्डैमा बलेनको लैरोमा सपोर्ट गरेपनि हामो्र छेत्रमा स्वतन्त्रलाई सारै हेपेउँ । पार्टिगतलाई तर्साउन भएपनि केही हद सम्म सवतन्त्रलाई भोट जानु पर्थ्यो ।
Nepali	Non-Hate	नया आउनै पर्छ। चाहे त्यो राप्रपा को रुपमा होस, रा.स्व.प को रुपमा होस अथवा बिबेकशिल साझा। कहिले होला? #nonotagain #NepalVotes2022
Hindi	Hate	राहुल गांधी ने दावा करते हुए कहा कि सरकार बनेगी तो कांग्रेस पार्टी की ही बनेगी. इस दौरान राहुल ने BJP पर भी निशाना साधा है. #GoaElections2022 #RahulGandhi #AssemblyElections2022 https://t.co/crw8q959wg
Hindi	Non-Hate	अमर उजाला दैनिक समाचार में हेड लाइन में प्रकाशित "मुर्दे से भी चुनाव में अशांति फैलाने का डर" के सम्बंध में खंडन। #UPPolice #AssemblyElections2022 #YourVoteMatters #AgelessDemocracy
		Evaluation
Nepali	Hate	तपाईको मुकुण्डो उधृन धेरै दिन बाकी छैन सर ।मातै्र क्रसर वालाहरुको काम फुक्का भएको दिन ।तपाईको चर्चाको राजनीति सिधिन्छ। अब उचित कानुन र नियमन वा हजुरको मुकुण्दो। No options for you. Time is running
Nepali	Non-Hate	हार्ने डर त्यसपछि राज्यकोषबाट रकम दुरुपयोग गर्न नपाइने भयले रवि लामिछाने माथि आक्रमणको प्रयास गरेको हुन गठबन्धनले । तोडफोड गर्दा प्रहरी र प्रशासन मुकदर्शक बन्नु उनिहरुलाई समर्थन गर्नु हो । #NoNotAgain
Hindi	Hate	योगी ने कहा कि कांग्रेस पहले जब सत्ता में थी तो आतंकियों को पे्ररित और पो्रत्साहित करती थी और ये हिंदू संगठनों पर झूठे मुकदमें दर्ज़ करते थे। https://t.co/ispuqj8BM7 #YogiAdityanath #UttarPradesh #UttarPradeshElections2022 #BJP #Congress https://t.co/jQPWPPNPZVD
Hindi	Non-Hate	उत्तर प्रदेश विधानसभा सामान्य निर्वाचन-2022 कल 10 मार्च-2022 को मतगणना के लिए व्यवस्थाओं के सम्बन्ध में पे्रस विज्ञपति जारी... @ECISVEEP @SpokespersonECI #ECI #AssemblyElections2022 https://t.co/vyC5hmeD4H

Figure 2: Examples from the dataset.

One_by_zero@NLU of Devanagari Script Languages 2025: Target Identification for Hate Speech Leveraging Transformer-based Approach

Dola Chakraborty, Jawad Hossain and **Mohammed Moshiul Hoque**
Department of Computer Science and Engineering
Chittagong University of Engineering & Technology, Chattogram-4349, Bangladesh
{u1904012, u1704039}@student.cuet.ac.bd, moshiul_240@cuet.ac.bd

Abstract

People often use written words to spread hate aimed at different groups that cannot be practically detected manually. Therefore, developing an automatic system capable of identifying hate speech is crucial. However, creating such a system in a low-resourced languages (LRLs) script like Devanagari becomes challenging. Hence, a shared task has been organized targeting hate speech identification in the Devanagari script. This work proposes a pre-trained transformer-based model to identify the target of hate speech, classifying it as directed toward an individual, organization, or community. We performed extensive experiments, exploring various machine learning (LR, SVM, MNB, GB, and ensemble), deep learning (CNN, LSTM, CNN+BiLSTM), and transformer-based models (IndicBERT, mBERT, MuRIL, XLM-R) to identify hate speech. Experimental results indicate that the IndicBERT model achieved the highest performance among all other models, obtaining a macro F1-score of 0.6785, which placed the team 6th in the task.

1 Introduction

The rapid evolution of social media has revolutionized global communication, enabling users to interact and exchange content instantly. As social media platforms have become central to online interaction, they have also become spaces where hate speech flourishes, often targeting specific individuals, organizations, or communities (Schmid et al., 2024). Addressing hate speech on digital platforms is essential for creating a secure, more inclusive online environment; however, the vast amount of content makes manual detection impractical. This challenge highlights the need for automated hate speech detection systems capable of accurately identifying targets within hateful language. However, hate speech often relies on context and subtle nuances in language, such as sarcasm, humor, or cultural references, making it challenging for automatic systems to identify accurately (Parihar et al., 2021).

In recent years, Natural Language Processing (NLP) has emerged as a promising solution to this problem, with significant advancements in hate speech detection for widely spoken languages (Lemmens et al., 2021). However, identifying specific targets of hate speech in low-resource languages (LRLs), especially those that use scripts like Devanagari (Hindi, Nepali), has received limited attention. The scarcity of resources and high-quality annotated datasets in Devanagari scripts is one of the critical barriers to effective hate speech detection in this script. Devanagari scripts' intricate syntax and semantics often lead to misinterpretations of hate speech, especially in cases involving indirect expressions, ambiguities, cultural allusions, or slang without an understanding of cultural and social context. Addressing these gaps, a shared task (Thapa et al., 2025) is organized at CHIPSAL@COLING2025 (Sarveswaran et al., 2025) that focuses on identifying the specific targets of hate speech within the Devanagari-script text. In this task, each instance of hate speech is categorized by its intended target, an individual, organization, or community, to deepen understanding of the scope and direction of hateful expressions in these languages. As participants in the task, the critical contributions of our work are outlined below.

- Developed a transformer-based model to categorize hate speech by its intended target: individual, organization, or community.
- Examined various baselines, including machine learning (ML), deep learning (DL), and transformers to perform the tasks.

2 Related Work

A wide range of studies have been conducted in NLP regarding hate speech. Dhanya and Balakrishnan (2021) explored the detection of hate speech

Proceedings of the First Workshop on Challenges in Processing South Asian Languages (CHiPSAL 2025), pages 327–333
January 19, 2025.

in various Asian languages, focusing on developing an automated system tailored for Malayalam. Shvets et al. (2021) worked on identifying sexism and racism in social media posts. Using GetTA Pair with BERT resulted in lower accuracy with 0.57 on the test set for exact matches but achieved a considerably higher accuracy of 0.82 for partial matches. The challenge of detecting hatred and insulting language in an LRL (Telugu), which is also code-mixed, was addressed by Farsi et al. (2024). They employed sentence BERT, achieving a macro F1-score of 0.70. Plaza-del Arco et al. (2021) used multi-task learning with sentiment, emotion, and target detection to recognize hate and offensive language. They implemented a multi-head, multi-task learning model based on BERT, which achieved the highest F1 score of 0.862. Farooqi et al. (2021) addressed hate speech detection on social media tweets, comments, and replies. They used code-mixed data (Hindi + English), and their system achieved a macro F1-score of 0.72 leveraging neural networks and ensemble transformer-based models (IndicBERT, XLM-ROBERTA, Multilingual BERT). A study by Joshi and Joshi (2023) assessed the effectiveness of several sentence-BERT models, including Bengali-SBERT, Gujarati-SBERT, Assamese-BERT, and L3Cube Indic-SBERT, which demonstrated state-of-the-art performance in detecting hate speech across Indian languages. Alam et al. (2024) conducted hate speech detection in Tamil on social media, specifically targeting caste and migration status. They explored various ML, DL, and transformer-based models, including M-BERT, XLM-R, and Tamil BERT. Notably, the M-BERT model achieved a standout macro F1-score of 0.80, marking the highest performance among the models tested. Mossie and Wang (2020) conducted vulnerable community identification on social media posts and comments in both Amharic and English text. The RNN-GRU model outperformed others, achieving an accuracy of 0.92. Singh et al. (2023) implemented the XLM-Roberta-base model on multilingual text data from the 'CrisisHateMM' dataset related to the Russia-Ukraine conflict, achieved the highest performance in detecting hate speech and identifying targets (individual, community, organization) across both Sub-task 1 (text-embedded image hate speech detection) and Sub-task 2 (target detection), with F1 scores of 84.62 and 69.73, respectively. Another notable work emphasizes hate speech detection in Marathi by Velankar et al. (2022) using the L3Cube-MahaHate dataset with 25,000 tweets where monolingual models like MahaBERT (0.909 accuracy for binary) and MahaRoBERTa (0.903 for 4-class) outperformed multilingual BERT variants. Karim et al. (2021) conducted hate speech detection in Bangla, using 8,087 labeled examples from Facebook, YouTube comments, and newspapers, and achieved an 88% F1-score with DeepHateExplainer, an ensemble of Bangla BERT-base, mBERT, and XLM-RoBERTa.

Numerous studies focus on identifying hate speech but lack target-specific classifications, especially for Nepali tweets. There is a vacuum in target identification in Nepali-language detection since most research has been on code-mixed Hindi-English or only Hindi scripts. This work addresses the gaps by including Hindi and Nepali tweets in the Devanagari script. Focusing on target identification in the Devanagari scripts, this work incorporates culturally relevant patterns to enhance the detection of nuanced hate speech.

3 Task and Dataset Description

In the shared task[1], we focus on identifying specific targets within hate speech written in the Devanagari script (Thapa et al., 2025). The task aims to classify each instance of hate speech according to its intended target: *Individual (InD)*, *Organization (OrG)*, and *Community (CoM)*. According to (Jafri et al., 2024), the definition of class is defined as:

- **Individual (InD):** Refers to hateful acts towards specific individuals, such as a self-reliant person targeted.
- **Organization (OrG):** Denotes hate targeted to institutions or groups of people formed to achieve specific goals.
- **Community (CoM):** Indicates instances where hate speech targets communities or larger socioeconomic groups.

The dataset (Jafri et al., 2024, 2023; Thapa et al., 2023; Rauniyar et al., 2023; Ojha, 2019; Kulkarni et al., 2021; Aralikatte et al., 2021) is developed for identifying the target of hate speech, comprises a variety of social media tweets containing hate speech directed toward individuals, organizations, and communities. This task aims to detect and

[1]https://github.com/therealthapa/chipsal24

prevent hate speech directed at individuals, organizations, and communities. The primary goal is to foster a safer and more respectful social media environment. Appendix A provides statistical details of the dataset, outlining key metrics and distributions.

4 Methodology

Figure 1 shows a schematic process in detecting hate speech, illustrating each major phase.

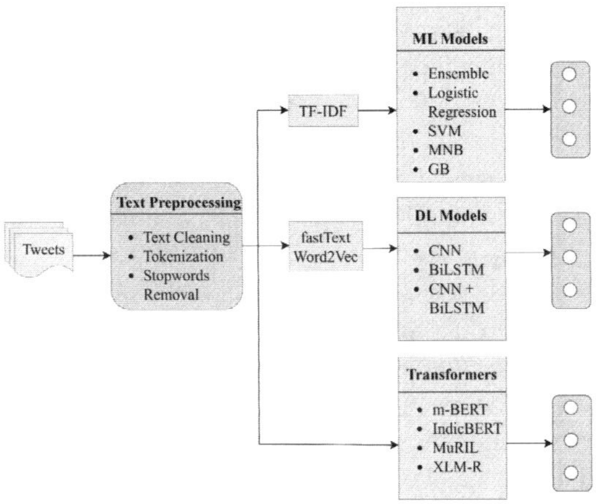

Figure 1: Schematic process of the target identification for hate speech.

4.1 Data Pre-processing

The dataset comprises tweets with substantial unnecessary and redundant content. The tweets contain emojis, unwanted spaces, symbols, punctuations, and URLs. To enhance data quality and handle class imbalance, we implemented a robust preprocessing pipeline that involves text preprocessing and oversampling. The dataset is refined by removing emojis, extraneous symbols, unnecessary punctuation, and URLs that do not significantly aid in identifying the target class. The tweets are then tokenized, with Hindi and Nepali stopwords systematically removed, resulting in a dataset containing only meaningful and relevant information. Appendix B presents the statistics of the training dataset after oversampling, highlighting key changes in data distribution.

4.2 Feature Extraction

We employed distinct feature extraction techniques for ML and DL models, optimizing each approach for its specific strengths in text data comprehension. To optimize performance, the feature set is restricted to the top 5000 terms, balancing the need for interpretability and computational efficiency. Word2Vec and FastText embeddings are employed for DL models, with each embedding represented in a 300-dimensional vector space. These embeddings capture semantic relationships between words, crucial for understanding context in the nuanced language of hate speech. Word2Vec offers continuous representations, while FastText incorporates subword information, making it particularly effective for processing morphologically complex languages like Hindi and Nepali.

4.3 ML Models

Various machine learning models are leveraged for target identification of hate speech. Logistic Regression (LR), Support Vector Machine (SVM), Multinomial Naive Bayes (MNB), and Gradient Boosting Classifier (GBC) were implemented. LR is set with a maximum iteration of 1000 for convergence. We also performed hyperparameter tuning for the SVM using "GridSearchCV" to identify the optimal configuration. An ensemble model using a Voting Classifier combining LR, SVM, MNB, and GBC with soft voting was used to enhance classification accuracy. Each model is configured to optimize performance: LR with a maximum iteration of 1000 for convergence, SVM with probability enabled for soft voting, MNB operates on TF-IDF vectorized term frequencies, and GBC refines predictions on complex samples. This ensemble leverages the strengths of each model to improve target identification.

4.4 DL Models

Three DL models, CNN, BiLSTM, and CNN+BiLSTM, were employed for the task. The CNN model utilizes an embedding layer with pre-trained word vectors, followed by a 1D convolutional layer with 128 filters and a kernel size of 5, along with max pooling and global max pooling layers to extract features and reduce dimensionality. It includes a dense layer with 64 neurons and a dropout rate of 0.5, culminating in a sigmoid activation output for binary classification. The BiLSTM model also begins with an embedding layer and employs a bidirectional LSTM layer with 64 units, leveraging forward and backward context. This is followed by global max pooling and a dense layer structure with dropout. The CNN-BiLSTM model integrates both architectures, featuring a convolutional layer for local pattern extraction and a bidirectional

LSTM for contextual understanding. All these three models are compiled with the 'Adam' optimizer and trained using 'binary_crossentropy' loss for 5 epochs.

4.5 Transformers

We utilized various pre-trained transformer-based models from HuggingFace[2] to identify the one that performs best for our task. We employed transformer-based models such as m-BERT, IndicBERT, MuRIL, and XLM-R. IndicBERT outperformed all other ML, DL, and transformer-based models by achieving the highest macro F1 score.

IndicBERT is a pre-trained multilingual language model designed to process multiple Indic languages and English. It is trained on the IndicCorp v2 dataset and evaluated against the IndicXTREME benchmark, showcasing its robustness in understanding diverse linguistic contexts. With a parameter count of 278 million, the model supports 23 Indic languages, enhancing its versatility in natural language processing tasks. The fine-tuned model architecture comprises a pre-trained IndicBERT with three output labels. IndicBERT-MLM utilizes a vanilla BERT architecture trained with the Masked Language Model.

Table 1 demonstrates the hyperparameters that are fine-tuned to attain best performance of the IndicBERT model.

Hyperparameter	**Value**
Optimizer	AdamW
Learning Rate	2e-5
Batch Size	16
Max Length	128
Weight Decay	0.05
Epochs	3

Table 1: Hyperparameter setup for transformer-based models

The hyperparameters are fine-tuned through extensive experimentation. Various learning rates, including 1e-5 and 5e-5, are tested, along with different batch sizes such as 4, 8, and 32, to evaluate performance. The maximum sequence length is set to 128 for optimal model generalization. Multiple epoch configurations, such as 5, 10, and 15, are implemented. After thorough trials, the model performs best with these selected hyperparameters.

[2]https://huggingface.co/

5 Results and Discussion

Table 2 illustrates the performance of the various ML, DL, and transformer-based models employed on the test set. The model's performance is evaluated using the macro F1-score. Among ML models, the LR model achieved the highest macro F1-score of 0.5267, while the ensemble model closely follows with a score of 0.5220. The ensemble model highlights potential challenges in integrating diverse ML models such as LR, MNB, and GB. The other ML models had an F1 score slightly lower than this value. DL models exhibited inferior performance compared to ML models. The CNN model with FastText embeddings yields a lower macro F1-score of 0.2175, while the BiLSTM model achieved a macro F1-score of 0.4587. The ensemble of CNN and BiLSTM achieved a higher F1-score of 0.5046. IndicBERT and MuRIL outperformed ML and DL models by achieving a macro F1-score of 0.6785 among transformer-based models. The XLM-R model also obtained a moderate result with a 0.6608 macro F1 Score. IndicBERT is the best model due to its higher precision value than MuRIL.

Model	**P**	**R**	**F1**
Ensemble	0.52	0.52	0.52
LR	0.53	0.53	0.53
SVM	0.46	0.47	0.46
MNB	0.51	0.52	0.51
GB	0.48	0.47	0.47
CNN	0.16	0.33	0.22
BiLSTM	0.46	0.46	0.46
CNN + BiLSTM	0.50	0.51	0.50
m-BERT	0.59	0.58	0.58
IndicBERT	**0.69**	**0.67**	**0.68**
MuRIL	0.68	0.68	0.68
XLM-R	0.63	0.63	0.63

Table 2: Performance of various ML, DL, Transformer-based models on the test set. P (Precision), R (Recall), F1 (macro F1-score)

The results highlight the superiority of transformer-based models in handling linguistic diversity while considering the limitations of conventional DL approaches, particularly in capturing the rich semantic information for LRLs needed for accurate classification. Lack of pre-trained models in ML/DL specially tailored for LRLs can be a key reason for such poor performence. A detailed error analysis of the best-performed model, both quantitative and qualitative, is presented below to offer a comprehensive understanding of the proposed model's performance.

Quantitative Analysis: An in-depth quantitative error analysis is done using the confusion matrix (Figure 2). The confusion matrix depicts that a total of 345 samples are classified correctly out of 475 samples. A total of 34 samples from the *InD* class are misclassified as *OrG*, while 18 are mistaken for *CoM*. Similarly, 34 samples from the *OrG* class are misclassified as *InD*, with an additional 13 misclassified as *CoM*. Meanwhile, 19 samples from the *CoM* class are misclassified as *InD*, and 12 as *OrG*. The misclassification can be traced to the initial class imbalance in the dataset. Though oversampling is performed, new feature patterns are not integrated, leading to a bias toward the limited features. This residual bias potentially impacts its ability to generalize effectively across all classes.

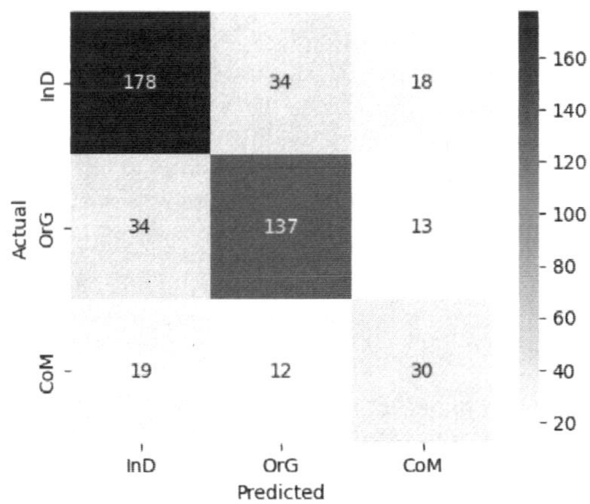

Figure 2: Confusion matrix of the best-performed model (IndicBERT).

Qualitative Analysis: A comparison of actual labels and predicted labels on a particular tweet is illustrated in Figure 3. The first three samples are predicted correctly as their actual classes. However, the fourth sample is incorrectly predicted. It is meant to target a community, but our model wrongly predicts the sample as *InD*.

The misclassifications likely occur due to the inherent challenges in context understanding and the overlap of semantic features between the classes. Even with IndicBERT, which excels in multilingual tasks, subtle contextual cues in the Devanagari script may cause confusion between classes.

Tweets	**True Label**	**Predicted Label**
कही बर्षमा कांग्रेस भित्र माओबादी मात्रे बाकी रलान जस्तो छ, राजीनामा राजीनामा, भनष्कासन गनष थाले कांग्रेभस	OrG	OrG
कस्ता पार्टी सभापति हुन्, हँसियाहथौडामा भाेट नहाले कारबाही रे । मारेके	InD	InD
नेपाली जनता श्रीलंकाको जनता बन्न समय लाग्छ। नेपाली जनताले दुख भोग्न पुगेको छैन।	CoM	CoM
सबै मिली सत्रे लाई हराऔँ	CoM	InD

Figure 3: Some predicted outputs by the IndicBERT.

6 Conclusion

This study evaluates several ML, DL, and transformer-based models for identifying hate speech targets in Hindi and Nepali tweets written in Devanagari script. While traditional ML methods like LR and ensemble provided valuable insights, they struggled to capture complex semantic relationships. DL models also faced challenges with feature representation in the Devanagari script and obtained poor results. However, IndicBERT outperformed all other ML and DL approaches among transformer-based models, achieving the highest F1-score of 0.6785 by effectively capturing the nuances of the Devanagari script. Future work can explore advanced embeddings, hybrid models, or ensemble multiple transformers for enhanced performance in hate speech detection.

7 Limitations

The current work poses several constraints: (i) The presented method relies on the pre-trained IndicBERT, which may require further fine-tuning and modification to capture contextual patterns better. (ii) The dataset is imbalanced, and to address this, we applied the oversampling technique, resampling the minority class. However, this approach may limit the model's ability to learn diverse patterns, impacting its performance. New NLP augmentation techniques can be more helpful in further investigation. (iii) DL models' performance can be investigated further, exploring alternative embeddings and classifiers.

References

Md Alam, Hasan Mesbaul Ali Taher, Jawad Hossain, Shawly Ahsan, and Mohammed Moshiul Hoque. 2024. Cuet_nlp_manning@ lt-edi 2024: Transformer-based approach on caste and migration hate speech detection. In *Proceedings of the Fourth Workshop on Language Technology for Equality, Diversity, Inclusion*, pages 238–243.

Rahul Aralikatte, Miryam De Lhoneux, Anoop Kunchukuttan, and Anders Søgaard. 2021. Itihasa: A large-scale corpus for sanskrit to english translation. In *Proceedings of the 8th Workshop on Asian Translation (WAT2021)*, pages 191–197.

L. K. Dhanya and Kannan Balakrishnan. 2021. Hate speech detection in asian languages: a survey. In *2021 International Conference on Communication, Control and Information Sciences (ICCISc)*, volume 1. IEEE.

Zaki Mustafa Farooqi, Sreyan Ghosh, and Rajiv Ratn Shah. 2021. Leveraging transformers for hate speech detection in conversational code-mixed tweets. *arXiv preprint arXiv:2112.09986*.

Salman Farsi, Asrarul Eusha, Jawad Hossain, Shawly Ahsan, Avishek Das, and Mohammed Moshiul Hoque. 2024. Cuet_binary_hackers@ dravidianlangtech eacl2024: Hate and offensive language detection in telugu code-mixed text using sentence similarity bert. In *Proceedings of the Fourth Workshop on Speech, Vision, and Language Technologies for Dravidian Languages*, pages 193–199.

Farhan Ahmad Jafri, Kritesh Rauniyar, Surendrabikram Thapa, Mohammad Aman Siddiqui, Matloob Khushi, and Usman Naseem. 2024. Chunav: Analyzing hindi hate speech and targeted groups in indian election discourse. *ACM Transactions on Asian and Low-Resource Language Information Processing*.

Farhan Ahmad Jafri, Mohammad Aman Siddiqui, Surendrabikram Thapa, Kritesh Rauniyar, Usman Naseem, and Imran Razzak. 2023. Uncovering political hate speech during indian election campaign: A new low-resource dataset and baselines.

Ananya Joshi and Raviraj Joshi. 2023. Harnessing pretrained sentence transformers for offensive language detection in indian languages. *arXiv preprint arXiv:2310.02249*.

Md. Rezaul Karim, Sumon Kanti Dey, Tanhim Islam, Sagor Sarker, Mehadi Hasan Menon, Kabir Hossain, Md. Azam Hossain, and Stefan Decker. 2021. Deephateexplainer: Explainable hate speech detection in under-resourced bengali language. In *2021 IEEE 8th International Conference on Data Science and Advanced Analytics (DSAA)*, pages 1–10.

Atharva Kulkarni, Meet Mandhane, Manali Likhitkar, Gayatri Kshirsagar, and Raviraj Joshi. 2021. L3cubemahasent: A marathi tweet-based sentiment analysis dataset. In *Proceedings of the Eleventh Workshop on Computational Approaches to Subjectivity, Sentiment and Social Media Analysis*, pages 213–220.

Jens Lemmens, Ilia Markov, and Walter Daelemans. 2021. Improving hate speech type and target detection with hateful metaphor features. In *Proceedings of the Fourth Workshop on NLP for Internet Freedom: Censorship, Disinformation, and Propaganda*.

Zewdie Mossie and Jenq-Haur Wang. 2020. Vulnerable community identification using hate speech detection on social media. *Information Processing & Management*, 57(3):102087.

Atul Kr Ojha. 2019. English-bhojpuri smt system: Insights from the karaka model. *arXiv preprint arXiv:1905.02239*.

Anil Singh Parihar, Surendrabikram Thapa, and Sushruti Mishra. 2021. Hate speech detection using natural language processing: Applications and challenges. In *2021 5th International Conference on Trends in Electronics and Informatics (ICOEI)*, pages 1302–1308. IEEE.

Flor Miriam Plaza-del Arco, Sercan Halat, Sebastian Padó, and Roman Klinger. 2021. Multi-task learning with sentiment, emotion, and target detection to recognize hate speech and offensive language. *arXiv preprint arXiv:2109.10255*.

Kritesh Rauniyar, Sweta Poudel, Shuvam Shiwakoti, Surendrabikram Thapa, Junaid Rashid, Jungeun Kim, Muhammad Imran, and Usman Naseem. 2023. Multi-aspect annotation and analysis of nepali tweets on anti-establishment election discourse. *IEEE Access*.

Kengatharaiyer Sarveswaran, Bal Krishna Bal, Surendrabikram Thapa, Ashwini Vaidya, and Sana Shams. 2025. A brief overview of the first workshop on challenges in processing south asian languages (chipsal). In *Proceedings of the First Workshop on Challenges in Processing South Asian Languages (CHiPSAL)*.

Ursula Kristin Schmid, Anna Sophie Kümpel, and Diana Rieger. 2024. *How social media users perceive different forms of online hate speech: A qualitative multi-method study*, volume 26.

Alexander Shvets et al. 2021. Targets and aspects in social media hate speech. In *Proceedings of the 5th Workshop on Online Abuse and Harms (WOAH 2021)*.

Karanpreet Singh, Vajratiya Vajrobol, and Nitisha Aggarwal. 2023. Iic_team@ multimodal hate speech event detection 2023: Detection of hate speech and targets using xlm-roberta-base. In *Proceedings of the 6th Workshop on Challenges and Applications of Automated Extraction of Socio-political Events from Text*.

Surendrabikram Thapa, Kritesh Rauniyar, Farhan Ahmad Jafri, Surabhi Adhikari, Kengatharaiyer Sarveswaran, Bal Krishna Bal, Hariram Veeramani, and Usman Naseem. 2025. Natural language understanding of devanagari script languages: Language identification, hate speech and its target detection. In *Proceedings of the First Workshop on Challenges in Processing South Asian Languages (CHiPSAL)*.

Surendrabikram Thapa, Kritesh Rauniyar, Shuvam Shiwakoti, Sweta Poudel, Usman Naseem, and Mehwish Nasim. 2023. Nehate: Large-scale annotated data shedding light on hate speech in nepali local election discourse. In *ECAI 2023*, pages 2346–2353. IOS Press.

Abhishek Velankar, Hrushikesh Patil, Amol Gore, Shubham Salunke, and Raviraj Joshi. 2022. L3cube-mahahate: A tweet-based marathi hate speech detection dataset and bert models. *arXiv preprint arXiv:2203.13778*.

A Appendix

Classes	Train	Valid	Test	T_W	T_{UW}
InD	1074	230	230	42438	15681
OrG	856	183	184	31181	11722
CoM	284	61	61	10564	5182
Total	2214	474	475	84183	25731

Table A.1: Dataset Statistics for Train, Validation, and Test Sets. T_W and T_{UW} denotes total words and total unique words, respectively

Table A.1 demonstrates the statistics of the dataset. The dataset comprises a total of 3163 instances of hate speech. The training dataset consists of 2214 samples. In addition, the validation dataset includes 474 tweets, while the test set contains 475 tweets, which will be used in the final evaluation to assess the model's generalization to unseen data. The datasets are highly imbalanced, with the individual class containing substantially more instances than the organization and community classes.

B Appendix

Analyzing the dataset reveals a substantial class imbalance, with instances of the class *InD* being the most prevalent, while *OrG* and *CoM* classes are significantly underrepresented. To address this, we employed an oversampling technique specifically targeting the minority classes. We accomplished this by replicating samples from these underrepresented classes until the number of instances in each class was comparable. This approach ensures that the model obtains sufficient samples from each class, minimizing the risk of bias toward the majority class. Table B.1 shows the number of training instances after applying the oversampling technique.

Oversampling can lead to bias by artificially inflating the representation of minority classes. Since it just duplicates existing minority class examples instead of generating truly novel samples, the new observations do not provide additional informative details about under-represented classes. This reduces the model's ability to generalize to unseen data and increases the risk of overfitting. To overcome this problem new data augmentation techniques introduced in NLP can be used in further analysis for better results. Methods like back translation, synonym replacement, lexical substitution, noise injection can enhance linguistic diversity and make models robust to minor changes. For target identification in hate speech in the Devanagari script, context-aware substitution and adversarial methods can help to reduce bias and improve generalization.

Classes	Train	T_W	T_{UW}
Individual	1074	29471	11963
Organization	1074	27831	6931
Communication	1074	27886	3773
Total	3222	85188	18187

Table B.1: Statistics of training dataset after oversampling

Paramananda@NLU of Devanagari Script Languages 2025: Detection of Language, Hate Speech and Targets using FastText and BERT

Darwin Acharya
Kathmandu University
acharyadarwin5@gmail.com

Sundeep Dawadi
Kathmandu University
sundeepdwd@gmail.com

Shivram Saud
Kathmandu University
saudshivram373@gmail.com

Sunil Regmi
Kathmandu University
sunil.regmi@ku.edu.np

Abstract

This paper presents a comparative analysis of FastText and BERT-based approaches for Natural Language Understanding (NLU) tasks in Devanagari script languages. We evaluate these models on three critical tasks: language identification, hate speech detection, and target identification across five languages: Nepali, Marathi, Sanskrit, Bhojpuri, and Hindi. Our experiments, although with a raw tweet dataset but extracting only the Devanagari script, demonstrate that while both models achieve exceptional performance in language identification (F1 scores > 0.99), they show varying effectiveness in hate speech detection and target identification tasks. FastText with augmented data outperforms BERT in hate speech detection (F1 score: 0.8552 vs. 0.5763), while BERT shows superior performance in target identification (F1 score: 0.5785 vs. 0.4898). These findings contribute to the growing body of research on NLU for low-resource languages and provide insights into model selection for specific tasks in Devanagari script processing.

1 Introduction

The proliferation of digital content in Devanagari script languages has created an urgent need for robust Natural Language Understanding (NLU) tools (Wilie et al., 2020). These tools are essential for content moderation, ensuring safe online spaces, and preserving linguistic diversity in digital platforms (Parihar et al., 2021; Kumar et al., 2024). However, processing Devanagari script languages presents unique challenges due to their complex character sets, morphological richness, and limited computational resources (Sarveswaran et al., 2025; Thapa et al., 2025).

This research addresses these challenges through two primary approaches. Firstly, the implementation of FastText (Joulin et al., 2017), known for its efficiency in handling Devanagari text data (Bansod, 2023; GitHub), and secondly, the utilization of pre-trained BERT-based Multilingual Cased models (Devlin et al., 2019) fine-tuned for specific tasks.

Our work focuses on providing a comprehensive comparison of traditional and transformer-based approaches, establishing baseline performances for three crucial NLU tasks, and identifying optimal model configurations for FastText Devanagari script processing tasks.

2 Related Work

Recent research in Devanagari script processing has focused on developing robust language identification systems and hate speech detection mechanisms (Kumbhar and Thakre, 2024; Rauniyar et al., 2023). Language identification and hate speech detection in low-resource languages, particularly those using the Devanagari script, have garnered significant research attention due to the increasing digital content in these languages. Traditional methods for language identification often relied on statistical models and n-gram analyses. With the advent of deep learning, more sophisticated models have emerged, offering improved performance (Bansod, 2023).

In the context of Indic languages, AI4Bharat's IndicLID (Devlin et al., 2019) leveraged FastText-based models fine-tuned on multiple Indian languages for language identification. Their models demonstrated high precision, recall, and F1-scores, with significant throughput suitable for large-scale applications. For instance, the IndicLID-FTN-4-dim model achieved an F1-score of 0.99 and an accuracy of 0.98, outperforming models like CLD3 and NLLB in terms of throughput and model size.

Thapa et al. (Thapa et al., 2023a) conducted the Multimodal Hate Speech Event Detection shared task at CASE 2023, providing valuable insights into various methodologies for hate speech detection. The methods from different participants re-

Proceedings of the First Workshop on Challenges in Processing South Asian Languages (CHiPSAL 2025), pages 334–338
January 19, 2025.

vealed interesting approaches, with transformer-based methods proving to be more effective. Most participants utilized BERT-based variations to extract textual features from the dataset (Hürriyetoğlu et al., 2023).

Bansod (Bansod, 2023) explored hate speech detection in Hindi using various embedding methods, including FastText, GloVe, and transformer-based embeddings like DistilBERT and MuRIL. The study found that transformer-based models, particularly when fine-tuned with low learning rates and class weights, achieved macro F1-scores in the range of 70–75%. The research highlighted challenges such as the model's difficulty in detecting sarcasm, understanding veiled references, and the need for background knowledge to interpret certain types of hate speech.

These studies underscore the importance of model selection, data augmentation, and handling linguistic nuances in low-resource languages. They highlight the challenges posed by unbalanced datasets, code-mixed languages, sarcasm, and the necessity for comprehensive datasets that capture the diversity of language use on online platforms. The collective findings contribute to the growing body of research on natural language understanding for Devanagari script languages and provide insights into optimal model configurations for specific tasks in this domain.

The theoretical foundations of our approach build upon the FastText architecture introduced by Joulin et al. (Joulin et al., 2017) and enhanced by Bojanowski et al. (Bojanowski et al., 2017) with subword information. The BERT-based component utilizes the multilingual model developed by Devlin et al. (Devlin et al., 2019), which has shown remarkable effectiveness in cross-lingual tasks.

3 Methodology

In this section, we outline our methodology in a step-by-step manner.

3.1 Task and Dataset Description

The shared task comprised of three specific subtasks: Sub-Task A involved classifying text into five distinct Devanagari languages. Sub-Task B focused on the binary classification challenge of determining whether a given text contained hate speech or not. Sub-Task C focused on identifying the target of hate speech.

3.1.1 Sub-Task A: Language Identification

This problem involved classifying text into five distinct Devanagari languages- Nepali, Marathi, Sanskrit, Bhojpuri, and Hindi - labeled as 0 through 4. The dataset comprised a total of 52,422 training samples, 11,233 evaluation data, and 11,234 test data.

3.1.2 Sub-Task B: Hate Speech Detection

Sub-task B is focused on binary classification of hate speech labeled as 0 ('non-hate') and 1 ('hate'). The dataset comprised a total of 19,019 training samples of text, 4,076 evaluation data, and 4,076 test data.

3.1.3 Sub-Task C: Target Identification

Sub-Task C focused on identifying the targets of hate speech i.e., for whom the hate speech was delivered. The dataset for this sub-task comprised of a total of 2,214 training samples, 474 evaluation data, and 475 test data. There are three classes in the dataset 'individual', 'organization', and 'community' labeled as 0, 1, and 2 respectively.

Dataset Description: Our study utilizes a comprehensive dataset (CodaLab), comprising sentences in five Devanagari script languages. The dataset incorporates diverse sources, including the CHUNAV dataset for Hindi hate speech (Jafri et al., 2024), the Political Hate Speech Corpus (Jafri et al., 2023), the Nehate Nepali hate speech dataset (Thapa et al., 2023b), the Multi-aspect Nepali tweet corpus (Rauniyar et al., 2023), the English-Bhojpuri parallel corpus (Ojha, 2019), the L3CubeMahaSent Marathi dataset (Kulkarni et al., 2021), and the Itihasa Sanskrit-English corpus (Aralikatte et al., 2021).

3.2 Preprocessing of Data

Initially, we cleaned the provided dataset into three sets: training, evaluation, and testing. Using a custom approach defined manually with the Python regular expression library, we extracted only the Devanagari text from the dataset, completely ignoring URLs, emojis, hashtags, mentions, digits, and punctuation, as they were considered irrelevant to the classification problem.

3.3 Data Augmentation

To balance the instances of the 'hate' class in Sub-Task B, the samples from Sub-Task C were merged with Sub-Task B and labeled as 'hate' (label 1).

This was feasible because all the samples in Sub-Task C represented hate tweets but targeted different groups so after augmenting the data we removed the duplicates.

3.4 Model Architecture and Training

Because the deep learning model can learn the complex distribution characteristics of data through deep artificial neural networks and nonlinearity, especially the use of deep learning in tasks related to text data has attracted more and more attention (Zhang et al., 2018).

3.4.1 FastText Implementation

FastText is a library for efficient learning of word representations and sentence classification and obtains performance on par with recently proposed methods inspired by deep learning while being much faster (FastText; Joulin et al., 2017) . It requires minimal preprocessing to preserve linguistic nuances. We have trained the fastText model for Sub-Task A, B, and C. The Hyperparameters we set were Epochs: 500 Learning rate: 1 Embedding dimension: 100 Word N-gram: 1 Bucket size: 10,000. For Task B, we implemented data augmentation strategies for FastText to assess the impact of additional training data, following methodologies validated in recent studies (Bansod, 2023; GitHub). This highly improved the performance of the model which is later discussed in the result section.

3.4.2 BERT Implementation

BERT (Bidirectional Encoder Representations from Transformers) (Devlin et al., 2019). All three sub-tasks were fine-tuned on BERT Base Multilingual Uncased and BERT Base Uncased with a constant learning rate of 1e-4 and a batch size of 32, while the number of epochs was varied across 5, 10, and 20.

4 Results and Analysis

This section is dedicated to a comparative detailed analysis of the proposed models on all three subtasks. We conducted controlled experiments for each task, maintaining consistent evaluation metrics across models. The performance metrics in Table 1 show the F1 score of each model and provide insight into their effectiveness.

Task	Method	F1 Score (Test)
Language Identification	FastText	0.9917
	BERT	**0.9939**
Hate Speech Detection	FastText	0.6159
	FastText (aug)	**0.8552**
	BERT	0.5763
Target Identification	FastText	0.4898
	BERT	**0.5785**

Table 1: F1 Scores for different NLU Tasks in Devanagari Script

4.1 Quantitative Results

4.2 Analysis

The results reveal distinct model strengths across various Devanagari language processing tasks:

1. **Language Identification:** Both FastText and BERT performed exceptionally well, achieving near-perfect F1 scores (0.9917 and 0.9939, respectively). These results align with previous findings in Indic language processing (GitHub), demonstrating that both models effectively differentiate between Nepali, Marathi, Sanskrit, Bhojpuri, and Hindi.

2. **Hate Speech Detection:** The performance of the models diverged significantly. FastText, when combined with data augmentation, achieved a notable improvement in F1 score from 0.6159 to 0.8552, outperforming BERT substantially. BERT, despite its capacity for deep contextual understanding, struggled with this task, displaying an F1 score of only 0.5763. This underperformance, coupled with signs of overfitting (an evaluation score of 0.88 but a lower test score), indicates that BERT's generalization ability is limited when faced with sparse hate speech datasets.

3. **Target Identification:** For this more nuanced task, BERT outperformed FastText, with F1 scores of 0.5785 versus 0.4898, respectively. This suggests that BERT's contextual embeddings are better suited to identifying and distinguishing complex targets, such as individuals, organizations, and communities, within text. Tuning FastText hyperparameters yielded only minor improvements (±2%), emphasizing its robustness but also its limitations in handling contextual nuances.

5 Conclusion and Future Work

This study provides an in-depth comparative analysis of FastText and BERT models for processing Devanagari script languages. Key findings include:

1. **LanguageIdentification:** Both models excel in distinguishing among Devanagari languages, indicating their robustness in handling script-based variations.

2. **Hate Speech Detection:** FastText, particularly when augmented with additional data, outperforms BERT, highlighting the importance of data volume and diversity. BERT's tendency to overfit suggests a need for more rigorous fine-tuning, especially for low-resource hate speech datasets.

3. **Target Identification:** BERT's superior performance in this task underscores the advantage of leveraging contextual embeddings to capture subtle, nuanced relationships.

Future Directions:

Exploring hybrid approaches that integrate the strengths of both models FastText and BERT could improve overall performance. Investigating script-specific pre-processing techniques to enhance model accuracy. Applying transfer learning techniques to better adapt models to low-resource Devanagari languages, could potentially reduce the need for extensive data augmentation.

6 Acknowledgments

We thank the organizers of CHiPSAL@COLING 2025 (Sarveswaran et al., 2025; Thapa et al., 2025) for providing the datasets and their support throughout this research.

References

Rahul Aralikatte, Miryam De Lhoneux, Anoop Kunchukuttan, and Anders Søgaard. 2021. Itihasa: A large-scale corpus for sanskrit to english translation. In *Proceedings of the 8th Workshop on Asian Translation (WAT2021)*, pages 191–197.

Pranjali Prakash Bansod. 2023. Hate Speech Detection in Hindi. Master's thesis, Master's Projects.

Piotr Bojanowski, Edouard Grave, Armand Joulin, and Tomas Mikolov. 2017. Enriching word vectors with subword information. *Transactions of the Association for Computational Linguistics*, 5:135–146.

CodaLab. CHIPSAL@COLING 2025 Competition. https://codalab.lisn.upsaclay.fr/competitions/20000#participate-get_data.

Jacob Devlin, Ming-Wei Chang, Kenton Lee, and Kristina Toutanova. 2019. BERT: Pre-training of deep bidirectional transformers for language understanding. In *Proceedings of the 2019 Conference of the North American Chapter of the Association for Computational Linguistics: Human Language Technologies, Volume 1 (Long and Short Papers)*, pages 4171–4186, Minneapolis, Minnesota. Association for Computational Linguistics.

FastText. Supervised-tutorial. https://fasttext.cc/docs/en/supervised-tutorial.html. (accessed October 30, 2024).

GitHub. AI4Bharat/IndicLID. https://github.com/AI4Bharat/IndicLID.

Ali Hürriyetoğlu, Hristo Tanev, Osman Mutlu, Surendrabikram Thapa, Fiona Anting Tan, and Erdem Yörük. 2023. Challenges and applications of automated extraction of socio-political events from text (CASE 2023): Workshop and shared task report. In *Proceedings of the 6th Workshop on Challenges and Applications of Automated Extraction of Socio-political Events from Text*, pages 167–175, Varna, Bulgaria. INCOMA Ltd., Shoumen, Bulgaria.

Farhan Ahmad Jafri, Kritesh Rauniyar, Surendrabikram Thapa, Mohammad Aman Siddiqui, Matloob Khushi, and Usman Naseem. 2024. Chunav: Analyzing hindi hate speech and targeted groups in indian election discourse. *ACM Transactions on Asian and Low-Resource Language Information Processing*.

Farhan Ahmad Jafri, Mohammad Aman Siddiqui, Surendrabikram Thapa, Kritesh Rauniyar, Usman Naseem, and Imran Razzak. 2023. Uncovering political hate speech during indian election campaign: A new low-resource dataset and baselines.

Armand Joulin, Edouard Grave, Piotr Bojanowski, and Tomas Mikolov. 2017. Bag of tricks for efficient text classification. In *Proceedings of the 15th Conference of the European Chapter of the Association for Computational Linguistics: Volume 2, Short Papers*, pages 427–431, Valencia, Spain. Association for Computational Linguistics.

Atharva Kulkarni, Meet Mandhane, Manali Likhitkar, Gayatri Kshirsagar, and Raviraj Joshi. 2021. L3cubemahasent: A marathi tweet-based sentiment analysis dataset. In *Proceedings of the Eleventh Workshop on Computational Approaches to Subjectivity, Sentiment and Social Media Analysis*, pages 213–220.

Deepak Kumar, Yousef Anees AbuHashem, and Zakir Durumeric. 2024. Watch your language: Investigating content moderation with large language models. In *Proceedings of the International AAAI Conference on Web and Social Media*, volume 18, pages 865–878.

Madhuri Kumbhar and Kalpana Thakre. 2024. Language identification and transliteration approaches for code-mixed text. *Journal of Engineering Science & Technology Review*, 17(1).

Atul Kr Ojha. 2019. English-bhojpuri smt system: Insights from the karaka model. *arXiv preprint arXiv:1905.02239*.

Anil Singh Parihar, Surendrabikram Thapa, and Sushruti Mishra. 2021. Hate Speech Detection Using Natural Language Processing: Applications and Challenges. In *2021 5th International Conference on Trends in Electronics and Informatics (ICOEI)*, pages 1302–1308.

Kritesh Rauniyar, Sweta Poudel, Shuvam Shiwakoti, Surendrabikram Thapa, Junaid Rashid, Jungeun Kim, Muhammad Imran, and Usman Naseem. 2023. Multi-aspect annotation and analysis of nepali tweets on anti-establishment election discourse. *IEEE Access*.

Kengatharaiyer Sarveswaran, Bal Krishna Bal, Surendrabikram Thapa, Ashwini Vaidya, and Sana Shams. 2025. A brief overview of the first workshop on challenges in processing south asian languages (chipsal). In *Proceedings of the First Workshop on Challenges in Processing South Asian Languages (CHiPSAL)*.

Surendrabikram Thapa, Farhan Ahmad Jafri, Ali Hürriyetoğlu, Francielle Vargas, Roy Ka-Wei Lee, and Usman Naseem. 2023a. Multimodal hate speech event detection: Shared task 4, case 2023. In *Proceedings of the Workshop on Challenges and Applications of Social Media Analysis (CASE 2023)*. Association for Computational Linguistics.

Surendrabikram Thapa, Kritesh Rauniyar, Farhan Ahmad Jafri, Surabhi Adhikari, Kengatharaiyer Sarveswaran, Bal Krishna Bal, Hariram Veeramani, and Usman Naseem. 2025. Natural language understanding of devanagari script languages: Language identification, hate speech and its target detection. In *Proceedings of the First Workshop on Challenges in Processing South Asian Languages (CHiPSAL)*.

Surendrabikram Thapa, Kritesh Rauniyar, Shuvam Shiwakoti, Sweta Poudel, Usman Naseem, and Mehwish Nasim. 2023b. Nehate: Large-scale annotated data shedding light on hate speech in nepali local election discourse. In *ECAI 2023*, pages 2346–2353. IOS Press.

Bryan Wilie, Karissa Vincentio, Genta Indra Winata, Samuel Cahyawijaya, Xiaohong Li, Zhi Yuan Lim, Sidik Soleman, Rahmad Mahendra, Pascale Fung, Syafri Bahar, et al. 2020. Indonlu: Benchmark and resources for evaluating indonesian natural language understanding. In *Proceedings of the 1st Conference of the Asia-Pacific Chapter of the Association for Computational Linguistics and the 10th International Joint Conference on Natural Language Processing*, pages 843–857.

L. Zhang, S. Wang, and B. Liu. 2018. Deep learning for sentiment analysis: A survey. *Wiley Interdisciplinary Reviews: Data Mining and Knowledge Discovery*, 8(4):e1253.

SKPD Emergency@NLU of Devanagari Script Languages 2025: Devanagari Script Classification using CBOW Embeddings with Attention-Enhanced BiLSTM

Shubham Shakya[1,2], Saral Sainju[1,3], Subham Krishna Shrestha[1,4], Prekshya Dawadi[1,5], Shreya Khatiwada[1,6]

[1]Department of Computer Science and Engineering, Kathmandu University

Emails: {[2]ss46041720, [3]ss42041720, [4]ss50041720,[5]pd12041720, [6]sk29041720}@student.ku.edu.np

All authors contributed equally to this work.

Correspondence: shubham.shakyaa@gmail.com

Abstract

Devanagari script, encompassing languages such as Nepali, Marathi, Sanskrit, Bhojpuri and Hindi, involves challenges for identification due to its overlapping character sets and lexical characteristics. To address this, we propose a method that utilizes Continuous Bag of Words (CBOW) embeddings integrated with attention-enhanced Bidirectional Long Short-Term Memory (BiLSTM) network. Our methodology involves meticulous data preprocessing and generation of word embeddings to better the model's ability. The proposed method achieves an overall accuracy of 99%, significantly outperforming character level identification approaches. The results reveal high precision across most language pairs, though minor classification confusions persist between closely related languages. Our findings demonstrate the robustness of the CBOW-BiLSTM model for Devanagari script classification and highlights the importance of accurate language identification in preserving linguistic diversity in multilingual environments.

Keywords: Language Identification, Devanagari Script, Natural Language Processing, Neural Networks

1 Introduction

Devanagari Script, part of the Brahmic family of scripts, is widely used in regions such as India, Nepal, Tibet, and Southeast Asia (Mhaiskar, 2014). Often referred to simply as 'Nagari', it has historical significance, with some attributing the name to the writing system of 'city people', while others believe it originates from the Nagar Brahmans of Gujarat (Lambert, 1953). Today, Devanagari serves as the standardized writing system for several major South Asian languages, including Hindi, Nepali, Sanskrit, Bhojpuri, and Marathi. The volume of text data produced in these languages is substantial and continues to grow with the expansion of digital content.

In multilingual contexts, accurate language identification is a critical preliminary step for many natural language processing (NLP) systems. A system trained to classify Nepali text, for example, would struggle to handle Marathi documents effectively, and a Hindi-to-Bhojpuri translation system would likely fail if it were provided with Sanskrit data. This makes precise language identification essential for ensuring the proper functioning of NLP applications. However, identifying languages within the Devanagari script poses unique challenges. These languages share a large character set and exhibit many similarities, while having significant variation in writing styles and grammar (Kopparapu and Vijayalaxmi, 2014). This complexity creates obstacles to developing reliable language identification systems, particularly when distinguishing between languages like Bhojpuri and Hindi, which share extensive lexical overlap.

To address these challenges, this study, which is a part of the first task of the challenges in processing south asian languages (CHIPSAL) workshop at COLING'24, focuses on the identification of five languages—Nepali, Marathi, Sanskrit, Bhojpuri, and Hindi—within the Devanagari script. The goal is to develop a model capable of accurately distinguishing between these languages despite their close linguistic relationships. By implementing a bidirectional Long Short-Term Memory (BiLSTM) network (Graves et al., 2014), we aim to capture the contextual information crucial for distinguishing between languages in the same script. BiLSTM networks have demonstrated success in various NLP tasks, and their ability to process text in both forward and backward directions makes them particularly suited to tasks involving complex language structures.

As digital text in Nepali, Marathi, Sanskrit, Bhojpuri, and Hindi grows, accurate language identification becomes essential. Our study addresses this need by creating a robust framework for identify-

Proceedings of the First Workshop on Challenges in Processing South Asian Languages (CHiPSAL 2025), pages 339–343
January 19, 2025.

ing languages in the Devanagari script, highlighting the importance of preserving the linguistic diversity and cultural significance each language represents.

2 Related Works

This section reviews the existing study that addresses the challenges and methods used in language identification, mainly those that utilized the Devanagari scripts.

In the earlier period, the problem of language identification was approached by methods that utilized n-gram models. These models are foundational but have limitations when it comes to distinguishing between languages that have similar vocabularies.(Cavnar and Trenkle, 1994) showed the ability of n-gram models in language identification but acknowledged their shortcomings in highly overlapping languages. This limitation is particularly pronounced in Devanagari Scripts as different languages share extensive lexical similarities.

There has been a shift towards machine learning and deep learning techniques in order to improve the language identification accuracy. For example, (Joshi et al., 2020) analyzed the characters and word embeddings for Devanagari text classification, demonstrating the method including ResNet's success in recognizing the linguistic intricacies which performed better than the convolutional neural network which is the current state of the art.

Bidirectional Long Short-Term Memory networks have emerged as a promising avenue for solving the problem of Language Identification. (Bedyakin et al., 2021) work on offensive language identification in low-resource language using BiLSTM networks illustrates the model's effectiveness in handling unique linguistic characteristics. Our approach also aims to use BiLSTM networks for language identification between languages that share lexical similarities. Overall, the current research on language classification among the languages that use the Devanagari script is focused on developing robust and accurate techniques for script recognition, segmentation, and language identification. The diversity of Devanagari-based languages and the complexity of the script itself continue to drive research in this area. However, the specific task of classifying languages such as Hindi, Nepali, Marathi, Sanskrit, and Bhojpuri within the Devanagari script remains an unexplored area that requires further investigation.

3 Methodology

This section describes our approach to Devanagari script classification using CBOW embeddings with an attention-enhanced BiLSTM model. Our methodology comprises of four main components: data preprocessing, word embedding generation, neural network architecture and model training.

3.1 Data Preprocessing

In this study, we utilized publicly available datasets, includeing (Jafri et al., 2024), (Jafri et al., 2023), (Thapa et al., 2023), (Rauniyar et al., 2023), (Ojha, 2019), (Kulkarni et al., 2021), (Aralikatte et al., 2021) to ensure transparency and reproducibility. The preprocessing pipeline consists of several steps to clean and standardize the Devanagari text data.

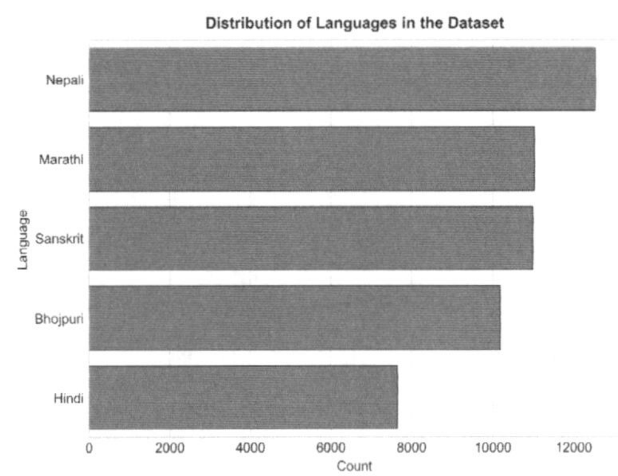

Figure 1: Distribution of Language in the Dataset

3.1.1 Text Cleaning

The dataset used for this research consists of 52,422 Devanagari-script text samples labeled by class as shown in Figure 1. First, the dataset was preprocessed to ensure data quality. Any missing text entries were removed. Non-Devanagari characters, numerals, and punctuation marks were eliminated using regular expressions. Each text entry was then stripped of whitespace resulting in a clean corpus of Devanagari text data.

3.1.2 Data Splitting

The preprocessed dataset was split into training and testing sets using an 80:20 ratio. For the final model training after hyper-parameter tuning, the entire dataset was used for model training. Evaluation was performed on a separate hold-out dataset.

Layer	Details
Input Layer	FastText Embeddings (Dimension: 100)
Bi-LSTM	LSTM (Input: 100, Hidden Units: 256, Layers: 3, Bidirectional: True)
Attention	Self-Attention (3 Linear Transformations: Wa, Ua, Va, Hidden Size: 512)
Output Layer	Fully Connected (Input: 512, Output: 5)

Table 1: Component configuration parameters for the model architecture.

3.2 Word Embedding Generation

In this research, two distinct methods for generating word embeddings were explored: Continuous Bag of Words (CBOW) model and a character-level encoding approach. Each method offers unique advantages and challenges in capturing the semantic richness of the Devanagari script.

3.2.1 Continious Bag of Words (CBOW)

The Continuous Bag of Words (CBOW) model is a predictive model used in natural language processing that captures contextual information by predicting a target word based on its surrounding words (Xia, 2023). In our implementation, we utilized FastText to train the CBOW model on a corpus of Devanagari text. The embedding dimension was set to 50 and embedding length of sentences was limited to 100 by either padding or truncating. This model generates dense vector representations of words which is effective in tasks like text classification and sentiment analysis (Xiong et al., 2019).

3.2.2 Character Level Encoding

Another approach explored in this research was character-level encoding. Each character of the text was converted into its Unicode code point, allowing for a straightforward numerical representation.We used this method to generate tensors of these code points, with a maximum sequence length of 100 characters. While this method provided a simplistic representation of the text, it did not capture the semantic relationships between characters as effectively as the CBOW embeddings which resulted in lower accuracy as shown in Table 4

3.3 Neural Network Architecture and Training

The Devanagari text classification model combines FastText embeddings with a Bidirectional Long Short-Term Memory (BiLSTM) network and an attention mechanism to capture features in each input sequence. The architecture is shown in table 1 First, each word in the text is transformed into a dense vector using FastText embeddings, which carry rich linguistic information. These vectors are processed by a bidirectional LSTM layer that captures context from both directions, essential for Devanagari script, where meaning is influenced by surrounding words. An attention layer then assigns weights to each word's hidden state to focus on the most relevant parts of the sequence, which allows the model to focus on specific parts of the input sequence (Zhang and Chu, 2023). This context vector is finally passed through a fully connected layer to output class probabilities. The model is trained using Cross-Entropy Loss and the Adam optimizer as shown in table 2, refining its weights across multiple epochs to improve accuracy in classifying Devanagari text.

Parameter	Value
Batch Size	32
Learning Rate	0.001
Epochs	10
Optimizer	Adam
Loss Function	Cross-Entropy

Table 2: Training parameters for the model.

4 Results

4.1 Model Performance

Our attention-enhanced BiLSTM model with CBOW embeddings demonstrated strong performance in Devanagari script classification. Figure 3 presents the detailed classification metrics for our proposed model.

4.2 Embedding Strategy Comparison

The results shown in table 4 demonstrate that both embeddings achieved comparable performance, significantly outperforming the character encoding approach. The superior performance of word embeddings can be attributed to their ability to capture semantic relationships and contextual information

Class	Precision	Recall	F1-Score	Support
Nepali	0.99	1.00	0.99	2688
Marathi	0.99	0.96	0.98	2365
Sanskrit	1.00	1.00	1.00	2356
Bhojpuri	0.96	0.99	0.97	2183
Hindi	0.94	0.93	0.93	1642
Accuracy	0.99			
Macro Avg	0.98	0.98	0.98	11234
Weighted Avg	0.98	0.98	0.98	11234

Table 3: Classification report showing precision, recall, f1-score, and support for each class.

Embedding Method	Accuracy
CBOW	99%
Skip-gram	97%
Character Encoding	72%

Table 4: Accuracy of different embedding methods.

in the Devanagari script, while character-level encoding fails to capture these higher-level linguistic patterns.

4.3 Error Analysis

We conducted a detailed error analysis to understand the model's classification behavior across different languages. Figure 2 presents the confusion matrix of our model's predictions.

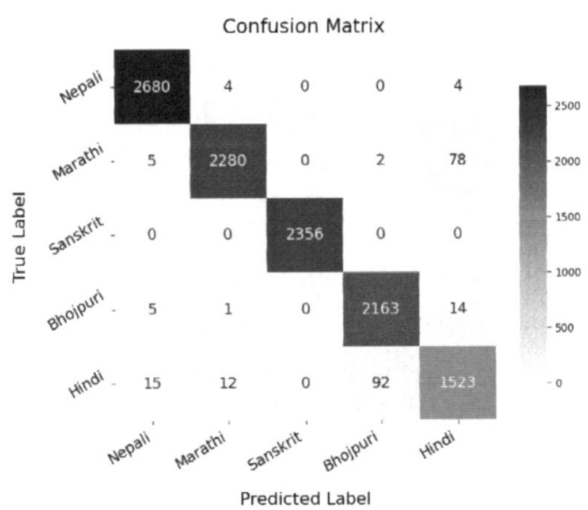

Figure 2: Confusion Matrix

Analysis of the matrix reveals several key patterns. Sanskrit achieved perfect classification with zero misclassifications, while Nepali showed robust performance with only 8 misclassifications. The most significant confusions occurred between Hindi-Bhojpuri (92 cases) and Marathi-Hindi (78 cases), likely due to their linguistic similarities. These patterns suggest that while the model excels at distinguishing languages with distinct characteristics, it faces some challenges with closely related language pairs.

4.4 Limitation and Future Enhancements

While the CBOW-BiLSTM model performs well, it faces challenges distinguishing closely related languages like Hindi and Bhojpuri due to their linguistic similarities. The character-level encoding method also underperforms compared to CBOW embeddings, as it lacks semantic depth. Future improvements could involve using transformer-based models to better handle these nuances and expanding the dataset to include more language variations and multi-modal data, such as handwritten text, to enhance accuracy and generalization.

5 Conclusion

This paper presents a practical and effective approach for identifying languages in the Devanagari script, a crucial task in today's multilingual world. By using CBOW embeddings combined with an attention-enhanced BiLSTM model, we show that our method can accurately distinguish between Nepali, Marathi, Sanskrit, Bhojpuri, and Hindi, providing a boost in precision over traditional techniques. Our findings highlights the value of a well-rounded preprocessing process and the role of attention mechanisms in improving performance for tasks involving Devanagari text. Overall, we believe our approach offers a flexible framework that can inspire further research, particularly in tackling the complex challenges of multilingual and mixed-language text in Devanagari.

References

Rahul Aralikatte, Miryam De Lhoneux, Anoop Kunchukuttan, and Anders Søgaard. 2021. Itihasa: A large-scale corpus for sanskrit to english translation. In *Proceedings of the 8th Workshop on Asian Translation (WAT2021)*, pages 191–197.

R. Bedyakin, M. Htsts, and N. Mikhaylovskiy. 2021. Low-resource spoken language identification using self-attentive pooling and deep 1d time-channel separable convolutions. *Proceedings of the 2021*, pages 1012–1020.

W. B. Cavnar and J. M. Trenkle. 1994. N-gram-based text categorization. In *Proceedings of SDAIR-94, 3rd Annual Symposium on Document Analysis and Information Retrieval*, pages 161–175.

A. Graves, N. Jaitly, and A. Mohamed. 2014. Hybrid speech recognition with deep bidirectional lstm. In *2013 IEEE Workshop on Automatic Speech Recognition and Understanding*, pages 273–278.

Farhan Ahmad Jafri, Kritesh Rauniyar, Surendrabikram Thapa, Mohammad Aman Siddiqui, Matloob Khushi, and Usman Naseem. 2024. Chunav: Analyzing hindi hate speech and targeted groups in indian election discourse. *ACM Transactions on Asian and Low-Resource Language Information Processing*.

Farhan Ahmad Jafri, Mohammad Aman Siddiqui, Surendrabikram Thapa, Kritesh Rauniyar, Usman Naseem, and Imran Razzak. 2023. Uncovering political hate speech during indian election campaign: A new low-resource dataset and baselines.

A. Joshi, P. Solanki, and M. Joshi. 2020. Language identification of devanagari text using embedding-based approaches. In P. K. Pattnaik and S. Rautaray, editors, *Progress in Computing, Analytics and Networking*, pages 167–176. Springer, Singapore.

S. K. Kopparapu and K. Vijayalaxmi. 2014. *Challenges in Optical Character Recognition of Devanagari and Related Indic Scripts*. Springer, India.

Atharva Kulkarni, Meet Mandhane, Manali Likhitkar, Gayatri Kshirsagar, and Raviraj Joshi. 2021. L3cubemahasent: A marathi tweet-based sentiment analysis dataset. In *Proceedings of the Eleventh Workshop on Computational Approaches to Subjectivity, Sentiment and Social Media Analysis*, pages 213–220.

C. M. Lambert. 1953. A new study of the devanagari script: Its development and historical context. *Journal of the Royal Asiatic Society of Great Britain & Ireland*, 85(1):45–58.

M. Mhaiskar. 2014. A comprehensive study of brahmic scripts: Their origin, spread, and development. *Journal of South Asian Studies*, 30(2):123–145.

Atul Kr Ojha. 2019. English-bhojpuri smt system: Insights from the karaka model. *arXiv preprint arXiv:1905.02239*.

Kritesh Rauniyar, Sweta Poudel, Shuvam Shiwakoti, Surendrabikram Thapa, Junaid Rashid, Jungeun Kim, Muhammad Imran, and Usman Naseem. 2023. Multi-aspect annotation and analysis of nepali tweets on anti-establishment election discourse. *IEEE Access*.

Kengatharaiyer Sarveswaran, Bal Krishna Bal, Surendrabikram Thapa, Ashwini Vaidya, and Sana Shams. 2025. A brief overview of the first workshop on challenges in processing south asian languages (chipsal). In *Proceedings of the First Workshop on Challenges in Processing South Asian Languages (CHiPSAL)*.

N. Taghizadeh and H. Faili. 2020. Cross-lingual adaptation using universal dependencies. *arXiv*.

Surendrabikram Thapa, Kritesh Rauniyar, Farhan Ahmad Jafri, Surabhi Adhikari, Kengatharaiyer Sarveswaran, Bal Krishna Bal, Hariram Veeramani, and Usman Naseem. 2025. Natural language understanding of devanagari script languages: Language identification, hate speech and its target detection. In *Proceedings of the First Workshop on Challenges in Processing South Asian Languages (CHiPSAL)*.

Surendrabikram Thapa, Kritesh Rauniyar, Shuvam Shiwakoti, Sweta Poudel, Usman Naseem, and Mehwish Nasim. 2023. Nehate: Large-scale annotated data shedding light on hate speech in nepali local election discourse. In *ECAI 2023*, pages 2346–2353. IOS Press.

H. Xia. 2023. Continuous-bag-of-words and skip-gram for word vector training and text classification. *Journal of Physics: Conference Series*, 2634:012052.

Zeyu Xiong, Qiangqiang Shen, Yueshan Xiong, YijieWang, and Weizi Li. 2019. New generation model of word vector representation based on cbow or skip-gram. *Computers, Materials amp; Continua*, 60(1):259–273.

H. Zhang and P. Chu. 2023. Prediction study based on tcn-bilstm-sa time series model. *Atlantis Highlights in Intelligent Systems*, pages 192–197.

Author Index

Association for Computational Linguistics
209 N. Eighth Street
Stroudsburg, Pennsylvania 18360

ISBN 979-8-3313-1360-9

CURRAN ASSOCIATES INC.
proceedings.com